Russia and the Idea of the West

Russia and the Idea of the West

GORBACHEV, INTELLECTUALS, AND THE END OF THE COLD WAR

Robert D. English

Columbia University Press   NEW YORK

Columbia University Press
Publishers Since 1893
New York   Chichester, West Sussex

Copyright © 2000 Columbia University Press

Library of Congress Cataloging-in-Publication Data
English, Robert (Robert D.)
Russia and the idea of the West : Gorbachev, intellectuals, and the end of the Cold War
Robert English.
p.cm.
Includes bibliographical references and index.
ISBN 0-231-11058-8 (cl) — ISBN 0-231-11059-6 (pa)
1. Soviet Union—Politics and government—1953-1985—Philosophy. 2. Soviet
Union—Politics and government—1985-1991—Philosophy. 3. Intellectuals—
Soviet Union—Political activity. 4. Soviet Union—relations—United States.
5. United States—Relations—Soviet Union. 6. Soviet Union—Relations—Europe,
Western. 7. Europe, Western—Relations—Soviet Union. I. Title.

DK274.E54 2000
303.48'24701821—dc21   00-024327

Printed in the United States of America
Designed by Audrey Smith

c 10 9 8 7 6 5 4 3 2 1
p 10 9 8 7 6 5 4 3 2 1

For Magda, Dave, Zhenya, and Bob

Contents

Preface: An Intellectual History   ix

Introduction: Intellectuals, Ideas, and Identity in the
Sources of International Change   1

1. The Origins and Nature of Old Thinking   17

2. Leaders, Society, and Intellectuals During the Thaw   49

3. Intellectuals and the World: From the Secret Speech
    to the Prague Spring   81

4. The Dynamics of New Thinking in the Era of Stagnation   117

5. Advance and Retreat: New Thinking in the Time
    of Crisis and Transition   159

6. The New Thinking Comes to Power   193

Conclusion: Reflections on the Origins and Fate of
New Thinking   229

Notes   *241*

Bibliography   *345*

Index   *375*

Preface: An Intellectual History

This book was conceived in the heady early days of perestroika with the intention of exploring a seemingly simple question: What was the source of the so-called "new thinking" that, already in 1987–88, was radically transforming both the theory and practice of Soviet international relations? With an undergraduate education focused on Russian and especially East European history, followed by a master's degree in international affairs and six years' subsequent work in defense and arms–control analysis, I began the formal study of political science with an eclectic and admittedly unsystematic perspective on Soviet politics. And it was a perspective that two years of training in preparation for thesis research did little to "systematize." For Princeton, in its wisdom, allowed me to divide my coursework among the Departments of Politics, History, and the Woodrow Wilson School. Encouraged simultaneously to explore the nature of the international and domestic systems, to appreciate both the influence of culture and the innovation of leadership, and to understand the complex sources of previous reform epochs in Russian and Soviet politics, I was ultimately on my own in searching for the nexus of power and ideology in perestroika.

This "benign neglect" was something I initially regretted as my Moscow fieldwork began in earnest in mid-1989. I envied my exchange colleagues their fine-tuned theories and specific research assignments, which contrasted sharply with my admittedly vague focus on "within-system reformers" and my research mission–then little better defined than to talk to as many people as possible, and read as much as I could, about foreign affairs. But this regret soon turned to appreciation because, with so much in flux (from policy itself to the people and ideas behind it, and the opportunities to explore both) a looser "orienting framework" allowed me continually to learn, adapt, and innovate.

These conditions, with the added circumstance of my wife's work as a correspondent for *Time*, then *Newsweek* and the *Wall Street Journal*, were invaluable, in both enriching and prolonging my stay in Moscow (through late-1991). This gave me the time to work in the archives of the USSR Foreign Ministry and the closed, *spetskhran* collections of several foreign-policy institutes. It enabled me to travel widely, in both provincial Russia and such regional centers of early reformist thought as Tallinn and Tbilisi (and to view the collapse of empire from the periphery as well as the metropole). Most of all, it allowed me the opportunity to conduct nearly 400 interviews with more than 100 different individuals. They ranged from Brezhnev-era Politburo members Petr Shelest and Gennady Voronov to such perestroika-era notables as Mikhail Gorbachev, Eduard Shevardnadze, Alexander Yakovlev, Yegor Ligachev, and Sergei Akhromeyev. But even more important were meetings with dozens of lesser-known apparatchiks and academics–foreign-affairs analysts, economists, historians, philosophers, scientists, artists, writers, and diplomats. These interviews–and the unpublished studies and memoranda to which they led, together with numerous classified reports, published articles, and memoirs–would constitute the core of my research.

Time and again, long afternoons or evenings spent reliving little-known events of the 1950s or reconstructing closed-door debates of the 1960s and 1970s uncovered the myriad episodes and experiences that contributed to the emergence of new thinking. Scientists recalled their earliest concerns about the environment; economists described their first exposure to Yugoslav "self-management" or their first reading of Paul Samuelson; historians recounted their thaw-era research in Poland and Italy; philosophers and sociologists led me to samizdat lectures and the works of obscure scholars in institutes far beyond Moscow. Some policy analysts, diplomats, and even military officers eventually opened their personal archives to me. Others opened the door to an ever-widening circle of interlocutors, and thus to an ever-growing appreciation of the social as well as intellectual dimensions of the new thinkers as a diverse but unified community of "Westernizing" reformers.

Little of this would have emerged had I begun with a narrowly structured model and rigid research plan. Even less would it have been possible had I followed the advice of one senior Sovietologist who, in a predeparture briefing, urged me to conduct my interviews via a standardized questionnaire. What little that would have gained me in quantifiability would have cost much in qualitative terms. Only a free-flowing and wide-ranging approach, going deeply into the particular experiences of each individual while building on the insights gleaned from others, could have yielded so much. For not until months into the process–only when I had acquired a large evidentiary base and thus begun to see the contours of a little-known intellectual history–did I even know which questions to ask.

Throughout, there was a growing sense of urgency as a shifting political climate affected the accessibility or volubility of some interlocutors, while mortality began to take its toll on others. Many were the "Children of the 20th Party Congress," that landmark event in post-Stalin liberalization, who by the late 1980s were well into their sixties. Others survive, and I was able to supplement my original research–and better place it in political-historical context–with extended return visits to the "new" Russia during the parliamentary elections of December 1993 and the presidential contest of June/July 1996. Readers of the chapters that follow will judge for themselves the extent to which I have found that proper context.

For this preface, there remains only to acknowledge the many institutions and individuals who made this project possible. The International Research and Exchanges Board supported my first, critical academic year in Moscow; the USSR Academy of Sciences extended my research privileges for two more; and the Princeton Society of Fellows and Center of International Studies supported the writing of a dissertation. Allegheny College funded subsequent research in Moscow that was vital in revising this book in manuscript.

Among numerous Russian-Soviet advisers and friends, special thanks are owed Georgy Arbatov, Alexander Bessmertnykh, Nikolai Bukharin, Anatoly Chernyaev, Gennady Gerasimov, Viktor Girshfeld, Vladimir Kovalevsky, Tatyana Kutkovets, Igor Malashenko, Merab Mamardashvili, Daniil Melamid, Constantine Pleshakov, Yuri Senokosov, Vladimir Tikhonov, Alexander Tsipko, Yuri Zamoshkin, and Rostislav Zolotaryev. I am also most grateful for the personal and intellectual comradeship of Julie Newton, Michael Kraus, and Allison

Stanger, and for the warmth and wisdom of three generations of the Pestretsova family–Anka, Tanya, and Tyotya Anna.

Academic advisers who, from diverse perspectives, each lent their time and sage advice are Richard Wortman, Fred Greenstein, and Dick Ullman. Others commented on various parts of the manuscript at various stages of its completion: Nancy Bermeo, Nikolai Biryukov, Craige Champion, Robert Herman, Howard Tamashiro, Vladislav Zubok, and three anonymous reviewers of Columbia University Press. Two whose guidance was exceptionally important, in both the inception and completion of the project, are Jim McAdams and Bill Wohlforth. But my greatest scholarly debt is to two senior mentors, Bob Tucker and Steve Cohen, who prepared me superbly for the study of Russia: sharing their deep knowledge and unsurpassed insights into Soviet politics, they lent me the best possible "intellectual armor" but sent me off to contend alone–free to survey the flanks and pursue various quixotic charges until, through the "fog" of upheaval and change, I also saw the continuities at which they had been pointing all along.

But in fact I did not contend alone, and my deepest debt is to my wife, Liza. Together we interviewed presidents and prostitutes, spoke at conferences and surveyed kolkhozy, crossed the Armenian-Azerbaijani frontier and braved the no-man's-land of Tskhinvali–always discussing, often arguing, sometimes even agreeing. From the barricades of Riga and Dubosary to the parliaments of Tallinn and Yerevan, from the cafes of Tbilisi to the corridors of Staraya Ploshchad, this has been, in every sense, a journey we made together.

Robert D. English
September 1999

Russia and the Idea of the West

Introduction: Intellectuals, Ideas, and Identity in the Sources of International Change

> It is only by studying the minds of men that we shall understand the causes of anything. —James Joll, *1914: The Unspoken Assumptions*

In the early 1980s, superpower relations were at their lowest ebb since the Berlin and Cuban crises of the early 1960s. The painstaking gains of arms control were unraveling with "palisades of missiles" rising on earth and "space strike weapons" soon to enter the heavens amid mutual accusations of treaty violation and deceit. Détente's diplomatic and economic ties had withered in the aftermath of Angola and Afghanistan, and Soviet and U.S. proxies were now at war on three continents. Moscow saw an adversary engaged in reckless provocations and sweeping challenges to its legitimate interests, launching a massive arms race that at best sought to exhaust the USSR, and at worst was actually readying for nuclear attack. Its citizens were barraged with parallel images of Nazi and NATO aggression; Kremlin propaganda shrieked of a dying imperialism preparing "to take with it all life on earth."

The view from Washington was not dissimilar—that of an "evil empire" increasingly repressive at home and aggressive abroad. Though ultimately destined for "the ash can of history," the USSR was still on the march. Administration officials exposed its plots, denounced its barbarity, and debated its plans for nuclear war. Some more thoughtful analysts, though less alarmist, still viewed Soviet global power as on an upward trajectory. Others saw a chance for modest reform but, noting the strength of military-industrial interests and the depth of imperial commitments, agreed that there was little hope of détente's revival.

None foresaw what soon occurred, the rise of a dynamic Soviet leader who, launching an ambitious perestroika at home, took even more radical steps abroad under the banner of *novoe myshlenie*—new thinking. In rapid sequence, Mikhail Gorbachev silenced the skeptics by opening his country to the world, unilaterally slashing arms, withdrawing from Afghanistan and other third world outposts, peacefully relinquishing the "outer" East European empire, and—in a final test of fealty to democratic, universal human values—ceding the "inner" empire as well. Striving, in his words, to "rejoin the path of world civilization," Gorbachev overturned nearly 50 years of cold war confrontation in just five.

How can this truly epochal change be explained? Was the cold war's end essentially just the overdue retreat of an overextended, bankrupt empire? Or, anything but inevitable, was it instead largely the handiwork of a rare visionary statesman whose very accession was an event of remarkably good fortune? Or does credit properly belong not to the inexorable dictates of power, nor to the innovation of leadership, but rather to institutions—namely, the détente-era international ties and supporting domestic networks that altered ideas and "incentive structures" in favor of major foreign-policy change?

These categories of explanation, which dominate the literature on the cold war's end, each highlight important aspects of new thinking's late development and subsequent implementation; in short, the cold war "endgame." None, however, adequately addresses a critical, earlier, process that made such an endgame possible: the emergence, over the preceding two decades, of a Soviet intellectual elite holding sharply unorthodox beliefs about their country's development and proper place in the world community.

The new thinking's global-integrationist outlook, rooted in the cultural thaw, domestic liberalization, and burgeoning foreign ties of the early post-Stalin era, had begun coalescing as a powerful alternative worldview by the mid-to-late 1960s. Shared by philosophers and physicists, economists, political scientists, and historians, this diverse policy-academic elite constituted a "Westernizing" minority within the Soviet intelligentsia. Numbering perhaps in the hundreds, the most active of its ranks—a few dozen—were already promoting a broad range of foreign and domestic reforms by the early 1970s; that is, prior to the full flowering of détente and more than a decade before the sharp worsening of problems and subsequent accession of Gorbachev in 1985. Also in advance of his accession, Gorbachev came under the influence of these ideas and, together with his core group of political allies, embraced the new-thinking *weltanschauung* and the new thinkers' ambitious agenda *before* his boldest steps of the later 1980s. So while crisis and leadership transition were vital preconditions, so was an earlier intellectual change—the rise of a global, "Westernizing" identity among a liberal policy-academic elite—a sine qua non of the cold war's sudden and peaceful end.

Crisis, Leadership, and Ideas in the Cold War's End

Power-centered approaches, which emphasize Soviet economic woes and consequent difficulty in continuing the arms race and maintaining empire, highlight some of the problems bedeviling Moscow in the mid-to-late 1980s. But they also describe well the problems of the late 1970s and, absent perestroika, largely the same dilemma Moscow would still be facing in the late 1990s. Neorealist theory, stressing the primacy of power in an anarchical international system, tells less about when and how a state will adjust to decline.[1] In the Soviet case, as will be seen, in addition to continuing the status quo indefinitely, there was also a reactionary alternative to liberalization; increasingly repressive at home and confrontational abroad, it was arguably an equally likely choice in 1985. "Crisis" may indeed have created an opportunity for reform, but it also emboldened powerful reactionaries; it was probably a necessary condition for some kind of major change, but certainly an insufficient one for the new thinking's triumph.[2]

Dynamic, innovative leadership was thus central to when, and how, crisis was addressed in the USSR. Even this is an understatement, for it is nearly impossible to imagine any of Gorbachev's competitors for the general secretaryship even undertaking, much less carrying through, his bold domestic and foreign reforms. Yet Gorbachev did not act alone. He was supported by a few, like-minded, senior colleagues (principally Alexander Yakovlev and Eduard Shevardnadze), who together relied heavily—for general inspiration and specific advice—on the new-thinking pioneers noted above.

The latters' role was vital, for they empowered leaders with ideas and information. If Gorbachev was indispensable in the launching and implementation of radical reforms, the new thinkers were similarly critical in their conception.[3]

The third broad approach noted above, encompassing various neoliberal and institutional analyses, does address the missing link in this causal chain. Drawing on theories of regimes and the international spread of norms, some stress the constructive influence of Soviet participation in arms control and other détente-era ties. These contacts fostered "transnational learning" and "epistemic communities" of experts promoting cooperative approaches to international affairs.[4] In such accounts, ideas do matter, but in often narrow or instrumental terms that do not capture the breadth, depth, and long genesis of new thinking.[5] Other analyses focus on one or another foreign-policy issue and the specialists directly concerned, and so cannot take full account of the earlier, underlying links among diverse reformist individuals (policy analysts, scientists, academics, even dissidents) and reform ideas (political, economic, social) that formed the vital broader context of new thinking in *all* fields.[6] Most also assume a rationality at odds with Soviet reality, i.e., the influence of "incentive structures" favoring reform initiatives when in fact they were mostly weighted against change and, in numerous instances, it was at the risk of privilege or career that individuals motivated by *ideals* pioneered key innovations.[7]

In short, while offering useful insights into the new thinking's late development and subsequent implementation, neoliberal approaches are limited by frameworks that—due to their largely instrumental conception of ideas—neglect the broader social-intellectual context, and often miscast the real political context, in which they actually emerged. Simply put, can the ideas of Soviet physicists be understood through their participation in disarmament fora abroad, overlooking their earlier efforts at home in the fight to de-Stalinize and "globalize" the social sciences? Can the beliefs of foreign-affairs experts be analyzed via their role in détente-era exchanges while ignoring their patronage of Moscow's avant-garde theater or reading of samizdat historical and cultural works? Can economists who sought global integration be viewed as students of the capitalist West without attention to their study of East European reforms, of the market experience of the Soviet 1920s, and of pioneering prerevolutionary Russian economists? And can the motives of these and many other diverse reformers be understood absent appreciation of their strong professional and personal ties, their shared hopes in the thaw era and common anguish over the crushing of the Prague Spring?

Analyzing the Origins of New Thinking: The Elites-Identity Framework

The first step toward an analytical framework that can address these questions is a redefinition of both the agents of intellectual change and the substance of their ideas. As suggested above, the ranks of the new thinkers were not limited to a narrow group of security specialists but comprised a broad cohort of social and natural scientists, students of culture and the humanities, ranging from academics to apparatchiks. The new thinking, too, has seen several definitions. Early ones, which listed such elements as "defense sufficiency" or "mutual security," were soon seen only to have enumerated the policies flowing from what was indeed a deeper new *thinking*. Later definitions—as a belief system, ideology, or operational code—agree that the ideas at issue were not such peripheral ones but rather the most basic "philosophical" beliefs about the nature of world politics.[8] With varying emphases, most include the elevation of universal over class values, and the rejection of inevitable East-West hostility, as central tenets.

The problem lies not with what is included in such definitions, but what is left out. For in discarding longtime core tenets, new thinking did not just posit an end to conflict with the West or the desirability of cooperation with the liberal international community. It argued that the USSR was, or should be, a *member* of that community. Thus I argue that the new thinking is best viewed as a watershed in national identity—not in opposition to, but in unity with the West—and so entailing a sharply different conception of Soviet national interests in world politics. Put simply, a diverse group of specialist elites, on the basis of their knowledge and experience over the preceding two decades, had by the early 1970s embraced a distinct "Westernizing" set of beliefs and political orientation that would play an indispensable role in shaping

Gorbachev's reforms. By privileging two factors—the paradigmatic and constitutive nature of belief change in reference to international "others," and the central role of intellectuals in that process—the elites-identity framework helps to answer the questions posed above and so offers a better model for analysis of intellectual-political change in the USSR.[9]

If the nation is a self-conscious community of people bound by a common culture and understanding of their past and future—a distinct "historical narrative"—then its identity is that which explains "Who are we, what do we collectively aspire to . . . and what most distinguishes us from the rest of the world?"[10] If a nation is shaped (and a state legitimized) by the symbols, norms, and beliefs that comprise the "map" of its political culture, then national identity provides the "compass" that guides the nation (state) in world affairs.[11] It includes a distinct sense of mission or purpose, possibly a messianic individualism, leadership of a cultural or ethnic bloc, or membership in some other political or economic grouping of states.[12] Identity powerfully influences the interplay of deep-rooted cultural and fast-changing material factors in deciding how national interests—and so international behavior—are determined.[13]

National identity is not immutable. It can change in a slow process of cultural evolution or more rapidly during such socioeconomic upheavals as industrialization.[14] But even when "imposed" from abroad—as after military defeat and foreign occupation—a key role in the rise of a new identity is played by intellectuals, the "secular priesthood" of the nation.[15] Whether in reaction to their personal alienation,[16] or to their professional insight into the nature of crisis,[17] it is intellectuals who lead the assault on a hegemonic identity and are the "storytellers in the invention of [a new] nationality."[18] Their role is even more vital in dictatorial systems where the state controls discourse over history and politics, imposing an identity from above through its monopoly over education, the media, and scholarship. In many such cases, where intellectuals have been the agents of large-scale belief change, several factors stand out as crucial.

First, the *prerequisites* of change include both an opening to foreign ideas and information, and the emergence of particular elite congregations in which these ideas are debated and an intellectual "critical mass" can accumulate. In Franco's Spain, the two were met in several ministries where the rise of a modern,

"European" identity paved the way for democratization. For the deradicalization of some Latin American Marxists, the conditions were found abroad; political exile in Italy, wrote one, "affected us as much as the Cuban revolution. . . . It was there [reading Gramsci and cementing close ties to Eurocommunists] that I changed my political perspective."[19] In post-Mao China, the journal *World Economic Herald,* through articles, seminars, and other ties with Western political and business figures, became "an important source of foreign ideas [and] helped set the agenda" for the prodemocracy movement.[20] In the case of Soviet new thinking, as will be seen, a handful of research centers and editorial boards constituted strikingly similar "networks . . . where the diffusion of foreign ideas" was greatly encouraged.[21]

Second, the *process* of identity change combines learning on two levels: *comparative-interactive* learning, wherein foreign ties facilitate a shift in intellectuals' essential "self-categorization" of the nation among allies and adversaries; and *social* learning, in which growing numbers of intellectuals, from diverse professions, are drawn into an informal domestic community. In other words, international links serve not only as conduits for ideas, but also as "reference groups" vital to realignment of identity vis-à-vis other states.[22] Simultaneously, rethinking of "external" identity prompts reappraisal of fundamental internal issues as well, thus further widening the circle of those involved.[23] Again, the Chinese case illustrates this two-level process: writers and journalists who began with a tentative opening to foreign ideas soon turned to a searching critique of their own society; economists and scientists who first sought expanded ties abroad later pushed for broader domestic liberalization; they were the "ideological entrepreneurs" who constructed a new "global" Chinese identity.[24] And so foreign "transaction flows"—the ties that "link people across space so as to form a new community"[25]—foster similar ties at home by "building bridges" among diverse actors and interests. Common aspirations for a reformed domestic society, and shared beliefs about its place in the international community, "create the basis of a new identity" among critically thinking intellectuals.[26]

The transformation of national identity, particularly in a closed-dictatorial system, is rarely a linear process. Periods of gradual change are punctuated by intervals of rapid intellectual upheaval.[27]

These can result from such external shocks as economic collapse or military defeat. Or the regime itself can unwittingly encourage rethinking of core beliefs, via permission of such signal cultural events as the 1988 televising of *The Yellow River Elegy* with its indictment of Chinese isolation, or the 1962 publication of *One Day in the Life of Ivan Denisovich* and other explosive critiques of the Stalinist legacy. The crackdowns that followed—the Tienanmen massacre and subsequent repressions in China, or the crushing of the Prague Spring and stifling of dissent in the USSR—provided still more powerful "cognitive punches" by revealing the limits of reform and exposing the brutal essence of the existing system.[28] But even as it suppresses open debate, such reaction only heightens the importance of informal intellectual congregations and catalyzes the development of a new identity.

To show that beliefs and identity ultimately matter, their impact on policy must be demonstrated. For *novoe myshlenie,* the new thinking, this means that the ideas of an intellectual elite influenced leaders in ways that were not just epiphenomenal to steps necessitated by the crises of the mid-1980s. This will be shown presently, but first it is important to ask why these crises arose in the first place.[29] It has been noted that, for all the attention to new thinking, little has been paid to "the motivated interests that held the old pathologies in power for so long."[30] Can the problems that Gorbachev inherited be explained mainly by the material interests of a Brezhnevist great-power bureaucratism? To what extent were they also a "pathological" product of social and cultural constraints rooted in the Stalinist experience, or earlier? To answer these questions, the elites-identity model directs attention back to the "basic values, cognitions and emotional commitments" of the once-hegemonic identity—how it was initially learned and subsequently socialized—and so to the sociointellectual context in which an alternative identity would later contend.[31] Therefore, as outlined in the chapter summaries that follow, analysis of the new thinking necessarily begins with examination of the old.

The Persistence of Old Thinking

One of the least-studied revelations of glasnost, but a vital one for Soviet foreign-policy studies, is how important ideology really

was. Soviet leaders may have been concerned first to preserve imperial gains and, by the 1970s, to maintain a sort of superpower con-
dominium. But at critical junctures—from wasted chances to
improve East-West ties, to provocative ventures that mortally
wounded them—ideological motives were important. And these
can be understood only via the unique circumstances that made the
old thinking, the "hostile-isolationist" identity, so tenacious.
Chapter 1 reviews these circumstances, from the contention of early
Westernizing and Slavophile intellectual currents, through the
upheavals of revolution, war, and consolidation of Bolshevik rule
that decimated the old "European" elite, to the Stalinist synthesis
of doctrinaire Leninist anticapitalism and traditional Russian
nationalist xenophobia.

The generation that came of age in these turbulent decades was
repeatedly terrorized, ceaselessly propagandized, and effectively isolated from most challenges to Stalinist dogma on the outside world.
Not surprisingly, Stalin's successors parted only slowly, and never
completely, with the fears, mistrust, and residual revolutionary
ambition of their formative years. From Cuba to Afghanistan, hostile-isolationist beliefs and values periodically reasserted themselves.
Of course, it was this Stalin-trained cohort that ruled until 1985. But
even among a second echelon of officialdom, once removed from
the early traumas and so presumably shaped more by Khrushchev's
reforms, the old thinking was strong—largely because the system
was so thoroughly ideologized. "Peaceful coexistence" notwithstanding, Leninist tenets of Western hostility and a divided world
remained intact. Privilege and career depended on fealty to this
dogma; information was controlled and manipulated on this basis;
and even language and categories of analysis were built upon its precepts.[32] In such overt and covert ways, old thinking permeated
Soviet identity in ways that far outlived the early tragedies and triumphs upon which it was built.

The Origins of New Thinking

So the thaw era, for most of the Soviet elite, did not go terribly
far in undoing more than a generation of hostile-isolationist
thought. But for some others, it did. Chapter 2 explores how intellectual life changed radically for those who would later mature as

new thinkers. Most came of age in the thaw's emancipatory atmosphere, which found many studying in Moscow or other urban centers where openness and diversity were greatest. They listened to unsanctioned poets and read unpublished manuscripts, discussed Orwell and Gramsci, and debated issues from the Party's past complicity in the terror to its current policy toward Hungary and Yugoslavia. And when new foreign-affairs institutes were established, exchanges with the West begun, and opportunities for working abroad (or in Moscow's corridors of power) were created—all with unprecedented access to ideas and information—they were prominent among the beneficiaries.

Part of this story is already familiar. What I emphasize, later in chapter 2 and in chapter 3, is how these changes combined to nurture a reformist policy-academic elite that differed sharply from the majority of careerists still dominated by Stalin's oxymoronically termed "proletarian intelligentsia."[33] Drawing on recent memoirs and interviews as well as earlier writings, I show this process beginning with the assault of historians and writers on core hostile-isolationist beliefs that launched an implicit debate over Russia's place in world civilization. Also seen is how the influences noted, from exchanges with the West to study of reforms in Eastern Europe, prompted new ideas in fields from foreign affairs and economics to the environment. From Pugwash seminars and Polish sociology to the Prague Spring, these diverse sources had, by the late 1960s, brought many to an increasingly social-democratic outlook that sought their country's integration with the liberal international community.

What the early new thinkers also shared—despite their often-divergent career paths in the humanities or natural sciences, from academia to the apparat—was a *social* identity as members of a liberal-reformist domestic community. Rooted in their common early experience and professional ties, these links grew stronger in a few key intellectual congregations: institutes, editorial boards, and consultant groups. They were also seen as liberals rallied in defense of reform, and each other, when reaction surged in the later 1960s. Historians and philosophers, ousted from university posts for faulting dogmas, found refuge at academic institutes with the help of former classmates. Critics of cultural chauvinism were shielded from the harshest punitive blows by their apparatchik allies.

International-affairs analysts, scientists, and even some military officers defended those under siege for questioning Stalin's foreign or economic policies. And this diverse community openly united in protest against the reactionaries' attempts to rehabilitate Stalin himself.

The Mobilization of New Thinking

With the invasion of Czechoslovakia in 1968, there began a difficult period that has usually been viewed as a hiatus in the evolution of new thinking. In fact, as argued in chapter 4, this is better seen as a time of consolidation and advance. The hard-line turn abroad and at home, while pushing many into silence or cynicism, was a critical watershed for others. For the Prague Spring had encouraged and united reformist intellectuals like nothing else since Khrushchev's "secret speech" in 1956; its defeat now prompted more radical rethinking of the country's problems and potential solutions. And it was in the late 1960s and early 1970s—*before* the brief flowering of détente—that some of the most important new ideas emerged. Drawing on internal reports and limited-circulation studies, as well as interviews and memoirs, I show this sharp break with old thinking (and frank criticism of official policy) in many fields: on security and relations with the United States; on policy toward Europe and Asia; on the economy, technology, and the environment; and on cultural freedom and concern over rising Russian nationalism.

Détente was clearly a powerful boost to such innovation. But the key conceptual breakthroughs usually traced to this period were often nearly a decade old. While reform ideas continued to develop, what stands out even more from the mid-to-late 1970s are vigorous new efforts to put them into practice. In chapters 4 and 5, this "mobilization" is detailed—first in analyses and proposals to improve East-West relations further, and later, as reform opportunities were missed and Soviet policy began undermining détente, in appeals to halt the slide back toward confrontation. Crucially, this mobilization also fostered links between the new thinkers and a small group of reform-minded senior Party officials whose emergent leader was Gorbachev.

The Triumph of New Thinking

Together, the proponents of change struggled through the difficult years of transition from 1982 to 1985, as detailed in chapters 5 and 6. Here I also show how the strength of a reactionary leadership faction made a status-quo foreign policy, or even a hard-line turn, a likely outcome. That Gorbachev was initially primarily concerned to reverse domestic decline is clear. But this concern, coupled with a rare intellect (particularly for a member of the Politburo) and broad exposure to reformist influences (a thaw-era Moscow University education, independent European travel, extensive private study) had already led him to early and fruitful interaction with a broad range of new-thinking ideas and individuals. These ranged from Yakovlev, the apparat-academic in Western exile, and Shevardnadze, the innovative Georgian party boss, to a growing circle of reformist economists, scientists, and foreign-policy experts. The members of this "brain trust"—whose ties to Gorbachev worried Politburo conservatives and delayed his accession—were not only the future leader's private tutors on specific international and domestic issues. They were also, in an important sense, the "ambassadors" to Gorbachev of a larger reformist intellectual elite.

Once in office, Gorbachev and his allies relied heavily on these and other new-thinking advisers. And while his reforms did have unintended consequences, it is incorrect to view his foreign policy as mainly reacting to events gone out of control.[34] As shown in chapter 6, Gorbachev's most critical steps abroad were *preceded* by a principled commitment to core new-thinking values. And this came, not in 1989, but as early as 1986. That watershed year began with a sweeping reappraisal of international affairs, even more radical than could be expressed at the reformist 27th Party Congress in February. April brought Chernobyl, another "cognitive punch" to remaining dogmas about security and relations with the world community. By summer, Gorbachev had taken the lead in crafting the radical disarmament plan unveiled at Reykjavik in October. These, together with an intensive series of meetings with Western leaders and intellectuals, brought Gorbachev and his allies to broad acceptance of new thinking's global, democratic, integrationist principles no later than 1987. The "proof" of this commitment may have come only with acquiescence in the tumultuous changes of 1989 and after.

But that commitment—to bury the hostile-isolationist outlook that underlay decades of cold war—was decisively made at least two years earlier.[35]

The Lessons of New Thinking

A decade on, the epoch of perestroika, the cold war's sudden end, and the myriad subsequent changes (and continuities) in the politics of Russia and the international system continue to reverberate in a vast new (and not-so-new) literature on the lessons of new thinking for Sovietology, for foreign policy studies, and for international relations theory. I address some of these at some length in my conclusion, discussing them only after the reader has had the opportunity to sift the evidence and interpretation presented in the chapters that follow. But for now, by way of summary, and as points to be borne in mind as that argumentation is considered, I offer the following.

First, as to U.S. foreign policy: the view that "strength won the cold war" is, at best, greatly oversimplified. The early 1980s Western military buildup, and particularly the U.S. turn toward aggressively challenging the USSR, made the accession of a genuinely reformist leadership much more difficult. The effort to tilt the military balance sharply in the West's favor certainly heightened Soviet perceptions of deepening problems and a need for change. But rarely is it recognized that such change could, and arguably almost did, take the form of a repressive-confrontational turn at home and abroad. Liberalization was hardly "necessary," and collapse was anything but imminent; when it did come, it was an unintended by-product of reforms, not something that their preconditions had preordained.

For their part, critics on the Left must acknowledge that a long-term policy of containment and measured emphasis on maintaining Western power contributed to the perception of some in Moscow that confrontation was fruitless and that there was need for systemic reforms. An eroding position in the global competition was indeed one factor in their embrace of new thinking. But most of this thinking *preceded* the Reagan challenge, a gamble that did as much to complicate as to accelerate reform. Foreign-policy liberals were a distinct minority in a political system dominated by old thinkers. A different leader, heeding different (and, in 1985, far more prevalent) advice, almost certainly would have chosen a different and more dangerous course. In short, the argument that "Star Wars brought the Soviets to their knees" reflects a lapse in basic counterfactual reasoning, if not an even more deterministic triumphalism.[36]

Thus, a second lesson concerns the intersection of power and ideas in shaping major international change. Clearly, power mattered. The steady erosion in the USSR's relative power and growing difficulty in maintaining military-imperial commitments were significant factors in the emergence of new thinking. Decline was a stimulus of both political and intellectual change—albeit, as noted, in both reformist *and* reactionary directions. But the new thinking's main impetus lay elsewhere, in the long-term rise of a new policy-academic elite whose "Westernizing" identity was rooted in the cultural thaw, domestic liberalization, and burgeoning international ties of the first post-Stalin decades. For what ensued, in terms of foreign policy lessons, the détente of the 1960s and 1970s was probably more consequential than the confrontation of the 1980s. In terms of international relations theory, intellectual change was also a key variable in shaping the cold war's peaceful end; declining power may have been the immediate catalyst of a turn in Soviet foreign policy, but rising ideas were predominant in determining its direction.

In short, ideas mattered, too. They were not merely epiphenomenal or incidental to considerations of power; nor can their impact be grasped in mainly instrumental terms. Ideas mattered as deeply held beliefs that moved many to promote reforms at risk to their personal or institutional interests (and, for the old thinking with which the new contended, to cling to hostile-isolationist policies that ultimately undermined the USSR's bases of power). Moreover, the new thinking was not just a narrow set of precepts on national security acquired in less than a decade, but a broader array of beliefs and values shaping national identity that developed over a full generation.

Further, essential in this development were the links between international and domestic sources of change; exposure to contemporary Western political and social ideas was important, but so was study of European leftist thought, debate over other socialist models, and rethinking of earlier Soviet and Russian experience; international "specialists' communities" were influential in certain areas, but even more important was the coalescence of a domestic community that united reformers across diverse fields. The ties among historians, philosophers, economists, and foreign-affairs specialists were vital in simultaneously strengthening new thinking's conceptual foundation while broadening its social base among critically minded Soviet intellectuals.

Analytical models that isolate one or another of these dimensions—though contributing much to understanding particular aspects of Gorbachev's reforms—cannot, by definition, capture the critical, larger process of social-intellectual change that was the rise of new thinking. Ironically, it was some of the now much-criticized "area studies" Sovietologists, with their characterization of "within-system reformers" or the evocative "children of the 20th Party Congress," who had it right.[37] And not simply because their terms were evocative, but for *what* they evoked: a broad reformist elite sharing a common intellectual development and commitment to fulfilling the early post-Stalin era promise of liberalizing, humanizing, and opening their country to the world.[38]

I ∎
The Origins and Nature of Old Thinking

A cleansing of the collective memory was carried out . . . through the physical annihilation of living witnesses to history. Systematic terror destroyed one stratum after another of the Russian intelligentsia. . . . After this, regular purges began of the new generation of humanists. And each time the nation was deprived of a portion of its collective memory, of part of its history, and in its place there took hold a remembrance of something that had never actually happened—an artificial memory.   Alexander Nekrich, *Foresake Fear*

A mass psychosis was rampant. . . . Who was guilty for the fact that we lived so badly, worse than anyone else? At first the spies were the guilty ones. Then the foreigners. Various internal aliens . . . and finally, the Jews. . . .   Raisa Orlova, *Memoirs*

To understand the emergence of new thinking, it is first necessary to apprehend the old. Major intellectual change is a very complex and difficult process, even on an individual level. When it is the core beliefs of larger groups or elites are at issue—as in the case of new thinking—then attention to the processes by which "basic values, cognitions and emotional commitments" are learned is doubly important.[1] And when the old worldview emerged from the traumatic experiences of war, terror, and socioeconomic upheaval, of strict isolation and overweening ideological indoctrination, then appreciation of the cultural and social inertia with which new beliefs and values had to contend is even more essential.

The old thinking was a worldview or identity built upon several precepts that governed "definitions, perceptions and diagnoses" of the USSR and its place in the world.[2] First was that of a world irretrievably split into irreconcilable camps; second was belief in capitalism's innate hostility and abiding threat to socialism; and third was a faith in Soviet superiority—its expansion and ultimate triumph over the West—in an amalgam of Russian messianism and Bolshevik internationalism. This identity is summarized in its essentials as "hostile isolationism."[3]

Xenophobia had deep roots in traditional, peasant Russia, and even the "Europeanized" intelligentsia was sharply divided over the Western path of development. But it was only after the Bolshevik revolution of 1917, with the ensuing civil war and foreign intervention, that such Leninist concepts as a two-camp world and "hostile capitalist encirclement" seemed emphatically confirmed in mortal combat. Simultaneously, such non-Leninist currents as "great-power chauvinism" surged to the fore.

In the 1920s, intellectual life regained a margin of freedom; while pressure on the old Westernized elite was great, it was not yet murderous. In the Stalinist 1930s, what remained of this elite was largely liquidated. New cadres lacking worldly exposure were brought up in the hothouse of xenophobia and Russian nationalism. Trained in isolation from foreign ideas and cultures, they began professional life in a cauldron of terror predicated on ceaseless Western plots. They knew only an outside world of capitalist exploitation and aggression. Their own world, a maelstrom of intrigue in which they fought to survive, fostered a political culture of "combat" and "conspiracy."[4] And so their inner world—values, symbolic attachments, ways of speech and thought—was also "radically restructured."[5] Thus, while building on isolationist, anti-Western currents from both the recent Bolshevik and the distant tsarist past, Stalinism raised both to unprecedented heights in forging the hostile-isolationist identity.

A generation that came of age in the civil war, and made their careers under Stalin, dominated the political-intellectual elite through the mid 1980s. It would be wrong to argue that, 30 years after Stalin's death, his ideology remained the chief determinant of policy; by then it was rather more like "imperial preservation." But neither was the old worldview entirely spent, for its beliefs and values continued to shape the identity and international outlook of Soviet elites. The paranoid extremes had faded, and Brezhnev's

"offensive détente" was far removed from Stalin's cold war. But the old thinking's core isolationist, anti-Western precepts remained strong enough to block any more significant East-West rapprochement than détente and eventually to undermine even what modest progress had been achieved. And that is why, in a critical sense, Gorbachev's new thinking had to contend less with Brezhnev's legacy than that of Lenin and Stalin.

The West and Russia Under the Old Regime

More than a century before asking "What is to be done?" Russia's thinkers were already struggling with another of their country's seemingly eternal questions: "Where is Russia's place between East and West?" This question came to the fore in the early eighteenth century with the changes wrought by Peter the Great (1683–1725). Hitherto politically, culturally, and economically backward—as Renaissance Europe progressed toward the Enlightenment, mere survival pushed old Muscovy in the opposite direction—pre-Petrine Russia remained a realm apart from the West. But in the space of two decades, Russia's first emperor forcibly injected Russia into the European balance of power and no less forcefully opened his country to European ways.

For a great majority of Russians—the rural masses—Peter's "revolution from above" was a huge step *away* from progress and enlightenment; the peasants were largely ignored except where, in support of a growing military-bureaucratic state, ever more of them were bound into serfdom. But even for those at whom Peter's Westernizing efforts were aimed—the nobility—the results were ambiguous at best. The fierce resistance that met forced changes in dress, manners, and worship are well known, as was the opposition of those required to accompany the tsar's court from ancient, "Asian" Moscow to Saint Petersburg, Russia's new "window on Europe." More central to Peter's efforts, but equally contradictory in impact, were his requirements that the nobility be educated and pursue civil or military careers. While grants of land (and serfs) benefited them materially and freed them for lives of service to the state, the freedoms that they lost were no less consequential. For even as their European counterparts gained liberties vis-à-vis the crown that were vital to future political and economic development, the

Russian nobility was now bound to the autocracy no less than the peasants were to the soil.

The intent of Peter's reforms was not to create slaves but rather to transform his nobility from an uncultured, hedonistic, inward-looking class into a modern, educated, dynamic estate dedicated to uplifting Russia. But a by-product of that transformation was a growing cleavage between this increasingly "European" elite and the traditional, xenophobic peasant masses. As the former changed, the latter increasingly regarded them as an "alien race" of "foreigners" in their own land.[6] Still, Peter's concern was with the elite, and here his success in remaking their outlook and ethos was great. So great, in fact, that exactly a century later it was the nobility pushing the autocracy toward further Europeanization.

The Napoleonic Wars brought more Russians into prolonged, intimate contact with Europe than ever before. For some—the long-suffering peasants and footsoldiers—the main impact was to reinforce their traditional xenophobia.[7] But others—the officers who occupied Paris—were impressed by the contrast between its freedoms and prosperity and the "bestiality and arbitrariness" that greeted them at home. Some of them, the "Decembrists," rebelled in 1825.[8] In the near term, their revolt brought only more repression under "Iron Tsar" Nicholas I (1825–55). But it also heralded growing opinion for change inspired by European examples.[9] By the end of Nicholas's reign, these pressures together with Russia's problems had grown so overwhelming that his successor, Alexander II, launched a series of "Great Reforms" that included the abolition of serfdom. The proximate cause may have been defeat in the Crimean War (and fear of peasant revolt). But Western influence was felt in equally powerful if more indirect ways. For example, serfdom had become the shame of most educated Russians, while European models were the inspiration for decades of quiet study that preceded Alexander's legal, military, and other reforms.[10]

But with the autocracy essentially unchanged and socioeconomic progress still lagging, Russia remained apart from a Europe that had become the critical reference point of a growing intelligentsia. For some of them—the Westernizers—Russia's proper path was clear.

> In Europe, in most civilized countries, institutions have developed by stages; everything that exists there has its sources and roots in the past; the Middle Ages still serve, more or less, as the basis of everything that constitutes the social, civic and political life of the European states. Russia had no Middle Ages; everything that is to prosper there must be borrowed from abroad.[11]

For others—the Slavophiles—further Europeanization could only harm Russia's unique civilization. "In the foundation of the Western state: violence, slavery and hostility. In the foundation of the Russian state: free will, liberty and peace."[12] The Slavophiles drew a sharp contrast between the spiritual-collectivist-Christian East and the materialist-individualist-atheist West.

Despite their antithetical goals for Russia, as social-political thinkers the two groups had much in common. The Slavophiles, European-educated and cultured, were in many ways no less "Westernized" than the Westernizers. Both sought to reform Russia's stifling autocracy. Both rethought fundamental aspects of their programs as utopian dreams collided with the harsh realities of Russia's domestic and foreign situation. And, especially toward the end of the nineteenth century, both exhibited a common political culture marked by intolerance and extremism.

Fundamental elements of Slavophilism were indeed borrowed from European, primarily German, thinkers, from the idea of the "organic" nation to reverence for the traditional peasant commune.[13] The latter, Westernizer critics charged, falsely idealized a pre-Petrine rural harmony. Even more harshly criticized was the attempt to make a virtue of Russia's backwardness quite out of touch with Russia's real socioeconomic problems and possibilities. Some of these charges were borne out in the 1870s, when the Populists, "Slavophiles in rebellion," went directly to the people in seeking to inspire a kind of pastoral semisocialism. The movement failed, and the unkindest cut—more painful than police repression—was that the peasants themselves rejected the "repentant nobles" who sought to enlighten them.

Later Slavophilism seemed to lose its bearings. Partly in reaction to Russia's foreign woes—from the Crimean debacle (1853–55) and revolt in Poland (1863) to the diplomatic defeat that followed military victory in the Balkans (1878)—the West now seemed to threaten more than just spiritual infection.

> In the future Europe will be divided into two camps: on one side Russia, with all Orthodox, Slavic tribes (not excluding Greece), on the other—the entire Protestant, Catholic, and even Muhammadan and Jewish Europe put together. Therefore Russia must care only about the strengthening of its own Orthodox-Slavic camp.[14]

Into this increasingly Manichaean view of international politics, there now entered a conspiratorial outlook: "It is high time for Russian diplomacy to become finally convinced that everything that is happening in Europe is nothing but a plot against us, against the natural moral and political influence of Russia on the Balkan peninsula, against its most legitimate claims and interests."[15] In this way, Slavophilism approached Pan-Slavism, a movement whose late-nineteenth-century rise coincided with a surge of xenophobia and anti-Semitism in Russia. Nikolai Danilevsky wrote that for Russia to follow Europe would be "contrary to all history [and to] the internal consciousness and strivings of her people."[16] But where early Slavophiles preached a *universalistic* messianism—Europe would eventually join Russia on the one, true path—Danilevsky saw the Slavs as a distinct "cultural-historical type" with a *separate* destiny. Many Slavophiles also now embraced the Pan-Slav goal of an expansionist foreign policy.[17]

Simultaneously, the views of many Westernizers were also in flux. Dostoevsky, once an ardent admirer of Europe, came to foresee an apocalyptic clash following which "there will remain on the continent but one colossus. . . . The future of Europe belongs to Russia."[18] Beyond the collision of imperial interests, close encounters with European life were often disillusioning because "it was more the imaginary West than the real West that they admired."[19] Such was the case with the early Westernizer Alexander Herzen, who, in European exile, grew disgusted by petty bourgeois attitudes under which "the ideal of the knight was altered into the ideal of the small shopkeeper."[20] Peter's opening to the West, which Herzen once hailed, he later described as "a civilization that had been ordered from abroad and bore upon it a German trademark."[21] This distaste for European materialism and individualism—the founda-

tion of the liberties and prosperity that they sought for Russia—echoed through much of later Westernizer thought, culminating in the early-twentieth-century views of the *Vekhi* (Signposts) group of political philosophers. Peter Struve judged bourgeois democracy deeply flawed, while Nikolai Berdyaev argued that capitalism "dehumanizes human life, turns man into . . . an article of merchandise."[22] Thus, in their search for a "more Russian" path of development, many Westernizers took a large step toward the Slavophile outlook.

In large part, as the *Vekhi* authors themselves argued, the evolution of both currents was explained by a common intellectual culture of intolerance and extremism: "The Russian elite tended to convert Western ideas and notions into absolutes whose validity was not to be questioned."[23] As Berdyaev later wrote,

> What was scientific theory in the West, a hypothesis or in any case a relative truth, partial, making no claim to be universal, became among the Russian intelligentsia a dogma, a sort of religious revelation. Russians are always inclined to take things in a totalitarian sense; the skeptical criticism of Western peoples is alien to them.[24]

The liberalism that tolerated private greed for public good, or venal governance for the sake of political stability, was anathema to those engaged in "a passionate search for ethical ideals."[25] The "down-to-earth, non-spiritual way of life revolts the Russian intellectual," who is chiefly distinguished by his "otherworldliness, his eschatological dream about . . . a coming kingdom of justice."[26]

By the 1890s, some believed that such a society could be created only through Marxism, and educated youth were "universally absorbed" in the new philosophy.[27] While backward, semifeudal Russia was a poor candidate for proletarian revolution, many were drawn to Marxism's "Europeanness," its appearance as a radical successor to Westernism (as Populism had been a radical offshoot of Slavophilism). Marxism *was* Western thought, and Russian Social Democrats certainly saw themselves as scientific, progressive, Western thinkers.[28] But Marxism's rise in Russia can be fully understood only in light of certain non- or anti-Western characteristics of the intelligentsia's political culture.

Some, paradoxically, were attracted to Marxism because of its portrayal of capitalist horrors that they hoped Russia could escape.[29] Its scorn for bourgeois society and "philistine" values, and its messianic promise to overturn the world for a radiant future, were also appealing. Neither early socialism nor Western liberalism offered the utopian sweep so attractive to "the characteristically Russian search for an integral outlook which will give an answer to all the questions of life."[30] But even if sharing this cultural affinity for the new philosophy, Russia's Marxists also had serious differences. And it is in viewing these differences that the greater complexity of Russian Marxism's relationship with the West is revealed.

Europe-oriented Marxists, of primarily Menshevik affiliation, were surprised by Bolshevik leader Vladimir Lenin's praise of the early Populists and his messianic claim that, by deposing the tsar, backward Russia would leap to the head of the world proletariat, Asian *and* European.[31] With Lenin's focus on heroic individuals, a "vanguard party," and the necessity of accelerating the historical process, more orthodox Marxists found his variant a perversion. Already in 1909, *Vekhi* author Semyon Frank noted that in Bolshevism the "all-consuming populist spirit has swallowed up and assimilated Marxist theory."[32]

This cleavage is seen by contrasting the views of Lenin and Georgy Plekhanov, the "father of Russian Marxism." While Plekhanov had only contempt for the reactionary peasants—and saw the village commune revered by the Slavophiles not as primitive socialism but the bulwark of "Asiatic despotism"—Lenin rated the peasantry highly as revolutionary allies. Where Plekhanov stood for cooperation with Western-oriented liberals, Lenin detested and rejected them. And while Plekhanov unapologetically argued that Russia needed much more "Westernization" before the precondi-tions of socialism would be achieved, Lenin worked tirelessly to accelerate revolution. Such "Jacobin" impulses, Plekhanov warned, would lead to a despotic "Peruvian socialism." Bolshevism, said Plekhanov's Menshevik ally Yuli Martov, was something "Asiatic."[33]

Lenin split irrevocably with most European Social Democrats when they supported their countries' efforts in World War I. In *State and Revolution*—which elaborated a rationale for taking power and establishing a proletarian dictatorship—Lenin excoriated them as "traitors" and "lackies of the bourgeoisie," guilty of "selling their birthright for a mess of pottage."[34] In *Imperialism: The Highest Stage of Capitalism*, Lenin attacked the resurgence of European national-ism and called for international workers' solidarity. But in so doing,

he also laid the foundation for the later "two-camp" worldview; while Marx had seen capitalism as promoting international stability, Lenin held that it was necessarily imperialist, with war inevitably growing out of the struggle over markets and resources.[35]

Russia was changing rapidly in the twilight of the old regime: economic growth accelerated; the autocracy granted a parliament and rudimentary constitution; and even the peasants' world of poverty and ignorance began changing with efforts to break down the old communal structures and create a class of independent farmers. These years saw "the most enthusiastic and unqualified Westernism in Russia's history," whose economic representative was a growing middle class and whose political supporters were the liberal Cadets (Constitutional Democrats).[36] Many believe that Russia had now decisively embarked on the European path of development, a path that promised success had World War I not intervened.

But "enthusiastic Westernizers" were still a small minority atop an impoverished working class and angry peasantry. Much of the intelligentsia, too, was skeptical of European models, and felt a deep foreboding about Russia's future. Influenced by the apocalyptic views of religious philosopher (and political Westernizer) Vladimir Solovyev, for example, the "Scythian" writers emphasized Russia's Asian identity—savage and chaotic—in confrontation with Europe.[37]

> You're millions. We're hordes and hordes and hordes.
> Just you try and fight with us!
> Yes, we're Scythians! Yes, we're Asiatics!
> With slant and greedy eyes![38]

In the coming decades, the tumult of revolution and war together with the mistakes, compromises, and ambitions of the country's new leaders would bring Russia's "Asiatic" heritage to the fore and sweep away a still-fragile Westernism.

International and National in Revolution and War

Although the most "national" of Russian Social Democrats, the Bolsheviks were still dedicated Marxists whose horizons remained broadly international. The collapse of the old order was the spark that would set Europe aflame, and the building of socialism would be a worldwide enterprise. Their faith in European revolution was so strong that little thought was given to how a socialist state might interact with capitalist neighbors. Leon Trotsky, the first Bolshevik commissar of foreign affairs, reflected this optimism in his comment that "all there is to do here is to publish the secret treaties. Then I will close the shop."[39]

But instead of revolution abroad, war came at home. With Russia's collapse, Germany occupied Ukraine and threatened the heart of the new Soviet state. Then in early 1918, even as the Bolsheviks swallowed the bitter Brest peace, there began a civil war that would last three bloody years and include the Western allies' intervention. And even as civil war raged, another foreign conflict—with Poland—further threatened the new regime.

It was during this time, as the Bolsheviks doubted their very survival, that the first precepts of Soviet international relations theory were enunciated. Their state suffered in a "hostile capitalist encirclement," a hostility that Lenin's *Imperialism* had explained was inherent in capitalism and so made long-term coexistence "unthinkable."[40] And while official policy could shift rapidly—from confrontation to "peaceful coexistence" abroad, and from harsh "War Communism" to the liberal New Economic Policy (NEP) at home—the years of revolution and war left a deep impression. In many Party and intellectual quarters, Marxist internationalism was supplanted by an increasingly anti-Western Russian nationalism.

While Lenin's Marxism did draw on various traditions of Russian radicalism, he was nevertheless a confirmed internationalist; chauvinism was "alien to Lenin's makeup."[41] Save the legacy of Russia's early revolutionaries, he found little to admire in a history of oppression and backwardness. The old empire was a "prison of nations" whom Lenin promised self-determination.[42] And while deposing the tsar would propel Russia into "the vanguard of the world proletariat," this would be only temporary; socialism's success in Russia was "unthinkable" without aid from revolution in Europe.[43]

Stalin, even before the revolution, offered a different view. It could be Russia that "blazes the trail to socialism" and "the outworn idea that Europe alone can show us the way" should be discarded.[44] After October, such views were echoed by other top

Bolsheviks. Mikhail Pokrovsky claimed that Russian workers—superior to the English or Germans—had made Moscow a "Mecca" for other nations.[45] In conflict with White and later Polish armies, "Rally around Russia" drowned out proletarian solidarity in the Bolshevik lexicon. The memory of 1812 was invoked as the regime sought support through an unabashed appeal to Russian national pride. And as the wars were won, historical parallels were proudly drawn; Pokrovsky and Mikhail Kalinin compared Lenin to Peter the Great, while Karl Radek argued that "our Civil War was always national, it was a regathering of Russian lands."[46]

Radek's was an allusion to Ivan Kalita's fourteenth-century "gathering of lands" that had forged the early Muscovite state. In the event, the Bolsheviks "regathered" not only Russia proper but most of the old empire as well. Here, in subjugating the non-Russian periphery, latent national-imperial attitudes were revealed. Pokrovsky wept upon learning that the Brest peace would leave Ukraine under its own national government.[47] The criticism that greeted Lenin's decision not to fight to keep Finland was parodied by Lenin himself: "Those were good fisheries and you gave them up!" "Scratch certain communists," he added, "and you find a Great Russian Chauvinist."[48] Nikolai Bukharin argued that self-determination was fine for Hottentots, Bushmen, Negroes and Hindus," but not for the Finnish or Polish bourgeoisie.[49] Lenin, recognizing Russia's weakness, counseled patience: "We shall conquer power, wait awhile, and then go as far as you want."[50]

Still, Lenin and Bukharin were probably the least nationalistic of the Bolsheviks. For them, it was not a matter of rebuilding the Russian empire but of liberating others from bourgeois oppression. But for those charged with extending Soviet power to the periphery—exporting a *Russian* revolution to non-Russian lands—the distinction was easily lost.[51] Their task was huge: creating proletarian rule where there was no proletariat, and establishing a Bolshevik regime where the Party had minimal support at best and where cadres even had to be imported from Moscow.[52]

Not surprisingly, nationalism came to the fore. Many Bolsheviks continued the tsarist practice of identifying peoples as Russians or *inorodtsy* ("other races" or "peoples").[53] Most regarded the new "federation" as a Russian (*Rossiiskoe*) state, like the old empire, and some even noted the parallel with approval; Sergo Ordzhonikidze, criticized for his heavy-handed treatment of national minorities, argued that "even obtuse Russian tsarism" understood the need for a strong central administration.[54] National hubris did serve a tactical purpose as patriotism was used to rally popular support; we must be "national," argued Anatoly Lunacharsky, or risk appearing as "a band of conquerors in a foreign country." But more than just tactics was behind Lunacharsky's exuberant claim that Dostoevsky had been "a Russian national prophet" who correctly foresaw that Russia was to be "the liberator of all humanity."[55]

In early 1918, Maxim Gorky lamented the rise of "Moscow Neo-Slavophilism" and criticized Bolshevik policy as "profoundly national" for glorifying backward, barbaric Russia while turning away from advanced, cultured Europe.[56] "Neo-Slavophilism" was widespread among the cultural elite as writers of diverse perspectives celebrated various anti-Western, imperial, and messianic themes. The avant-garde Left of poet Vladimir Mayakovsky rejoiced in revolutionary destruction and joyfully anticipated building a new world. As for Russia's neighbors, Mayakovsky predicted the following: "The Germans will look on in confusion at the Russian banner flapping in the Berlin sky while the Turkish sultan will see the day on which the Russian shield will be glimpsed over the gates of Constantinople."[57] Boris Pilnyak extolled the revolution not for its promise of a new future but as a return to Russia's pre-Petrine past, for its elemental peasant fury and rejection of decadent Europe. He and other "Scythian" writers celebrated Russia's Asian heritage, "a whirlwind that will overwhelm the old West."[58] These writers were close to the "Eurasian" historical-cultural school that rejected "kowtowing before Europe" and viewed Bolshevism positively as a product of Russia's Asian half.[59]

Writers such as Gorky, sympathetic to the revolution but firmly oriented toward Europe, worried that the new Bolshevik culture was "organically tied to . . . Russian prerevolutionary culture."[60] But others, less concerned about cultural life than that of the state, saw a different sort of continuity, and hailed it. Poet Valery Briusov wrote, "This ancient space is once more closed up under a common banner."[61] Such views were reflected in the *Smena vekh* (Change of Signposts) movement launched by a 1921 symposium of emigré writers who urged the old intelligentsia, Cadets, and former Whites to support the new regime in rebuilding Russia.[62] Rather than a destructive alien ideology, Bolshevism was now seen as a deeply national movement that was restoring a mighty imperial state.[63] Nikolai Ustrialov, the *Smena vekh* leader, wrote that Russia must be "powerful, great, and frightful to her enemies. The rest will follow of itself."[64] Others saw Bolshevism working toward Russia's "historical objectives—the advance to the Bosporus, hegemony among the Slavs, pressure on India . . . the cleaving of new roads to the open sea."[65]

This celebration of imperial revival—not Mayakovsky's passion for revolution nor Pilnyak's longing for old Russia—drew far-Right support for the Bolsheviks. *Vekhi* author Sergei Bulgakov noted that for reactionaries, "the very thought of a Cadetized [liberal-democratic] Russia is abominable . . . the Bolsheviks are better."[66] Cadet leader Pavel Miliukov wrote that "two extremes, the Red and the Black, came together and seemed to understand each other better than their opponents from the moderate center."[67] Lenin himself confirmed the impact of these right-wing currents at the 11th Party Congress in 1922: "We must say frankly that the things Ustrialov speaks about are possible. History knows all kinds of metamorphoses. *Smenavekhites* echo the sentiments of [the many officials] who manage our New Economic Policy. This is the real and main danger."[68] While Lenin was stressing the danger of NEP's degenerating into capitalism, others at the congress worried more about a revival of Russian chauvinism. Ukrainian Mykola Skrypnik argued that *Smenavekhites* in the government behaved as if the new Soviet state were simply "Russia, One and Indivisible."[69]

Smena vekh also profited from official encouragement and even support. In the early 1920s, many of its prominent emigrés returned to sow their views on fertile soil. *Smena vekh* writings were subsidized, imported, and distributed by the Party, whose bureaus were often among the subscribers.[70] And in their own speeches and editorials, the Bolsheviks found much to praise. Lunacharsky hailed the "knights of *Smena vekh*," former Whites who "took arms against us because they saw us as the ruiners of Russia," but who now realize that Bolshevism "serves the interests of Russia as a great power."[71]

By their 12th congress in 1923, resurgent Russian nationalism had become a burning question for the Bolsheviks. Delegates from Georgia, Ukraine, and Turkestan protested policies of "Russification" and "colonization."[72] They accused the Kremlin of ignoring local party bodies, denigrating national customs and languages, and building center-periphery ties that resembled imperial exploitation.[73] "Young Russian comrades," sent by Moscow, ran roughshod over local cadres and behaved like "tsarist gendarmes."[74] As Lenin saw it, the problem was that "Great-power prejudices, imbibed along with their mothers' milk, were instinctive for many." But the Party was also at fault for encouraging "former tsarist officials" whose imperial attitudes influenced "Soviet workers who do not understand the national question."[75] Stalin, too, gave a report critical of chauvinism, noting that "*Smenavekhism* has gained a mass of supporters" and that "creeping" chauvinism was changing "the spirit, the very soul, of our [Party] workers."[76]

Stalin's congress report, though accurate, was hardly sincere.[77] As nationalities commissar, he had been responsible for some of the worst abuse of non-Russians.[78] And now as the Party's general secretary, said Skrypnik, "Stalin is implanting *Smena vekh's* 'one and indivisible' yearnings in our apparatus." If Stalin prevaricated, others did not in describing a Russian "Gulliver with the Lilliputians—Armenians, Georgians, Muslims, Azerbaijanis—all underfoot."[79] A majority of delegates agreed; Bukharin noted that when Russian chauvinism was faulted, the hall was "nearly silent," but when the national minorities were criticized, "thunderous applause rang out."[80]

Bowing to Lenin's authority, the congress passed a resolution against chauvinism. But little changed in practice. Instead, especially after Lenin's death in 1924, the Russian national line in political-intellectual life grew stronger. In history, "a totally new and Russocentric genealogy emerged."[81] Literature, too, was soon "howling in a 'genuine Russian' fashion," lamented Bukharin.[82] Minority Communists who protested Russian chauvinism were demoted, expelled, or even arrested for "nationalist deviations."

Outwardly, this was a time of calm and progress. The NEP economy was recovering strongly and relations with the West were improving. But the changes described above had troubling implications for the future. As Grigory Zinoviev warned,

> Great-Russian chauvinism . . . is backed up by 300 years of monarchy and imperialistic policies, tsarist policies, the entire foreign policy of tsarism. . . . When you are showered with compliments from the camp of the Smenavekhites, who say: "Yes, we're for the Comintern, because the Comintern does the bidding of the

Kremlin and puts into practice the idea of Russia, One and Indivisible" . . . that is dangerous.[83]

Lenin, too, had worried that "the infinitesimal percentage of . . . sovietized workers will drown in that tide of chauvinistic Great-Russian riffraff like a fly in milk."[84]

In fact, the danger was even greater. The old attitudes alone portended a return to the earlier empire: chauvinistic, somewhat expansionist, but not intrinsically anti-Western. Most purveyors of old-regime beliefs were educated elites who saw Russia as part of Europe.[85] But the new "sovietised workers" were tempered by no such Westernization. Ill-educated, xenophobic, and militant, they had emerged from the bitter crucible of war—with capitalist aggressors abroad and class enemies at home. And the danger was no longer that they would "drown in the tide of chauvinsim," for their ranks so swelled, especially after Lenin's death, that they became a tide in themselves. Rather, it was that the two would merge, joining the most militant and xenophobic element in Bolshevism with the most chauvinistic and illiberal strain of traditional imperialism—the "red and the black"—in a more powerful and dangerous new current.

Forging a New Bolshevik Elite

In early 1927, noting the Faustian bargain that the Bolsheviks had earlier struck with Russian nationalism, Bukharin warned:

> Smenavekhism's "National Russian" aspect was . . . a bridge that enabled a part of the bourgeois intelligentsia to be reconciled with the Soviet system system. . . . That we Bolsheviks had gathered Russia together in the fashion of Ivan Kalita was regarded in a positive light by the Smenavekhites. We tried to use them, direct them, lead them. . . . However, it happens that . . . the steering wheel is slipping from our hands.[86]

Political control was not the issue, for the Party's command was firm. Neither was the restoration of capitalism Bukharin's main concern, for he himself was now the main exponent of NEP. Rather it was the return of old attitudes and beliefs. As Lenin observed, "a vanquished nation imposes its culture upon the conqueror."[87] A duel of cultures was now under way, one fought over the central issue of how the new Soviet state was understood—its relation to the old empire, and its place in the world.

> For the old *intelligentsia* who offered their services to the regime, it was a natural continuation of old Russia. For the overwhelming *masses* of people who did not accept the new ideology or adopted it only superficially . . . the new state was likewise . . . simply the Russian empire under a new sign.[88]

But the Russia of the intelligentsia was very different from that of the masses. And the attitudes of the latter, by dint of sheer numbers, were a growing force in the Party. These "half-peasants, half-workers [brought with them] a bunch of rural . . . prejudices."[89] Most worrisome to those still faithful to Marxism's internationalist heritage, these prejudices included "a xenophobic attitude toward neighboring ethnic groups and foreign nations."[90] As early as 1922, Zinoviev noted that the new members' impact was "more and more apparent in the countryside, at provincial conferences, and now . . . even at party congresses."[91] And as the Party swelled, its ethos was increasingly marked by anti-Westernism and anti-intellectualism.[92] Unlike "bourgeois" nationalists, the new members had few ties to Europe or Russia's complex intellectual traditions. And unlike the Bolshevik elite minority, the unsophisticated new majority partook little of NEP high culture and its burgeoning ties to progressive Western currents. Instead, their essential outlook was formed in the separate world of old peasant Russia.[93]

The new Party members' "animalistic nationalism" was only heightened in the civil war.[94] Whether seen as a triumphant trial by fire that the Bolsheviks had always sought, or as a tragedy that derailed the peaceful construction of socialism, the changes it wrought were decisive.[95] By 1921, "the archetypal Communist was no longer a shabbily dressed intellectual, but rather a leather-jacketed commissar with a Mauser at his hip . . . poorly educated, theoretically unsophisticated, direct, resourceful, often brutal."[96]

How did this commissar view the world? The Party's patriotic wartime themes were broadly compatible with his Russocentrism and xenophobia, the symbiosis of which is seen in the impact of wartime propaganda. The civil war was depicted not as a struggle between opposing groups of Russians, but mainly as an outside attempt to unseat a popular national government. Russia was suffering a foreign invasion, and the Whites were little more than pawns of the entente.[97]

Many who began Party careers at this time saw that "our country was being attacked from all sides,"[98] that the danger of a foreign-based "counter-revolutionary coup, about which Soviet propaganda trumpeted every day, seemed a reality,"[99] and that war was "thrust on us by the bourgeoisie, our own [and that of] the world at large, which was instigating counterrevolution and intervention against us."[100] As for the Polish war, it was depicted as the " 'Third Campaign of the Entente,' and that Poland concerted its actions with the White generals in order to restore tsarism."[101] Famine, too, was thrust upon Russia: "If it weren't for the cursed Allies and the blockade, we'd have food enough for all."[102] And when the Kronstadt sailors rose up in 1921—with the civil war won and foreign intervention past—it was still labeled a "White conspiracy," and Bolshevik propaganda trumpeted "fiendish calumny," that blamed the revolt on capitalist intrigue.[103]

Similarly, failed revolutions in Germany and Hungary were "betrayals" that further eroded a thin internationalist veneer to reveal a powerful anti-Western Russian nationalism beneath.[104] Altogether, the pervasive imagery of "hidden enemies, saboteurs [and] spies" fostered the "triumph of a new mentality."[105] An observer recalled the outlook of a typical new Party official "from the masses": "Revolution can only conquer by the generous use of the sword . . . morality and sentiment are bourgeois superstitions. His conception of Socialism is puerile; his information of the world at large of the scantiest. His arguments echo the familiar editorials of the official press."[106]

By 1921, these new members "from the masses" made up a majority of the Party. And while many were soon purged, their numbers rose even more sharply in the "Leninist levy" that followed the leader's death in 1924.[107] Their "puerile" views of socialism, "warfare" ethos, and crude anti-Westernism changed the Bolshevik Party radically. These "Genghis Khans with telephones" were often not only opponents of NEP and supporters of War Communist methods, but also receptive to the imagery of "internal and external enemies" that later justified a much harsher antiforeign turn.[108] And it was during the relative calm of the 1920s that they received the education and training that constituted the third key element—beyond their native "rural prejudices" and subsequent experience of civil war—in shaping the outlook and identity of a new elite.

The possibilities of this education were already limited by what had occurred during the revolution and after, when Russia's liberal-Westernizing tradition suffered a severe blow. The flower of the intelligentsia was mostly opposed to the Bolsheviks, and many emigrated; others supported the Whites and, with their defeat and flight, also found themselves abroad. Thousands also perished, some from privation and disease, others in the Red Terror. Scientists, scholars, lawyers, and engineers suffered disproportionately for their class origins. The Bolsheviks soon eased their hostile stance toward those bourgeois professionals who remained because their skills were badly needed. But then and after, the leeway permitted the chauvinist-imperial segment of the old elite was far greater than that allowed its liberal-democratic elements. In 1922, even as the "knights of *Smena vekh*" were returning, some 150 prominent writers, philosophers, lawyers, and other professionals were deported.[109] At one stroke, the Bolsheviks got rid of their most serious liberal critics and sent a chill through those who remained.

The NEP period has been described as the "golden age of Soviet science."[110] Although largely true in the natural sciences, for the humanities and social sciences it was a time of increasing intimidation and loss of intellectual freedom. The wartime ban on the non-Bolshevik press was relaxed, but mainly to permit views neutral or sympathetic to the regime.[111] *Glavlit*, the censorship organ set up in 1922, began imposing strict controls in 1925.[112] Non-Marxist societies in fields such as psychology and economics were banned. University teaching of sociology and history was brought under tight control.[113] And the Academy of Sciences, under fire for its "foreign" orientation, suffered a loss of international contacts and a drain of talent abroad.[114]

Non-Bolshevik scholars were also attacked by militant *Komsomol* groups who objected to the remaining "bourgeois" content of their lessons as well as to the nonproletariat element in teaching faculties and student bodies.[115] In response, thousands of teachers were fired and tens of thousands of students expelled solely on the basis of class. At the same time, admissions practices were changed to increase the percentage of proletarian students while reducing those of bourgeois origin.[116]

In tracing the fate of Russia's Westernizing tradition, this purge of "socially alien" elements is critical. The Bolsheviks meant to forge a new intelligentsia, and even the small tolerance shown the old one was to be only temporary. Lenin defended "bourgeois specialists" against their most radical critics, for the proletariat still had many skills to learn from their former masters.[117] But this reflected no affection for the old intelligentsia; on the contrary, Lenin once cursed the "lackeys of capital who fancy themselves the nation's brain. In fact they are not the brain but the shit."[118] They would be tolerated only so long as they abjured politics, and even then only until a new "proletarian intelligentsia" was ready to replace them.

To hasten this, the Bolsheviks did more than just favor the proletariat in access to higher education. *Rabfaki* (workers' faculties) were created, offering poorly prepared students a crash catch-up course, as adjuncts to most institutes.[119] Trade schools were opened, and *politgramota* (Marxist-Leninist "political literacy") was taught through a broad network of Party organs. The worldview cultivated in all this training was harsh and anti-Western.

"Everyone who joined the Party learned Marxist-Leninist science by studying Bukharin's . . . *The ABC of Communism*," recalled one graduate of political training during the 1920s.[120] Written by Bukharin and Yevgeny Preobrazhensky as a popular version of the 1918 Party program, *The ABC of Communism* was the most widely read political work in Soviet Russia. Reflecting the harsh War Communist ethos, it offered Marxism in a nutshell, a ruthless domestic program, and a chilling world outlook. Peaceful coexistence? "We might just as well hope by petting a tiger to persuade the animal to live upon grass and to leave cattle alone . . . capitalism cannot exist without a policy of conquest, spoilation, violence and war."[121] America, led by the "trickster Wilson," heads a "robber alliance" known as the League of Nations [sic]. "Its agents blow up bridges, throw bombs at communists. . . . The imperialists of the whole world hurled their forces against the Russian proletariat."[122]

Another veteran of 1920s training recalled the day a Party official admitted him to the Komsomol (the Communist Youth League):

> He gave me *The ABC of Communism*, by Nikolai Bukharin, and told me: "This contains all the wisdom of humanity. You must study it from cover to cover." I read the book through in several days and began to study it with the group. The simplicity of its concepts shocked me. . . . We received [its] ideas enthusiastically. . . . To put the manifesto into practice we would sacrifice everything, even our lives.[123]

This epiphany took place in 1922, a year *after* the Party, and Bukharin in particular, had embraced NEP at home and coexistence abroad. In fact, at this time *The ABC* was still gaining influence. Its strident view of capitalism's hostility and unremitting aggression would eventually see 18 Russian editions; it became the "Bible of Communism" for millions, enduring well into the 1930s.[124]

Similar views were cultivated in higher education—including the military and industrial academies—though the level of knowledge and sophistication was considerably higher at a few institutions such as the Communist Academy and the Institute of Red Professors. There, students were taught by leading Party intellectuals, such as Pokrovsky, and they also produced major research works—some of significant quality, but much highly slanted and crudely anti-Western.[125] At these elite institutes, Bukharin and his NEP-oriented *Historical Materialism* (1921) attracted many students,[126] though they, too, struggled with "a political culture . . . of polemic and purge" that quickly transformed their schools into the "intellectual equivalent of an armed camp."[127] At most other institutions, Stalin's *Foundations of Leninism* (1924) was more widely read, and his thinly disguised chauvinism and view of "politics as combat" were far more popular.[128]

In general, a majority of the new Bolsheviks were less influenced by NEP's brief intellectual-cultural revival than by the synthesis of old Russian nationalism and new anti-Westernism so prominent in their experience of the early-to-mid 1920s. A striking example of this symbiosis is seen in a lecture, given by a former tsarist general, at the Soviet General Staff College. Since Peter the Great, he argued,

> the Russian empire has been irresistibly drawn toward . . . the Indian Ocean. And Russian expansion . . . has always been blocked by the British. [We fought] in Persia and Central Asia . . . but the British Empire stood always behind our adversaries. The victories

of Russian armies in the Balkans were frustrated by British intrigue. You will ask why I am telling you this when the revolution has cast out imperialism . . . to liberate oppressed peoples. . . . But the most serious obstacle in the way of this liberation is British imperialism. If we want to give the peoples of Asia their freedom, we have to break the power of British imperialism. It is still our deadliest enemy.[129]

Enemies, Terror, and the Conspiracy Worldview

By the later 1920s, the decade of the moderate NEP, this deadly enemy was the capitalist power whose good graces—and economic investment—the Foreign Commissariat most assiduously sought. More important than a turn in policy, however, was a change in the political climate, and consequent expectations and outlook, of many in the Party. By 1927, a decade since the revolution and seven years since the end of the civil war, the attitudes born of that era had moderated with time and the intervening calm in foreign and domestic life.

The earlier beliefs were hardly gone. On the contrary, for many the "military-heroic" epoch remained their defining experience. Moreover, the view of a divided world, with capitalism's inherent aggression making indefinite coexistence impossible, remained the official ideology—written, broadcast, and taught. Just as NEP (whatever its successes) remained ideologically tenuous because its capitalistic aspects clashed with so many fundamental beliefs and so much painful experience, so, too, did peaceful coexistence. Still, the salience of these contradiction eased with the years of foreign calm and domestic progress.

The *vydvizhentsy*, the new generation now occupying the Party's middle- and upper-middle ranks, were focused mainly on NEP's domestic priorities.[130] Though their experience rendered them of two political mindsets, continued calm portended further deradicalization. But when this calm ended, the old attitudes quickly resurfaced and helped decide a leadership struggle in favor of the contender—Stalin—who best exploited latent Russian-national, antiforeign attitudes. And under Stalin's terror, the subsequent decade took the hostile-isolationist identity to new heights.

NEP's (and Bukharin's) immediate problem was a slump in growth, a serious dilemma given the Bolsheviks' shared commitment to swift industrialization. NEP's critics, particularly Trotsky and the "left opposition," had never been reconciled to the restoration of private markets. Now it seemed that these methods could not even deliver rapid development. With their martial spirit, they saw NEP's domestic focus as sacrificing the ultimate goal of world revolution.

So long as Stalin supported NEP, its continuation was not seriously at issue. But even as he stood by Bukharin, Stalin differed on several points whose importance would soon grow. One was his case for the viability of "socialism in one country," which was doctrinally opposite Trotsky's emphasis on world revolution as a necessity for Soviet survival. Another was his stress on foreign threats, a theme that linked domestic and foreign policy via the need for heavy military industrialization.[131] So despite his support of NEP, Stalin was simultaneously stressing a position that—depending on the imminence of a foreign threat—called the long-term possibilities of peaceful coexistence into question. And a threat was already materializing.

In early 1927, the decimation of Chinese Communists was trumpeted by the Left as a revolutionary "betrayal." Worse, the Soviet Union itself was now vulnerable because the fiasco "freed the imperialists' hands for war against the USSR."[132] Shortly thereafter, a sense of real crisis developed following London's severing of relations with Moscow and the assassination of the Soviet ambassador to Poland. While troubling, these events did not stem from any concerted effort by the country's enemies. But this was increasingly the view in Moscow as arguments were heard that "the breathing spell was ending" and "war was inevitable in the near future."[133] There now ensued a "war scare" that would strongly influence the pivotal 15th Party Congress in December 1927.

The war scare sharply changed the political atmosphere and revived fears reminiscent of the civil war era: "hostile capitalist encirclement" soon became the "ever-present background to politics."[134] Even some in the leadership reportedly believed that war was imminent.[135] Many young cadres—the executors of NEP and coexistence policies—once again felt keenly the loss of "revolutionary spirit" and the compromises required for "living on neighborly terms" with capitalism.[136] On the congress's eve, the left opposition (demonstrating their own public support) staged large rallies denouncing betrayal of world revolution.

Both Stalin and Trotsky thus had their constituencies. Both "socialism in one country" and "world revolution" were predicated on a foreign threat.[137] Yet Stalin defeated Trotsky, in part because his stance better reflected the simplistic, Russocentric views of the Party majority. Stalin did not deny that European revolution was ultimately necessary to ensure security; rather he argued that the road to Europe lay through a mighty Russia. Trotsky, in fact, was the enemy of world revolution; his "disbelief" in Russia's ability to build socialism on its own created a "spirit of capitulation" that would "extinguish foreign workers' hope for the victory of socialism in Russia, which would in turn delay the outbreak of revolution in other countries."[138] In this way, Stalin's appeal to latent nationalism scored a "triumph of subtle phrasing and satisfied almost everybody," recalled one observer. His "casuistry covered two different mental attitudes—that of those who believed in a revolutionary international policy and that of those who favored a strategy of withdrawal."[139] But while wooing the former, Stalin clearly emphasized the views of the latter; the choice was between being "an appendage of the future revolution in the West . . . without any independent power" or "an independent power, capable of doing battle against the capitalist world."[140]

Stalin also profited from the "siege mentality" that, while dormant through years of peace, flared anew during the war crisis. Many *vydvizhentsy* suppressed doubts over the political struggles in order to maintain Party unity in the face of a perceived threat; the "forces of counterrevolution" seemed near, and so, "like many others, I supported [Stalin] only because I hoped thus to end the sapping struggle . . . only as a measure necessary to insure the safety of the state."[141] Nikita Khrushchev, a first-time voting delegate at the congress, recalled another view of how the issues appeared to many new provincial elites: "I don't remember exactly what the differences were. . . . Rightists, opportunists, right-leftists, deviationists— these people were all moving in basically the same political direction, and our group was against them."[142] The fantastic belief that various opposition currents were all "basically the same" reflects the ignorance of the new Bolsheviks that played to Stalin's advantage;

so, too, did their fear of Western aggression: "I thought to myself, "Here is a man who knows how to direct our minds and our energies toward the priority goals of industrializing our country and assuring the impregnability of our Homeland's borders against the capitalist world."[143]

Over the years 1928 to 1933, as Stalin now bested Bukharin and NEP yielded to violent collectivization and forced industrialization, struggle with "enemies" became the hallmark of politics. In the *Shakhty* and *Prompartiia* cases, show trials were used to expose the "wrecking" of domestic and foreign plotters. These cases also marked the end of cooperation with bourgeois specialists and the severing of ties abroad.[144] Experts in agriculture, industry, and medicine were accused of sabotage. Entire fields were declared "bourgeois" and their leading figures disgraced. And there followed "an unbelievable display of obscurantism and attacks on anything sophisticated or refined" while "everywhere the status of cranks and militant ignoramuses rose sharply."[145] Just as science had no need of "groveling" before the West, neither had culture and the humanities, and so artists and writers were cut off from foreign ties. The avant-garde in literature and theater suffered as national-patriotic themes rose and Russians became the "first among equals" of the Soviet peoples.

Russocentrism also soared in philosophy and history. Tsars from Ivan the Terrible to Peter the Great were hailed for building a mighty state in struggle with traitors and foreign aggressors, while Marxists from Engels to Pokrovsky were criticized for misunderstanding the progressive role of tsarist imperialism. Tellingly, the recent past, too, was reinterpreted: the civil war even supplanted the October Revolution as Bolshevism's most important "legitimizing" triumph.[146] Leninism was not repudiated, but Stalin's constituency among the *vydvizhentsy* grasped simple historical analogies better than complex Marxist theories about capital or markets. Hence, his infamous 1931 speech to Soviet industrial managers:

> To reduce the tempo is to lag behind. And laggards are beaten. No, we don't want that! The history of old Russia consisted, among other things, in continual beatings for her backwardness. She was beaten by the Mongolian khans. Beaten by the Turkish Beys. Beaten by the Swedish feudals. Beaten by the Polish-Lithuanian nobles. Beaten by the Anglo-French capitalists. Beaten by the Japanese barons. Beaten by them all—for her backwardness.[147]

The themes of "external and internal enemies," and the methods of "exposing" conspiracy, together reached their apogee in the great purge trials of 1936–38. Nearly a decade in rehearsal, show trials were now employed on a grand scale to reveal sinister plots linking political, industrial, and military elites to foreign imperialists. The terror swiftly struck down tens of thousands—and would soon engulf millions—as "the apparently inexplicable turmoil . . . represented a permanent threat to the security of virtually any Soviet citizen."[148] But this turmoil, and the accompanying "frenzy in the Bolshevik mentality," was indeed explicable in the context of the traditional popular culture and especially of those beliefs and fears cultivated since 1917.[149] Among the new industrial workers, subjected to endless "campaigns and mobilizations . . . predicated on emotional appeals against class enemies, both inside and outside the country," the regime fostered a new social (and political) identity in which "the exertions of every worker at the bench were inscribed in an international struggle."[150] The *vydvizhentsy,* too, even more relentlessly propagandized and terrorized, could not help "rationalizing the regime's internal conflicts through the representation of a 'struggle' with 'enemies.' "[151] Like the workers, these future political and academic elites were also a class being created largely ex nihilo, and so their still-malleable identity was shaped by "the unpredictable, incomprehensible, and treacherous daily reality of the system [that] fed perceptions of omnipresent conspiracy."[152]

On the whole, "Stalin engineered the revolution of belief with substantial success."[153] Central to this was "a paranoid political culture, galvanized by themes of external encirclement, internal subversion and pervasive treachery."[154] So deeply ingrained were such attitudes that most arrested innocents saw their cases as isolated "mistakes" that did not undermine broader belief in the existence of nefarious foreign and domestic plots against the USSR. When the terror's scope and contradictions no longer permitted blind belief, equally improbable rationalizations were found.[155] And at its height, Soviet people received what they had lacked since Bukharin's fall: a primer to serve as the new Bolshevik catechism. The *Short Course,* published in 1938, outdid *The ABC* in its demonization of the West and in its portrayal of politics—foreign and domestic—as mortal combat.[156] Its impact was great; Soviet society had by now been "well prepared" for a treatise that "brought the outward speech and inner thought of everyone—from the plumber to the professor—down to one [primitive] level."[157] Naturally, the *Short Course* also revised *The ABC* entirely in its lionization of Stalin.

In fact, Stalin was probably more successful in cementing paranoid, antiforeign beliefs than in canonizing himself. In many accounts, the doubts that persisted more often centered on the Stalinist personality cult than the Stalinist worldview. One survivor recalled that, even after his father's arrest, it was the time of the "brightest hopes of my youth." Though skeptical of Stalin's infallibility, his view of the world was dominated by the fact of a hostile capitalist encirclement: "If we don't fulfill the plan we'll be defenseless, we'll perish, we won't be able to fight if attacked—this was absolutely clear. . . . Stalin stood for rapid industrialization and he achieved it . . . for me, his correctness was beyond question."[158]

As always, ignorance was critical in cultivating such views. "The regime's monopoly on information," in the judgment of a rare survey of popular attitudes during the Stalin era, was central to success in creating a view of "America [and the capitalist West in general] as aggressive and bent on world domination." In most cases there was "complete acceptance of official propaganda with regard to foreign affairs . . . foreign news as put out by the regime is accepted more readily than domestic news, chiefly because the Soviet citizen has a scant basis on which to check the inaccuracy of what he reads about foreign countries."[159] Khrushchev, as one of the new elite, put it more bluntly: "We'd been cut off, we didn't know anything."[160]

Khrushchev's recollections are important not only because he would be Stalin's successor, but because he was a typical member of the *vydvizhentsy* who would dominate official life for 30 years. But they would not reach the top just yet; in the terror, the vacancies they filled were not those of the old Bolsheviks but of a second generation who had worked closely with them. And it was by annihilating these second-echelon leaders that Stalin severed most remaining links to the Party's Western, social-democratic heritage.

This transformation of the elite was repeated in all fields that had any bearing on the world abroad; cultural, scientific, military, and diplomatic circles were ruthlessly purged. As consequential as Bukharin's fall was that of the young "Red Professors" close to him and his views. Similarly, the 1939 dismissal of Foreign Commissar Maxim Litvinov rid Stalin of an advocate of ties to the democratic West (and eased rapprochement with Hitler), but the diplomatic purge that followed served the larger purpose of making room for newcomers ignorant of the world by liquidating Litvinov's "Europeanized" corps.[161]

Despite the many anti-Western aspects of their beliefs, the old generation had been drawn to Marxism by its "Europeanness."

> It came from Europe, blew in from there with the scent of the new, fresh and alluring, not our moldy, homegrown ways. Marxism . . . promised that we would not stay semi-Asiatic but instead . . . become a Western country . . . the West beckoned us. Our group read every history of Western civilization and culture, surveys of foreign life in the thick journals, and painstakingly searched for any traces of a Western current in Russian history.[162]

By contrast, the *vydvizhentsy* came to the 1920s defined by rural prejudices and regime propaganda. NEP had hardly eliminated early beliefs based on xenophobia, nationalism, and War Communist militancy. And Stalinism now raised them to new heights. While their elders, however radical, were products of Petrine-European Russia, the new elite was "reminiscent of the ruling class of Muscovy in the XVI century."[163]

> The Old Bolsheviks . . . were able to modify the distortion [of their propaganda] because of their own education and personal residence abroad. However, the new generation . . . lacked the knowledge and sophistication of their predecessors . . . had little contact with foreigners and foreign societies, and . . . lived in a most rigidly controlled community.[164]

Bukharin, notwithstanding his early radicalism, was always a thoughtful student of Europe. For him and his "Red Professors," the rise of fascism and the destruction of German culture were deeply troubling.[165] For the mass of *vydvizhentsy*, who knew little of Europe and understood only the Stalinist view that all capitalist states were equally hostile, the Nazis' triumph over the Social Democrats mattered little.

The War and After: Opening, and Iron Curtain

Beyond exposing Stalin's tragically erroneous equation of fascism and social democracy, World War II cracked his wall of isolation and gave many Soviet citizens their first glimpses of the outside world in a generation. The very fact of alliance with the democratic West was crucial, far more corrosive of official views than had been the brief and cynical alignment with Hitler; this, after all, was genuine alliance in a life-and-death struggle. Moreover, it brought tangible images that countered the decades of invective. Negative propaganda eased, and even some positive views were permitted. For example, U.S. films were now sometimes shown, to significant effect.[166] Even greater was the impact of lend-lease aid: airplanes, automobiles, foodstuffs, and other goods that conveyed impressions of a land of plenty.[167]

But perhaps most eye-opening were the personal observations of Soviets whom the war brought to Europe—the soldiers who fought to Berlin, and the occupying forces and support personnel who followed.[168] They were "amazed to learn that, over there, it was nothing like what we'd been told for so many years before the war. They lived more dignified, richer, and freer lives than we did."[169]

> The contrast between our standard of living and Europe's, which millions of soldiers had seen, was a moral and psychological blow that wasn't easy to take even though we'd triumphed. . . . Millions of them were telling millions more what they, the victors, had seen there, in Europe.[170]

These soldiers "represented danger number one for the Stalinist regime."[171] And in confronting this danger, Stalin as always was mindful of history. This time the lesson was that of the Decembrist officers who had rebelled against the autocracy after tasting European liberties in the post-Napoleonic occupation of Paris.[172] Stalin had good reason to fear when his agents reported on such private conversations as the following between generals Vasily Grodov and Filipp Rybalchenko:

RYBALCHENKO: Everyone says that there's going to be war.

GRODOV: Those conferences in Paris and America went nowhere. . . .

RYBALCHENKO: It's awful how our prestige is falling . . . nobody's for us.

GRODOV: What's there to do Filipp? . . . Maybe get out of here, go abroad somewhere? . . .

RYBALCHENKO: Before, other countries helped us.

GRODOV: Look at what we've come to! Now they give us nothing. . . .

RYBALCHENKO: There's no chance for better, we're completely isolated.

GRODOV: What we need is real democracy.[173]

These officers were shot, and millions of returning prisoners of war were treated little better. Since, by Stalin's order, falling into enemy hands was treasonous, soldiers not only were driven to fight desperately but were also subject to arrest when they returned from captivity (civilians who had lived, however briefly, under German occupation were also subject to investigation and arrest).[174] Many of these, too, were shot or sentenced to hard labor, but most were later released after passing through brutal "filtering" camps where they were warned: " 'Keep silent. You whiled away your time in captivity on fascist grub.' And they did keep quiet."[175]

But even had they not, a generation of hostile beliefs could not be undone in a few years. Triumph at such a terrible price suppressed many doubts and stirred national-patriotic feelings that were often far from liberal or magnanimous.

> For a long time I remained an incorrigible "Red Imperialist." In my consciousness ripened a symbiosis, highly typical for the period, of Soviet patriotism and Russian nationalism. Perhaps the main proof of Stalin's genius for me were his annexations. After, we got back everything we had lost of the former great Russia, and had added more. We stretched from the Elbe River to the China Sea. They were all real victories, and victors are not judged.[176]

Stalin's authority grew, and for most, even apart from official glorification of his genius, the fact of the surprise German attack itself seemed to confirm his correctness in warning of enemies and forcing spartan five-year plans.[177] For others, "the absence of a second European front until June, 1944, was a primary cause of [the post-Stalin generation's] enduring mistrust of the West."[178] And among the political elite, as Litvinov frankly warned, storm clouds hovered because of "the ideological conception prevailing [in Moscow] that conflict between the communist and capitalist worlds is inevitable."[179]

Perhaps most ordinary Soviets came out of the war with more positive than negative new impressions of the West, together with hope that alliance could continue and contribute to a better life at home. In the event, Stalin quickly dashed these hopes with familiar methods: a return to rigid isolation, a new barrage of hostile propaganda, and the build-up to another round of terror. As before, intellectuals were seen as most dangerous to the control of minds. The creative professions were struck first, with Stalin's henchman Andrei Zhdanov viciously attacking writers Akhmatova and Zoshchenko and composers Shostakovich and Khachaturian.[180] Soon it was "impossible to find a single work of postwar literature where there are not clear or concealed enemies: the black-and-white schemas of those years simply could not exist without them."[181] Such lines as these, from popular writer Konstantin Simonov, were a warning to the naive:

> To many of us it seemed, especially toward the end of the war, that, yes, the last shot will have been heard and everything would change. Of course, in a way, people are right: everything has changed, there is peace, the cannons are silent. . . . But they thought that there would be friends all around for the rest of their life. And all around there are enemies.[182]

A particular threat to the hostile-isolationist worldview came from some specialists in politics and economics. In mid 1945, Petr Fedoseyev, editor of the Party's main theoretical journal *Bolshevik*, wrote that the capitalist world included "peace-loving" states as well as naked imperialists, and that the USSR could make common cause with the former.[183] In 1946, Yevgeny Varga, director of the Moscow Institute of World Economy and World Politics (and a Comintern survivor) began arguing that postwar capitalism could regulate its contradictions and that popular forces in the West could restrain imperialist tendencies.[184]

Such views were permitted a brief latitude because Stalin—at least publicly—sought continuation of the wartime alliance. But his private plans for cementing power in Eastern Europe and hostility toward the West pointed to cold war instead, and ideas such as Varga's were soon under attack. Zhdanov's 1947 address at the founding of the Cominform represented Stalin's "official declaration of permanent cold war against the West."[185] And as that war grew hotter with the Berlin and Korean crises, Stalin had the pretext for an even harsher crackdown at home. There ensued a campaign against "kowtowing" and "servility before the West," and the demonization of all things foreign. "Friends and enemies, they and us, the red and the white, the positive and the negative heroes: this is the basis of our . . . confrontational, mythologized consciousness."[186] "Rationality yielded to emotional aggressiveness in an atmosphere of mass psychosis."[187] A new wave of Russocentrism in philosophy and history surpassed even that of the 1930s. This chauvinism—and its perversion of Marxism—reached record heights in the unlikely field of linguistics, Stalin's latest pastime:

> No one who does not know Russian and cannot read the works of the Russian intellect in the original can call himself a scholar. . . . It may be seen in the history of mankind how . . . the world's languages succeed one another. Latin was the language of antiquity . . . French was the language of feudalism. English became the language of imperialism. And if we look into the future, we see the Russian language emerging as the world language of socialism.[188]

Writers and journalists who praised anything foreign did so at their risk, while scholars who tried to publish abroad or even correspond with foreign colleagues were in peril. Cybernetics, genetics, and other fields were attacked for "idealistic" and "bourgeois-reactionary" trends.[189] The international isolation of Soviet intellectual life was virtually complete.

In 1949, Varga's institute was closed for harboring "no few state criminals and traitors to the motherland," and Varga himself was found guilty of authoring the anti-Leninist idea of "capitalist planning."[190] To correct these errors, Stalin's 1952 *Economic Problems of Socialism in the USSR* made it clear that "inter-imperialist rivalries" remained severe and crisis unavoidable. Capitalism's aggression was untamable, and so war was inevitable. To end this threat, "it is necessary to abolish imperialism [i.e., defeat the West]."[191]

Jews were a particular target, at Varga's institute and throughout the academic world. By 1950, *cosmopolitan* was the official term for things foreign, anti-Russian, and traitorous; unofficially it was a synonym for *Jewish*. In late 1952, the exposure of a "plot" by mainly Jewish doctors to assassinate Soviet leaders signaled a new round of terror. Only Stalin's death in March 1953 halted the planned unmasking of more "internal and external enemies."

■

By most accounts, Stalin's postwar campaign to demonize the West was broadly successful. Even among the best informed, a "majority . . . were deformed by pervasive ideology, propaganda and fear."[192] For those who knew less of the world, Stalin's cold war rationale was not seriously questioned. Physicist Andrei Sakharov recalled the paranoid, militarized atmosphere that caused him and other scientists to be "possessed by a true war psychology" so intense that they shut their eyes to the brutal tableau of convict labor employed on their projects.[193] And even many of those who had glimpsed Western prosperity were still inclined to blame "the machinations of a hostile encirclement" for Soviet backwardness:

> This is what caused such dissatisfaction with the results of the war and resentment of the allies who, it appeared, were solely responsible not only for the growing international tensions (as the initiators of the cold war) but also for our domestic difficulties. And so doubts emerged as to whether the war had really been pursued "to a victorious end" and sometimes you even heard that "It was a mistake, that we didn't crush our 'allies' after taking Berlin. We should have driven them into the English Channel. Then America wouldn't be saber-rattling now."[194]

As confrontation worsened abroad, and hopes for a better life at home were dashed with announcement of a new five-year plan reminiscent of the militant 1930s, "people's attention was successfully distracted from analysis of the real causes of social ills and directed along the false trail of a search for 'enemies.' "[195] Party committees and work collectives resounded with such comments as

> "The peace is over, war is coming, and so of course prices are rising. They're trying to hide it from us, but we know what's what. Prices always go up before a war" . . . "America has broken the peace treaty with Russia, there'll soon be war. They say that the first echelons have already reached Simferopol, that there are wounded. . . ." . . . "I heard that war is already under way in China and Greece, where America and England have intervened. And tomorrow or the next day they'll attack the Soviet Union."[196]

2 ■

Leaders, Society, and Intellectuals
During the Thaw

Decades of political and cultural isolation, the sickness of living in a permanently surrounded "besieged fortress," left their mark. But there began a psychological and ideological liberation from this legacy [and] we started to see the other world not as an inevitable future conquest . . . but as an integral part of our own culture.
—Elena Zubkova, *Obshchestvo i reformy*

It is difficult to imagine how hard it is to crawl out from under the pile of communist dogmas in which you have believed and that have long guided your actions.   —Petro Grigorienko, *Memoirs*

The decade following Stalin's death in 1953—popularly known as the "thaw" era—was a critical turning point in Soviet history. The period of Nikita Khrushchev's rule, through 1964, saw the country's first major liberalizing change in more than 30 years. The long nightmare ended, society's rejuvenation began, and efforts were launched to mitigate Stalin's legacies both at home and abroad.

The defining moment of Khrushchev's leadership was his "secret speech" to the 20th Party Congress in 1956. While the terror had been halted and some positive initial steps taken, Khrushchev's sweeping denunciation of Stalin's crimes now knocked the tyrant from the pedestal he had occupied for an entire generation and paved the way for a more searching reappraisal of his politics. In domestic affairs, this led to freedom and rehabilitation for millions, economic changes to benefit society instead of the militarized state, a cultural rebirth, and considerable truth-telling about Soviet history, politics, and the world.

The 20th congress was also a turning point in foreign policy. Although they had ended the Korean War, managed a tenuous rapprochement with Yugoslavia, and begun diplomatic engagement with the West, Stalin's heirs had not yet permitted any serious reappraisal of the hostile-isolationist "old thinking." But at the congress, Khrushchev took an important step in that direction by formally rejecting the Stalinist thesis of an inevitable, apocalyptic clash with capitalism and embracing instead a philosophy of "peaceful coexistence." In one sense, this was simply a concession to the fact that, in the nuclear era, major war would be so destructive that there could be no victors. But even if born of necessity, peaceful coexistence soon led to a broader engagement with the West that saw significant progress: a climate of real détente, the Limited Test Ban Treaty of 1963, and cuts in the Soviet armed forces. Still, the boldest changes would come only after the nuclear lesson had been relearned—this time not in theory but practice—through the Berlin crisis of 1961 and a trip to the brink of Armageddon over Cuba in 1962.

Change was difficult for several reasons. Psychologically, for leaders raised in revolution and war, and long steeped in the "hostile capitalist encirclement," acceptance of a radically different worldview came only with great difficulty—if at all. Khrushchev's own rethinking was a slow and contradictory process, and he was the boldest of Stalin's successors. Politically, the military-industrial-bureaucratic interests vested in Stalinist policies were very strong. The West, too, was slow to respond to Khrushchev's changes in a way that could have strengthened him vis-à-vis these forces.[1] And doctrinally, peaceful coexistence was still only a first step away from old thinking. It did mean deflating grossly exaggerated threats and ending the extreme demonization of capitalist adversaries. But they remained adversaries, for peaceful coexistence did not touch the bedrock principle of a world divided into antagonistic camps. The rivals could no longer go directly to war, but the international class struggle would continue, and even *intensify*, as they competed and confronted each other diplomatically, economically, and even militarily, in old venues and new ones such as the third world.[2] Thus an important step was taken, but meaningful East-West rapprochement was stymied by the distrust and fear that were so deeply rooted in the hostile-isolationist identity. And so Khrushchev's foreign-policy record was decidedly mixed, with progress toward détente darkened by such actions as the invasion of Hungary as well as the Berlin and Cuban crises.

But this era's importance for Soviet international relations cannot be measured exclusively or even primarily by specific foreign-policy steps. For it was in tandem with the liberalization of domestic life that Khrushchev made his most vital contributions to a broad rethinking of the hostile-isolationist outlook. Intellectual life was dramatically transformed by an awakening of critical thought, study, and debate, one aspect of which was a modest but extremely consequential new opening to the West.

Millions were engaged by the literary-cultural thaw, which encouraged reflection not only on Stalin's domestic abuses but also on the USSR's place in world civilization. Tens of thousands, from students and scholars to diplomats and journalists, were especially stimulated by new critical freedoms and access to diverse ideas and information. And hundreds of intellectuals—historians, writers, economists, scientists, and policy analysts of all stripes—benefited from burgeoning ties abroad and new or rejuvenated research centers at home that now permitted remarkably frank examination of most domestic and foreign issues. In these "elite congregations," encouraged by the broader climate of reform, began the systematic study of international affairs, something that had simply not existed for nearly 30 years.

In the short time of the thaw, much progress was made in intellectual circles toward dismantling old beliefs and laying the foundation of a liberal, reformist orientation in foreign and domestic affairs. But the process was still in its infancy, and the academic-cultural hierarchy was still dominated by an older, conservative generation. These conservatives would soon triumph with the overthrow of the thaw and subsequent partial re-Stalinization of political-intellectual life. But they could not halt the emergence of a diverse and critically minded new elite—"redolent of the classical Russian intelligentsia"[3]—one important segment of which was now embarked on the path of a revived "Westernism."

Stalin's Successors Face the World:
Change and Continuity

Analyses of the Soviet 1950s offer a number of explanations for the "secret speech" and launching of de-Stalinization. These include a leadership struggle, fear of the terror's repetition, a desire to exonerate Party innocents, the need to stimulate a moribund economy, and genuine moral revulsion at past horrors. Just what measure of these factors moved Khrushchev is difficult to determine; however, the main impetus clearly lay in domestic problems and was not primarily driven by rejection of Stalin's legacy in foreign affairs. His successors mostly lacked Stalin's near-pathological drive toward confrontation with "enemies," and they were worried by the simmering conflicts and unsettled disputes that ringed their borders. Also, the imperative to get the country moving economically and the dangers of the nuclear era engendered some important changes. But the post-Stalin leaders still largely retained the Manichaean outlook of a world sharply divided into mutually hostile camps of socialism and capitalism-imperialism.

The duality of their approach to Stalin's international legacy was seen in his successors' first major actions. In June 1953, riots in East Germany were crushed by Soviet tanks; in July, secret police chief Lavrenty Beria—who had advocated permitting German reunification—was removed from the leadership and later shot on Stalinesque charges that he had been an imperialist agent guilty of economic sabotage and seeking to restore capitalism in Russia. That same month, however, Soviet pressure on the Chinese produced an armistice that ended the Korean War.

To see the sources and limits of change in the first post-Stalin decade, it is important to understand the political-psychological context in which the new leadership entered the international arena. The postwar order they had anticipated was not one of long-term cooperation with erstwhile capitalist allies. Instead, Khrushchev noted a widespread belief that Western Europe would, on its own, turn socialist; first, "Germany would stage a revolution and follow the path of creating a proletarian state. . . . All of us thought it would happen . . . we thought the war had created the most favorable conditions [and] had the same hopes for France and Italy."[4] This did not happen because the United States, having grown rich on the war, suppressed the tide of socialism. Instead, the imperialist powers launched an anti-Soviet cold war that threatened to turn hot; at Stalin's death, "we believed that America would invade the Soviet Union and we would go to war."[5]

These views are striking not only for their exaggerated expectations of socialist revolution and fears of U.S. aggression, but also for the particular historical patterns in which they reasoned. Postwar foreign relations were seen as evolving in a repetition of events earlier in the century. Recalled Khrushchev, "Just as Russia came out of World War I, made the revolution, and established Soviet power, so after the catastrophe of World War II, Europe too might become Soviet."[6] But like the entente in 1918–20, the United States in 1945–50 was seen charging about Europe to crush Communist gains, raising a blockade against the USSR, and poising to intervene.

These fears made sense, given Stalin's successors' ignorance of life abroad, their worldview built around a distorted understanding of Western aggression during and after the civil war, and a grotesque fantasy of capitalism's hostility from the 1930s on. A Politburo member since 1939, Khrushchev came to power in the 1950s with virtually no worldly exposure; his only "foreign" experience—aside from youthful toil in factories and mines built or owned by Western capitalists—were postwar visits to Soviet-occupied Poland and Austria.[7] Instead of firsthand knowledge, he had the usual background of one of the *vydvizhentsy*: War Communist militancy, political education in the aggressive spirit of *The ABC* and The *Short Course*, and a rapid career rise in Stalin's "hostile capitalist encirclement." During the terror, Khrushchev was "looking everywhere for enemies—in sporting groups, in the Komsomol, among specialists at the Moscow City Council . . . in all this Khrushchev comes off looking very, very bad. [But] at that time he was young, really fired up, and he sincerely believed that there were enemies all around."[8] Khrushchev's wife, who taught *politgramota* to semi-literate workers, echoed millions of *vydvizhentsy* in recalling the 1930s as the best and "most active" years of political and social life.[9]

Since foreign policy was terra incognita for Khrushchev in the early 1950s, he initially deferred to those of his colleagues with greater international experience. Andrei Vyshinsky, the jurist-cum-foreign-minister who built his career on the theory of forced confessions and the practice of exposing imperialist plots as Stalin's show-trial prosecutor, was quickly replaced by Vyacheslav Molotov.[10] That this was a "relative improvement" suggests how far the new leaders had to travel to de-Stalinize their outlook.[11] Molotov, whose second term as minister lasted through 1955, "lived in a Stalinist world, where war was expected to break out at any moment."[12] Molotov himself later recalled that his main task as Stalin's minister had been "to extend the frontiers of our Fatherland as far as possible." Viewing East-West confrontation as normal, the very term *cold war* baffled him: "The cold war—I don't like that expression. . . . Just what does 'cold war' mean? Strained relations? It was really their doing, although we were on the offensive. Of course they were furious at us, but we had to consolidate our conquests [and] drive out capitalism. So that's the 'cold war.' "[13] Molotov also judged antiwar efforts "very dangerous. We have to think about preparations for new wars. It will come to that. And we've got to be ready." In fact, he looked forward to a third world war—one that would "finish off imperialism for good."[14]

Khrushchev recalled his initial respect for Molotov's knowledge and experience—that theirs was a "good, trusting relationship."[15] Beyond Khrushchev's inexperience, this trust is explained by the fact that he still shared Molotov's harsh Stalinist worldview:

> We persisted in believing the delusion perpetrated by Stalin that we were surrounded by enemies, that we had to do battle against them. . . . You must realize that for many, many years it was drilled into us that we should not make the slightest concession to the West. . . . We looked at things a bit suspiciously . . . we continued to see the world through [Stalin's] eyes and do things according to his style and way of thinking.[16]

The first sign of change in this outlook came from Georgy Malenkov, not Khrushchev. In March 1954, he argued for better East-West ties because nuclear war would mean "the destruction of world civilization" and also sought a shift in economic priorities from heavy industry to consumer goods.[17] Though Malenkov was forced to recant, Soviet policy soon turned in an encouraging direction, and 1954–55 saw such progress as territorial settlements or peace treaties with Finland, Turkey, and Austria.

Equally important, this diplomacy drew Stalin's successors out onto the world stage. Recollections of early visits to Vienna,

Geneva, and London offer revealing, even touching, accounts of the fear, confusion, and ideological orthodoxy with which they found their way in the international arena.[18] There was the anxiety of a self-confessed "country bumpkin" whose "European debut" was among leaders educated at Oxford and the Sorbonne.[19] But Khrushchev and his colleagues were also deeply suspicious of Western intentions and haunted by fears that they would be "intimidated" or "get confused," that "the first time we came into contact with the outside world our enemies would smash us into pieces."[20] Stalin's warning still rang in their ears: "When I'm gone, the imperialistic powers will wring your necks like chickens." So this early summitry, while producing few concrete gains, at least helped ease the terrors: "We were encouraged, realizing that our enemies feared us as much as we feared them."[21]

At the 20th Party Congress in 1956, Khrushchev embraced a position like Malenkov's of two years earlier: that war was no longer inevitable and the new priority must be "peaceful competition" with capitalism.[22] A concession to nuclear reality, this also invited a broader rethinking of East-West relations by discarding the axiom of a violent clash between social systems. Still, coexistence was defined as "a specific form of class struggle," and antagonism was enshrined as "the defining characteristic" of the modern era. Khrushchev's doctrinal changes left intact the core of the hostile-isolationist identity—a divided world—and with the struggle between social systems now "intensifying," emphasis remained on confrontation rather than cooperation.[23]

In any case, these doctrinal changes competed with events such as turmoil in Eastern Europe in shaping the leadership's post-Stalin outlook. Although the 1956 invasion of Hungary can be seen as a simple act of "imperial preservation," it is vital to understand that Khrushchev and his colleagues viewed the crisis through the ideological lens of old thinking—as something instigated by the West and so proof of capitalism's hostility to socialism. Adzhubei recalled the leaders' horror at the specter of "a NATO bridgehead" deep in the socialist camp. High-level analyses echoed Stalin in arguing that the uprising was the work of "enemies, not only internal, but external ones too."[24] In private remarks, Khrushchev declared that "anti-Soviet elements have taken up arms against the [socialist] camp and the Soviet Union . . . the West is seeking a revision of the results of

World War II, and has started in Hungary, and will then go on to crush each socialist state in Europe one by one."[25] Khrushchev's own memoirs describe the Hungarian revolt as "export of counter-revolution." Fear of Western attack was strong enough to prompt troop deployments in a "covering action" so as to block an anticipated NATO thrust through neutral Austria.[26]

Post-1956 events showed change and continuity in the Soviet leaders' outlook.[27] In 1959, Khrushchev visited the United States for "a firsthand look at our number one capitalist enemy." Respect for U.S. strength coexisted with old images: "We'd read Gorky's description of capitalist America in *The Yellow Devil*, as well as Ilf and Petrov's *One-Storied America*, and we knew all about its perversions."[28] The impact of his visit was mixed. On the one hand, as his son Sergei recalled, America's wealth and dynamism so impressed Khrushchev that "he paid careful heed to its experience and even measured our own against it." At the same time, he found much to confirm America's "perversions"—its social weakness and political aggressiveness—and so for very long was "unable . . . to rid himself of the 'image of the enemy.' "[29]

This image was also reflected in several domestic episodes. In 1958, Boris Pasternak received the Nobel Prize for literature after *Dr. Zhivago*, which had been rejected at home, was published in the West. For Khrushchev, the matter was obvious: "They gave Pasternak the Nobel Prize? Then they clearly did it to spite our country, to spite [me] personally."[30] In 1963, he was enraged by a *Mosfilm* production about U.S. bomber pilots who defied a command to strike the USSR: "How can this be, showing our potential adversaries as chivalrous knights, humanitarians, refusing an order to bomb Russia! What sort of ideological message does this film send? Did Soviet filmmakers do this, or was the production paid for by the Americans?"[31] While allowing much liberalization, Khrushchev remained suspicious of intellectuals and deeply distrustful of the West. And despite considerable progress, he "could not fully break down the Stalinist precept of mistrust of things foreign. The iron curtain was raised but some very vigilant comrades were standing nearby."[32]

Post–20th congress events must also be seen in the broader context of renewed faith in Soviet economic prospects. However pathetic, in hindsight, was the campaign to "catch up and surpass

America," confidence at the time ran high. The drive to cultivate "virgin lands," begun in the mid 1950s, saw great enthusiasm and encouraging early results. In 1957, Khrushchev pledged to overtake the United States in production of meat, milk, and butter, and later that year the first sputnik prompted an enormous burst of pride and faith in the evident superiority of Soviet science. In 1961, the year of Yuri Gagarin's historic space flight, a new Party program promised that the current generation of Soviet people would live under Communism (that is, by the 1980s). While in a narrow sense faithful to the idea of peaceful competition, such hubris served also to reinforce the split between rival "camps" by justifying continued isolation from the world economy and by trumpeting socialism's impending triumph over a declining capitalist West.

These hopes were also fed by events in the third world, a region that Stalin had largely ignored. But Khrushchev, viewing a surge of anticolonial struggle, saw allies in the global contest with capitalism. He courted new Asian and African leaders and fairly rejoiced in the revolutionary spirit that brought back "the old days of the Comintern" and seemed capable of "bringing imperialism to its knees."[33] But it was revolution in Latin America, specifically Cuba, where this ideological romance and rejuvenation of faith in global triumph over capitalism was most clearly seen. Khrushchev's admiration for young Fidel and Che—true revolutionaries, not inheritors of a once revolutionary but now ossified state—was great. Similar enthusiasm was seen in the normally staid Anastas Mikoyan, who, upon visiting Cuba, was "boiling over" with excitement: "Yes, this is a real revolution. . . . I feel as if I've returned to my youth."[34] These were the emotions that, together with obvious geopolitical aims, fed the disastrous 1962 decision to place nuclear missiles in Cuba.

It was also in the late 1950s that a rift in the socialist camp grew. Chinese objections to rapprochement with Tito and to de-Stalinization, especially after Hungary, were followed by criticism of moves to improve ties with the United States. Mao Zedong's militant "anti-imperialism" was an ideological challenge that Soviet leaders took very seriously: "At every stage in relations with the United States, he [Khrushchev] looked constantly over his shoulder to check the expression on the face of the Chinese sphinx."[35] Central Committee and Foreign Ministry staffers recall their bosses' obsession with Mao's attacks.[36] Until 1961, when the rift opened wide, attempts to contain it and guard Soviet "ideological flanks" retarded progress on ties with the West. At every step, "Khrushchev felt the icy breath of the Maoist revolution at his back,"[37] and Chinese criticism hung "like a sword of Damocles" over U.S.-Soviet relations.[38] "The thesis that peaceful coexistence is a form of class struggle emerged as an attempt to bring our positions closer to Maoism: the idea that you could have both peaceful coexistence *and* class struggle."[39]

For much of the thaw era, Mao's "Stalinist critique" of their policies, and his challenge to their leadership of world socialism, had a malevolent impact on insecure Soviet leaders. For all their private scorn, Mao was arguably the world's greatest living revolutionary. One diplomat recalled, "Now [they] had to compete with the Chinese . . . and the result was a resuscitated militancy in . . . foreign policy."[40]

> It was incredibly hard to renounce the old dogmas and preconceptions . . . having taken a few brave steps forward in practice and theory, [our leaders] then fell ill with what I would call the syndrome of "revolutionary inadequacy." This showed up when almost immediately we began looking for a way to "compensate" in our revolutionary "theology" for those steps that had been taken toward realism in theory and practice.[41]

Still, Khrushchev's final two years in power saw a real turn in thinking about East-West relations, at least on the part of Khrushchev himself. Catalyzed by the danger of the Cuban crisis, motivated by a sharp economic slump, and freed from fears of Mao's criticism by an increasingly open rift with China, he now took bolder steps.[42] These included deep, unilateral troop cuts and a drive for improved ties with the West that produced the 1963 Limited Test Ban Treaty, the first major nuclear accord. But by this time, Khrushchev's days in office were numbered. And while his ouster resulted mainly from a backlash of threatened domestic interests, neither did Khrushchev's successors—those same "vigilant comrades"—share his evolution toward East-West rapprochement. Some sought at least a partial re-Stalinization of Soviet foreign relations.

Immediately after Khrushchev's removal in October 1964, hawks in the Soviet leadership sought a turn away from peaceful

coexistence and renewed emphasis on military might and the solidarity of a militant socialist camp. At the November 7 reception for
foreign Communist leaders in Moscow, Defense Minister Rodion
Malinovsky "made a vicious anti-American toast . . . and then told
Zhou Enlai 'Let's drink to Soviet-Chinese friendship; we've gotten
rid of our Nikita Sergeyevich, you do the same with Mao Zedong,
and our relations will be splendid."[43] Malinovsky's sentiments—as
defense minister in a time of troop cuts—were not surprising. More
so were the views of others whose positions were not so closely tied
to military-industrial interests. For example, in 1965 Alexander
Shelepin drafted a speech for the new general secretary, Leonid
Brezhnev, that was "nothing less than a demand in the spirit of open
neo-Stalinism for a complete reconsideration of all policy under
Khrushchev." In foreign affairs, this meant

> returning to the party line on world revolution and renouncing
> peaceful coexistence . . . restoring friendly relations with Mao
> Zedong by unequivocally accepting his [praise of Stalin] and his
> common strategy for the communist movement; to restore the
> previous characterization of . . . Yugoslavia as a "hotbed of revi-
> sionism and reformism" . . . and much else in the same spirit.[44]

Perhaps more surprising were the views Alexei Kosygin, the
Kremlin's strongest economic reformer, who sought to restore
"friendship and alliance with China which, he understood, would
lead to a definite, sharp deterioration in our relations with the
West." Just after Khrushchev's fall, Foreign Minister Andrei
Gromyko criticized a pro-détente speech prepared for Kosygin by
young Central Committee staffers:

> What've you slipped into this speech—peaceful coexistence with
> the West, the 20th Congress, criticism of Stalin? It's got to be
> redone in the spirit of our new policy—the harsh struggle against
> American imperialism, which is trying to smother the Vietnamese
> revolution—and to say warm things about our unshakable friend-
> ship with the Chinese people.[45]

In fact, that friendship proved very shakable, in part due to such
indiscretions as Malinovsky's, but mainly because Mao's price for
reconciliation was too high. His demand for coequal status as a
leader of world Communism and his eagerness to risk war were too

much for Soviet pride and common sense to swallow. In the later 1960s, the impact on Soviet policy of Chinese militancy was reversed as Mao's extremism "restrained our own 'Maoists' and to some extent slowed the shift toward neo-Stalinism."[46]

There is no doubt that Khrushchev's singular leadership was mainly responsible for de-Stalinization and the thaw-era progress in Soviet-Western relations. As seen, the differences between him and most others in the post-Stalin leadership were great. All the same, in de-Stalinizing foreign relations, Khrushchev, too, was hampered by the dictator's political and psychological legacies. As Khrushchev himself once observed, "There's a Stalinist in each of you, there's even some Stalinist in me."[47]

Society, De-Stalinization, and Cracks in the Iron Curtain

If Stalin's successors could not break decisively with the hostile-isolationist outlook, they could and did create the conditions for the rise of a different identity in a post-Stalin generation. Some of these changes came immediately, such as the end of the terror. Others came gradually, flowing from the liberalization that unfolded, in fits and starts, over the entire thaw era. Critical in fostering radically new beliefs and values was a tentative opening to the outside world that began dismantling the legacies of an entire generation's aberrant existence as "inhabitants of an eternally surrounded, besieged fortress."[48]

This process began with a reduction in the anti-Western propaganda that had pervaded the Stalinist epoch, and reached a hysterical climax in the postwar years. The curbing of xenophobic images flowed from the decision to end the terror and, in particular, to halt the new repressions that Stalin had planned in the so-called Doctors' Plot, which, by familiar script, was tied to imperialist agents and their Soviet hirelings. With the most negative images of the West in abeyance, the stage was set for more positive ones that came with the easing of diplomatic isolation in 1954–55. As their leaders traveled to summits in Belgrade, Vienna, and London—and as foreign leaders visited Moscow—the psychology of encirclement began to break down, and people started to see their country not as a "besieged fortress" but as a normal participant in international relations. An early milestone in this process was the 1955 Geneva summit, where Soviet leaders attended a gathering of major world powers for the first time since Postdam, a full decade earlier.

Of even greater impact on the popular outlook were changes that offered more intimate exposure to life beyond Soviet borders. World literature, hitherto extremely limited, now became widely available. The journal *Inostrannaia Literatura* (Foreign Literature) was launched in 1955 and soon became one of the most widely read publications.[49] Western authors appeared in other journals, too, as well as in ever-larger Russian editions. These books sold rapidly while many Soviet authors gathered dust on the shelves, a preference that was also reflected in library borrowing. The great interest in foreign life was also seen in the immediate popularity of *Za Rubezhom* (Abroad), a weekly digest of articles from the foreign press that was begun in 1960.[50] An *Inostrannaia Literatura* editor recalled that publishing foreign authors meant

> opening up that world by whose light those dull-witted chauvinistic concepts of exclusiveness had to fade. "Only in our country . . . " No, as it turns out, it's not only in our country. Then it began to appear that there was not even as much in our country as we had thought.[51]

This world was further opened via knowledge of foreign languages. Already by 1957, some 65 percent of students in higher education were studying English. In 1961, foreign-language study in secondary education was expanded and the creation of a large network of special foreign-language schools was begun.[52]

In the immediate post–20th congress years, the USSR reached cultural exchange agreements with many Western countries; for example, with Belgium and Norway in 1957 and with France in 1958. Later that year, terms of an exchange were also reached with the United States. Covering a wide range of scientific, educational, sport, and tourist activities, most of these fruits were restricted to the Soviet elite. At the same time, others reached much further. Part of the U.S.-Soviet exchange was agreement on more-or-less annual visits of U.S. exhibitions. Extremely popular, their displays, discussions, and distribution of books, journals, and pamphlets drew millions of visitors during the Khrushchev years alone.[53]

Foreign culture now became a strong presence in Soviet intellectual life. Western theater and movies, museum and art exchanges, all grew increasingly accessible and wildly popular. The USSR became a true member of the world "cultural circuit," sending delegations to fairs and exhibitions abroad and hosting such gatherings as the International Youth Festival of 1957 and the semi-annual Moscow International Film Festival, begun in 1959. Tourism's growth was important as well. Though only a few thousand Soviets went abroad annually—mostly to Eastern Europe—just a few years before there had been almost no such travel. Moreover, Western visitors now flooded Soviet cities. From the U.S. alone, from a mere 43 tourists in 1953, some 2,000 visited in 1956; within a decade, the number had risen to more than 20,000 per year.[54] The roughly *two million* foreigners who visited annually by the mid-to-late 1960s became a real presence in Soviet urban (chiefly, Moscow and Leningrad) life.[55] So, too, were the increasing numbers of foreign students.

The impact of all these changes was tremendous. Just a few years after Stalin's death, Moscow was transformed from a stagnant, isolated "big village" into an increasingly vibrant international capital alive with exotic sights and sounds and pulsating with new ideas and lively discussions.[56] As one Muscovite recalled, an atmosphere of "springtime, hope and expectation" now grew:

> There was the World Youth Festival in Moscow in 1957, then the American exhibition in 1958 [*sic*]—the first swallows from the West in our entire Soviet history. All this talk of "putrefying capitalism" became ridiculous. . . . Then [came] foreign tourists and [consumer] goods imported from the West. Moscow was transformed [from a] crime-ridden slum [into] a city whose inhabitants thronged the bookshops, crowded into halls where poets gave public readings and packed the *Sovremennik* Theater. The music drifting through the windows on summer evenings was no longer . . . ersatz pop, but jazz and rock 'n' roll.[57]

Such changes were most keenly felt in major cities, where, it should be noted, a growing percentage of the Soviet population now lived; internal migration saw the USSR become a predominantly urban society by the mid 1960s.[58] At the same time, many aspects of the thaw reached well into the provinces. Readers of central newspapers nationwide devoured expanding coverage of foreign life that now balanced monochromatic political reporting with cultural, economic, and human-interest stories offering subtler and increasingly positive images of the West.[59] Across the country—not only in Moscow or Leningrad—subscribers to "thick" journals could now sample Western literature, diaries of foreign travel, and criticism of cultural and economic isolation in many new or newly enlivened publications.[60]

Moreover, advances in communications now contributed to the opening and diversification of Soviet life.[61] A huge expansion in postal and telephone service, as well as increased domestic travel, brought the country closer together. Records, tape recorders, and other audio technologies appeared, further spreading Western music and words. Especially great was the impact of radio and television. Expansion of the latter was particularly rapid; from just over two million sets nationwide in 1958, there were 16 million by the mid 1960s and 30 million by the end of the decade.[62] Easing the isolation so conducive to xenophobia, television beamed unprecedented views of foreign cities, leaders, and people.

Foreign radio broadcasts, too, blanketed the country. The BBC's Russian Service had started in 1946; then came Voice of America in 1947, to be followed by other U.S., Swedish, and German programs in the 1950s.[63] Private ownership of shortwave radios, and so access to foreign news and commentary, grew swiftly during the thaw era, and, by some estimates, millions were regular listeners by the mid 1960s.[64] Jamming was pursued, but even in large cities—where these efforts were focused—its success was limited; much of the country received foreign broadcasts freely. By all accounts, their impact was tremendous, becoming a major source of news on domestic as well as foreign events: "Is it possible to speak of absence of freedom of information in a country where tens of millions of people listen to Western radio?"[65]

Altogether, the pace and breadth of the USSR's post-Stalin opening to the world—after a generation of strict isolation and harsh xenophobia—were remarkable. Still, this influence must not be viewed in solely one-dimensional terms; the impact of foreign exposure was closely tied to domestic changes—a parallel opening to the truth about the country's own political, social, and economic life, past and present.

The link between openness at home and abroad was seen in the rethinking that followed the end of the terror and subsequent revelations about Stalin's crimes. Even without the cascade of information about the West that would follow, the exposure of the terror system and the lies that had fueled it challenged a linchpin of the Stalinist outlook by "automatically destroying belief in the infamous show trials of 1937–1938."[66] If millions had been falsely accused of involvement in fascist or imperialist conspiracies, then had there really existed any such conspiracies at all? And if the West had not been weaving endless aggressive plots against the Soviet state, then was the "imperialist threat" really so great?

Beyond such questions, there indeed followed a cascade of information about the outside world. But even before the country's opening, such information began spreading from internal sources—the multitudes who had glimpsed foreign life during the war and postwar occupations. As already noted, Stalin acted decisively and cruelly to contain such ideas. But with the terror's end, these witnesses began to talk. And with the emptying of the camps, many more returned to society with their own stories and images of life abroad.[67]

The link between revelations in domestic and foreign issues was also seen in more explicit discussion of the economy. During the war, Allied aid had meant that images of Western prosperity (ranging from tasty sausages to modern Studebakers) could not be avoided, but propaganda had countered that such bounty was enjoyed only by a very few. America was indeed the land of the super-rich, but also of huge disparities, with the masses living in poverty, sickness, and insecurity; by many accounts, a majority believed that, on the whole, the lot of the Soviet worker was better than that of his Western counterpart.[68] Similarly, propaganda and the terror concealed the true condition of the Russian countryside and successfully created an image of rural progress for many city dwellers.[69]

This myth was one of the first exposed in the thaw. The continuing rural disaster that was the legacy of Stalin's brutal collectivization of agriculture was revealed in some of the first post-Stalin exposés. Popular and professional literature soon featured fairly honest comparisons of the Soviet and Western economies, including data on growth and labor productivity.[70] Khrushchev's decision to publicize such bitter truths stemmed from a belief that the airing of problems, and a halt to Stalinist abuses, would free socialism's potential to leap past capitalism. For specialists, the proliferation of data opened the door to a deeper critique of the Soviet economy and a reexamination of Western experience. For others, admission of such failures twenty years after the construction of socialism had been declared "essentially complete" was a crushing blow. Even for the faithful, Khrushchev's revelation of such backwardness (though coupled with a pledge to close the gap quickly) set the stage for even greater disillusion when the economy faltered less than a decade later.

For the moment, such questions lay mainly in the future. In the early thaw years, reappraisal of Soviet socialism and its relations with the West was just beginning. Khrushchev's faith in economic miracles was widely shared.[71] The Hungarian revolt stirred no broad concern, and explanations of the West's perfidy were generally believed.[72] Most also shared their leaders' outrage over Pasternak's "betrayal" for publishing abroad.[73] Enthusiasm for the Cuban Revolution was enormous.[74] The image of a divided world and hostile West was deeply ingrained in the popular psyche, and the process of its rethinking had only begun. "People suddenly had to think independently," which was "an unimaginable task, completely at odds with the kind of life to which we'd become accustomed."[75] Still, the seeds of change had been planted: "One tear after another appeared in the iron curtain. It split and started to slide apart. Truthful information gave birth to questions. . . . Society was undergoing a . . . tumultuous reassessment of values."[76]

Intellectuals, De-Stalinization, and the Revival of Critical Thought

For one particular group in Soviet society—intellectuals—this "tumultuous reassessment of values" prompted by the country's early opening was felt especially keenly. It is natural that writers, historians, economists, scientists, and political analysts of all types—those whose professions were most directly affected by the country's stance toward the outside world—would be most vitally concerned with such issues. The next chapter will examine in detail these specialists' rethinking of the West during the thaw decade and for several years beyond.

But first it is necessary to see the broader context in which this rethinking took place, for intellectuals' conditions of life and work probably changed more radically during the thaw than those of any other group in society.[77] Intellectuals had hardly been isolated from the complex impact of the war—the surge of patriotism and apparent vindication of Stalin's prewar policies, followed by new questions and expectations.[78] Nor had the terror, and now its cessation, left them unaffected, for the educated elites had been struck even harder than society at large. But what came next was equally critical: a huge growth in access to ideas and information, much broader exposure to the world and the West in particular, and greatly liberalized conditions of inquiry and debate. These transformed the intellectual milieu radically; from being one of the most dogmatically regimented and terrorized segments of society, Soviet intellectuals were given real freedom to think and question for the first time in an entire generation.

For them, the signals of change began immediately after Stalin's death. Exposure of the phony "Doctors' Plot," an ebb in antiforeign propaganda, and an abrupt halt to "moaning and groaning" over the departed leader hinted at change.[79] Beria's removal was seen as a positive step, even as he was unmasked as another "agent of imperialism."[80] Then the months passed with no new "campaigns" in science or ideology. Colleagues no longer vanished from universities and institutes, and there began instead a few rehabilitations and the return of those most recently arrested.

The waning of fear and anticipation of change prompted a "spiritual emancipation."[81] An atmosphere of tentative freedom and renewed hope emerged in which questions—some new, others long-dormant—were posed with increasing boldness. Everywhere, "groups of like-minded people came together."[82] In private homes and small meetings, from discussions "on Moscow streets" to "endless nocturnal conversations," Stalin's legacies began to be confronted.[83] Some spoke up at public lectures; others gathered in the basement of the Lenin Library to discuss the sensations now appearing in the press:

> I learned to recognize the faces of some of the men who spent their days in the smoking room . . . graduate students, scholars, journalists. Formal introductions were avoided. On Wednesdays, the days *Literaturnaya Gazeta* came out, the crowd grew larger. [When] *Novy Mir*, the daring monthly journal, hit the stands, the crowds grew larger still.[84]

As so often in the past, censorship meant that political issues were first broached via the surrogate of literature. In 1953, *Novy Mir* published Vladimir Pomerantsev's sensational "On Sincerity in Literature," a slashing attack on the prevalence of lies and hypocrisy in Soviet cultural—and, by extension, political—life.[85] In 1954, Ilya Ehrenburg's novella *The Thaw* foresaw even broader changes ahead.[86]

The intellectual awakening was particularly evident at centers of higher education, especially Moscow State University (MGU). Very quickly, "the protective shell of lethargy, silence and fear began to crack open."[87] Graduate students and young faculty challenged Stalinist dogmas in the philosophy department, while journalism students formed groups to reexamine the works of Lenin and Marx.[88] History students searched the past for alternatives to Stalin's militarized "barracks communism," while physicists looking to the future protested the orthodox presentation of such "bourgeois" theories as relativity and quantum mechanics.[89] With students whose outlook was marked less by terror than by the flush of victory and hopes for postwar change, and who now encountered everything from Western social thought to foreign classmates, the fact that the universities became centers of "radicalism, zeal and creativity" was no surprise.[90]

"We acquired a lifelong habit of self-education to make up for what was lacking in our university programs."[91] Some poured their energies into study groups; others privately devoured rare volumes of Russian and early Soviet history.[92] Many recall the impact of certain older professors, liberals of NEP or prerevolutionary vintage who had survived Stalin to provide a living link with the old intelligentsia.[93] While formal curricula were little changed in the first post-Stalin years, Stalinist dogmas were challenged by a bold new spirit of inquiry. In fact, the very resistance of old dogmas to this spirit provoked "a positive . . . energy of antagonism and dispute."[94] At MGU, the clash of old and new created a "general atmosphere of dialogue and discourse [which generated] sparks of inspiration, enlightenment and creativity."[95]

The still-cautious awakening of the first post-Stalin years was given a powerful new impetus by Khrushchev's "secret speech" in February 1956. His sweeping exposure of Stalin's crimes caused an uproar in the thousands of Party organizations where the speech was read. Debate centered first on the terror and Party members' guilt in having remained silent or joined in the denunciations that had fueled repression.[96] But discussion soon went beyond repentance, to question the very essence of the system.

> We heard about Bonifatsi Kedrov speaking out at the Institute of Philosophy. . . . We heard about the speech of the chess grandmaster Mikhail Botvinnik. About the speech of Yuri Orlov at the Institute of Theoretical Physics. About the speeches at the Institute of Eastern Studies. People talked about the social basis for "the cult of the personality," about the kind of system that was capable of producing this cult.[97]

The leadership, deeply divided over the wisdom of even Khrushchev's limited unmasking of Stalin, moved to halt the questions that inevitably flowed from their decidedly un-Marxist explanation that one evil individual bore all responsibility. Orlov and his colleagues at the Institute of Theoretical-Experimental Physics, having called for "total democratization," were expelled from the Party, fired from their jobs, and denounced by *Pravda* for "singing in Socialist-Revolutionary and Menshevik voices."[98] Such steps intimidated many, but did not halt the questions. Indeed, the leadership's reluctance to draw what many saw as the obvious conclusions of its own admissions, and its determination to limit discussion to a narrow and self-serving denunciation of Stalin's personal guilt, served instead to provoke a much wider debate.

In October 1956, a Writers' Union meeting to discuss an anti-Stalin novel drew an overflow crowd that enthusiastically cheered a call to "sweep away" Stalinist functionaries and "fight this battle to the end." Even some workers and soldiers were stirred: "Official speakers were heckled at factory meetings and unauthorized wall newspapers appeared in the naval barracks at Kronstadt and Vladivostock."[99] "Semi-legal" university groups now proliferated, and an initiative to unite students in Moscow and Leningrad was launched.[100] Official student bulletins grew increasingly critical, while new, unsanctioned journals also appeared. And the *Komsomol* soon split between a dogmatic-careerist group and another that openly called for further glasnost and democratization.[101]

Foreign issues, too, now rose in prominence; the rapprochement with Tito sparked interest in Yugoslav reforms and many were especially concerned by events in Hungary. While public opinion generally supported the crackdown, many students and young intellectuals did not.[102] Committees were formed, "solidarity" meetings held, and leaflets distributed in support of the Hungarians.[103] "During the very same days and hours [that we were struggling with Stalinism], in Budapest they toppled the cast-iron statue of Stalin and rallied by a memorial to the Polish General Bem who had fought for Hungary's freedom in 1848. That's where the popular revolution began."[104]

Some of this activity even spilled out into Moscow's streets. A statue of Mayakovsky became the site where "young people, mainly students, assembled almost every evening to read the poems of forgotten or repressed writers." These gatherings turned into an "open-air club" for literary-political discussions.[105] Most often, such debates went on in private *kompanii*, groups which served as "publishing houses, speakers bureaus . . . seminars in literature, history, philosophy, linguistics, economics, genetics, physics, music and art," wrote one participant. "Just about every evening, I would walk through the dark corridor of some communal flat and open the door of a crowded, smoky room. . . . Old *politzeki* [political prisoners] would be shouting something at young philologists, middle-aged physicists would be locked in hot debates with young poets."[106]

Much the same was under way at many scientific centers. Igor Tamm, director of the Physics Institute's weapons-research program, briefed his staff on foreign radio broadcasts and "passionately" denounced chauvinism: "Science is universal. It is a vital part of the world's cultural heritage."[107] Peter Kapitsa, the Cambridge-trained physicist who refused military work, criticized academic isolation; judging Soviet social sciences "scholastic and dogmatic" in comparison with Western studies, he also pushed for international cooperation in the peaceful uses of atomic energy.[108] Kapitsa opened his doors to informal seminars and speakers on wide-ranging topics.[109] Humanities institutes, too, now awakened:

> The Institute of History had Nekrich while we [at the Institute of Philosophy] had Grigory Pomerantz on the personality cult, Merab Mamardashvili on European social and political thought, Zinoviev . . . and many others in seminars on questions of ideology

and politics. The debates between younger scholars and old Stalinists were tremendous.[110]

A number of research institutes soon became centers where social and political issues could be discussed in relative freedom. Economists, historians, poets, and musicians too bold for public audiences were invited to present their work. Seminars and conferences, "regardless of their designated subjects, became arenas for the discussion of political issues."[111]

Intellectual "Oases" and Study of the World

After 1956, much of this discussion was conducted at various new research centers where foreign affairs were precisely the "designated subjects" of inquiry. As Khrushchev's "secret speech" unmasked Stalin, Mikoyan's 20th congress address began to do the same for Stalinism in academic life. "Comprehensive evaluation" and "deep study" came second to propaganda, Mikoyan found, with the result that "we seriously lag" in analyzing both capitalist and non-capitalist development."[112] Soon the Institute of World Economy and World Politics, closed by Stalin in 1949 due to Varga's too-positive views of capitalism's prospects, was revived as the Institute of World Economy and International Relations (IMEMO). Varga returned as senior member of a staff comprised largely of young, newly graduated economists and historians. Over the next decade, a number of other foreign affairs institutes were established under the aegis of the Academy of Sciences: the Institute of the Economy of the World Socialist System (IEMSS); the Institute of the International Workers' Movement (IMRD); Institutes of Africa, Latin America, and the Far East; and the Institute of the USA.[113]

Several other centers dedicated to international political or economic issues were also created at this time. The journal *Problemy Mira i Sotsializma* (Problems of Peace and Socialism), whose Prague-based editorial staff included European, American, and third-world Marxists, was established in 1958.[114] In 1961, the Central Committee's first international affairs consultant group began work, a staff comprised of young scholar-journalists from outside the Party apparatus.[115] The Institute of Economics and Industrial Organization (popularly known, for its location, as the Novosibirsk

Institute) was created in 1961; the Central Economic-Mathematical Institute (TsEMI) was established in 1963.

It is difficult to overstate the importance of these new institutes. For decades, there had barely existed any centers for serious research into world affairs. Most such work was seen as redundant, since national development was viewed in universal, class terms, and Lenin's *Imperialism* set the framework for study of international politics and economics. Under Lenin, even as academic study of international relations was growing and diversifying in the West, Soviet scholars suffered the gradual imposition of orthodoxy and loss of ties to foreign thought. Under Stalin, *Imperialism*—a doctrinaire but still serious work—was supplanted by the crude formulas of the *Short Course*, while most remaining pockets of critical foreign-affairs thought were crushed.[116] But now, in a postwar world of unanticipated complexity, some in the leadership felt hampered by their own ignorance.[117] Thus it was a need for fresh perspectives and talent that underlay the creation or rejuvenation of foreign-affairs research and advisory groups, "a need to employ intellectuals to assist . . . leaders who couldn't write, speak, or develop a political strategy."[118]

At the centers where young specialists gathered, vital "oases of creative thought" soon emerged.[119] The Prague journal *Problemy Mira i Sotsializma* became "a center of new ideas and free discussion of all socio-political issues . . . for many of us, it was where new thinking began."[120] In its heyday during the early 1960s, the staff variously included talented young liberals such as philosophers Ivan Frolov and Merab Mamardashvili, historian Yuri Karyakin, economist Oleg Bogomolov, and foreign-policy specialists Georgy Arbatov, Nikolai Inozemtsev, Vadim Zagladin, Georgy Shakhnazarov, and Anatoly Chernyaev.[121] One Prague veteran recalled that this "critical mass" and the "constant, freewheeling debates" it encouraged were as important as was the exposure to new ideas.[122] Another noted that "unlike us, the foreign communists had not been cut off from real Marxism, from social democratic traditions. . . . Our debates with the French and Italians were very important . . . the European socialists certainly influenced us much more than we influenced them."[123]

The influence of the Chinese was important too, but in a different way; their views were so dogmatic—"What's the problem, you don't even like the *word* revolution?"—that it helped push

Soviet staff members even further in the opposite direction.[124] Their growing identification with the "non-communist left, and especially with Western social democracy,"[125] was also facilitated by the liberal leadership of editor Alexei Rumyantsev. An Academy of Sciences official who had most recently aided in the reopening of Varga's old institute, Rumyantsev was a scholar-publicist of NEP-era vintage (and outlook) who encouraged an openness and diversity unheard of for a Soviet institution.[126]

And so Rumyantsev, who also carefully guarded his charges' freedoms and fended off the periodic attempts of "Central Committee inspectors" to rein in his liberal haven, was a strong reformist mentor.[127] "He gave us the impetus, and in return we gave him a constant stream of ideas and proposals."[128] The Prague setting was also important, a "cosmopolitan paradise compared to Moscow. Culturally it was far more interesting, it was *Europe* after all. . . . I had many friends and colleagues . . . and was usually speaking French, Italian and English."[129] Chernyaev, who would later serve as Gorbachev's chief foreign-policy aide during the perestroika years, summarized his experience at the journal:

> It was a totally non-Soviet environment. . . . We were exposed to a huge amount of information on the outside world. And from all that, the idea of imperialist aggression, that the West posed a real threat to the Soviet Union, it instantly disappeared. In Prague people simply found themselves in totally different surroundings, we could take off our ideological blinders. And we turned out to be normal people who could look at the world and our own country normally.[130]

Closely linked to *Problemy Mira i Sotsializma*, both through ideas and individuals, were the new Central Committee consultant groups. Much like postgraduate work for those who had studied in Prague, these groups were a pipeline into the Party apparatus, where such "aliens" had hitherto been unknown.[131] "Praguers" including Arbatov, Gerasimov, Chernyaev, Bogomolov, Shakhnazarov, and Zagladin—together with other original thinkers such as Bovin, Burlatsky, Yakovlev, Lev Delusin, Nikolai Shishlin, and Yuri Krasin—worked in one of the two Central Committee "international" departments or, somewhat later, in those for ideology, propaganda, and culture. Burlatsky, who was recruited by Yuri

Andropov to head the first consultant team (in Andropov's Department for Liaison with Ruling Communist and Workers' Parties—i.e., with Eastern Europe and China), recalled that its members "stood out by virtue of their independent minds, unusual talents, and thirst for change."[132]

Although this "massive intellectual breakthrough into the centers of power" had little impact on policy, its impact on the staffers themselves was great. As Arbatov recalled,

> We wrote documents (drafts of Central Committee decisions; memoranda for our leaders; the leaders' speeches, and so on). At the closing stages of a major product, everyone involved would gather in Andropov's office, and an interesting and productive workshop would begin. Lively discussions developed, turning these sessions into stimulating theoretical and political seminars. . . . Andropov [had] the following rule . . . "In this room you can come clean and speak absolutely openly—don't hide your opinions."[133]

Bovin recalled this experience as "the best school of my life—dealing with large political issues, arguing with my colleagues, working with politicians, reading all kinds of scholarly and Western literature."[134]

These recollections highlight two factors above all others that made the Prague journal and the Central Committee groups so important: a "critical mass" of talented minds free to debate critically; and broad access to ideas and information, that is, the tools to do so. The latter was as vital as the former since new analytical centers alone were not enough to remedy ideological paralysis. The weight of ignorance noted in the case of Yugoslavia was no less problematic in other efforts to de-Stalinize foreign policy, such as the first steps toward serious arms control. As recalled by a young Foreign Ministry staffer, "Facts . . . were ignored in favor of simplistic propaganda appeals. Soviet diplomats needed . . . basic documents on disarmament, a record of proposals and negotiations over the years, material that was easy to obtain in the West but had not been collected in Moscow."[135]

In diplomacy, de-Stalinization gradually eased the twin legacies that had long stymied an objective view of the West: crippling ideological strictures and extreme secrecy. Here Khrushchev's opening had a reciprocal effect as quantitative growth in the country's foreign relations combined with qualitative change in their conduct.[136] No longer confined to terrorized embassy ghettos, diplomats now engaged in broad contacts with foreign political, cultural, and business figures. They began seeing the West "with new eyes" and, cautiously, reported back to Moscow what they learned.[137]

Staffers of the new Central Committee groups were among the beneficiaries of this diversification of information, but so—to a somewhat lesser extent—were those who stood just outside the apparat. A parallel "opening" was under way throughout the system of foreign-policy analysis, such as at the Moscow State Institute of International Relations, where future diplomats, journalists, and scholars were trained.

> My second education was conducted in the special section of the library where Western newspapers, magazines, and books were kept. . . . What I read there began to give me a better understanding of the world [and raised] doubt about the validity of many things I had been taught. . . . My understanding of recent history took a quantum leap.[138]

A virtual information explosion occurred over the thaw years, as the data and sources available to researchers grew exponentially. Economists and area specialists, experts in diplomacy, trade, and international law, reveled in a wholesale opening to Western science and scholarship. Subscriptions to foreign journals soared, institutes set up translation bureaus for pertinent foreign literature, and summary-abstracts of contemporary Western studies reached an ever-broader circle of Soviet academic and policy specialists. Foreign media, almanacs, statistical yearbooks, and other reference works appeared in more and more libraries of research and higher-education institutions.[139] Specialists' access to domestic sources expanded greatly too, as once-closed archives were opened and voluminous diplomatic, demographic, economic, and other data became more widely available.[140] This broke the "hypercentralized" control of information and challenged the "one-dimensional" analyses that had persisted after 1953, practices that had continued "nourishing the Stalinist mentality" even after the tyrant's death.[141]

This opening was buttressed by the renewal of contacts abroad. Pursuant to the new agreements noted earlier, Soviet scholars began attending foreign conferences and participating in academic exchanges. Their numbers were small at the outset—only about 500 Soviets visited the United States on such exchanges in 1958—but less than a decade later more than ten times as many would travel annually to the United States and other Western countries for research, study, seminars, and conferences.[142] The vehicles were many: exchanges of graduate students and senior scholars, UNESCO fora, delegations to regular gatherings such as the Pugwash and Dartmouth meetings on international security, and attendance at academic conventions in political science, sociology, and other fields.[143]

It is difficult to overstate the devastating impact that firsthand exposure to the West had on old beliefs and stereotypes. The correlation between participants in thaw-era exchanges and those who later emerged as prominent "Westernizing" reformers is strong.[144] The experiences of most of them—whether political, cultural, or scientific figures—echo the following recollection of a writer's first trip abroad (to the 1962 Youth Festival in Finland):

> We'd been repeatedly warned about CIA treachery and the many agents who were descending on Helsinki . . . but nothing happened. We reveled in the strolling, multilingual crowds, traded badges and other souvenirs . . . it was so pleasant to make friends, to hear all about their lives. . . . I didn't see any reason for secrecy. . . . These trips astonished me. In many ways, whatever I am was formed then—in these new associations, in understanding new values and new people.[145]

In describing this initial stage in the evolution of new thinking, it would be premature to speak of "transnational communities" of Soviet and Western professionals; such associations, and other constructive changes, would emerge somewhat later. For the moment, direct exposure to the West had a more "destructive" impact, at least insofar as the old beliefs and values were concerned:

> By the 1960s we'd come a long way, but there was still far to go. We still didn't know the world. I remember my first trip to the U.S., and how quickly I realized that 90, maybe 99 percent of all that I had written was wrong. I'd read everything, we had facts and information, but we didn't yet *understand*.[146]

Though travel to the West was predominantly a privilege of reliable senior specialists, Soviet delegations were now increasingly penetrated by younger, better-educated, reform-minded analysts. Many more visited Eastern Europe, but here, too, the contrasts with Soviet life and exposure to Western ideas were great. There was, as already noted, the "cosmopolitan paradise" of Prague, but other young analysts went to Hungary and Yugoslavia and found them of even greater interest.

> I was deeply impressed by Yugoslavia's economic reforms, above all by decentralization, rejection of rigid planning, and by their firms' emphasis on the domestic market [with] free access to foreign markets. . . . Food shops resembled those in the West and their industrial products . . . were already approaching world standards. . . . The country's spirit was ruled by "modernism," a striving for everything contemporary and new.[147]

By the early 1960s, exposure to foreign diversity together with the intellectual liberties permitted within these new analytical groups began their transformation into nascent centers of new thinking. The Novosibirsk Institute, "gathering the best young scholars" in an atmosphere of creative freedom, quickly evolved into "the new school" of political economy.[148] The Central Economic-Mathematical Institute, originally a "grab-bag of poorly schooled, undereducated political economists, Marxist-Leninists, mathematicians, physicists, chemists and historians," began its rise to become the leading center of Western-oriented market reformism.[149] And a revived IMEMO, notwithstanding "serious mistakes [such as] euphoria for quickly overtaking the West . . . soon became the 'incubator' for a new generation of international economists . . . and foreign-policy experts."

> Dogmas about capitalist stagnation, total impoverishment of the Western working class, and others were rejected while new concepts came into political circulation [such as] European integration . . . multiple paths of third-world development . . . and so on. There emerged new research methods and an objective look at [the West].[150]

The Rebirth of the Russian Intelligentsia

The study of these and other "new concepts," and particularly the "objective look at the West," will be examined in detail over the next two chapters. But here it is crucial to emphasize again the broader context in which these changes were occurring. And that context, as much of the above is meant to illustrate, was the birth of a new intelligentsia. To understand both the phenomenon—and its neglect in most Western analyses of post-Stalin change—it is important to clarify a definition.

The intelligentsia, in historic terms, was a group in Russian society characterized by its vital interest in sociopolitical issues. It was outwardly heterogenous; with members drawn from the sons and daughters of the nobility, clergy, bourgeoisie, and peasantry, it crossed Marxist class boundaries as well as those of the traditional Russian estates. Its members also differed sharply on their prescriptions for Russia, as seen in chapter 1. What they had in common was what defined them as *intelligenty*: a deep concern about the country's social and political problems, a passionate interest in its history, culture, and place in world civilization, and a dedication to the reform of a stifling autocracy.

In speaking of an intelligentsia in the post-Stalin context, many analyses alter its traditional meaning in one of two ways. First are those that use it as synonymous for all those engaged in intellectual professions or even simply possessing higher education.[151] While the rapid growth in the latter that such statistics reveal was an important aspect of thaw-era social change, a quantitative definition overlooks the critical qualitative distinction between a minority of true intellectuals and the majority who, if not "militant ignoramuses," were at best "professionally useless people."[152]

Other definitions are too restrictive, either denying the status of *intelligent* to any but those who openly defied the regime, or dividing the intelligentsia into subgroups such as the *technical, creative,* or *Party* intelligentsias. But by emphasizing differences of occupation or official status, the unofficial interests and concerns shared by scientists, writers, economists, and historians—Party and non-Party alike—are obscured, if not lost altogether. And a view that recognizes only the boldest public dissidents as *intelligenty* ignores the significance of less-public or private dissidence, and so imposes an oversimplified heroes-conformists dichotomy on what in fact was a wide spectrum of reformist thought and activity.[153]

During the thaw, critically minded Soviets devoured new portrayals of foreign life and culture in such liberal journals as *Novy Mir,* they pondered questions about the origins of Stalin's "besieged fortress" raised by such works as Alexander Solzhenitsyn's *One Day in the Life of Ivan Denisovich*. Just as physicists Tamm and Kapitsa pronounced science a "universal" heritage and called for international cooperation, so did historian Mikhail Gefter criticize scholarly isolation and call for a "worldwide historical canvas."[154] Even as Party-sanctioned conferences resounded with calls to air the truth about the 1939 pact with Hitler and Stalin's wartime bungling, hundreds attended General Petro Grigorienko's unsanctioned lectures on the same issues at Moscow University.[155] For Arbatov, a future member of the Central Committee, just as for future dissident Raisa Orlova, early work as translator-reviewers of foreign literature was instrumental in shedding dogmas about the West.[156] The heated debates under way in numerous *kompanii* of students, nonconformist poets, and gulag survivors were echoed in the private "salons" of prominent journalists and writers, senior scholars of the Academy of Sciences, and young Party officials.[157] Meanwhile, Party and non-Party researchers alike pored over newly accessible literature on Russia and liberalism, revolution, and the West.[158] For all these and many other diverse thinkers, the thaw was, above all, a time of intellectual liberation:

> Freeing myself from the blinders of the Party, from severely two-dimensional criteria—"ours or alien, there is no middle course"—I was losing my fear of ideological taboos, my distrust of idealism and liberalism. . . . For the first time, I read Berdyaev . . . Semyon Frank, Vernadsky, Camus, Sartre, Schweitzer, Martin Luther King Jr., Robert Ardrey. My discoveries astonished me. Probably the students of Galileo experienced the same joy as they escaped the cramped, tightly locked universe of Ptolemy.[159]

For some, as seen, the path lay directly through new Western ties. For many others—not just those at the Prague journal *Problemy Mira i Sotsializma*—it went through Eastern Europe. Those who visited after the invasion of Hungary were shocked by the anger they encountered.[160] Others were moved by the *Hungarian Diary* of Polish journalist Wiktor Woroszylski, a "sincere and passionate outcry of the soul."[161] In all fields, Soviet scholars found their East European colleagues increasingly critical of Leninism as well as Stalinism. Many discovered the works of Lukacs, Gramsci, and Djilas analyzing not only the past tragedies of

Bolshevism, but also the continuing tragedy of Stalinism and its imperial-isolationist legacies.[162] Economists and political scientists envied the decentralization and opening of the Yugoslav system, while philosophers followed Belgrade's emerging Marxist-humanist currents. Historians enjoyed new access in Warsaw archives, and social scientists followed closely the growing diversity, greatly influenced by Western studies, in Polish scholarly literature.[163]

The vital intellectual background to all the experiences described above—whatever the field of study or the nature of its specialists' exposure to Western thought—was a broader cultural revival, one that engaged all circles of critically minded Soviets. From idealistic students to cynical veterans, a growing "cult of culture" heralded a new passion for the humanism of classical Russian and foreign literature, and thence to contemporary Western currents.[164] Dostoevsky and Yesenin led to Sartre, Camus, Hemingway, and Martin Luther King. "But King learned from Gandhi, and Gandhi from Tolstoy, whose ideas returned to Russia like a boomerang."[165] In another recollection, "After decades of cowering, a genuine humanitarian Russian culture was reborn . . . a culture represented not only by several dozen morally irreproachable dissident-heroes, but also by a whole generation of potential reformers."[166]

The fans of folksingers Bulat Okudzhava and Vladimir Vysotsky included not only students and artists, but also young Central Committee staffers. The latter not only patronized director Yuri Lyubimov's avant-garde *Taganka* theater, but also introduced him to their boss Andropov and helped defend him from conservative attacks.[167] The reformist apparatchiks were also avid consumers of the same samizdat that circulated widely among liberal intellectuals. They, too, read anti-Stalinist works from Solzhenitsyn to Orwell. They also read Gnedin on Stalin's decimation of the diplomatic corps and the end of Litvinov's policy of cooperation with the Western democracies in favor of the pact with Hitler.[168] It was the same "Party intellectuals" who pushed for publication of Roy Medvedev's anti-Stalinist classic *Let History Judge*, and, failing that, helped protect him from reprisals.[169] "People simply needed to hear the truth. Therefore they seized eagerly upon . . . Varga's works in the field of political economy, on the economic notes of Academician Agagebyan [*sic*], and on Djilas's essay. . . . I myself launched into circulation . . . Avtorkhanov's *Tekhnologiya Vlasti*."[170] The works noted here illustrate well the interests and concerns shared by reform-minded individuals in Soviet officialdom and the wider circles of creative, scholarly, and "unofficial" intellectuals. The former were not only consumers of the ideas that were vital to the evolving outlook of so many liberal thinkers, they were themselves also producers: Novosibirsk Institute director Abel Aganbegyan, for example, in his above-mentioned critique of economic centralization and militarization; and Varga, in his controversial analysis of postwar capitalism.[171]

■

Now, alongside legions of the so-called *proletarian intelligentsia* (Stalin's terrorized pseudointellectual servitors), there arose a new, critically minded, anti-isolationist, increasingly Western-oriented current—an *intelligentsia* in the fullest sense of the term. They were "a social group . . . of great intellectual and practical strength . . . unorganized but numerous and fairly united in spirit."[172] And notwithstanding their diversity, the members of this new intelligentsia were increasingly aware of their identity as such. "Self-conscious about Russian history and the role of the intelligentsia in it,"[173] this meant many came to understand the efforts of their nineteenth-century predecessors as an important point of reference for themselves.[174]

Another historical reference point was the early twentieth century. This was, in the first place, because the goals of thaw-era reformers so resembled, and in many areas drew explicitly upon, the NEP model of a more liberal market socialism. But NEP's resonance was also broader, for the changes of the thaw had already returned Russian intellectual life to a situation not seen since the early 1920s. During the early NEP years, a diversity of opinion and tolerance of debate existed that in many ways was similar to that of the late 1950s and early 1960s.

There was, however, one crucial difference: the vectors of change were opposite. The brief cultural flowering of the 1920s, after the traumas of revolution and war, saw growing restrictions on intellectual life and increasing repression of liberal, Western-oriented thought. The later thaw, although it followed the even greater traumas of Stalinism, and notwithstanding many setbacks and reversals, brought ever-increasing diversity to intellectual life and so rapid growth in the integrationist, "Westernizing" outlook.

3 ■

Intellectuals and the World: From the Secret Speech to the Prague Spring

The "generation of 1966" consisted of "establishment" people. Instead of half-scholars, it included doctors of science; instead of poets who had never published a single line, it included longtime members of the Union of Soviet Writers; instead of "persons with no specific occupation" it included old Bolsheviks, officers, actors and artists. For many of them, the years 1953–56 had also been decisive. But they still had hopes for improvement, and it was not until the unmistakable regression toward Stalinization in 1965–66 that their inner dissent was strengthened and their protest provoked.
—Andrei Amalrik, *Notes of a Revolutionary*

I suffered terribly over Prague. I condemned it in my soul, to my friends, and told my little schoolgirl daughter "Remember this—a great country has covered itself with shame and won't be forgiven."
—Anatoly Chernyaev, *Shest' let s Gorbachevym*

The era of post-Stalin reforms is usually seen as strictly tied to, and bounded by, the years of the Khrushchev leadership beginning soon after Stalin's death in 1953 and ending with Khrushchev's removal in 1964. But in terms of the new thinking's rise—the transformation of beliefs and identity among a particular intellectual elite—the most important changes began in earnest only with Khrushchev's "secret speech" in 1956, and they continued well beyond his fall—until the new Brezhnev leadership moved strongly against reform after strangling the Prague Spring in 1968.

Notwithstanding some early steps, Khrushchev's main reform efforts began with his assault on Stalin, and on a conservative-Stalinist majority in the leadership, at the 20th congress. The

Stalinists fought back and nearly ousted Khrushchev in the affair of the "Anti-Party Group" of 1957. Narrowly victorious, Khrushchev pushed ahead. By the 22nd congress, in 1961, he brought an even bolder de-Stalinization campaign into the open. This time there were many anti-Stalin speeches, not just one, and they were public, not secret. Stalin's body was pointedly removed from the Lenin mausoleum, and there now followed in literature and the media an honest, searching critique of Stalinism and its legacies.

Though never without contradictions and reversals, this was also the period of Khrushchev's most important reform efforts in three areas: cultural-intellectual life, administration and the economy, and international affairs. Experimentation, diversity, and a general liberalizing trend dominated. In foreign policy, particularly after the Berlin and Cuban crises of 1961–62, Khrushchev embarked much more resolutely on the path of peaceful coexistence that he had proclaimed six years earlier. Critically, in all three areas, reforms were *not* undone immediately after Khrushchev's fall from power in October 1964. Conservative forces were emboldened, but in important ways the thaw epoch continued, and many of Khrushchev's changes would not come under serious assault until after the Czechoslovak crisis of 1968. This was particularly true of the intellectual revival so vital in the inception of new thinking.

The preceding chapter viewed the main outlines of the USSR's initial opening to its own past and present, and to the world. There were broad changes in society and culture, new freedoms and diversity in intellectual life that began a reconnection with foreign thought and practice, and institutional changes that established regular interchange with the West and new centers for the specialized study of international politics and economics. By the end of Khrushchev's rule, these changes had already gone far toward the revival of an active, critical-thinking intelligentsia.

This chapter focuses more closely on intellectual life in the three fields noted above—culture and history, economics and society, and international relations—to trace the roots of new thinking mainly from the changes following the 20th congress in 1956 through the onset of a sharp conservative turn after 1968. It will show how growing scholarly-analytic freedoms at home and expanding ties abroad rapidly eroded hostile-isolationist beliefs. In all three fields, a push to reintegrate with the international community was strong. In the humanities and social sciences, foreign experience became a critical reference point. For specialists in economics and foreign policy, Western models grew increasingly influential.

It has been argued that these various currents dominated a new intelligentsia. It is also important to understand that their diverse proponents were not simply motivated by related concerns, or engaged in parallel pursuits, but in a critical sense *were united in one common pursuit*. This was so, first, because their seemingly disparate professional priorities—international or domestic affairs, social, economic, or cultural policy—were inextricably linked. Just as the fundamental problem of a centralized-militarized system confront-ed reformers in both foreign and economic affairs, so did the revival of Soviet literature and philosophy necessitate similar rethinking of ties to foreign cultures. The reformist intellectuals examined here are often referred to as "Children of the 20th Congress," but rarely is it understood how the logic of their inquiries, not just their shared anti-Stalinism, indeed made them a member of similar intellectual fraternity. Moreover, they were also joined by personal and profes-sional bonds; the educational and career links among reformist his-torians and economists, philosophers and physicists, policy analysts and Party apparatchiks, were strong. And it was these personal-pro-fessional ties, together with their shared beliefs, that fostered a dis-tinct social identity and fortified the "neo-Westernizers" in the dif-ficult years after 1968.

Intellectuals Against Isolationism: Culture, Philosophy, and History

The post-Stalin protest against isolationism came swiftly in the field of literature and culture. Led by the flagship reformist journal, *Novy Mir*, prominent authors and critics attacked the overweening "Soviet nationalism" and Russian chauvinism that had rendered cultural life self-congratulatory, barren, and ritualistic. Konstantin Simonov, *Novy Mir* editor from 1954 to 1956, criticized both the suppression of non-Russian cultures within the USSR as well as the country's broader isolation from foreign cultures.[1] Simonov pub-lished a number of European authors, and his successor, Alexander Tvardovsky, furthered the opening to Western thought.[2] Ilya Ehrenburg's 1958 article "Rereading Chekhov" recalled the shame of the Dreyfus affair (over its anti-Semitism and scapegoating of others for one's own failures) in a veiled defense of Pasternak and a broad attack on the Stalinist system.[3] Ehrenburg deplored the system's legacy of "ferocious and absurd censorship . . . extreme anti-semitism and national chauvinism."[4] In memoirs serialized over 1960–62, he appraised Western culture. "I am prepared," he wrote, "to render homage not only to Shakespeare and Cervantes, but to Picasso, Chaplin and Hemingway, and I do not feel that this degrades me. Unending talk about one's superiority is [a sign of] an inferiority complex."[5]

Essayist Yefim Dorosh also faulted Stalin's cultural iron curtain and argued that "nations, like people, cannot live in isolation, and the more boldly a nation draws from outside, the healthier it will be."[6] Beyond such principled critiques, other works challenged hostile-isolationist beliefs more directly by portraying the West in a new, positive light. Viktor Nekrasov's 1958 "First Acquaintance," the diary of a trip to France and Italy, offered complex, sympathetic portraits. Further, Nekrasov not only revealed that most progressive Europeans deplored Soviet actions in Hungary, but also allowed that he, too, found the official justifications unconvincing.[7] Ehrenburg's influential memoirs gave an even more detailed picture of European life, drawn from his extensive travels. His portrayal of cultural and social diversity, praise for artists and writers vilified in Moscow, and admiration for European intellectuals were widely read and discussed.[8] Ehrenburg also offered some harsh comparisons; even Spain, though poor, was "a very great country, it has succeeded in preserving its youthful ardor despite all of the efforts of inquisitors and parasites . . . in this country live people, real, live people."[9] The contrast with Russia, whose people had been bled by parasites and had the life squeezed out of them by the grand inquisitor Stalin, was clear.

The best-known writers of the thaw era dealt primarily with Stalin's domestic legacies; for example, Vladimir Dudintsev's *Not by Bread Alone* attacked the arbitrary bureaucratic system that suppressed initiative and destroyed creativity.[10] But the most sensational such theme—the gulag and the millions who had labored and perished in the camps, as depicted in Solzhenitsyn's *One Day in the Life of Ivan Denisovich*—also raised the issue of Stalinism's domestic-foreign nexus. The question was devastatingly simple, as already noted: If so many had been wrongly condemned for involvement in nonexistent capitalist plots, then what *was* the truth about capitalism's "threat" to socialism? Other works raised questions about the country's ties to the West through history and culture; the heresy of Pasternak's *Dr. Zhivago*, for example, lay in its sympathetic portrayal of the old "European" intelligentsia whose traditions were destroyed in the revolution and civil war. Yevgeny Yevtushenko's 1961 poem *Babi Yar*, an attack on the policy that hid the mainly Jewish identity of those massacred at the Ukrainian site, was also an implicit criticism of the chauvinism that sought to isolate the fate of Soviet Jews and other persecuted peoples from the broader European tragedy of fascism and anti-Semitism.[11]

By the mid 1960s, the literary avant-garde was dominated by Yevtushenko and other young writers such as Andrei Voznesensky, Bella Akhmadulina, and Vasily Aksenov. Though also focused mainly on domestic themes, they stood in sharp contrast to a generation of Stalinist literary figures by virtue of their increasingly Western orientation. Some admired and consciously emulated Proust, Joyce, and T. S. Eliot.[12] Others found inspiration not only in the newly permitted works of pre-Stalin Russian masters—Bulgakov, Gumilev, Tsvetaeva, and Mandelstam—but also in Kafka, Brecht, Hemingway, and other now-widely read Western authors. Culturally, the country was "making an exit from Asia, attaching itself to Europe."[13]

Despite this movement's youth, the role played by some notable older-generation figures in fostering the country's opening must also be stressed. Unlike a majority of their contemporaries, these few stood out by virtue of experience that set them apart from most Stalin-era intellectuals, tying them instead to an earlier epoch or rendering them particularly critical of the Stalinist outlook. Simonov, the first thaw-era *Novy Mir* editor, was a poet-essayist whose patriotic wartime writings won Stalin's favor. Later, on visits to Europe and the United States, Simonov was deeply struck by the contrast between life at home and abroad. With new eyes, he critically viewed the onset of cold war and the campaign against "kowtowing" before the West, contrasting legitimate national pride with "superficial patriotism, kvas-bottle patriotism . . . self-glorification and the rejection of all things foreign simply because they are foreign."[14] Simonov was especially pained by Stalin's imperial treatment of Yugoslavia; he had formed close ties with Partisan leaders and greatly admired Yugoslavia and its people.[15]

Tvardovsky, Simonov's successor at *Novy Mir*, was another formerly orthodox writer who had gained fame through his wartime works. The turning point in his outlook came with the revelation of Stalin's crimes. While sponsoring many reformist works, his passion was the gulag theme and his main battles with the old guard were over Solzhenitsyn and other "camp writers."[16] Although focused on the terror, dogmas about the world abroad that justified repressions at home did not escape Tvardovsky's scrutiny. In 1963, Vasily Terkin, the famed soldier of Tvardovsky's wartime verse, passed on to "the other world" in a poem that ridiculed militant isolationism and suggested that the socialist paradise was really closer to hell:

> You couldn't be expected to know: there's this world where
>   we are
> And then there's the other, the bourgeois one, of course.
> Each has its walls beneath a common ceiling:
> Two such worlds, two systems, and the border under
>   lock and key.
>
> . . .
>
> But wait: Even in the stillness beyond the grave
> Do labor and capital exist? And the struggle too,
>   and all the rest?
>
> . . .
>
> That's a big subject. Here's the chief thing to remember:
> In this place beyond the grave, our world is the best and
>   most advanced.
>
> . . .
>
> In the first place, the discipline there is weak compared
>   with ours.
> The picture is: Over here—a marching column, over there
>   —a mob.[17]

Ehrenburg, like Simonov and Tvardovsky, was a conformist writer for most of the Stalin era. His later (re)emergence as a leading critic of cultural isolation stemmed from his extensive European experience—that of a self-described intellectual "formed in pre-revolutionary times."[18]

Closely tied to the cultural thaw was a revival of philosophy, and here, too, a critical role was played by a few old-intelligentsia exemplars. Even before the 20th congress sanctioned fresh scholarly approaches, a postwar generation was encouraged by prominent elders such as Valentin Asmus, Bonifatsy Kedrov, and Konstantin Bakradze. Specializing respectively in formal logic, philosophy of science, and the history of philosophy, all were born around the turn of the century and schooled in a rich, prerevolutionary tradition. They were Marxists, but also nondogmatic thinkers who rejected the crude schemas of the *Short Course* and instilled in students the critical faculties that would ultimately lead many to non- and anti-Marxist views. Thus the rejuvenation of philosophy was "powerfully abetted by the survival of a group of older scholars . . . a link to an earlier tradition of Russian work . . . reaching back into the nineteenth century.[19]

This rejuvenation was already in evidence at MGU even before the events of 1956. Motivated by such teachers as Asmus, I. S. Narsky, and Teodor Oizerman—in whose lectures and seminars the discussion went far beyond what was then publishable—students sought answers "by going back to the real Marx."[20] Others were impressed by earlier, non-Marxist Russian thought.[21] "Courses on contemporary bourgeois philosophy became extremely popular with all students," particularly as access to original texts expanded around the time of the 20th congress.[22] There ensued a "revolt of the young" among the new generation of philosophers.[23] Students of logic, including future luminaries Evald Ilyenkov, Alexander Zinoviev, Boris Grushin, and Merab Mamardashvili, extended their criticism beyond the *Short Course*'s "barren" dialectics to fault the limitations of both Lenin's and Marx's systems of knowledge.[24] Students of the history of Russian philosophy, notably Yuri Karyakin and Yevgeny Plimak, "openly criticized their professors . . . for falsifying historical facts, for crudely lumping together the views of Russian revolutionary democrats as Marxism, and for their sterile, tongue-tied lectures."[25]

Many suffered for their boldness, especially in the backlash that followed the rebellion in Hungary. Some, such as Zinoviev, retreated into safer niches such as mathematical logic and continued at the university. Others, including Ilyenkov, found refuge at the Institute of

Philosophy under the old liberal Kedrov. Still others turned to sociology (Grushin), history and literature (Karyakin), or quietly continued their philosophy in scholarly-publicistic jobs (Mamardashvili). In these pursuits, they were aided by influential party liberals such as Alexei Rumyantsev.[26] Support for the victims of the university "pogrom" also came in the form of protests from prominent foreign Communists, among them Palmiro Togliatti and Todor Pavlov.[27]

This intercession from abroad on behalf of Moscow's bold student-philosophers highlights an important foreign link in the post-Stalin revival of philosophy. It was no coincidence that Togliatti spoke up for the new generation of Soviet philosophers, for it was the same tradition of European Marxism that encouraged both political de-Stalinization among European Communist parties and philosophical de-Stalinization in the Soviet Union. Especially after 1956, many Soviet intellectuals were particularly taken by the writings of Antonio Gramsci, Georg Lukacs, Herbert Marcuse, Robert Garaudy, Robert Havemann, Ernst Bloch, and others. For a time, the views of these writers dominated many private discussions of political, cultural, and social issues. Though still not widely published, such works became familiar to many. Students pored over scarce copies of Lukacs and debated the arguments of reformist Hungarian intellectuals, especially during and after 1956.[28] The literary intelligentsia shared scarce foreign journals and limited-circulation translations to discuss Lukacs, Gramsci, and Marcuse on matters of culture and society.[29] Specialists studied the significance of these early "Euro-Communist" critiques, drawing on the new opportunity to do research abroad as well as access to once-closed *spetskhran* library collections.[30]

The excitement these works elicited in Moscow is not hard to understand. At a time when reformism dominated the political agenda, and interest in the early, "humanistic" Marx ran high, these European critics pointed the way toward "socialism with a human face." Moreover, their writings were directly relevant to the fate of Bolshevism. Gramsci's warnings of the Party's becoming a "Byzantine-Bonapartist authority," with Marxism degenerating into "crude materialism," resonated loudly, as did the concern of Lukacs and Marcuse for the fate of democracy and culture under "proletarian" dictatorship.[31] The European Marxists also challenged specific Stalinist policies. Lukacs's prewar arguments for broad anti-fascist cooperation in Europe were published in 1956. Gramsci's *Prison Notebooks*, in which he equated Russian national Bolshevism with "social fascism," were also widely read by Soviet intellectuals. As one recalled, "Gramsci laid bare the imperial-chauvinistic essence of Stalin's foreign policy."[32] Moreover, the Italians now argued that such attitudes lived on; defending German Communist Havemann from attacks over his criticism of ideological intrusions on science, *L'Unita* warned that "the habit of describing as enemies of the people and agents of imperialism all comrades who dissent is a characteristic of Stalin."[33]

But even more important than particular criticisms of the hostile-isolationist posture was that, through the European Left, new Soviet intellectuals were returning to an old Russian tradition of broad engagement with Western social and political thought. In one recollection,

> It was the steady awakening of our intelligentsia to 20th century philosophy and a renewed link to world civilization and modern Western ideas. Ilyenkov came at it through Marx, Feuerbach, Kant and Hegel. For others the path was through Gramsci and Lukacs. . . . I was always closer to sociology, to Freud, Heidegger . . . Sartre and Camus.[34]

By the mid 1960s, many Soviet intellectuals were well-versed in the leading currents of contemporary Western thought.[35] Their sources included foreign books newly published in Russian translation and an increasingly diverse East European scholarship, particularly Polish and Yugoslav, which itself drew heavily on Western thought.[36] Specialists enjoyed ever-broader access to Western books and journals in their libraries and research institutes; others became familiar with such works through scores of ostensibly critical review articles in Soviet journals.[37]

Greatly influenced by the writings of Erich Fromm, Jean-Paul Sartre, Karl Jaspers, and Teilhard de Chardin, as well as the early Marx, young Soviet philosophers turned their attention away from sterile fields such as historical materialism and dialectics and toward sensitive topics such as consciousness, alienation, and the individual. New "existential" and "pragmatic" trends, inspired by Sartre, Bertrand Russell, and John Dewey, emerged.[38] Still, such themes remained highly sensitive, and while some significant works were published toward the end of the thaw, the boldest ideas were restricted to lectures, seminars, and conferences.[39]

Other branches of philosophical-cultural studies also joined in the assault on old thinking. The Tartu Semiotics School, pioneered by Yuri Lotman in the 1960s, offered a critique of the Manichaean worldview and contributed much to the creation of "a common cultural space between Russian and the West."[40] Meanwhile, a common "scientific space" was the goal of some philosophers of science who, viewing the wreckage that a militant, class approach had wrought in fields such as genetics and cybernetics, revived earlier debates over the intrusion of ideology.[41] More than just scientific integrity, the principle at issue was the essential unity of all scholarly inquiry—bourgeois or socialist—and thus even esoteric arguments over dialectics were directly relevant to the assault on intellectual isolation.[42]

Perhaps even more significant for intellectuals' rethinking of isolation, and their attitude toward the core question of Russia's place in the world, was the de-Stalinization of historical studies. Philosophy played a role here, too—raising basic questions about the Marxist historical process.[43] This, together with the airing of long-hidden truths and the broader opening to the world, encouraged many historians to respond boldly to Mikhail Gefter's call for a "perestroika" of Soviet historiography. Gefter noted approvingly the growing breadth of Western scholarship and urged his colleagues to work toward creation of a "worldwide historical canvas."[44] While the revival of historical studies included diverse trends, a central theme united most: the shedding of exclusivist, national-chauvinist dogmas and the revival of the "Westernizing" tradition.

In 1962, a conference of historians erupted in an "academic rebellion." The Stalinists were confronted by an "alliance between the younger generation of historians and . . . veterans from the pre-Stalin period."[45] Some questioned Stalinist views of tsarist history, namely Russian colonialism's supposedly "progressive" role and the denigration of the non-Russians' struggle for independence. This new anti-imperial, anti-chauvinist current was accompanied by renewed interest in the still-banned works of the once-preeminent Marxist historian Mikhail Pokrovsky. Moreover, its controversial implications for views of the state-building process—both tsarist and Soviet—were obvious as a dispute was already under way over the rehabilitation of Ukrainian Communists condemned as "nationalist-deviationist" by Stalin.[46]

In 1964, under Gefter, a section on methodology was created at the Institute of History. For several years, during which time the institute's Party committee was dominated by anti-Stalinists and supported by influential liberals such as Rumyantsev in the Academy of Sciences, Gefter's section mounted a strong challenge to the "Whiggish" historical schemas of the *Short Course*.[47] Motivated in part by the failure of anti-colonial movements to hasten capitalism's downfall, Gefter's seminars drew in not only historians but also philosophers, ethnographers, and economists—Soviet *and* Western—to reconsider fundamental issues of the world-historical process. Directly or indirectly, they raised questions concerning everything from the "inevitability" of 1917 and 1929 to the correctness of Khrushchev's policy toward the third world.[48]

Other historians turned to a more distant past for lessons relevant to the present. Karyakin and Plimak, a decade after being forced out of MGU's Philosophy Department, published a study of Radishchev, the eighteenth-century critic of autocracy. Drawing on foreign as well as domestic sources, they disputed the view that Radishchev's ideas were of purely Russian origin by illustrating the impact on his thought of Western liberalism and the Enlightenment.[49] Less fortunate was Andrei Amalrik, whose thesis about Norman influence on ninth-century Russia was rejected for contradicting dogmas of Russian uniqueness.[50] More successful was Natan Eidelman, who now began his influential work on the autocracy and its challengers—from the Decembrists in the early nineteenth century to liberals in the early twentieth—to explore the sources of change and the role of Russia's European ties.[51] The "Aesopian" message of such works—emphasizing reform of the autocratic system and the importance of Western models—was not lost on Eidelman's many readers.[52]

A third historiographical current confronted Stalin's foreign policy head on. Joining the samizdat memoirs of Yevgeny Gnedin were the published ones of another "old-school" diplomat, Ivan Maisky, that openly faulted Stalin's paranoid suspicions for delays in forming alliances with the West at the outset of World War II.[53] Even more controversial was Alexander Nekrich's 1965 book *June*

22, 1941, which not only detailed Stalin's responsibility for the USSR's unpreparedness and huge losses, but also cast Western policies in a more favorable light.[54] Nekrich noted that in 1940 and 1941, before the Nazi invasion of Russia, the United States and Britain offered aid, alliance, and warnings of impending attack. Stalin's "spy mania," belief in Western "intrigue," and "special suspicion" of Anglo-American intentions meant such offers languished. Instead, as Nekrich repeatedly stressed, the USSR continued supplying Hitler with critical raw materials and foodstuffs, even as Germany ravaged the continent and bombarded England.[55]

Nekrich too answered Gefter's appeal for integration with foreign studies by drawing extensively on Western works. And while postwar foreign policy was not explicitly addressed, a positive appraisal of Allied prewar actions implicitly challenged the official line—that the hostilities of the cold war derived solely from "Anglo-American imperialism." Nekrich's revisionism touched even archvillain Churchill, who was seen addressing Parliament just hours after the Nazi attack, giving a strongly pro-Russia speech and promising aid, even as Stalin was immobilized by shock and most Soviet people still knew nothing of the invasion.[56]

Economy, Society, and Isolation: Early Critiques of the Stalinist System

In contrast to the assault on cultural-academic isolation that was launched and sustained by the intelligentsia, often at odds with Party conservatives, the critique of economic isolation and other aspects of the centralized-command system was inspired by the Party itself. Not surprisingly, change here appeared far more urgent to the leadership as it faced the need to invigorate the economy and move the country out of the rut of Stalinist stagnation.

Though economic difficulties were known to all, at Stalin's death few even in the top leadership fully grasped the depth of the continuing rural tragedy. Stalin's legacies included a divided country in which the cities lived by benefit of horribly unequal terms of exchange with the countryside. Moreover, as seen, much of the urban population was ignorant of real conditions in the village due to restrictions on internal travel and communications, harsh sanctions against criticism, and incessant propaganda images of rural

prosperity.[57] Stalin's successors were soon apprised of the true state
of affairs. The revival of oligarchic rule eased the rigid compart-
mentalization of information and the shroud of lies was stripped
away. Khrushchev, with his early experience in Ukraine, where collectivization's toll had been particularly high, was more sensitive to
the state of agriculture than most of his Politburo (Presidium) colleagues who had worked mainly in industry.[58] And even though
official statistics continued to exaggerate economic progress by
individual sectors, the overall picture was clear enough; more than
20 years after collectivization, production in many areas was still
below NEP levels, or even those of prerevolutionary times.

In September 1953, a Central Committee plenum publicly criticized the "appalling" state of agriculture. Some modest but positive
steps followed; rural incomes rose as farm prices were raised, taxes
lowered, and private plots revived. The plenum's long-term impact
was even greater, its critical line prompting bold new writings that
pilloried the Stalinist system and laid bare its legacies—backwardness, stifled initiative, and widespread rural poverty.[59]

At this early stage, economic debate was dominated by the
exposés of novelists and journalists. A more analytical critique still
lay in the future; economics, like all social sciences, was just beginning to recover from the long Stalinist nightmare in which critical
study had been replaced by lies, commands, and exhortations.[60]
Also, many economists succumbed to the enthusiasm of the mid
1950s, the belief that, by simply stripping away Stalinist abuses, the
economy could be induced to make a great leap forward. The
apparent success of the Virgin Lands campaign, the reported
surge in growth rates, and pride in technological feats such as
Sputnik seduced intellectuals no less than society at large. Many
were caught up in Khrushchev's euphoria for overtaking America,
and the illusory nature of early gains would become fully clear
only toward the end of the decade. Such enthusiasm, as noted
above, led to steps that would bring unintended consequences.
Mikoyan's address at the 20th congress criticizing the primitive
state of Soviet scholarship rejuvenated economic studies too. The
leadership's desire to improve policy-relevant studies, coupled
with confidence in the essential soundness of the system, engendered a new openness that soon transformed Soviet economics
radically.

This openness came first to study of the domestic economy. Specialists set upon much new information—voluminous census data, information on investment and resources, and detailed statistics on industrial and labor productivity.[61] Moreover, Khrushchev's faith in the superiority of the Soviet system facilitated an opening to foreign studies; although he was motivated less by desire to adopt capitalist methods than by hubris that sought to challenge and defeat rival bourgeois theories, much Western literature become available to Soviet analysts in the thaw era.[62]

Equally important was the broader context of economic discourse raised by the challenge to the West. Not just by opening the country to foreign thought and practice, but by explicitly raising the United States as the marker by which progress would be measured, Khrushchev set a new frame of reference for younger economists. And their gaze would turn increasingly Westward.[63]

> In one sense, just as important as the opening of the country was that Khrushchev set the goal of catching up with the West. . . . He was focused on our radiant future, but specialists now turned more attention to the other side, our current backwardness. . . . We looked at how others were solving problems that we couldn't, and we focused on the West in a way that we would not have done if [Khrushchev] hadn't made it our reference point.[64]

With these changes in both the conduct and content of inquiry, Soviet economic science developed rapidly in the mid-to-late 1950s. Many postwar, post-Stalin graduates now began advancing in the field. With experience and an outlook that differed sharply from their Stalin-era seniors, they would form an entirely new generation of economists. An examination of their rise points up several important factors.

As in other fields, one of these factors was the influence of a few scholars of pre-Stalin vintage, economists schooled in the diversity of NEP traditions, or even those of the prerevolutionary era. Tatyana Zaslavskaya recalled that her mentor was Vladimir Vezhner, an advocate of reforming the collective farms' economic and social structures. Attacked in Stalin's *Economic Problems of Socialism in the USSR*, Vezhner was one of those who provided a "human bridge" between the 1920s and the 1950s–60s.[65] Abel Aganbegyan described similarly the impact of two other Stalin-era survivors: Vasily

Nemchinov, a veteran of the old *zemstvo* statistical offices that performed a vital research function in Russia's pre-1917 capitalist development; and Viktor Novozhilov, "a man of the Russian intelligentsia in the best sense of that word."[66]

> [Novozhilov] had a broad cultural outlook, knew several languages, and was well versed in contemporary world literature on economics. . . . He was an original thinker who was accused of being a non-Marxist, a cosmopolitan, of borrowing his ideas from bourgeois science. . . . He suffered for this: he was deprived of his professorship and . . . could only get hourly-paid work.[67]

Another pioneer was Leonid Kantorovich, a 1920s graduate of Leningrad University whose seminal work on modeling was published only in 1959, some 20 years after it was written.[68] Of all the Stalin-era survivors, his impact on the new generation was the greatest and his genius in mathematical economics was recognized by a Nobel Prize. Even some who had not survived still influenced debate through their work—for example, Alexander Chayanov, and his *The Theory of Peasant Cooperatives*, an NEP-era treatise on the noncoercive development of collective farming. While none of these older scholars openly advocated a market system, they sought changes that would reintroduce certain of its aspects, such as rational prices, profit-and-loss accounting, and producer independence. Moreover, all were notable for their intellectual honesty, scholarly accuracy, and originality. These were qualities that would eventually lead their students, through study and experience, toward efforts to reintegrate with world economic theory and practice.

Another early formative experience shared by many of the post-Stalin economists was a harsh collision with Soviet reality. Zaslavskaya, for example, recalled her first rural fieldwork, on the condition of collective farms in Soviet Kirghizia, in the mid 1950s:

> I was looking through the books and saw . . . a mistake, that pay per work-day was figured in fractions of a kopeck. "No, that's correct," the director said. "But how can they live on that? It only adds up to a few rubles a year!" "Oh that's not so important, they're still the nomadic tribesmen that they've always been. Each of them has a herd [of goats] up in the mountains somewhere, and every now and then they disappear to tend them." I had absolutely no idea . . . the situation was positively feudal.[69]

Meanwhile Aganbegyan, working in the Council of Ministers' Committee on Labor, encountered "astonishing" data: "Even after industrialization more than half our workers . . . were employed as manual laborers. Our published [statistics] distorted the picture."[70] In 1957, Zaslavskaya and a colleague ran up against the limits of the new openness. Assigned to compare U.S.-Soviet labor performance, they found that the former was some five times more productive than the latter. This brought a harsh reprimand when it turned out that Khrushchev himself would only permit the admission of a threefold difference.[71]

A third key factor in the development of post-Stalin economic thought was the haven provided by new institutes that "brought together all the best younger economists."[72] Most influential were the Novosibirsk Institute of Economics and Industrial Organization, set up in 1961, and the Central Economic-Mathematical Institute (TsEMI), founded in 1963.[73] The Novosibirsk Institute, particularly under director Aganbegyan, was a key center of reformist economic and socioeconomic research, the cradle of such pioneering sociologists as Zaslavskaya, Vladimir Shubkin, and Vladimir Shlapentokh.[74] TsEMI, though dedicated to technical modeling and planning studies, soon became a school of Western-oriented economic research, "the breeding ground of marketeers, of anti-Marxists, the Austrian school. . . . We were students of Kantorovich, Nemchinov . . . Pareto, Leontiev . . . Keynes, Koopmans, Hayek, Marshall. . . ."[75]

By the end of the 1950s, the economy entered a sharp downturn as the half-measures of the first post-Stalin years failed to address systemic ills. The superficial success of grandiose projects such as the Virgin Lands, and pride in achievements such as Sputnik, could no longer hide the danger signs of falling productivity and growth rates. Armed now with extensive data, analysis, and relevant experience—from earlier Russian and Soviet practice, from ongoing East European experiments, and from Western market models—Soviet economists advanced several critiques that all pointed toward a need for serious reform.

The first of these critiques was an attempt to improve planning. Proceeding from analysis of persistent bottlenecks, shortages, and hoarding, it was recognized that the antiquated system in which thousands of bureaucrats juggled millions of supply, production, and resource-allocation decisions simply could not manage a modern economy. "Optimal planing" sought to improve central administration. A minimum goal was the use of computers to perform better and faster the numerous calculations still done exclusively by hand, while a broader objective was the employment of forecasting techniques and mathematical models that would enable the system to be more efficient, dynamic, and adaptable.

Decades earlier, Soviet economists had done pioneering work in this field. Most prominent was Kantorovich, whose early studies either were not understood or were rejected as "bourgeois deviations." Such charges were motivated by optimal planning's echo of the Austrian school's "maximum efficiency" credo, and from the models' reliance on some semblance of rational prices that clashed with the Marxist labor theory of value.[76] Ironically, it was the opening to foreign studies that revived Soviet mathematical economics as "news of [such] work by American scientists filtered through to the USSR."[77]

The impact of "optimal planning" on the development of Soviet economic thought was a mixed blessing. For a time, it fostered illusions that the centrally planned system could be induced to operate efficiently. But it also stimulated analyses that eventually led back to the market; reliance on rational prices was only a first such step. Moreover, exposure to Western literature revealed not only the possibilities of planning, but also its limits. Finally, the field's early promise to "improve the system without changing anything," together with its complexity and inaccessibility to most ideologues (much like the Tartu semioticians' analysis of Stalinist culture), afforded it a sanctuary that permitted more radical critiques to develop in relative safety.[78] And these critiques were uniformly pro-market.[79]

Still, the main impetus for market reforms was simply that Soviet economic woes contrasted ever more sharply with Western success. The United States refused to follow its predicted decline but instead, particularly with the Keynsian policies of the early 1960s, surged ahead strongly. Also impressive were the vigorous postwar recoveries of capitalist Japan and West Germany. Perhaps most immediately relevant to Soviet experience were the successes of new market reforms in socialist Hungary and Yugoslavia.[80]

Reform ideas proliferated widely. Yuri Chernichenko advocated decentralization of agriculture and development of a rural market, while Grigory Khanin studied the market's role under socialism.[81]

In 1965, *Pravda* editor Rumyantsev published Yevsei Liberman's calls for decentralization and enterprise autonomy.[82] Probably the era's best-known reformist economic manifesto—Gennady Lisichkin's *Plan and Market*—was published in 1966.[83] Otto Latsis, another prominent perestroika-era reformer, recalled that by the early 1960s "the urgent necessity of market reforms [was agreed by] all serious economists."[84]

Beyond the optimal planning and market critiques, a third important current that emerged from thaw-era studies of socioeconomic issues was sociology. As a science devoted to the study of social groups, their interrelations and problems, sociology posed an automatic challenge to Marxism-Leninism's class-based approach to society. Though Soviet sociology had flowered in the early 1920s, its inherently critical stance toward the new regime was regarded by Lenin with suspicion and increasing hostility. Under Stalin, this "bourgeois" field was simply banned.

As with economics, sociology's revival had both domestic and foreign origins. The domestic spur came as young scholars studied firsthand the economics of agricultural (and, later, industrial) life and soon encountered severe social problems and divisions whose existence had long been denied and largely hidden from scholarly scrutiny.[85] Impetus from abroad came as the opening of scholarship gave access to important foreign literature—both Western and that of the more liberal East European countries—in a field that lacked theoretical and empirical foundations.[86]

Though denied an independent place in higher education, sociology gained several institutional bases in the thaw era.[87] Even before the Novosibirsk Institute was created in 1961, a Sociological Association had been founded in 1958, and such centers as the Public Opinion Research Institute at the newspaper *Komsomolskaia Pravda* and the Laboratory for Concrete Social Research at Leningrad University also emerged. Since sociology pointed toward broad socioeconomic liberalization, it was strongly supported by reformist intellectuals in other fields, such as philosophers Zinoviev and Kedrov and economists Kantorovich, Aganbegyan, and Shatalin.[88] The Institute for Concrete Social Research, whose first director was Rumyantsev, was established in 1968. During its brief heyday, it was home to a remarkable collection of original thinkers, including Levada, Lisichkin, Zamoshkin, Davydov, Burlatsky, Karpinsky, and Igor Kon.[89]

Sociology too contributed to new thinking about Russia and the West, first via research that exploded myths about Soviet society and its uniqueness, exposing social problems and divisions no less serious than under capitalism.[90] Sociology also brought many specialists better understanding of Western realities, further eroding stereotyped views of class-torn, crime-plagued societies.[91] And increasingly, via ostensibly denunciatory analyses of Western society and bourgeois scholarship, it spread these insights among specialists and the broader reading public.[92]

By the mid 1960s, the evident failures of Khrushchev's economic policies, following a decade of relative scholarly freedom and openness, encouraged the coalescence of a strong "Westernizing" socioeconomic critique. Slow growth and agricultural stagnation were clearly chronic woes, and the beginning of large-scale grain imports sharply highlighted the system's inferiority vis-à-vis the capitalist West. These problems provided a strong impetus to market reformers. A vivid example was a 1965 closed-session report by Novosibirsk director Aganbegyan that circulated in specialist, and soon samizdat, circles. Judging the state of the economy "extremely disturbing," he broke taboos by noting falling growth, inflation and unemployment, as well as a decline in real living standards.[93] The fault lay in Stalinist methods, and solutions were to be found in enterprise autonomy, rational prices, and other marketizing steps. Not only did Aganbegyan measure socialist progress by the capitalist yardstick; because official data were "a lie," Soviet economists relied on the capitalists' data about their own economy. While the Soviet Central Statistical Administration distorted facts, "the U.S. Central Intelligence Agency . . . gave an absolutely accurate assessment of the Soviet economy."[94]

Aganbegyan also lamented the underdeveloped state of Soviet foreign trade.[95] That reforms must include broad participation in the "international division of labor" was now recognized by most serious specialists.[96] As recalled by Nikolai Shmelev,

It was impossible to study the international economy seriously without concluding that our country must become a real participant in it. . . . We discussed ways of expanding our foreign trade, we envied East European and especially Yugoslav experience . . . and we even studied ways to move toward convertibility of the ruble.[97]

Growing economic woes and near-unanimity among serious specialists convinced some in the post-Khrushchev leadership that changes were necessary. As modest as they were, however, the "Kosygin reforms" of 1965–66 were doomed by half-hearted implementation and bureaucratic resistance. Still, the late thaw period is less notable for what did not change than for what did—the outlook of leading social scientists. Just a decade earlier, many had believed in the essential soundness of the Soviet system, its prospects for outpacing capitalism, and the inevitability of the world's division into separate camps. Now such beliefs were fading, as was the underlying hostile-isolationist precept of a permanent Western threat. Aganbegyan broached the latter indirectly but boldly—contradicting official claims—in noting that, with an economy only half as large, Soviet military spending was roughly equal to that of the United States. Moreover, of 100 million workers nationwide, an astonishing 30 to 40 million were employed in defense industries.[98] Others put the matter even more bluntly; Vladimir Shkredov's 1967 *Economics and Law* argued that "a new stage has been reached in which the social system and . . . the state no longer face external dangers . . . there are no excuses therefore for delaying the indispensable rethinking and reorganizing of the system."[99]

Isolation, Integration, and International Relations

This repudiation of Stalinism's core tenet was obviously central to the reappraisal of international relations. Thus, in a critical sense, the preceding discussions of revived cultural-historical and socioeconomic thought have already sketched the broader foundation of new thinking. This section will focus more narrowly on the evolving views of the *mezhdunarodniki*, those policy analysts, journalists, scholars, and others particularly concerned with foreign affairs. Although many of their ideas about war, peace, and international change have been closely studied, their evolution in the context of an emergent reformist intelligentsia has not.[100] Yet it was from the same intellectual milieu that new foreign-affairs thought arose;

future *mezhdunarodniki* partook of the same university discussions and institute seminars, read the same works and debated the same questions of history and culture, and pondered the same links between domestic and international problems. Thus it is only as an integral part of the broader "Westernizing" intellectual current that the rise of new thinking about foreign affairs can be fully understood.

Here, too, the impact of a few veterans of pre-Stalin experience was great. Arbatov and Burlatsky were among those shaped by work in the mid-to-late 1950s under Otto Kuusinen, drafting *The Essentials of Marxism-Leninism*, a textbook meant to replace such Stalin-era works as the *Short Course*.[101] While luminaries, including the philosopher Asmus, also consulted on the project, none so influenced the younger participants as Kuusinen himself. He was a Finn by nationality and veteran of early social-democratic politics, and his original views cleared minds "dirtied and dulled" by Stalinist dogmas:

> Kuusinen was a live exemplar of the . . . distant traditions of the European workers' movement, of early "left" social democracy and mature Leninism, of the best [pre-Stalin] period of the Comintern. . . . Highly cultured, he also . . . wrote poetry, composed music . . . and surveyed literature.[102]

Many important revisions to dogmas about the West came from young specialists affiliated with Kuusinen (and later, with the consultant group of Kuusinen's political ally Andropov), with Rumyantsev at *Problemy Mira i Sotsializma* in Prague, and on the new staff at IMEMO, the resurrection of Varga's old institute. Arbatov, echoing the postwar views of Varga, called attention to the masses' "vital interest" in international affairs and the moderating impact of public opinion on Western foreign policies.[103] Eduard Arab-Olgy, who joined Arbatov in Prague, published a "global roundtable" on overpopulation.[104] *Problemy Mira i Sotsializma* certainly featured much orthodoxy, but it also published a whole host of heretofore heretical perspectives. These included the diverse views of West European Marxists, on issues from integration and the Common Market to the benefits of a multiparty electoral system.[105] Another young "Praguer," Alexander Galkin, questioned the stereotype of Wall Street militarism and, at one of Gefter's history seminars, dismissed the dogma of inevitable revolution in capitalist countries by noting that "the Western proletariat has more to lose than its chains."[106]

Galkin and other *mezhdunarodniki*, including Anatoly Chernyaev and Yuri Krasin, were increasingly drawn to social-democratic critiques.[107] Some even managed to attended such elite foreign gatherings as the 1966 Stockholm Socialist International; others were struck by the writings of Willy Brandt and Olof Palme.[108] Another young analyst, Vladimir Lukin, wrote a dissertation on Asian social democracy that warned against hopes for revolution in the third world, noting that regional leaders criticized Soviet foreign policy and rejected the Soviet model for its "cruelty" and "lack of humanism."[109] Chernyaev echoed this caution at a Moscow conference on the world revolutionary movement and also suggested that, far from finished, European social democracy had more than a little to teach the USSR.[110]

Increasingly, these and other specialists called for reintegration with foreign scholarship and creation of a true Soviet political-science discipline.[111] In the field of international-relations theory— aided by broad exposure to Western literature—such integration was already well under way. Translations became widely available to Soviet specialists, including the works of Bernard Brodie, Henry Kissinger, George Kennan, and Thomas Schelling.[112] As in other fields, the impact of Western thought was strong.[113] New ideas were also spread through objective, often positive, reviews; Gennady Gerasimov introduced Soviet readers to the work of Schelling and others on game theory, while Yuri Krasin assessed bipolarity via John Herz's *International Politics in the Atomic Age*.[114] Some turned to balance-of-power theory and a more "realist" view of international relations.[115] Proceeding from the nuclear stalemate and Europe's division into blocs, Soviet writings increasingly equated the United States and the USSR as leaders of similar state systems.[116] Globally a balance held, the historian-*mezhdunarodnik* Karyakin argued, and it was one that neither could nor should upset.[117] Perhaps the most influential Western realist was Hans Morgenthau, author of *Politics Among Nations*, the subject of a widely read though unpublished study by Alexei Obukhev.[118] A young Foreign Ministry staffer, Obukhev had earlier spent a year at the University of Chicago in the early 1960s and studied under Morgenthau.

I studied conceptual works by American authors who wrote on theoretical aspects of foreign policy. In other words, I was doing what Americans call "political science." Today we regard it as a well-established discipline but back then that was something new to us. Speaking about Soviet authors . . . I haven't yet found anything comparable, say, to *Politics Among Nations* by Hans Morgenthau.[119]

Mention of the youthful experiences of Foreign Ministry staffers such as Obukhev highlights another segment of the new Soviet *mezhdunarodniki*: the diplomats. In the 1930s, as seen, the diplomatic corps was purged with particular ruthlessness. As a specialized profession whose stock in trade was knowledge of the outside world, Stalin decimated the first Bolshevik generation of broadly educated, Europe-oriented diplomats. Andrei Gromyko, who succeeded Molotov as foreign minister in 1955, fit the typical profile of the successor generation: a young economist-propagandist trained in agronomy, plucked from an academic career for a crash course in Stalinist diplomacy. His wartime appointment to one of the most important positions in the entire diplomatic service—first secretary of the Soviet embassy in Washington—was Gromyko's first posting abroad and also his first time ever outside Soviet borders.[120]

In contrast, the post-Stalin generation of Soviet diplomats stood out by virtue of their better training, greater worldliness, and broader outlook as products of the general thaw-era opening to the West. The Moscow State Institute of International Relations (MGIMO), which was created late in the war and became the chief school for diplomats, also underwent important changes in the postwar and post-Stalin years. Foreign students, mainly from the new "people's democracies," were now admitted. Over 1954–58, separate departments for study of the West and training in foreign trade were established, followed by an international-law department in 1968.[121] Access to foreign media and scholarly literature was eased, and advanced students now did original research on previously restricted topics such as arms control.[122]

Simultaneously, diplomatic work abroad was radically transformed over the post-Stalin years. Change here came first with the easing of fears over personal security and the relaxation of xenophobic ideological strictures. As recalled by Georgy Kornienko, who would later rise to first deputy foreign minister, with Stalin's death, the fear that pervaded diplomatic work went away . . . and with it the highly dogmatic outlook that possessed even those who dealt intimately with the West. . . . The demand to fit everything into extreme ideological formulas now eased [and] we saw the world with new eyes. . . . This began to be reflected in reports and analyses.[123]

These changes, combined with the broader thaw-era activization of Soviet foreign relations, transformed the experience of a new generation of diplomats. Foreign contacts expanded qualitatively as well as quantitatively. No longer confined to fear-ridden embassy compounds, diplomats engaged in a broad new range of political, trade, and cultural duties. Those in East Berlin, for example, became acquainted with survivors of the old German Social Democratic Party. Learning of their heroic struggles with Nazism— and their fate under the Gestapo-NKVD collaboration that followed the Hitler-Stalin Pact in 1939—they were struck by the contrast between the "more democratic" traditions of German social democracy and the dogmatic, Moscow-trained Communists promoted by Stalin.[124] And many younger diplomats cringed at the "imperial" behavior of Soviet ambassadors as the practice of naming unqualified Party officials to top foreign posts continued and caused increasing friction with the diplomatic corps' growing professionalization from below.[125]

Boris Ilyichev, a young diplomat posted to Indonesia in the mid 1960s, recalled Ambassador Nikolai Mikhailov, a "hidebound party functionary" who rose swiftly under Stalin before his "exile" to diplomacy. Reflecting the Party leadership's enthusiasm for expanding Soviet influence in the developing world, Mikhailov crudely attempted to cultivate the Indonesian Communist Party toward Moscow's line: "His entire approach to the fraternal party's leadership strongly smacked of Comintern directives. 'Every time we meet,' [Indonesian Communist] chairman Adit told me in Moscow one day, 'he teaches me the ABC of Marxism-Leninism.' "[126] Ilyichev also recalled 1965 as "The beginning of my political awakening and the refutation . . . of dogmas made out to be Marxist-Leninist ideals." The crushing of the Indonesian Communist Party in the coup of that year little impressed senior Soviet officials, who still "held the legacy of the Comintern sacred. . . . As for us junior

Party officials, we sensed that something historically inevitable . . . was taking place."

> My view . . . was strongly influenced by a brilliant paper which Anatoly Chernyaev delivered to a theoretical seminar in the ID [International Department of the Central Committee]. . . . By the standards of the time, the paper was a bold political analysis of the situation in fraternal parties. It warned against what befell us years later.[127]

The experience of those who served in the West was even more eye-opening. In London, diplomats pursued a broad range of activities that kept them in frequent contact with not only all manner of political, business, and cultural figures, but also Russian emigrés— from the sisters of Boris Pasternak to the "White" anti-Bolshevik emigré great-great grandson of tsarist Admiral Nakhimov. Moreover, as one diplomat wrote,

> We in London (like our colleagues in other foreign capitals, I suppose) had a rare opportunity to read samizdat and emigre publications . . . hardly anybody withstood the temptation of tasting the forbidden fruit. [I myself collected] an entire library . . . the Bible, the Koran, Pasternak, Solzhenitsyn, Okujava, Daniel, Sinyavsky, Alliluyeva, and much else.[128]

Another diplomat recalled, "Sooner or later, those who worked in the West for any length of time all came to the conclusion that our system was just no good [*ne deesposobnaia*]. But we weren't able to do anything [to improve relations with the West]."[129]

Beyond such general trends in the experience of Soviet diplomats, a change of particular importance came with the inception of arms control. It has already been seen how the shift from propagandistic calls for "general and complete disarmament" to serious negotiations required the easing of controls on information and the studying of Western theory and policy. Higher standards of knowledge and professionalism were needed for training a new corps of less ideological, more businesslike "Americanists." Equally influential was the experience gained in extensive bilateral and multilateral talks. A strong current favoring arms control emerged among midlevel ministry officials. Georgy Kornienko recalled the situation in the mid 1960s when the United States first proposed limiting strategic defenses:

Our leaders really couldn't understand these issues. . . . When the subject was first broached, the initiative came from bureaucrats . . . in the Ministry of Foreign Affairs, those who worked on the United States and studied disarmament issues; and though they weren't technical experts, they'd read American publications and understood these concepts, so they started to think.[130]

Disarmament concerns were also uppermost for a third group of *mezhdunarodniki*: scientists. Among the earliest critics of ideology's intrusion on scholarship, scientists also led in calling for integration with foreign cultural and economic life.[131] Prominent were senior figures, such as Tamm and Kapitsa, whose outlook was shaped by experience abroad before Stalin's forced isolation. Another was Lev Artsimovich, schooled under NEP, a pioneer in plasma physics who also pioneered the revival of international scientific ties.[132] Their "cosmopolitan" views influenced a younger generation—whose best-known representative was Sakharov—that matured during the war.[133] But it was the opening to the West that had the greatest impact. The anti-nuclear activism of Linus Pauling and Robert Oppenheimer, for example, made a great impression on Sakharov's thinking.[134] Yevgeny Velikhov and Roald Sagdeyev, of a still-younger cohort, in turn credited not only the influence of such exemplars as Artsimovich and Sakharov in the evolution of their ideas, but also the broad foreign interchange that came with the thaw.[135]

Leading scientists, along with many others, were struck by what they saw in "closed" screenings of such satirical or apocalyptic films as *On the Beach* and *Doctor Strangelove*.[136] Their new exposure to a broad range of Western views—together with their professional expertise on nuclear-technical issues—led many to a rethinking of international confrontation, especially when the Soviet leadership entered serious arms talks.[137] Attention swiftly turned from building bombs to the possibilities of their reduction or elimination. Some, such as Sakharov, had privately studied such issues as the effects of atmospheric nuclear testing, while others were now formally charged with exploring strategic problems as technical advisers to the new negotiations.[138] Moreover, thanks to the thaw, scientists also participated in new international fora dedicated to issues of peace and security: Pugwash and Dartmouth conferences, UN-sponsored meetings (and, later, those of the United Nations

Association of the USA), the Soviet-American Disarmament Study groups, and several others.[139]

Such exchanges went far in breaking down stereotypes and forging common understanding.[140] They were also instrumental in spreading Western strategic concepts.[141] Significantly, the first Soviet analyst to embrace openly the logic of limiting strategic defenses was a *political* scientist. Gennady Gerasimov, drawing on U.S. critiques of defensive systems, presented in 1965 the logic that, seven years later, would be enshrined in perhaps the most important arms-control agreement of the nuclear age—the ABM (anti-ballistic missile) Treaty.[142] In 1967, when the United States first formally proposed such limitations—which the USSR initially rejected— Artsimovich contradicted his government's position in an address to the Pugwash conference of that year in Sweden.[143] Sakharov's searching 1968 samizdat memorandum, *Reflections on Progress, Coexistence, and Intellectual Freedom,* also called for limiting ABM systems as part of a broader plea for sweeping domestic reforms and international cooperation.[144]

Soviet Intellectuals and the Prague Spring

By the mid-to-late 1960s, the various reformist critiques outlined above were coalescing into a single coherent and vigorous intellectual current. The priorities of writers and artists were not identical to those of economists and sociologists, just as the immediate concerns of philosophers and historians differed from those of scientists and policy analysts. But all sought similar liberalization in economic, social, and political life. Moreover, most were united by an increasingly Western orientation in foreign policy—and a "Westernizer" social identity at home—that saw their country's future in expanding Khrushchev's early steps toward broad integration with foreign economic, scientific, and cultural life.

> Analyzing [East European] reforms . . . we concluded that many of them could be . . . adopted in our country. We studied the rapid integration of Western Europe, deeply envious of the Common Market and its contrast with the slow, bureaucratic functioning of CEMA [the Council for Economic Mutual Assistance]. We thought about acquiring . . . modern technology and joining in the

greatest achievements of world culture. In other words, we dreamed of reforming Russia.[145]

For this new intelligentsia, "the children of the 20th congress," Stalinist beliefs about a "hostile capitalist encirclement" had long since disappeared, and even Leninist tenets on the irreconcilability of capitalism and socialism were broadly questioned.[146] Sakharov raised these issues openly in his 1968 *Reflections* memorandum. "The division of mankind threatens it with disaster," he began, and "in the face of these perils, any action increasing the division of mankind, any preaching of the incompatibility of world ideologies and nations is madness and a crime."[147] Sakharov saw salvation in a steady "convergence" of the socialist and capitalist systems.[148]

To be sure, many reformist intellectuals retained a broadly Marxist outlook. But theirs was less the Marx of class struggle and revolution and more the Marx of broader humanistic interests and concern for mankind's alienation. It was a Marxism that led back to a European tradition of social-democratic reformism. And, given the Stalinist legacy, it led to a search for "socialism with a human face," to reforms of an arbitrary, militarized, hypercentralized system that would unleash society's potential for economic vitality, cultural diversity, and international harmony. For most liberals, these goals were embodied in the model of the Prague Spring.

With the hindsight of August 1968, the Brezhnev regime's intolerance of substantial reforms anywhere in its socialist camp suggests that the end of the thaw began with Khrushchev's removal in October 1964. But the perception then was very different. Khrushchev's fall was greeted by many with optimism; his cultural intolerance had grown oppressive, for example, and his "hare-brained schemes" were seen as the main impediment to economic reform.[149] Although conservatives were emboldened by the change at the top, the view of most liberals at the time was that a fight was now under way for "Brezhnev's soul," and that the outcome was not at all preordained. Accordingly, they boldly joined the struggle.

The conservative resurgence was first felt incrementally, in actions such as the expulsion from the Party of outspoken liberals such as Karyakin.[150] Hard-line voices grew louder, from dogmatic ideologists to military writers who largely ignored Khrushchev's coexistence-and-disarmament priorities in a renewed emphasis on international class struggle and the winnability of nuclear war.[151] Sergei Trapeznikov, a rigid neo-Stalinist, became Brezhnev's adviser for academic-scientific affairs. In 1965, as Rumyantsev was forced from *Pravda*, Trapeznikov declared the 1930s "one of the most brilliant periods" in Soviet history;[152] also sacked were reformist *Pravda* writers Lisichkin, Chernichenko, and Yegor Yakovlev.[153]

The liberals responded vigorously. Tvardovsky fought and won many battles with *Novy Mir*'s censors and, as seen, important reformist works in all fields were published in the years 1965 to 1968. Announcement of the "Kosygin reforms" in 1965 raised hopes, as did a 1966 address in which Brezhnev criticized those who would limit the social sciences to a purely "propagandistic" role.[154] When conservatives began pushing for Stalin's rehabilitation, many prominent scientists, writers, and other intellectuals protested directly to Brezhnev.[155] The 1966 trial for "anti-Soviet slander" of writers Andrei Sinyavsky and Yuli Daniel prompted other protests.[156] Another diverse group—including Rumyantsev, Maisky, Central Committee staffer Chernyaev, and military historian Col. Vyacheslav Dashichev—supported Nekrich at various stages of the battle over his controversial *June 22, 1941*.[157] In 1967, Burlatsky and Karpinsky published another strong appeal for cultural-intellectual freedom.[158]

However ominous the signs of a neo-Stalinist resurgence, the hopes of Soviet liberals rose even further with the inception of the Czechoslovak reforms. As an intelligentsia-led movement, presided over by the Communist Party in a "fraternal" country historically friendly to Russia, the Prague Spring's impact on Soviet intellectuals was enormous. It was an experiment that united the many political, economic, and social reforms that they sought for the USSR, a concrete model for further de-Stalinization.

> The political and economic system [they] were trying to transform had been created as the mirror image of ours. Therefore, Czechoslovakia's experience [was] transferable to our country. My best-case scenario went something like this: After reforms, Czechoslovakia's workers would be given incentives . . . factory managers would . . . see value in innovation, writers would be allowed to publish. As labor, management and the intelligentsia united, economic indicators would shoot up. Impressed by the Czech economic miracle, Soviet leaders would attempt similar reforms.[159]

Interest in East European reforms had been strong since the late 1950s, as already noted. By the mid 1960s, the writings of Yugoslav, Hungarian, and Czechoslovak reformers were known to their Soviet counterparts. Prominent were the works of Janos Kornai and Ota Sik, the latter becoming the chief economic theorist of the Prague Spring. In 1967 and 1968, the professional and personal links between Soviet and Czech reformers grew even stronger.[160] Moreover, Soviet interest went far beyond narrow specialists' circles. Solzhenitsyn's "Open Letter" to the 1967 Congress of Czechoslovak Writers was "one of the brightest and hottest sparks" for Soviet reformism.[161] The Prague Spring was also central in stimulating Sakharov's *Reflections*.[162] In general, liberal intellectuals were transfixed by the experiment under way in Prague.[163]

The reformers followed events through the Soviet press, in the interested and often sympathetic coverage of *Problemy Mira i Sotsializma*, and through Czech articles in official Russian translations. As the Soviet media turned hostile, foreign radio broadcasts were monitored. Other interested Russians turned to Czechoslovak sources; some already knew Czech while others now learned it, translating news from the "fraternal" papers *Literarni Listy* and *Rude Pravo* for themselves and colleagues.[164] Writings on Czechoslovakia became the most popular samizdat items, a notable example being the Czechoslovak Communist Party's *Action Program*.[165] Analysis of East European reformism had figured prominently in the samizdat journal *Politicheskii Dnevuik* (Political Diary) since the mid 1960s; in 1968, Czechoslovakia completely dominated the bulletin.

"Prague became the Mecca of the Soviet opposition,"[166] literally as well as figuratively. Leading the way were staffers of *Problemy Mira i Sotsializma*. "Those on the scene were naturally most excited . . . but even those of us who had worked in Prague somewhat earlier were caught up in events. . . . We all had Czech friends and contacts, we couldn't help our enthusiasm."[167] With censorship tightening, Soviet "Praguers" such as Vladimir Lukin also provided a vital personal link for interested Muscovites.

> Pavel Litvinov and I recalled an . . . episode from early 1968. I returned to Moscow from Prague on business and met with a friend, P. Yakir, who asked me to report on events in Czechoslovakia. We agreed to meet at his apartment. . . . I cau-

tioned that only our friends should be present [but] when I
arrived, literally all of dissident Moscow was there in his home. I
couldn't back out, and there ensued a lecture with questions and
answers . . . that was followed by a [typical] Moscow "kitchen" discussion.[168]

In short, "the entire Moscow liberal intelligentsia was preoccupied
with the Prague Spring." Many were skeptical of the Kremlin's tolerance, but most were hopeful and all were uplifted. "In the early
summer of 1968, there were few anti-socialists among the Moscow
intelligentsia . . . we believed again."[169]

Given such hopes, the crushing of the Prague Spring in late
August was a painful blow, a powerful "cognitive punch" toward
further rethinking of domestic and international politics. One emotion appears in nearly every intellectual's recollection of the time:
"Burning shame, shame for the policy of our country"; "The shame
of our complicity . . . our servility"; "Such deep shame . . . that I
had to turn away upon meeting Czech friends and colleagues";
"The shameful . . . suicide of socialism." All were "ashamed of being
part of a barbarian country that had clubbed its enlightened neighbor."[170]

This view of the Prague Spring's demise—the brutal invasion of
a progressive neighbor—dominated Soviet liberals' assessments of
their government's action. Over the twelve thaw years since the
crushing of the Hungarian revolt, their outlook had changed considerably. The justification that was widely though passively accepted in 1956—blaming Western instigation and a NATO threat to the
socialist camp—was broadly rejected in 1968.[171] Instead it was seen
as an act of pure imperialism, and some went so far as to place events
in a particular historical context.

Solzhenitsyn, drawing a parallel to tsarist Russia's crushing of a
Polish rebellion in 1863, argued that the country needed "a new
Herzen"—that was to say, a Russian patriot willing to denounce
Soviet imperialism.[172] Bard Alexander Galich, in his *St. Petersburg
Romance*, allegorically raised the legacy of the Decembrists, the offi-
cer-noblemen who, in search of reforms, rose up against the autocracy in 1825.[173] His refrain—"Dare you come to the square, when
that hour strikes?"—took on special meaning when a demonstration
was indeed staged on Red Square four days later.[174] Among the pro-

testers' banners was one that read "For your freedom and ours," a slogan that hailed from the Poles' nineteenth-century fight for independence from the tsarist empire and now challenged twentieth-century Russians to reject imperialism.[175]

Though only seven protesters answered the challenge to "come to the square" literally, many protested in other ways. Lukin, the young "Praguer," whose meeting with prominent dissidents was described above, openly criticized the invasion and was promptly sent home to Moscow.[176] *Izvestiia* correspondents Vladlen Krivosheyev and Boris Orlov not only refused to report the Kremlin's version of events, but actually tried to communicate their dissent both in the media and directly to the Soviet leadership, for which they, too, were punished.[177] Central Committee staffer Alexander Bovin, who had been so bold as to warn his Czech friends of an imminent invasion at the July meeting of Soviet and Czechoslovak leaders, also protested directly to Brezhnev.[178] And poet Yevgeny Yevtushenko, in a telegram to Brezhnev, called the invasion "a tragic mistake" that "detracts from our prestige in the eyes of the world and our own."[179]

Protests took other forms as well. Tvardovsky, for example, refused orders for the Party committee at *Novy Mir* to pass a resolution endorsing the invasion.[180] Such statements were orchestrated in Party organizations throughout the country, from farms and factories to academic institutes. Gefter walked out of the room at the Institute of History when the vote was called, an act of defiance that would further cripple his career.[181] Yegor Yakovlev, then the editor of *Zhurnalist*, provocatively published the liberal Czech press law and was promptly fired.[182] Central Committee staffer Shakhnazarov refused to join the "brigade" set up to provide publicistic support for the invasion, and he, too, was punished.[183]

Bovin and Shakhnazarov were not the only young apparatchiks who shared in the "deep dismay" that enveloped liberal opinion.[184] Throughout the Central Committee's International Department and other sections of the apparat, as well as in the new foreign-affairs institutes and elsewhere, were many who had together caught the "virus" of the Prague Spring, hopes of democratizing, modernizing, and further opening Soviet society.[185] And these dozens of the elite "Party intelligentsia" joined the hundreds of other reformist writers, scholars, and scientists (and thousands of other critical thinkers) in sympathy with the goals of thoroughgoing domestic and international change. Importantly, this sympathy did not evaporate with the shock of August 1968. While the ensuing crackdown on reformist activity forced upon many a stark choice—conformism or nonconformism, even dissidence—many who chose the former retained their ideals and made quiet but valuable contributions from within the system.

Arbatov "rescued" Lukin and gave him a home at his new USA Institute, as he had recently done for Boris Nikiforov, a legal scholar persecuted for refusing to serve on the puppet jury that condemned Sinyavsky and Daniel.[186] Shatalin, expelled from the Party for a highly critical report on the economy, was "saved" by Academy of Sciences president Mstislav Keldysh.[187] Alexander Yakovlev, then a midlevel official in the Ideology Department of the Central Committee and later Gorbachev's main perestroika ally, helped soften the blow to Karpinsky and Burlatsky after their article in defense of intellectual freedom angered powerful conservatives.[188] The pair soon landed at the new Institute of Concrete Social Research, along with other fired reformers such as Levada and Lisichkin, through the efforts of the still-influential but weakened Rumyantsev. The former *Problemy Mira i Sotsializma* and *Pravda* editor also aided such "semidissidents" as Karyakin and Gefter by employing them informally as researchers and speechwriters.[189]

Rumyantsev, now a vice president of the Academy of Sciences, was aided in establishing the new institute by his former Prague assistant Anatoly Chernyaev, who had become an analyst in the Central Committee's International Department.[190] In 1969, Chernyaev also helped create the Institute of Scientific Information on the Social Sciences (INION) and facilitated the appointment of Lev Delusin, his erstwhile Prague colleague, as director. Another veteran of the Burlatsky-Arbatov Central Committee consultant group under Andropov, Delusin in turn hired such liberal staffers as the fired *Izvestiia* correspondent Boris Orlov, and the budding dissident Ludmilla Alexeyeva, before being forced out himself just a year later.[191] Other such instances, of small steps in defense of embattled reformers and reformism, were numerous.[192]

■

The suppression of the Prague Spring and the subsequent crackdown on liberal intellectuals engendered a wide range of responses. A very few protested openly, and a great many did nothing, but between these extremes there was a variety of milder protests and subtler forms of opposition, from less-public criticism to the defense of colleagues and friends who had risked their positions and privileges. Such quiet resistance naturally attracted less attention. But it was equally noteworthy for its demonstration of the broad acceptance among post-Stalin intellectuals, both within and without the Party apparatus, of the reformist, integrationist, "Westernizing" beliefs that were the core of new thinking.

Certainly for many, the end of the Prague Spring was also the end of hopes for liberalizing change, a deep disillusion that led to conformism and cynical careerism. But others drew the opposite conclusion: that the Prague Spring had shown that reforms *were* possible, but only under an enlightened leader that many "awaited as if for the coming of the Messiah."[193] For these intellectuals, the Prague Spring acquired a kind of mythological status that, while sustaining, was also not unproblematic. Cut off before it had a chance to succeed, the Czech perestroika was also denied the opportunity to fail. Soviet liberals viewing the arrested Czech and Soviet reforms did not see the contradictions, inconsistencies, and often utopian aspects of their own hopes.[194] Their naïveté—if only leaders had the will, then reforms would "work without a hitch"— would be a severe handicap to a later leader's search for "socialism with a human face."[195]

But the reverse of illusion was inspiration, and here the legacy of the Prague Spring and the Russian thaw was undeniably positive. Like a latter-day NEP, they offered concrete models for future reformers. Writing in the gloom of post–Prague Spring reaction, the journalist and former Komsomol official Karpinsky optimistically foresaw the following:

> Our tanks in Prague were, if you will, an anachronism, an "inadequate" weapon. They "fired" at ideas. With no hope of hitting the target. . . . With a fist to the jaw of thinking society, they thought they had knocked out and "captured" its thinking processes. [But these] new times are percolating into the apparatus and forming a

layer of party intellectuals . . . an arm of the intelligentsia, its "parliamentary fraction" within the administrative structure. This fraction will inevitably grow, constituting a hidden opposition. [One day it will triumph and then we will] take consolation in the fact that our cause had not perished, that it had "awakened" new layers within the Party intelligentsia who would repeat the attempt with more success.[196]

4 ■
The Dynamics of New Thinking in the Era of Stagnation

> Formulated without regard for real interests and opportunities, and based on the prejudices, ambitions and illusions [of members of the Politburo] . . . foreign policy increasingly lost touch with what has happening in the outside world. . . . By the mid-1970s, they seriously thought that they'd already won the "cold war" and that they had every reason to anticipate a new redivision of the world.
> —Andrei Grachev, *Kremlevskaia khronika*

> We reformers dreamed of ending . . . the division between East and West, of halting the insanity of the arms race and ending the "Cold War." —Alexander Yakovlev, *Gor'kaia chasha*

For Soviet new thinking, the long rule of Leonid Brezhnev was a distinctly contradictory period. In part it was a time of great hopes, of the maturation and activization of reformist thought in foreign (and domestic) affairs, boosted by an extensive new thaw in East-West relations. But it was also the "era of stagnation," a time when the country's mounting problems were largely ignored. At home, urgently needed changes were rejected as socioeconomic ills grew increasingly critical. Abroad, an expansionist course eventually undermined détente and accelerated a perilous and ruinously expensive arms race.

As seen, for many the post-Khrushchev era began with anticipation of "more consistent pursuit of the 20th Congress line." The new leadership's first major initiative was a plan for economic reform, and even though conservatives soon went on the offensive, liberals fought back and, among other successes, helped defeat an effort to rehabilitate Stalin. Only the crushing of the Prague Spring experiment in 1968 ended hopes for similar near-term liberalization of the Soviet system. Anti-Western rhetoric now grew, while official pronouncements even qualified Khrushchev's unequivocal rejection of nuclear war.

But just a few years later, a new détente blossomed. The centerpiece was arms control, particularly the 1972 SALT (Strategic Arms Limitation Talks) and ABM treaties. These breakthroughs led to expanded Soviet-Western ties in many other areas, from trade agreements to new academic, cultural, and scientific exchanges. Symbolically, perhaps, the apogee of détente was a joint Apollo-Soyuz spaceflight in 1975. Substantively, the high point was reached with the Helsinki Accords of the Conference on Security and Cooperation in Europe (CSCE) that same year. With all these steps, the détente of the 1970s went considerably farther than had the earlier epoch of "peaceful coexistence."

But in other ways, Brezhnev's "thaw" was notably more limited than Khrushchev's. From the outset, ideological controls remained much tighter. The media and culture were never so openly bold or experimental as they had been a decade before. Outwardly, at least, the Party enforced stricter orthodoxy in intellectual life. Dissidence was harshly repressed and periodic conservative attacks kept reformist-Westernizing thought on the defensive. Instead, the Party tolerated or even encouraged a growing anti-Western, Russian national current. In an effort to counter new foreign influences, themes of "vigilance," militarization, and a virtual cult of the Great Patriotic War were assiduously fostered.

By the mid-to-late 1970s, even as Western military programs slowed, development of new Soviet nuclear and conventional forces accelerated. Simultaneously, emboldened by U.S. recognition of its superpower status and strategic parity, the Kremlin embarked on a new course of activism in the third world. Soviet leaders, encouraged by a glut of petrodollars while the West endured recession at home and the United States suffered a post-Vietnam hesitancy abroad, appeared convinced that the tide of history had indeed turned. But within a few years, their military-political assertiveness had soured détente. The high Brezhnev era ended as it had begun, with a foreign invasion; the 1979 dispatch of a "limited contingent" of troops to Afghanistan was the final nail in détente's coffin. Though Brezhnev would live for three more years, his near-complete physical and mental incapacity made this a time of political paralysis. With no leadership worthy of the name, the country sputtered on autopilot.

The prevailing Western interpretation of Soviet foreign-policy thought during this period has been that most analysts in the USSR shared, and often encouraged, their leaders' confidence that "the correlation of forces" had shifted in Moscow's favor; global assertiveness would be tolerated by a declining West, it was believed, and only with the crises of the decade's end did Soviet analysts reconsider the lessons of détente. In fact, among the community of new thinkers, the experience of the 1970s was very different. For them, the main impact of détente was not to bolster an expansionist course, but rather to subject it to increasing criticism.

Already by the late 1960s, the social and natural sciences had been distinguished by a growing anti-isolationist, Western-oriented current. By the early-mid 1970s, building on this early progress and now propelled by extensive new foreign ties, liberal specialists from diverse fields called for a much broader rapprochement abroad (and extensive reforms at home). But their efforts went largely unheeded, and by decade's end simply saving the modest gains of détente prompted even bolder critiques. By this time, however, Brezhnev was almost completely infirm. Reformist pleas were ignored, reactionary voices grew ominously louder, and the Kremlin's "hegemonic, great-power" policies ultimately left a nearly bankrupt and absurdly militarized country in confrontation with most of the world.[1]

The Brezhnev Cohort: Old Thinking's Last Hostages

One of the most important insights into Brezhnev-era politics since the inception of glasnost is that ideology loomed much larger than was previously understood. Certainly the hubris of the Khrushchev years—faith in socialism's rapid ascendance over capitalism—was supplanted by a cynicism in which preservation of the Stalinist system at home, the empire abroad, and the powerful interests vested therein were central. But many accounts also stress the enduring influence of the hostile-isolationist outlook:

For us, one factor always blocked the development of stable relations with the United States and the West as a whole—the primacy of an irreconcilable "ideological struggle" between the two socio-political systems. Any agreement, any attempt to improve our relations with the USA, would immediately run into this obstacle.[2]

In the Middle East, a senior diplomat recalled, fealty to its "historical mission" and "an orthodox and dogmatic mode of thinking" propelled the Kremlin toward superpower confrontation.[3] In Vietnam, wrote Anatoly Dobrynin, longtime ambassador to the United States, these beliefs prolonged war "to the detriment of our own basic interests."[4] And in Africa, the warnings of pro-détente advisers about the danger posed to East-West ties by intervention in regional conflicts were trumped by ideologues' arguments that "Angola was reminiscent of Spain in 1935, we couldn't just stand aside and ignore our [internationalist] duty."[5] Others recall their leaders' dogmatism in various specific episodes. For example, early in the Brezhnev era—more than a decade after Stalin's death opened the world to his successors—Soviet President Nikolai Podgorny visited Austria and, viewing the bounty of Viennese markets, remarked, "Look how well they set things up for my visit."[6] A decade later, celebrating an apparent socialist tide in the third world, General Secretary Brezhnev exclaimed, "See, even in the jungles they want to follow Lenin!"[7]

Such beliefs would seem comical were it not for their role in the tragedy of renewed confrontation and an accelerating arms race. And even the few instances cited among many such revelations since the inception of glasnost reveal the several ways in which the hostile-isolationist identity contributed to détente's demise. One was through ignorance of the West and belief in its abiding threat to the USSR. Another was enduring faith in the expansion and ultimate triumph of socialism. And a third, in many accounts the most salient, was an ideological insecurity or "complex of revolutionary inadequacy" that drove expansion abroad in an effort to bolster legitimacy at home—both in the eyes of the Soviet people and, more importantly, in the minds of the leaders themselves.[8]

Many of these "servitors of an archaic ideological cult" were not so much cynics as captives of the "myths, prejudices, and unrealized hopes" of the Lenin and, especially, Stalin epochs.[9] Fealty to dogmas served not only to rationalize their hold on power, but also to justify their—and their country's—bitter experience. Critically, in each of its aspects noted above, old thinking was perpetuated by the systematic distortion of reality. An "ideocracy" reigned, an ideological system that operated on several levels and served multiple functions.[10] Information and assessments were overtly bent through the prism of dogma, while perceptions and beliefs were covertly molded by ideology's monopoly over the symbols, language, and terms of analysis—the broader discourse—of politics.[11] Exaggerations of socialism's prospects, and imperialism's threats, were consciously advanced to please bosses and further careers.[12] But many also subconsciously distorted facts in order to "reaffirm the centrality of their experience and to explain to their colleagues developments abroad within a common framework of reference."[13]

The persistence of the hostile-isolationist identity must also be seen in the context of the elite's path to power. While many analysts of Soviet politics emphasize the differences in the backgrounds of the Khrushchev and Brezhnev cohorts, the similarities were probably even more salient. Though one group was still maturing while the other launched careers—over the bitter years of 1918 to 1921— they drew similar lessons from the epoch of civil war, class war, and foreign intervention. Both were also profoundly shaped by World War II and, most important, they shared Stalin's pre- and postwar "hostile capitalist encirclement" as a central formative experience. *The ABC* was supplanted by the *Short Course*, but both cultivated fear and loathing of the West.

Moreover, both generations of elites—ill-educated, anti-intellectual, and xenophobic—belonged to successive waves of *vydvizhentsy* largely drawn from Russia's rural masses. As with Khrushchev, Brezhnev's first exposure to "a totally different world" was the humiliation and envy of a poor youth in a factory town run by French, Belgians, and Poles.

> It was as if they were a different breed of people—well-fed, well-groomed, and arrogant. An engineer dressed in a formal peak cap and coat with a velvet collar would never shake hands with a worker, and the worker approaching an engineer or foreman was obliged to take off his hat. We worker's children could only look at "the clean public" strolling to the sounds of a string orchestra from behind the railings of the town park.[14]

From the tensions of the late 1920s through the terror of the 1930s, and thence to wartime service as political-ideological officers, many Brezhnev-era elites needed little encouragement to embrace Stalin's cold war precepts.[15] In contrast to the Decembrist officers who returned from the post–Napoleonic War occupation of Paris imbued with reformist ideas, Brezhnev's reaction to the suggestion of his assignment to the French capital in 1945 was "I'll climb the Eiffel Tower and spit on all of Europe!"[16] Nor, despite the subsequent post-Stalin thaw, could these critical formative experiences be quickly overcome.

The enduring influence of Marxism-Leninism as the source of legitimacy and language of politics, together with an ingrained Stalinist outlook, produced in the Brezhnev leadership a deep distrust of the West and a lasting susceptibility to "revolutionary" appeals and expansionist policies. Notwithstanding his sometime reliance on a younger group of aide-speechwriters (which included Arbatov, Bovin, and other reform-minded specialists), Brezhnev himself remained psychologically dependent on—and far more comfortable with—his own generation of more dogmatic, orthodox advisers. They ensured that his

> declarations, proposals or formulations conformed to Marxism's "holy writ." This obviously troubled Brezhnev greatly when he became general secretary. He thought that to do something "un-Marxist" now was impermissible—the entire party, the whole world, was watching him. Leonid Ilyich was very weak in [matters of] theory and felt this keenly.[17]

These advisers included Boris Ponomarev, the conservative head of the International Department, and the dogmatic Ideology Secretary Mikhail Suslov, both Stalin-era "Red Professors."[18] But equally influential, especially early in Brezhnev's reign, were trusted associates who had built careers alongside their patron. Viktor Golikov was a "committed Stalinist" and self-styled "theoretician on all issues [including] ideology and foreign affairs."[19] Another old crony, who became the bête noire of Soviet liberalism, was Sergei Trapeznikov, an unrepentant Stalinist whom Brezhnev named to head the Central Committee department overseeing the Academy of Sciences.[20] For Trapeznikov, anti-intellectual campaigns were reenactments of "the real battle for socialism"—

Stalin's brutal collectivization—whose pain and glory were always with him in the form of a disfigurement inflicted by pitchfork-wielding peasants.[21] Mediocrities at best, these were the men whom Brezhnev regarded as "real experts in politics, economics, and Marxism."[22]

The USSR's situation in the late 1970s has been characterized as that of a not-atypical "overextended" power. But Soviet overextension was so severe—it is now evident that the military-imperial appetite consumed more than a quarter of the country's wealth—that neither international, power-centered analyses, nor domestic, interest-group models, offer adequate explanation.[23] And it was at that moment, when "retrenchment" was so long overdue, that the final, ruinous foreign adventure in Afghanistan was launched.

Documents reveal that the leadership was well aware of the international outcry that would follow an invasion, as well as of the danger of the military quagmire that soon resulted.[24] While the actual decision to intervene remains shrouded in mystery, evidence shows that old thinking again played a key role. This it did directly, through grossly inflated assessments of a Western threat.[25] It also operated indirectly, through the call of "internationalist duty" to support a revolutionary movement proclaiming its "socialist orientation."[26] As with Czechoslovakia a decade earlier, there was also the tendency in a crisis to fall back on a familiar, simplified, black-and-white interpretation of events. In their dotage, this tendency on the part of the Brezhnev gerontocracy was only heightened—as was reflected in Defense Minister Ustinov's bizarre suggestion that they should defend Afghan "socialism" by "arming the working class."[27]

Brezhnev and his colleagues were simultaneously the inheritors and hostages of a vast "command-administrative" system at home and an empire abroad, and their policies were largely driven by the goal of preserving that legacy. But they were also captives of another legacy, the hostile-isolationist outlook of a divided world and threatening capitalist West. It was the latter, as well as the former, that limited and eventually doomed the second post-Stalin détente. And it was their liberation from the latter that prepared a new generation of thinkers for a more decisive break with the Stalinist (and Leninist) heritage.

Intellectual Life Under Brezhnev: Public Conformism, Private Reformism

Paradoxically, the era of conservatism began with a small reformist victory. As already seen, attempts to raise Stalin back to his pedestal were fought off in efforts that involved the entire liberal intelligentsia, uniting Party intellectuals and senior academicians with writers, artists, and future dissidents.[28] But despite its symbolic significance, the thwarting of Stalin's full rehabilitation was a rearguard action at best, a small battle in a losing war against conservatism and reaction. The neo-Stalinists eventually triumphed on nearly all fronts—ending hopes of economic reform, aligning with resurgent Russian nationalism, and clamping down on intellectual freedom and openness.

The "highlights" of this period were grim. *Novy Mir* editor Alexander Tvardovsky, long under siege, was fired in 1970. Alexei Rumyantsev, who had provided a haven for many reformers fired in the first round of conservative attacks, was now defeated himself; his sociology institute was crushed in 1971–72, and he and his staff of prominent liberals were dismissed en masse. Similar purges swept other institutes. Tellingly, in 1973 the minister of defense, along with the minister of foreign affairs and the KGB director, were elevated to full Politburo status.

For Yuri Andropov, as KGB chief, his days of sponsoring creative young scholar-analysts were long past. He carried out his new charge—repressing dissidence—with a thoroughness that sent chills through the liberal intelligentsia. Meanwhile, the last of his 1960s consultant group now dispersed. Some, such as Alexander Bovin and Gennady Gerasimov, worked in journalism. Others, such as Fedor Burlatsky, Ivan Frolov, and Lev Delusin, moved between academic and scholar-publicist jobs. Georgy Arbatov and Oleg Bogomolov now headed their own research institutes.

Though most remaining idealistic hopes had been crushed, a different and ultimately more important kind of progress began in earnest. There now ensued much more serious study of the outside world—the slow but steady accumulation of knowledge and insight about foreign political, social, and economic life that went well beyond that of the thaw era. Over time, it became clear that efforts to quash reformism, by crushing the few arenas where it had blossomed and casting its exponents away, had failed. Like seeds scattered to the wind, reformist ideas germinated and grew wherever these liberal thinkers landed.

At the Institute of World Economy and International Relations (IMEMO), new director Nikolai Inozemtsev quickly shaped his staff into perhaps the leading critical think tank. Arbatov, whose USA Institute (renamed the USA-Canada Institute, or ISKAN, in 1974) was founded only in 1967, gathered a diverse group of analysts that included independent-minded officers on loan from the Soviet general staff. Bogomolov became director of the new Institute of the Economy of the World Socialist System (IEMSS) after the drama of 1968 made it clear that Eastern Europe required more serious study. In 1969, the Institute of Scientific Information on the Social Sciences (INION) was created and, under Delusin's brief directorship, began its vital work of disseminating Western scholarship as well as conducting its own research on such topics as social democracy. Novosibirsk and the Central Economic-Mathematical Institute (TsEMI) continued their development into centers of original socioeconomic thought. Even the Central Committee apparatus slowly changed; Shakhnazarov, Chernyaev, Yakovlev, Nikolai Shishlin, Vadim Zagladin, and other reform-minded analysts—the now-middle-aged "children of the 20th Congress"—were joined by a modest influx of younger liberals, "the children of détente."[29]

The steady growth of reformist, anti-isolationist thought was also aided by two other developments. The first was a sharp deterioration in relations with China, to the point of armed conflict; this forced a deeper rethinking of the two-camp outlook and, in some instances, also offered analysts an ostensibly socialist state that could be studied and criticized with direct relevance for the USSR. Second, and more important, was the rise of détente with the West; though accompanied by a tightening of ideological orthodoxy at home, détente provided specialists their broadest access to the West in 50 years.

The scope of this new opening swiftly dwarfed that of the thaw era. Academic exchanges, conferences, international science and policy fora, and diplomatic and cultural negotiations were soon a full order of magnitude greater than under Khrushchev. This interchange developed on other levels, too, as Western media and scholarship in the humanities as well as the natural and social sciences became widely available to Soviet analysts. Their influence grew evident as political science, economics, and international relations began debating foreign concepts with growing frequency and seriousness, while the boldest and most original new works moved rapidly toward broader integration with Western scholarship.

As in their studies, so, too, in their conclusions; the early-mid 1970s saw many calling not just for expanded intercourse with the West, but also for more radical changes that would move their country toward broader integration with the liberal international community. However, amid the prevailing orthodoxy, the reformist-integrationist views of many philosophers, economists, sociologists, scientists, and political analysts of all sorts were not always readily visible, especially from afar. Some could be found in specialized literature, others in classified or limited-circulation publications; and it is in these venues, including analyses for various state ministries or reports to the Central Committee, that some of the boldest reform proposals were seen.

This maturation and mobilization of new thinking early in the Brezhnev era could not have occurred without the foundation laid under Khrushchev. In nearly all its aspects—from the evolution of particular ideas and the impact of specific individuals, to the role of key institutes—détente-era new thinking was an organic outgrowth of thaw-era changes. By the late 1960s, the changes had already gone so far that, as noted earlier, a new hard line could not halt, and in some instances further stimulated, reformist thought. But neither could the progress of the 1970s have advanced as rapidly as it did without the new impetus of détente. As Arbatov noted, a "majority of our specialists" had yet to overcome "pervasive ideology . . . propaganda and fear." Speaking for himself he recalled that, when named to head the USA Institute,

> my knowledge was insufficiently deep. . . . I had never been to the United States. I had no contacts or acquaintances among Americans . . . [but] harder to acquire than acquaintances . . . was a feeling for the country, a partly rational, partly intuitive sense that we could only acquire through regular professional contact with a wide variety of specialists from the United States and with representatives from government and business.[30]

Thanks to such contacts, less than a decade later this situation was reversed. Victor Kremenyuk, one of Arbatov's ISKAN deputies, recalled that "it became easier for us to talk to Americans than to our own Central Committee."[31] Anatoly Dobrynin, the longtime Soviet ambassador to Washington, noted the "deep respect, even love" for the United States that developed among some specialists in the Foreign Ministry: "Often we felt more at home in Washington than in Moscow. After all, who could we talk to back there? Nobody really, except Arbatov and Primakov.[32]

The same held for those in fields from economics to nuclear physics. And as their country stagnated, the early new thinkers saw the way out in deeper rapprochement with the West. Some shed their Marxist ideals altogether, seeing the USSR's future in adoption of radical market reforms at home and embrace of the liberal order abroad. Others retained the hopes of the 20th congress, though now of more social-democratic than socialist orientation, with Khrushchev's confrontational coexistence replaced by a desire for broader cooperation. For both—whether they envisioned an eventual "convergence" of socioeconomic systems, or their country's evolution from one to the other—Leninist-Stalinist dogmas of a divided world and hostile West were supplanted by an increasingly "global" outlook.

Politics, Science, and Society: The Emergence of a Global Outlook

The orientation toward global concerns and "universal human" (*obshchechelovecheskie*) values that replaced a class-based worldview as the cornerstone of new thinking, while usually seen as a phenomenon of the mid-to-late 1980s, in fact preceded perestroika by more than a decade. Its rise was difficult to perceive from afar, in part due to the Aesopian or "subterranean" nature of much original intellectual life under Brezhnev. But Western understanding of these changes was also hampered by approaches that, focusing on separate fields (for example, economics, sociology, history) or specific policy areas (security, trade, the third world), could not appreciate the totality of an emerging global critique that was visible only in the links *across* these fields and issue areas.

This "dispersion" was a stagnation-era necessity, for it also concealed the new thinking's breadth from ideological watchdogs quick to crush any more frontal attack (such as Sakharov's) on their dogma. But it simultaneously contributed much to new thinking's strength, informally uniting diverse individuals and ideas in an increasingly coherent critique of the hostile-isolationist identity. Sociologists and political scientists discussed literary-cultural affairs. Economists, philosophers, and historians debated issues of science and ethics. And analysts of modern China or the third world looked back to earlier historical and economic trends. In some cases, the same individuals performed pathbreaking work in various fields; in others, leading thinkers were former classmates or colleagues at academic institutes and journals. It was these personal ties and this intellectual cross-fertilization that, together with détente's exposure to foreign life, powerfully abetted the rise of a global outlook during the era of stagnation.

The rebirth of genuine political and sociological inquiry over the first post-Stalin decade was described in the preceding chapter. Over the post-Prague decade, even greater strides were taken toward less ideological, less class-bound analysis of domestic and foreign affairs. Fedor Burlatsky and Georgy Shakhnazarov, who pioneered the establishment of Soviet political science in the mid 1960s, continued to lead with studies that pushed the frontiers of their infant field much further. In his 1970 book *Lenin, the State, and Politics* Burlatsky confronted the gap between socialist ideals and Soviet reality by borrowing Western concepts of the "political system" or "regime" as distinct from formal institutions. He cited the example of Hungary, where social and economic changes since 1956 were significant notwithstanding unaltered Party-state structures. The changes were viewed positively, of course, and his praise of Hungarian reforms suggested a model for the USSR.[33] Shakhnazarov, in his 1972 *Socialist Democracy*, cautiously called attention to an absence of real democracy and stressed the need for greater freedom of information.[34] Anatoly Butenko, in *The Theory and Practice of Building Socialism*, held that a lack of democracy, together with oversized, overcentralized industry, was to blame for Soviet and East European socioeconomic woes.[35]

While Burlatsky and Shakhnazarov were well versed in foreign literature, others benefited from a proliferation of Russian-language reviews of Western scholarship. Continuing a practice begun in the early 1960s, an overall critical orientation permitted such works to pass the censors while conveying much about Western theory as well as the reality of Western political life.[36] Venyamin Chirkin, another of Burlatsky's collaborators, noted that "the polemic with bourgeois conceptions" helped to stimulate "the formation of a new branch of knowledge."[37] Beyond politics and the state, another now-invigorated branch of knowledge was the study of modern society. "As a result of participating in international conferences and having access to Western literature," Soviet sociology drew closer to foreign scholarship in both its methods and conclusions.[38] Broad professional and personal ties to the West prompted a fresh look at Soviet society and appreciation of the problems common to both socialism and capitalism. They also encouraged a search for solutions that drew on others' experience. This was seen in the works of such pioneers as Boris Grushin, Yuri Levada, Igor Kon, Vladimir Yadov, and Andrei Zdravomyslov, on such issues as labor, youth, sex, values, and even public opinion on domestic and foreign affairs.[39]

This "rapprochement" between conceptions of socialist and capitalist society, and a new understanding of Western life, necessarily influenced views of international relations. Political systems that creatively studied and sought solutions to their domestic ills—many of which plagued Soviet society too—appeared less a threat and more a source of ideas for Soviet reform.[40] Moreover, as the global character of modern social processes was understood, class-based, conflict-centered views of international relations receded even further.[41] And as Soviet thinkers looked to the future, they found orthodox models increasingly barren, and foreign thought increasingly useful.[42] Debates over "limits to growth," "postindustrial society," and other issues raised by Western "futurology" now figured prominently in their writings.[43] Though often still couched in the jargon of capitalism's crisis and socialism's superiority, the new thinkers rapidly embraced global concerns, interdependence, and even ideas of "convergence."

In this, an important pioneer was a domestic, not foreign, thinker—Andrei Sakharov. As Burlatsky recalled, "I'd never read anything like it from a Soviet author. It was a real manifesto of liberalism, free thought, a totally new and unique perspective on . . . the contemporary world."[44] The "manifesto" was Sakharov's 1968 samizdat memorandum *Progress, Peaceful Coexistence, and Intellectual Freedom.* Burlatsky credits it in the conception of his own bold 1970 proposal on "Planning Universal Peace."[45] Almost every significant new thinker has similar memories of the impact of Sakharov's pathbreaking discussion of nuclear dangers, the environment, overpopulation, and human rights.[46]

Yet a year before Sakharov's essay, overpopulation had been addressed by Gennady Gerasimov. His 1967 tract, *Will the World Become Too Crowded?*, drew on Western authors such as Kenneth Boulding and Bernard Brodie to place this issue on the Soviet agenda. Gerasimov faulted Soviet writers who held that overpopulation threatened only "bourgeois" societies, chided those who found sinister meaning in the term *birth control,* and implicitly criticized Stalinist policies by denouncing those of fascist Germany and South Africa for encouraging high birth rates under a "supremacist" ideology.[47] His 1968 article "For the Sake of a Woman's Health" contrasted the availability of contraception in the West with the single choice—abortion—facing most Soviet women.[48]

One of the pioneers of Soviet environmentalism was Grigory Khozin, a military-aviation writer who, at Arbatov's invitation, joined the USA Institute in 1969 as a space-policy specialist.[49] His *In Defense of the Planet*, though critical of the West, was probably the first open, full-scale analytical work to raise serious (albeit indirect) questions about Soviet policy.[50] He later described how research on the U.S. space program drew his attention to congressional and public oversight of science, including environmental issues:

> I saw the same technical-legal system that managed space research now turn to the environment. Ecology became a big issue, it was "small is beautiful," and that was impressive in contrast with the "gigantomania" that prevailed here. . . . You had this incredible scientific-industrial machine that now came under the Environmental Protection Agency, the Clean Air Act, the Wildlife Fund, and so on. . . . There wasn't—and couldn't have been—anything like that here.[51]

Like many others—from Zamoshkin, a leader in objective study of the West, to Artsimovich, the pioneer of Soviet scientists' involvement in arms control—Khozin was influenced by diverse new

Western ties.[52] These ranged from study of such works as those by the Club of Rome to personal meetings with U.S. scholars.[53]

One global thinker, whose outlook was formed well before the détente-era opening that was so crucial to younger specialists, was Peter Kapitsa. A physicist of world renown, Kapitsa spent the pre-war years at Cambridge University and later suffered for his principled refusal to lend his talents to nuclear weapons. Kapitsa merits comparison with Sakharov as a scientific-intellectual figure of great authority and global orientation. But in contrast to Sakharov's early strong devotion—and later harsh opposition—to the Soviet regime, Kapitsa's career was one of consistent efforts to effect reforms from within the system.[54]

Even under Stalin, Kapitsa fought for scientific integrity. In the 1960s and 1970s, he continually pressed the authorities on issues such as the environment, arms control, censorship, and international scholarly cooperation.[55] Kapitsa's years abroad were central in the formation of his outlook, as were his diverse Western contacts, his knowledge of foreign languages, and his concern over social and cultural issues. Kapitsa's iconoclasm brought more harassment in the post-Stalin years, and his views came to wider attention only via his participation in a series of debates in the early 1970s.[56] These were the roundtable discussions of global problems published in the journal *Voprosy Filosofii* (Philosophical Issues).

Ivan Frolov—another veteran of the Prague journal *Problemy Mira i Sotsializma* and a colleague of Arbatov, Burlatsky, Gerasimov, et al. in Andropov's consultant group of the early 1960s—became editor of *Voprosy Filosofii* in 1968.[57] Under his stewardship, which lasted until 1977, the journal went far beyond the usual range of Soviet philosophical concerns. But Frolov's greatest success was the 1972–73 debates that prominently featured Kapitsa in airing pressing international issues.[58]

Kapitsa's contributions to the roundtable on "Man and His Habitat" startled many. He stressed the "global nature" of economic, social, and ecological problems, ridiculed those who saw separate "socialist" and "bourgeois" approaches to them, and argued that they could be solved only by "the combined efforts of all humanity." While acknowledging the Kremlin's stated commitment to halting the pollution of Lake Baikal, Kapitsa also cited the U.S. program to restore the Great Lakes. And he blasted militarism, stressing the inadmissibility of any nuclear exchange and noting in amazement that "to this day you find people who think that if you take cover in a shelter filtered against radioactive fallout, then you'll survive."[59]

Kapitsa's frankness emboldened other roundtable participants. Khozin endorsed the U.S. idea of an international environmental center, arguing that, since the world was a "communal apartment," ecological problems demanded "the united efforts of all states."[60] IMEMO analyst A. E. Medunin criticized Soviet environmental "backwardness" and also injected an economic concern; noting the West's emphasis on clean technologies, he argued that "in 5–7 years, only those . . . technologies that cause minimal pollution will be competitive on foreign markets."[61] Cyberneticist Axel Berg took issues of technological progress a step further, praising Western programs for computer development and lamenting the attitude of "Bolsheviks . . . who think that to use [foreign models] plays into the hands of counterrevolution."[62]

With this, the debate touched on central issues of economic growth that were directly addressed in another roundtable on "The Interrelation of the Natural and Social Sciences." Nikolai Dubinin, director of the Institute of Genetics, saw a danger of pollution-induced genetic mutations and argued that Soviet technology's harmful impact on the environment resulted from "a 'ministerial' approach to exploiting natural resources." A system emphasizing quantity over quality lacked "a value-centered approach" to progress.[63] Nikolai Fedorenko, director of TsEMI and a champion of computer-mathematical models to aid planning, now stressed the limitations of his own field. Positive long-term development had social as well as economic aspects: "We can tell how many power stations there will be," but regarding culture and lifestyle "there are many questions that [central planning] cannot answer."[64]

Berg continued this critique by noting that Soviet science neglected methods "accepted and practiced throughout the world." Though one remedy for producers' ignorance of consumers' needs was better sociological research and polling, Berg also hinted that this was no substitute for direct market input.[65] Leonid Kantorovich—though he, too, could not quite say so explicitly—made the same point by questioning the dogma that the role of the market in determining prices disappears in a socialist economy. A pioneer of models to improve planning, Kantorovich nevertheless echoed Fedorenko in noting the limits of central administration. He lamented the budget distortions caused by arbitrary pricing and argued that "correct technological and production decisions, and a proper balance of productive forces, depend on correct prices."[66]

Frolov also published anti-materialist, non-Marxist views, ostensibly pure philosophical arguments that were in fact linked to the same issues of society and world civilization. In a roundtable on "Science, Ethics, and Humanism," Frolov's sometime coauthor Merab Mamardashvili wrote that science "was not just a sum of knowledge, but a constant expansion of the means for man's understanding of the world and himself in it. . . . Knowledge exists in science only as something that constantly produces a different knowledge and is in permanent transition."[67] Yuri Zamoshkin echoed this heretical, metaphysical conception of science, arguing against a "pragmatic, overly narrow . . . expedient" view that led to "administrative" approaches to issues of science and society. In fact, simply posing the question of scientific ethics implied a false separation: "The problem of science's value orientation is above all the problem of the value orientation of society."[68] In the context of so much discussion of the ills of Soviet science, Zamoshkin thus suggested that the underlying problem was a sickness in the "value orientation" of Soviet society.

Conservatism, Nationalism, and the Debate Over Russia in World Civilization

For their daring, Frolov and his staff were subjected to fierce conservative attack.[69] And though he hung on as editor of *Voprosy Filosofii* for several more years, Frolov's fate was foreshadowed by that of the early liberal tribune, *Novy Mir*, and its editor Alexander Tvardovsky.[70] By the mid 1970s, the journal's latitude had been sharply curtailed, whereas others of increasingly chauvinistic, anti-Western orientation flourished. Everywhere reaction triumphed over reformism.

In 1971, Vasily Ukraintsev became director of the Institute of Philosophy. "The bastard quickly put his house in order," one observer recalled, "clamping down on original thought and driving out outstanding scholars such as [Alexander] Zinoviev."[71] In 1972, an even more devastating purge struck the Institute of Concrete Social Research; director Rumyantsev and some 140 staffers, including Burlatsky, Karpinsky, Levada, and Zamoshkin, were fired in one stroke.[72] Rumyantsev was replaced by Mikhail Rutkeyevich, a pseudo scholar known by liberals as "the bulldozer" for his approach to critical thought.[73] There now ensued "a wholesale crackdown on the Moscow intelligentsia managed by that 'little Zhdanov' Yagodkin."[74] The crackdown struck even liberals formerly protected by their positions on the Central Committee staff. Shakhnazarov was disciplined, even though his published works were more cautious than those of his fellow political-science traveler Burlatsky.[75] Alexander Bovin, one of the last of Andropov's original consultant group still in the apparat, was fired in 1972.[76] A year later, after openly criticizing resurgent Russian nationalism, Alexander Yakovlev was dismissed from his post in the Propaganda Department and sent on a ten-year diplomatic exile to Canada.[77]

Many other new thinkers now endured a kind of internal exile, shuttling between various institutes and journals. Burlatsky was one such "intellectual gypsy," changing jobs five times over the early Brezhnev years. After the 1972 pogrom of Rumyantsev's sociology institute, he spent two years at the Institute of State and Law before joining his frequent collaborator Alexander Galkin and other beleaguered liberals at the Institute of Social Sciences to ride out the remainder of the Brezhnev era.[78]

Reflecting on this difficult period, IMEMO analyst Viktor Sheinis noted that "notwithstanding how minor were the departures from established ideological canons," it was amazing

> how quickly repression ensued, how rapidly fortifications and prison cells were rebuilt on "the front of ideological struggle." . . . The Central Committee's science department, headed by S. Trapeznikov, energetically . . . crushed research groups that had taken the first steps toward rebirth of real social studies. . . . "Ideological diversion" came back into the political lexicon, an invention of Stalin's that revived the medieval concept of the devil seducing man into sin.[79]

Of course, despite important parallels, the differences between this "ideological struggle" and Stalin's were great. Prisons were infre-

quently used and security could be had for the price of outward conformity. Echoes of the past were often heard, as in a new treatise by
the old xenophobe Mark Mitin. But this time he "received no help
from shouting mobs that filled the galleries of academic halls [under
Stalin]."[80]

The harshest sanctions were reserved for open dissidents and
human-rights campaigners. Private criticism was generally tolerated,
but even the smallest hint of public or organized dissent was swiftly
punished. Loss of travel privileges was a frequent sanction whose victims included such persistent critics as the economist Shatalin and
philosopher Mamardashvili. Others ranged from Alexander
Pumpyansky, a *Komsomolskaia Pravda* correspondent (and glasnost-
era editor of the liberal weekly *Novoe Vremya*), for "blackening
Soviet reality" by writing about U.S. millionaires, to Alexander
Lebed (Gorbachev's last ambassador to Czechoslovakia), for characterizing that same reality as "an experiment."[81] In 1975, historian
Gefter was forced into retirement. That same year, the KGB brought
a more serious case against scholar-publicists Len Karpinsky, Otto
Latsis, and Igor Klyamkin. The three, guilty of sharing private writings that found their way into a draft samizdat almanac, endured reprimands, expulsion from the Party, or loss of employment.[82] Just a
few years earlier, allies within the apparat had often intervened to
mitigate such cases (for example, Alexander Yakovlev in the 1967
Burlatsky-Karpinsky affair).[83] But by the mid 1970s, such "Party liberals" were either gone or under heavy pressure themselves.[84]

By such tactics, the regime sought to isolate the boldest critical
thinkers from others who sympathized. The former would be punished and the latter co-opted through job security and privileges, a
tactic that effectively squelched any wider stirrings among the
broadly conservative ranks of the professional-educated class.[85]
Those unwilling to break openly with the system had few choices.
Some gave up and withdrew in cynicism. Others wrote "for the
drawer" or made quiet efforts to effect change from inside. They
protected friends, published in Aesopian language, and expressed
themselves more openly only in limited-circulation journals and
classified studies. Still others retreated to "the provinces" to escape
the scrutiny of Moscow. Liberal economists and sociologists sought
refuge in Novosibirsk, for example, while philosophers and histori-

ans found greater freedom in regional centers such as Tartu, Tbilisi, and Kiev.[86]

But even in Moscow, notwithstanding the hard-liners' offensive, some latitude remained for reformist-integrationist thought. This was so because, in searching for a post-Khrushchev identity and direction for the country, the Brezhnev leadership found itself trapped between Scylla and Charybdis. Officially, the now-embarrassing 1961 Party Program was supplanted by a declaration of "developed socialism," the supposed attainment of a qualitatively new stage in the march toward Communism.[87] But the very enunciation of a new formation only opened the door to critical analysis of its actual characteristics. Moreover, the evident hollowness of the new model and steady worsening of socioeconomic ills encouraged another ideological competitor—Russian nationalism—that rekindled the reformers' challenge to reaction in new venues, even as it was extinguished in old ones.

As previously noted, new thinking was not the only growing thaw-era intellectual current: there was also a Russian national or "neo-Slavophile" current. Initially less prominent than "neo-Westernism," it had a potential (if not actual) elite following that was much larger.[88] Like their nineteenth-century predecessors, these competing currents had common roots in dissatisfaction with the reigning "autocracy." For example, both neo-Westernism and neo-Slavophilism were stimulated by the exposure of Stalinism's rural catastrophe. But while the former saw solutions in market incentives and structures, the latter's prescription was the opposite. The neo-Slavophiles emphasized the *cultural* tragedy of collectivization, the destruction of traditional, religious, communal life. Both were shocked by poverty, alcoholism, family breakdown, and ecological despoilation. But while the neo-Westernizers looked forward to a "modernizing" technological and social transformation of rural life, the neo-Slavophiles sought a return to a "premodern" past.

The philosophy underlying this goal—a general belief in the uniqueness of Russian civilization, that Russia was not properly destined to follow the Western path—was what united many otherwise diverse nationalists. Some were official writers or scholars, while others belonged to unofficial groups and circulated works in samizdat.[89] Some emphasized Orthodox Christianity; others grew openly and aggressively neo-Stalinist. Some saw the West's main threat to be in its bourgeois values; others feared its military might. Some wanted to expand Russia's role as a global-imperial power; others sought its retreat into the isolation of a separate cultural and social world.[90]

Like their nineteenth-century predecessors, many neo-Slavophiles indulged in romanticism (as did some enthusiastic but naïve neo-Westernizers). Theirs was mostly a sincere protest against social and cultural decline, though the past they recalled was a much-idealized one. Moreover, their "program" was long on ideology and short on specifics (unlike that of the neo-Westernizers).[91] But a more serious problem was neo-Slavophilism's relationship to Stalinism. Though it was Stalin who had destroyed their idealized pastoral harmony, it was also Stalin who swept away the hated European, cosmopolitan aspects of Bolshevism and promoted Russian nationalism.[92] So in this respect—and certainly in their dislike of the West and Brezhnev's flirtation with it through détente—even benign neo-Slavophilism found itself uncomfortably close to something far more malignant.[93]

The nineteenth-century parallel is also useful in viewing the evolution of neo-Slavophilism. Just as its predecessor's early inclusive, universal, humanitarian ideals degenerated into the exclusive, chauvinistic, xenophobic hostility of Pan-Slavism, so would neo-Slavophilism follow a similar path.[94] Some of its own early supporters would migrate toward increasingly virulent (or just increasingly open) anti-Semitic, anti-Western attitudes. The movement would also be influenced by its attraction of adherents whose outlook contained few of the positive, and many of the negative, aspects of Russian nationalism. The latter included some defiantly reactionary, neo-Stalinist members of Soviet officialdom.[95]

Therein lay the dilemma that nationalism presented. The declaration of "developed socialism" had *not* been inspirational.[96] Some openly described its "essence" as including "Oblomov-like laziness . . . money-grubbing greed . . . drunken debauchery [and] religious fanaticism."[97] With such a hollow ideology, the temptation was strong to embrace nationalism as an alternative source of support. This temptation was all the greater because such attitudes were deeply ingrained in the Brezhnev generation. Russian nationalism was integral to the hostile-isolationist identity so persistent among those schooled in Stalin's chauvinist 1930s, in genuine wartime patriotism, and in the extreme Russocentrism of the postwar years. But openly embracing reactionary nationalism was highly problematic because it directly contradicted the regime's internationalist basis of legitimacy.[98] Yakovlev's attack on "Great-Russian chauvinism" was particularly awkward for emphasizing that such ideas were absolutely anti-Marxist and anti-Leninist.[99]

Thus official ambivalence permitted both neo-Slavophiles and neo-Westernizers some latitude as the two engaged in a debate about the past that was transparently aimed at the country's present identity and future direction. Alexander Yanov argued that the nineteenth-century Slavophiles failed because they rejected European democracy and humanism for a utopian myth of Russia's cultural uniqueness.[100] The neo-Slavophiles answered that it was their critics whose model was idealized and unrealistic: "Was not the Westernizers' idea of transplanting European ways onto Russian soil a utopian one?"[101] Yanov invoked authorities such as Pokrovsky and even Lenin to brand the nineteenth-century Slavophiles "kvas-bottle patriots" and "apologists for [the messianic idea of] a Third Rome." The early Westernizers, by contrast, "had imbibed 50 years of European thought from Goethe to Georges Sand, from Kant to Fourier."[102]

Though this particular exchange was soon halted, the larger debate went on. Neo-Slavophilism continued to enjoy official tolerance and unofficial support, while the neo-Westernizers fought back in samizdat,[103] private lectures,[104] and—cautiously—in the open literature as well. Through the latter can be seen how a historical debate expanded to draw in specialists from other fields in an indirect but broader indictment of the old thinking.[105] For some, the Marxist-humanist critique was again the starting point. In *Novy Mir*, Grigory Vodolazov recalled Gramsci's view that "a revolution is not necessarily proletariat and Communist, even if a wave of popular revolt has placed in power men who call themselves communists."[106] In modernizing a backward country, the tendency exists "to render the problem very simply. All 'subtleties' are eliminated . . . from the complication of transition stages . . . the solution to the problem is laid out in straight lines [leading to] barbed wire . . . prisons, concentration camps."[107] In part, Vodolazov was responding to a call for broader reassessment of Soviet historiography than that which had initially followed Stalin's death. This call had come in a symposium, edited by Gefter, that amounted to a "manifesto of legal Marxism."[108] This symposium, and a later one on "multi-structurality," raised basic questions of historical development— from the origins of European nations to the rise of socialism.[109] As the *Short Course's* crude but still-prevalent model of progression through Marx's five "formations" was challenged, discussion inevitably led back to "the accursed question" of Russia's path between East and West.[110] Gefter, like Vodolazov, was not addressing Soviet history per se, but his argument's relevance to the Stalin and post-Stalin periods was clear: "It is an historical paradox that one-sided, accelerated growth of a new formation 'takes it back' again and again to where it started."[111]

Views similar to Vodolazov's and Gefter's, on the danger of premature revolution and "accelerated" development, resonated far beyond the domain of historians. Area experts now used their subjects as a "mirror" for the USSR.[112] For example, Vladimir Lukin analyzed China to argue the perils of totalitarian ideology in transforming a backward "peasant-statocratic" society.[113] By the 1970s, as ties with China worsened and those with the third world grew, these socialist or "socialist oriented" states provided grist for an indirect debate about the USSR. And beyond bureaucratism, elite corruption, and economic failure, analysts also found suggestive parallels to Soviet foreign policy.[114] Yuri Ostrovityanov and Antonina Sterbalova cited Engels's injunction against labeling as socialist the "crying anachronism" of a system marked by "chauvinism . . . national isolationism, and the resurgence of old despotic methods."[115] Sheinis, viewing "revolutionary" elites of the third world, criticized their "foreign-policy strivings which are not related to real social needs," but lead instead to "arms build-up and militarization that ruin the national economy."[116]

These arguments about developmental paths were also tied to another aspect of debate about Russia and the West. The view of Gefter's 1969 symposium as a manifesto of "legal Marxism" appropriately linked it to the political-philosophical debates of early-twentieth-century Russia, in particular to Berdyaev and the *Vekhi* writers (whose views on Europe and Russia were now widely read).[117] These earlier authors—liberals, former Marxists, or Marxists of Menshevik, social-democratic leanings—had criticized the radical intelligentsia for their ignorance of Western values and institutions, and for not understanding Russia's need for further economic, social, and cultural development along the European path before there was any possibility of building socialism.[118] Lyudmila Nikitich of the Institute of Social Sciences recalled:

> I read *Vekhi*, Berdyaev and the others in our *spetskhran*. It was all there. Berdyaev's story of the Russian who goes to France and finds that "there's no freedom" because nothing changes and there's no struggle underway, *that* was the naivete and the impatience of our radicals. By 1918 [Semyon] Frank already foresaw everything that would happen to us later. . . . Berdyaev's culture and spirituality was such a contrast to Lenin, who rejected Kantian ethics and the individual, and for whom the only morality was whatever advanced communism, as he said at the Komsomol Congress. . . . For me, Berdyaev was superior even to Gramsci as an inspirational thinker, and you know that my field is Italian Marxism![119]

By the mid 1970s, many understood that under Stalin the country had not only suffered an unfortunate "distortion" in building socialism, but that his attempted leap forward had instead thrown it back onto a primitive, "Asiatic-despotic" developmental path. Others questioned "utopian leaps" more generally and so suggested (intentionally or otherwise) that the wrong turn had been made even earlier, with Russia's break from Europe in 1917.[120] In either case, the remedy was a return to Western civilization. As Tsipko argued, building a humanistic socialist society required "assimilation of all the achievements of civilization and culture."[121] This was the theme that linked the anti-utopian philosophers with historians such as Gefter, political analysts such as Burlatsky, and third world experts such as Sheinis. From diverse perspectives, they all arrived at one conclusion: that Russia must return to the mainstream of world civilization.

Sheinis wrote that all nations were advancing, by various paths, "toward the formation of one international community, the basic features and main values of which . . . cannot be anything but universal."[122] Mamardashvili argued that "the main task before social thinkers . . . is reuniting our motherland with its European destiny . . . our minds still tend toward the old images of encirclement, of 'enemies.' . . . [But] it must be remembered that Russia is indivisibly part of European civilization."[123] Gefter put it thus in a 1977 samizdat essay:

> The past forty years have brought gigantic changes to all human endeavors. The strengthening of the West through fundamental economic changes and the [postwar] revival of "bourgeois democracy," the self-collapse of colonial empires and the rise of the third world, the explosion of science . . . all this and more . . . raises the question of the identity, the oneness of humanity. Planetary shifts, calamities, and fears all knock at our door. Khrushchev . . . cracked the door open. But the "thaw" bogged down largely because we hung on to the anachronism of our exclusive, universalistic path [which led directly to] the Berlin Wall and the Caribbean crisis. . . . The centuries and millennia of civilization's variety, of its arrhythmia, take on new meaning: they are drawing us toward one universal human norm [*obshchechelovecheskaia norma*].[124]

Autarky Versus Integration: Economic Thought at Home and Abroad

Implicitly, underlying much of the early "global" thinking described above were economic concerns. Whether focused on science and the environment, China and the third world, or Russia's historical development, all were greatly influenced by the manifest failures of the Soviet system. By now economists well understood these failures, of course, and two strong reform currents emerged in the 1970s. One, aided by vast new experience studying Western models, was to marketize the economy. The other was to join the world economy, to end autarky and integrate with the "international division of labor." As in other fields, the two currents were intimately connected in their conception, in the politics and personalities of their elaboration, and in their broad implications for policy.

The need for serious economic change was already understood in the years of the thaw, for the ills of the Stalinist system—from apathetic workers to shortages, bottlenecks, and stifling bureaucracy—had been well aired in the media and specialized literature. But it is a mistake to see a straight line between the reformist thought of the early 1960s and the late 1970s, for there were critical differences, too. The thaw saw many bold diagnoses but fewer concrete remedies—mainly general ideas of "market socialism." Many early reformers were "political" economists, weak in quantitative analysis and guided instead by an NEP legacy that was increasingly irrelevant to a modern industrial economy. Moreover, their outlook was largely domestic, their only foreign models being the chimera of self-management and the inspirational but often impractical theories of Lange, Sik, and Brus.

By contrast, the new cohort who studied and began their careers in the 1960s were a different breed. Trained in a more sophisticated world of mathematical models and rigorous empirical analysis, they were steeped in Western theory (and Western critiques of the Soviet economy).[125] Their foreign models were Samuelson, Keynes, and Friedman.[126] It is not entirely incorrect to group the younger generation of reformist economists together with its elders in the broad category of "market socialists," as is often done. But now the emphasis was increasingly on *market* at the expense of *socialist*.

Thus the greatest difference was the extent to which the younger economists were oriented toward the West. Having imbibed neoclassical theory early, many followed advances in macroeconomic and econometric analysis. Given computers to improve planning, they soon found its limitations and used their new tools to examine market alternatives instead. Eastern Europe remained a testing ground, but interest in such "socialist" models as Yugoslav self-management was supplanted by study of such "capitalist" innovations as those in Hungarian agriculture.[127] Still, their gaze remained fixed on the West and its success in encouraging growth, managing business cycles, and stimulating scientific innovation. Reformist institutes became "breeding grounds for marketeers and anti-Marxists."[128] While their works retained a socialist veneer, their ideas were increasingly based on purely economic criteria. Nikolai Shmelev later described this outlook as "everything that is economically efficient is moral."[129] And it was the "immoral" capitalist world where economic efficiency and popular well-being were greatest.

By the mid 1970s, this new cohort was well represented not only in the main establishments of economic research—Novosibirsk, TsEMI, and the Institute of Economics—but also at leading institutes of foreign-policy studies such as IMEMO, ISKAN, and

IEMSS. How did they see their system's performance during the high Brezhnev era? Judging primarily by the open writings of the latter institutes—those most closely scrutinized in the West—it appears they held a quite favorable view. Soviet economic woes were not ignored but, viewed in the relative context of the broader "global correlation of forces," optimism seemed high.[130] For example, an ISKAN study saw the fall of the Bretton Woods order as sharply worsening Western difficulties.[131] A major IMEMO study, while noting Western scientific prowess, argued that this could not mitigate capitalism's contradictions. On the contrary, it increased domestic social strains and also heightened inter-imperialist rivalries.[132] Ideologues naturally emphasized "a qualitative shift in the general crisis of capitalism," but it appeared that many liberal analysts, too, were bullish on Soviet prospects vis-à-vis the West. The consensus at IMEMO seemed to be that "capitalism had entered a new and more troubled phase of its development."[133]

But elsewhere, institute directors Inozemtsev, Arbatov, and Bogomolov were considerably less optimistic. In other writings they emphasized the gathering "scientific-technological revolution," stressed Soviet weakness, and argued for drawing on Western experience to keep pace.[134] Far from simply following the official détente policy of cautiously expanding certain East-West ties, the directors were echoing research by their own staffs, and those of other institutes, that painted a far gloomier picture of the Soviet economy and the global balance of economic forces. And in many classified or limited-circulation studies, these problems, and the necessary remedies, were laid out in much starker terms.[135]

For example, in contrast to limits on honest data in the open literature, specialized publications reported alarming statistics on a Soviet lag in everything from living standards to technology.[136] Some of them detailed problems in scientific, social, and environmental aspects of development, or stressed capitalism's success in these areas.[137] Others argued that solutions lay not just in expanded exchanges or purchases of Western goods, but in broad adoption of Western methods.[138] By the mid 1970s, official recognition of the fact that a global "scientific-technological revolution" was indeed under way permitted a certain latitude for concerns about its success in the USSR (and, beyond the economy, its impact on society, the environment, and military security). But the mainstream literature was still dominated by optimistic views of this revolution's contribution to "developed socialism" at home and Soviet power abroad.[139] In the open press, reformers could only hint that technological change posed challenges that—without far-reaching reform—the Soviet economy could not possibly surmount. In private, they fairly trumpeted a warning.[140]

In 1972, Shatalin initiated a high-level study group that reported on *Scientific-Technological Progress and its Socio-Economic Impact Through the Year 1990.* Their farsighted study was ignored.[141] Shortly thereafter, Kosygin invited top experts—including Aganbegyan, Fedorenko, Arbatov, Inozemtsev, and Bogomolov—to discuss the economy. But when anyone argued the need for substantial change, Kosygin attacked them viciously.[142] In 1973, with a decision to hold a Central Committee plenum on scientific-technological issues, many of the same experts were tapped to draft a report. Again they called for substantial reforms, again they were ignored, and the idea for a plenum simply "sank like a stone."[143]

Whereas the USSR's international technological lag was uppermost in some reformers' early détente-era appeals to the leadership, others stressed domestic concerns even more emphatically. Again, this is seen in specialized literature, where analysts could go beyond such cautious arguments as Kantorovich's on the problem of irrational prices in *Voprosy Filosofii.* For example, Shatalin hit hard on the price issue and on the sensitive question of incentives and pay differentials.[144] His TsEMI colleague Nikolai Petrakov and IEMSS analyst Nikolai Shmelev both advocated financial and decision-making autonomy for production enterprises.[145] Others promoted Hungary's market-cooperative experiments or even a revamping of Lenin's original cooperative ideas.[146] Novosibirsk director Aganbegyan warned of severe socioeconomic ills in various national regions.[147] And in 1975, TsEMI director Fedorenko presented an in-depth, classified report on Soviet economic problems and prospects so stark that it left his listeners stunned.[148]

Taken together, these analyses shouted of a looming crisis. While the general need for market reforms had been long understood—and many ideas for change in one or another sector were now advanced—probably no critique was so bold and no proposals so sweeping as those of Shmelev. Already in 1970, he was advocating that enterprises operate on a self-financing, cost-accounting (*khozraschet*) basis. With détente, he joined the strong supporters of East-West trade.

Shmelev's arguments were unique in several important respects. First, he did not limit them to economic gains but offered a theoretical justification as well; for socialism "there have not been, and are not now, any objective developmental factors that require autarky."[149] Second, he refuted warnings of sinister capitalist motives; the West sought trade for the same reason that the USSR should, namely "the advantages of the international division of labor [i.e. classical gains from trade] which are the foundation of our deep, mutual interest."[150] Third, the sort of trade Shmelev envisioned was not simply access to Western markets or the purchase of specific technologies, but a means to transform completely the domestic system. This it would do by opening the economy to foreign contacts and competition, essentially forcing it to adopt decentralizing measures and market practices across the board.

Shmelev's proposals toward this end were concrete. First, foreign trade must not be a state monopoly. Rather, "spontaneous" ties should be fostered "by giving production enterprises and firms the right of direct access to the foreign market."[151] Second, joint ventures and broad foreign investment should be encouraged.[152] Third, steps must be taken toward internal and ultimately external currency convertibility.[153] This would mean transition to world market prices, to be bolstered by a further step: membership in international organizations such as the IMF, the World Bank, and GATT.[154] Taken together, the implications of Shmelev's ideas were clear; the end of state control over prices, exchange rates, and international ties would make most central planning impossible, while forcing newly independent enterprises to learn from and compete with foreign producers.

At least officially, the Soviet leadership was all for expanding trade and contacts with the West. In 1973, Brezhnev stated, "We have no plans for autarky [but instead seek] growth of broad cooperation with the outside world."[155] But others stressed trade's limits, warned of Western economic and ideological manipulation, and argued that the country must remain "an independent economic unit."[156] Of course, the leadership knew exactly where Shmelev was pointing and had no intention of taking even his first step toward "internationalization" of the Soviet economy. As one high-level Party declaration argued,

> The state monopoly on foreign trade is the best way to meet the needs of a planned, socialist economy [without which] it is impossible to preserve socialism's economic independence, operate a planned economy, and preserve state and national interests. . . . We maintain a high state of vigilance against abuse of economic cooperation by class enemies.[157]

By the time of this statement, 1977, hopes for an East-West trade boom had already been dashed, in part due to a U.S. congressional amendment tying favorable trade status to human rights, as well as by the pall cast over East-West relations by Soviet activism in the third world. But as Shmelev saw it, the real problem was a Soviet decision not to take advantage of détente's opportunities to assist in economic reform, but to use them instead as a stopgap measure to avoid it. As he had warned as early as 1975,

> The USSR lags behind the other CEMA states and even some developing countries in the use of promising international economic cooperation. . . . The biggest growth so far [has been in] grain imports made possible by Western credits. So now we have a trade deficit with the West. In 1973–74 another factor emerged [namely] a rise in world prices of raw materials and oil which led to a sharp rise in our hard currency earnings. . . . However, this situation is temporary and is not likely to last beyond the 1980s.[158]

Just as the appeals of Inozemtsev, Arbatov, and others for urgent measures to redress the country's growing technological lag fell on deaf ears—at least among the senior leadership—so, too, did Shmelev's warnings about using the glut of oil money to avoid change. The country enjoyed an illusory prosperity that blinded the aging Politburo and even emboldened it to launch the foreign adventures that helped bury détente. And this, in turn, aided reactionary tendencies with predictable results for reformist thinkers. Economists who persisted in offering unwanted advice were subject to the same sanctions suffered by outspoken intellectuals in other fields.[159]

Still, the new thinkers did not give up. On the contrary, in the specialized literature they pushed reformist proposals harder than ever. IEMSS continued to hold up East European success in attract-

ing foreign investment as a model for the USSR.[160] Vladimir
Tikhonov, who had promoted the revival of NEP-style cooperatives, now called for "fundamental changes" in agriculture.[161]
IMEMO admired the Common Market's environmental programs
and held out the United States and Japan as models for technological growth.[162] And ISKAN produced scores of laudatory studies of
the U.S. economy, on topics from automation and civilian uses of
space technology to housing construction and scrap-metal recy-
cling.[163]

Toward decade's end, hopes for reform were probably lower
than even at its troubled beginning. Still, the stagnation era saw
great changes in thinking about the USSR's economic place in the
world. A highly professional cohort of specialists had matured, and
their experience studying the West made the desire to join it very
strong. Their vision of the Soviet future was generally that of a
social-democratic type welfare state and full participant in the
"international division of labor."[164] The salience of capitalist-social-
ist differences faded and Western "threats" were simply no longer
an issue. Informed by neoclassical precepts of mutual gains from
trade, the USSR's overriding interest in fully joining the global
economy was simply a given.

International Relations and the West: Coexistence, Cooperation, and Conciliation

This section focuses on the *mezhdunarodniki*, the most specialized students and practitioners of international relations: area
experts, policy analysts, technical advisers, diplomats, and others
directly concerned with foreign affairs. While the preceding sections
have shown the broad conceptual underpinnings of new thinking
on international relations—and also explored some of the main
issues and individuals involved—they have not examined closely the
most pressing East-West problems. In the 1970s, the most critical of
these was probably nuclear arms control.

For new thinkers, the first post-thaw years were distressing in
their retreat from Khrushchev's near-categorical rejection of "sur-
vivable" nuclear war. This was indirectly seen in such statements as
Brezhnev's that "in combat against any aggressor, the Soviet Union
will achieve victory," and directly in military pronouncements that

even from the ashes of nuclear war, socialism would arise triumphant with capitalism defeated forever.[165] Briefly silenced, the resumption of U.S.-Soviet arms talks emboldened liberals such as Burlatsky with his heretical claim that peace was "an absolute value," higher than class and other interests.[166] With the success of the 1972 SALT and ABM treaties, others joined in. Bovin rejected the formula that war could be a rational continuation of policy; he argued that "further growth of nuclear arsenals loses . . . meaning and decreases rather than increases security."[167] Arbatov echoed this; he warned hawks (on both sides) that striving for superiority would only prompt "efforts to build up power by the opposing side—in other words, unrestrained military rivalry and armed conflict."[168] To those who still emphasized capitalism's aggressive designs, Burlatsky answered that Western democracy "virtually precluded" resort to nuclear war.[169]

Such views enjoyed a brief prominence during the early-to-mid 1970s—though more militaristic voices were hardly silenced—because détente's heyday was the time of greatest influence on Brezhnev of such reformist advisers as Arbatov, Inozemtsev, and Bovin (and because Brezhnev the "realist" temporarily eclipsed Brezhnev the "ideologue").[170] But behind such public statements, détente and arms control brought far more radical changes to the outlook of many experts than was visible from afar. This they did by utterly transforming their conditions of study and work—through exposure to vast new sources of data, to foreign theoretical and policy studies, and through broad new ties with their Western counterparts. The impact of such changes in other fields has been seen, but for many *mezhdunarodniki* it came somewhat later. Arbatov explains this via his own experience, with the example that as late as 1968 even he, director of the new USA Institute, still had not a single American acquaintance because "given the restrictions of the times . . . I didn't even have the right to initiate such contacts."[171]

Arms control, addressing as it did the holy of holies—the country's nuclear forces—was an area of highest secrecy. Earlier negotiations (such as on the 1963 Limited Test Ban Treaty) brought in some scientists and other civilian advisers, to enlightening effect. But beyond the military, detailed knowledge of strategic capabilities remained extremely limited and there existed nothing even remotely like an independent analytical center. Still, as seen earlier, some scholar-publicists and Foreign Ministry staffers familiar with Western strategic thought played a vital role in urging the leadership to begin talks on nuclear limitations as the Soviet buildup attained strategic parity (on top of conventional superiority) with the United States and NATO. Even so, the Politburo was still not fully committed to concluding a treaty, and Stalin's legacy weighed heavily on Soviet participants as the first SALT talks began in 1969. "When Brezhnev saw us off [to Helsinki] he really didn't have anything of substance to say on the issues but mainly spoke about how we should behave ourselves: 'You watch your step there, don't forget that the Lubyanka [KGB headquarters and prison] isn't far away.' "[172]

As talks progressed, this cloud hanging over Soviet negotiators largely passed and the "psychological climate . . . changed a great deal."[173] But they soon collided with other Stalinist legacies that encouraged deeper rethinking of their Western counterparts and the political systems that they represented. One such legacy was paranoid secretiveness, which led to such embarrassing episodes as the following:

> Once my American colleague at the UN disarmament commission, where at [our own] initiative the discussion concerned cuts in naval forces, asked me to specify the size of the Soviet fleet. I had no data on this. He showed me a list of Soviet warships . . . in an American publication and asked me to confirm it. That I could not do. He then said that under such circumstances he would not even discuss the matter, let alone enter into negotiations.[174]

Soviet diplomats felt humiliation at their dependence on open Western sources, such as the International Institute for Strategic Studies (IISS) or the Stockholm International Peace Research Institute (SIPRI), for data on their own country's forces.[175] They also envied the broad initiative permitted their U.S. counterparts: "[A Soviet] negotiator, even a very high-ranking one, could not know whether a 'bargaining position' even existed or whether there was another position to fall back on; he simply lacked the data required for [such a] judgment."[176] Gradually, mutual respect and trust were built, "not only during negotiating sessions but also [in] conversations at home, intervals, or 'walks in the woods.' "[177] Moreover, understanding grew that "our enduring supersecrecy and spy mania" was not only a problem for arms control—as an obstacle to agreement on treaty verification provisions—but symptomatic of a much deeper malady of the Soviet system.[178]

During détente, experts in European and, especially, American affairs emerged as a special corps among Soviet diplomats. The latter worked in the ministry's U.S.A. section in Moscow or studied in "Dobrynin's School," the Soviet embassy in Washington.[179] Arms negotiators were a particular elite; others worked on broader political, economic, and cultural ties.[180] Many *zapadniki* ("Westernizers," a telling self-appellation) developed a high regard for the United States and a deep commitment to furthering détente.[181] As Alexander Bessmyrtnykh recalled, "We developed great admiration for the West, for the United States . . . respect for the country, its strengths, its people. I can't say that it was all 'new thinking,' we were what you call realists, but strongly dedicated to arms control and to improving Soviet-American relations."[182]

Détente similarly affected another segment of the *mezhdunarodniki*—Soviet scientists—who were now increasingly drawn in to East-West relations and arms control. Some knew the issues from work in weapons design or as advisers to the negotiations. Others took part in Pugwash meetings, UN committees on disarmament and nuclear energy, or other international fora on global security issues. An even larger group participated in scores of new foreign exchanges in fields from nuclear physics to medicine.[183] Natural scientists had long been prominent among politically active Soviet intellectuals.[184] Due in part to the critical, non-ideological nature of their work as well as the tradition of exemplars from Kapitsa to Artsimovich, their détente-era experiences only heightened awareness of the folly of isolation and "raised the consciousness of Soviet scientists about their role in their own society and the world."[185]

In this consciousness-raising, Sakharov's influence was particularly important. Notwithstanding his growing official ostracism, détente only increased the resonance of his early arguments on coexistence and human rights. For some, such as Sagdeyev, the latter was as important as the former as understanding grew that scientific integrity was inseparable from broader intellectual and individual liberties.[186] Others found Sakharov's views on East-West relations particularly persuasive; Goldansky, who shared a hospital room with him for several days in 1973, recalled "endless hours" of debate over foreign policy.[187] But for Goldansky and many others, a breakthrough only came with participation in the Pugwash movement:

> I first went to the meeting in Munich in 1977, then Bulgaria in 1978 and Mexico in 1979. It was highly impressive . . . the foreign participants had such command of the scientific and political issues. I learned about non-proliferation, testing and other matters . . . it broadened my horizons in every way.[188]

Sagdeyev, who first attended a Pugwash meeting at Artsimovich's invitation in 1970, described his involvement as having "played a central role in my thinking." But he also noted that, over the decade of détente, Pugwash was gradually "displaced" by new exchanges that drew in many more Soviet participants.[189] Boris Raushenbakh, a pioneer of Soviet rocketry (and a camp survivor) described his work on the 1975 Apollo-Soyuz joint spaceflight as important to his evolving views on U.S.-Soviet cooperation.[190] Cardiologist Yevgeny Chazov wrote of the "mutual sympathy and individual friendships" that arose among U.S. and Soviet physicians.[191] Perhaps the most influential perestroika-era Soviet scientist was Yevgeny Velikhov, who (in addition to insights on global security gained from weapons-design work) credited his broad détente-era experience with international exchanges on fusion and other physics problems. "I had many foreign colleagues and friends . . . and so realized very early that we live in one world. You know, I probably had more American contacts than anybody else here except Arbatov."[192]

The benefits of détente were equally great for the core group of *mezhdunarodniki*—the scholar-publicists of international-relations and foreign policy. The 1970s saw a huge increase in the information and contacts available to Soviet analysts. INION, founded only in 1969, was soon distributing hundreds of reviews, summaries, and translations of Western foreign-policy studies.[193] Subscriptions to foreign journals soared, and institute libraries quickly filled with specialized Western literature. Access was also eased to Western media and to restricted "White TASS" reportage.[194] For the hundreds of young analysts who joined ISKAN, IMEMO, and other institutes in the 1970s, the hypersecrecy (and consequent ignorance) of an earlier generation was largely unknown.[195]

Military-related information remained under tighter control, but civilian analysts relied on the same SIPRI and IISS data books that Soviet negotiators used.[196] Moreover, among closed institute publications there now appeared many dispassionate, detailed analyses of defense issues. Some reviewed U.S. missile programs or naval doctrine.[197] Others examined NATO nuclear cooperation or issues of defense-economic conversion.[198] All drew overwhelmingly on Western sources or simply presented Western views, the latter ranging from a State Department study on the global effects of nuclear war to lectures on threat assessment and defense planning by Pentagon advisor Alain Enthoven.[199]

This rapid growth in military studies was abetted by ties to scientific-diplomatic expertise. Senior *institutchiki* took part in Pugwash and other international fora alongside scientists and military officers.[200] Military and diplomatic officials were increasingly frequent visitors to ISKAN.[201] In 1978, IMEMO became the coordinating institution for the U.S.-Soviet Joint Committee on International Issues that united scientists with policy analysts under the two countries' academies of science.[202] From being nonexistent just a few years earlier, strategic studies became central to both institutes' work; ISKAN's Military Department grew with the addition of reform-minded officers on loan from the general staff, and IMEMO's military research section (whose very existence was still concealed as the "Department of Technical-Economic Research") managed to combine contract work for the Defense Ministry with the hiring of "semi-dissident" officer-analysts.[203]

It was not long before this growth in access and expertise was reflected in critical analyses.[204] Vitaly Shlykov, a retired officer working at IMEMO, questioned dogmas about NATO forces and the rationale for such massive, expensive Soviet armies.[205] Study of NATO economics showed an alliance divided by business squabbles and unable to agree even on weapons standardization.[206] Shlykov also questioned projections of the West's mobilization potential that were central to assessments of a conventional-arms threat to the East: "Once I examined NATO plans and resources, I saw that our assumptions were ridiculously exaggerated and that our own capabilities were ten times greater."[207] Meanwhile, his colleague Alexei Arbatov (the son of ISKAN director Georgy Arbatov) reviewed the U.S. nuclear threat; analyzing the U.S. *Trident* and B-1 programs, he downplayed Moscow's view of them as first-strike weapons, while acknowledging the U.S. position that they were meant to counter the huge Soviet land-based missile force.[208] ISKAN analyst Yevgeny Kutovoi, examining Western views of the Soviet military buildup, warned that "any steps capable of upsetting the existing balance . . . could have very serious consequences."[209]

Regional studies, too, grew bolder. Viewing the recent Sino-American rapprochement, ISKAN analyst Vladimir Lukin questioned the official anti-Chinese (and anti-American) line; while faulting Mao for "splitting" socialist unity and blocking Soviet influence, the USSR itself was actually more to blame. Improved Sino-American relations had "an objective foundation" in Soviet behavior; the United States had "reconsidered the Chinese military threat" because Peking was "no longer . . . inclined to send troops beyond its borders." The United States, too, had greatly reduced its military presence in Asia, as Lukin detailed, while Soviet deployments in the region, particularly opposite China, had only grown.[210] Asia was also the subject of an even bolder proposal by IMEMO analyst (and retired army colonel) Viktor Girshfeld.[211]

> The Soviet Union can even undertake unilateral arms and troop reductions without danger of upsetting the balance. On the contrary, this will lead to similar reductions [by the United States and NATO]. . . . And to normalize our relations with China, these [cuts] could be up to one-half of our conventional and two-thirds of our strategic forces.[212]

Analysts also rethought dogmas about Europe. Boris Orlov, the former *Izvestiia* correspondent rescued by Delusin and Chernyaev, published several original works on social democracy.[213] Their subjects ranged from the politics of Willy Brandt to the phenomenon of neofascism; he admired the former and judged the latter a fringe phenomenon that was decidedly not part of a broader "revanchist" threat, as officially depicted.[214] Another who cautiously reappraised the Federal Republic of Germany and its foreign policy was IMEMO analyst Daniil Proektor.[215] Such works reflected a broader rethinking of Western Europe and the progress of its integration. Over the mid-to-late 1970s, IMEMO produced many studies viewing European political and economic union in an increasingly favorable, even glowing light.[216]

To the Summit and Back: The Peaks and Valleys of Détente

Europe was the setting of détente's other main diplomatic breakthrough—the CSCE. It was also the locus of an internal debate that, as with the ongoing struggle over arms control, pitted old thinkers against new thinkers in a battle that concerned domestic as much as international affairs, and whose near-term significance for foreign policy was matched by its long-term implications for the cause of reform and the country's overall path of development.

While the idea of a pan-European agreement went back decades, it rose to the top of the Soviet diplomatic agenda only in the early 1970s. This was due in large part to the efforts of midlevel diplomats-*zapadniki* concerned to broaden the momentum of détente—principally Lev Mendelevich and Anatoly Kovalev—and was also enthusiastically supported by new thinkers in the apparat, academia, and journalism.[217] Just the first round in an envisioned permanent (to date, ongoing) process of negotiation, the Helsinki agreement of 1975 was, for the leading states of the two blocs, a compromise; the East sought formal recognition of Europe's postwar borders, while the West sought to open those same borders to the freer flow of individuals, information, and ideas.

Brezhnev, concerned primarily with the former (and also with his chances for the Nobel Peace Prize), signed the Final Act "without really reading it through."[218] Other Politburo members looked at it closely and did not like what they saw. The CSCE became "a highly contested topic inside the country, the subject of an acute ideological and political struggle."[219] Suslov, in particular, detected "a threat to the steel and concrete dogmata of the communist ideals." He subsequently "blacklisted" Kovalev, who had worked most assiduously for Moscow's acceptance of Helsinki's human-rights provisions.[220]

Yet it was precisely those provisions that encouraged many new thinkers. In the CSCE, they saw, rather than simply de jure confirmation of a de facto geopolitical reality, a new impetus for détente that would extend beyond superpower summitry to encourage domestic reforms, a gradual liberalization of the Communist system, and humanization of Soviet society. At home, some worked to incorporate Helsinki's humanitarian strictures into Soviet domestic law.[221] Others went even further, edging close to Sakharov and the dissidents' concerns in seeking greater protection of human rights or broader openness and steps toward real democratization of political life.[222] In short, Helsinki provided an enormous boost to liberals' hopes of forging a meaningful Soviet "Westpolitik."[223]

Thus, by the mid 1970s, reformist thought had gone far beyond mere revival of "peaceful coexistence" to the broad theoretical conception of—and numerous concrete proposals toward—deeper integration with the West. But while thinking rapidly advanced, practice stagnated or retreated. Socioeconomic problems at home, and throughout the bloc, worsened as reform opportunities were squandered. Abroad, détente's diplomatic gains seemed to encourage not conciliation but expansionism. Trade talks floundered, human-rights disputes grew, and an aging Politburo seemed to draw all the wrong lessons from the experience of the early-to-mid 1970s. And so what appeared so promising in 1975 was clearly unraveling only a year or two later. In response, leading new thinkers turned to even more active measures to save détente.

Even as their influence on an increasingly skeptical and infirm Brezhnev waned while that of militaristic-nationalistic forces grew, reformist advisers such as Arbatov and Inozemtsev struggled to revive and advance the arms-control process.[224] Others appealed for a reversal of provocative steps, such as the decision to deploy a new generation of missiles targeted on Europe or to construct a massive new radar in violation of the ABM Treaty.[225] In these efforts they failed, but Soviet scientists did successfully block an even more dangerous (and expensive) military initiative—that of a vast strategic defense system akin to the later U.S. "Star Wars" program.[226]

The signing of the SALT II Treaty in 1979 brought a ray of hope, and Soviet liberals again spoke out publicly in strong support of arms control. Beyond criticism of the still-prevalent formula that war "was simply a continuation of policy by other means," the domestic need for deep arms cuts was now stressed.[227] Central Committee aide Shakhnazarov, IMEMO analysts Oleg Bykov and Rachik Faramazian, and IEMSS analyst Boris Gorizontov noted weapons production's environmental harm, the need to convert military industry to civilian needs, and even compared the arms race to "eating one's own skin to ward off starvation."[228] Elsewhere, IMEMO director Inozemtsev renewed his calls, in public writings and even stronger, private appeals to the leadership, for integration with the global economy.[229] ISKAN echoed this in a continuing flow of laudatory studies of the U.S. economy; simultaneously, in a report to the Central Committee, director Arbatov returned to arms control and the confrontation heightened by Moscow's military buildup. Renewed superpower tensions could be eased only by greater Soviet openness and an "authoritative, public explanation of our positions." The problem was that

> extreme secrecy leads to deadlock in relations with the USA [and permits] their military-industrial complex to take the arms race to yet another level while weakening the position of those [American] forces in favor of lowering the level of military confrontation and defense outlays. A lack of clarity and openness regarding the intentions of one side always fuels suspicion and fear, encourages worst-case scenarios, and complicates the chances for agreement.[230]

Meanwhile, IEMSS analyst Dashichev tied détente to Eastern Europe. In a strongly implied criticism of the USSR's increasingly confrontational course with the West, and its efforts to enforce such a policy throughout the bloc, Dashichev stressed Eastern Europe's "special need for good relations" with Western neighbors.[231] Unlike the autarkic USSR, "easing international tensions is vital" for states like Poland and Hungary, due to economic and geographic realities. Despite Poland's foreign-debt crisis, Dashichev argued "the necessity of widening cooperation in the international division of labor," assessed East-West economic ties as "on the whole, positive," and even suggested that East European experience could help "draw the USSR into" such exchange.[232] In general, "the independence and initiative" of smaller socialist states could moderate tensions [i.e., Soviet intransigence]."[233] IEMSS director Bogomolov sent up a report warning that, without radical reforms, Eastern Europe—and, by implication, the USSR—was "doomed to economic and social degradation and crisis." Integration must be

> an organic process (i.e., free movement of people, ideas and capital across borders) . . . the internationalization process, which Lenin considered the most critical indicator and precondition of mankind's progress, has stopped. The main reason for this is that ruthless centralization inevitably leads to withdrawal and isolation, autarky. . . . And monopoly, as Lenin taught, always leads to rot.[234]

■

A Russian proverb tells that "a fish rots from the head," and this was certainly true of Soviet politics at the beginning of the 1980s. Despite the emergence of a reformist intellectual elite—many of whose members now vigorously promoted a sharp "Westernizing" turn in the country's course—an aging leadership was unable to accept even minor changes. The rapid decay in domestic and international life was directly tied to a growing decrepitude at the top. Politically and ideologically opposed to change even in the best of times, the Brezhnev cohort was increasingly paralyzed by a literal physical rot. Reformist efforts now went far beyond even those at the height of the thaw era. But the new thinkers would endure another five years of rejection until arrival of a leader willing and able to put their ideas into practice.

5 ▪

Advance and Retreat: New Thinking in the Time of Crisis and Transition

> GENERAL SECRETARY CHERNENKO: As you know, we have decided to readmit [Stalin's Foreign Minister] Molotov to the ranks of the CPSU. . . .
>
> DEFENSE MINISTER USTINOV: In my opinion, Malenkov and Kaganovich should [also] be readmitted. . . . No matter what they say, Stalin is our history. No single enemy ever harmed us so much as Khrushchev did with his policy toward the past of our party and our state, and toward Stalin. . . .
>
> PRIME MINISTER TIKHONOV: Yes, if not for Khrushchev they would never have been expelled from the party. He besmirched us and our policies in the eyes of the whole world. . . .
>
> FOREIGN MINISTER GROMYKO: He irreparably damaged the Soviet Union's positive image . . . thanks to him this so-called "Eurocommunism" was born. . . .
>
> USTINOV: Shouldn't we restore the name Stalingrad to Volgograd? Millions of people would support this. . . .
>
> GORBACHEV: This proposal has both positive and negative aspects.
>
> —Politburo meeting, July 12, 1984

By the early 1980s, the Soviet Union was in serious trouble. The economy, stagnant for more than a decade save for sales of weapons and raw materials abroad, and of vodka at home, sputtered as the flow of petrodollars that had sustained it now suddenly slowed. Socially, rising absenteeism, alcoholism, and mortality rates were just the most obvious symptoms of decay. Internationally, the "limited contingent" of troops sent into Afghanistan in December 1979 had fallen into a quagmire that brought worldwide condemnation not seen since Stalin's attacks on Finland and Poland in 1939. Soon the latter was again in rebellion, and only the imposition of martial law in December 1981 managed to "save socialism" from the Polish workers. The world watched nervously as Soviet military might continued to grow; by 1983, large deployments of new nuclear and conventional forces had firmly united Washington, London, Bonn, Tokyo, and Peking against Moscow.[1]

The Soviet peoples suffered as food, housing, and health care were sacrificed to superpower ambitions. Better insulated against material privations than most of their compatriots, liberal intellectuals suffered in another way, watching with distress as the gains of détente now quickly evaporated. Despite its limitations, the preceding decade had seemed a steady preparation for broader integration with the West: economic, political, and cultural. Now these hopes were dashed as their country slid back into self-inflicted isolation. As with the burial of the thaw by Soviet tanks in Prague, the death of détente marked by Soviet tanks in Kabul (and along the Polish border) prompted much despair among reformers.[2]

But now the distress was far greater. In part, this was because the détente era had not simply repeated an earlier cycle but had built on the gains of the thaw to develop reformist, integrationist views much further. The infant new thinking of the 1960s had, for many specialists, reached maturity by the mid-1970s. Moreover, the alternatives were now fewer. Brezhnev had earlier been able to reject both the paths of reform and reaction, of broader integration or tighter isolation, because the system still had enormous reserves for a middle, "muddle-through" course. By the early 1980s, it was increasingly obvious that the status quo in fact meant decline. In his semi-conscious dotage, Brezhnev could not grasp this. But those who were still politically conscious—reformers and reactionaries alike—understood that their country was approaching a crossroads.

Accordingly, a struggle ensued over the Soviet future, and it raged over the prolonged transition period from 1980 to 1985.[3] First, prompted by the Afghan and Polish crises, liberals in 1980–81 launched a push for change on all fronts, domestic and foreign, that reached far beyond Brezhnev's modest détente toward broad international integration. Senior reactionaries in the Party—bureaucratically and ideologically tied to the Stalinist system and hostile-isolationist identity, and never comfortable with even the limited détente of the 1970s—responded with attacks that kept reformers on the defensive for much of 1982. Liberals rebounded again in 1983 as Brezhnev's successor Andropov began modest reforms. But his tenure was too brief, and his horizons too limited, to realize significant change at home and halt the momentum of confrontation abroad built up over "Star Wars," Euromissiles, and the KAL 007 tragedy.[4] By 1984, the country was back on automatic pilot and Andropov was succeeded by the Brezhnev-like Konstantin Chernenko.

The Politburo had again put off urgent decisions by electing another aged, do-nothing leader. But reactionaries were not idle; throughout 1984 they exploited the vacuum at the top to strengthen their positions and mount a new offensive intended to vanquish the reformers once and for all. As domestic and foreign problems grew, the old thinkers—by virtue of their powerful places in the militarized Party-state system—seemed to hold all the cards. But the new thinkers, whose only institutional base was their fragile, academic-advisory posts that now came under fierce attack, had the power of ideas—a promising yet untried reform agenda. Their appeals, however, fell on mostly deaf ears, and defeat would have been certain were it not for a group of younger, reform-minded officials promoted under Andropov. Sharing a belief that *tak zhit' nel'zia*, Mikhail Gorbachev and several allies seized upon the new thinkers' agenda.[5] They quietly prepared for sweeping changes to come, even as the cold war reached an intensity not seen in decades.

Crisis and Activization: New Thinking to Save Détente

Notwithstanding their early awareness of looming political, social, and economic crises at home and throughout the socialist camp, many new thinkers, too, were taken aback by how quickly these problems exploded in 1980–81. Despite their own unheeded warnings of the danger to détente posed by continuing military buildup and muscle-flexing abroad, they were only slightly less shocked than the leadership at the speed with which not only the developed West, but much of the developing world too, united against the USSR. Some lamented the loss of a decade's work and hoped that "reality would prevail" upon conservative Western leaders, such as Ronald Reagan and Margaret Thatcher, to modify their new hard line.[6] Others took genuine offense at the West's "anti-

Soviet crusade" and defended Moscow's positions more than just half-heartedly. Such at least were the reactions of some liberals in the mass media, which gave little inkling of their less-visible reformist efforts. But it was just this public conformity that provided new thinkers the latitude to do their "real work"—private criticism and a renewed push for change.[7]

IEMSS director Bogomolov, whose jeremiad about socialism's "rot" was the last and boldest warning of the 1970s, began the 1980s with the same abandon. Less than a month after the invasion of Afghanistan, he sent the Central Committee and KGB an analysis of détente's demise, which, he argued, had actually begun much earlier, with the "shock effect" on the West of Soviet meddling in Africa. "Subsequent events . . . in the Arab world, our military support of Vietnam in Kampuchea and other similar actions led to further escalation of tensions. [In] Afghanistan our policy apparently went beyond admissible bounds."[8]

Militarily, the USSR now faced "a protracted war against Afghan rebels in extremely unfavorable circumstances." Politically, the invasion's backlash was even more negative.

> The USSR's influence on the non-aligned movement, especially on the Moslem world, has suffered considerably. . . . Détente has been blocked and political prerequisites for limiting the arms race have been eliminated. . . . Economic and technological pressure on the Soviet Union has grown sharply. . . . [There is] growing distrust of Soviet policy and departure from it on the part of Yugoslavia, Romania and [North] Korea. Even the Hungarian and Polish press . . . openly reveal [dissatisfaction] with Soviet action. . . . [C]urtailment of our military activity in the Third World could contribute to a gradual return to a policy of détente . . . if crisis situations do not spread to other regions, especially to Eastern Europe.[9]

Crisis in Eastern Europe, specifically Poland, was the topic of another IEMSS report a year later. Their earlier warnings having proved correct, institute analysts now examined the Solidarity-Communist Party confrontation that paralyzed Poland in 1981. But now the criticism of Soviet policy, and danger to the USSR itself, was spelled out even more bluntly.[10]

First and foremost, Poland's crisis was *not* the result of malign Western influence but had deep domestic roots.[11] The economy labored under an archaic model little changed since its postwar imposition by Stalin. Indebtedness to the West was not the problem; on the contrary, Poland had been granted credit on highly favorable terms. The fault lay instead with overcentralization, bureaucracy, and "gigantic, prestige projects" that squandered foreign loans. Neither was private farming to blame; it was poor price-allocation decisions that plagued agriculture, not the "vestiges of capitalism." In fact, foreign ties had created the opportunity for "a systematic *perestroika*" of the economy, but the Party had done nothing.[12] As a result, shortages of food, housing, and health care bred social unrest. Deficits led to "a black market and speculation, bribe-taking, corruption, and the use of public office for private gain." But instead of reforming, the Polish leadership "grew increasingly distant from the masses . . . socialist democracy acquired a formal character, the party-state apparatus swelled . . . bureaucracy and lawlessness grew [together with] the hypertrophy of the role of the First Secretary and his entourage."[13]

Beyond these obvious parallels to Soviet woes, the IEMSS report also warned that the Polish crisis was fast coming to resemble Lenin's definition of a "revolutionary situation." Finally, blaming decades of Moscow's *diktat* for the crisis and calling for "new methods of mutual relations," the authors cautioned against repressive measures; if reforms were not undertaken soon, it would mean "the death of socialism."[14]

In contrast to Bogomolov's brutally honest (and consequently ineffectual) critique, Arbatov trod more cautiously in the first post-Afghanistan years. With ISKAN and he personally so closely identified with "a failed détente policy"—and thus, like Inozemtsev and IMEMO, busy fending off conservatives' attacks—Arbatov sought influence through his personal ties to the leadership. But his efforts to convince Brezhnev of the SS-20 folly and other "mistakes" came to naught due to the latter's near-total mental incapacity and the attendant devolution of power to Defense Minister Dmitri Ustinov and the military. A subsequent appeal to Arbatov's former boss Andropov, to support a proposed nuclear-free zone in Central Europe, also failed. "What do you want me to do," Andropov testily replied, "quarrel with Ustinov on your account?"[15] In late 1980, Arbatov joined with Inosemtsev and Bovin in an effort to shape preparations of the next five-year plan (for 1981–85) in a reformist direction. Privately characterizing the draft plan as "utter fiction," their concerns were swept aside by Brezhnev and other conservatives as "defamatory."[16]

Elsewhere, Inozemtsev focused on the international economy in his recommendations to Brezhnev and the senior leadership. "Courageously," in light of his own worsening health and an isolationist mood that now saw East-West trade as economically and politically subversive, Inozemtsev continued to argue that "the organic participation of the USSR in the international division of labor" was necessary, given technological change and "the unifying tendency . . . of one world economy."[17] But these appeals, too, went unheeded, and as confrontation worsened and détente unraveled completely, gloom settled over IMEMO and the other reformist institutes. This atmosphere was illustrated in a 1981 analysis by Donald Maclean, the onetime British spy and a longtime member of Inozemtsev's staff. Maclean bemoaned the "unqualified" Brezhnev leadership's narrow international horizons and its "one-sided conception of the role in world politics of . . . armed forces."[18] Instead of a modest nuclear deterrent, the Soviet Union was "continually adding to overkill capacity," which brought only "seriously harmful consequences."

> The latest instance of this is the introduction, now well advanced, of a new generation of nuclear rockets targeted upon Western Europe . . . unless the Soviet Union changes its policy [the net result will be] a rise in the level of nuclear confrontation in Europe with no corresponding advantage. [Here] it is much easier to understand the behaviour . . . of the United States than the Soviet Union.[19]

The same held for conventional forces, where the USSR had "a sizeable advantage" over the West and so should agree to "disproportionately large reductions of its own forces." In Asia, too, common sense "pointed clearly towards restitution of the [Kurile] islands as a relatively small price to pay for a much larger gain."[20]

Though Maclean's reflections were not widely circulated at the time, that his views were widely shared is seen even in some of the open foreign-policy literature of 1980–81.[21] Alexander Bovin, writing in the authoritative Party journal *Kommunist*, abandoned his earlier optimism over Soviet influence in the third world and now cautiously echoed Bogomolov on Moscow's blame for the collapse of détente; Bovin obliquely acknowledged that Afghanistan was a blunder by citing Lenin's warning against "ill-considered, hasty steps" that boosted Western hard-liners.[22] The same point, on the harm to Soviet foreign relations caused by excessive activism abroad, was also emphasized by Arbatov and Burlatsky.[23]

In the closed or specialist-only literature, as seen in a frank IMEMO overview of Western foreign policies, such arguments could be made without need of resort to historical analogies or subtle allusions.[24] Beyond the problem of Soviet expansionism, other fundamental questions were raised about the position of the third world in East-West relations. Viktor Sheinis challenged the prevailing class-based schema that saw many developing states as socialist or "socialist-oriented."[25] Another IMEMO analysis called attention to their changing economic strategies: a turn toward consumer production and small manufacturing, and away from the "catch up fast policy" (*politika dogoniaiushchego razvitiia*).[26] An ISKAN report noted that while the USSR still pushed military sales and mammoth industrial projects, the United States was responding to the third world's new priorities by facilitating technology transfer, encouraging multilateral aid and private investment, and by shifting emphasis to "basic human needs."[27]

Indirect (and sometimes direct) criticism of Soviet behavior extended to other regional issues as well. On Asia, for example, Vladimir Lukin furthered his 1970s arguments in a review of changing U.S. policy in the region. U.S. President Reagan's anti-Communist crusade was duly noted, but so were Chinese, Japanese, and the ASEAN states' fears of Soviet and Vietnamese expansion that drove them to cooperate with the United States.[28] On Europe, analysts of social democracy such as IMEMO's Daniil Proektor, Central Committee staffer Anatoly Chernyaev, and Institute of Social Sciences analyst Alexander Galkin continued their nuanced critiques of West European political, economic, and security policy.[29] On defense and arms control, in contrast to an increasingly harsh official line, there appeared a number of objective, even sympathetic ISKAN reviews of U.S. and European perspectives on nuclear issues.[30]

Specialists also pushed harder than ever for serious economic change, from adoption of cooperative or private enterprise modeled on East European innovations to pursuit of joint ventures with the West.[31] But equally noteworthy was that socioeconomic problems—and ideas for reform—raised still more sensitive issues about the nature of socialism (and capitalism). Stagnation, caused by rampant bureaucracy and rigid centralization, was seen as a *systemic* problem of "developed socialism." Boris Kurashvili, of the Institute of State and Law, wrote that the ministerial system, essentially unchanged since the 1930s and entirely inappropriate to a modern economy, required "radical" reforms.[32] But reform must not again be confused with "pseudo-reform," for needed now was a *perestroika* of the entire state mechanism.[33] Shakhnazarov, Kurashvili, and others suggested that the core issue was one of democratization.[34] IEMSS analyst Anatoly Butenko also linked democratization to economic reform; echoing his institute colleagues who saw a "revolutionary situation" looming in Eastern Europe, he described a basic "contradiction" between centralized, authoritarian structures and the need for popular initiative and participation.[35]

These diagnoses all rejected the official view that the West—through vestiges of the bourgeois past, or intrigues of the capitalist present—was largely to blame for socialism's woes. However, foreshadowing a division among some reformers that would grow acute under Gorbachev's perestroika, Butenko and Kurashvili harked back to a NEPish vision of Party-led social activization, while Shakhnazarov and Burlatsky looked forward to broader economic and political freedoms.[36] The former looked inward to an essentially Leninist or anti-Stalinist model of *socialist democracy*, while the latter searched outward for increasingly liberal or *social democratic* solutions to stagnation at home and confrontation abroad.[37]

Simultaneously, the worsening of this confrontation in the years 1980 to 1982 provided additional impetus for global-integrationist thought by shaking some of the leadership, and consequently public discourse, out of their confident complacency on military rivalry and the nuclear dilemma. As Brezhnev now pronounced the idea of nuclear victory to be "dangerous madness" and the Party renewed a no-first-use pledge, military and other issues of the global agenda came to the fore.[38] Now many of the concerns raised by Sakharov in 1968, Burlatsky in 1970, and Frolov in 1973—dissident or semi-dissident ideas at that time—entered the mainstream of Soviet thought.

In 1981, Frolov and International Department deputy Zagladin published *Contemporary Global Problems,* which raised issues from "limits to growth" and depletion of resources to the early, "human-istic" Marx's concerns about mankind and alienation.[39] Also in 1981, and under the same title, Inozemtsev edited an IMEMO volume that surveyed the entire range of pressing global issues in a new light. Backwardness, overpopulation, the environment, hunger, energy, natural resources, and nuclear confrontation were viewed as "universal-human" (*obshchechelovecheskie*) problems whose solution required greater East-West cooperation.[40]

Here, as well as in Shakhnazarov's 1981 book *The Coming World Order* and Burlatsky's 1982 article "The Philosophy of Peace," the nuclear danger was the primary concern.[41] For Shakhnazarov and Zagladin—at least formally—the superiority of the socialist approach to global issues was manifest.[42] Yet their reference to the humanistic concerns of the early Marx marked a qualitative shift in the context of discussion, and their stature as "prominent ideolo-gists" gave the field of globalistics a legitimacy that it had previous-ly lacked.[43] The new middle ground—criticizing Soviet liberals for "an uncritical attitude toward Western works" but also faulting Soviet conservatives for being "insufficiently aware of the nature and depth" of global problems—was an important step toward new thinking in the open literature.[44]

Less prominent ideologists were now correspondingly freer to push the limits even further and risk an "uncritical attitude toward Western works." For example, IEMSS staffer Alexander Tsipko's *Some Philosophical Aspects of the Theory of Socialism* cast Soviet socioeconomic problems in a radically new light.[45] Breaking with the more materialist analysis of his erstwhile coauthor Butenko, Tsipko emphasized "moral and spiritual" problems, "the autonomy of the individual," and "free choice" in socioeconomic develop-ment. Tsipko, too, stressed the universal-human nature of these concerns; he cited the Club of Rome, which Shakhnazarov had crit-icized as "Malthusian," in analyzing the "limits to growth" that constrained both capitalist *and* socialist economies.[46] But common limits existed in the "spiritual-psychological" realm as well; echoing the early *Vekhi* authors (see chapter 1), Tsipko warned against forced leaps in societal development.

> In society, as in nature, there are many interconnected social-psy-chological systems upon whose balance everything depends. To this day these systems are incompletely understood. Therefore,

destruction of even one of the links of such systems, such as rejection of some tradition or form of social organization, can have unforeseen consequences for the entire system. "In matters of culture," as Lenin noted, "haste and grand designs" are more harmful than anything.[47]

While Tsipko cited Lenin in praise of the NEP, Burlatsky quoted Engels in support of new thinking on nuclear issues; there would come a time, Engels had noted, when technology would make waging war "unthinkable."[48] Burlatsky stressed global interdependence and repeated the formulation of his 1970 program, that peace was an "absolute value."[49] Moreover, Burlatsky downplayed capitalism's supposed militarism and emphasized the "dialectics" of the arms race, an action-reaction spiral that had acquired a momentum of its own quite apart from the goals and intentions of either side.

An attempt to halt this spiral, to forge professional ties and mutual understanding, lay behind another important development of Brezhnev's final years. Building on longstanding Pugwash contacts as well as the U.S. and Soviet academies of science exchanges of the 1970s, international gatherings on issues of global concern now grew in prominence. Even as some scientific ties were curtailed in the bitter post-Afghanistan climate, others soon expanded—particularly those in the field of nuclear arms control.[50] Beyond the official Committee on International Security and Arms Control (CISAC), led on the Soviet side by Inozemtsev, these included new nonofficial links with such U.S. groups as the National Resources Defense Council and the Federation of American Scientists. Velikhov now brought Roald Sagdeyev and other Soviet physicists into informal U.S.-Soviet discussions of anti-satellite weapons, a test ban, and other issues; as Sagdeyev recalled, "we were becoming more and more active in non-governmental forms of arms control."[51] Their nongovernmental nature was critical as such fora allowed Soviet specialists greater freedom to explore issues without the official constraints of formal Pugwash presentations.

In 1981, American physician Bernard Lown and the Kremlin's head doctor Yevgeny Chazov founded International Physicians for the Prevention of Nuclear War.[52] Also that year, Arbatov joined the Independent Commission on Disarmament and Security (the

Palme Commission). In these and other such venues, nonscientists, too, "became familiar with various American points of view on . . . foreign, military and economic policy, and they became valuable sources of our education."[53] In 1982, when Velikhov became director of the Soviet CISAC delegation, the number and range of Soviet participants grew still further. As Sagdeyev described, "I met all the great guys—Panovsky, Garwin, Wiesner and Townes—and the discussions were extremely enlightening."[54] ISKAN deputy director Andrei Kokoshin noted the impact of new Westrern ideas (and older, long-supressed Soviet ones) on notions of "nonoffensive defense"[55] And ISKAN director Arbatov recalled how the Palme Commission influenced his thinking:

> For several years I was in constant contact . . . with people who were unusually perceptive and original thinkers. I had to argue with them and find points of common ground. . . . In the midst of once-again tense international relations, new ideas and thoughts were born from collective experience in open, honest, and sometimes heated debate . . . [such as] the idea of "common security" [and] a new approach to nuclear arms.[56]

New Thinking Under Fire

But without support from the Soviet leadership, the emboldened new thinking of 1980–82 remained in a precarious state, a new foreign-policy agenda at odds with an essentially unchanged official line. As East-West relations continued to deteriorate, liberals' positions grew increasingly tenuous; their calls for conciliation sounded increasingly dissonant in an environment of heightened confrontation and militancy. Only a sharp turn at the top could rescue the new thinking from this highly vulnerable position.

But the decrepit Brezhnev was incapable of any bold moves, either toward reform *or* reaction.[57] His incapacity, and the decline or death of others in the core Politburo group that had steered the 1970s course of limited détente abroad and muddle-through at home, began shifting power in the senior leadership toward foreign-policy hawks.[58] The influence of Defense Minister Ustinov and the military grew, partly at the expense of Foreign Minister Gromyko, who was viewed by some as the main executor of a failed détente.[59] Also increasing with the growing immobility at the top—on secondary if not primary policy matters—was the weight of hard-line "second echelon" Politburo members, such as the Moscow Party boss Viktor Grishin and the International Department head Boris Ponomarev, together with senior Central Committee old thinkers such as Propaganda and Ideology chief Mikhail Zimyanin, Science and Education tsar Sergei Trapeznikov, and *Kommunist* editor Richard Kosolapov.[60] In 1982, as Brezhnev neared death, these reactionaries launched a concerted attack on the new thinkers.

For example, Arbatov fell afoul of Ponomarev for his Palme Commission activity; he also provoked Suslov's ire for sponsoring publication of the commission's report in Moscow.[61] The military harshly criticized Chazov for publicizing his views on the nuclear danger—"demoralizing the Soviet people at a time of great danger."[62] Burlatsky and others who championed nonideological approaches to the arms race were also attacked, and, in late 1982, the old Stalinist Trapeznikov promulgated new, "utterly dogmatic" directives for Academy of Sciences' institutes—a "club" to beat recalcitrant liberals.[63]

More than just scattered attacks, these efforts soon coalesced into a major counteroffensive that took aim at the three most "Westernized" institutes: IMEMO, ISKAN and IEMSS. The first blow, in early 1982, fell upon IMEMO. When an investigation of criminal activity over a relatively trivial matter—the disposal of old furniture—failed to produce serious *kompromat* (compromising material), the big guns were rolled out. In April, the KGB arrested two young staffers for dissident activity and there ensued a drawn-out attempt to purge IMEMO at the highest level and destroy its influence.[64]

The arrested, Andrei Fadin and Pavel Kudyukin, belonged to a group that had circulated leaflets denouncing the official line on events in Poland and praising Solidarity, the independent trade union. They also put out a samizdat journal that drew in others, such as left-wing dissident Boris Kagarlitsky.[65] Such incidents had occurred before and "ordinarily . . . did not have any serious consequences for the institute or its directors." But this time the affair offered a pretext for investigation by a special Party commission, chaired by Grishin and Zimyanin.[66] They found that IMEMO, in part due to "zionist elements," was in a state of "ideological collapse" and had "disoriented the leadership of the country as to the processes underway in the world." That the institute was recognized abroad as a reformist, pro-détente bastion at a time of worsening U.S.-Soviet relations fueled the further charge that IMEMO was being "praised by our enemies."[67]

The victims of this witchhunt, along with some senior IMEMO officials, included director Inozemtsev, whose death in 1982 was hastened by the ordeal.[68] Another casualty was IMEMO's strong public reformism on international affairs; for nearly a year, such views disappeared from the institute's journal.[69] Arbatov and Bovin eventually raised the case with Brezhnev in one of the now-rare moments "when you could have a serious talk with him." Brezhnev, apparently unaware of the matter but sympathetic to his long-time adviser Inozemtsev, promptly phoned Grishin and told him to call the witchhunt off.[70]

Bogomolov also came under fire at this time. Just as the collapse of détente provided ammunition to attack IMEMO and ISKAN, problems in Eastern Europe fueled attacks on IEMSS. For example, the institute's frank criticism of the Polish (and, by extension, Soviet) leadership brought down the wrath of reactionaries in the Central Committee apparatus. Bogomolov was reprimanded by Konstantin Rusakov, chief of the Department for Liaison with Communist and Workers' Parties. Punishments meted out to analysts in the Polish section at IEMSS ranged from suspension of travel privileges to loss of their jobs.[71] Though their warnings had proven absolutely correct, their diagnosis of Polish problems, and harsh criticism of the Polish Communist Party, hit too close to home for Soviet conservatives to tolerate. Conservatives also struck at ISKAN, viewing it as a collective of dubious loyalties because of Arbatov's sheltering of outspoken liberals fired from other positions in academia and journalism. Their suspicions were further fueled by incidents such as that involving two ISKAN analysts who were dismissed on orders from the Central Committee for their too-accurate speculation on Soviet arms-negotiations positions in an interview with *Newsweek*.[72]

As superpower ties worsened during 1982, ISKAN suffered as the main institutional bastion of détente,[73] and soon after Brezhnev's death in November, Arbatov began to feel even more heat. The proximate cause was a memo he had written in December to Andropov, the new general secretary. Continuing a longstanding practice of informally advising his former Central Committee boss, Arbatov now found his recommendations for liberal cultural-scientific policies rejected and was told henceforth to keep his views to himself.[74] Bovin, another former subordinate of Andropov's, was similarly reprimanded.[75] Arbatov, recalling that already in January 1982 he had been sharply criticized by Suslov, believes that Andropov was seeking to shore up his support among Politburo reactionaries: "They were pressing him from all sides, especially from the right, and he was not always able or willing, to resist this pressure."[76]

In early 1983, Arbatov was summoned to the KGB headquarters to explain his alleged criticism of the Soviet leadership to a group of visiting Americans.[77] In May, he and Bovin received a stinging public reprimand at a plenum of the Central Committee (of which both had been members since 1981):

> Everything was going routinely when suddenly, in the section of the plenum report on counterpropaganda and the need "to denounce those who, consciously or unconsciously, act as a mouthpiece for foreign interests [*poet s chuzhogo golosa*] by spreading all kinds of gossip and rumors," Andropov interrupted the speaker. . . . And in the dead silence of the shocked auditorium, he sharply said the following: "Yes, by the way. I know that there are people sitting in this hall who, in conversation with foreigners, give out information that is unnecessary or even harmful to us. I am not going to name names just now, these comrades themselves know whom I have in mind. And let them remember, this is their final warning."[78]

General Secretary Yuri Andropov: Reformism Revived

Arbatov is surely correct in attributing this episode, at least in part, to Andropov's perceived need to distance himself publicly from the most visible reformers as he consolidated power in a tense international and domestic environment.[79] But it was power that Andropov sought precisely in order to begin long-overdue reforms. As such, his clash with Arbatov highlights a central dilemma of Andropov's reign: initiating change in an ossified, militarized Party-state system, and doing so against a growing tide of reaction and a backdrop of collapsing East-West relations.

Beyond conservative resistance, Andropov's efforts were hamstrung by other factors: his own limited horizons; foreign-policy crises beyond his control; and, above all, his brevity of tenure. Andropov was general secretary for only 15 months—from November 1982 through February 1984—and his active period was even briefer, some nine months, before he entered the Kremlin hospital from which he would not emerge alive. Yet during these nine months, Andropov undertook more than Brezhnev had over the preceding nine years. He sponsored several economic innovations—"experiments" in enterprise autonomy and decentralized management—and also took small steps toward defusing confrontation with the United States and ending the Afghan war.[80] Although in hindsight these can be seen as inadequate half-measures, they were reasonably bold in the climate and context of 1983. Moreover, they were linked to what would be Andropov's most lasting contribution: shaking the country out of its torpor, openly airing problems, and beginning the political-personnel changes that would later facilitate the inception of perestroika.

In general, Andropov's term was a time of renewed hopes and revived activity for Soviet reformers. Though his direction of the KGB and suppression of dissidence had hardly endeared him to liberals, those who knew him from his even earlier sponsorship of innovative thinking were cautiously optimistic. At a minimum, the era of stagnation seemed to have ended as Andropov took charge with great vigor; he denounced idleness, drunkenness, and corruption, began retiring old Brezhnev-era cadres, and announced his intention to get the country moving again. "We must soberly realize where we find ourselves," he warned.[81] In June 1983, summoning the first Central Committee ideology plenum since 1961, he stated:

> We cannot be satisfied with our pace in shifting the economy onto the rails of intensive development. . . . It is obvious that in searching for ways to solve new tasks, we were not energetic enough, that we often resorted to half measures and could not overcome the accumulated inertia quickly enough. We must now make up for our neglect.[82]

To address the backlog of problems, Andropov sought to tap the country's scientific expertise, stating in his plenum address that "we have not adequately studied the society in which we live and work, and have not fully revealed the laws which govern it, particularly the economic ones."[83] His priority was domestic (primarily economic) affairs, and specialists were now invited to submit their analyses and proposals. Scores responded to the call, including leading reformers ignored under Brezhnev.[84]

Some, such as the oft-persecuted Moscow economist Stanislav Shatalin, were asked to offer their ideas directly to Andropov.[85] Others, such as the Novosibirsk reformers, focused mainly on further refining their critiques; it was at this time, for example, that Tatyana Zaslavskaya's analysis of the socioeconomic divisions underlying stagnation—the famous "Novosibirsk memorandum"— was quietly drafted.[86] Among others who injected their views into the open debate was Academy of Social Sciences director Vadim Medvedev; his *Administration of Socialist Production* argued for decentralizing, marketizing reforms as boldly as anything seen in the mainstream literature for a decade.[87] Medvedev soon replaced Trapeznikov, the long-serving Brezhnev crony and open neo-Stalinist, as head of the Central Committee department overseeing Academy of Sciences institutes.

Early in 1983, Andropov gained Politburo approval to convene a plenum on scientific-technological (i.e., economic) issues; in preparation, work began to assemble and analyze the proposals now pouring into the Central Committee.[88] And in connection with this initiative, Andropov began what were arguably the most important changes of his brief tenure, promoting several younger officials and putting them in charge of plenum preparations. Mikhail Gorbachev, whose leadership responsibilities grew rapidly, was appointed to manage the project. He was assisted by Nikolai Ryzhkov, a senior Gosplan deputy and long-time industrial manager, who was also named to head the newly created Central Committee Economics Department.[89]

Other members of Andropov's young team, distinguished by their energy and distance from corruption, were Viktor Chebrikov, Vitaly Vorotnikov, and Yegor Ligachev. The latter, Party boss of the Tomsk region, was brought to Moscow to head the Party Organizations Department of the Central Committee and charged with replacing many provincial Brezhnev-era holdovers.[90] Another important appointment was Lev Tolkunev, a protégé of Andropov's from his 1960s Central Committee consultant group, as editor of *Izvestiia*. In general, editors were encouraged to confront problems more openly and honestly, and this produced a modest critical margin in the press and much greater critical freedom in specialist writings.[91] Together, these personnel and political changes were Andropov's main levers in the effort to overcome inertia and fierce conservative resistance in the Party-state apparatus.

In foreign policy, Andropov faced tasks no less daunting. He had inherited bad superpower relations and a U.S. counterpart disinclined to compromise. On the "Euromissile" issue, the two sides had already set themselves on a collision course; SS-20 deployments were far advanced, and NATO's counterdeployments were set to begin in late 1983. Andropov was also confronted by such complications as Reagan's "Star Wars" in March, the Korean airliner tragedy in September, and the U.S. invasion of Grenada in October.[92]

Still, Andropov undertook several initiatives in an attempt to arrest the slide; he announced a halt in testing of the Soviet anti-satellite system, for example, and proposed a moratorium on further deployment of SS-20s if NATO would cancel its plans for new ballistic and cruise missiles. Andropov also undertook the first serious Soviet effort to prepare for withdrawal from Afghanistan.[93] But these modest steps were unsuccessful, and with the KAL airliner tragedy and the failure of efforts to block NATO rearmament, relations virtually collapsed. The invective on both sides reached a pitch not seen since the early cold war.[94]

Although clearly a victim of circumstances, Andropov was hardly blameless. Certainly his inherited Afghanistan dilemma was at least partly of his own making. He also ignored advice to take a conciliatory public line on KAL 007, and allowed himself to be persuaded that an ultimatum on Euromissiles would be successful owing to anti-war sentiment in Western Europe.[95] When it failed, there seemed no choice but to follow through (at least temporarily) on his threat to abandon the Geneva arms talks. With better luck and more time, Andropov's foreign policy might have evolved differently. But circumstances dictated otherwise, and in any case—if he is judged by his own beliefs and inclinations—Andropov was hardly a new thinker.[96] Only bolder steps would have made a real difference, and these could come only from a different leader.

But while his gestures to the West were quite limited, his suggestions to Soviet foreign-policy analysts were far more consequential. Already in November 1982, just days before taking office, Andropov echoed the new thinkers' critique of Soviet support for radical regimes in the third world by arguing that "It is one thing to proclaim socialism . . . and quite another to build it."[97] Further, suggesting a need to demilitarize foreign policy and put domestic affairs first, he noted that "we exercise our main influence on the world revolutionary process through economic policy."[98] Finally, in summoning specialists to search for new solutions, Andropov encouraged study not only of other socialist countries, but of "world" experience in general.[99]

This was all the encouragement that the new thinkers needed. After lying low to weather conservative attacks at the bitter end of Brezhnev's reign, the "year of Andropov" saw another vigorous push for foreign-policy change.[100] It began with a qualitative reappraisal of the main adversary. For example, a 1983 ISKAN study of the U.S. economy bluntly contradicted the official line:

> The basic mass of business interests are not and cannot be drawn into the arms race. . . . The basic interests of the overwhelming majority of US firms depend on mass production for civilian markets, with the normal functioning of which militarization of the economy increasingly interferes.[101]

Shmelev extended this analysis to the international level, arguing that modern capitalism bred not cutthroat and violent competition, but cooperation and stability.[102] Many works now cast Western political-economic life in an increasingly positive light, essentially bringing to broader attention the views developed in the restricted or specialized literature of the 1970s. Notably, in early 1984, the deputy head of the International Department, Zagladin, contradicted the views of Ponomarev, his chief, by criticizing as "premature" the arguments of "some Marxist scholars that the general crisis of capitalism has entered a new stage."[103]

With an open reassessment of the capitalist West, there also came a variety of new (or revived) ideas for easing the confrontation. Burlatsky, for example, offered a proposal for international cooperation in a revision of his 1970 "Planirovanie" address.[104] Building on his earlier study of the international arms trade, Foreign Ministry staffer Andrei Kozyrev published a plan to limit weapons sales; here, in an open Soviet source, he revealed for the first time data on Soviet participation in this trade that showed that, as of the 1970s, the USSR had become the world's largest weapons exporter.[105] IEMSS analyst Yevgeny Ambartsumov raised the link between domestic- and foreign-policy reforms; joining his colleague Butenko's critique of socialism's systemic "crisis," Ambartsumov drew an explicit parallel to 1921 and called for another NEP.[106] Though stressing domestic problems, the fact that NEP had also seen a turn from confrontation to peaceful coexistence abroad was the clear subtext of Ambartsumov's argument, particularly in the context of the renewed cold war of 1983–84.

Perhaps the most important publication of this period was Shakhnazarov's article "The Logic of Political Thinking in the Nuclear Era."[107] Moved by new insight into the "upside-down logic" of Soviet military policy acquired via special access to Warsaw Pact data—and though debate with senior military officials— Shakhnazarov now revised his earlier arguments in several critical ways.[108] First, the nuclear dilemma now necessitated a "transformed worldview," a shift to a "new way of thinking" (*k novomu obrazu myshleniia*). Its central tenet was that each side "is forced to consider the security of the other as its own." Attempts to gain security unilaterally could only provoke a corresponding buildup that lessened security for all; "only collective security is possible in the nuclear era."[109] A second tenet of Shakhnazarov's new thinking was de-ideologizing international relations. The old belief that "however passionate the ideological dispute and whatever the methods employed in it, they don't threaten the human race," was now found deeply flawed.[110]

Further discarding his earlier ridicule of Western futurology as a "fiasco" and his scorn for Western globalistics as "Malthusian," Shakhnazarov now stressed poverty, the environment, and other problems that, if not solved, threatened consequences "no less dangerous than those of thermonuclear war." These problems, moreover, could be addressed only through "the collective efforts" of all nations.[111] Shakhnazarov also sought to reconcile class with universal priorities, arguing that "Marxism-Leninism . . . has never opposed class interests to universal-human ones." Given the dangers of confrontation, the latter must now take precedence or else risk "extremely negative consequences."[112]

While exploring such theoretical innovations, attention also turned to the two most pressing concrete foreign-policy issues: the existing military debacle in Afghanistan, and a possible future military debacle in outer space. Regarding the former, 1983–84 saw the Afghan war seriously addressed for the first time since 1980. As noted above, Andropov began work toward ending the conflict. Simultaneously, and almost surely with his tolerance or even approval, criticism of the war was now manifested in a number of ways.[113]

Ambartsumov, in a historical analogy even subtler than his NEP argument, warned of "danger . . . when messianism becomes the official ideology of a superpower." Ostensibly criticizing the U.S. invasion of Grenada, Ambartsumov noted that such a superpower "really believes that it makes the world happy, that it brings progress and culture. . . . Lev Tolstoy exposed the inhumanity of this 'civilizing mission' in chapter 18 of *Hadzhi Murat* which was banned by tsarist censorship."[114] Educated readers knew that Tolstoy's work had in fact been banned for heroically depicting the resistance of Muslim *basmachi* to tsarist imperialism.

At this time, Afghan veteran Col. Leonid Shershnev sent the Politburo his analysis of the war: "The inhuman actions of Soviet soldiers against civilians are systematic and widespread, manifested in plunder . . . destruction of homes . . . desecration of mosques . . . and lack of respect for customs and traditions. As a result, we have been drawn in to a war with the people and it is hopeless."[115] Shershnev, like some other critics, was handled gently for his dissidence. Less fortunate was Lt. Col. Vladimir Kovalevsky, a teacher at the Frunze Military Academy, who "went so far in his lectures as to compare the presence of our troops in Afghanistan with the activities of the USA in Vietnam."[116] Kovalevsky's case "raised considerable alarm" in the army's Main Political Administration because, as the Party moved to expel him, some 10 percent of the student body—nearly all of Kovalevsky's pupils—signed petitions to the academy administration in support of their teacher.[117] It was no coincidence that, soon after Andropov's death, Kovalevsky was indeed fired and kicked out of the Party.[118]

For all its intractability, the Afghan dilemma was a straightforward one. From dissident officers to soldiers' mothers, all understood well that the war was a disaster and must be ended. Much more complex was the issue of strategic weaponry, particularly in space, and here the ideas and initiatives of specialists would prove much more critical.

With the announcement of the U.S. "Star Wars" initiative in March 1983, a familiar Soviet response soon followed. Beyond the rhetorical reply—outrage over Washington's flouting of the ABM Treaty and dire warnings of the program's dangers—the policy response was reflexive: If the Americans build it, so shall we.[119] Further, all other arms talks would be held hostage to the space issue, which became the subject of an enormous Soviet propaganda campaign. As part of the latter, a group of prominent scientists would, it was felt, be useful in the battle for world public opinion. And so the Committee of Soviet Scientists in Defense of Peace and Against the Nuclear Threat was formed two months later.

Unfortunately for partisans of orthodoxy, these prominent scientists were the same ones who, for more than a decade, had been broadening their outlook in various international exchanges. Many were also closely involved in the numerous informal U.S.-Soviet arms control discussions of the late 1970s and early 1980s.[120] The result was that, while initially echoing the official condemnation of U.S. policy, the Soviet Scientists' committee quickly began charting another course.

Almost immediately after the committee's founding, in May 1983, its senior members Velikhov and Kokoshin sent Andropov a report arguing SDI's impracticality and opposing "the hysterical Gromyko policy" of loud propaganda and the threat of a tit-for-tat military reply.[121] Here, at the very outset of its work, the committee had already produced what would be perhaps its most important contribution to the strategic debates of the mid 1980s: the idea of an "asymmetric response," ignoring the cry for absolute parity in favor of a realistic assessment of what SDI could actually do and, if necessary, adoption of simple, low-cost countermeasures to preserve the Soviet deterrent.[122]

Led by Velikhov and Sagdeyev, the scientists' committee also took the initiative to advise Andropov on such matters as anti-satellite weapons and nuclear testing.[123] Meanwhile, other, less-prominent committee members publicized heretofore little-addressed issues such as the detailed climactic and other effects a nuclear exchange would cause.[124] Said one, "We took the issues seriously and came to our own conclusions, such as on the effects of nuclear winter or the possibility of accidental nuclear war. . . . We didn't take instructions from the government, it was the other way around."[125] In the words of another, "what started as another marionette organization, to carry out the leadership's directives, soon began operating as an independent group of specialists. . . . It is in a scientist's nature to question, and we knew the West well by this time."[126]

New Leadership for New Thinking

The emboldened foreign-policy discussions of 1983 were aided by the greater critical freedoms permitted under Andropov and encouraged by the expectation of change that enveloped Soviet intellectuals and much of society at large. Still, the new thinking remained somewhat apart. While exploring modest reforms, Andropov himself was no new thinker. A hard official line mainly prevailed and foreign relations continued to deteriorate during his tenure as Andropov's priority remained domestic change. Similarly, his main long-term contribution to reform—the inception of a study project and creation of a team of young reformers to manage it—was also primarily domestic and economic in focus. But for one member of that team, Mikhail Gorbachev, domestic and foreign-policy reformism grew increasingly linked.

Gorbachev was clearly the leader of Andropov's young protégés. By 1983 he was already a full member of the Politburo, held much greater responsibilities than Andropov's other promotees, and it soon became apparent that he was being groomed for eventual succession. But Gorbachev stood out from the other members of Andropov's team in another important respect; alone among them, he built strong ties to the boldest foreign-policy reformers. Some became unofficial advisers, while others influenced his thinking through writings that he avidly consumed. Gorbachev grew personally close to a number of leading new thinkers during the post-Brezhnev interregnum, forging political and intellectual bonds that would be of critical importance after 1985.

Gorbachev also stood out among the leadership—including the other young reformers—by virtue of his education and early experience. As seen earlier, he and his wife Raisa witnessed first-hand the transforming events of the early thaw era at Moscow State University (MGU), a crucible of debate and original thought that in those years graduated many future leading reformers in all fields—history, economics, philosophy, and science.[127] Gorbachev's subsequent career showed an intolerance of complacency, waste, and stagnation, an open, searching mind, and a reformist bent that contrasted sharply with the overwhelming majority of Party careerists.[128]

These traits were manifested in his record as a dynamic, innovative Party official in his native Stavropol region.[129] They were also seen, and to a certain extent shaped, by Gorbachev's interest in East European reform experience, including the Prague Spring.[130] In an important sense, the latter began long before 1968, in his acquaintance with one of the movement's future leaders, Zdenek Mlynar, at MGU in the early-to-mid 1950s. They drew close—"He is Raisa's and my friend, one of our closest friends during our whole life"—and in 1967 Mlynar paid the couple a highly unusual visit in Stavropol.[131] For two days, they discussed the problems and prospects of reform in their respective countries. And so the crushing of the Prague Spring a year later was deeply disillusioning, though, as Gorbachev admits, he partly shared in the perception of a threat to the socialist camp and participated in the rituals of support for the invasion.[132] The full force of 1968, as "a major impulse to my critical thinking," came only a year later, when Gorbachev, as a member of a Party delegation, visited Czechoslovakia and found a country still seething in the invasion's aftermath. Nearly everywhere the group went, the people—from shopfloor workers up to Communist Party leaders—criticized or snubbed the Soviet visitors.

> People just turned away from us . . . for me it was a shock. Suddenly I understood that, for global strategic and ideological reasons, we had crushed something that had [in fact] ripened within society itself. From that time on, I thought more and more . . . and came to the distressing conclusion that something was really wrong with us.[133]

By the 1970s, such reflections were also fueled by travel in the West that followed his promotion to first secretary of the Party bureau at Stavropol. By many accounts, Gorbachev's visits over the next decade to Italy, France (twice), Germany, Belgium, and the Netherlands—some on Party business, others mainly as a tourist—had an enormous impact on his intellectual evolution.[134] Chernyaev, who accompanied Gorbachev on a 1972 trip to Belgium and Holland, recalled that he "stood out from all the other local party bosses by virtue of his unusual passion for change, to correct, to improve."[135] Gorbachev himself described the familiar shock, of a first-time visitor to the West, at the standard of living. But also impressive was "the functioning of a civil society." Having met people ranging from German students and French farmers to Italian workers, the "openness and relaxed, free, and critical discussion" he encountered "shook my faith in the superiority of socialist democracy."[136] Soon, with Gorbachev's promotion to the Central Committee, came other opportunities to gain a "different perspective on socialism. We could order so-called 'white' books off a special list from Progress publishers. That's how I read G. Boffa's three-volume *History of the USSR*, the works of Togliatti, the collection *Dubcek's Drama*, the books of Gramsci, Garaudy, and the articles of Brandt and Mitterand."[137]

In Stavropol, Gorbachev also developed a close relationship with the leader of the neighboring Georgian Republic, Eduard Shevardnadze, probably the most reformist republican leader of the 1970s. The two frequently met, cooperating on practical matters and comparing reform ideas and experience. They also lamented their country's decline and agreed, "Everything's rotten. It's all got to change."[138] In 1978, Gorbachev took the bold step of sending a report to the Central Committee arguing for far-reaching changes in agriculture.[139]

A year later, with Andropov's support, Gorbachev was Central Committee secretary for agriculture and a candidate Politburo member. Back in Moscow again after more than 20 years, he wasted no time in seeking out the country's best minds for new ideas. Beginning a practice unheard of for a high official of the Party, Gorbachev summoned leading reform economists—including Aganbegyan, Zaslavskaya, and Tikhonov—for a series of private seminars.[140] Significantly, these began nearly five years before such "semi-dissident" scholars were formally tapped under Andropov. Tikhonov later described Gorbachev's special interest in, and considerable knowledge of, the NEP experience as a model for future reforms.[141] Zaslavskaya recalled a 1982 meeting with Gorbachev in which they discussed "a *perestroika* of the economic system."[142]

Toward the end of Brezhnev's reign, Gorbachev also began forging ties with leading foreign-policy new thinkers. Velikhov described their association as beginning in earnest in 1981, over the subject of computers and Gorbachev's interest in streamlining agricultural planning. But soon their discussions turned to foreign policy and ideas for breaking the nuclear stalemate.[143] A similar breadth of interests is recalled by Chernyaev, who at that time was an assistant to International Department head Boris Ponomarev. Chernyaev described his boss's anger at "this upstart, who's supposed to be working on agriculture, sticking his nose where it doesn't belong."[144]

Chernyaev emphasizes three aspects of Gorbachev's early outlook on international affairs. One was an interest in (and openness with) foreigners "that none of his colleagues permitted themselves."[145] Another was his interest in social democracy and admiration for the social democratic-leaning European Communist Parties.[146] And a third was his disgust at the rigid, Comintern-style domination (*kominternovshchina*) that prevailed in intrabloc relations. Revealingly, Zagladin recalled Gorbachev's complaint on this issue:

> We have to deal with [the socialist countries] as equals. And we've got to wonder why the strong, influential parties all turn away from us, to various "deviations," while the small, insignificant ones remain orthodox and faithful. And by what criteria is a party considered "good"? Our main concern is that they support [the Soviet line]. To talk about equality here is simply absurd.[147]

By the early 1980s, Gorbachev had established ties with many liberal foreign-policy thinkers in the Moscow establishment. For example, according to Yevgeny Primakov, Inozemtsev and Gorbachev developed "implicit trust" and saw "eye to eye."[148] Frolov recalled Gorbachev telling him that "he'd been reading works on global problems for 15 years."[149] And Shakhnazarov described how Gorbachev "really surprised me once. Back when he was still agriculture secretary we met in the corridor, and he said that he'd read my book *The Coming World Order* and that he really liked it."[150]

On practical policy issues, Velikhov's and Arbatov's influence on Gorbachev was apparently strongest—the former on arms control, and the latter on broader East-West relations. Beginning in 1983, with his appointment to head the Supreme Soviet's international-affairs committee, Gorbachev's foreign activity expanded greatly and he drew increasingly on Arbatov and Velikhov for advice. Both played important preparatory roles in his May 1983 visit to Canada.[151] As Sagdeyev writes, "My friends Arbatov and Velikhov were already considered members of Gorbachev's team."[152]

Gorbachev's Canadian trip was also decisive in bringing another member to this team—Alexander Yakovlev. During the visit, Gorbachev spent considerable time with Yakovlev, then in his tenth year of ambassadorial exile for having run afoul of resurgent Russian-national chauvinism. The two now renewed their earlier acquaintance and found that they were "kindred spirits."[153] "Tossing out the official program and forgetting about Canadian agriculture, they spent hours talking about Russia."[154] These talks "had a decisive impact" on Gorbachev, helping him "to understand in much greater depth the processes occurring in the Western world [as well as] questions of democratization, freedom, and glasnost. As Gorbachev later told me . . . Yakovlev expounded his vision of development in the Soviet Union and the world as a whole, suggesting ways of improving our society."[155] In Yakovlev's own summary, "We spoke completely frankly about everything . . . the main idea was that society must change, it must be built on different principles—all that was there. It's clear that these thoughts didn't just appear spontaneously, accidentally, in March of 1985."[156]

For Yakovlev, having observed détente's demise and much else from his vantage point in the West, these thoughts were already quite radical. Earlier known as a reformist apparatchik for efforts that also played a part in his banishment, the subsequent evolution of his worldview is revealed in an essay that he had completed in 1983 just prior to Gorbachev's visit.[157] In it, Yakovlev lambastes stagnation and militarization while emphasizing all the concerns of a broad, new-thinking agenda. These included: criticism of dogmatic social thought and of belief in the infallibility of one's own model; admiration for the market, as a practical *and* ethical socioeconomic institution, and scorn for an outdated view of primitive capitalism; concern over global problems and praise for Western futurology; lamentation over the revolutionary destruction of avant-garde expression and Russia's lost place in world culture; and, finally, an appeal for recovery of "fundamental values" and establishment of a "worldwide humanism."[158]

Immediately after Gorbachev's return from Canada, Yakovlev's long exile ended and he was named director of IMEMO. The institute, cowed by the attacks of 1982 and rudderless since the death that year of Inozemtsev, quickly revived under Yakovlev's direction. Recalled one staffer, "He'd lived in the West for 10 years, it was incredible experience, and his guidance helped us overcome the remaining dogmas."[159] Yakovlev "assigned his researchers the work of John K. Galbraith on post-industrial societies, that of Wassily Leontiev on growth, and that of Daniel Bell on the end of ideology."[160] Soon IMEMO was producing studies that proposed creation of Soviet-Western joint ventures and warned that, without radical economic reform, the country would sink to the status of the third world in 15 years.[161]

Yakovlev himself credits IMEMO's staff in the institute's revival, recalling that now he "was listening to smart people."[162] One of those, military-affairs analyst Sergei Blagovolin, had just completed a doctoral thesis on NATO, essentially arguing the economic and political folly of a Soviet policy that sought to match the combined might of all the country's potential adversaries.[163] "Yakovlev read it, called me in, and asked: 'If you take out the anti-imperialist jargon, do you realize what you've written? That we're at a dead end!' " A report based on this research, and many other similar memos, became part of "a steady flow of information to Gorbachev."[164] Yakovlev's own characterization is that "we were collecting heresies."[165]

For the most part, these ideas remained separate from the official plenum preparations that proceeded simultaneously. The latter, as noted, had an overwhelmingly domestic focus, and foreign-policy "heresies" were mostly a matter of private discussion and analysis among Gorbachev, Yakovlev, Arbatov, Velikhov, and a few others.[166] This group, described by Sagdeyev as "Gorbachev's team," was distinct from the "Andropov team" assembling reform proposals through the Central Committee apparatus. Still, at Gorbachev's direction, some of the former were brought into the latter. As noted by Vadim Medvedev, in addition to domestic analyses, "other comrades contributed their international experience."[167]

By early 1984, the plenum project had distilled numerous studies and proposals down to 110 separate documents. These, Gorbachev recalled, were "the conclusions of academicians, writers, prominent specialists, and public figures . . . the materials were prepared for a special Central Committee plenum on issues of scientific-technological progress, and your humble servant was assigned to give the main report. But that plenum was never held."[168]

The Neo-Stalinists Bid for Power

That plenum was not held because its reformist goals were opposed by powerful conservatives. Already under fire because of Andropov's campaigns against stagnation and corruption, and threatened by the retirement of status-quo cadres, the old guard knew exactly where his "experiments" were heading—to the erosion of their main power base in the economy as decentralizing, anti-bureaucratic innovations were adopted. Initially sent reeling by Andropov's vigorous start, they quickly regrouped, and by late 1983, with Andropov's health failing, they struck back. Beginning with renewed attacks on the most reformist individuals and institutes, the hard-liners' counteroffensive grew so broad as to reveal deep domestic and foreign-policy divisions at the highest levels. By 1984, with Andropov's death and the accession of Chernenko, they struck even harder.

While Chernenko's words pledged continuity with Andropov's initiatives, his deeds represented mostly a return to the muddle-through, conservative course of his long-time patron Brezhnev.[169] But Chernenko's political and physical weakness soon created another vacuum at the top that enabled officials far more reactionary than he to seize the initiative. Like the reformers, they, too, understood the long-run bankruptcy of a Brezhnevite, do-nothing course. But instead of liberalizing domestic and foreign-policy changes, they sought a return to older, "proven methods" of tight control at home and confrontation abroad.[170]

Chernenko's own antipathy toward serious reforms had been

revealed back at the Central Committee plenum of June 1983. From the same rostrum where Andropov lamented the "inertia" and "half-measures" of the past, and called on the country's specialists to tackle old problems with new approaches, Chernenko took a different tack. He assailed the Novosibirsk Institute, for example, and also criticized TsEMI, "of which we expected much . . . but from whom we have yet to see any major concrete research."[171] Although these and other reformist institutes had revived under Andropov, under Chernenko they again came under siege. For example, the security investigation that ensued after Zaslavskaya's "Novosibirsk memorandum" leaked to the West in 1983 was now followed by renewed ideological pressure on her and her boss Aganbegyan.

The reactionaries also struck against IEMSS. Butenko and Ambartsumov, the theorists of socialism's contradictions and crises, were subjected to fierce attacks orchestrated by Richard Kosolapov, editor of *Kommunist*. Butenko was forced to recant in early 1984; Ambartsumov was demolished in an article in *Kommunist* later that year.[172] Another IEMSS analyst, the *Vekhi*-admiring Tsipko, also came to grief. His globally oriented, pro-NEP book *Some Philosophical Aspects of the Theory of Socialism* had been published, under Andropov, only after two years of struggling with the censors. Now, under Chernenko, a full-blown scandal ensued; all remaining copies of the book were recalled and Tsipko's editor at the Nauka publishing house was fired.[173] Tsipko was savaged in various academic fora as Kosolapov prepared the coup de grâce for a forthcoming issue of *Kommunist*.[174] Only the intervention of Gorbachev, who had read and admired the book, saved Tsipko from annihilation.[175]

Foreign-policy specialists were also beleaguered. Reformist analysts in the Central Committee were dismayed by a new directive that—limiting apparat positions to those who had chaired local Party committees—now favored conservative hacks over qualified area experts.[176] IMEMO director Yakovlev clashed repeatedly with Grishin, the Moscow Party boss, and Zimyanin, the ideology secretary, who had been Inozemtsev's main tormenters.[177] Arbatov, too, felt renewed heat. In addition to the usual criticism, hard-liners now had the pretext of a security breach (like the Novosibirsk report, only this case was far more serious) with which to beat Arbatov's institute. Their pretext was the affair of ISKAN staffer Vladimir

Potashov, who was arrested by the KGB for providing the CIA with classified information concerning Moscow's positions on key issues in U.S.-Soviet relations.[178]

These relations were in fact fast approaching a nadir as Andropov succumbed to his final illness in late 1983 and early 1984. The repercussions of KAL 007 continued to grow, followed by the failure of Moscow's Euromissile gambit, the deployment of new NATO missiles, and the Soviet walkout from the Geneva arms talks. Now, more than just attacking the new thinkers, resurgent hard-liners brought top-level foreign-policy disputes into the open. For example, after Gromyko defended détente's gains with reference to Lenin's flexibility toward the West, the chief of the general staff, Nikolai Ogarkov, answered with a broadside pointing out that Lenin's disarmament policies of the 1920s had ultimately failed.[179] An even louder anti-détente voice was that of Politburo member Grigory Romanov, who pronounced détente dead and warned darkly of NATO preparations for a first strike against the USSR.[180]

In the summer of 1984, as the date of the long-scheduled visit of East German leader Erich Honecker to the FRG approached, another policy dispute was on public display. Supporters of détente such as Bovin and Zagladin wrote (tellingly, in the *Izvestiia* of Andropov protégé Lev Tolkunev) in support of Honecker's visit; they argued for efforts to normalize East-West relations, including expanded trade, and downplayed the significance of the Christian Democrats' triumph in recent West German elections. Others (writing mainly in the conservative Victor Afanasyev's *Pravda*) took a harder line, depicting the FRG as a revanchist pawn of the United States and warning of economic leverage that Bonn could use to "ideologically disarm" the East.[181] The debate ended in a victory for the hard-liners as Honecker's visit was abruptly canceled.

At its peak, Soviet propaganda reached a pitch unseen since early in the cold war. Scenes of World War II filled television and movie screens, Reagan was compared to Hitler, and NATO's attack plans were "exposed." A large increase in the defense budget was publicly announced and civil-defense preparations were heightened.[182] Privately, responding to directives for closer attention to Western nuclear activities, KGB residents abroad deluged Moscow with intelligence that reportedly convinced many in the leadership

that war was imminent.[183] Writing in early 1984, Kosolapov depicted the West as a doomed, fevered maniac:

> Swallowed up in the abyss of its general crisis, capitalism becomes
> especially dangerous. In ancient times, slave-holders and feudal
> lords ordered that their wives, servants and slaves be buried with
> them when they died. In our times, capitalism, in leaving the his-
> torical scene, is ready to take with it all life on earth.[184]

Nobody with memories of the earlier cold war could miss the
Stalinist echo—the infamous thesis that as socialism grows stronger,
its enemies become more devious and desperate—in Kosolapov's
diatribe.[185] But such gross inflation of the Western threat raised an
even earlier parallel with the Stalinist past—with 1927–28, when war-
scare propaganda helped hard-line forces to triumph in a domestic
power struggle. In 1983–84, the threat was not Anglo-American
invasion but a NATO nuclear strike.[186] As Gorbachev later
described it, "things were near a boiling point, it worried us.
Wherever you went, you encountered the same questions. When
will the war come? Will there be war or not?"[187]

The extent to which the Soviet leadership may have succumbed
to a largely self-generated war scare remains unclear. No doubt, as
in the late 1920s, a heightened foreign threat served hard-line interests in a struggle that was primarily domestic; the main goal of its
exponents was to squelch reforms and gain power at home. Still,
these reactionaries had a long-term foreign agenda that was anything but conciliatory. Confrontation abroad served not only the
immediate purpose of gaining power, but also that of tightening
control and strengthening the hard-liners' positions in the militarized Party-state system.

All the same, the extreme cold-war imagery evoked by the hard-
liners cannot be fully understood solely in terms of a domestic power
struggle while ignoring their beliefs, values, and core identity. The
perceived Stalinist legacy of order and discipline certainly had broad
appeal in a time of physical and spiritual decay; but suggestions of
skewed domestic priorities, immense new sacrifice, and even war
were arguably counterproductive, not only in society at large but
among the broad middle ranks of Party and managerial elites.[188]
That a group of older, Stalin-trained reactionaries in the top leadership reflexively invoked earlier images—from anti-foreign, anti-

Semitic echoes of the postwar campaign against "cosmopolitanism" to Kosolapov's view of capitalism lashing out from "the abyss of its general crisis"—is certainly revealing.[189]

So, too, were the directives that Trapeznikov had recently issued to Soviet research institutes. These praised "the economic debate of 1951, and Stalin's contribution to it" as a model of analysis for the current period.[190] One side in that earlier debate—which concerned foreign affairs more than economics—argued that World War II had eased capitalism's aggressiveness and ended its hostile encirclement of the USSR, thus permitting a relaxation of the country's fortress-like isolation. But these views were demolished by Stalin whose "contribution to the debate," his 1952 *Economic Problems of Socialism in the USSR*, was a primer for relentless cold war.[191] That there were deep ideological and emotional ties to the Stalinist worldview at work in 1983–84, and not just near-term political considerations, is also revealed in a series of steps that, more ominously than at any time since the mid 1960s, pointed again toward the tyrant's rehabilitation. These included awarding a state prize to an openly Stalinist novel,[192] Stalin's reappearance in television and films,[193] and a decision to readmit Stalin's faithful lieutenant Vyacheslav Molotov to the Communist Party. At the Politburo meeting that discussed this step (and the further one of readmitting Malenkov and Kaganovich), the old guard—Chernenko, Ustinov, Gromyko, and Tikhonov—engaged in an orgy of Khrushchev-bashing and nostalgia for Stalin.[194]

At the same time that Stalin's aged henchman was being rehabilitated, Yakovlev recalls, a legal case was in the works against "28 specialists at various Moscow institutes."[195] Thus, by late 1984, reformers and new thinkers were threatened not only with another "theoretical" defeat, but by a broader academic purge that would silence their unwanted voices once and for all. And the reactionaries sought not only victory on the academic front; they were also preparing specific steps for a hard-line turn in policy. For example, the announced 14 percent hike in military spending was dwarfed by an increase of 45 percent that was now incorporated in preparations for the next five-year plan (for the period 1986–90).[196] The implications such a sharp turn held for both domestic and foreign policy are obvious.

But the permanence of such a turn would remain in doubt so long as transition and turnover continued at the top. Thus it was important to cement hard-line policies by decisions of a Party congress. Here the reactionaries "were in a race with death." As Arbatov recalls, "their bets were on the 27th CPSU Congress, which was [scheduled] for early 1986. But by late 1984 . . . it grew clear that Chernenko probably would not last [so they pushed through] a decision . . . to advance the congress' date."[197]

But the most important decision for the country's future was the choice of a new general secretary, one healthy enough to see major changes through and chart a long-run course. And here, despite the "inevitability" of reforms that many detect in hindsight, much of the preceding suggests that a liberalizing course was anything but inevitable. In late 1984, with Andropov gone, Chernenko dying, and Gromyko weakened, hard-liners such as Ustinov, Grishin, Tikhonov, and the ascendant Romanov appeared to have the upper hand. As Yakovlev recalled, "With the exception of Gorbachev, all the members of the party-state leadership at that time leaned toward non-democratic methods, a return to the system of camps, prisons and prohibitions. They wanted to crush anyone whose political or philosophical views went beyond the boundaries of Marxism."[198]

Yakovlev's reference to "camps, prisons and prohibitions" is probably exaggerated, for there is little evidence that a literal return to Stalinist methods was planned. But the reactionaries clearly sought hard-line policies at home and an even more confrontational turn abroad, a course that can certainly be characterized as neo-Stalinist. Had this course been chosen, moreover, the resultant sharpening of foreign and domestic crises might indeed have eventually led to a truly "Stalinist" outcome.

∎

The years 1980–84 were, in many respects, a time of culminations. The policies of offensive détente abroad and muddle-through at home, after decades of tinkering and delay, seemed nearly spent. At least to those whose concerns extended beyond the immediate future, it increasingly appeared that the country was fast approaching a crossroads. The choice, for many, seemed increasingly stark: either back to older, proven methods; or forward to new, untried ones.

To the great fortune of the entire world, and against powerful opposition, the latter course was chosen. Gorbachev's succession, and the subsequent development of his policies, will be examined in the chapter that follows. In reviewing the events of 1980–84, most important was that, despite a surge of reaction, the reformist cause advanced and a reformer moved into position to take power. Moreover, of all Andropov's reformist protégés, Gorbachev was certainly the one with the most far-reaching goals for changing the Soviet system and society. Under his dynamic leadership, the post-Brezhnev era would finally begin.

As much as for his bold domestic agenda, Gorbachev also stood out as the only one of the reformers in the leadership who was close to the new thinking. All desired an end to the arms race, but only Gorbachev possessed the interest, experience, and intellectual ties to new-thinking ideas and individuals that would prove absolutely essential in winding down nearly 70 years of Soviet-Western hostility, isolation, and cold war in less than five.

6 ▪

The New Thinking Comes to Power

Russia is tired of living apart from, at odds with, the strong half of the world, tired of pumping up her muscles while living hand to mouth. . . . She wants to live well, freely, to enjoy life, to learn about others and show off herself. Now many are asking what perestroika was, where has it taken us. . . . The answer is simple; it is yet another Russian march to the West, but on a much greater scale than all those before. Peter only opened a window on Europe, but we're knocking down the walls. Both those that divided us from Europe, and those that cut us off from America and Japan.

—Georgy Shakhnazarov, *Tsena svobody*

We are merging into . . . the common stream of world civilization.
—Mikhail Gorbachev, *The Crimea Article*

Once he took office, the pace and breadth of Gorbachev's changes not only shocked foreign observers and distressed Soviet conservatives, but also surprised Gorbachev's own comrades from the original "Andropov team" of reformers. In domestic life, his call for a major reformation was followed by broad liberalization, glasnost, and by 1989, a radically transformed political system. And in foreign policy, his changes were equally unexpected and similarly bold. Initial moves, such as halting nuclear tests in August 1985 and a grand disarmament plan in January 1986, were soon followed by even more substantial steps: acceptance of unprecedented military-verification measures in mid 1986; agreement to eliminate all medium-range nuclear missiles in 1987; deep, unilateral conventional force cuts in 1988; and, by early 1989, a complete exit from Afghanistan (as well as disengagement from other conflicts in the third world). Later in 1989, if any still doubted that the cold war had ended, the iron curtain came down on its final act.

In seeking the reasons for this historic turn, it is impossible to ignore the centrality of the economic woes that made vast foreign-military commitments increasingly difficult to maintain. Reform at home clearly necessitated tranquillity abroad to free the requisite attention and resources. Still, domestic crisis is only part of the explanation of the cold war's end—the more obvious, but arguably less important, part; economic decline was probably a necessary, but certainly not sufficient, condition for what ensued. A primary focus on Soviet weakness at home and declining relative power abroad underrates the impact of ideas and values—the new thinking—which was not merely a rationalizing factor, but a facilitating, and ultimately even a prime motivating force behind Gorbachev's changes.

The inadequacy of a predominantly balance-of-power explanation is seen in, and to a great extent flows from, its view of what essentially happened in the years 1985 to 1989: a withdrawal from empire. For the new thinkers, this was only half, and clearly the less critical half, of their agenda. They sought less a withdrawal than a reengagement—a return to Europe and the reestablishment of broad, vital ties with the West. Rejecting the Leninist-Stalinist precepts of a divided world and innate capitalist hostility in favor of admiration for Western political and economic freedoms, they accordingly embraced liberal priorities over socialist ones, universal-human values over class ones. Their "global" identity rejected isolation in favor of integration with "the common stream of world civilization."

This intellectual component is seen in a study of exactly what happened after March 1985. Here what stands out is Gorbachev's reliance on key reformist advisers: Yakovlev, Arbatov, Aganbegyan, Velikhov, Chernyaev, Shakhnazarov, and others—prominent members of a broad, Western-oriented current of the intelligentsia developing since the thaw era. Initially accepting key elements but not yet the totality of new thinking, Gorbachev soon embraced its integrationist core, which *only then* made possible the changes that ended the cold war. A close look at the domestic politics of Soviet foreign policy over 1985–87 also shows that there was no "inevitability" to conciliation and retreat from empire; from the start, powerful conservative interests resisted change, soon to be joined by many of Gorbachev's erstwhile allies in earlier, modest domestic reforms. Gorbachev, Shevardnadze, and Yakovlev fought long and hard to transform Soviet international relations. The new thinking was inevitable only in their minds; in the political arena, it could easily have been halted at any number of turns.

That it was not is explained by Gorbachev's principled accept-ance of the new identity and by the strong support of reformist, anti-isolationist intellectuals, particularly that of his core new-think-ing advisers. In the eyes of Soviet conservatives, the country's broad turn toward the West resulted from "a conspiracy of academi-cians."[1] It was indeed something remarkable for Soviet high poli-tics, a leader who soon found his main base of support not in the Party, military, or industry, but in the liberal intelligentsia. As earli-er chapters have shown, the new thinking was ready, and its propo-nents eager, by the late 1970s. However, bitterly opposed by pow-erful reactionary interests, it stood no chance of influencing policy except through a reformist leader. But Mikhail Gorbachev, a bold and ambitious leader in his own right, grew equally dependent—intellectually and politically—on the new thinkers.

A Reformer Takes Charge

Strictly speaking, of course, there was no inevitability to pere-stroika. As bad as domestic problems had grown in the early 1980s—the USSR was now experiencing zero economic growth, rising mor-tality, and other negative phenomena unprecedented for a devel-oped, industrialized state—popular pressures remained negligible and a liberalizing turn was hardly preordained. In a dictatorial sys-tem, the seemingly "objective" demands of the situation and popu-lar desires matter far less than the subjective goals and perceptions of leaders. As many former top Soviet officials acknowledge, includ-ing Gorbachev's detractors from both the Left and the Right, he could have sat idle and enjoyed his reign in regal comfort.[2]

But by early 1985, this option was fading: two powerful groups in the top leadership now agreed that something must change—that continuation of the status quo was no longer acceptable. More ger-mane to the issue of perestroika's "inevitability" was that one of these groups, as seen in the preceding chapter, sought a hard-line, even neo-Stalinist turn at home and abroad. This group had its contenders for succession: Victor Grishin, the Moscow Party boss or, perhaps, Grigory Romanov, the Central Committee secretary for military and heavy industry. One or both apparently launched serious bids to succeed Chernenko.[3] Gorbachev, despite (or perhaps because of) his grooming by Andropov and his leadership of the reformist faction in the Party, was "feared and distrusted by the old guard."[4] They regarded him as "a mysterious, alien, even hostile figure."[5] Suspicious of his energy and intelligence, and jealous of the international attention he had begun to attract, they were mainly worried about the extent of changes that Gorbachev might seek to implement should he attain the general secretaryship.

Having stymied Andropov's dying wish that Gorbachev succeed him in early 1984, the anti-reformists also took other steps to block his rise during the brief reign of Chernenko.[6] They maneuvered to lower his growing public profile, to bypass his authority, and compromise his position as the Party's evident number two figure.[7] In light of these efforts—and given the overall conservative correlation of forces in the top leadership—Gorbachev's election to succeed Chernenko in March 1985 appears to have defied the odds, an outcome that participant-witnesses explain in several ways. Ligachev, who after 1983 managed replacement of Brezhnev-era regional officials, emphasizes the impact of his own promotees. He argues that their demands for change, which he organized in a last-minute lobbying campaign on Gorbachev's behalf, were most critical.[8] While certainly important, Ligachev's portrayal of this as the decisive factor, and of his own role in sealing the outcome, is likely exaggerated. So, too, is his depiction of the Central Committee as the critical forum; its plenum did formally elect Gorbachev, as it technically decided all major issues, but only *after* the Politburo had issued its own decisive "recommendation."[9]

Another view stresses the role of Foreign Minister Andrei Gromyko, who spoke out on Gorbachev's behalf in both the Politburo and the Central Committee.[10] As Ryzhkov described the fateful Politburo meeting, pro- and anti-Gorbachev factions faced off warily, "like football players on the field before a match," whereupon Gromyko preempted the reactionaries by quickly speaking up to nominate Gorbachev.[11] Gromyko's step, argue long-time associates, was motivated by his high professionalism and distaste for the corruption of Brezhnev and his cronies.[12] Gromyko was no new thinker, but of all the Brezhnev-era holdovers he was probably the most distressed at the country's rapid decline and plunging international prestige.[13]

Others agree that Gromyko's support of Gorbachev was critical, but argue that his key endorsement came a year earlier, in February 1984. At that time, upon Chernenko's accession, it was agreed that Gorbachev would chair the Central Committee Secretariat and, in Chernenko's absence, the Politburo, too. With this, Gorbachev became something of an heir-apparent. Romanov, Grishin, and Prime Minister Nikolai Tikhonov fought the arrangement, but Gromyko brokered a compromise: Let Gorbachev try and "we'll see how it goes. We can take up this question again later."[14]

Beyond such efforts on Gorbachev's behalf, any analysis of his succession must also acknowledge the role of chance. At the time of the fateful decision, another Politburo hard-liner and Gorbachev opponent, Vladimir Shcherbitsky, was abroad and unable to vote.[15] Perhaps also fortuitous was the death, in December 1984, of Defense Minister Ustinov. Given Gromyko's long-standing deference to Ustinov and the military, it is hard to imagine him playing his described role as kingmaker had Ustinov been present and active. Ustinov, a champion of the armed forces since his appointment as Stalin's armaments commissar in 1941, reportedly disliked and distrusted Gorbachev.[16] But his sudden death changed the alignment of power sharply; had Ustinov lived just three months more and outlasted Chernenko, a different outcome in March 1985 is not difficult to imagine.[17]

Given some interplay of these factors, when Chernenko died, on March 10, Gorbachev ultimately seemed the best choice—clearly the most intelligent, energetic, and capable—and so was unenthusiastically supported by a slight majority of the old guard.[18] But their acceptance of him, grudging as it was, was eased by Gorbachev's concealing the extent of his ambitions for change behind a moderate, Andropov-like image.[19] Gorbachev's contacts with liberal intellectuals were known to his colleagues, but he kept them low-profile.[20] He made no secret of his desire for reform, but suggested nothing so drastic as he would soon undertake. On foreign policy, his early-1980s statements were ambiguous, with important hints of change but also enough old rhetoric to allay suspicion and make credible Gromyko's famous warning to Soviet adversaries that behind Gorbachev's smile lay "iron teeth." Those wavering between reform and reaction, the critical Politburo swing votes, later felt that they had been deceived. One of them, Geidar Aliev, complained that "he didn't turn out to be the man that we'd voted for" (*On stal ne tem, kakym on byl*).[21]

The extent of Gorbachev's initial ideas for reform and the subsequent expansion of his ambitions, particularly in foreign policy, will be examined presently. What was unambiguous in March 1985 was that Gorbachev represented a distinctly new generation. More than 30 years after Stalin's death, the country would now have its first genuinely post-Stalin leader, one whose career and outlook were shaped not by the terror, triumphs, and tragedies of the 1930s and 1940s, but by the thaw and détente of the 1950s, 1960s, and 1970s.

One important change that came with a younger leader was the fading salience of World War II. Sergei Akhromeyev, who at the time of Gorbachev's accession was the chief of the General Staff, later noted that "the burden of wartime experience" had left the older generation obsessed with military preparedness, while the young turned more easily to "political means" of ensuring security. Gorbachev, in particular, "was not daunted by obstacles which were a nearly insurmountable wall before the older generation."

> Well before 1985 it was quite clear that Gorbachev, Ryzhkov, Ligachev, Shevardnadze and Medvedev looked at things rather differently (some more, some less) than the earlier leadership—at our Soviet reality, at relations between capitalist and socialist countries, at socialist internationalism, and at maintaining security and supporting the country's defense capability.[22]

Maclean, the spy-cum-IMEMO analyst, writing in 1981, also saw a generational shift ahead, but he traced the Brezhnev cohort's outlook to back before the war, to their rise in the terror of the 1930s: "They were politically unqualified people with little knowledge either of the cultural and political heritage of mankind or of the contemporary world. [They replaced] the revolutionary intellectuals destroyed or paralysed in the purges." The new generation, by contrast, was better educated, more professional, and much freer of the "cult of force . . . chauvinism and anti-intellectualism" that marked the old.[23]

These differences in experience and worldview were shared, to a certain degree, by all members of the post-Brezhnev generation. What few understood at the time was the extent to which the "intellectual" factor described by Maclean set Gorbachev apart from others in his cohort much more than it did all of them from the Brezhnev generation. As seen in the preceding chapter, the breadth of his interests and outlook contributed to Gorbachev's receptivity, nearly a decade before taking office, to the ideas of some of the country's most original political minds. In some combination, Gorbachev's personal, intellectual qualities, together with this early study of reform ideas and his ties to leading new thinkers, produced a leader who already possessed far-reaching, even radical ambitions for change in early 1985.

In hindsight, these intentions were visible in various public statements prior to his accession. For example, in an address on December 10, 1984, Gorbachev spoke not only of the need for perestroika and glasnost, but also echoed Andropov's 1982 suggestion for demilitarizing foreign policy by arguing that the Soviet Union's "main influence" in the world lay in the example of its economic achievements.[24] A week later, during his much-publicized visit to London, he raised yet another theme that would become prominent later—that of Russia as a member of a "common European home."[25]

Still, few then perceived in Gorbachev's new words the deeds that were to follow, and his public positions retained enough orthodoxy not to stir a majority of the old guard against him.[26] But privately, his intimates knew that Gorbachev's plans were far bolder. In 1983, for example, when Oleg Kalugin (a KGB general who would later turn dissident) visited Alexander Yakovlev (his colleague on a thaw-era exchange at Columbia University and now the new IMEMO director) and lamented the USSR's international decline, Yakovlev was encouraging: "Just wait, if Gorbachev comes to power there will be really big changes."[27] Later that year, as Gorbachev rose under Andropov, "We [liberal Central Committee] international department consultants saw that we now had support on high."[28] And by 1984, now well aware of both Gorbachev's origi-

nality and Chernenko's infirmity, reformers privately wished the latter a swift end and rejoiced that "now there's hope for Russia."[29]

The Domestic Roots of New Thinking: Economic

Once in power, Gorbachev quickly showed that he was indeed
planning big changes. In his address at the now-famous April plenum
of the Central Committee, he diagnosed the country's ills and
emphasized the need for reforms, speaking even more sharply than
had Andropov. He denounced an "inability to tell the truth" and
"false idealization of reality," decrying "serious shortcomings" in the
Party and "irresponsibility and waste" in the economy. Sounding the
themes of Aganbegyan, Zaslavskaya, and Tikhonov, Gorbachev
called for "flexible" pricing, along with greater independence, and
"strict cost-accounting" (*khozraschet*) for enterprises.[30]

These, Gorbachev knew, required an improved international
environment, for the country could not properly address its domestic priorities in circumstances of continuing foreign confrontation.
Those priorities, he soon learned, were even more urgent than he
had imagined. Two weeks after taking office, Gorbachev was officially briefed on defense issues by General Akhromeyev, at which
time he first learned the "true" size of the military budget and its
share of the national product (supposedly some 16.5 percent).[31]
From his own experience, particularly in agriculture, Gorbachev
knew that the military burden was huge.[32] But only as general secretary did he now become privy to detailed figures on the bloated
defense sector and the bankrupt remainder of the economy that put
the need for rapid change in an even more urgent light.[33]

To ease this crushing burden, to stave off domestic crisis and
break the deadlock in international relations, Gorbachev quickly
made clear that a sharp foreign-policy turn lay ahead. At Chernenko's
funeral in mid-March, he met with East European leaders to
announce that relations would now be based on full equality—and
also to warn that Moscow would no longer prop up failing regimes.[34]
At the April plenum, he suggested that military doctrine must
become more defensive and its forces limited to the criteria of "sufficiency."[35] In July, he met with top military brass and served notice
of impending cuts in their once-sacred budgets.[36] In August, in
hopes of a reciprocal U.S. step, Gorbachev halted nuclear tests with

a unilateral moratorium that would last 18 months. And in October, he argued that the time had come to dissolve military blocs and suggested Soviet readiness to make disproportionately large cuts in its huge conventional forces.[37]

These steps generated considerable unease in the Soviet military-industrial complex—even open criticism.[38] Though concrete policy changes were still few, the course Gorbachev now plotted was very troubling for powerful vested interests. Equally worrisome was that his moves were bold and unilateral, originating with Gorbachev himself and either bypassing or only formally consulting long-established ministry and Central Committee channels. Akhromeyev noted Gorbachev's "skeptical attitude toward generals and admirals." The latter, concerned, wondered "just how is he deciding defense issues"?[39]

The answer is that Gorbachev was working with the same informal advisers, the same "brain trust," that he had gathered in the early 1980s.[40] Roald Sagdeyev recalls his own membership in "the gang of four" (himself, fellow physicist and arms-control expert Yevgeny Velikhov, and foreign-policy analysts Georgy Arbatov and Yevgeny Primakov) that Gorbachev relied upon heavily during his first year in office.[41] Primakov soon replaced Yakovlev as director of IMEMO (Yakovlev was promoted to a Central Committee secretaryship—see below), but he continued his predecessor's practice of using the institute as an analytical base for reports to Gorbachev that argued for greater international economic and political integration.[42]

Meanwhile, at Arbatov's suggestion, Sagdeyev sent a memorandum urging not only the policy of asymmetric response (one Gorbachev soon adopted—eschewing a new competition in space weapons for low-cost measures to preserve the Soviet deterrent) but also suggesting ways to go even further, de-linking SDI from other nuclear issues in order to achieve cuts in offensive weapons.[43]

Arbatov, unofficially serving as Gorbachev's main foreign-policy adviser, coordinated the inputs of others as well as offering his own analyses.[44] Just three weeks after Gorbachev's election, he produced a 40-page memo, "Toward a Revised Approach to Foreign Policy," that surveyed problems from arms control and Eastern Europe to technological backwardness and Soviet international isolation.[45] He argued, in particular, for an immediate withdrawal from

Afghanistan, conciliatory steps toward Western Europe and China (including unilateral reductions in the huge Soviet conventional forces arrayed against them), and the return to Japan of the Kurile Islands (in dispute since their seizure by the USSR at the end of World War II).[46]

Apprised of this unusual activity, conservatives worried that Gorbachev was listening to outsiders instead of "experienced" ministry and Central Committee officials.[47] But what conservatives viewed with alarm, Eduard Shevardnadze considered a boon. Shevardnadze, named foreign minister in July 1985, described Arbatov's role in debunking the inflated threats presented by "experienced" officials in favor of a calmer, more realistic assessment of the military balance.

> On disarmament, I recall our discussions with Arbatov and other [institute] experts . . . their contribution was crucial. I knew that we had to go forward but I had no real data or numbers. The Arbatov institute had been studying this, they had accurate [Western] sources, and their information was extremely useful.[48]

Gorbachev's decision to replace the aged Gromyko with his colleague and confidant (*edinomyshlennik*) Shevardnadze was another signal of bold changes ahead.[49] Had Gorbachev simply sought to "put his personal stamp" on foreign relations (as many believed) and remove a figure too closely tied to past policies, any one of several Foreign Ministry deputies could have been promoted. By appointing Shevardnadze, Gorbachev not only gained a minister of great personal loyalty and one whose reformist credentials rivaled his own.[50] He also appointed an individual who, while lacking diplomatic experience, shared with him an outlook and set of priorities on a number of issues directly relevant to foreign policy. As long-time bosses of primarily agricultural regions, they stood out from others in the leadership for their meager industrial experience and weak links to the military-industrial complex. Indeed, their lack of ties to the key Moscow constituencies that constituted the power base of most previous Soviet leaders was remarkable.[51] Shevardnadze had spent his entire career in Georgia, while Gorbachev's relatively brief tenure in the capital had been dominated by his stewardship of agriculture.[52] Instead of the favored industrial sectors and artificial prosperity of Moscow, they were closer to the country's "real conditions," particularly its disastrous collective farms.[53] These, in private, Gorbachev scorned as a system of "serfdom."[54]

Thus, even without the benefit of precise statistics, Gorbachev and Shevardnadze knew better than others in the top leadership the true impact of skewed economic priorities. Further, their native Caucasian regions, as key southern transit bases, were geographically and politically close to Afghanistan. Georgia, in particular, was a point through which many dead and wounded soldiers returned home, a situation that weighed heavily on republican leaders.[55] Fittingly, it was during one of their annual meetings at the Georgian resort of Pitsunda that Gorbachev and Shevardnadze first learned of the invasion.[56]

Shevardnadze also shared Gorbachev's concern over Eastern Europe, though the two arrived at their views from different vantages. Gorbachev's early distaste for "Comintern-style" bloc relations, and his admiration for West European Communist Parties that leaned toward social democracy, have already been described.[57] By 1985, according to Akhromeyev, his now-considerable international experience had convinced Gorbachev that only by "radically transforming" the confrontation of European blocs could he develop "normal political and economic relations with the West . . . one of his main goals."[58] In contrast to Gorbachev's increasingly "global" perspective, Shevardnadze's views on Eastern Europe had rather more "provincial" roots. They were, first, those of a republican leader who had studied Hungarian reforms for their application in Georgia.[59] But his was also the outlook of the "governor" of a "Russian colony" that had long chafed under Moscow's control, and so one who understood intrinsically the long-term untenability of imperial diktat—and the likelihood of recurrent crises—in Eastern Europe.[60]

Their Afghan and East European priorities were reflected in Gorbachev's and Shevardnadze's early steps. In one of his first actions as leader, without even waiting for Central Committee approval, Gorbachev ordered preparation of a plan for near-term withdrawal from Afghanistan.[61] By the summer of 1985, criticism of the war had become a serious issue in the press.[62] That fall, in a secret meeting with Afghan leader Babrak Karmal, Gorbachev argued the following:

Every day 10 of our boys die in Afghanistan. There is no hope that the Afghans themselves will defend their revolution. This "revolution" has no mass support. Our recommendations: a sharp turn toward free-market capitalism, restoration of Afghan-Islamic values, and power-sharing with the opposition.[63]

Gorbachev also wasted no time in making his intentions for Eastern Europe clear. At the time of Chernenko's funeral, as noted above, he met privately with East European Party bosses to inform them that the Brezhnev doctrine was dead and henceforth they would sink or swim on their own. Later, at his reception with world leaders, Gorbachev greeted the East Europeans briefly and formally—in marked contrast to his warm reception of the Italian Communist Party secretary Alessandro Natta (whom he already knew and admired, and who provocatively asked if the USSR "was still following Lenin or coming back to Kautsky?")[64]

Meanwhile, Shevardnadze consulted reformist East European experts such as IEMSS director Oleg Bogomolov.

> I hadn't yet mastered all the fundamentals . . . but Bogomolov was already saying that without serious change, crises are to be expected. He told me that he'd done a very serious report on Eastern Europe. It was lying around somewhere in the Central Committee. I got it, read it, and everything became clear. He didn't draw such conclusions as "we have to remove Honecker or Zhivkov." But that tensions would grow, that these countries were essentially our satellites, that the mechanism of cooperation had collapsed and that no kind of equality was ever achieved, all that was there.[65]

Despite these preparatory steps, 1985 saw little real progress on Afghanistan and Eastern Europe due to several key obstacles. Even more problematic than Western intransigence was resistance from Soviet "allies," both in the regions in question as well as in Moscow ministries.[66] In Afghanistan, Gorbachev faced a Vietnam-like dilemma of abandoning an unpopular regime propped up by the Soviet Union for the better part of a decade. In East Europe, an area of much greater strategic importance and far deeper political, economic, and ideological commitment, the inertia was even stronger. Efforts to persuade hard-line East European leaders to reform failed, while Soviet conservatives were equally stubborn.[67] For example, Oleg Rakhmanin, head of the Central Committee department for relations with socialist countries, defied Gorbachev's new aims by publicly reaffirming the Brezhnev doctrine, denouncing any changes in bloc relations, and stressing cohesion at the expense of sovereignty.[68]

It was not only reactionary Brezhnev-era officials who clung to the old dogmas, however; some of them also persisted in the minds of reform leaders Shevardnadze and Gorbachev themselves. In late 1985, though moving toward the view of a complex, interdependent world, Gorbachev's outlook was "still strongly infected with ideological, class-based mythology."[69] As Shevardnadze noted, "We [still] believed that America was the center of global imperialism."[70] This dissonance is seen in Chernyaev's observations of Gorbachev's private meetings: one moment he would appraise the West thoughtfully, recognizing that its leaders, too, understood the imperative of arms control, and even argue that Leninism had erred in rejecting "bourgeois" Western morals; but shortly thereafter, with apparently equal sincerity, Gorbachev would insist that international relations were also shaped by class struggle and affirm the need to support regimes in Angola, Ethiopia, and Mozambique "that have taken the anti-imperialist path."[71] Here, concering Western policies toward the developing world, his skepticism was particularly deep:

> Gorbachev became very interested in the issue of Third-World debt. He assigned specialists to analyze and assess the problem. And he grew furious when, every time, they concluded that this was a serious problem of contemporary international economics, one that you couldn't simply blame on imperialist plunder.[72]

The arguments of the economists—Aganbegyan, Shmelev, Shatalin, and others—would eventually persuade Gorbachev. But at this time, he proceeded primarily from the belief "that he could end the Cold War solely by cutting weapons and halting the arms race."[73] Still, whatever the contradictions of his worldview in 1985, Gorbachev's commitment to ending the nuclear dilemma was firm; overriding opposition in the Politburo, and ignoring the skepticism of even some liberal advisers, he pushed through a decision to hold the Geneva Summit in November 1985.[74] U.S.-Soviet talks had resumed immediately after Gorbachev took office, but positions had not changed since the Soviet walkout under Andropov, and the prospects for progress remained bleak. But Gorbachev insisted in the hope that a face-to-face meeting with Reagan might break the deadlock.

When it did not, Gorbachev soon took a large step forward with his grand disarmament plan of January 1986. Here were offered the first major Soviet concessions on nuclear weapons: agreement to eliminate medium-range missiles and to set aside the issue of French and British forces; and a proposal for 50 percent cuts in strategic weapons, including the sacred SS-18 heavy missiles. Such sweeping reductions could only distress entrenched military-industrial interests, but the cause for concern seemed slight as few believed the proposals would ever be accepted. The plan was, in fact, too broad to be immediately, practically negotiable. So the military brass grudgingly signed on to the proposal with the expectation that, like so many before, it would serve propaganda and nothing more.[75]

It was, tellingly, almost precisely these 1986 proposals that would later be enshrined in the INF (Intermediate-Range Nuclear Forces) and START (Strategic Arms Reduction Talks) treaties. Gorbachev, in contrast to the hard-liners, offered the plan in earnest. A close observer's impression at the time was that "he has already decided, come what may, to end the arms race. He's taking this gamble because [he believes that] nobody is going to attack us even if we disarm completely."[76]

But even though Gorbachev's perception of foreign threats was fading and new ideas for enhancing security were gaining, it also appears that at this early stage the economic motive remained paramount. As Shevardnadze recalled, the reformers felt almost desperate to halt U.S. advances: "The point at issue was to stop the arms race. It was true that the Americans were ahead of us on some weapons. But there was no stopping them unless we signed an agreement."[77] Still, if this were all that had driven new thinking, further progress would have been highly unlikely since domestic resistance now grew even more determined. Reactionaries such as Shcherbitsky, who had opposed the Geneva Summit, felt vindicated when it failed to produce anything more than a declaration of nuclear war's inadmissibility, and emboldened when even Akhromeyev, the chief of the general staff, publicly expressed his skepticism.[78] Privately, hard-liners fought hard against proposals that were based on anything but strict numerical parity.[79]

But despite such resistance, Gorbachev and Shevardnadze pushed ahead. Over 1986, in almost inverse proportion to growing opposition at home, the new thinking was rapidly transformed, first from heretical ideas to the conceptual base of a new international posture, then to important early steps toward translating these concepts into concrete policies. An essential factor in this progress was a powerful intellectual push.

The Domestic Roots of New Thinking: Intellectual

As Gorbachev argued from the outset of perestroika, foreign policy would henceforth serve the interests of domestic reform, thereby reversing priorities that had stood for much of Soviet (and, before it, Russian) history. But now, as he began his second year in office, Soviet foreign policy acquired another domestic nexus, one driven less by economic than intellectual forces. As early reforms stalled and conservative resistance grew, Gorbachev fought to broaden perestroika's base by reaching beyond the Party. His weapon was glasnost—truth-telling, about both past and present, that sought to mobilize society in the cause of change. Initially, through most of 1986, this openness touched mainly domestic, not foreign, affairs. But even at this early stage, it had dramatic implications for the new thinking. For Gorbachev's new policy brought him much closer to glasnost's most eager recipients—the country's liberal intellectuals—who were not only supporters of domestic reform, but also the bastion of an anti-isolationist, Western-oriented identity.

This change was seen in several ways. Now Gorbachev met more and more frequently with writers and cultural figures, as well as economists, historians, and other scholars, to hear their views and rally their support.[80] This he received, in backing for change abroad as well as at home. For example, long-time liberals such as Bogomolov, Shakhnazarov, and Bovin rebutted Rakhmanin in strong defense of Gorbachev's proposed transformation of bloc relations.[81] Simultaneously, civilian defense specialists mounted a challenge to the military's public monopoly on foreign-policy issues, both in support of Gorbachev's initiatives and to push them even further.[82] In return for this support, Gorbachev defended the boldest reform thinkers: civilian prerogatives to debate military-security affairs were expanded,[83] and domestic reformers were now even more strongly encouraged.[84]

The cause of glasnost in the media, and of rethinking long-established dogmas more generally, received a huge boost with the appointment in late 1985 of Alexander Yakovlev as Central Committee Secretary for Ideology.[85] Yakovlev, an admirer of Western political and economic liberties (if not always of Western leaders) and probably the strongest proponent of democratization in Gorbachev's inner circle, had advanced rapidly since his return to head IMEMO in 1983.[86] Following membership in the Academy of Sciences and the Central Committee, Yakovlev now assumed a post commensurate with his influence as Gorbachev's preeminent domestic and foreign-policy adviser.[87] At this time, in late 1985, he had just completed a memorandum calling for broad reform measures and decrying the world's division into antagonistic camps (while also advocating a division of the CPSU into two competing parties).[88] Liberal intellectuals correctly viewed Yakovlev as their greatest champion among the top leaders,[89] and conservatives grew properly concerned at the growing influence of this "agent of the West."[90]

Over 1986, Yakovlev's promotion was followed by many other personnel changes that increased the influence of liberal, anti-isolationist intellectuals. The head of the Central Committee department for ties with socialist states, the hard-liner Rakhmanin, was fired, together with the dogmatic *Kommunist* editor Richard Kosolapov. Their places were taken by the "globalists" Shakhnazarov and Frolov, who now drew closer to Gorbachev's inner circle of advisers. In March, Boris Ponomarev was replaced as head of the Central Committee's International Department by Anatoly Dobrynin, the long-time Soviet ambassador to the United Sates. Soon thereafter a number of notable liberals, including the recently persecuted Tsipko, joined Dobrynin's department as staffers or consultants. Under Yakovlev's department, a new sector on human rights was created, headed by the liberal Andrei Grachev and staffed by the likes of the new-thinking ISKAN analyst Igor Malashenko.[91]

Similar changes were under way at the Foreign Ministry. Vladimir Lukin, the ISKAN Asia specialist, left the institute to join Shevardnadze's team, and Andrei Kozyrev, the arms-trade critic, was promoted to head the ministry's International Organizations Department. Long-time centrists such as Deputy Minister Georgy Kornienko were dismayed as Shevardnadze's liberal turn soon left them defending what were now conservative positions.[92] Their influence waned, and that of more innovative or flexible deputies (such as Anatoly Kovalev, Victor Karpov, Anatoly Adamashin, and Lev Mendelevich) grew accordingly.[93] Meanwhile, Shevardnadze not only consulted informally with outside experts including Bogomolov, Arbatov, and Velikhov, he also created a formal Academic Consultative Council that would regularly inject the views of outside experts—such as those of Vyacheslav Dashichev on German reunification—into the ministry.[94] In early 1986, Shevardnadze also created a new Arms Control and Disarmament Division and, in so doing, "threw open the doors to youth, to new ideas" that had long been germinating within the ministry.[95] "Shevardnadze had an allergy to words like 'class struggle' and 'proletarian internationalism.' He always said 'Don't be afraid, speak up.' You could never imagine someone saying to Gromyko, 'Andrei Andreyevich, I don't agree.' "[96]

Another critical appointment, made in early February 1986, was that of Gorbachev's personal foreign-policy aide. Replacing the Brezhnev-era holdover Andrei Alexandrov-Agentov, at the urging of Yakovlev and Arbatov, was Anatoly Chernyaev, the long-time International Department liberal, sometime student of social democracy, and quiet defender of persecuted independent thinkers. Chernyaev, in turn, soon acquainted Gorbachev with some of the latter (such as the anti-isolationist, semi-dissident historian Mikhail Gefter) and with the fate of Soviet historical studies under the reign of the reactionary Trapeznikov.[97]

Though still largely unappreciated in the West, the promotion of so many new-thinking advisers, together with the growing influence of liberal, anti-isolationist ideas in intellectual life more generally, began to shift the "critical mass" in foreign-policy thought. In early 1986, in connection with the upcoming 27th Party Congress (25 February–6 March), Gorbachev, Yakovlev, and Shevardnadze sat down to tackle "the philosophy of foreign policy."[98] They were joined by Raisa Gorbacheva—increasingly a "fully fledged participant" in policy discussions—and supported by the inputs of many liberal academics.[99] "Scientists, scholars, experts and managers laid their proposals before Mikhail Sergeyevich Gorbachev, driven by the general pent-up desire for change."[100] One who did not volunteer his input, but was specially invited to contribute, was Tsipko. Still something of an "untouchable heretic" in high Party circles, Tsipko was approached by Gorbachev's assistant for ideology, Georgy Smirnov, to prepare a report drawing on his early-1980s ideas about NEP-style cooperation and the primacy of universal-human values.[101]

Shevardnadze recalled the "incredible difficulty" with which the group accepted the view of an integral world over one divided by social systems; in their near-daily sessions, he "observed Gorbachev's ideas heading into dangerous, uncharted waters."[102] In fact, though uncharted for Soviet politics, they had good directions; as Yakovlev noted, they were guided by "the leading minds of the century—Einstein, Kapitsa, Russell and Sakharov"—as they "threw out the [Stalinist] psychology of a besieged fortress."[103]

Gorbachev, too, recalled the days that he, Yakovlev, and Shevardnadze spent wrestling over rejection of Lenin's basic precept of a divided world:

> We were at Zavidovo [a government dacha] working on the report and we really quarreled—for a day and a half we even stopped speaking to each other. What was the argument about? About . . . the fact that we live in an interdependent, contradictory, but ultimately integral world. No, the new thinking wasn't just some policy shift, it required a major conceptual breakthrough.[104]

This breakthrough was largely (but not completely) reflected in the congress' documents. The worst contradictions of the Khrushchev-era CPSU Program—that peaceful coexistence is another form of class struggle, and that nuclear war, while not inevitable, would nevertheless see socialism's triumph should it occur—were absent from the new one.[105] Not surprisingly, Gorbachev's report was the far bolder document.[106] Here was found emphasis on global problems, interdependence, cooperation, and an integral world, as well as on the political means of ensuring security and "reasonable sufficiency" in defense.

These changes did not come easily. The report generated fierce opposition and the final document contained more than a few compromises with the old thinking. These compromises gave it a schizophrenic character, with new-thinking concepts coexisting uneasily with passages on "American aggression" and "imperialism." A reference to Afghanistan as a "bleeding wound," deleted by conservatives in draft, was restored only at the last minute upon the insistence of Shevardnadze and Gorbachev.[107] Ponomarev, the veteran International Department head whose role was now much diminished (he would be replaced by Dobrynin after the congress), fought particularly hard.[108]

> PONOMAREV: What's this "new thinking?" Our thinking is already correct! Let the Americans change their thinking.
>
> CHERNYAEV: But look at what Gorbachev's been saying, it's quite clear that he's referring to our thinking.
>
> PONOMAREV: As far as what he said in Paris and Geneva, that's [propaganda] for them, for the West . . . and as for peaceful coexistence, we outlined that [back at] the 19th Party Congress under Stalin. So what's new here?
>
> CHERNYAEV: [Stalin, Khrushchev, Brezhnev], nobody believed them. But they trust Gorbachev because he's begun to make our deeds match our words.
>
> PONOMAREV: . . . What are you trying to do to our foreign policy? Didn't we open up outer space? Didn't we create the ICBM? Are you against [the use of military] force, which is the only language that imperialism understands?[109]

In reflecting on the congress, Gorbachev proudly recalled "what Yakovlev, Shevardnadze and I accomplished, how we began it all" against such determined opposition.[110] Nevertheless, despite this critical breakthrough, the new thinking was indeed just beginning its conquest of the old.

> Speaking these words, and even putting them in Party documents, we did not yet understand that we had struck a mortal blow at our entire "theory of development" since 1917. If the world is interdependent and interconnected, then mankind is one, our priority must be universal problems, and class confrontation and violence as the motor of history are unacceptable. We did not immediately recognize this. Then came the deideologization of foreign policy. Introducing this term, we justified it to our "guardians of purity" by trying to separate the supposedly objective fact of confrontation between the two systems from "purely" diplomatic relations. But real-life experience soon foiled this clever trick.[111]

This experience came in several ways. One was Gorbachev's now-intensive private study of international relations. His "insatiable thirst for knowledge" led him to read everything from Western political science to the memoirs of Western leaders such as Churchill, works long available to the elite in classified, "white book" translations.[112] Gorbachev also broadened his reading at others' advice. On philosophical issues, his wife, Raisa, introduced him to the integrationist, social democratic-leaning ideas of "semi-dissident" Moscow scholars.[113] On policy matters, Arbatov offered the works of the Palme Commission and other European social-democratic writings on disarmament and "common security."[114] With his interests now going beyond specific arms-reduction proposals to their underlying conceptions of international security, to the basic issues of survival, civilization, and human development on the eve of the twenty-first century, Gorbachev also reviewed writings from the Einstein-Russell manifesto of 1955 to the more recent works of the Pugwash scientists' movement.[115]

Also in early 1986, Gorbachev began to meet with various representatives of foreign countries—both official and unofficial—with increasing frequency. His immediate goal was to show perestroika's seriousness and deflate exaggerated fears of "the Soviet threat."[116] In this he generally succeeded, but the meetings' greater impact was on Gorbachev himself. Chernyaev describes them as the way he "came to know the other world," one of the most critical influences on Gorbachev's evolving outlook; Gorbachev himself recalls "a great school" that enabled him to "feel the moods and hear the thoughts and ideas of an international intellectual elite."[117]

His interlocutors included representatives of world culture, and their humanistic concerns made a "deep impression."[118] Equally consequential were Gorbachev's discussions with foreign leaders and statesmen. For example, it was his early meeting with the French president, François Mitterand, that helped propel Gorbachev toward Geneva. With opposition to the summit strong in Moscow, Gorbachev asked if the United States was really intent on bankrupting the USSR through an arms race. Mitterand's answer—that Reagan was not merely a pawn of U.S. militarists but in fact a vital leader committed to ending the nuclear stalemate—provided crucial encouragement.[119] Over 1986, in meetings with figures ranging from former U.S. president Richard Nixon to scores of U.S. and European parliamentarians, Gorbachev heard many similar arguments and numerous appeals for more concrete Soviet steps to improve East-West relations.

But on deeper, "philosophical" matters relating to international (and domestic) affairs, perhaps no foreign statesman had so great an impact on Gorbachev as the Spanish prime minister, Felipe Gonzalez. From their first meeting in early 1986, the two established a rapport and mutual understanding that provided much impetus in Gorbachev's evolution toward an essentially social-democratic outlook. Recalling their first encounter several years later, Gorbachev said that "you were the only one that we could share opinions with candidly."[120] As Gorbachev's "comrade in the socialist movement"—and, more importantly, as the leader of a country that was completing its own transition away from decades of dictatorship—Gorbachev paid close heed to Gonzalez's arguments. These ranged from the importance of real democracy to the necessity of a free market (and foreign investment) in order to achieve socialist goals.[121] Gonzalez also criticized Lenin harshly, for sins that included a lack of humanism, suppression of legality, and his responsibility for the world's division into antagonistic camps.[122]

Also influential were Gorbachev's audiences with members of the international scientific community. From a delegation of Nobel Prize recipients to representatives of Western science and arms-control groups, Gorbachev found many of their arguments "impossible to ignore."[123] These included praise for his arms initiatives, but also criticism of Soviet stubbornness on issues such as the ongoing dispute over arms-control treaty violations.

Groups such as the Union of Concerned Scientists and the Federation of American Scientists urged bolder steps, such as delinking SDI from negotiations over strategic weaponry.[124] Here, as well as on issues of secrecy and a test ban, the pressure of international scientific opinion aided Soviet liberals, who were urging the same actions. Joining forces with U.S. physicist Frank von Hippel and other members of the National Resources Defense Council, Velikhov won approval for an unprecedented verification project at U.S. and Soviet nuclear test sites.[125] Meanwhile, Arbatov, Chernyaev, and Dobrynin seized on an appeal from the International Physicians for the Prevention of Nuclear War to lobby

Gorbachev for extending the moratorium on nuclear testing, due to expire in mid 1986.[126]

A separate but near-constant issue in his conversations with foreign scientists, at least until December 1986, was the fate of their esteemed and still-exiled colleague Andrei Sakharov.[127] The "Sakharov affair" was important in at least two different ways: first, as a critical, long-standing Soviet-Western issue of trust and liberalization in and of itself; and second, as a continual reminder of Sakharov's own arguments—for democratization and human rights at home, and for disarmament and peaceful coexistence abroad.[128] Gorbachev, reflecting on the evolution of new thinking, credited

> the dissident movement, whose influence extended to a substantial part of the creative intellectuals . . . and even to [members] of the economic and party governmental apparatus. The external factor also played an increasingly powerful role in the promotion of . . . a humanistic dimension as a major component of normal international relations.[129]

Viewing the acceleration of all this activity over the post-congress months, during mid-1986, conservatives were aghast. The influence of Yakovlev and other hated liberals, the emergence of glasnost and the attendant spread of subversive ideas from abroad and dissident thought at home, and Gorbachev's own embrace of increasingly bold positions all amounted, in their eyes, to a hijacking of perestroika. As one recalled, up to this point political influence had been divided between the *praktiki*, those with traditional Party-management experience, and the *akademiki*. The latter, beyond Yakovlev and other members of Gorbachev's "brain trust," also included several "highly politicized research organizations of a pro-Western orientation," such as Arbatov's ISKAN and Primakov's IMEMO.[130] In this view, the *akademiki*, mostly alien to the Party apparatus and only "at home in intelligentsia circles," were easily "neutralized" by the majority *praktiki*. But Gorbachev, interested only in power, switched allegiance from the Ligachev-led *praktiki* to the Yakovlev-dominated *akademiki*.[131] With this fateful shift, perestroika became "a revolution from above, a project conceived by a liberal scholarly elite and carried out by a small group of the top party *nomenklatura*."[132]

This interpretation of events—apart from its view of a lurking anti-Soviet conspiracy and its portrayal of Gorbachev as both an unprincipled power seeker and a hapless pawn in the sway of Yakovlev & Co.—is largely correct.[133] They *were* in fact the *akademiki,* and the scornful characterization of them as "a new generation of pro-Western civilizers of our Fatherland" is cynically accurate.[134] And Gorbachev did reach out to the liberal intelligentsia in order to broaden his support. But this was a move in the cause of reform, not just a grab at power for its own sake. Gorbachev's intellectual search of 1985–86, in tandem with his search for political allies, increasingly led him to those who were not only the boldest domestic reformers, but the boldest foreign-policy reformers as well.[135] In Chernyaev's view, the fact that new-thinking intellectuals became Gorbachev's main domestic support "forced him" to confront, and ultimately accept, the essentials of their liberal-integrationist *weltanschauung.*[136]

As swiftly as this rethinking had proceeded over the first post-congress months, the second half of 1986 saw even more rapid change. Chernyaev noted that Gorbachev now showed a new determination: "Sometime in the spring of 1986 he set a task for himself" of achieving a decisive breakthrough in foreign relations.[137] This determination sprang, in Gorbachev's characterization, from yet another "real-life experience."

The Domestic Roots of New Thinking: Openness, Democracy, and International Trust

That experience, in the spring of 1986, was the Chernobyl tragedy, the deadly reactor explosion and fire that cost thousands of lives and billions of rubles. The impact of Chernobyl on the new thinking, and on the broader evolution of perestroika, is difficult to overestimate; its effect "on both domestic and foreign policy . . . was tremendous."[138] The disaster consumed the leadership for nearly three months. The government—with a Politburo crisis committee, constant meetings and reports, and a summoning of all available civilian and military resources—was on a virtual wartime footing. Participants recall mobilization of a frantic pace and grave intensity "seen only in the years of the Great Patriotic War."[139]

More than just another economic setback, Chernobyl gave a broader impetus to domestic reforms by further exposing the backwardness and corruption of the Stalinist system, particularly the failures of central planning with its haste, sloppiness, and disregard of "the human element." But the tragedy also gave a powerful boost to the already rapidly advancing cause of new thinking: "It was a tremendous shock . . . that raised our view of security to an entirely new plane of understanding."[140] This it did by dramatically illustrating the urgency of arms control. Gorbachev recalled Chernobyl's fallout "touching the hearts" of the people, while Akhromeyev saw it reaching "their minds and souls . . . the nuclear danger was no longer abstract but something palpable and concrete."[141]

Gorbachev added that Chernobyl "mercilessly reminded us" of what nuclear war would really mean, although in fact there was nothing quite like it in Soviet memory.[142] Many have compared its impact to that of World War II. But unlike Hitler's sudden and devastating strike of 1941, whose enduring lesson was to build up forces and heighten vigilance, Chernobyl's message was the opposite; traditional military principles such as surprise, superiority, and even parity lost meaning when even a small reactor accident could wreak such havoc.

Equally vital was Chernobyl's impetus to appreciation of the world's oneness. This understanding was driven home by the cloud of radiation blowing freely across the iron curtain, and by the realization that since all of Europe was crowded with nuclear and chemical plants, the result of any hostilities there would resemble a nuclear war. As Gorbachev argued, even a limited conflict "would mean so many Chernobyls that you can't even imagine."[143] Already accepted in theory, the understanding of an integral, non class-divided world was given practical meaning by the outpouring of international aid and sympathy—"an unprecedented campaign of solidarity"—that, briefly, also approached a level unseen since World War II. This support, despite the ill will caused by initial Soviet secrecy (and consequently some anti-Soviet parading in the West), was a vote of confidence in Gorbachev's reforms, reinforcing the primacy of global concerns and the cause of openness and East-West cooperation.[144] As Shevardnadze recalled, it "tore the blindfold from our eyes" and "convinced us that morality and politics could not diverge."[145]

For Shevardnadze, Gorbachev, and others fighting to improve foreign ties, the shame of having initially misinformed their foreign supporters about the disaster (as they themselves were misinformed by their military-industrial complex) and so inadvertently aided a cover-up was a ramifying experience.[146] It was "outright sabotage of the new thinking [and of] the trust we had worked so hard to build." They had been "betrayed," and not by the West but by their own hard-liners.[147] But the end result was the opposite of what the hard-liners had hoped for.

In policy terms, Chernobyl's positive fallout followed quickly. As Velikhov described, it pushed Gorbachev toward "a great, instinctive leap to break the old cycle" of secrecy, stubbornness, and deadlocked negotiations.[148] By May, Soviet delegates to the Stockholm talks on conventional forces had new instructions—to accept unprecedented on-site verification measures—and by July a treaty was completed. At this time, Gorbachev also requested an "interim" summit, before the next scheduled U.S.-Soviet gathering, which became the famous Reykjavik conclave of October 1986.

There Gorbachev shocked Reagan and his advisers—but not those who understood the seriousness of his January proposal—with huge concessions in a bid for total nuclear disarmament. Agreement foundered on only one issue: Gorbachev's insistence on modest limits to SDI, which Reagan rejected.[149] But there was no more mistaking the sincerity and radicalness of Gorbachev's intentions. The genesis of Reykjavik, and the underlying shift in Gorbachev's view of international security, are seen in various deliberations from the summer and early fall of 1986.[150] In one, Chernyaev responded to Gorbachev's request for a critique of the latest proposal generated by the apparatus:

> It proceeds from the old view: "If there is war, the two sides must have equal abilities to destroy each other." What's contained here is the arithmetic, not the algebra, of contemporary world politics. It fails to reflect your intention [to achieve a breakthrough]. It must begin with the need to liquidate all nuclear weapons. [On strategic forces] it should stress our idea of a 50 percent cut as a first step. In contrast to our earlier positions, the reductions need not be contingent on agreement over SDI. Otherwise it will be another dead end. [On INF] we must not begin with an interim but optimal variant: liquidate all medium-range missiles in Europe. . . . This {ministry} proposal again raises a scare over French and English forces. But it is impossible to imagine any circumstances . . .

under which they would push the [nuclear] button against us. Here we are only frightening ourselves and raise anew the obstacle that has blocked European disarmament for a decade.[151]

Gorbachev's Reykjavik proposals, together with a broad push along fronts from a defensive restructuring of doctrine and forces to opening up Soviet society to the world, provoked enormous high-level opposition over the second half of 1986. The summit concessions were bitterly contested, and Akhromeyev nearly resigned over the issue.[152] A new doctrine of "reasonable sufficiency," which Gorbachev had warned was coming nearly two years earlier, caused near-rebellion among senior officers.[153] Meanwhile, the military-industrial complex pushed hard for a Soviet version of "Star Wars."[154] And KGB director Viktor Chebrikov—who had earlier warned that glasnost was allowing the spread of dangerous foreign influences—now argued that "Western intelligence services are intensifying their efforts to subvert Soviet authors," who were already showing "oppositional, revisionist tendencies."[155]

The scales had fallen hard from conservatives' eyes as they were presented with policies that they had earlier, grudgingly, endorsed with no expectation that they would ever be implemented. The military, in particular, had been "entrapped by their own gambit."[156] The Politburo now became an open battleground, but Gorbachev was unyielding:

He fought off all the arguments against [his new proposals] with a critical, rhetorical question: "What are you doing, still preparing to fight a nuclear war? Well I'm not, and everything else follows from that. . . . If we still want to conquer the world, then let's decide how to arm ourselves further and outdo the Americans. But then that'll be it, and everything we've been saying about a new policy has to go on the trash heap."[157]

Hard-line security interests, responsible for an earlier "betrayal" in the Chernobyl cover-up, now tried again to "sabotage" the new thinking; espionage charges leveled at U.S. journalist Nicholas Daniloff in August, at best a massive overreaction to the earlier arrest of a low-level Soviet agent in the United States, threatened to derail the summit at which the radical proposals they had been unable to halt would soon be presented.[158] But once again, the attempt back-fired; intense, last-minute negotiations by Shevardnadze allowed the

Reykjavik summit to proceed and left the new thinkers angrier at their own hard-liners than at the West.

This was so in spite of the summit's ostensible failure. Even as Gorbachev publicly criticized Western refusal to join in real nuclear disarmament (and some Western politicians' misportrayal of the Reykjavik negotiations), his private discussions revealed a far-reaching rethinking of fundamental East-West issues whose significance was much greater than the immediate success or failure of any particular policy initiative. This can be seen in the record of Gorbachev's post-Reykjavik debate with Margaret Thatcher, a firm proponent of Britain's independent nuclear forces and of Western reliance on nuclear deterrence in general. Thatcher, whose arguments led to a "sharp turn" (*silnyi povorot*) in Gorbachev's thinking, stubbornly focused on unresolved differences that made broader disarmament impossible.[159] As Gorbachev summarized for the Politburo,

> She focused on trust. She said, "The USSR has squandered the West's faith and we don't trust you. You take grave actions lightly: Hungary, Czechoslovakia, Afghanistan. We couldn't imagine that you'd invade Czechoslovakia, but you did. The same with Afghanistan. We're afraid of you. If you remove your INF, and the Americans do too, then we'll be completely defenseless before [your huge armies]." That's how she sees it. She thinks we haven't rejected the "Brezhnev doctrine." Comrades, we have to think this over. We can't ignore these arguments.[160]

Gorbachev later ascribed an even deeper significance to the private arguments of Thatcher and other European leaders. Even if the Afghan war were ended, the USSR's conventional superiority reduced, and other issues resolved, they stressed that the problem of trust would still remain:

> "You have no democracy, so there's no control over the government. It does what it wants. You stress the will of your people, that they don't want war, but they're denied the means to express this will. Let's say we trust you personally, but if you're gone tomorrow, then what?" . . . We had to think long and hard to grasp that human rights are an extraterritorial, universal, all-human value, and to understand that [without democracy] we'd never achieve real trust in foreign relations.[161]

In fact, this "long and hard" rethinking, at least on the part of Gorbachev and close advisers such as Yakovlev and Chernyaev, was already well-advanced, and the greater significance of the argument with Thatcher was that it served as a vehicle to place on the Politburo agenda that which had long since been on the personal agenda of most new thinkers. For it was in the aftermath of Chernobyl (in April of 1986), not of Reykjavik (later, in October), that Gorbachev took the most important step in placing human rights at the center of Soviet foreign-policy concerns. This can be seen in his address to an extraordinary Foreign Ministry conference in May. There, in a particularly bold speech that did not appear in print until a year later (and then only in summary form), Gorbachev criticized old-thinking behavior across the board.[162] Though offering the still-obligatory reference to the United States as the "locomotive of imperialism," nearly everywhere else he emphasized Soviet shortcomings. These included the lack of progress on a withdrawal from Afghanistan as well as ideological opposition to the settlement of other conflicts in the third world. He also criticized "panicked" reporting on the progress of SDI and other threat assessments that supported unnecessary (and unaffordable) military expenditures, a paternal attitude toward East European states as if the USSR were "running a kindergarten for little children," and an approach to China that still viewed relations "though the prism of the 1960s."[163]

But the centerpiece of Gorbachev's broadside was to insist on a "radical restructuring" of the underlying approach to foreign policy. The new priorities included facilitating economic integration, expanding cultural ties, cooperating in the fight against terrorism, and, above all, raising the profile of "humanitarian issues."

> The very words "human rights" are put in quotation marks and we speak of so-called human rights, as if our own revolution had nothing to do with human rights. . . . But would there even have been a revolution if such rights had been observed in the old society? We need to reject decisively this outdated approach to the problem . . . and view it more broadly, particularly with regard to such specific issues as reunification of families, exit and entry visas . . . all this is part of the process of building trust.[164]

Thus, in the immediate aftermath of Chernobyl (Gorbachev also asked, "If peaceful use of the atom carries such risks, then what does that say about nuclear war?"), Gorbachev's address reflected a heightened understanding of the link between trust abroad and democracy at home, a growing belief among the leaders of new thinking that Soviet interests lay in broader rapprochement with the West and deeper liberalization of Soviet society.[165]

This understanding grew, in part, from Chernobyl's lessons of openness and international cooperation. But it was driven home even more forcefully by the "betrayal" of the Chernobyl cover-up and the attempted "sabotage" of Reykjavik. Now, with conservatives bitterly fighting foreign-policy change in top party councils, the new thinkers could not avoid a searching reappraisal of just who their "friends" and "enemies" really were.[166] It was not only that, in values and beliefs, the reformers now found themselves closer to the Western democracies than the cruel system and policies that Soviet conservatives fought so tenaciously to preserve. The new thinkers were also pushed across a critical threshold by the realization that, in immediate policy terms, their more problematic adversaries were not Western leaders but their own, Soviet, hard-liners.

The situation in Eastern Europe also encouraged this rethinking. There, reactionary Party leaders not only rejected appeals to reform, but some now went so far as to criticize perestroika openly and even to censor the glasnost-infected Soviet media, previously freely available in their countries. The war in Afghanistan also furthered reappraisal of "friends" and "enemies," highlighting as it did the link between democracy at home and trust abroad. Distressed that after nearly two years of perestroika the war's end was still not in sight, Gorbachev and Shevardnadze publicly blamed the West for the stalled Geneva talks; but privately, they considered the demands of the Afghan government—and its supporters in the Soviet leadership—an even greater source of frustration. With intimates, Shevardnadze vented his anger at regimes that did not "stand for anything" nor have "any real support among their people."[167]

Domestic politics were also central in raising the issue of democratization. By late 1986, perestroika still had little success on the critical economic front. Resistance to domestic reforms exceeded even that for foreign policy, and now pushed Gorbachev and Yakovlev toward the remarkable political liberalization that culminated in the free elections and new legislature of 1989.[168] Like glasnost, it was intended to mobilize society and help Gorbachev's domestic initiatives overcome conservative opposition. But also like glasnost, democratization in practice served to reinforce the link between perestroika at home and new thinking abroad. Even if its initial impetus is seen in domestic-instrumental terms, its international-ideological significance was soon equally vital.

In fact, as shown above, the intellectual link between democratization at home and trust abroad was present from the outset; the "vector of causality" ran not in one but both directions. Accepting the idea of an integral world, the new thinkers quickly realized that "the Cold War could not be ended . . . if we continued to exclude human rights and democracy from the political process, that there can't be any special socialist type of democracy, that it must be the same for the East as in the West."[169]

Thus, no later than early 1987 the third and most critical domestic nexus of new thinking was falling into place. Following its early (and continuing) economic impetus, and Gorbachev's subsequent embrace of the liberal intelligentsia who stood for Westernizing reforms abroad as well as at home, the leaders of new thinking now came to a more fundamental, near-Kantian view on the domestic roots of international trust and cooperation. With this watershed, the reform process entered an even more rapid and intense phase of development. Domestic and foreign change grew increasingly interconnected as various separate, tactical reform objectives were supplanted by a broader, strategic, integrationist goal: for the Soviet Union "to become a normal member of the international community."[170]

1987–89: The Endgame of New Thinking

In most interpretations, 1987–89 was the period of the new thinking's main development. Now there appeared the harshest critiques of Soviet foreign policy past, and the boldest designs for its future.[171] Above all, the present saw Gorbachev's most radical policy changes: deep cuts in nuclear and conventional arms, withdrawal from Afghanistan, and acceptance of Socialism's collapse in Eastern Europe.[172]

These were the steps that definitively ended the cold war. But the view that they can be understood mainly in the immediate context of their undertaking—the domestic and foreign crises of the late 1980s—is deeply flawed. While important, these problems alone were insufficient for the policy breakthrough that ensued. This, as seen above, could proceed only after a prior conceptual break-through among the leaders of new thinking. By late 1986, this intel-lectual turn was nearly complete; the next two years, rather than the inception or design of new thinking, were the time of its imple-mentation and execution.

Gorbachev's, Shevardnadze's, and Yakovlev's paths to a new worldview have already been seen:[173] the early experience that inclined them to bolder domestic and foreign-policy reforms from the outset of perestroika; their reliance on the most innovative, Western-oriented specialists and advisers; and their rapid estrange-ment from Soviet conservatives as they embraced the broader inte-grationist goals espoused by Soviet and Western scientists, states-men, and intellectuals.[174] With this conceptual shift largely com-plete, work on their boldest policy changes followed immediately.

By late 1986, Gorbachev had openly rejected most of the remaining "old thinking" of the 27th Party Congress documents that had seemed so bold only eight months before. In November, he declared that "the interests of societal development and all-human values take precedence over the interests of any particular class."[175] Accordingly, he now laid increasing emphasis on open-ness, human rights, and democratization, even calling for secret, multicandidate elections to all Party posts, and to many govern-ment positions, too.[176] These words were accompanied by deeds: glasnost in all areas accelerated rapidly over 1987; the unjamming of foreign radio broadcasts began; and political prisoners were freed en masse. One of the first and most notable of these was Andrei Sakharov. In December 1986, Gorbachev phoned him to convey the decision personally and to bid Sakharov, "Go back to your patriotic work."[177]

This work consisted of pushing hard on all reform fronts, including arms control. By February 1987, adopting the position long argued by Sakharov and now-growing numbers of other Soviet specialists, Gorbachev again overruled Politburo opposition and dropped the SDI linkage in nuclear arms talks.[178] This, along with acceptance of unprecedentedly intrusive verification measures, removed the final obstacles to deep cuts in offensive weapons.[179] The INF treaty was completed later that year, and the door was now open to the major strategic reductions that followed next.

Gorbachev and Shevardnadze also decided, against much resistance, to proceed with an Afghan settlement "in the shortest possible time."[180] Karmal was replaced by the more flexible Najibullah and, in 1987, Shevardnadze informed his U.S. counterpart that Soviet withdrawal was imminent, with or without U.S. help.[181]

Simultaneously, Gorbachev took rapid steps toward the changes in Eastern Europe that would play out so suddenly in 1989. Just as he had shocked the military by making good on an early commitment to restructure doctrine, Gorbachev now shocked the East European leaders whom he had warned back in 1985 to "change or go." At a closed meeting in late 1986, he startled the other Party chiefs with "an incredibly harsh assessment of relations among socialist states and the situation of the camp as a whole." The existing order was "leading to disaster" that could be halted only by radical change in domestic and foreign policy.[182] He insisted that the East Europeans reform their systems and find popular legitimacy; they could no longer rely on Moscow's support of the old order, he said.[183]

By 1986, Shevardnadze had the Foreign Ministry studying variants for troop withdrawals from Eastern Europe. Gorbachev, at a Politburo meeting, asked Defense Minister Yazov: "What are you waiting for? For them to ask you to leave?"[184] Though they did not foresee the bloc's sudden collapse, there was a growing understanding among the new thinkers that these countries would inevitably evolve toward the West.[185] Indeed, the events of 1989 might not have been inevitable—or at least would not have unfolded so precipitously —if East European leaders had heeded Gorbachev's call to perestroika. In any case, it was now exclusively their own affair; Gorbachev, chipping away at the old foundations of stability, made it clear that these regimes must find new bases of support without reliance on the Soviet army.

Though principal decisions had now been taken on all central foreign-policy issues, the results of these decisions would not be fully evident for another two or three years. The reasons for this lag are several. On arms control, there remained the task of negotiating and implementing agreements, which continued to be extremely complex even when offering highly concessionary terms. In Eastern Europe, Gorbachev provided the impetus, but the pace of change— or non-change—was dictated by conservative leaders there.[186] But even more significant was the resistance of Soviet conservatives;

political opposition to the new thinking now grew stronger than ever, and continued progress was "hellishly difficult."[187]

This resistance consisted, in part, of ministerial-military obstruction of everything from an Afghan settlement to the INF treaty.[188] Though more problematic than before, this was not new. What was new, beginning in 1987, were high-level *public* attacks on the philosophy of new thinking. For example, some in the military command now denounced growing "pacifism" and openly clung to the notion of victory in nuclear war.[189] In an even more direct challenge to the new, global outlook, Ligachev boldly reaffirmed the old line in mid 1988: "We proceed from the class nature of international relations," he asserted; talk of any other approach "only confuses the Soviet people and our friends abroad."[190]

Given such public, high-level dissent, together with the fact that Gorbachev's sincerity was not definitively "tested" until the events of late 1989, skeptics of the new thinking qua thinking argue that the crucial policy steps were those of the period immediately preceding and accompanying these momentous changes.[191] While properly stressing the contingency and even chaos that accompanied their implementation, this view overlooks the critical fact that for Gorbachev and his main allies, the key decisions-in-principle on Afghanistan, arms control, and even Eastern Europe had been taken more than two years earlier. As Chernyaev emphasizes, as long as Gorbachev was chairing the Politburo, it was "simply impossible even to suggest" any sort of intervention to halt events in Eastern Europe.[192]

Still, for skeptical realists, the actual turning point came only with Soviet acquiescence in a major shift of the European balance of power. Accordingly, they are left perplexed by "the diplomatic equivalent of unconditional surrender"—Gorbachev's 1990 acceptance of a reunified Germany's membership in the Western alliance—a move they can explain only by invoking various situational factors (domestic political rivalries, the need for Western aid, confusion over the terms of agreement, and so forth).[193] But with an understanding of Gorbachev's by-now deep and principled commitment to the new thinking, there is little mystery; while hardly denying the complexities of the situation facing the Soviet leadership in 1989–90, Gorbachev the "idealist" was ultimately moved by appeal to those principles—democracy, self-determination, and the "grand vision" of integration with the West.[194]

And so the public debates of 1987–89 reflected less a dispute over policy than a struggle for power. The leaders of new thinking had already crossed their Rubicon by late 1986, and there was little chance of turning back so long as Gorbachev remained at the helm (something that, as soon seen, was hardly guaranteed). The disputes within the Politburo and the Central Committee were at least as contentious as those seen in the press. However, it was no longer these bodies that were deciding foreign policy, but—repeatedly overruling their conservative colleagues' objections—Yakovlev, Shevardnadze and Gorbachev alone.

■

As sudden and painful as was the collapse of socialism abroad, a far more difficult test of the new thinking came with the challenge of separatism at home. In January 1991, after simmering for more than two years, this issue boiled over in an outburst of hard-line brutality in the Baltic republics. The killings, and Gorbachev's hesitancy in condemning those responsible, brought a surge of anger and disgust from Soviet liberals (already increasingly disillusioned by Gorbachev's rejection of more radical economic reforms the previous fall). Chernyaev, Gorbachev's close aide since early 1986, reflected these emotions in a letter of resignation stressing the vital linkage between democracy and human rights at home, and cooperation and trust abroad.

> Your choice is clear: either say that you won't permit even one inch of the Soviet Union to break away and that you will employ all means, including tanks, to prevent it; or admit that this was tragic, that you didn't order these actions, and that you condemn those who used force . . . . If it's the latter, *perestroika* can recover although [nothing] can change how these events are seen around the world and in Western political circles. . . . [The] most important thing is being destroyed, that which was achieved through the policy of new thinking—trust . . . . Those who warned that new thinking was just something that would be tossed out at an opportune moment are rejoicing. Can't you imagine the feelings of Bush, Baker and others who sincerely trusted you?[195]

Though Gorbachev soon spoke out unequivocally against those responsible for bloodshed, his ambivalence continued. This was only partly due to his own much stronger attachment to the domestic than foreign "empire." Even more important was Gorbachev's fear of hard-line opinion, that of the Soviet military as well as that of the Russian people.[196] The danger of the former was very real, although, as the attempted putsch of August 1991 demonstrated, Gorbachev's effort to co-opt the hard-liners ultimately backfired as they conspired against him. But Gorbachev's fear of the latter—of public opinion— proved much exaggerated, as he overestimated Russians' concern for the "empire" and perhaps underestimated the enlightening impact of his own policies. Chernyaev's letter continued:

> You began the return of our country to civilization, but it rejected your precept of "one and indivisible." You've often told me and other comrades that the Russians would never forgive the "collapse of empire." But Yeltsin, in the name of Russia, is doing this with impunity. And few Russians are protesting.[197]

In conclusion, Chernyaev summarized the anguish felt by him and legions of other veteran liberals as the policies they had directly or indirectly done so much to support now seemed in danger of collapsing.

> I suffered terribly over Prague . . . and didn't hide my distress at the invasion of Afghanistan, even though I was no more responsible for that policy than any other apparat staffer. But I have been directly involved in the policy of the past five years, one that excluded a repetition of 1968 or 1979. But now it's turned out otherwise. And I cannot support a policy that requires me to betray my very essence.[198]

Ultimately, neither could Gorbachev. His brief flirtation with the conservatives ended in a turn back to his reformist base and, over the spring and summer of 1991, with redoubled efforts toward a liberalized Soviet federation. Dedicated to humanizing his country, Gorbachev had become equally committed to its integration with the liberal international community. These goals were joined, conceptually, in new thinking's embrace of the organic link between democracy at home and trust abroad. They were also joined, politically and personally, in Gorbachev's complex reliance on the core ideas and key individuals (notwithstanding their later alienation) of the liberal-Westernizing intelligentsia.

> Gorbachev found himself strongly under their influence . . . and could not ignore the fact that the most intelligent part of society

and of the party too, which had earlier sympathized with or even supported dissidents, already had reconstructed itself [*perestroilis'*] ideologically. And it was precisely this group that became the main, if not exclusive, base of Gorbachev's support. In short, Gorbachev himself was forced to change in an atmosphere now freed from overweening ideological control.[199]

Gorbachev came to power a committed reformer for whom peaceful coexistence and ending the arms race were axiomatic to reviving the Soviet economy. New thinking's second domestic nexus—intellectual—came as his already considerable ties to Western-oriented scientists, scholars, and policy analysts grew critical to both his changing political base and his evolving world outlook. The new thinking's third and most far-reaching domestic nexus came with the understanding that good, enduring relations abroad meant broad democratization at home. By late 1986, with this conceptual turn complete, the leaders of new thinking were moving swiftly to put these ideas into practice.

Against high-level domestic opposition, the next two years saw the swift demilitarization of foreign policy and equally rapid opening of Soviet society to the world. In 1989, when their commitment to the deeper democratic nexus of foreign policy was challenged in Eastern Europe, the leaders of new thinking chose principle over power. In 1991, this challenge visited the USSR itself. Gorbachev, fighting resurgent Soviet reactionaries as well as his own deep allegiance to the Union, hesitated but again chose the path of new thinking.

The familiar Soviet-era response—an angry insistence on others' noninterference in Soviet internal affairs, and the drawing of a sharp distinction between domestic and foreign policy—was no longer conceivable. For Gorbachev had moved well beyond the modest original objectives of "peaceful coexistence." Having embraced the global, integrationist, "Westernizing" identity, his far more ambitious goal was now for his country to join "the common stream of world civilization."[200]

Conclusion: Reflections on the Origins and Fate of New Thinking

> Even a dyed-in-the-wool materialist would have to agree that "In the beginning was the Word," the suggestion. . . the idea.
> —Leonid Kornilov, *Lenoid Il'ich ne znal, chto zapuskaet mekhanizm perestroiki*

This book began with a review of the dangerous state of superpower relations in the early 1980s. So rapidly and completely did Gorbachev transform those relations that what might have been has faded from memory, and what did occur has taken on near-inevitability in hindsight, a deterministic bias that pervades even some serious analyses in subtle ways. So it is useful to reflect on where the paths not taken in 1985 could have led.[1] Between continuing the status quo (a path whose support was dwindling) or making a sharp reactionary turn (with its obviously perilous implications for a very different ending to the cold war) there was a third, and perhaps most likely, option of resuming the modest changes initiated by Andropov in 1982–83. Domestically, various streamlining and anticorruption measures could have slowed decline and prolonged the life of the old system well into the next century. Internationally, the USSR might have quit Afghanistan and ceded other contests in the third world—but surely not so easily as it did—while a precarious nuclear confrontation would likely continue.[2] In this scenario, the Soviet condition, at best, might today resemble a protracted "Ottoman-style" imperial retreat, with dissent, repression, and eventually rebellion erupting in Eastern Europe and perhaps the Caucasus and the Baltics as well. At worst, a more defiant USSR might only now be entering its terminal crisis, which could see it stumble into conflicts with Turkey or China abroad, with an ultimately swift but violent "Romanian-style" finale awaiting it at home. And Romania, of course, possessed neither an international empire nor a global, nuclear arsenal.[3]

Thus, perhaps ironically for a study stressing the importance of intellectual change, I begin by affirming that the pessimistic expectations some realist, power-centered analyses were well-founded. Those that foresaw the likelihood of a conflictual resolution to the dilemma of Soviet international decline were in fact correct.[4] Their failing lay, rather, in an inability to foresee, or contribute much to understanding, how ideas and leadership could combine to overcome these difficult odds. Without appreciation of the complex sources of intellectual and social change that nurtured the steady rise of a "Westernizing" identity among a diverse policy-academic elite, the process by which its ideas managed to capture an innovative leader and help propel a remarkable series of foreign (and domestic) reforms is simply incomprehensible. To reiterate, decline played a minor role in the long-term rise of new thinking and a major one in catalyzing the change that brought it to power. But that change could easily have gone in a very different direction; that it did not was thanks to an earlier intellectual transformation whose origins lie largely beyond the reach of materialist, international-level explanations.

Nor have most attempts to integrate domestic-level factors—modified realist or neoliberal-institutionalist—been much more successful in explaining the triumph of new thinking. A prominent example of the former, Snyder's "defensive realist" interpretation of Soviet overextension, details well the forces that stood for continuity of a hostile international posture (and its supporting ideological "myths") through powerful military-industrial interests. But the forces that ultimately produced change remain vague, and their influence undemonstrated.[5] Economic necessity, foreign-policy failures, and a growing intelligentsia are all cited. But *what* economic necessity and *which* policy failures? To repeat the question that neo-realism cannot answer, why not 10 years earlier, or 10 years later? The difference in the 1980s apparently lay in Gorbachev's "successful learning about grand strategy."[6] But how and when this learning occurred—particularly the intelligentsia's beliefs and Gorbachev's ties to this admittedly key "constituency"—are addressed only briefly, and not without the inevitability of hindsight. Yet by their own recourse to learning and leadership, such arguments themselves suggest that ideas were indeed more than epiphenomenal, and that Gorbachev's new thinking was not merely a rationalization of the inevitable.

The interplay of ideas and leadership are examined much more closely in the noted works of Mendelson and Checkel. The former, an invaluable study of Soviet policy making in the invasion, occupation, and eventual withdrawal from Afghanistan, faults both power-centered and learning-based explanations in stressing, instead, the *process* of mobilization for major policy change.[7] But the centrality of politics notwithstanding, the decline of Soviet power over the decade under review—and consequent difficulty in sustaining global confrontation—was manifestly more significant than that revealed in a focus on just one aspect of the confrontation. And so was learning; though downplayed as a causal variable, ideas are in fact central to her model in that they constituted the very expertise of the "expert communities" (and the source of their influence over Gorbachev, via a reformist agenda of which Afghanistan was just one part) whose "empowerment" is given primary emphasis.

Checkel considers the new thinking more broadly, and so goes rather further, in capturing the new thinkers as a larger group of specialists concerned with a wider array of interconnected foreign-policy problems. But his approach—a policy "windows" and "entrepreneurs" model—leads to emphasis on divergent institutional interests when common ideological interests were even more salient, particularly in the new thinking's critical earlier development.[8] It was during this earlier development, about which Checkel, too, has much less to say, that enterprising reformers pioneered the most important ideological innovations—often *against* their institutional and personal interests.

Both of the above approaches, notwithstanding efforts "to capture the full array of factors affecting a complex process of change," essentially take the existence of reformist ideas for granted;[9] both contribute less to understanding such ideas' origins than they do to analyzing their implementation.

By contrast, it is approaches that privilege the normative over the instrumental aspects of ideas that better capture the nature of new thinking as a long-term intellectual phenomenon as well as the contingencies of its near-term influence over leadership.[10] For example, rather than viewing détente as a time when Moscow for-eign-policy analysts were imbued with confidence about Soviet power and its prospects in global rivalry with the United States, Risse-Kappen emphasizes instead a period of specialists' coopera-tion with their Western counterparts that facilitated the transna-tional diffusion of liberal ideas about global security.[11] Evangelista, focusing closely on Soviet scientists and other arms-control experts, traces important steps in this process back more than a decade ear-lier.[12] And Herman, taking the wider view of a community of liber-al-Westernizing reformers, argues for reconceptualizing this process as a fundamental transformation in identity.[13] My attempt to build on these pioneering efforts has led in two directions: first back, to an even earlier and broader understanding of that community and the sources of liberalizing intellectual change; and then forward, to demonstrate as concretely as possible its real influence on the Gorbachev leadership.

But even if I have succeeded in showing that long-term intel-lectual and social (even cultural) change was a decisive factor in when and how the cold war ended, so what? What does it con-tribute to the broader theoretical and methodological concerns of the study of international relations? Many scholars committed to general theory building, through the application of deductively derived hypotheses over multiple cases, argue that an empirically driven, single-case study contributes little to that enterprise. In response, I would raise several points.[14] The first is that such a clear-ly inductive study offers an important test of deductive hypotheses. If we are concerned about the validity of theory, we must then also be concerned about more than just plausibility or general consis-tency with long-term outcomes. Tests of postulated causal mecha-nisms are essential if theory is to contribute to a progressive research program, generating useful hypotheses and even offering some pre-dictive value. In other words, it is not only important that a theory "get it right," but that it do so for the right reasons.[15] Admittedly, the in-depth, single-case study can usually trump multiple-case, par-simony-seeking analyses in the particulars, and the cause of scholar-ly progress is ill-served by "empirical ad hocism."[16] But the other extreme—dismissing close, inductive empirical analysis as "mere history"—is equally unproductive and parochial.

Such either/or arguments on the lessons of the cold war's

end—often posing stark contrasts between international-structural-material and domestic-ideational-cultural factors—are now yielding to more fruitful interaction between different types of analysis.[17] Wohlforth, a "neoclassical" realist whose state-of-the-debate critique is probably the most trenchant and constructive to date, argues for both greater theoretical precision and better empirical research.[18] His own analysis of great-power decline is filtered through the lens of leaders' and elites' perceptions—and one with which, ultimately, my main disagreement in interpreting the cold war *finale* is over the relative weighting of material and ideational factors.[19] But having admitted such domestic-level variables as elite perceptions, intelligentsia beliefs, or specialists' expertise into their models, neither neorealists nor neoliberals can avoid the necessity of exploring, in much greater detail than we have yet seen, the sources of those perceptions, beliefs, and expertise.[20] Without such investigation, theory remains limited to mere plausibility, and its relevance largely restricted to the cold war's endgame.

But beyond modifying well-established neorealist and neoliberal models, a second and perhaps more important contribution of the elites-identity framework is to an understanding of the broader relevance of ideas in political change. Many questions need study: on the interplay of domestic and international sources of ideas, on the impact of cultural-historical as well as institutional factors, and above all on the social dimensions of intellectual change and ideological innovation.[21] Strict constructivists may view the case of new thinking as a contribution to general theory on the role of beliefs, norms, and identity in broad political-historical change. Caution is in order here, too, for just as we have seen how neoliberal-institutional models derived from Western political experience can obscure as much as they reveal when applied in contexts as different as the Soviet political system before perestroika, so, too, with ideational models of large-scale international change.[22]

Still, at a minimum, the case of Soviet new thinking suggests some directions for middle-range theorizing about the processes of political liberalization and international opening in other dictatorial systems and ideologized polities.[23] Following on the examples noted in the introduction, fruitful comparisons are suggested with cases of democratic transition in Latin America (where key elite-intellectual congregations and foreign reference groups played an apparently similar role), or with contemporary China (where a once-terrorized society and isolationist party dictatorship are undergoing wrenching reforms, with a xenophobic ideology challenged by a Western-influenced and global-oriented intellectual elite).[24] The potential of such study for linking the domestic and international levels of analysis is great.[25]

And in all such cases, the methodological-empirical injunction is particularly important. By definition, closed-dictatorial systems yield their (and their societies') secrets only grudgingly, and informal intellectuals' groupings and closed-door debates are, by their very nature, especially difficult to reconstruct. But that hardly makes them less important than other, more easily accessible types of evidence. As Herrmann argues, "Logic will not substitute for evidence. Rigorous data analysis cannot replace careful data collection, which requires both area expertise and attention to contextual assumptions."[26] Such research makes it possible to explore causation and not just correlation, and to gain much-needed insight into the complex intersection of material and intellectual forces. Drawing on cases of political reform in southern Europe and in Latin America, Bermeo stresses that beliefs and values

> emerge from earthly experiences and earthly observations in identifiable situations and institutions. Using biographical and historical sources to reconstruct what key elites observed and experienced can enable us to understand when political learning takes place and why it takes a particular form.[27]

Finally, on the lessons of new thinking for post-Soviet Russia. The myriad changes that the country has undergone since 1991 have been deeply traumatic and, for many observers, the bright but brief flowering of Westernizing ideas and policies now seems a distant, increasingly irrelevant or even aberrant episode. A period of gradual reestrangement from the West has now lasted longer than that of perestroika's rapid rapprochement, with strains in these relations steadily worsening in tandem with Russia's deepening economic crisis. By 1999, tensions over issues from IMF policy and ties with Iran to NATO expansion and crisis in Kosovo-Serbia had reached an intensity that made Yeltsin's earlier characterization of an emergent "cold peace" seem an understatement. Official anti-American voices had grown louder than at any time since the early 1980s, while elite (and, by some reports, popular) anti-Western, Russian nationalist sentiments were more widespread than they had been in decades. To place these events in some broader context—including that of this study's findings—several observations should be made.

First, the resurgence of a Russian national "neo-Slavophile" current should come as no surprise. As I have frequently emphasized, the "neo-Westernizing" political-philosophical current was always in a minority—even among Soviet intellectuals, much less educated society more broadly, and certainly among the general public.[28] It came to power thanks to a confluence of domestic and international changes that—together with the force of its ideas and the unity of its advocates—gave it unique influence over an innovative leader. Thus even in the best of circumstances, it was to be expected that democratization, the inclusion of these other voices and opinions in the political process, would temper the "extremes" of the conciliatory-integrationist policies that ended the cold war.[29] And circumstances, to put it mildly, have not been the best.

Widespread poverty and immiseration, an arrogant oligarchy presiding over rampant corruption, and collapsing systems of health, education, and welfare—these are the fruits of Russia's market experiment for most ordinary citizens. Many educated Russians, at least those with the time and means for reflection, see even worse—a humiliated former superpower for whom the tragedy of vanished international prestige is now supplanted by the specter of an already truncated state's internal fracturing. Even those still admiring of the West, and faulting primarily their own leaders for Russia's catastrophe, naturally question the efficacy of some Western models (and the prescriptions tied to much Western aid) in the Russian political-cultural context. And everywhere there is enormous gloom, disappointment, and resentment at expectations falsely raised and promises long unfulfilled (As in the last century, many were enamored of a West that was "more imaginary than real").[30] In this context, skepticism of "alien" models and a turn toward "native" Russian values is hardly surprising. The wonder, perhaps, is why Russian opinion and Russian policies have not turned more sharply anti-Western.

Because, in fact, they have not. For all the rhetorical excesses of some Russian officials, Russia's international behavior has generally been responsible and cooperative. For all the anti-Western fury of some intellectuals, educated opinion remains broadly committed to liberal values and acceptance as a "normal" Western state. And for all their suffering in the national humiliation and immiseration in which they perceive Western leaders as complicit, ordinary Russians remain surprisingly well disposed toward Western peoples and societies. As always, it is tempting to conflate attitudes critical of certain Western policies with attitudes of deeper anti-Westernism. And as usual, the vitriol of a vocal minority gains disproportionate attention. Russian policy makers, too, pander to these minorities, and play on wounded national pride, for political gain. Still, given Western and especially U.S. policies that sometimes seem almost calculated to offend Russian dignity and interests (most notably NATO expansion, but also threatened abrogation of the ABM treaty, discriminatory trade practices, and a whole host of other issues), Russia's perseverance has been remarkable. It is this not-unreasonable perspective—that *the West has rejected them,* and not the reverse, with thoughtful Russians still desiring meaningful integration and genuine partnership—that is either absent or underemphasized in most recent commentary.[31]

Again, the elites-identity framework is helpful in understanding the continuity as well as change in a broadly Western orientation, and in avoiding the interpretive extremes that have been so evident. For if the new thinking was built on a generation-long process of transformation in fundamental beliefs and values, followed by a decade-long period of glasnost and international openness, then it is not something that should vanish so rapidly even in the face of enormous difficulties (any more than did the old thinking, which endured over two decades of "disconfirming experience"). Certainly, as a transformation driven primarily by intellectuals, it is significant that many of the new thinking's pioneers have left the scene. Some have died (notably, just among those interviewed for this study, historians Gefter and Edelman, commentator Karpinsky, philosopher Mamardashvili, economists Shatalin and Tikhonov, political scientist Zamoshkin, and ethnographer-politician Starovoitova), while others have retired or otherwise lost political influence in Russia (Gorbachev, Shevardnadze, Yakovlev, Arbatov, Bogomolov, Kozyrev, Aganbegyan, Zaslavskaya, Sagdeev). Among those that remain prominent, most are considered to have migrated from the camp of the liberal new thinkers to that of the realist "state-builders" (*derzhavniki*) concerned primarily with Russia's status and influence as a great power. The latter include economist Grigory Yavlinsky, parliamentary foreign-policy experts Vladimir Lukin and Alexei Arbatov, and the former foreign minister and prime minister Yevgeny Primakov.

This categorization flows from the now-familiar typology of contemporary Russian foreign-policy opinion as consisting of three main groups: Westernizing liberals, great-power statists, and anti-Western nationalists. While perhaps a useful shorthand for making sense of today's political debates, this typology is less helpful in gaining a deeper understanding of how Russian international-relations thought has evolved since 1991. This is so, in part, because it suggests a clear distinction between the first two groups, when in fact their differences are not really so sharp and their similarities are probably even more salient. Like the Westernizers, the statists want to see Russia as a "normal" member of the liberal international order. The circumstances of Russia's crises—particular threats to the integrity of the federation as well as an emergent "arc of instability" stretching from Central Asia to the Caucasus—are seen as necessitating reassertion of Russian influence in the region. Similarly, economic needs coupled with the understandable desire to continue playing a prominent role in major international issues lie behind the ties with Iran and other "pariah" states that many anti-Russian voices in the West find so troubling. The same desire—not some supposed resurgent cultural-historical imperative—has much to do with Russia's policy in the Balkans (see below). For all the rhetoric about a "Eurasian" political-cultural orientation, it is clear that a majority of statists seek recognition of Russia as a member of the European or Western club of great powers.[32] Its course may have shifted disappointingly since 1991, and Russia may presently be foundering on its shoals, but evidence is strong that most thoughtful Russians still seek inclusion in "the common stream of world civilization."[33]

But proceding from a near-caricature of the new thinkers as naive idealists,[34] many realist analysts miss this underlying continuity between liberal-Westernizing and statist-great power thought. Thus they insist on an either/or distinction in rejecting—according to their theoretical precepts—the apparent contradiction of a realist-like defense of national interests being driven by liberal ideals. And they make an even more fundamental mistake in claiming that a more assertive, "realist" line in Russian foreign policy *since* the cold war's end somehow invalidates "idealist" or ideational arguments about *how* the cold war ended.[35] Both material and intellectual factors were important before 1991, and both remain so after. And no account that emphasizes one to the near-exclusion of the other—or that overlooks the ever-growing salience of domestic politics—can be satisfactory.

In this new calculus of Russian foreign–policy making, the importance of understanding the role of not just ideas per se, but of *identity*, also remains. This is seen in a final illustration regarding the international problem that, as of this writing, found Russia and the West at most serious odds—the crisis in Kosovo-Yugoslavia. How to interpret Moscow's support of Serbia? Given that Russia's economic and geostrategic interests in the region are negligible, it would appear from the realist perspective to be a particularly odd choice of issue upon which to have taken a stance that, since 1993, has cost Russia so much in international influence and prestige. A domestic-politics perspective finds the answer in a democratized Russia's foreign relations necessarily reflecting broad attitudes of sympathy for their "orthodox brethren" and "historic allies" in Serbia. But such arguments based on cultural-historical continuity forget the fact that Russia's prerevolutionary foreign policy was motivated overwhelmingly by autocratic-imperial interests (which led to more frequent "betrayal" than support of Serbia); they also overlook the intervening Soviet decades during which Yugoslavia (with only brief exceptions) was widely demonized.[36] As recently as 1989, on the eve of Yugoslavia's collapse, popular attitudes were governed by general ignorance of the Balkans, while most elites perceived Yugoslavia as politically, economically, and even culturally part of the West.

Yet the dominant perception in today's Russia *is* very different, and the explanation of this rapid change—and the policies that have flowed from it—lies in appreciation of the domestic politics of national identity since perestroika. It was probably inevitable, as argued above, that the difficulties of Russia's latest attempt at rapid Westernization would lead many back to a search for meaning and identity in "traditional" Russian beliefs and values. What was *not* inevitable was the triumph of one or another, often tendentious, interpretation of those historical traditions. What a closer examination of recent Russian attitudes toward the Balkans reveals is a fairly contingent process in which a minority of nationalist intellectuals and publicists effectively filled a broad vacuum of knowledge and understanding with their particular, highly distorted, interpretation of past and present events—the myth of a centuries-old alliance with Russia's Orthodox "Serbian brethren."[37] Liberal intellectuals, discredited by the difficulties of Westernization and defensively seeking to buttress their own "patriotic" credentials, were frequently silent or even complicit in what, during its early stages, seemed a modest concession to the nationalists, unlikely to produce such tragic consequences for both the peoples of Yugoslavia and for Russia's international prestige.[38] With identity in flux, the "secular priesthood" of the national idea—by omission as well as commission—succeeded magnificently in creating a largely "invented tradition." Then, with the escalation of the Kosovo crisis to the bombing of Serbia, that issue was suddenly, directly, yoked to another, one about which Russian liberals *were* genuinely and deeply concerned: the expansion of NATO.[39]

It is noteworthy that much recent scholarship on post-Soviet politics has turned to an explicit focus on the importance of identities in transition.[40] This is only to be welcomed, even if much of it is simply driven by Russians' and other former Soviet nationalities' own near-obsessive emphasis on identity.[41] Understandably, for a people that historically has lacked a strong sense of itself apart from its empire, analysts across the political spectrum debate the path to a unifying "national idea." But interpreting these debates without a critical comparative-theoretical perspective presents several hazards. One is treating contemporary Russian events as sui generis, with an accompanying tendency to slip into historical-cultural determinism. On the other extreme is the danger of repeating the error of much earlier Sovietology in treating 1991—like 1917—as a *stunde null*, or clear break with the past.[42] For if there is any overriding lesson from the case of new thinking for understanding contemporary Russian debates over identity, the "national idea," and the country's place in world civilization, it is for judicious appreciation of both material and ideational forces.

The pressures of the international system are powerful, but not determinant, while politics remains a fluid and contingent process.

Culture changes only slowly, yet change it does. Identity is not infinitely malleable, but it is significantly so. And within this matrix of forces, particularly in a time of large-scale socioeconomic transformation, the importance of intellectual innovation and enlightened leadership is as great as ever. So far, in the post-Gorbachev era, such leadership has been notably lacking—and not only in Russia. Its continued absence, or reassertion, will be critical in determining the fate of Russia's beleaguered Westernizers for decades to come.

■

Notes

Introduction

1. The most persuasive "neoclassical" realist interpretation of the cold war's end is William C. Wohlforth, "Realism and the End of the Cold War, *International Security* 19, no. 3 (1994–95): 91–129; see also Wohlforth, *The Elusive Balance: Power and Perceptions During the Cold War* (Ithaca: Cornell University Press, 1993). For various critiques see also Richard Ned Lebow and Thomas Risse-Kappen, eds., *International Relations Theory and the End of the Cold War* (New York: Columbia University Press, 1995).

2. Contrary to one realist's claim, the USSR was not "coming apart at the seams" in the mid 1980s; see Stephen M. Walt, "The Gorbachev Interlude and International Relations Theory," *Diplomatic History* 21, no. 3 (1997): 476. It was the unintended side effects of reform—not its preconditions—that led to Soviet collapse. So the term *crisis*, which I use reservedly, must be understood in relative terms. On the prereform system's considerable reserves, and capacity to continue up to 20 years under the status quo, see Michael Ellman and Vladimir Kontorovich, eds., *The Disintegration of the Soviet Economic System* (London: Routledge, 1992).

3. Two important leader-centered analyses, one a diplomatic history and the other a political biography, both credit the new thinkers' influence but examine their origins only briefly; see Raymond L. Garthoff, *The Great Transition: American-Soviet Relations and the End of the Cold War* (Washington, DC: Brookings Institution, 1994), and Archie Brown, *The Gorbachev Factor* (New York: Oxford University Press, 1996). Leadership—in this case its failures—is also central to Jerry F. Hough, *Democratization and Revolution in the USSR, 1985–1991* (Washington, DC: Brookings Institution, 1997). See also Janice Gross Stein, "Political Learning by Doing: Gorbachev as Uncommitted Thinker and Motivated Learner," *International Organization* 48, no. 2 (1994): 155–83.

4. See for example Steven Weber, "Interactive Learning in U.S.-Soviet Arms Control," in George W. Breslauer and Philip E. Tetlock, eds., *Learning in U.S. and Soviet Foreign Policy* (Boulder, CO: Westview Press,

1991), pp. 784–824, and Emanuel Adler, "The Emergence of Cooperation: National Epistemic Communities and the International Evolution of the Idea of Nuclear Arms Control," *International Organization* 46, no. 1 (1992): 101–46.

5. Noting the profound differences in Soviet politics that limit the appropriateness of the epistemic community model—with its narrow, technical criteria for membership as well as leaders' presumed dependence on such expertise—is Robert G. Herman, "Identity, Norms, and National Security: The Soviet Foreign Policy Revolution and the End of the Cold War," in Peter J. Katzenstein, ed., *The Culture of National Security: Norms and Identity in World Politics* (New York: Columbia University Press, 1996), p. 284. More broadly relevant to the authoritarian Soviet system is the model of a "principled issue network." See Kathryn Sikkink, "Human Rights, Principled Issue Networks, and Sovereignty in Latin America," *International Organization* 47, no. 3 (1993): 411–44.

6. Such a single-issue study that accordingly emphasizes the *implementation* of one foreign-policy initiative over its *origins* within a broader new-thinking agenda is Sarah E. Mendelson, *Changing Course: Ideas, Politics, and the Soviet Withdrawal from Afghanistan* (Princeton: Princeton University Press, 1998). By contrast, detailed attention to the origins of ideational change buttresses what is far and away the most persuasive application of a transnational learning model, Matthew Evangelista's *Unarmed Forces: The Transnational Movement to End the Cold War* (Ithaca: Cornell University Press, 1999). This work stands out for its great empirical depth and historical reach, and I draw on it extensively in my later chapters and conclusion.

7. On "incentives" to promote reform, see George Breslauer, "Explaining Soviet Policy Changes: Politics, Ideology, and Learning," in Breslauer, ed., *Soviet Policy in Africa: From the Old to the New Thinking* (Berkeley: University of California Press, 1992), p. 207. See also the "policy entrepreneur-policy window" model of Jeffrey T. Checkel, *Ideas and International Political Change: Soviet/Russian Behavior and the End of the Cold War* (New Haven: Yale University Press, 1997).

8. Steven Kull, *Burying Lenin: The Revolution in Soviet Ideology and Foreign Policy* (Boulder, CO: Westview Press, 1992); Douglas Blum, "The Soviet Foreign Policy Belief System: Beliefs, Politics, and Foreign Policy Outcomes," *International Studies Quarterly* 37, no. 4 (1993): 373–94.

9. Here I am indebted to Herman's "ideas and identity" framework, though I propose a broader and earlier definition of the new thinking and new thinkers. See Herman, "Identity, Norms, and National Security."

10. Samuel S. Kim and Lowell Dittmer, "Whither China's Quest for National Identity?" in Dittmer and Kim, eds., *China's Quest for National*

Identity (Ithaca: Cornell University Press, 1993), p. 279. On historical "narratives," see Robert Gildea, *The Past in French History* (New Haven: Yale University Press, 1994), and Benedict Anderson, *Imagined Communities: Reflections on the Origin and Spread of Nationalism* (London: Verso, 1983).

11. On the "map-compass" image of the relationship between culture and identity, see T. K. Fitzgerald, *Metaphors of Identity* (Albany: State University of New York Press, 1993), p. 186.

12. Anthony Giddens, *Modernity and Self-Identity* (Stanford: Stanford University Press, 1991).

13. "Identities define attitudes toward one's surroundings that operate as important constraints for political decisions" and "powerfully influence actual behavior, especially in crisis situations that require existential choices based as much on emotion as on reason." Konrad H. Jarausch, "Reshaping German Identities," in Jarausch, ed., *After Unity: Reconfiguring German Identities* (Providence, RI: Berghahn Books, 1997), p. 4.

14. Ernest Gellner, *Nations and Nationalism* (Ithaca: Cornell University Press, 1983).

15. See Thomas U. Berger, "Norms, Identity, and National Security in Germany and Japan," in Katzenstein, ed., *The Culture of National Security*, pp. 317–56.

16. Liah Greenfeld, *Nationalism: Five Roads to Modernity* (Cambridge: Harvard University Press, 1992).

17. A "crisis of self-definition" occurs when intellectuals perceive that the developmental path embodied in a given identity has manifestly failed; see Dittmer and Kim, "In Search of a Theory of National Identity," in Dittmer and Kim, eds., *China's Quest for National Identity*, p. 29. The "hegemonic" identity then confronts "incurable contradictions" and "gross discrepancies" with reality; Antonio Gramsci, *Selections from the Prison Notebooks*, eds. Quintin Hoare and Geoffrey Nowell Smith (New York: International Publishers, 1971), pp. 210, 276.

18. Harold James, *A German Identity, 1770–1990* (New York: Routledge, 1989), p. 8; also Eric Hobsbawm and Terence Ranger, eds., *The Invention of Tradition* (New York: Cambridge University Press, 1983).

19. On Spain and Latin America, see Nancy Bermeo, "Democracy and the Lessons of Dictatorship," *Comparative Politics* 24, no. 3 (1992): 273–92 (quote from pp. 284–85; brackets in the original).

20. Li Cheng and Lynn T. White, "China's Technocratic Movement and the *World Economic Herald*," *Modern China* 17, no. 3 (1991): 342–89.

21. Bermeo, "Democracy and the Lessons of Dictatorship," pp. 283–84. As noted above, Sikkink's study of how international norms shaped democratization in some Latin American states via "principled issue networks" closely parallels the manner in which ideas and intellectuals influ-

enced perestroika in the USSR; see Sikkink, "Human Rights, Principled Issue Networks, and Sovereignty in Latin America."

22. Concerning the impact of foreign "reference groups" on identity, see Daniel Druckman, "Nationalism, Patriotism, and Group Loyalty: A Social Psychological Perspective," *Mershon International Studies Review* 38, supp. 1 (1994): 60–62. On competing socialist, third world, and global identities in China, see Merle Goldman, Perry Link, and Su Wei, "China's Intellectuals in the Deng Era: Loss of Identity with the State," in Dittmer and Kim, eds., *China's Quest for National Identity*, pp. 125–53.

23. On the link between "external" identity and domestic politics, see Michael Barnett, "Identity and Alliances in the Middle East," in Katzenstein, ed., *The Culture of National Security*, pp. 412–13.

24. Lynn White and Li Cheng, "China Coast Identities: Regional, National, and Global," in Dittmer and Kim, eds., *China's Quest for National Identity*, p. 170. On the early 1980s emergence of currents from Marxist humanism to liberalism—"virtually the whole range of modern Western thought found a receptive audience in China's institutes of higher learning"—see Tu Wei-ming, "Intellectual Effervescence in China," *Daedalus* 121, no. 2 (1992): 259.

25. John Hall, "Ideas and the Social Sciences," in Judith Goldstein and Robert O. Keohane, eds., *Ideas and Foreign Policy: Beliefs, Institutions, and Political Change* (Ithaca: Cornell University Press, 1993), p. 51. On "transaction flows," see Emanuel Adler and Michael N. Barnett, "Governing Anarchy: A Research Agenda for the Study of Security Communities," *Ethics and International Affairs* 10 (1996): 66–71.

26. Mark Blyth, "Any More Bright Ideas? The Ideational Turn of Comparative Political Economy," *Comparative Politics* 29, no. 2 (1997): 264.

27. On alternation between incremental and "punctuated" learning see Peter A. Hall, "Policy Paradigms, Social Learning, and the State: The Case of Economic Policymaking in Britain," *Comparative Politics* 25, no. 3 (1993): 277. See also Emanuel Adler, "Cognitive Evolution: A Dynamic Approach for the Study of International Relations and Their Progress," in Adler and Beverly Crawford, *Progress in Postwar International Relations* (New York: Columbia University Press, 1991).

28. A "cognitive punch" is a crisis or event that accelerates "reevaluation and change from one set of collective understandings or 'paradigms' to another." See Adler, "Cognitive Evolution," p. 55.

29. Or, why they were not recognized as such and addressed a decade earlier.

30. Richard K. Herrmann, "Policy-Relevant Theory and the Challenge of Diagnosis: The End of the Cold War as a Case Study," *Political Psychology* 15, no. 1 (1994): 134.

31. Sidney Verba, "Comparative Political Culture," in Lucien Pye and Sidney Verba, *Political Culture and Political Development* (Princeton: Princeton University Press, 1965), p. 515. On "social constraints," see Philip E. Converse, "The Nature of Belief Systems in Mass Publics," in David E. Apter, ed., *Ideology and Discontent* (New York: Free Press, 1964), p. 207.

32. Concerning how political elites are "constrained by the symbolic myths which their predecessors created," see Alastair Iain Johnston, "Thinking about Strategic Culture," *International Security* 19, no. 4 (1995): 40; studies of "discursive practices" and "rhetorical momentum" are also reviewed in Albert S. Yee, "The Causal Effects of Ideas on Politics," *International Organization* 50, no. 1 (1996): 94–101.

33. This point needs emphasis, for while some analyses define the new thinkers too narrowly, others essentially go to an opposite extreme in viewing the entire post-Stalin "urban intelligentsia"—which was in fact broadly conservative, as was a majority of the post-Stalin elite—as a strong reform constituency. See Moshe Lewin, *The Gorbachev Phenomenon: An Historical Interpretation* (London: Hutchinson Radius, 1988) for an influential elaboration of this view, which is adopted in Hough, *Democratization and Revolution*, and Jack Snyder, *Myths of Empire: Domestic Politics and International Ambition* (Ithaca: Cornell University Press, 1991). Generational change was hardly a sufficient condition for major reform; nor was it—save in an indirect sense—even a necessary one.

34. A view of Gorbachev as less the sorcerer than his apprentice is Coit D. Blacker, *Hostage to Revolution: Gorbachev and Soviet Security Policy, 1985–1991* (New York: Council on Foreign Relations Press, 1993).

35. On this point, see Robert Legvold, "Observations on International Order: A Comment on MacFarland and Adomeit," *Post-Soviet Affairs* 10, no. 3 (1994): 273–75.

36. See Richard Pipes, "Misinterpreting the Cold War: The Hardliners Had it Right," *Foreign Affairs* 74, no. 1 (1995): 154–60, and Peter Schweizer, *Victory: The Reagan Administration's Secret Strategy that Hastened the Collapse of the Soviet Union* (New York: Atlantic Monthly Press, 1994).

37. See Stephen F. Cohen, *Rethinking the Soviet Experience: Politics and History Since 1917* (New York: Oxford University Press, 1985), chapter 5.

38. Notable for its early appreciation of the new thinking's breadth in terms accurately suggestive of a Kuhnian paradigm shift—"Literally every dimension of policy is affected . . . [it] has tumbled forth on all levels at once"—was Robert Legvold, "The Revolution in Soviet Foreign Policy," *Foreign Affairs* 68, no. 1 (1989): 82–98. Other perceptive early studies, upon which I draw in subsequent chapters, include Stephen Shenfield, *The*

Nuclear Predicament: Explorations in Soviet Ideology (London: Routledge & Kegan Paul, 1987), and Alan Lynch, *The Soviet Study of International Relations* (New York: Cambridge University Press, 1987). Another inspirational early work—whose idiosyncrasies are balanced by many original insights—is Jerry Hough, *Russia and the West: Gorbachev and the Politics of Reform* (New York: Simon & Schuster, 1988).

1. The Origins and Nature of Old Thinking

1. Verba, "Comparative Political Culture," p. 515.

2. Alexander George, "The 'Operational Code': A Neglected Approach to the Study of Political Leaders and Decision-Making," in Erik P. Hoffmann and Frederic J. Fleron Jr., eds., *The Conduct of Soviet Foreign Policy* (New York: Aldine, 1980), pp. 165–90.

3. A similar "revolutionary-imperial paradigm" is analyzed in Vladislav Zubok and Constantine Pleshakov, *Inside the Kremlin's Cold War: From Stalin to Khrushchev* (Cambridge: Harvard University Press, 1996), p. 4, passim.

4. Gabor T. Rittersporn, "The Omnipresent Conspiracy: On Soviet Imagery of Politics and Social Relations in the 1930s," in J. Arch Getty and Roberta T. Manning, eds., *Stalinist Terror: New Perspectives* (New York: Cambridge University Press, 1993), p. 100.

5. Caryl Emerson, "New Words, New Epochs, Old Thoughts," *The Russian Review* 55, no. 3 (1996): 358.

6. Nicholas Berdyaev, *The Origin of Russian Communism* (Ann Arbor: University of Michigan Press, 1972), pp. 110, 135.

7. A. V. Buganov, *Russkaia istoriia v pamiati krest'ian XIX veka i natsional'noe samosoznanie* (Moscow: Institut Etnologii i Antropologii, 1992).

8. J. N. Westwood, *Endurance and Endeavor: Russian History, 1812–1986* (New York: Oxford University Press, 1987), p. 33. One veteran of Paris recalled that "seeing the insipid life at St. Petersburg and the deprecation of [Europe's] every progressive step was unbearable. We were a hundred years behind them."

9. Both were seen in the case of Peter Chaadaev, whose criticism led to his imprisonment and a forced recantation. He wrote that "we have given nothing to the world, we have taken nothing from the world; we have not added a single idea to the mass of human ideas; we have contributed nothing to the progress of the human spirit. And we have disfigured everything we have touched of that progress." See Peter Chaadaev, *Philosophical Letters and Apology of a Madman* (Knoxville: University of Tennessee Press, 1969), p. 41.

10. See Bruce Lincoln, *In the Vanguard of Reform: Russia's Enlightened Bureaucrats* (De Kalb: University of Northern Illinois Press, 1982), and Richard S. Wortman, *The Development of a Russian Legal Consciousness* (Chicago: University of Chicago Press, 1976).

11. Nicholas Turgenev, cited in Robert F. Byrnes, "Attitudes toward the West," in Ivo J. Lederer, ed., *Russian Foreign Policy* (New Haven: Yale University Press, 1962), pp. 116–17.

12. Konstantin Aksakov, cited in Nicholas Riasanovsky, *Russia and the West in the Teaching of the Slavophiles* (Cambridge: Harvard University Press, 1952), p. 76.

13. See Thomas G. Masaryk, *The Spirit of Russia* vol. 1 (London: Allen & Unwin, 1955).

14. Ivan Aksakov, cited in Riasanovsky, *Russia and the West in the Teaching of the Slavophiles*, p. 85.

15. Ibid., p. 84.

16. N. Danilevskii, *Rossiia i Evropa. vzgliad na kul'turnye i politicheskie otnosheniia slavianskogo mira k germano-romanskomu* (Sanktpeterburg: Tovarishchestvo Obshchestvennaia Pol'za, 1871), p. 69.

17. On Slavophilism's "secularization" and drift toward Pan-Slavism-imperialism, see Donald W. Treadgold, *The West in Russia and China*, vol. 1 (New York: Cambridge University Press, 1973), pp. 197–99.

18. Cited in Mikhail Agursky, *The Third Rome: National Bolshevism in the USSR* (Boulder, CO: Westview Press, 1987), p. 51.

19. Frederick C. Barghoorn, "Some Russian Images of the West," in Cyril E. Black, ed., *The Transformation of Russian Society.* (Cambridge: Harvard University Press, 1960), p. 576.

20. Berdyaev, *Origin of Russian Communism*, p. 34.

21. Abbott Gleason, *Young Russia: The Genesis of Russian Radicalism in the 1860s.* (New York: Viking, 1980), p. 55.

22. Berdyaev, *Origin of Russian Communism*, pp. 185–86.

23. Mark Raeff, *Origins of the Russian Intelligentsia: The Eighteenth Century Nobility.* (New York: Harcourt, Brace & World), 1966, p. 167.

24. Berdyaev, *Origin of Russian Communism*, p. 21.

25. Andrzej Walicki, *History of Russian Thought* (Stanford: Stanford University Press, 1979), p. xiv.

26. S. N. Bulgakov, "Geroizm i podvizhnichestvo," in *Vekhi. Sbornik Statei o Russkoi Intelligentsii* (Moscow: Novosti, 1990), pp. 32–33. This tendency has been explained by the intelligentsia's lack of political influence and consequent situation in permanent opposition: "To overcome their alienation" they "put all their energies . . . into ideas and doctrines aimed at . . . a radical transformation of reality." Raeff, *Origins of the Russian Intelligentsia*, pp. 170–71.

27. This was observed by Bolshevik leader Vladimir Lenin in "What Is to Be Done?" cited in Robert C. Tucker, ed., *The Lenin Anthology* (New York: Norton, 1975), p. 23.

28. Barghoorn, "Some Russian Images," pp. 578, 580–81.

29. In other words, contrary to Marx, as a reason to avoid or bypass the capitalist stage. In the 1870s, some Marxist works such as Engels's *Situation of the Working Class in England* were enthusiastically received in this way by Russian Populists.

30. Berdyaev, *Origin of Russian Communism*, p. 38.

31. As enunciated in Lenin's 1902 "What Is to Be Done?" whose title was pointedly borrowed from the 1863 Populist classic by Nikolai Chernyshevsky.

32. S. Frank, "Etiki nigilizma," in *Vekhi*, p. 162.

33. On these debates, see "Lenin and Revolution," in Tucker, ed., *Lenin Anthology*, pp. xxvi–xlvi.

34. Lenin, "The State and Revolution," in Tucker, *Lenin Anthology*, pp. 311–98.

35. After 1917, this argument implied inherent capitalist hostility toward a socialist state (see this chapter, below).

36. Barghoorn, "Some Russian Images," p. 58.

37. Walicki, *History of Russian Thought*, p. 374.

38. Alexander Blok, "Scythians," cited in Robert C. Tucker, *Stalin in Power: The Revolution from Above, 1928–1941* (New York: Norton, 1990), p. 33.

39. Cited in Adam B. Ulam, *Expansion and Coexistence: The History of Soviet Foreign Policy, 1917–1967* (New York: Praeger, 1968), p. 54.

40. Cited in Byrnes, "Attitudes Toward the West," p. 126.

41. Robert C. Tucker, *Stalin as Revolutionary: A Study in History and Personality* (New York: Norton, 1973), p. 246. A contrasting view, of Lenin as Russian nationalist, is Agursky, *Third Rome*.

42. Lenin, "The Right of Nations to Self-Determination," in Tucker, ed., *Lenin Anthology*, pp. 153–80. However, Lenin also criticized the "preservation of small nations at all costs" and the "petty-bourgeois idea of federalism." See his "On the National Pride of the Great Russians," ibid., pp. 196–99.

43. Tucker, *Stalin as Revolutionary*, p. 370.

44. Cited ibid., p. 174.

45. Mikhail Pokrovsky, *Russia in World History* (Ann Arbor: University of Michigan Press, 1970), p. 155.

46. Cited in Agursky, *Third Rome*, pp. 210, 218.

47. Ulam, *Expansion and Coexistence*, p. 60. This showed that "deep beneath the internationalist and socialist phraseology of the Bolsheviks lay their unconscious Russian nationalism."

48. *Vos'moi s"ezd RKP(b). Mart 1919. Stenografickeskii otchet* (Moscow: Izdatel'stvo Politicheskoi Literatury, 1959), pp. 52–53.

49. In other words, for peoples of the British Empire but not the Russian; cited in Ulam, *Expansion and Coexistence*, p. 104.

50. *Vos'moi s"ezd*, pp. 107–8.

51. Dmitri Furman, "Ostorozhno s imperiiami," *Vek XX i Mir*, no. 11 (1989): 7. For background, see Richard Pipes, *The Formation of the Soviet Union* (Cambridge: Harvard University Press, 1964).

52. See Stephen Blank, *The Sorcerer as Apprentice: Stalin as Commissar of Nationalities, 1917–1924* (Westport, CT: Greenwood Press, 1994).

53. Furman, "Ostorozhno s imperiiami," p. 7. See also *Dvenadtsatyi s"ezd RKP(b). Aprel' 1923. Stenograficheskii otchet* (Moscow: Izdatel'stvo Politicheskoi Literatury, 1968), pp. 571–78.

54. Tucker, *Stalin as Revolutionary*, p. 254.

55. Cited in Agursky, *Third Rome*, p. 206.

56. M. Gorky, *Untimely Thoughts*, ed. Herman Ermolaev (New York: Paul Eriksson, 1968), pp. 132, 141.

57. Cited in Agursky, *Third Rome*, p. 276.

58. A. A. Blok, *Dvenadtsat': Skify* (Moscow: Russkii Iazyk, 1982), p. 212.

59. N. A. Omel'chenko, "Spory o evraziistve. Opyt istoricheskoi rekonstruktsii," *Polis*, no. 3 (1992): 156.

60. D. Furman, "Nash put' k normal'noi kulture," in Iu. Afan'asiev, ed., *Inogo ne dano* (Moscow: Progress, 1988), p. 574.

61. As cited in Agursky, *Third Rome*, p. 178.

62. *Smena vekh*, 2nd ed. (Prague: 1922). The title was an allusion—and rebuttal—to the earlier *Vekhi* (Signposts) collection of liberal essays on Russian politics, culture, and the intelligentsia. *Smena vekh* adherents included Alexei Tolstoy, whose influential novel *The Road to Calvary* was a classic of the genre. Tolstoy also helped edit the *Smena vekh* journal *Nakanune* (On the eve).

63. See Hilde Hardeman, *Coming to Terms with the Soviet Regime: The "Changing Signposts" Movement Among Russian Emigres in the Early 1920s* (De Kalb: Northern Illinois University Press, 1994).

64. *Pod znakom revoliutsii* (Harbin: 1925), p. 277.

65. A. Bulatsel, cited in Agursky, *Third Rome*, p. 256.

66. S. Bulgakov, in *Iz glubiny. Sbornik statei o russkoi revoliutsii* (Moscow: Prospekt, 1988), pp. 124–29.

67. P. Miliukov, *Russia Today and Tomorrow* (New York: Macmillan, 1922), pp. 39–40.

68. *Odinnadtsatyi s"ezd RKP(b). Mart-aprel' 1922. Stenograficheskii otchet* (Moscow: Izdatel'stvo Politicheskoi Literatury, 1961), pp. 28–29.

69. Ibid., pp. 73–74. "Russia, One and Indivisible," a motto of the tsarist empire, was also a rallying cry of the White armies in the civil war.

70. These included the Paris-published weekly *Smena vekh*, the daily *Nakanune* (with its weekly literary supplement, edited by Tolstoy) based in Berlin, and the Soviet-published journal *Novaia Rossiia* (later *Rossiia*). Trotsky called for dissemination of *Smena vekh* literature among the army, too.

71. Cited in Agursky, *Third Rome*, p. 260.

72. See Skrypnik and Tsintsadze, in *Dvenadtsatyi s"ezd*, pp. 571, 584.

73. Ibid. See also the remarks of Khodzhanov, "Iz istorii obrazovaniia SSSR," *Izvestiia TsK KPSS*, no. 3 (1991): 175; Ibragimov, "Iz istorii obrazovaniia SSSR," *Izvestiia TsK KPSS* no. 4 (1991): 164–65; and Rakovskii, *Dvenadtsatyi s"ezd*, pp. 578–79.

74. Ibid., p. 578; Sultan-Galiev in "Iz istorii obrazovaniia SSSR," *Izvestiia TsK KPSS* no. 4 (1991): 163.

75. See remarks of Skrypnik, Yakovlev, and Ryskulov in *Dvenadtsatyi s"ezd*, pp. 511, 571, 597.

76. Ibid., pp. 484–85.

77. Lenin had recently dictated a letter critical of Russian chauvinism—and of Stalin—that was known to top Bolsheviks. Although Lenin was too ill to attend the congress, his authority forced Stalin to conform publicly. See "The Question of Nationalities and 'Autonomisation,'" in Tucker, ed., *Lenin Anthology*, pp. 719–24.

78. Stalin's behavior notwithstanding, the most momentous single act of Russian chauvinism was arguably Lenin's—ordering the violent annexation of non-Russian lands and the imposition of Bolshevik dictatorship.

79. "Iz istorii obrazovaniia SSSR," *Isvestiia TsK KPSS* no. 4 (1991): 167.

80. *Dvenadtsatyi s"ezd*, p. 614. Judging by the written record alone, a slight majority took anti-chauvinist positions. So Bukharin's observation illuminates the nationalistic views of the mass of delegates representing Party organizations throughout Russia.

81. This included a shift in emphasis, in Soviet historiography of European socialism, from the Paris Commune to the French Revolution, thereby justifying terror and elevating the more "national" model. See Katerina Clark, "Changing Historical Paradigms in Soviet Literature," in Thomas Lahusen, ed., *Late Soviet Culture: From Perestroika to Novostroika* (Durham: Duke University Press, 1993), p. 297.

82. Cited in Agursky, *Third Rome*, p. 330.

83. *Dvenadtsatyi s"ezd*, p. 603.

84. Cited in Tucker, ed., *Lenin Anthology*, p. 720.

85. On support of nineteenth-century imperialism as "an emblem of European status" stemming from a "deeply felt need to assert Russia's

membership in the European community," see Alfred J. Rieber, "Russian Imperialism: Popular, Emblematic, Ambiguous," *Russian Review* 53, no. 3 (1994): 333–34.

86. Cited in Agursky, *Third Rome*, p. 330.

87. Cited in Tucker, *Stalin as Revolutionary*, p. 527.

88. Furman, "Ostorozhno s imperiiami," p. 6 (italics added).

89. *Odinnatsatyi s"ezd*, p. 386. See also Moshe Lewin, *The Making of the Soviet System: Essays in the Social History of Interwar Russia* (New York: New Press, 1985), pp. 258–61, 274–77.

90. Robert Daniels, "Russian Political Culture and the Post-Revolutionary Impasse," *Russian Review* 46, no. 2 (1987): 170. On anti-foreign attitudes and conspiracy theories, see also Buganov, *Russkaia istoriia v pamiati krest'ian*; Savelii Dudakov, *Istoriia odnogo mifa. ocherki Russkoi literatury XIX–XX vv.* (Moscow: Nauka, 1993); and G. Fedotov, "Rossiia i svoboda," *Znamia* no. 12 (1989): 214.

91. *Odinnadtsatyi s"ezd*, p. 386.

92. "*Intelligentnost'* was more a synonym for cowardly liberalism and softness than proletarian firmness." See Roy Medvedev, *Let History Judge: The Origins and Consequences of Stalinism*, revised and expanded ed. (New York: Columbia University Press, 1989), p. 87.

93. On these attitudes and beliefs, see also Cathy A. Frierson, *Peasant Icons: Representations of Rural People in Late-Nineteenth-Century Russia* (New York: Oxford University Press, 1993).

94. On "animalistic nationalism," see Furman, "Nash put,'" p. 575.

95. For these contrasting interpretations, see respectively Shelia Fitzpatrick, "The Civil War as a Formative Experience," in Abbott Gleason, Peter Kenez, and Richard Stites, eds., *Bolshevik Culture: Experiment and Order in the Russian Revolution* (Bloomington: Indiana University Press, 1985), and Stephen F. Cohen, *Bukharin and the Bolshevik Revolution: A Political Biography, 1888–1938* (New York: Oxford University Press, 1971), pp. 129–33, 186–90, 276.

96. Geoffrey Hosking, *The First Socialist Society: A History of the USSR From Within* (Cambridge: Harvard University Press, 1985), p. 84.

97. On the manipulation of symbols and information to cultivate an "enemy image" of the bourgeois West, see Victoria E. Bonnell, "The Representation of Politics and the Politics of Representation," *Russian Review* 47, no. 3 (1988): 315–22.

98. Alexander Barmine, *One Who Survived* (New York: Putnam's Sons, 1945), p. 52.

99. Petro Grigorienko, *Memoirs* (New York: Norton, 1982), p. 20.

100. Nikita Khrushchev, *Khrushchev Remembers* (Boston: Little, Brown, 1970), p. 17.

101. In reality, the Poles, hardly wishing to help restore their archenemy imperial Russia, explicitly timed their campaign so as *not* to aid the Whites. Citation from Alexander Solzhenitsyn et al., *From Under the Rubble* (Boston: Little, Brown, 1975), p. 132.

102. Alexander Berkman, *The Bolshevik Myth* (New York: Boni & Liveright, 1925), p. 63. See also Barmine, *One Who Survived*, p. 66.

103. Berkman, *Bolshevik Myth*, p. 303.

104. N. V. Zagladin, *Istoriia uspekhov i neudach Sovetskoi diplomatii* (Moscow: Mezhdunarodnye Otnosheniia, 1990), p. 55. See also V. Sirotkin, "Rizhskii mir," *Mezhdunarodnaia zhizn'* no. 8, 1988, p. 132.

105. Vladimir Brovkin, "Workers' Unrest and the Bolsheviks' Response in 1919," *Slavic Review* 49, no. 3 (1990): 373. See also David Joravsky, "Cultural Revolution and the Fortress Mentality," in Gleason et al., *Bolshevik Culture*, pp. 93–113, and Roger Pethybridge, *The Social Prelude to Stalinism* (New York: St. Martin's, 1974), p. 122.

106. Berkman, *Bolshevk Myth*, p. 206.

107. Party membership soared to 800,000 in 1925, and to more than 1.3 million by 1928; T. H. Rigby, *Communist Party Membership in the USSR, 1917–1967* (Princeton: Princeton University Press, 1968), p. 52.

108. "Genghis Khans with telephones" was Bukharin's characterization, cited in V. Sirotkin, "Ot grazhdanskoi voiny k grazhdanskomu miru," in Afan'asiev, *Inogo ne dano*, p. 391.

109. Joravsky, "Cultural Revolution," p. 99. See also L. A. Kogan, " 'Vyslat' za granitsu bezzhalostno' (Novoe ob izgnanii dukhovnoi elity)," *Voprosy Filosofii* no. 9 (1993): 61–84.

110. Zhores Medvedev, *Soviet Science* (New York: Norton, 1978), pp. 11–13.

111. Peter Kenez, *The Birth of the Propaganda State: Soviet Methods of Mass Mobilization, 1917–1929* (New York: Cambridge University Press, 1985).

112. Pethybridge, *The Social Prelude to Stalinism*, p. 178.

113. Ibid., pp. 72–118; Larry Holmes, *The Kremlin and the Schoolhouse* (Bloomington: Indiana University Press, 1991), pp. 79–80; A. I. Gukovskii, "Kak ia stal istorikom," *Istoriia SSSR* no. 6 (1965): 87.

114. Alexander Vucinich, *Empire of Knowledge: The Academy of Sciences of the USSR, 1917–1970* (Berkeley: University of California Press, 1984), pp. 77, 92–96, 108–9.

115. Holmes, *The Kremlin and the Schoolhouse*, p. 21.

116. Fitzpatrick, "The Civil War as a Formative Experience," pp. 97–100, 125–26. It should be noted that Soviet sources used the classifications *proletariat*, or *working class*, when a majority of these were closer to the peasantry in experience and outlook.

117. On "specialists," see Kendall E. Bailes, *Technology and Society Under Lenin and Stalin* (Princeton: Princeton University Press, 1978), p. 49. See also Cohen, *Bukharin and the Bolshevik Revolution*, p. 100.

118. Cited in Joravsky, "Cultural Revolution," p. 94.

119. Mervyn Matthews, *Education in the Soviet Union* (London: Allen & Unwin, 1982), pp. 98–99.

120. Khrushchev, *Khrushchev Remembers*, p. 30.

121. N. Bukharin and E. Preobrazhensky, *The ABC of Communism* (Ann Arbor: University of Michigan Press, 1966), pp. 127, 109.

122. Ibid., pp. 132–34, 163–64.

123. Grigorienko, *Memoirs*, p. 16.

124. Cohen, *Bukharin and the Bolshevik Revolution*, p. 84.

125. For example, the seven-volume series *Ten Years of the USSR's Capitalist Encirclement*, compiled at the Communist Academy, contained much important historical detail, even as its central thrust remained highly one-sided and propagandistic. See E. Pashukanis, M. Spektator, *Desiat' let kapitalisticheskogo okruzheniia SSSR. seriia v semi knigakh* (Moscow: Izdatel'stvo Kommunisticheskoi Akademii, 1928). On research at the Institute of Red Professors, see Gukovskii, "Kak ia stal istorikom."

126. Cohen, *Bukharin and the Bolshevik Revolution*, p. 219.

127. Michael S. Fox, "Political Culture, Purges, and Proletarianization at the Institute of Red Professors, 1921–1929," *Russian Review* 52, no. 1 (1993): 36, 39.

128. See "Foundations of Leninism" in Joseph Stalin, *Problems of Leninism* (Moscow: Foreign Languages Publishing, 1953), pp. 15–112. Of all the post-1924 syntheses of Leninism, "Stalin's work had the greatest success." See Tucker, *Stalin as Revolutionary*, pp. 315–16.

129. Barmine, *One Who Survived*, pp. 85–86.

130. The *vydvizhentsy*, literally "those moving up" rapidly in the Party.

131. In 1923, Stalin argued that "the wolves of imperialism who encircle us are not dozing. There is not a moment when our enemies do not try to seize hold of every little crack in order to slip through and harm us." Cited in Hough, *Russia and the West*, p. 56.

132. Michal Reiman, *The Birth of Stalinism: The USSR on the Eve of the "Second Revolution"* (Bloomington: Indiana University Press, 1987), p. 21.

133. Rykov and Voroshilov as cited in ibid, p. 157.

134. Evgeny Gnedin, *Vykhod iz labirinta* (New York: Chalidze, 1982), p. 59.

135. Ibid., p. 60. In June, Foreign Commissar Georgy Chicherin told the Politburo that it was distorting the situation and that there was "no immediate danger of war." Reiman, *Birth of Stalinism*, pp. 15–16.

136. Barmine, *One Who Survived*, pp. 130–31. A skeptical view of NEP's long-term possibilities, even absent the manipulation of foreign threats, is Shelia Fitzpatrick, "Cultural Revolution as Class War," in Fitzpatrick, ed., *Cultural Revolution in Russia, 1928–1931* (Bloomington: Indiana University Press, 1978), pp. 18–19.

137. "Each side supported their arguments by exaggerating the foreign threat or by accusing the other of incorrectly assessing the international situation." Gnedin, *Vykhod iz labirinta*, p. 59.

138. Tucker, *Stalin as Revolutionary*, pp. 385–86.

139. Barmine, *One Who Survived*, p. 163.

140. Tucker, *Stalin as Revolutionary*, p. 388. See also Lewin, *Making of the Soviet System*, p. 274.

141. Barmine, *One Who Survived*, pp. 164, 168–69.

142. Khrushchev, *Khrushchev Remembers*, p. 39.

143. Ibid., p. 37.

144. See Medvedev, *Soviet Science*, chapter 3.

145. Respectively, M. Lewin, "Society, State, and Ideology During the First Five-Year Plan," and David Joravsky, "The Construction of the Stalinist Psyche," both in Fitzpatrick, ed., *Cultural Revolution in Russia*, pp. 68–69, 108.

146. Clark, "Changing Historical Paradigms in Soviet Literature," p. 297.

147. I. V. Stalin, "O zadachakh khoziaistvennikov (rech' 4 fevraliia 1931 g.)," in Stalin, *Sochineniia* vol. 13 (Moscow: Izdatel'stvo Politicheskoi Literatury, 1951), p. 38.

148. Rittersporn, "Omnipresent Conspiracy," p. 100.

149. Ibid., p. 115. On the "frenzy," see Joravsky, "The Construction of the Stalinist Psyche," pp. 108–9.

150. Stephen Kotkin, "Coercion and Identity: Workers' Lives in Stalin's Showcase City," in Lewis H. Siegelbaum and Ronald Grigor Suny, eds., *Making Workers Soviet: Power, Class, and Identity* (Ithaca: Cornell University Press, 1994), pp. 279–80.

151. Rittersporn, "Omnipresent Conspiracy," p. 109.

152. Ibid., p. 115. On the indoctrination of elites and intellectuals, a classic remains Jacques Ellul, *Propaganda: The Formation of Men's Attitudes* (New York: Knopf, 1965).

153. Tucker, *Stalin in Power*, p. 549. Rittersporn judges that "everything points to the assumption that Soviet citizens of the epoch were inclined to lend credit to the regime's propaganda about the subversive activities of plotters and foreign agents." See "Omnipresent Conspiracy," p. 100.

154. Steve Smith, "Russian Workers and the Politics of Social Identity," *Russian Review* 56, no. 1 (1997), p. 6.

155. See Eugenia S. Ginzburg, *Journey Into the Whirlwind* (New York: Harcourt Brace Jovanovich, 1967).

156. *History of the Communist Party of the Soviet Union (Bolshevik) Short Course* (Moscow: Foreign Languages Publishing, 1945).

157. A. S. Cherniaev, *Moia zhizn' i moe vremia* (Moscow: Mezhdunarodnye Otnosheniia, 1995), p. 74.

158. Konst. Simonov, *Glazami cheloveka moego pokoleniia. Razmyshleniia o I. V. Staline* (Moscow: Novosti, 1990), pp. 37–38; also Aleksei Adzhubei, *Te desiat' let* (Moscow: Sovetskaia Rossiia, 1989); E. A. Evtushenko, *Avtobiografiia* (London: Flegon Press, 1964); Raisa Orlova, *Memoirs* (New York: Random House, 1983); Lev Navrozov, "Kak videlsia Stalin sovetskomu bol'shinstvu," *Izvestiia*, 2 July 1992.

159. Raymond A. Bauer, Alex Inkeles, and Clyde Kluckhohn, *How the Soviet System Works* (Cambridge: Harvard University Press, 1959), pp. 124–25, 133. These are the findings of the Harvard Project on the Soviet Social System, a survey of Soviet wartime refugees and emigrés.

160. Khrushchev, *Khrushchev Remembers*, p. 79.

161. Typical was Andrei Gromko, a peasant-born, Stalin-trained agronomist transferred to diplomatic service during the terror; see A. A. Gromyko, *Pamiatnoe* (Moscow: Politizdat, 1990), vol. 1. On the breadth and diversity of the NEP-era diplomats, see Gnedin, *Vykhod iz labirinta*, pp. 33–35; Gnedin, *Katastrofa i vtoroe rozhdenide. Memuarnye zapiski* (Amsterdam: Fond imeni Gertsena, 1977), pp. 17, 50–61, 89–91.

162. N. Valentinov, *Vstrechi s Leninym* (New York, n.d.), p. 50.

163. G. P. Fedotov, "Russia and Freedom," *Review of Politics* 8, no. 1 (1946), p. 34.

164. Byrnes, "Attitudes Toward the West," p. 131.

165. See Cohen, *Bukharin and the Bolshevik Revolution*, pp. 360–63.

166. See the case of *Mission to Moscow*, whose pro-Stalin line was partly undermined by its glimpses of U.S. freedoms and prosperity, as discussed in Hough, *Russia and the West*, p. 272.

167. "O lend-lize 50 let spustia," *Izvestiia*, 6 April 1992.

168. "Everywhere I saw full granaries, well-fed cows, horses and other animals, fine brick houses." See Mikhail Semiryaga, "The Russians in Berlin, 1945," *International Affairs* (Moscow) no. 11 (1994): 99.

169. E. S. Seniavskaia, *Frontovoe pokolonie. 1941–1945. Istoriko-psikhologicheskoe issledovanie* (Moscow: Institut Rossiiskoi Istorii, 1995), p. 164.

170. Simonov, *Glazami cheloveka moego pokoleniia*, pp. 91–92.

171. Aleksandr M. Nekrich, "The Socio-Political Effects of Khrushchev: His Impact on Soviet Intellectual Life," in R. F. Miller and F. Fehrer, eds., *Khrushchev and the Communist World* (London: Croom Helm, 1984), p. 85.

172. Seniavskaia, *Frontovoe pokolenie*, pp. 91–92.

173. "Podslushali i rasstreliali . . . " *Izvestiia*, 16 July 1992.

174. Aleksandr N. Iakovlev, *Po moshcham i elei* (Moscow: Izdatel'stvo "Evraziia," 1995), pp. 135–56.

175. "Prisoners of War," *Moscow News* no. 19 (1990): 8–9.

176. Kopelev, *Ease My Sorrows* (New York: Random House, 1983), p. 14.

177. Orlova, *Memoirs*, p. 223. See also the many letters, memoirs, Party committee transcripts, and other sources cited in E. Iu. Zubkova, *Obshchestvo i reformy. 1945–1964* (Moscow: Rossiia Molodaia, 1993).

178. S. F. Akhromeev and G. M. Kornienko, *Glazami marshala i diplomata. Kriticheskii vzgliad na vneshniuiu politiku SSSR do i posle 1985 goda* (Moscow: Mezhdunarodnye Otnosheniia, 1992), p. 62. See also Cherniaev, *Moia zhizn' i moe vremia*, p. 149.

179. Cited in Robert G. Kaiser, *Cold Winter, Cold War* (New York: Stein & Day, 1974), pp. 12–13.

180. Iu. S. Aksenov, "Poslevoennyi Stalinizm: udar po intelligentsii," *Kentavr* 1, no. 1 (1991) 80–89.

181. Evgeny Dobrenko, "The Literature of the Zhdanov Era: Mentality, Mythology, Lexicon," in Lahusen, ed., *Late Soviet Culture*, p. 133.

182. Cited in ibid., pp. 131–32.

183. See the discussion in Hough, *Russia and the West*, p. 60.

184. Wohlforth, *Elusive Balance*, chapter 4.

185. Robert C. Tucker, *The Soviet Poltical Mind*, (New York: Norton, 1971), p. 228.

186. Dobrenko, "The Literature of the Zhdanov Era," p. 132. See also M. Gefter, "Sud'ba Khrushcheva: istoriia odnogo neusvoennogo uroka," *Oktiabr'* no. 1 (1989): 176.

187. Zubkova, *Obshchestvo i reformy*, p. 88.

188. From an article in *Literaturnaia Gazeta* of 1949, cited in Klaus Mehnert, *Stalin Versus Marx: The Stalinist Historical Doctrine* (London: Allen & Unwin, 1952), p. 64. Mehnert's classic offers a striking picture of the ascendance of extreme Russocentrism in postwar philosophy and historiography.

189. Medvedev, *Soviet Science*, pp. 42–57.

190. Aksenov, "Poslevoennyi Stalinizm," p. 85.

191. Joseph Stalin, *Economic Problems of Socialism in the USSR* (New York: International, 1952), p. 30.

192. Georgy Arbatov, *The System* (New York: Times Books, 1992), p. 292. Arbatov, the son of a trade official, spent several childhood years in Western Europe. Rigid Stalinist thinking is seen even among those, such as diplomats, who had the benefit of prolonged residence abroad; see N. V.

Novikov, *Vospominaniia diplomata. Zapiski 1938–1947* (Moscow: Politizdat, 1989).

193. Andrei Sakharov, *Memoirs* (New York: Vintage, 1992), pp. 113–14, 116.

194. Zubkova, *Obshchestvo i reformy*, p. 68.

195. Ibid., p. 91.

196. Ibid., p. 43.

2. Leaders, Society, and Intellectuals During the Thaw

1. For this view, and the links between domestic and international politics, see Alexander Yanov, "In the Grip of the Adversarial Paradigm: The Case of Nikita Sergeevich Khrushchev in Retrospect," in Robert O. Crummey, ed., *Reform in Russia and the USSR* (Urbana: University of Illinois Press, 1989), pp. 156–81.

2. On Khrushchev-era foreign policy, and the persistence of the "revolutionary-imperial paradigm" among the post-Stalin leadership, see Zubok and Pleshakov, *Inside the Kremlin's Cold War*.

3. Roger D. Markwick, "Catalyst of Historiography, Marxism, and Dissidence: The Sector of Methodology of the Institute of History, Soviet Academy of Sciences, 1964–68," *Europe-Asia Studies* 46, no. 4 (1994): 580.

4. Nikita Khrushchev, *Khrushchev Remembers: The Glasnost Tapes* (Boston: Little, Brown, 1990), p. 99.

5. Ibid., p. 100.

6. Ibid.

7. On this background, see Khrushchev's own memoirs and those of close observers such as his son-in-law Adzhubei, *Te desiat' let*, and Central Committee consultant Fedor Burlatskii, *Vozhdi i sovetniki. O Khrushcheve, Andropove i ne tol'ko o nikh* (Moscow: Politizdat, 1990).

8. This was the judgment of Nikolai Yegorychev, the Party boss in Moscow during the thaw, upon reviewing Khrushchev's late-1930s tenure in the same post. See "Beseda s Egorychevym N. G.," in *Neizvestnaia Rossiia XX Vek* (Moscow: Istoricheskoe Nasledie, 1992), pp. 294–95.

9. The brief memoir of Nina Khrushcheva appears in Adzhubei, *Te desiat' let*, pp. 39–46 (citation from p. 45).

10. On Vyshinsky, see Arkady Vaksberg, *Stalin's Prosecutor: The Life of Andrei Vyshinsky* (New York: Grove Weidenfeld, 1990).

11. "Relative improvement" is the characterization of Joseph L. Nogee and Robert H. Donaldson, *Soviet Foreign Policy Since World War II*, 3rd ed. (New York: Macmillan, 1988), p. 106.

12. Khrushchev, *Glasnost Tapes*, p. 69.

13. F. Chuiev, *Sto sorok besed s Molotovym* (Moscow: Terra, 1991), pp. 14, 86. Molotov even dreamed of regaining Alaska, though "the time for that job hasn't come yet" (p. 100). He also proudly accepted the characterization of his "salami tactics" for slicing off Europe in pieces: "We haven't come up with a better policy yet—and it so happens that it tastes pretty good" (p. 104).

14. Ibid., pp. 90, 95.

15. Khrushchev, *Glasnost Tapes*, p. 87.

16. Khrushchev, *Khrushchev Remembers*, p. 343.

17. E. Iu. Zubkova, "Lidery i sud'by: 'posadnik' Georgiia Mal'enkova," *Polis* no. 5 (1991): 181–88. Malenkov had already broached a reappraisal of foreign policy priorities in 1953; on his motives and subsequent fate, see Zubok and Pleshakov, *Inside the Kremlin's Cold War*, pp. 163–69.

18. In addition to the sources cited below, see also Sergei Khrushchev, *Khrushchev on Khrushchev* (Boston: Little, Brown, 1990); Arkady Shevchenko, *Breaking with Moscow* (New York: Knopf, 1985); and an interview with Vladimir Semichastny, Komsomol first secretary (1958–59) and KGB director (1961–67), "Ia by spravilsia s liuboi rabotoi," *Ogoniok* no. 25 (1989): 24–26.

19. Khrushchev said that his was "the working man's Cambridge." Burlatskii, *Vozhdi i sovetniki*, pp. 62–63.

20. Khrushchev, *Glasnost Tapes*, pp. 79–80; Khrushchev, *Khrushchev Remembers*, p. 375.

21. Khrushchev, *Khrushchev Remembers*, pp. 392, 400. Adzhubei's account of a 1955 trip of Soviet journalists to the U.S.—the first such visit in a decade—parallels the international debut of Soviet leaders; he recalls a predeparture meeting with Molotov, for example, who warned them of such dangers as Coca-Cola, "the embodiment of American imperialism." Adzhubei, *Te desiat' let*, p. 120.

22. Khrushchev, *Glasnost Tapes*, p. 80.

23. The "cognitive dissonance" of the new formulation was later described by the perestroika-era foreign minister Eduard Shevardnadze: "I honestly cannot understand how to get closer to someone while at the same time conducting an implacable struggle against him." Eduard Shevardnadze, *Moi vybor* (Moscow: Novosti, 1991), p. 152.

24. Adzhubei, *Te desiat' let*, pp. 152–53. Khrushchev saw the hand of Allen Dulles and an effort to effect the policy of "rollback." See Zubok and Pleshakov, *Inside the Kremlin's Cold War*, pp. 186–87.

25. Veljko Micunovic, *Moscow Diary* (London: Chatto & Windus, 1980), p. 127.

26. See, respectively, Khrushchev, *Khrushchev Remembers*, p. 428, and Khrushchev, *Glasnost Tapes*, p. 125.

27. The trauma of 1956, and its enduring impact on the Kremlin, was great. As the Prague Spring unfolded in 1968, KGB chief (and future general secretary) Yuri Andropov warned where it could lead by recalling Budapest: "He compared Hungary to a fine Arabian mare—while you admire her, she can kick out your teeth." Valery Musatov, *New Times* (Moscow) no. 16 (1992): 38. As ambassador to Hungary in 1956, Andropov had come—literally—under fire and thereafter suffered from what intimates termed a "Hungarian complex," deep fear at what could result from any relaxation of Soviet control in Eastern Europe. G. A. Arbatov, *Zatianuvsheesia vyzdorovlenie (1953–1985 gg.) Svidetel'stvo sovremennika* (Moscow: Mezhdunarodnye Otnosheniia, 1991), p. 310.

28. Khrushchev, *Khrushchev Remembers: The Last Testament*. Boston: Little, Brown, 1974. pp. 369, 373. Maxim Gorky's *The City of the Yellow Devil* and Ilf and Petrov's *One-Storied America* were satirical but typically harsh and distorted portrayals of capitalism.

29. Sergei Khrushchev, *Khrushchev on Khrushchev*, p. 24.

30. Adzhubei, *Te desiat' let*, p. 175.

31. Ibid., p. 177.

32. Sergei Khrushchev, *Khrushchev on Khrushchev*, p. 26.

33. Zubok and Pleshakov, *Inside the Kremlin's Cold War*, pp. 206, 208.

34. N. S. Leonov, *Likholet'e. Sekretnye missii* (Moscow: Mezhdunarodnye Otnosheniia, 1995), p. 55.

35. Burlatskii, *Vozhdi i sovetniki*, p. 241.

36. See the recollections of Alexander Bovin in *Izvestiia*, 8 February 1989, and Vadim Zagladin in *N. S. Khrushchev. 1894–1971* (Moscow: Rossiiskii Gosudarstvennyi Gumanitarnyi Universitet, 1994), pp. 86–88.

37. Zubok and Pleshakov, *Inside the Kremlin's Cold War*, p. 229.

38. Burlatskii, *Vozhdi i sovetniki*, p. 241.

39. *Izvestiia*, 8 February 1989 (italics added).

40. Shevchenko, *Breaking with Moscow*, p. 93.

41. Arbatov, *Zatianuvsheesia vyzdorovlenie*, p. 187.

42. Vasily Kuznetsov, then deputy foreign minister, said that during the crisis "we were so terrified that we shat in our pants." *Lektsiia G. M. Kornienko o dogovore po PRO 1972 g.*, 17 November 1989 [unpublished transcript], p. 5. On the impact of the first large-scale purchases of U.S. grain necessitated by the "food crisis" of 1963, see Adzhubei, *Te desiat' let*, p. 287.

43. Arbatov, *Zatianuvsheesia vyzdorovlenie*, pp. 112–13.

44. Burlatskii, *Vozhdi i sovetniki*, pp. 284–85.

45. Ibid., pp. 316–18.

46. *Izvestiia*, 8 February 1989.

47. Cited in Cohen, *Rethinking the Soviet Experience*, p. 111.

48. Zubkova, *Obshchestvo i reformy*, p. 158.

49. Vladimir Shlapentokh, *Public and Private Life of the Soviet People* (New York: Oxford University Press, 1989), p. 149. *Internatsional'naia Literatura*, an earlier journal, was closed by Stalin in 1943 because "there was no need to spread foreign ideas at all." Orlova, *Memoirs*, p. 114.

50. Shlapentokh, *Public and Private*, p. 143; see also pp. 149–50 on reading/borrowing patterns in regional Soviet libraries. The specialized foreign-affairs journal *Mezhdunarodnaia Zhizn'* (International life) was also begun in 1954 and was quite lively and original over the years 1956 to 1966.

51. Orlova, *Memoirs*, p. 226.

52. *Education in the USSR* (New York: U.S. Department of Health, Education, and Welfare, 1957), p. 74. See also Matthews, *Education in the Soviet Union*, p. 28.

53. Yale Richmond, *U.S.-Soviet Cultural Exchanges, 1958–1986: Who Wins?* (Boulder, CO: Westview Press, 1987), pp. 26–28, 35–41, 71–72. See also Robert F. Byrnes, *Soviet-American Academic Exchanges, 1958–1975* (Bloomington: Indiana University Press, 1976), p. 58.

54. Byrnes, *Academic Exchanges*, pp. 60–61.

55. *United Nations Statistical Yearbook* (New York: United Nations, 1956, 1965, 1967).

56. This was the characterization of former Czech exchange student Zdenek Mlynar, interview in *L'Unita*, cited in *FBIS-SOV*, 9 April 1985.

57. Vladimir Bukovskii, *To Build a Castle: My Life as a Dissenter* (Washington, DC: Ethics and Public Policy Center, 1977), p. 139.

58. Lewin, *Gorbachev Phenomenon*, pp. 32–43.

59. Shlapentokh, *Public and Private*, pp. 140–43; Adzhubei, *Te desiat' let*, p. 200.

60. On the literary explosion, and on central journals including *Druzhba Narodov, Iunost', Moskva, Teatr', Voprosy Literatury* and *Inostrannaia Literatura*, as well as regional ones such as *Neva, Sever, Don, Pod"em, Volga* and *Ural*, see Sergei Chuprinin, "Nastaiushchee nastoiashchee, ili razmyshlenie u paradnogo pod"iezda," *Ogoniok* no. 42 (1987): 9–11.

61. S. Frederick Starr, "New Communications Technologies and Civil Society," in Loren R. Graham, ed., *Science and the Soviet Social Order* (Cambridge: Harvard University Press, 1990), pp. 19–50.

62. Ibid., pp. 33–34.

63. Ludmilla Alexeyeva, *U.S. Broadcasting to the Soviet Union* (New York: U.S. Helsinki Watch Committee, 1986), p. 9; Alex Inkeles, *Social Change in Soviet Russia* (Cambridge: Harvard University Press, 1968), pp. 354–55, 462.

64. Starr, "New Communications Technologies," pp. 37–38; Inkeles, *Social Change*, p. 344. From only one million privately-owned shortwave radios in 1947, and four million in the late 1950s, by the late 1960s there were nearly 30 million by some estimates.

65. Bukovskii, *To Build a Castle*, p. 354.

66. Z. L. Serebriakova, in *N. S. Khrushchev. 1894–1971*, p. 54.

67. Kopelev, *Ease My Sorrows*, pp. 106–24.

68. Simonov, *Glazami cheloveka moego pokoleniia*, passim; see also Bauer, Inkeles, and Kluckhohn, *How the Soviet System Works*, chapters 12–14, 19–20.

69. E. Mal'tsev, "Ne izmeniaia sebe," *Literaturnaia Gazeta*, 18 February 1987, p. 8; Orlova, *Memoirs*, p. 222.

70. Tatyana Zaslavskaya, *The Second Socialist Revolution: An Alternative Soviet Strategy* (London: Tauris, 1990), p. 44.

71. B. A. Grushin, V. V. Chikin, *Ispoved' pokoleniia* (Moscow: Molodaia Gvardia, 1962), pp. 116–28, 150–52. See also Arbatov, *Zatianuvsheesia vyzdorovlenie*, pp. 73–74; Adzhubei, *Te desiat' let*, pp. 164, 240.

72. Aron Katsenelinboigin, *The Soviet Union: Empire, Nation, and System* (New Brunswick, NJ: Transactions, 1990), p. 333; see also Shevchenko, *Breaking with Moscow*, p. 80.

73. Ludmilla Alexeyeva and Paul Goldberg, *The Thaw Generation: Coming of Age in the Post-Stalin Era* (Boston: Little, Brown, 1990), p. 113.

74. Egor Gaidar, *Dni porazhenii i pobed* (Moscow: Vagrius, 1996), pp. 15–17.

75. Nekrich, *Forsake Fear: Memoirs of an Historian* (Boston: Unwin Hyman, 1991), p. 78.

76. Orlova, *Memoirs*, p. 227.

77. With the obvious exception of the millions of camp inmates who were released and rehabilitated.

78. For veterans and future Gorbachev advisers Alexander Yakovlev, Georgy Shakhnazarov, Georgy Arbatov, and Anatoly Chernyaev, the war led to insights into society's grotesque militarization, the nature of Soviet imperialism, and aspects of Western life: Aleksandr Iakovlev, *Muki prochteniia bytiia. Perestroika: nadezhdy i real'nosti* (Moscow: Novosti, 1991) p. 28; Georgii Shakhnazarov, "Vo mnogom poteriannaia zhizn'," *Sobesednik* no. 11, 1992, p. 5; Arbatov, *Zatianuvsheesia vyzdorovlenie*, p. 369; Cherniaev, *Moia zhizn' i moe vremia*, chapters 4–5.

79. Katsenelinboigin, *Empire, Nation, and System*, p. 107.

80. Mikhail Nenashev, *Zalozhnik vremeni: Zametki. Razmyshleniia. Svidetel'stva* (Moscow: Progress-Kul'tura, 1993), p. 32.

81. Nekrich, "The Socio-Political Effects of Khrushchev," p. 90.

82. Iakovlev, *Muki prochteniia bytiia*, p. 30.

83. Orlova, *Memoirs*, pp. 200–208, 239–40; also Alexeyeva and Goldberg, *Thaw Generation*, pp. 70–77.

84. Ibid., p. 72.

85. V. Pomerantsev, "Ob iskrennosti v literature," *Novy Mir* no. 12, 1953, pp. 218–45.

86. Il'ia Erenburg, "Ottepel'," *Znamia* no. 5 (1954): 14–87.

87. R. M. Gorbacheva, *Ia nadieius'* (Moscow: Novosti, 1991), p. 75.

88. V. I. Korovinkov, "Nachalo i pervyi pogrom," *Voprosy Filosofii* no. 2 (1990): 65–67; Zubkova, *Obshchestvo i reformy*, pp. 137–45.

89. N. N. Pokrovskii, "V prostranstve i vremeni," introduction to Natan Eidel'man, *"Revoliutsiia sverkhu" v Rossii* (Moscow: Kniga, 1989), pp. 3–5; interview with Yevgeny Velikhov, "Chernobyl Remains on Our Mind," in Stephen F. Cohen and Katrina vanden Heuvel, *Voices of Glasnost: Interviews With Gorbachev's Reformers* (New York: Norton, 1989), p. 157.

90. Gorbacheva, *Ia nadieius'*, p. 77. On Western sources, see Korovinkov, "Nachalo i pervyi pogrom," p. 65; see also the recollections of philosophy student Ivan Frolov in Hough, *Russia and the West*, p. 30.

91. Adzhubei, *Te desiat' let*, p. 52; Zubkova, *Obshchestvo i reformy*, pp. 138–39.

92. On young Mikhail Gorbachev's interest in the debates of the 1920s, see Tatyana Zaslavskaya, "Socialism with a Human Face," in Cohen and vanden Heuvel, *Voices of Glasnost*, p. 119. See also the recollections of his Law Department classmate Zdenek Mlynar, then a Czech exchange student at MGU and later a leader of the Prague Spring reforms, in *FBIS-SOV*, 9 April 1985.

93. Cherniaev, *Moia zhizn' i moe vremia*, pp. 201–11. See also the interviews with Nikolai Shmelev and Yuri Afanasyev in Cohen and vanden Heuvel, *Voices of Glasnost*, pp. 98, 141; Shevchenko, *Breaking With Moscow*, pp. 71–73. Arbatov, like Shevchenko a postwar graduate of the Moscow State Institute of International Relations, recalled teachers who were "the best of what was left of a brilliant galaxy of Russian scholars of the old school." See Artbatov, *The System*, p. 33.

94. Merab Mamardashvili, *Kak ia ponimaiu filosofiiu* (Moscow: Progress, 1990), p. 35. Mamardashvili and Raisa Gorbacheva were classmates in MGU's philosophy faculty; Gorbacheva, *Ia nadieius'*, p. 66. "Coming from provincial Southern Russia, Mikhail and Raisa . . . were drawn to Moscow's intelligentsia and Bohemian circles." Andrei Grachev, *Kremlevskaia khronika* (Moscow: EKSMO, 1994) p. 156.

95. Mamardashvili, *Kak ia ponimaiu filosofiiu*, p. 35. For similar recollections of Leningrad State University, see Nenashev, *Zalozhnik vremeni*, pp. 32–33.

96. See for example "Recriminations: Party Writers Discuss the Past," meeting of the Soviet Writers' Union, March 1956, in Stephen F. Cohen, ed., *An End to Silence: Uncensored Opinion in the Soviet Union* (New York: Norton, 1982), pp. 105–14.

97. Orlova, *Memoirs*, p. 196.

98. Alexeyeva and Goldberg, *Thaw Generation*, pp. 85–86.

99. Dina R. Spechler, *Permitted Dissent in the USSR* (New York: Praeger, 1982), pp. 65–66. The work under discussion was Vladimir Dudintsev's *Not by Bread Alone*.

100. Nekrich, "The Socio-Political Effects of Khrushchev," p. 89; Zubkova, *Obshchestvo i reformy*, p. 152.

101. Boris Kagarlitsky, *The Thinking Reed: Intellectuals and the Soviet State from 1917 to the Present* (London: Verso, 1988), p. 145; Zubkova, *Obshchestvo i reformy*, p. 140. See also David Burg, "Observations on Soviet University Students," in Richard Pipes, ed., *The Russian Intelligentsia* (New York: Columbia University Press, 1961), p. 90.

102. Including Anatoly Kovalev, a young Soviet diplomat in Hungary, whose liberalism (and literary flair) would later recommend him to Gorbachev. In the aftermath of the invasion, he penned the following: "Everyone is seething with rebellion, here in Budapest of November 1956. A five year-old girl hurls snow at a tank—she is a daughter of her nation." From "Politik poroi obiazan skhodit' s tribuny pod skrip svoikh botinok," *Novaia Gazeta*, 22 April 1996. See also A. G. Kovalev, *Azbuka diplomatii*, revised and expanded ed. (Moscow: Interpraks, 1993).

103. Kagarlitsky, *Thinking Reed*, pp. 145–47; see also various documents cited in George Saunders, ed., *Samizdat: Voices of the Soviet Opposition* (New York: Monad Press , 1974), pp. 235–45.

104. Zubkova, *Obshchestvo i reformy*, p. 153. The Hungarian rebellion of 1848, like those of the Poles in 1830–31 and 1863, was crushed by tsarist troops.

105. Bukovskii, *To Build a Castle*, p. 143.

106. Alexeyeva and Goldberg, *Thaw Generation*, pp. 83–84.

107. Sakharov, *Memoirs*, pp. 123, 127.

108. P. L. Kapitsa, *Pis'ma o nauke* (Moscow: Moskovskii Rabochii, 1989), pp. 304–19, 324–28, 342–43.

109. For various accounts of these influential meetings, see Vladimir Shlapentokh, *Soviet Intellectuals and Political Power: The Post-Stalin Era* (London: Tauris, 1990), p. 112; Medvedev, *Soviet Science*, pp. 130–34; Adzhubei, *Te desiat' let*, pp. 35–36.

110. Yuri Senokosov (author's interview: Moscow, 30 March 1990). Detail on the activities of historian Nekrich, philosopher Mamardashvili, and many others follows in chapter 3.

111. Shlapentokh, *Soviet Intellectuals*, p. 119. On the appearances of Alexander Galich, folk singer and social critic, at the Novosibirsk Institute, see Alexeyeva and Goldberg, *Thaw Generation*, p. 239.

112. Cited in Jerry Hough, "The Evolution in the Soviet World View," *World Politics* 32, no. 4 (1980): 512. Mikoyan's criticism of Stalin's catechismal *Economic Problems of Socialism in the USSR* made a great impression and, especially among younger scholars, began the swift erosion of many Stalinist dogmas; see Shevchenko, *Breaking with Moscow*, p. 74.

113. Georgy Arbatov, an early IMEMO researcher, in 1967 became the first director of the Institute of the USA, later expanded as the Institute of the USA and Canada (ISKAN).

114. This "international" journal, loosely managed by the Party's Central Committee, was officially established to replace the diktat of Stalin's defunct Cominform with a new organ reflecting the now-permitted diversity of international Communist and Socialist Parties.

115. Under the Department for Liaison with Ruling Communist and Workers' Parties, run by Yuri Andropov, one of two Central Committee "International" Departments. The other, headed by Boris Ponomarev, handled relations with Western (nonruling) Communist Parties and movements. A consultant group was soon created for this department, too. See Burlatskii, *Vozhdi i sovetnki*, p. 259.

116. By 1949, only foreign-policy sections of the dogmatic, oft-purged history institutes approximated centers for the study of international affairs, and the only regional institute was that of oriental affairs, which Mikoyan criticized in his 20th congress address as "still slumbering to this day."

117. On how this ignorance and ideological orthodoxy hampered rapprochement with Yugoslavia, see Khrushchev, *Khrushchev Remembers*, pp. 377–78.

118. Burlatskii, *Vozhdi i sovetniki*, p. 258.

119. Arbatov, *Zatianuvsheesia vyzdorovlenie*, p. 49.

120. Gennady Gerasimov (author's interview: Moscow, 22 December 1990).

121. Other Prague veterans included Vladimir Lukin, Gennady Gerasimov, and Yevgeny Ambartsumov, all prominent in the development of new thinking and examined in subsequent chapters.

122. Maria Pavlova-Silvanskaya (author's interview: Moscow, 16 May 1991). Frolov noted the personal ties cemented by this experience, that former staffers remained a close-knit fraternity whose members thereafter referred to each other as Praguers (*Prazhany*); see *Moskovskii Komsomol'ets*, 7 January 1990.

123. Gennady Gerasimov (author's interview: Moscow, 22 December 1990).

124. Cherniaev, *Moia zhizn' i moe vremia*, p. 230. Chernyaev also recalled that "a compliment from one of [the Europeans] was considered the highest praise" (p. 227).

125. Grachev, *Kremlevskaia khronika*, p. 61.

126. Rumyantsev, who would later play an instrumental role in founding other reformist institutes and also served briefly as editor of *Pravda*, was a strong anti-Stalinist who began his career helping manage the transition from War Communism's forced grain requisitioning to NEP's tax-in-kind. He recalled this experience, and the debates of the 1920s (including his study of authors such as Plekhanov, Kautsky, and Berdyaev), as most important in the development of his views (author's interview: Moscow, 8 May 1991).

127. Merab Mamardashvili (author's interview: Tbilisi, 17 April 1990).

128. Ivan Frolov, interview in *La Repubblica*, cited in *FBIS-SOV*, 19 April 1989, p. 83.

129. Merab Mamardashvili (author's interview: Tbilisi, 18 April 1990). Regarding Mamardashvili's erudition and popularity—in the context of Prague's social-personal freedoms that Moscow lacked—one former colleague recalled a ditty composed in the early 1960s: "*V molodosti my vse greshili, no bol'she vsekh—Mamardashvili*" (In our youth we sinned, one and all—but Mamardashvili, most of all).

130. Anatoly Chernyaev (author's interview: Princeton, 22 February 1993).

131. Arbatov called Prague a "prep school" for the Party apparatus; *Zatianuvsheesia vyzdorovlenie*, p. 36.

132. Burlatskii, *Vozhdi i sovetniki*, p. 257.

133. Arbatov, *The System*, pp. 85–86.

134. See interview with Alexander Bovin in Cohen and vanden Heuvel, *Voices of Glasnost*, p. 213.

135. Shevchenko, *Breaking with Moscow*, pp. 80–81. Further, "my job was to monitor the London negotiations [but] I had no access to the . . . cables . . . sent to the Ministry, and without them . . . it was impossible. I complained [and was] reminded of the rule that only first secretaries or above were permitted access to such information." (p. 83)

136. In just the first post-Stalin decade, diplomatic relations were established (or reestablished) with 57 states, including Austria, Denmark, Finland, Japan, Australia, Switzerland, and West Germany.

137. Georgy Kornienko (author's interview: Moscow, 1 March 1989).

138. Shevchenko, *Breaking with Moscow*, p. 71.

139. Noting the influence of official "classified" translations of Western books, journals, and news media, one former Soviet scholar referred to such literature as a kind of regime-sponsored samizdat that had unintended consequences similar to those of dissident literature; see Nekrich, *Forsake Fear*, p. 120.

140. Zaslavskaya, *The Second Socialist Revolution*, p. 44.

141. Vladislav M. Zubok, "Soviet Intelligence and the Cold War: The 'Small' Committee of Information, 1952–1953," *Cold War International History Project*, working paper no. 4, 1992, pp. 5–6, 15. This article examines the informational-analytical system that served Soviet foreign policy making from the late 1940s through the mid 1950s.

142. See Byrnes, *Academic Exchanges*, and Richmond, *Cultural Exchanges*, passim.

143. J. Rotblat, *Pugwash—the First Ten Years* (London: Heinemann, 1967).

144. Alumni of thaw-era exchanges include key Gorbachev adviser Alexander Yakovlev (Columbia University), publicist-diplomat Gennady Gerasimov (journalism exchange, Columbia and Princeton Universities), future arms negotiators Alexei Obukhev and Viktor Israelyan (Oxford and Cambridge Universities) and poet-editor Vitaly Korotich (UNESCO exchange, USA and Canada).

145. Vitaly Korotich, *Zal ozhidaniia* (New York: Liberty Publishing, 1991), pp. 59–61.

146. Viktor Kremenyuk, ISKAN deputy director (author's interview: Moscow, 19 December 1989).

147. Burlatskii, *Vozhdi i sovetniki*, p. 148. For similar recollections of Yugoslavia see Gaidar, *Dni porazhenii i pobed*, p. 18.

148. Zaslavskaya, "Socialism With a Human Face," in Cohen and van-den Heuvel, *Voices of Glasnost*, p. 116.

149. Stanislav Shatalin, " '500 dnei' i drugie dni moei zhizni," *Nezavisimaia Gazeta*, 31 March 1992.

150. Arbatov, *Zatianuvsheesia vyzdorovlenie*, pp. 73–74.

151. Defined to include all those with tertiary education, the intelligentsia numbered 10.7 million members in 1967, roughly double that of a decade earlier. See L. G. Churchward, *The Soviet Intelligentsia: An Essay on the Social Structure and Roles of Soviet Intellectuals During the 1960s* (London: Routledge, 1973), pp. 7–9; also I. E. Vorozheikin et al. eds., *Sovetskaia intelligentsia. Istoriia formirovaniia i rosta, 1917–1965* (Moscow: Mysl,' 1968).

152. Nekrich, *Forsake Fear*, p. 100.

153. And in so doing blinds itself to the rise of a broad intellectual current that would later play a vital role in political change. On interpretations

of the intelligentsia, and on thaw-era debates in particular as conceptual preparation for perestroika, see Markwick, "Catalyst of Historiography," pp. 579–96.

154. See Gefter's contribution to "O metodologicheskikh voprosakh istoricheskoi nauki," *Voprosy Istorii* no. 3 (1964): 47–48.

155. Grigorienko, *Memoirs*, pp. 334–39.

156. Arbatov reviewed English- and German-language political and economic works for limited-circulation translations; Orlova reviewed and translated French and English fiction. See Arbatov, *The System*, p. 34; Orlova, *Memoirs*, pp. 225–38.

157. On one such "salon" that included sociologist Boris Grushin, philosophers Merab Mamardashvili and Alexander Zinoviev, and Americanist Yuri Zamoshkin, see B. Grushin, "O liudakh, umevshikh zhit' pod vodoi," *Nezavisimaia Gazeta*, 31 October 1997. On another that included writer Daniil Granin, journalist Yegor Yakovlev, and Komsomol official Len Karpinsky, see Gaidar, *Dni porazhenii i pobed*, p. 18.

158. A former Central Committee staffer recalled that "in working on my dissertation, I was able to read still-forbidden works in the so-called *spetskhran* [special collection]—Berdyaev, Kropotkin, the diaries of Nicholas II, the memoirs of Miliukov, Gudkov, Denikin." See Nenashev, *Zalozhnik vremeni*, pp. 30–31.

159. Kopelev, *Ease My Sorrows*, p. 245.

160. Len Karpinsky, then a young Komsomol official, described "tense meetings with students" in Poland; see Cohen and vanden Heuvel, *Voices of Glasnost*, p. 287. Karpinsky later recalled that "we more or less understood that [unrest in Hungary and Poland] stemmed from domestic problems and was not really a matter [of Western] interference . . . but their rage at what they saw as pure Russian imperialism was extremely strong" (author's interview: Moscow, 11 June 1990).

161. On the *Hungarian Diary*, as well as her own experience in Poland, see Orlova, *Memoirs*, p. 240–44.

162. On the popularity of Gramsci, Lukacs, Sartre, and "non-dogmatic" Marxists see Kagarlitsky, *Thinking Reed*, p. 96.

163. The impact of East European scholarship on Soviet intellectuals is discussed in more detail in chapter 3. An account of one scholar's eye-opening experience in Poland—which ranged from broad archival access to second-hand bookstores openly selling such works as Orwell's *1984*—is Nekrich, *Forsake Fear*, pp. 87, 105–6, 123–35.

164. Cherniaev, *Moia zhizn' i moe vremia*, chapter 5. See also A. N. Iakovlev, *Gor'kaia chasha. Bol'shevizm i reformatsiia Rossii* (Iaroslavl': Verkhne-Volzhskoe Knizhnoe Izdatel'stvo, 1994), p. 10; Zubkova, *Obshchestvo i reformy*, chapters 2–3.

165. Andrei Amalrik, *Notes of a Revolutionary* (New York: Knopf, 1982), p. 26.

166. Grachev, *Kremlevskaia khronika*, p. 43.

167. Georgii Shakhnazarov, *Tsena svobody. Reformatsiia Gorbacheva glazami ego pomoshchnika* (Moscow: Rossika-Zevs, 1993), pp. 31–33. See also Burlatskii, *Vozhdi i sovetniki*, p. 254.

168. Gnedin's memoirs were among the thousands that flooded editorial offices in the mid 1960s. They were copied and shared widely in semi-legal fashion as manuscripts awaiting decision on publication—which few would see—but not yet banned, either. Many political and historical tracts circulated in this manner, early samizdat (self-published) works before the practice had the dissident connotations it would later acquire. On their circulation in the apparat, see Arbatov, *Zatianuvsheesia vyzdorovlenie*, pp. 20–21.

169. The long-time "open secret" of Medvedev's high-level patrons was revealed under perestroika; see his thanks to Shakhnazarov, Krasin, Delusin, and Burlatsky in Roy Medvedev, *Let History Judge*, revised and expanded ed. (New York: Columbia University Press, 1989), p. 19.

170. Grigorienko, *Memoirs*, p. 335.

171. Aganbegyan's 1965 report on "The Real State of the Economy" appears in Cohen, *End to Silence*, pp. 223–27; Abdurakhman Avtorkhanov's *Stalin and the Soviet Communist Party* (New York: Praeger, 1959), which circulated in the original Russian *Tekhnologiia Vlasti* (The technology of power), analyzed Stalin's rise with emphasis on the manipulation and exaggeration of foreign threats; senior Yugoslav Communist-turned-dissident Milovan Djilas's *New Class*, a critique of high-level corruption and bureaucratic degeneration, was widely read in liberal Moscow circles in the early 1960s.

172. Alexander Yakovlev, *The Fate of Marxism in Russia* (New Haven: Yale University Press, 1993), p. 111.

173. See the introduction to the symposium "Soviet Intelligentsia and Russian History," in *Survey* 19, no. 1 (1973): 2.

174. A notable example was Mamardashvili's "legendary" 1967 address on the role of the intelligentsia in contemporary society. See Merab Mamardashvili, "Medium ili vseobshchee chuvstvilishche?," *Literaturnaia Gazeta*, 17 July 1996.

3. Intellectuals and the World

1. K. M. Simonov, "O Sovetskoi khudozhestvennoi proze," *Vtoroi vsesoiuznyi s"ezd Sovetskikh piastel'ei* (Moscow: Sovetskii Pisatel,' 1956), p. 84; "Literaturnye zametki," *Novy Mir*, no. 12 (1956): 251.

2. See Dina Spechler, *Permitted Dissent*, pp. 39–40, 77–78. Credit is owed Spechler for attention to a number of publications as well as for various interpretative insights.

3. Erenburg, "Perechityvaia Chekhova," *Novy Mir*, nos. 5–6 (1959).

4. Spechler, *Permitted Dissent*, pp. 94–95.

5. Among various translations of Ehrenburg's *Liudy, gody, zhizn'* the above is cited from Ilya Ehrenburg, *Memoirs: 1921–1941* (Cleveland: World Publishing, 1963), p. 26.

6. Efim Dorosh, "Raigorod v fevrale," *Novy Mir*, no. 10 (1962): 20–21.

7. Viktor Nekrasov, "Pervoe znakomstvo," *Novy Mir*, no. 7 (1958): 152, 162–65; no. 8 (1958): 136.

8. On his "importance to millions of Soviet citizens who revered him for trying to sustain Russia's connection to European art and culture," see Joshua Rubinstein, *Tangled Loyalties: The Life and Times of Ilya Ehrenburg* (New York: Basic, 1996), chapters. 12–15 (citation from p. 2).

9. Ehrenburg, *Memoirs*, pp. 193–94.

10. V. Dudintsev, "Ne khlebom edinym," *Novy Mir*, nos. 8–10 (1956).

11. An even sharper commentary was Mikhail Romm's 1965 film *Ordinary Fascism*. Examining Nazi Germany, he used documentary scenes of militarism and mass rallies that any Soviet adult recognized as strongly reminiscent of Stalin's Russia. See Mira and Antonin J. Liehm, *The Most Important Art* (Berkeley: University of California Press, 1977), p. 315.

12. On these authors' "profound" impact see Evtushenko, *Avtobiografiia*, p. 73,

13. Mihajlo Mihajlov, *Moscow Summer* (New York: Farrar, Straus & Giroux, 1965), pp. 19–30, 87–88, 130 (citation from p. 168). Mihajlov, a Yugoslav specialist on Russian literature, accurately foresaw that "within the next two or three decades we shall probably witness a repetition of what occurred in the last century, a conflict between the new 'Slavophiles' and 'Westerners'" (pp. 154–55).

14. Simonov, *Glazami cheloveka moego pokoleniia*, pp. 84–93, 124. Kvas is a traditional Russian drink.

15. Ibid., pp. 149–57. After 1948, as polemics with Tito sharpened and xenophobia gripped Soviet cultural policy, Simonov's earlier pro-Yugoslav works were banned (as was Ehrenburg's *The Roads of Europe*).

16. On Tvardovsky and the "camp theme," see Vladimir Lakshin, *Solzhenitsyn, Tvardovsky, and Novy Mir* (Cambridge: Harvard University Press, 1980).

17. From "Tvardovsky's Satirical Romp through Purgatory" (translation of *Terkin na tom svete)* in *Current Digest of the Soviet Press* 15, no. 34 (1963): 24–25.

18. Ehrenburg, *Memoirs*, p. 79.

19. James Scanlan, *Marxism in the USSR* (Ithaca: Cornell University Press, 1985), p. 149.

20. Vladimir Smirnov, "M. K. Mamardashvili: Filosofiia soznaniia," *Kommunist* no. 8 (1991): 67. On the influence of Asmus, see N. V. Motroshilova, "Pamiati Professora," *Voprosy Filosofii* no. 5 (1988): 67–70, and Raisa Gorbacheva, *Ia nadeius'*, p. 74.

21. Mikhail Gorbachev recalled that study of the ethics of religious philosopher Vladimir Solovyev made a particularly strong impression; see Gorbachev, "Herman Phelger Lecture on the Rule of Law," *Stanford University Campus Report* no. 29, 13 May 1992. On MGU see also Mikhail Gorbachev and Zdenek Mlynar, *Dialog o perestroike, "Prazhskoi vesne" i o sotsializme* (unpublished MS), pp. 11–13.

22. Neli Motroshilova (author's interview: Moscow, 13 October 1990). Motroshilova studied at MGU in the mid 1950s, and worked from 1959 to 1989 at the Institute of Philosophy.

23. Nikolai Novikov, "Myslit' mozhno v kazhdoi tochki mira," *Izvestiia*, 25 November 1991.

24. F. T. Mikhailov, "Slovo ob Il'enkove," *Voprosy Filosofii*, no. 2 (1990): 57–58, 62–63; Korovnikov, "Nachalo i pervyi pogrom," pp. 68–69.

25. Smirnov, "Filosofiia soznaniia," pp. 66–67.

26. Rumyantsev, it will be recalled, edited the Prague journal *Problemy Mira i Sotsializma* in 1958–64. After a stint as editor of *Pravda* (1964–65) which was cut short because of his too-reformist views, he was transferred back to the Academy of Sciences, where he helped many of those fired find new positions and was also instrumental in establishing the Institute of the USA (1967), the Institute of Concrete Social Research (1968), and the Institute of Scientific Information on the Social Sciences (1969).

27. Korovnikov, "Nachalo i pervyi pogrom," p. 68.

28. Kagarlitsky, *Thinking Reed*, pp. 96, 145, 162, 305; see also Mihajlov, *Moscow Summer*, p. 23.

29. Alexeyeva and Goldberg, *Thaw Generation*, pp. 95, 236. On Marcuse, Lukacs, Garaudy, Erich Fromm, and C. Wright Mills, see also 1965–68 issues of Roy Medvedev's samizdat journal *Politicheskii Dnevnik* (Amsterdam: Alexander Herzen Foundation, 1972, 1975), issue nos. 9, 24, 31, 46, and 50.

30. One specialist on Italian Marxism, who had studied in Rome, wrote in the *Bulletin of Moscow University* in praise of parliamentary institutions and criticism of those who "underestimated bourgeois-democratic freedoms." See L. A. Nikitich, "Nekotorye voprosy sviazi borby za demokratiiu s borboi za sotsializm v trudakh Italianskikh Marksistov,"

Vestnik Moskovskogo Universiteta. Seriia VIII. Ekonomika, Filosofiia, no. 4 (1965): 57–66.

31. See especially Marcuse's *Soviet Marxism: A Critical Analysis* (New York: Vintage, 1961).

32. Evgeny Ambartsumov (author's interview: Moscow, 6 August 1991). See also Kagarlitsky, *Thinking Reed*, pp. 291–92.

33. Cited in Neil McInnes, "Havemann and the Dialectic," *Survey*, no. 62 (1967): 31.

34. Neli Motroshilova (author's interview: Moscow, 13 October 1990).

35. Shlapentokh, *Soviet Intellectuals*, pp. 71, 196; also Churchward, *The Soviet Intelligentsia*, pp. 57–58.

36. For example, the Polish sociologist Adam Schaff's 1965 book *Marxism and the Individual* drew on Sartre, Fromm, and even George Orwell to analyze socialism's failure to solve such problems as worker alienation and cultural emptiness; on Schaff, see Yakovlev, *Fate of Marxism in Russia*, p. 13. On the influence of Polish scholarship in general, see Vladimir Shlapentokh, *The Politics of Sociology in the Soviet Union* (Boulder, CO: Westview Press, 1987), pp. 16, 21, 38–39; regarding that of the Yugoslav *Praxis* group of humanistic Marxists, see S. F. Oduev, "Zametki o filosofskoi zhizni v Iugoslavii," *Voprosy Filsosfii*, no. 5 (1966): 157–61; also Scanlan, *Marxism in the USSR*, p. 173.

37. Yuri Zamoshkin recalled, "Such writings helped communicate ideas found in foreign scholarship—you'd just ignore the orthodox introduction and conclusion, and focus on the substance in between" (author's interview: Moscow, 15 February 1990). Zamoshkin, one of the less-known but most influential early new thinkers, authored many such "critical" reviews of Western thought as one of those "whose primary motive is to gain thereby an opportunity of studying and expounding it." Eugene Kamenka, "Philosophers in Moscow," *Survey*, no. 62 (1967): 20.

38. Louis Feuer, "Meeting the Philosophers," *Survey*, no. 51 (1964): 10–23; Mamardashvili, *Kak ia ponimaiu filosofiiu*, p. 57, 190–91. See also Mihajlov, *Moscow Summer*, pp. 23–30, 115, 151.

39. "It was really something back then. Six or seven hundred people would crowd the zoology auditorium at MGU to hear Merab [Mamardashvili] speak, and yet almost nobody outside the intelligentsia knew anything about it." Motroshilova (author's interview: Moscow, 13 October, 1990). On the "independent-minded, anti-Hegelian" arguments of Mamardashvili and Zinoviev at a 1958 Moscow conference, see Scanlan, *Marxism in the USSR*, p. 124. See also Iu. Davydov, *Trud i svoboda* (Moscow: Vysshaia Shkola, 1962), and M. Mamardashvili, *Formy i soderzhanie myshleniia* (Moscow: Vysshaia Shkola, 1968).

40. Valentina Polukhina, preface to Polukhina, Joe Andrew, and

Robert Reid, eds., *Literary Tradition and Practice in Russian Culture* (Amsterdam: Rodopi, 1993), p. ix. Regarding the semioticians' critique of Stalinism's "medieval" mindset, see Harriet Murav, "The Case Against Andrei Siniavskii: The Letter and the Law," *Russian Review* 53, no. 4 (1994): 552–53.

41. P. Kapitsa, "Teoriia, eksperiment, praktika," *Ekonomicheskaia Gazeta*, 26 March 1962; I. T. Frolov, M. K. Mamardashvili, "Soiuz nauki i demokratii," *Problemy Mira i Sotsializma*, no. 4 (1965): 47–55.

42. A. Bovin, "Nauka i mirovozzrenie," *Kommunist*, no. 5 (1960): 96–107. See also I. Frolov, *Genetika i dialektika* (Moscow: Nauka, 1968).

43. Scanlan, *Marxism in the USSR*, p. 207. See also the roundtable discussion "O metodologicheskikh voprosakh istoricheskoi nauki," in *Voprosy Istorii*, no. 3 (1964): 3–68.

44. M. Ia. Gefter, ibid., pp. 47–48. On his anti-isolationist theme from the 1960s on, see Gefter, *Iz tekh i etikh let* (Moscow: Progress, 1991), pp. 8–9, 67–85, 101–12, and passim. See also Len Karpinskii and Valerii Pisigin, *Zapovednik dlia dinozavrov. Stat'i poslednikh let* (Moscow: EPItsentr, 1996), pp. 72–78.

45. Kurt Marko, "History and the Historians," *Survey*, no. 56 (1965): 74–75. See also *Vsesoiuznoe soveshchanie istorikov. 18–21 dekabria 1962 g.* (Moscow: Nauka, 1964).

46. It did not require much imagination to see that the debate over tsarist imperialism was directly relevant to Stalin's foreign policy and the Sovietization of Eastern Europe. See also Nekrich, "The Socio-Political Effects of Khrushchev," p. 91. On Pokrovsky, see Marko, "History and the Historians," p. 78.

47. See Markwick, "Catalyst of Historiography," p. 579–96; Nekrich, *Forsake Fear*, p. 164.

48. In a 1965 paper at one of Gefter's seminars, A. L. Mongait exposed chauvinistic dogmas about "the unadulterated continuity of the Slav peoples," and in so doing suggested that "Soviet archaeologists, who . . . repudiated ideas of racial superiority advanced by Nazi scholars, were themselves unwittingly indulging in their own theory of Slav superiority." Markwick, "Catalyst of Historiography," pp. 583–84.

49. Iu. F. Kariakin, E. G. Plimak, *Zapretnaia mysl' obretaet svobodu* (Moscow: Nauka, 1966), pp. 77–139. Karyakin and Plimak examined non-Soviet interpretations ranging from *Vekhi* philosopher Berdyaev to Western historians Marc Raeff and Hans Rogger.

50. Amalrik, *Notes of a Revolutionary*, pp. xi–xii.

51. N. Ia. Eidel'man, *Tainye korrespondenty "Polarnoi zvezdy"* (Moscow: Mysl', 1966); Eidel'man, *Lunin* (Moscow: Molodaia Gvardiia, 1970). See also Pokrovskii, "V prostranstve i vremeni," pp. 6–7. For more

on both the liberals' and conservative-nationalists' use of history to debate contemporary politics, see Yitzhak M. Brudny, *Reinventing Russia: Russian Nationalism and the Soviet State, 1953–1991* (Cambridge: Harvard University Press, 1998), pp. 175–81.

52. On Eidelman's popularity, see Alexeyeva and Goldberg, *Thaw Generation*, pp. 242–43. Concerning his portrayal of Lunin the Decembrist, Westernizer, and "man of honor" as a model for contemporary Soviet intellectuals, see Mamardashvili, *Kak ia ponimaiu filosofiiu*, p. 193.

53. Published in *Novy Mir* in 1965, his translated memoirs appeared as Ivan Maisky, *Memoirs of a Soviet Ambassador: The War, 1939–1943* (New York: Scribner's, 1967). Maisky also intimated that Stalin had designs on Eastern Europe even during Russia's darkest hour, in December 1941 (p. 231).

54. Nekrich's book was published in English translation as Vladimir Petrov, *"June 22, 1941": Soviet Historians and the German Invasion* (Columbia: University of South Carolina Press, 1968).

55. Ibid., pp. 58–65, 138–39, 144–51, 174–81, 191–92, 197.

56. Ibid., p. 225.

57. One provincial youth who knew better was Mikhail Gorbachev. Zdenek Mlynar, the Czech exchange student who was his university classmate, recalled Gorbachev's open disgust at scenes of rural bounty presented in the highly popular film *The Kuban Cossacks*. See Mlynar in *FBIS-SOV*, 9 April 1985.

58. Khrushchev, *Khrushchev Remembers*, pp. 71–75, 228–44.

59. Dudintsev, "Ne khlebom edinym." See also Tikhon Zhuralev, "Kombainery," *Novy Mir*, no. 7 (1953); Sergei Zalygin, "Vesnoi nyneshnego goda," *Novy Mir*, no. 8 (1954); Vladimir Soloukhin, "Vladimirskie proselki," *Novy Mir*, no. 9 (1957).

60. Under Stalin, "the basic task of . . . economists was to consecrate the latest decisions of the party and its great leader as the height of wisdom. Economics became an integral part of ideology . . . required to fulfill, in essence, a priestly function." Katsenelinboigin, *Empire, Nation, and System*, p. 332.

61. Zaslavskaya, *Second Socialist Revolution*, p. 44

62. On the "great interest in Western economics," see Abel Aganbegyan, *Moving the Mountain* (London: Bantam, 1989), p. 128. On the publication in Russian of Paul Samuelson's *Economics*, see Arbatov, *Zatianuvsheesia vyzdorovlenie*, p. 73. On the impact of Samuelson and other Western works, see also Gaidar, *Dni porazhenii i pobed*, pp. 23–26.

63. Under Stalin, East-West comparisons were allowed only in raw output of such goods as steel and concrete. Economist M. Kabunin was

shot for revealing that Soviet agricultural productivity trailed that of the United States; see Katsenelinboigin, *Empire, Nation, and System*, pp. 392–93. Now, soon after Stalin's death, this "crime" was repeatedly committed by the Communist Party's first secretary.

64. Maria Pavlova-Silvanskaya (author's interview: Moscow, 16 May, 1991). Pavlova-Silvanskaya, who served in the mid 1960s on the staff of *Problemy Mira i Sotsializma* in Prague, joined Oleg Bogomolov's Institute of the Economy of the World Socialist System (IEMSS) soon after its creation, following the Prague Spring crackdown.

65. Teodor Shanin, "forward" to Zaslavskaya, *Second Socialist Revolution*, p. ix. On Vezhner's work, see also Moshe Lewin, *Political Undercurrents in Soviet Economic Debates* (Princeton: Princeton University Press, 1974), pp. 221–28.

66. The *zemstvos* were rural administrative bodies created after the emancipation of the serfs in 1861. Nemchinov's major early work was *The Development of Capitalism in Russia*. On Nemchinov and Novozhilov, see Aganbegyan, *Moving the Mountain*, pp. 129, 145–49 (citation from p. 148).

67. Ibid., p. 148. Others who returned from prison to play key roles in the revival of Soviet economics were Lev Mints, Albert Weinstein, Yakov Kvasha, and Viktor Krasovsky.

68. This was Kantorovich's *Ekonomicheskii raschet nailuchshego ispol'-zovannia resursov*, published in English as *The Best Use of Economic Resources* (Cambridge: Harvard University Press, 1965).

69. Tatyana Zaslavskaya (author's interview: Moscow, 17 April 1990).

70. Aganbegyan, *Moving the Mountain*, p. 127.

71. Zaslavskaya, "Socialism With a Human Face," p. 120.

72. Aganbegyan, *Moving the Mountain*, p. 140.

73. As with several other important new institutes, Alexei Rumyantsev played a key role in TsEMI's creation against conservative opposition; see Katsenelinboigin, *Empire, Nation, and System*, p. 420.

74. On Novosibirsk as a haven for original scholars from the intellectual and ideological "crowding" of Moscow, see R. G. Ivanovskii in *N. S. Khrushchev (1894–1970)*, pp. 64–66. See also Shlapentokh, *Politics of Sociology*, p. 32.

75. Shatalin, " '500 dnei' i drugie dni moei zhizni." Among the economic luminaries noted, Hayek—leader of the anti-Marxist "Austrian school"—argued that even a modest state role in the economy was "the road to serfdom." TsEMI alumni include prominent market advocates Stanislav Shatalin, Nikolai Petrakov, and Yegor Gaidar, as well as sociologists Yuri Levada and Boris Grushin. On TsEMI, see also Gaidar, *Dni porazhenii i pobed*, pp. 31–33 and passim.

76. Katsenelinboigin, *Empire, Nation, and System*, pp. 336–37. Real

prices for labor and capital had to be "smuggled" into economic models under the guise of "technical coefficients."

77. Aganbegyan, *Moving the Mountain*, p. 144. This included the input-output analysis pioneered by Russian emigré Wassily Leontief. See Katsenelinboigin, *Empire, Nation, and System*, pp. 335, 413.

78. "Protected by the technical language of their discipline . . . economists were able to address issues of fundamental political importance." See Peter Kneen, "The Background to *Perestroika*: 'Political Undercurrents' Reconsidered in the Light of Recent Events," in Nick Lampert and Gabor T. Rittersporn, eds., *Stalinism: Its Nature and Aftermath* (New York: Macmillan, 1992), p. 249.

79. Shatalin, " '500 dnei' i drugie dni moei zhizni."

80. Aganbegyan, *Moving the Montain*, p. 162.

81. Iuri Chernichenko, "Tselinnaia doroga" and "Russkaia phsenitsa," *Novy Mir*, no. 1 (1964) and no. 11 (1965). On Khanin's work, see Katsenelinboigin, *Empire, Nation, and System*, p. 400. Both Chernichenko and Khanin reemerged in the 1980s as leading advocates of radical economic reform.

82. On Liberman, see Eugene Zaleski, *Planning Reforms in the Soviet Union, 1962–1966* (Chapel Hill: University of North Carolina Press, 1967). It was for publicizing such proposals as Liberman's, as well as criticism of cultural policies, that caused Rumyantsev's removal as *Pravda* editor after less than one year.

83. Gennadii Lisichkin, *Plan i rynok* (Moscow: Ekonomika, 1966). On NEP as a reference for 1960s economic reformers, see Lewin, *Political Undercurrents in Soviet Economic Debates*.

84. Otto Latsis, " 'Izvestiia' znaiut, pochemu podderzhivaiut reformy," *Izvestiia*, 21 May 1993.

85. In addition to Zaslavskaya and the others previously noted, another who studied rural problems and wrote an original dissertation on the subject was Raisa Gorbacheva; see *New York Times*, 2 April 1987; also Gorbacheva, *Ia nadieius'*, p. 117.

86. On the influence of Polish scholarship, see Shlapentokh, *Politics of Sociology*, pp. 16, 21, 38–39.

87. This was "a dramatic and tortured process [since] the very word 'sociology' was invariable associated with 'bourgeois.' " See Grushin, "O liudakh, umevshikh zhit' pod vodoi."

88. Shlapentokh, *Politics of Sociology*, pp. 56, 74–76.

89. "Never before in the history of Soviet society had so many brilliant thinkers gathered in one room." Ibid., pp. 36–37.

90. B. Grushin and V. Chikin, *Vo imia shchastia chelovecheskogo* (Moscow: Molodaia Gvardiia, 1960); Grushin and Chikin, *Ispoved' pokolenia*.

91. See I. Kon, "Razmyshleniia ob Amerikanskoi intelligentsii," *Novy Mir*, no. 1 (1968): 173–93. Zamoshkin acknowledged the "one-sidedness" of his early writings about the United States while describing how his study of labor unions, anti-war activism, and the civil rights movement countered views of corporate greed, militarism, and racism and so "made me realize" that American individualism was the foundation of a dynamic and essentially healthy society. See Iu. A. Zamoshkin, "Za novyi podkhod k probleme individualizma," *Voprosy Filosofii*, no. 6 (1989): 3–16.

92. Zamoshkin, *Krizis burzhuaznogo individualizma i lichnost'* (Moscow: Nauka, 1966) is one example. Shlapentokh recalled that such "critical" reviews and analyses "served as a . . . means of familiarizing researchers with [Western thought and practice]. . . . In many cases such works were written for the purpose of disseminating this information, employing a critical orientation as a cover to obtain consent for publication." Shlapentokh, *Politics of Sociology*, p. 16.

93. Aganbegyan, "The Real State of the Economy," pp. 223–27 (citation from p. 224).

94. Ibid., pp. 226–27.

95. Ibid., p. 225.

96. See for example G. Arbatov, *Stroitel'stvo kommunizma i mirovoi revoliutsionnyi protsess* (Moscow: Nauka, 1966), p. 473.

97. Nikolai Shmelev (author's interview: Moscow, 23 January 1991). Shmelev, soon to become one of the Soviet Union's strongest advocates of radical market reforms, worked at IEMSS and, later, ISKAN.

98. Aganbegyan, "The Real State of the Economy," p. 225.

99. Lewin, *Political Undercurrents*, p. 241. Here Lewin summarizes the arguments of Shkredov's *Ekonomika i pravo* (Moscow: Ekonomika, 1967).

100. The classic on thaw-era international-relations thought remains William Zimmerman, *Soviet Perspectives on International Relations: 1956–1967* (Princeton: Princeton University Press, 1969), to which credit belongs for attention to many of the citations that follow.

101. Burlatskii, *Vozhdi i sovetniki*, pp. 32–43.

102. Arbatov, *Zatianuvsheesia vyzdorovlenie*, pp. 49–63 (citation from pp. 53–54). The Kuusinen-edited text, *Osnovy Marksizma-Leninizma* (Moscow: Politizdat, 1959) was criticized by conservatives for its "social-democratic tinge" and never gained wide acceptance.

103. Arbatov, "K voprosu o roli narodnykh mass v mezhdunarodnykh otnosheniiakh," *Mezhdunarodnaia Zhizn'*, no. 9 (1955): 64.

104. E. Arab-Olgy, "Is There a Danger of Overpopulation?" *World Marxist Review* (English translation of *Problemy Mira i Sotsializma*), no. 8 (1961): 38–49.

105. P. Joye, "Problems of Modern Capitalism," *World Marxist Review* no. 12 (1962): 58; E. Berlinguer, "Speech at the Plenum of the PCI," *World Marxist Review*, no. 9 (1963).

106. Markwick, "Catalyst of Historiography," p. 593, n. 48. On Western foreign-policy making, see A. A. Galkin, *O sovremennoi Sovetskoi diplomatii* (Moscow: Politizdat, 1963), p. 14.

107. Cherniaev, *Moia zhizn' i moe vremia*, pp. 238–39.

108. Ibid., p. 239. By this time, 1966, Chernyaev had left Prague and joined the influx of young specialists into the Central Committee apparatus.

109. V. Lukin, *Sotsial-demokratiia v Iuzhnoi i Iugo-Vostochnoi Azii* (Moscow, 1964), pp. 6–7, 18–22.

110. Institut Mirovogo Rabochego Dvizheniia, *Problemy rabochego dvizheniia* (Moscow: Mysl',' 1967).

111. A. Bovin, *Izvestiia*, 9 February 1962; F. Burlatskii, *Pravda*, 10 January 1965. Burlatsky and Georgy Shakhnazarov (another veteran of Prague and of Andropov's first Central Committee consultant group) together founded the Soviet Association of Political Sciences in 1965.

112. Zimmerman, *Soviet Perspectives*, pp. 52–55. A more exhaustive listing of "white book" special-edition translations produced between 1958 and 1968 includes works by political scientists and Sovietologists such as Sam Huntington, Zbigniew Brzezinski, Leonard Schapiro, Adam Ulam, Frederick Barghoorn, Ray Garthoff, Edward Crankshaw, John Armstrong, Guiseppe Boffa, and Klaus Mehnert. Also translated were studies or memoirs by Adlai Stevenson, Dean Acheson, John Foster Dulles, Konrad Adenauer, Charles DeGaulle, Willy Brandt, and Milovan Djilas; from *Spisok knig redaktsii Spetsizdanii, peredavaemykh v spravochnuiu biblioteku izdatel'stva "Progress"* (unpublished list).

113. See, for example, the impact of Stanley Hoffman on the IMEMO collection *Dvizhushchie sily vneshnei politiki SShA* (Moscow: Nauka, 1965) as noted in Zimmerman, *Soviet Perspectives*, pp. 70–71.

114. G. Gerasimov, "Teoriia igr i mezhdunarodnye otnosheniia," *Mirovaia Ekonomika i Mezhdunarodnye Otnosheniia* (hereafter *MEMO*), no. 7 (1966): 101–8; see also Krasin in *MEMO*, no. 5 (1960): 143–46.

115. On this point, see Zimmerman, *Soviet Perspectives*, pp. 242–74.

116. A. Butenko, "O zakonomernostiakh razvitiia sotsializma kak obshchestvennogo stroia i kak mirovoi sistemy," *MEMO*, no. 11 (1966): 84–91.

117. Y. Karyakin, "Allen Dulles Instead of Karl Marx," *World Marxist Review*, no. 4 (1962): 82–87.

118. Zimmerman, *Soviet Perspectives*, p. 105.

119. Interview with A. Obukhev in "Practicioners of Policy," *Vestnik MID*, no. 5 (1990): 74.

120. Gromyko, *Pamiatnoe*. Andrei Vyshinsky, the purge-trial prosecutor and one of Gromyko's predecessors as foreign minister, served for three years as deputy commissar of foreign affairs before making his first foreign visit in 1943. See V. Sokolov and A. Vaksberg, "Ministr inostrannykh del Andrei Vyshinskii," *Mezhdunarodnaia Zhizn'*, no. 6 (1991): 108.

121. See *Vse o MGIMO* (Moscow: MGIMO, 1991), p. 6.

122. Shevchenko, *Breaking with Moscow*, pp. 72–73.

123. Georgy Kornienko (author's interview: Moscow, 1 March 1989). Evidence from the Foreign Ministry archive confirms this change. For example, reviews of diplomatic reporting show a decrease in orthodox, formulaic interpretations and an increase in objective, purely informative analyses. The evidence of same could take up an entire chapter, but can also be concisely illustrated in quantitative terms. An analysis of reporting from the Soviet embassy in Washington—in samples of press-political reviews taken over the 1950s—shows a decline in citations of the *Daily Worker*, *People's World*, and other Communist newspapers from more than 50 percent in 1952, to 30 percent in 1955, and to only 13 percent in 1959. Simultaneously, reliance on the *New York Times*, the *Wall Street Journal*, and similar publications shows a corresponding increase over the same period. Samples from *Arkhiv Vneshnei Politiki SSSR, fond Referentura po S.Sh.A.*, "Khronika sobitii po voprosam vnutrennei politiki S.Sh.A.," opis. nos. 38, 41, 45 (1952, 1955, 1959).

124. Victor Karyagin, "Berlin After the War," *International Affairs* (Moscow), no. 9 (1991): 72–83. On joint Gestapo-NKVD persecution of German social democrats, Karyagin recalled that "I had neither read nor heard anything of the kind before."

125. Karyagin recalls Soviet Ambassador Abrasimov acting officially as the Soviet "high commissioner" in East Germany, even though the occupation had ended ten years earlier. Ibid., pp. 78–79.

126. Boris Ilyichev, "Indonesia, My Homeland," *International Affairs* (Moscow), no. 3 (1992): 109–10.

127. Ibid.: 112, 117. On Chernyaev's argument, see above, note 110.

128. Victor Karyagin, "Recollections of London," *International Affairs* (Moscow), no. 7 (1992): 77–86 (citation from 83). Another diplomat for whom England was "an incredibly broadening experience" was Viktor Israelyan, later a leading proponent of a chemical-weapons ban (author's interview: Moscow, 27 February 1990). Israelyan, like Obukhev, took part in a thaw-era academic exchange, with Cambridge University.

129. Viktor Beletskii, "Pri otkrytykh granitsakh my ne smozhem tiagat'sia s kapitalizmom," *Izvestiia*, 29 September 1992. Beletsky, a career Germanist, was later Soviet ambassador to the Netherlands.

130. Lektsiia G. M. Kornienko, p. 12.

131. In addition to the examples cited earlier, see also the early support of physicists Vladimir Ginzburg and Vitaly Goldansky for an honest discussion of Soviet history in Nekrich, *Forsake Fear*, pp. 101–2, 109–11.

132. B. B. Kadomtsev, ed., *Reminiscences about Academician Lev Artsimovich* (Moscow: Nauka, 1985). See pp. 128–34 (on childhood, education) and pp. 32–33, 52–62, 88–94 (on international scientific cooperation).

133. Sakharov, *Memoirs*, pp. 123, 127. On Artsimovich's acquaintance with the historian Eidelman, and with such victims of Stalin's "anti-cosmopolitan" campaign as Anna Akhmatova, Dmitri Shostakovich, and Mikhail Zoshchenko, see Kadomtsev, ed., *Reminiscences*, pp. 98, 122.

134. Ibid., pp. 97–100. See also Andrei Sakharov and Ernst Henry, "Scientists and the Danger of Nuclear War," in Cohen, *End to Silence*, p. 229.

135. Yevgeny Velikhov (author's interview: Moscow, 30 December 1993), and Roald Sagdeyev (author's interview: College Park, MD, 12 April 1997). Both were leading arms-control advocates under Gorbachev.

136. "They absolutely shocked us. And this was a real breakthrough toward new thinking because we began to understand that the same thing would happen to us, as to them, in a nuclear war." Vitaly Goldansky (Moscow: author's interview, 12 December 1990). See also Shakhnazarov, *Tsena svobody*, pp. 92–93.

137. On the particular influence of Soviet specialists' access to the ideas and information contained in the journal *Bulletin of the Atomic Scientists*, see Evangelista, *Unarmed Forces*, pp. 39–40, 84.

138. Sakharov, *Memoirs*, pp. 230, 267–68.

139. A superb treatment of Khrushchev- and early Brehznev-era exchanges is Evangelista, *Unarmed Forces*, pp. 25–67, 82–86, 131–47. See also Lawrence S. Wittner, *Resisting the Bomb: A History of the World Nuclear Disarmament Movement, 1947–1970*, vol 1. (Stanford: Stanford University Press, 1998) and Joseph Rotblat, *Scientists in the Quest for Peace: A History of the Pugwash Conferences* (Cambridge: Harvard University Press, 1972).

140. One revealing episode saw Artsimovich—publicly critical of the U.S. war in Vietnam—observing a U.S. campus protest in 1969 and remarking privately that "these young people should be made to work harder at their studies." See Kadomtsev, ed., *Reminiscences*, p. 55.

141. Evgeny P. Velikhov, "Nauka rabotaet na bez"iadernyi mir," *Mezhdnarodnaia Zhizn'*, no. 10 (1988): 49–53. See also Kadomtsev, ed., *Reminiscences*, pp. 84–87.

142. G. Gerasimov, "The First-Strike Theory," *International Affairs* (Moscow), no. 3 (1965): 39–45. Gerasimov recalled the impact on his thinking of Thomas Schelling, whose work he studied close-hand as a mid-1960s journalism exchange student visiting Columbia and Princeton Universities;

"It was one thing to read . . . Western theorists in Moscow, but quite another to be immersed in the literature, seminars and discussions." Gerasimov (author's interview: Moscow, 22 December 1990). Another former *Problemy Mira i Sotsializma* writer, Gerasimov became chief foreign-policy spokesman under Gorbachev.

143. L. A. Artsimovich, "New Ideas in Disarmament," in Kadomtsev, ed., *Reminiscences*, p. 153. Perhaps even more surprising was the *Pravda* article of another political scientist, Burlatsky, that looked favorably on talks to discuss limitations on both offensive *and* defensive weapons. See F. Burlatskii, "Problemy obshchechelovecheskie," *Pravda*, 15 February 1967. Credit for this reference is owed Evangelista, *Unarmed Forces*, pp. 197–98.

144. Sakharov, *Progress, Coexistence, and Intellectual Freedom* (London: Penguin, 1968), p. 35. Here Sakharov cites the arguments of Richard Garwin and Hans Bethe from a just-published article in *Scientific American*. Sakharov's manifesto was distributed to the presidium of the Academy of Sciences, whose members in turn shared it with friends and colleagues. See Vitalii Goldanskii, "Scientist, Thinker, Humanist," *Physics Today* 43, no. 8 (1990): 47–48. An important mass-circulation article in favor of limiting ABMs—but much more strongly argued than Burlatsky's of 1967—was Arbatov's 1969 *Izvestia* article that protrayed the U.S. position in a vey favorable light. See Iu. Arbatov, "S.Sh.A.: Bol'shie raketnye debaty," *Izvestia*, 15 April 1969.

145. Burlatskii, *Vozhdi i sovetniki*, p. 261.

146. Another term for this generation of liberals is the *shestidesiatniki*, literally "those of the sixties."

147. Sakharov, *Progress, Coexistence, and Intellectual Freedom*, p. 27.

148. Among many intelligentsia accounts of Sakharov's great influence, see Nekrich, *Forsake Fear*, p. 54.

149. Shakhnazarov, *Tsena svobody*, p. 34.

150. Karyakin wrote a bold defense of Solzhenitsyn, criticizing Stalinist-militant "barracks socialism," during a term in Prague; see his "Epizod is sovremennoi borby idei," *Problemy Mira i Sotsializma*, no. 9 (1964). Karyakin's ties to dissidents Roy Medvedev and Petr Yakir also irritated conservatives, as did samizdat circulation of his speech in memory of anti-Stalinist writer Andrei Platonov. See detail in Zhores Medvedev, *Andropov* (New York: Norton, 1983), pp. 47–48.

151. A 1964 report by Propaganda Secretary L. F. Ilyichev presented a manifesto for reimposing cultural orthodoxy. Ilyichev singled out Ehrenburg, Tvardovsky, and Yevtushenko for such sins as "contact with foreign authors . . . whose views are alien to us," "abstract humanism," and "carrying on a bohemian lifestyle and appearing intoxicated in public." See "S chistym serdtsem priniala politiku partii. Zapiska Sekretariia

TsK KPSS L. F. Il'icheva o tvorcheskoi intelligentsii," *Vestnik*, no. 6 (1966): 140–51.

152. Cited in Spechler, *Permitted Dissent*, pp. 217–18. Conservatives were angered by Rumyantsev's "The Party and the Intelligentsia," an article written with Karyakin's assistance, that argued for less ideological interference and more "free expression and contending opinions." *Pravda*, 21 February 1965.

153. Burlatskii, *Vozhdi i sovetniki*, pp. 253–54. Yakovlev, formerly *Izvestiia's* Prague correspondent, became perestroika-era editor of *Moscow News*, a leading reformist tribune.

154. Pravda, 30 March 1966.

155. Among those expressing "profound concern" were scientists Tamm, Kapitsa, Artsimovich, and Sakharov, historians Maisky and Nekrich, and writers Nekrasov, Dudintsev, and Ehrenburg. See "Establishment Intellectuals Protest to Brezhnev," in Cohen, *End to Silence*, pp. 177–79.

156. Kagarlitsky, *Thinking Reed*, pp. 188–90.

157. Nekrich, *Forsake Fear*, pp. 73, 181–89. See also the transcript of debate over Nekrich's book in Petrov, *Soviet Historians and the German Invasion*, pp. 250–61.

158. L. Karpinskii, F. Burlatskii, "Na puti k prem'ere," *Komsomol'skaia Pravda*, 30 June 1967.

159. Alexeyeva and Goldberg, *Thaw Generation*, p. 210.

160. Zdenek Mlynar, one of the Prague Spring leaders, visited his old MGU classmate Mikhail Gorbachev in the Stavropol region in 1967—a time when provincial officials were struggling to put some of Gennady Lisichkin's reform ideas into practice. See Mikhail Gorbachev, *Zhizn' i reformy*, vol. 1 (Moscow: Novosti, 1995), pp. 117–19. Lisichkin's *Plan and Market* was published in Prague in early 1968.

161. Vladimir Lukin, "Tanki na zakate leta," *Literaturnaia Gazeta*, 18 August 1993.

162. See Sakharov's letter to Alexander Dubcek in *Moskovskie Novosti*, no. 22 (1990).

163. A particularly detailed picture of this excitement is seen in Anatolii Agranovskii, "Aprel' v Prage. 1968 god," *Znamia*, no. 1 (1990): 167–91.

164. Alexeyeva and Goldberg, *Thaw Generation*, p. 210. See also Pavel Palazchenko, *My Years With Gorbachev and Shevardnadze: The Memoir of a Soviet Interpreter* (University Park: Pennsylvania State University Press, 1997), pp. 3–4.

165. Kagarlitsky, *Thinking Reed*, p. 199.

166. Ibid., p. 198.

167. Yevgeny Ambartsumov (author's interview: Moscow, 6 August 1991).

168. Lukin, "Tanki na zakate leta," p. 12. Pavel Litvinov was the grandson of Foreign Affairs Commissar Maxim Litvinov, fired by Stalin in 1939; Petr Yakir was the son of a Red Army hero shot in 1937.

169. Alexeyeva and Goldberg, *Thaw Generation*, pp. 208, 210. See also Amalrik, *Notes of a Revolutionary*, p. 55.

170. See, respectively, Arbatov, *Zatianuvsheesia vyzdorovlenie*, p. 143; Orlova, *Memoirs*, p. 317; Israelyan (author's interview: Moscow, 27 February 1990); Gefter, *Iz tekh i etikh let*, p. 35; Alexeyeva and Goldberg, *Thaw Generation*, p. 216.

171. Roy Medvedev, "A Refutation of the Soviet Invasion," in Cohen, *End to Silence*, pp. 281–92.

172. Orlvoa, *Memoirs*, p. 317.

173. Alexeyeva and Goldberg, *Thaw Generation*, pp. 217–19.

174. The square in Galich's song was Saint Petersburg's Senate Square, the rallying place of the Decembrists.

175. In 1863, as seen in chapter 1, most Russian liberals closed ranks with the autocracy as it turned out that their national-imperial attitudes overpowered their reformist beliefs; Herzen was a rare exception.

176. "Za granitsei nashi khodiat khmuro," *Komsomol'skaia Pravda*, 10 September 1991.

177. E. Maksimova, "Prikaz ne podchinilis,'" *Izvestiia*, 4 May 1990; "Togda, v avguste 68-go," *Literaturnaia Gazeta*, 13 December 1990, p. 3.

178. "Kto priglasili v Pragu Sovetskie tanki?," *Izvestiia*, 17 July 1992, p. 7; see also the interview with Bovin in "Bez illiuzii," *Sobesednik*, no. 6 (1990).

179. See Yevtushenko, "I Cannot Sleep," in Cohen, *End to Silence*, p. 279.

180. Spechler, *Permitted Dissent*, p. 224.

181. Gefter, *Iz tekh i etikh let*, p. 122.

182. "Avgust 68-go," *Izvestiia*, 20 August 1990.

183. Shakhnazarov, "Vo mnogom poteriannaia zhizn'." Shakhnazarov was "exiled" from work on European to Chinese affairs.

184. Ambartsumov (author's interview: Moscow, 6 August 1991).

185. Grachev, *Kremlevskaia khronika*, p. 61. See also Cherniaev, *Moia zhizn' i moe vremia*, p. 236.

186. An overview of these events appears in Strobe Talbott's introduction to Arbatov, *The System*, p. xv. See also Cohen and vanden Heuvel, *Voices of Glasnost*, pp. 311–12.

187. See the interview with Shatalin, "Tebe nado byt' prem'erom," in Andrei Karaulov, *Vokrug Kremlia. Kniga politicheskikh dialogov*, vol. 2 (Moscow: Novosti, 1992), pp. 306–7. Keldysh and other senior scientists also rose to Sakharov's defense, with some even supporting open publica-

tion of his *Reflections* memorandum; see Filipp Bobkov, *KGB i vlast'* (Moscow: Veteran MP, 1995), p. 282.

188. Len Karpinsky (author's interview: Moscow, 11 June 1990).

189. Shlapentokh, *Politics of Sociology*, p. 40; Shlapentokh, *Soviet Intellectuals*, p. 118.

190. Alexei Rumyantsev (author's interview: Moscow, 8 May 1991); Otto Latsis (author's interview: Moscow, 4 September 1991).

191. Alexeyeva and Goldberg, *Thaw Generation*, p. 236. Chernyaev also later helped establish a department at INION, headed by Orlov, on Western social democracy. Boris Orlov (author's interview: Moscow, 25 July 1991).

192. In a typical example, Shakhnazarov attempted—unsuccessfully— to help friends expelled from the Czech Communist Party; see Shakhnazarov, *Tsena svobody*, p. 106. Expelled from the Soviet Communist Party was the controversial historian Nekrich, who, after the Prague Spring, also faced an attempt to rescind his doctoral degree. He fought these efforts with support from the diplomat-historians Israelyan and Maisky (the latter had nominated Nekrich for membership in the Academy of Sciences), the military historian Dashichev, and IMEMO analyst Daniil Melamid (a long-time aide to Varga). Nekrich, *Forsake Fear*, pp. 228–29. Dashichev, who was soon retired from the army, later joined "Praguer" Oleg Bogomolov's Institute of the Economy of the World Socialist System (IEMSS) and emerged as a leading foreign-policy new thinker under perestroika.

193. Grachev, *Kremlevskaia khronika*, p. 43.

194. On the unworkability of the much-discussed "Liberman reforms," see Vladimir Mau, "The Road to *Perestroika*: Economics in the USSR and the Problems of Reforming the Soviet Economic Order," *Europe-Asia Studies* 48, no. 2 (1996): 211–13.

195. Under the influence of the exaggerated success of Yugoslavia's economic reforms, Latsis's confident prediction—that self-management in Soviet industry would "work without a hitch"—was fairly typical of the time. See *Novy Mir*, no. 4 (1967): 168.

196. L. Okunev (Len Karpinsky), "Words Are Also Deeds," in Cohen, *End to Silence*, pp. 306–10.

4. The Dynamics of New Thinking in the Era of Stagnation

1. This was military historian (and Nekrich defender) Vyacheslav Dashichev's characterization of how the USSR provoked "all the world's major powers . . . to align against it" and thereby created a geopolitical dilemma "unprecedented in history." See "Vostok-zapad: poisk novykh

otnoshenii," *Literaturnaia Gazeta*, 18 May 1988, p. 14. The preeminent analysis of détente-era diplomacy is Raymond L. Garthoff, *Détente and Confrontation: American-Soviet Relations From Nixon to Reagan* (Washington, DC: Brookings Institution, 1985).

2. Shevardnadze, *Moi vybor*, p. 151.

3. Victor Israelyan, *Inside the Kremlin During the Yom Kippur War* (University Park: Pennsylvania State University Press, 1995), pp. 57, 215.

4. Dobrynin, *In Confidence*, p. 140.

5. Arbatov, *Zatianuvsheesia vyzdorovlenie*, pp. 224–25.

6. Grachev, *Kremlevskaia khronika*, pp. 14–15.

7. Iakovlev, *Gor'kaia chasha*, p. 190.

8. "Revolutionary inadequacy" is Arbatov's characterization based on years near the ruling elite. For a "true believer's" perspective on the same, see Leonov, *Likholet'e*, pp. 140–41 and passim.

9. Grachev, *Kremlevskaia khronika*, pp. 15, 18, 36–37.

10. Shakhnazarov, *Tsena svobody*, p. 20.

11. "This mythology still provided images and symbols that informed [their] understanding of the world." Odd Arne Westad "Secrets of the Second World: The Russian Archives and the Reinterpretation of Cold War History," *Diplomatic History* 21, no. 2 (1997), p. 265. See also Nigel Gould-Davies, "Rethinking the Role of Ideology in International Politics During the Cold War," *Journal of Cold War Studies* 1, no. 1 (1999), pp. 90–109.

12. Viktor Afanas'iev, *4-aia Vlast' i 4 Genseka. Ot Brezhneva do Gorbacheva v "Pravde"* (Moscow: Izdatel'stvo KEDR, 1994), p. 41. See also Grachev, *Kremlevskaia khronika*, pp. 28–29, 54.

13. Westad, "Secrets," p. 265. See also Shakhnazarov, *Tsena svobody*, p. 351.

14. From the memoirs of Leonid Brezhnev, as cited in Hough, *Russia and the West*, p. 49.

15. An unrepentant old thinker—who recalled 1937 as "the happiest time of my life"—was Brezhnev's Politburo comrade Victor Grishin; see *Ot Khrushcheva do Gorbacheva. Politicheskie portrety piati genseka i A. N. Kosygina. Memuary* (Moscow: "ASPOL," 1996), pp. 92, 199–200, 282–86 (quote from p. 89).

16. As recalled by Politburo aide Vadim Pechenev in *Gorbachev: k vershinam vlasti* (Moscow: Gospodin Narod, 1991), p. 34. Significantly, Brezhnev was elevated to the Central Committee under Stalin in 1952.

17. Arbatov, *Zatianuvsheesia vyzdorovlenie*, p. 45. See also Dobrynin, *In Confidence*, p. 130, and Roy Medvedev, *Lichnost' i epokha: Politicheskii portret L. I. Brezhneva* (Moscow: Novosti, 1991).

18. On Suslov and other dogmatics, see Evgenii Chazov, *Zdorov'e i*

vlast.' Vospominaniia "kremlevskogo vracha" (Moscow: Novosti, 1992), pp. 80–91, 159–75; also Grachev, *Kremlevskaia khronika*, pp. 24–28.

19. Arbatov, *Zatianuvsheesia vyzdorovlenie*, p. 126.

20. A. S. Cherniaev, *Shest' let s Gorbachevym. Po dnevnikovym zapisiam* (Moscow: Progress-Kul'tura, 1993), p. 9.

21. The young Trapeznikov, a Party activist involved in the drive to collectivize agriculture, was injured when peasants put up violent resistance to being herded onto the new kolkhozy. On memories of this incident, see Burlatskii, *Vozhdi i sovetniki*, p. 129. On Suslov's role during the terror, particuarly in the postwar repression of Jews and other "cosmopolitans," see Iakovlev, *Po moshcham i elei*, pp. 181–82.

22. Arbatov, *The System*, p. 129.

23. See respectively Paul Kennedy, *The Rise and Fall of the Great Powers: Economic Change and Military Conflict From 1500 to 2000* (New York: Random House, 1987), and Snyder, *Myths of Empire*. The latter, comparing cases of modern imperialism, judges Soviet overexpansion "moderate" (p. 212). On the enormous burden of Soviet empire, see E. Aleksandrov and V. Kolbin, "Ekonomika strany podgrebena pod grudami oruzhiia," *Izvestiia*, 16 June 1992, and V. Selunin and G. Khanin, "Lukavaia tsifra," *Novy Mir* no. 2, 1987, pp. 181–201. See also Henry S. Rowen and Charles Wolf Jr., eds., *The Impoverished Superpower: Perestroika and the Soviet Military Burden* (San Francisco: ICS Press, 1988).

24. See the declassified Soviet documents cited in the *Cold War International History Project Bulletin* no. 4 (1994): 70–76.

25. On fears of a "U.S. forward base" aimed at the USSR's "soft underbelly," see Dobrynin, *In Confidence*, p. 441; on the belief that the new Afghan leader Hafizullah Amin was an "American agent," see Iakovlev, *Gor'kaia chasha*, p. 195. See also "Even a Spy Makes Mistakes," *Moscow News* no. 46 (1991); "The KGB and the Afghan Leaders," *New Times* (Moscow), no. 24 (1992): 36; Leonov, *Likholet'e*, pp. 201–7.

26. Alexander Bovin, then an aide-speechwriter to Brezhnev, recalled that the analogy of the Spanish Civil War was invoked again to color deliberations over Afghanistan; "Bez illiuzii," *Sobesednik*, no. 6 (1990): 10. See also K. M. Tsigalov, "Ne vse tak prosto," and G. Trofimenko, "Rukoi neposviashchennoi," both in *S.Sh. A.: Politika, Ekonomika, Ideologiia* no. 6 (1989): 62–68, 70–71.

27. Ustinov is cited in Arbatov, *Zatianuvsheesia vyzdorovlenie*, p. 230. The professional military's opposition to invasion is noted in V. I. Varennikov, "Afghanistan: podvodia itogi," *Ogoniok* no. 12 (1989): 6–8, 30–31, and also in "Kak prinimalos' reshenie," *Krasnaia Zvezda*, 18 November 1989.

28. In addition to the better-known 1966 attempt, Arbatov's role in

fighting another effort to rehabilitate Stalin in 1969 is described in *Nedelia*, no. 39 (1988) 20–21.

29. Together, in the view of Andrei Grachev (one of the "children of détente" who would rise quickly on the Central Committee staff under perestroika), they constituted the "social-democratic wing" of the Party apparat. See Grachev, *Kremlevskaia khronika*, p. 61. For insight into the diverse background of one of these younger-generation new thinkers, Igor Malashenko (an ISKAN analyst who later joined Grachev in the Central Committee), see his dissertation on "The Social Philosophy of Dante." I. E. Malashenko, *Sotsial'naia Filosofiia Dante* (Moscow: Izdatel'stvo MGU, 1980).

30. Arbatov, *The System*, pp. 289–90, 292.

31. Viktor Kremenyuk (author's interview: Moscow, 19 December 1989).

32. Anatoly Dobrynin (author's interview: New Jersey Turnpike, 14 June 1993). Yevgeny Primakov, who served first as Russian foreign minister and then prime minister over 1996–99, was then a senior IMEMO analyst and later the institute's director. See also Dobrynin, *In Confidence*, pp. 35, 605, and passim.

33. F. M. Burlatskii, *Lenin. Gosudarstvo. Politika* (Moscow: Nauka, 1970), p. 139.

34. G. Kh. Shakhnazarov, *Sotsialisticheskaia demokratiia. nekotorye voprosy teorii* (Moscow: Politizdat, 1972).

35. A. P. Butenko, ed., *Teoriia i praktika stroitel'stva sotsializma* (Moscow: Nauka, 1975). Butenko was an analyst at Oleg Bogomolov's Institute of the Economy of the World Socialist System.

36. Among major reviews of foreign scholarship were V. G. Kalenskii, *Politicheskaia nauka v S.Sh.A.. Kritika burzhuaznykh kontseptsii vlasti* (Moscow: Iuridicheskaia Literatura, 1969), and P. S. Gratsianskii, *Politicheskaia nauka vo Frantsii* (Moscow: Nauka, 1975). On other publications, and the work of the Soviet Association of Political Sciences, see Archie Brown, "Political Science in the USSR," *International Political Science Review* 7, no. 4 (1986): 451.

37. Cited in ibid., pp. 462–63. On the impact of Western studies, see also Ronald Hill, *Soviet Politics, Political Science and Reform* (London: Martin Robertson, 1980), pp. 161–62.

38. Shlapentokh, *Politics of Sociology*, pp. 31, 38–39, 264.

39. B. Grushin, *Mneniia o mire i mir mnenii* (Moscow: Politizdat, 1967); Iu. Levada, *Lektsii po sotsiologii*, 2 vols. (Moscow: Institut Konkretnykh Sotsial'nykh Issledovanii, 1969); V. Iadov, A. Zdravomyslov, et al., eds., *Man and His Work* (White Plains, NY: International Arts and Sciences Press, 1970); I. Kon, "Seks. Obshchestvo. Kul'tura," *Inostrannaia Literatura* no. 1 (1970): 243–55.

40. See A. A. Galkin. "Sotsial'naia struktura sovremennogo kapitalis-ticheskogo obshchestva i burzhuaznaia sotsiologiia," *Voprosy Filosofii*, no. 8 (1972): 63–73. Here Galkin explores views ranging from Herman Kahn and Norbert Weiner to Seymour Martin Lipset and Talcott Parsons.

41. F. M. Burlatskii and A. A. Galkin, *Sotsiologiia. Politika. Mezhdunarodnye otnosheniia* (Moscow: Mezhdunarodnye Otnosheniia, 1974). The authors note the impact of "general trends of humanity and the system of global interrelationships" (p. 318). In 1972, Shakhanzarov stressed "great-power relations" over class divisions; by 1974, he saw international relations as influenced by global movements and organizations in a "complex parallelogram of forces." See G. Shakhnazarov, " 'Great Powers' Approach to International Politics," *World Marxist Review*, no. 5 (1972): 110–18; Shakhnazarov, "K probleme sootnosheniia sil v mire," *Kommunist*, no. 3 (1974): 77–82.

42. On Alvin Toffler's *Future Shock*, see Burlatskii, *Novoe myshlenie* (Moscow: Politizdat, 1989), p. 8.

43. Iu. A. Zamoshkin, ed., *Amerikanskoe obshchestvennoe mnenie i politika* (Moscow: Nauka, 1978). The views studied here range from Daniel Bell on postindustrial society to Robert Dahl on the U.S. Congress. Zamoshkin also detailed opinion polls showing that only 4 percent of Americans ranked themselves upper or lower class, with 52 percent saying middle, and 41 percent working class. Following this, the obligatory conclusion on capitalism's social crisis—emphasized via a quotation from Gus Hall—appeared truly comical (pp. 249–91).

44. Burlatskii, *Vozhdi i sovetniki*, p. 346.

45. Peace was judged a "universal human value," above class and other interests. See "Planirovanie vseobshchego mira, utopiia ili real'nost'?" in Burlatskii, *Vozhdi i sovetniki*, pp. 344–45.

46. Virtually without exception, the "new thinkers" interviewed in this study recall Sakharov's essay as important in the evolution of their views. Those in the Party apparat had access through official channels, while others found it via Western sources. While the former acknowledge Sakharov's impact, many noted that his activism complicated their situation: "If you voiced a similar view, the conservatives said 'Ah, so you're repeating Sakharov, you're a Sakharovite!'" Alexander Yakovlev (author's interview: New York, 15 November 1991). Younger liberals were more unreservedly positive in assessing Sakharov's impact.

47. G. I. Gerasimov, *Stanet li tesno na zemnom share? Problema narodonaseleniia* (Moscow: Znanie, 1967), pp. 4–7, 14–18. Gerasimov, as noted, also pioneered Soviet criticism of missile defense programs.

48. "Radi zdorov'ia zhenshchiny," as cited in "V range posla," *Sobesednik* no. 23, 1990, p. 7.

49. Career highlights and biographical data on ISKAN staff can be found in Barbara L. Dash, *A Defector Reports* (Falls Church, VA: Delphic Associates, 1982), pp. 1–198.

50. G. S. Khozin, *V zashchitu planety. Mezhdunarodnoe sotrudnichestvo v oblasti okhrany okruzhaiushchoi sredy* (Moscow: Znanie, 1974).

51. Grigory Khozin (author's interview: Moscow, 12 September 1991).

52. On Artsimovich's attendance at a 1972 Club of Rome seminar, and discussion of Meadows's *The Limits to Growth* and environmental issues with his colleagues in Moscow, see Kadomtsev, *Reminiscences*, pp. 20–21.

53. Khozin recalled discussions with Marshall Shulman, George Rathjens, and Robert C. Tucker at U.S.-Soviet seminars in Pitsunda over 1970–71 (author's interview: Moscow, 12 September 1991). See also V. Vasil'ev, V. Pisarev, and G. Khozin, *Ekologiia i mezhdunarodnye otnosheniia* (Moscow: Mezhdunarodnye Otnosheniia, 1978), which draws on Daniel Meadows's *The Limits to Growth*, Richard Falk's *Future Worlds*, and Alvin Toffler's *Future Shock*. Khozin and his coauthors identified ecology as a "universal human problem" (*obshchechelovecheskaia problema*) and faulted Soviet subordination of environmental concerns to military-industrial goals as a "temporary" expedient that must be corrected (pp. 4, 220).

54. Though Kapitsa was criticized for not publicly denouncing Sakharov's 1980 internal exile to the city of Gorky, after his death it was learned that he had appealed directly to the Soviet leadership on Sakharov's behalf. See *Sovetskaia Kul'tura*, 21 May 1988, p. 6.

55. Kapitsa, *Pis'ma o nauke* (a collection of Kapitsa's wide-ranging *Letters on Science*). See especially those to Brezhnev on the pollution of Lake Baikal, to Kosygin on the alienation of Soviet workers, and to the historian Nekchina defending pre-1917 historian Klyuchevsky and criticizing Nekchina's position on the irreconcilability of bourgeois and socialist scholarship (pp. 347–48, 355–60). Kapitsa's private arguments parallel those of the public 1970 letter to Soviet leaders from Sakharov, Roy Medvedev, and Valentin Turchin; see "A Reformist Program for Democratization" in Cohen, *End to Silence*, pp. 317–27.

56. In a 1956 article, Kapitsa had advanced perhaps the earliest public Soviet critique of strategic defenses—a full decade before ABM limitations became U.S., much less Soviet, policy. See Peter Kapitsa, "The Paramount Task," *New Times*, no. 36 (1956): 10–11, and the discussion thereof in Evangelista, *Unarmed Forces*, pp. 132–33.

57. On the Marxist-humanist roots of Frolov's views, especially the influence of Erich Fromm and Jurgen Habermas, see "Vokrug sensatsii i bez nee," *Moskovskii Komsomol'ets*, 7 January 1990.

58. Frolov and Kapitsa—a philosopher and a physicist—both fought against Lysenkoism and so were also united in opposing the isolationism and chauvinism that were the hallmarks of Stalinist science. See Frolov's *Genetika i dialektika* and Kapitsa's *Eksperiment. Teoriia. Praktika* (Moscow: Nauka, 1974).

59. "Chelovek i sreda ego obitaniia," *Voprosy Filosofii* (hereafter *VF*), no. 2 (1973): 37–42. Given Moscow's civil-defense efforts, Kapitsa was clearly addressing Soviet as well as U.S. militarists.

60. G. S. Khozin, *VF*, no. 3 (1973): 71–73.

61. A. E. Medunin, *VF*, no. 4 (1973): 68–70.

62. A. I. Berg, *VF*, no. 12 (1973): 54–58. See also B. Grushin, "K analizu sposobov proizvodstva nauchnoi informatsii," *VF*, no. 12 (1973): 65–68.

63. N. P. Dubinin, *VF*, no. 9 (1973): 53–58.

64. N. P. Fedorenko, *VF*, no. 9 (1973): 46–50.

65. A. I. Berg, *VF*, no. 10 (1973): 42–45. Of course, "practiced throughout the world" was not central planning but development driven by market supply and demand.

66. L. V. Kantorovich, *VF*, no. 10 (1973): 39–41. "Correct prices" were those reflecting investments of capital and knowledge, i.e., as under capitalism, and so contradicting the Marxist labor theory of value.

67. M. K. Mamardashvili, *VF*, no. 8 (1973): 98–100.

68. Iu. A. Zamoshkin, *VF*, no. 8 (1973): 108–9.

69. After numerous battles with the "mastadons" of ideology, *VF* editorial board members Zamoshkin, Grushin, and Mamardashvili were fired in 1974; Grushin, "O liudakh, umevshikh zhit' pod vodoi," p. 5.

70. For violating "the ironclad canons of the Central Committee, [Frolov] got a thrashing. He was worked over, [denounced] by the Moscow Party Committee, and cast out to the fringes of the nomenklatura." See Viktor Gorlenko, "Dvoe s ulitsy 'Pravdy,'" *Literaturnaia Gazeta*, 20 November 1991, p. 3.

71. Neli Motroshilova (author's interview: Moscow, 13 November 1989). Philosopher Motroshilova, the wife of sociologist-Americanist Zamoshikin, was on the institute staff from 1959 to 1989.

72. Burlatskii, *Vozhdi i sovetniki*, p. 353.

73. Shlapentokh, *Politics of Sociology*, p. 54.

74. Motroshilova (author's interview: Moscow, 13 November 1989). V. N. Yagodkin was ideology secretary of the Moscow Party committee.

75. Shakhnazarov, unable to explore such topics as futurology so openly as the "outsider" Burlatsky, instead wrote science fiction and translated Orwell's *Nineteen Eighty-Four*. This, following earlier disputes over his support of singer-social critic Vladimir Vysotsky (and his nonsupport of the Czechoslovak invasion) eventually earned Shakhnazarov a two-year demo-

tion; see Arbatov, *The System*, p. 84; Shakhnazarov, *Tsena svobody*, pp. 33, 66–67; Shakhnazarov, "Vo mnogom poteriannaia zhizn,'" p. 5.

76. See the interview with Bovin in Cohen and vanden Heuvel, *Voices of Glasnost*, p. 217.

77. A. N. Iakovlev, "Protiv antiistorizma," *Literaturnaia Gazeta*, 15 November 1972. A typical reaction of the conservative elite to Yakovlev's "anti-Russian" article is seen in the memoirs of Viktor Afanasyev (who served as *Pravda* editor until Gorbachev replaced him with Ivan Frolov); Afanas'iev, *4-aia Vlast' i 4 Genseka*, p. 46.

78. Under the rectorship of Yuri Krasin—the former Central Committee consultant fired for his ties to Roy Medvedev—the Institute of Social Sciences became a stagnation-era liberal haven. Charged with training foreign communists and socialists (the similarly named but much more orthodox Academy of Social Sciences schooled Soviet communists), the level of discourse was considerably higher. With sophisticated students, instruction "could not be carried out in a dogmatic way but required new approaches—leftist thinkers, even semi-dissidents [were] invited to address the Eurocommunists [and] even write new textbooks." See Henry Hamman, "Soviet Defector on Origins of 'New Thinking,'" *Report on the USSR* (Radio Free Europe-Radio Liberty), 20 October 1989, pp. 14–16; Grushin, "O liudakh, umevshikh zhit' pod vodoi," p. 5. In addition to staffers Burlatsky, Galkin, and Zamoshkin, "semi-dissident" lecturers included Mamardashvili, Motroshilova, and Batalov. As a Central Committee (not Academy of Sciences) body, the institute was safe from Sergei Trapeznikov, the reactionary sciences overlord, and protected by Vadim Zagladin, Krasin's former colleague and deputy head of the Central Committee's International Department.

79. "Avgustovskaia zhatva," *Izvestiia*, 13 October 1989.

80. Vucinich, *Empire of Knowledge*, p. 360. The neo-Stalinist tract at issue was M. B. Mitin, *Sovremennye problemy teorii poznaniia dialekticheskogo materializma* (Moscow: Mysl,' 1970).

81. Grachev, *Kremlevskaia khronika*, p. 34; Arbatov, *The System*, p. 226.

82. Cohen and vanden Heuvel, *Voices of Glasnost*, pp. 292–93. Karpinsky attacked resurgent Stalinism in domestic and foreign policy, while Latsis analyzed NEP's demise and Stalin's rise; see L. Okunev (Len Karpinsky), "Words Are Also Deeds," pp. 299–310; Otto Lacis, *The Turning Point* (Moscow: Progress, 1990). See also Karpinskii and Pisigin, *Zapovednik dlia dinozavrov*, pp. 3–4.

83. Yakovlev's efforts were reconted by Karpinsky (author's interview: Moscow, 11 June 1990). On the similar efforts of Anatoly Chernyaev and Vadim Zagladin, see Burlatskii, *Vozhdi i sovetniki*, p. 353.

84. Reformist economist Nikolai Shmelev, who worked in the Central

Committee under Yakovlev, also left the apparatus for academia at this time.

85. Again, this point requires emphasis as a corrective to the popular misconception of generational change as *the* essential prerequisite for reform. Hough, in what might be termed the "jeans and jazz" view of post-Stalin sociointellectual change, argues that "anyone in contact with Moscow intellectuals knew that the great majority wanted Western democracy." This is a highly problematic claim, and one can only suspect that it follows from a mistaken assumption that the "Moscow intellectuals" who most frequently met with Western visitors in the pre-Gorbachev era were representative of Soviet intellectuals (or bureaucrats, with whom he oddly conflates them) as a whole. Elsewhere, having emphasized the nomenklatura's rational self-interest, Hough overlooks what pursuit of that interest dictated under the old system of hierarchy and shortage when he wonders why those who had envied Western "clothes, music and movies" in their 20s would, as privileged members of that hierarchy in their 50s, stand for anything but radical reform. See Hough, *Democratization and Revolution*, pp. 23, 51, and passim.

86. On Yuri Lotman's Tartu semiotics school, see Scanlan, *Marxism in the USSR*, pp. 313–17. Some of Mamardashvili's then-unpublishable works on philosophy and culture, including Tartu papers of 1970–71, appear in his *Kak ia ponimaiu filosofiiu*. Regional diversity in philosophy is discussed in Vucinich, *Empire of Knowledge*, p. 342. On sociology, including the Georgian Public Opinion Center sponsored by the innovative republican Party boss Eduard Shevardnadze, see Shlapentokh, *Politics of Sociology*, pp. 88–91, 185–88; see also Darrell Slider, "Party-Sponsored Public Opinion Research in the Soviet Union," *Journal of Politics* 47 (1985): 209–27.

87. Butenko recalled that the concept originated in confusion. Attempting to back away from the utopian 1961 Party Program and highlight unresolved socioeconomic problems, a group drafting Brezhnev's address for the 24th CPSU Congress in 1971 suggested the formulation that Soviet socialism was still in its early, *developing* stages. But Brezhnev impulsively decided that *developed* sounded better. Anatoly Butenko (author's interview: Moscow, 31 May 1991).

88. In one view, Russian nationalism began gaining strength during the mid 1960s and by the 1970s was the "dominant ideology" of educated Russians; Shlapentokh, *Soviet Intellectuals*, p. 223. On its growth over the Brezhnev era, see Brudny, *Reinventing Russia*, chapters. 3–4.

89. The leading nationalist journals were *Molodaia Gvardiia* (Young Guard), *Nash Sovremennik* (Our Contemporary), and *Oktiabr'* (October). See also John B. Dunlop, *The Faces of Contemporary Russian Nationalism* (Princeton: Princeton University Press, 1983); Alexander Yanov, *The Russian New Right* (Berkeley: University of California Press, 1978).

90. In addition to the above, see the various views in " 'I Am a Stalinist': A Meeting of Party Officials," in Cohen, *End to Silence*, pp. 158–61; also Shlapentokh, *Soviet Intellectuals*, p. 205.

91. With the exception of the Stalinists' preferred repressive-isolationist measures. On the lack of a neo-Slavophile economic program—beyond simply directing resources to Russia and away from the other republics— see Shlapentokh, *Soviet Intellectuals*, p. 214.

92. The term *cosmopolitan*, since Stalin's time an epithet for Jewish, now began appearing in nationalist writings.

93. Though some admired Stalin for exactly what he had been, others mainly felt nostalgia for an era of order and strict morality. See Cohen, *Rethinking the Soviet Experience*, pp. 124, 150.

94. A key difference between the nineteenth-century Slavophiles and their Brezhnev-era successors was that the former—through education, language, and culture—were steeped in the same Europe whose model they doubted for Russia. Most of the latter, by contrast, were products of Stalinist isolation and propaganda.

95. See "Varieties of Neo-Stalinism" in Cohen, *End to Silence*, pp. 170–76.

96. The new concept gave reformers a lever for analysis and criticism. See B. A. Grushin, *Sotsialisticheskii obraz zhizni. poniatie i vozmozhnye napravleniia issledovaniia* (Moscow: TsEMI, 1975); A. P. Butenko, A. S. Tsipko, and V. P. Kiselev, eds., *Sotsialisticheskii obraz zhizni. metodologicheskie problemy issledovaniia* (Moscow: IEMSS, 1975). Boris Grushin, another of those fired from the Institute of Concrete Social Research, landed for a time at TsEMI. Alexander Tsipko was a colleague of Butenko's at IEMSS.

97. Butenko, Tsipko, and Kiselev, *Sotsialisticheskii obraz zhizni*, p. 52. Though unclassified, only 150 copies of this book were printed.

98. And, as Yakovlev warned, because it would inflame the nationalisms of the non-Russian Soviet peoples. His underlying concern was that the leadership, "having exhausted all other reserves for its survival, was actively switching over" to a chauvinist-imperialist ideology "characteristic of national-socialism." See Aleksandr N. Iakovlev, "Vremia podtverdilo moi opaseniia," *Istochnik*, no. 1 (1997): 98.

99. Yanov, *New Russian Right*, p. 58.

100. A. Ianov, "Zagadka slavianofilskoi kritiki," *Voprosy Literatury*, no. 5 (1969): 91–116.

101. V. Kozhinov, "O glavnom v nasledii slavianofilov," *Voprosy Literatury*, no. 10 (1969): 118.

102. A. Ianov, "Otvet opponentam," *Voprosy Literatury*, no. 12 (1969): 80, 94–95. The Slavophiles also "consciously exploited national feelings . . . to serve despotism and reaction" (p. 100).

103. See the powerful 1970 anti-chauvinist essay "The Charms of the Whip," by Raisa Lert, a friend of historians Mikhail Gefter and Roy Medvedev, in Cohen, *End to Silence*, pp. 189–200.

104. Historian Natan Eidelman, the thaw-era pioneer in study of nineteenth-century Westernism (and, indirectly, its lessons for the twentieth), lectured to overflow audiences at Novosibirsk in the 1970s on Russia's "great reforms" of the 1860s and 1870s. See Pokrovskii, "V prostranstve i vremeni," pp. 8, 19.

105. In preparing the 1972 edition of *The History of the Second World War*, Defense Minister Grechko attacked Arbatov for criticizing the draft's exaggeration of U.S. "expansionism" and aid to Germany. See Rumiantsev et al. in *Moskovskie Novosti*, 9 April 1989; Arbatov, *Zatianuvsheesia vyzdorovlenie*, p. 380. On efforts to air the Hitler-Stalin pact, see V. K. Furaev, "Ob izuchenii istorii mezhdunarodnykh otnoshenii i vneshnei politiki SSSR," *Novaia i noveishaia istoriia*, no. 3 (1992): 6.

106. Cited in Kagarlitsky, *Thinking Reed*, p. 292.

107. G. Vodolazov, *Dialektika i revoliutsiia* (Moscow: Izdatel'stvo Moskovskogo Universiteta, 1975), p. 80.

108. M. Ia. Gefter, ed., *Istoricheskaia nauka i nekotorye problemy sovremennosti* (Moscow: Nauka, 1969). "Manifesto of Legal Marxism" is the characterization of Kagarlitsky, *Thinking Reed*, p. 291.

109. V. V. Adamov, ed., *Voprosy istorii kapitalisticheskoi rossii: problema mnogoukladnost'* (Sverdlovsk: Redaktsionno-Izdatel'skii Sovet Ural'skogo Universiteta, 1972).

110. Kagarlitsky, *Thinking Reed*, p. 292.

111. M. Ia. Gefter, "Mnogoukladnost'—kharakteristika tselogo," in Adamov, ed., *Voprosy istorii kapitalisticheskoi rossii*, p. 93.

112. This characterization belongs to Gilbert Rozman; see his *A Mirror for Socialism: Soviet Criticisms of China* (Princeton: Princeton University Press, 1985).

113. V. P. Lukin, " 'Ideologiia razvitiia' i massovoe soznanie v stranakh 'tret'ego mira,'" *Voprosy Filosofii*, no. 6 (1969): 35–46. Lukin published this immediately after joining the USA Institute, which followed his dismissal from the Prague journal *Problemy Mira i Sotsializma*.

114. On such Aesopian critiques of Soviet domestic issues, see Rozman, *Mirror for Socialism*; Jerry Hough, *Struggle for the Third World*; and Elizabeth Valkenier, *The Soviet Union and the Third World: An Economic Bind* (New York: Praeger, 1983).

115. Iu. Ostrovitianov and A. Sterbalova, "Sotsial'nyi 'genotip' Vostoka i perspektivy natsional'nykh gosudarstv," *Novy Mir*, no. 12 (1972): 216–17.

116. V. L. Sheinis, ed., *Tretii mir. strategiia razvitiia i upravlenie ekonomiki* (Moscow: Nauka, 1971), pp. 42–43. On Chinese militarism, see

Fedor Burlatskii, *Mao Tsze-dun* (Moscow: Mezhdunarodnye Otnosheniia, 1976), and Lev Delusin, *The Socio-Political Essence of Maoism* (Moscow: Progress, 1976).

117. Berdyaev had acquired "a clandestine following among Russian intellectuals as far back as Brezhnev's time." Archie Brown, *New Thinking in Soviet Politics* (New York: St. Martin's, 1992), p. 3. On interest in Berdyaev, see also Shlapentokh, *Soviet Intellectuals*, pp. 184, 196; Nenashev, *Zalozhnik vremeni*, pp. 30–31; M. Piskotin, "Nazyvat' veshchi svoimi imenami," *Narodnyi deputat*, no. 11 (1990): 46.

118. Berdyaev later expressed a fatalistic view on the role of Russian political culture in the state's path of development. But, in his view, it remained a great misfortune that Russia had broken with Europe.

119. Lyudmila Nikitich (author's interview: Moscow, 1 August 1991).

120. G. Vodolazov, *Ot Chernyshevskogo k Plekhanovu* (Moscow: Izdatel'stvo Moskovskogo Universiteta, 1969); A. Tsipko and V. Lukin, *Optimizm istorii* (Moscow: Molodaia Gvardiia, 1974); E. Batalov, *Filosofiia bunta* (Moscow: Politizdat, 1973). On Berdyaev and *Vekhi*, see also Tsipko in "Pochemu zabludilsia prizrak?," *Sobesednik*, no. 21 (1990): 6.

121. A. Tsipko, *Ideia sotsializma: vekha biografii* (Moscow: Nauka, 1976), p. 260.

122. Sheinis, *Tretii mir*, p. 271.

123. Mamardashvili, *Kak ia ponimaiu filosofiiu*, pp. 168–69, 183, 196.

124. "O proekte konstitutsii 1977 goda," in Gefter, *Iz tekh i etikh let*, pp. 67–68.

125. Katsenelinboigin, *Empire, Nation, and System*, pp. 335, 413.

126. Gaidar, *Dni porazhenii i pobed*, pp. 26–30. Like Arbatov and many others, Gaidar also worked as a translator-reviewer of foreign professional literature early in his career, at INION in the early 1970s.

127. Aganbegyan, *Moving the Mountain*, p. 162.

128. Here Stanislav Shatalin describes the Central Economic–Mathematical Institute (TsEMI) through which passed "nearly every smart, well-informed economist" in the country; Shatalin, " '500 dnei' i drugie dni moei zhizni." On TsEMI, see also Gaidar, *Dni porazhenii i pobed*, pp. 31–32.

129. Interview with Shmelev in Cohen and vanden Heuvel, *Voices of Glasnost*, p. 151.

130. The "correlation of forces" (*sootnoshenie sil*) included ideological, military, and other factors together with economic power (and potential). For definitions and views, see Allen Lynch, *The Soviet Study of International Relations* (New York: Cambridge University Press, 1987), pp. 89–103.

131. A. A. Kokoshin, *O burzhuaznykh prognozakh razvitiia mezhdunarodnykh otnoshenii* (Moscow: Mezhdunarodnye Otnosheniia, 1978), pp. 45–47.

132. Inozemtsev et al., *Politicheskaia ekonomika sovremennogo monopoliticheskogo kapitalizma* (Moscow: Mysl,' 1975), pp. 49–50.

133. Wohlforth, *Elusive Balance*, p. 210.

134. N. Inozemtsev, "O novom etape v razvitii mezhdunarodnykh otnoshenii," *Kommunist*, no. 13 (1973): 89–103; O. Bogomolov, "O vneshneikh ekonomicheskikh sviazakh SSSR," *Kommunist*, no. 5 (1974): 89–99. See also N. Inozemtsev, G. Arbatov, and V. Alkhinov in *Izvestiia*, 5 and 8 May 1973.

135. Limited-circulation fora permitted far greater latitude than the open press in offering frank information and assessment. Many of the works cited below bear the initials *dsp*, the abbreviation of *dlia sluzhebnogo pol'zovaniia* (for official use only). Others, not classified, were published only in tiny editions of between 50 and 200 copies. The distribution of both sorts of works was limited to the Central Committee, relevant ministries, and other specialized institutes (in whose closed or *spetskhran* library collections they generally remain).

136. E. I. Kapustin et al., *Osnovnye problemy ekonomicheskogo razvitiia SSSR v X piatiletke* (Moscow: IE, 1974) *dsp*; S. V. Pirogov, *Nauka v sisteme obshchestvennogo proizvodstva* (Moscow: IE, 1975).

137. O. T. Bogomolov, ed., *Problema razvitiia nauchno-tekhnicheskikh potentsialov stran-chlenov SEV* (Moscow: IEMSS, 1977) *dsp*; G. S. Khozin, *Razrabotka standartov kachestva vodnykh resursov v SShA* (Moscow: ISKAN, 1974) *dsp*; B. Komzin, *Materialy o sovremennom sostoianii i perspektivakh razvitiia nauki v glavnykh kapitalisticheskikh stranakh* (Moscow: IMEMO, 1976).

138. N. P. Shmelev, *Ekonomicheskaia strategiia zapada v otnoshenii stran sotsialisticheskogo sodruzhestva* (Moscow: IEMSS, 1974) *dsp*; A. N. Bykov, *Puti sovershenstvovaniia form i metodov nauchno-tekhnicheskogo obmena SSSR s zarubezhnymi stranami* (Moscow: IEMSS, 1974) *dsp*; V. Orlov and G. Khozin, *Amerikanskii podkhod k nauchno-tekhnicheskomu sotrudnichestvu s SSSR i k otsenke ego effektivnosti* (Moscow: ISKAN, 1977).

139. Robbin F. Laird and Erik P. Hoffmann, " 'The Scientific-Technological Revolution,' 'Developed Socialism,' and Soviet International Behavior," in Hoffman and Fleron, *Conduct of Soviet Foreign Policy*, pp. 386–405.

140. One classified study faulted mainstream Soviet writings for "inadequate analysis" of U.S. economic strength and for "hardly even mentioning" technological changes that increased the United States' international influence. See G. A. Trofimenko, A. A. Kokoshin, and A. V. Nikiforov, *Mezhdunarodnye pozitsii SShA v seredine 70-x godov* (Moscow: ISKAN, 1977) *dsp*, pp. 7–9. Note the contrast to Kokoshin's own open writings, as noted above.

141. Shatalin, " '500 dnei' i drugie dni moei zhizni."

142. Ibid. Further, "A chill fell over the room. I finally understood that with such 'bosses' as these, we were doomed . . . and Kosygin was the best of them!" See also Aganbegyan, *Moving the Mountain*, p. 151.

143. Arbatov, *Zatianuvsheesia vyzdorovlenie*, p. 155. The report was *Uskorenie nauchno-tekhnicheskogo progressa—korennaia strategicheskaia zadacha sovremennogo etapa razvitiia strany* (Moscow, 17 August 1973, unpublished MS).

144. S. S. Shatalin, *Tsennost' v sisteme ekonomicheskikh kategorii sotsializma* (Moscow: TsEMI, 1974); Shatalin, *Kompleksnyi prognoz narodnogo blagosostoianiia na 1978–1980 gg.* (Moscow: TsEMI, 1974) *dsp*.

145. Nikolai Shmelev, *Problemy ekonomicheskogo rosta razvivaiushchikhsia stran* (Moscow: Nauka, 1970), pp. 116–19; N. Ia. Petrakov, *Issledovanie sovremennogo sostoianiia i razrabotka predlozhenii po sovershenstvovaniiu sistemy khozrashchetnykh otnoshenii v promlyshennosti* (Moscow: TsEMI, 1974).

146. V. N. Starodubrovskaia, *Analiz opyta kooperativnogo dvizheniia v Vengrii na sovremennom etape* (Moscow: IEMSS, 1974) *dsp*; V. A. Tikhonov, *Problemy Leninskogo kooperativnogo plana v svete novoi konstitutsii SSSR* (Moscow: IE, 1978).

147. A. G. Aganbegian, *Sotsial'no-ekonomicheskie problemy razvitiia Sibiri v desiatoi piatiletke* (Moscow: IE, 1974).

148. For details of Fedorenko's report, and a KGB audience's response, see Leonov, *Likholet'e*, pp. 168–69.

149. N. Shmelev, "Vakhnyi faktor rosta ekonomiki," *MEMO*, no. 5 (1973): 145–46.

150. N. P. Shmelev, ed., *Osnovnye napravleniia zainteresovannosti zapada v razvitii ekonomicheskikh sviazei so stranami SEV* (Moscow: IEMSS, 1976) *dsp*, p. 146.

151. N. P. Shmelev, *Ekonomicheskie sviazi vostok-zapad. problemy i vozmozhnosti* (Moscow: Mysl', 1976); N. P. Shmelev and V. P. Karavaev, *Osobennosti podkhoda evropeiskikh stran SEV k problemam ekonomicheskikh otnoshenii s zapadom* (Moscow: IEMSS, 1975), pp. 29–30.

152. N. P. Shmelev, *Problemy i perspektivy ekonomicheskikh sviazei Sovetskogo soiuza so stranami zapada* (Moscow: IEMSS, 1975) *dsp*, p. 78; also Shmelev and Karavaev, *Osobennosti podkhoda*, pp. 26–29.

153. Ibid., p. 29; Shmelev, *Problemy*, p. 78.

154. Shmelev and Karavaev, *Osobennosti podkhoda*, pp. 31–33.

155. *Pravda*, 22 May 1973.

156. See Trade Minister K. Katushev, "Glavnoe napravlenie: o protsesse i ob"ektivnoi neobkhodimosti dal'neishego splocheniia stran sotsializma," *Problemy Mira i Sotsializma*, no. 8 (1973): 3–10.

157. Vysshaia Partiinaia Shkola pri TsK KPSS, *Sotsialisticheskaia*

Ekonomicheskaia Integratsiia. Uchebnoe Posobie (Moscow: Mysl,' 1977), pp. 314, 325.

158. Shmelev, *Problemy*, pp. 75–77.

159. Shatalin repeatedly exceeded the limits. Hounded from MGU for "ideologically unreliable lectures" and "bias toward vulgar Western theories," he was fired from TsEMI in 1976. In 1977, after a seminar in Paris, he was denounced to the KGB for "criminal ties to White emigres" and barred from Western travel. See, respectively, Gaidar, *Dni porazhenii i pobed*, p. 28; Shatalin, " '500 dnei' i drugie dni moei zhizni."

160. A. A. Bel'chuk and E. L. Iakovleva, *Opyt sotsialisticheskikh stran v privlechenii inostrannogo kapitala v forme smeshannykh obshchestv i vozmozhnosti ego ispol'zovaniia v SSSR* (Moscow: IEMSS, 1979).

161. V. A. Tikhonov, *Effektivnost' proizvodstva i spetsifika ee izmereniia primenitel'no k narodnokhoziastvennomu agropromyshlennomu kompleksu* (Moscow: IE, 1979).

162. See S. N. Nesterov, *Deiatel'nost "obshchego rynka" v oblasti okhrany okruzhaiushchoi sredy* (Moscow: IMEMO, 1979); S. M. Nikitin, *Predlozheniia po uskoreniiu nauchno-tekhnicheskogo progressa i povysheniiu effektivnosti proizvodztva v SSSR (s uchetom opyta SSSR, SShA i Iaponii)* (Moscow: IMEMO, 1979).

163. *Prognoza razvitiia avtomatizatsii proizvodstva v mashinostroenii v SShA* (Moscow: ISKAN, 1978); *O peredache tekhnicheskikh dostizhenii kosmicheskoi programmy SShA v grazhdanskie oblasti ekonomiki* (Moscow: ISKAN, 1979); *Opyt zhilishchnogo stroitelstva v SShA* (Moscow: ISKAN, 1979); *Spravka ob ispol'zovanii metallicheskogo skrapa v SShA* (Moscow: ISKAN, 1978).

164. See the interview with Shmelev in Cohen and vanden Heuvel, *Voices of Glasnost*, pp. 147–48.

165. See J. Somerville, *Soviet Marxism and Nuclear War* (London: Aldwych, 1981), p. 122.

166. See Burlatskii, "Planirovanie vseobshchevogo mira."

167. *Izvestiia*, 11 July 1973.

168. *Pravda*, 22 July 1973. See also Shakhnazarov on the declining importance of military power, in "K probleme sootnosheniia sil v mire," pp. 77–90.

169. F. M. Burlatskii, "O sistemnom podkhode k issledovaniiu vneshnei politiki," in *Mezhdunarodnye otnosheniia, politika i lichnost'* (Moscow: Sovetskaia Assotsiatsiia Politicheskikh Nauk, 1976), p. 79.

170. The role of reformist advisers is detailed in the memoirs of Arbatov, Chernyaev, Grachev, and other new thinkers. For confirmation (and criticism) of their influence on Brezhnev from other perspectives, see Leonov, *Likholet'e*, p. 138; Afanas'iev, *4-aia Vlast' i 4 Genseka*, p. 39. On the

"two Brezhnevs," see Cherniaev, *Moia zhizn' i moe vremia*, pp. 288–99, 305–7, 325; on the ascendance after 1975 of "the other Brezhnev," increasingly dogmatic and infirm, see Chazov, *Zdorov'e i vlast'*, pp. 87–90, 127–34.

171. Arbatov, *The System*, pp. 289–92.

172. *Lektsiia G. M. Kornienko*, p. 19.

173. Obukhev, "Practitioner of Policy," p. 75. The old ways did not disappear completely; because of his vigorous pursuit of agreement, Kornienko recalled, Defense Minister Grechko "seriously considered me to be some sort of an American agent." *Lektsiia G. M. Kornienko*, p. 14.

174. V. Israelian, "O diplomaticheskikh peregovorakh," *Mezhdunarodnaia Zhizn'*, no. 12 (1988): 88.

175. On this point, see also veteran arms negotiator Yuli Vorontsov, "The Military-Political Aspects of Security," *International Affairs* (Moscow), no. 10 (1988): 42.

176. Obukhev, "Practitioner of Policy," p. 75.

177. Ibid.

178. Israelian, "O diplomaticheskikh peregovorakh," p. 86.

179. "Dobrynin's school" is the characterization of Bessmertnykh, a member of that elite and foreign minister himself in 1990–91 (author's interview: Moscow, 30 December 1993).

180. Andrei Kozyrev, then a junior diplomat in the international-organizations section of the ministry (also a leading perestroika-era Westernizer and subsequently Yeltsin's first foreign minister), recalled his research in Western sources on the global arms trade as central in his rethinking of Soviet policy on the third world. See Kozyrev, "Osnovnaia opasnost'—v nomenklaturnom revanche," *Nezavisimaia Gazeta*, 10 August 1992.

181. Sergei Tarasenko, a junior member of "Dobrynin's school" and perestroika-era aide to Foreign Minister Eduard Shevardnadze, described "a rift between the *zapadniki* . . . and the others. The USA section became a separate ministry with MID. . . . You start to resemble the people, the country, where you work, and this was especially so for those who worked on the USA. It took a higher level of professionalism and culture, and such experience changes your outlook. I was there under Dobrynin in 1972–1978, I saw the oil crisis, Watergate, the bicentennial . . . we admired Camp David and thought 'how stupid that we cut ourselves off from so much.'" (author's interview: Moscow, 16 August 1991).

182. Bessmertnykh (author's interview: Moscow, 30 December 1993). Another Soviet diplomat faulted his pro-détente colleagues for absorbing "bourgeois values" while serving in the West; Stepan Chervonenko, "The Personnel Policy to Serve Perestroika," *International Affairs* (Moscow), no. 11 (1988): 56.

183. Again, the preeminent source on Soviet involvement in transnational disarmament efforts is Evangelista, *Unarmed Forces* (see esp. chapters 7–11 on Brezhnew-era activities).

184. Kapitsa, Tamm, Artsimovich, and Sagdeev were among those to author or sign protestations against Russian chauvinism and efforts to rehabilitate Stalin; see Cohen, *End to Silence*, pp. 177–82. See also Vera Rich, "He who would dissident be," *Nature* 263 (1976): 361–62.

185. Medvedev, *Soviet Science*, p. 63. See also Valentin Turchin, *The Inertia of Fear and the Scientific Worldview* (New York: Columbia University Press, 1981).

186. Roald Sagdeev (author's interview: College Park, MD, 12 April 1997).

187. Vitaly Goldansky (author's interview: Moscow, 12 December 1990). See also Goldanskii, "Scientist, Thinker, Humanist," *Physics Today* 43, no. 8 (1990): 47–48.

188. Vitaly Goldansky (author's interview: Moscow, 12 December 1990).

189. Roald Sagdeev (author's interview: College Park, MD: 12 April, 1997). See also Herbert F. York, *Making Weapons, Talking Peace: A Physicist's Odyssey from Hiroshima to Geneva* (New York: Basic, 1987), pp. 245–79.

190. Boris Raushenbakh (author's interview: Moscow, 20 March 1991). For Raushenbakh, the study of other civilizations was also central to surmounting "the way we were indoctrinated. 'He who isn't with us is against us.' 'If the enemy won't give up, destroy him.' These slogans hammered us all our lives. We have . . . the only correct theory, the best values. These were our norms of behavior toward other countries." See the interview with Raushenbakh, "Vse ne tak, rebiata," *Literaturnaia Gazeta*, 7 April 1990.

191. Chazov, *Zdorov'e i vlast'*, pp. 90–113 (quote from p. 99).

192. Yevgeny Velikhov (author's interview: Moscow, 30 December 1993). Sagdeev and later Velikhov both lobbied to end Sakharov's exile. On Sakharov's influence among scientists, see also Vladimir Fainberg, "Precursor of Perestroika," *Physics Today* 43, no. 8 (1990): 40–45.

193. See *Institute of Scientific Information on Social Sciences* (Moscow: INION, 1979) for detail on surveys, abstracts, and other publications of INION.

194. Dash, *Defector Reports*, pp. 13–15, 47–59.

195. Though "subterfuge" was still sometimes needed. Nikolai Biriukov, a 1969 MGIMO graduate and specialist in Western political philosophy, worked as a *Znanie* (Knowledge) Society lecturer to gain access to restricted sources, chiefly the "White TASS" wire service that included daily translations of foreign reportage and political commentary (author's

interview: Princeton, 10 November 1993). By the late 1970s, the staffs of IMEMO and ISKAN numbered about 800 and 400 respectively.

196. Andrei Kokoshin recalled such sources as "bibles" for ISKAN security analysts (author's interview: Moscow, 15 August 1991).

197. R. G. Tumkovskii, *Amerikanskie krylatye rakety* (Moscow: ISKAN, 1978) *dsp*; B. D. Iashin, *Voenno-morskaia politika SShA v 70-x godakh* (Moscow: ISKAN, 1977) *dsp*.

198. R. G. Tumkovskii, *SShA i strategicheskie sily Velikobritanii. k voprosu ob Amerikanskoi pomoshchi v modernizatsii angliskikh strategicheskikh sil* (Moscow: ISKAN, 1978) *dsp*; Iu. Bobrakov et al., *Voennoe proizvodstvo SShA i razriadka. ekonomicheskie aspekty problemy konversii* (Moscow: ISKAN, 1978) *dsp*.

199. *Rezultaty vypolnenie v SShA issledovanii po otsenke dlitel'nykh globalnykh effektov bol'shoi iadernoi voiny* (Moscow: ISKAN, 1978) *dsp*; *Razvitie strategicheskikh sil SShA na rubezhe 70x godov i priniatie reshenii po voennoi programme, Lektsia Enthoven A. M.* (Moscow: ISKAN, 1974) *dsp*.

200. In addition to attending the Pugwash meetings, Inozemtsev, Arbatov, and Primakov took part in the Soviet-American Disarmament Study groups with physicist Kapitsa, geneticist Dubinin, and other leading scientific and military figures: David Wright, *Notes on SADS Meetings* (unpublished paper, May 1993).

201. ISKAN analyst and retired colonel Lev Semeiko recalled that "in the West, Pugwash was seen as propaganda and wasn't taken too seriously . . . but for us it was very enriching. My first time was 1976. There were top foreign scientists, so many arguments and interesting ideas, in contrast to the boilerplate [*khaltura*] of our side's officially approved positions." Lev Semeiko (author's interview: Moscow, 2 February 1990).

202. Yevgeny Velikhov (author's interview: Moscow, 30 December 1993).

203. Insight on IMEMO's strategic studies comes from staffers Alexei Arbatov, Sergei Blagovolin, and Vitaly Shlykov (author's interviews: Moscow, 20 May, 13 August, and 4 September 1991).

204. Andrei Kokoshin recalled that there emerged "a culture of Western-style strategic thought" (author's interview: Moscow, 15 August 1991). Ironic evidence of this was the 1975 investigation and firing of ISKAN analysts Georgy Svyatov and Yuri Streltsov for too-accurately speculating on Soviet SALT negotiating positions in an interview with *Newseek*: see Dash, *Defector Reports*, pp. A-167, A-169.

205. Shlykov first drew close to civilian analysts while at the Defense Ministry's Institute of Military-Technical Information, for which IMEMO did contract work.

206. V. V. Shlykov, *NATO i sovmestnoe proizvodstvo vooruzhenii* (Moscow: IMEMO, 1970). See also V. V. Repinskii (Shlykov) , *NATO i voennyi biznes* (Moscow: Mezhdunarodnye Otnosheniia, 1970).

207. Vitaly Shlykov (author's interview: 13 August 1991). "Studying the problem from within [the military] I understood: we don't see reality, we're caught up instead in nonsense of our own creation, nonsense that is both wasteful and ineffective." See the interview with Shlykov, "Mertvye dengi na sluchai voiny," *Demokraticheskaia Rossiia*, no. 13 (1991).

208. A. G. Arbatov, *Novye programmy strategicheskikh vooruzhennykh sil SShA* (Moscow: IMEMO, 1977) *dsp* (esp. pp. 15, 91–92).

209. E. G. Kutovoi, *Teoreticheskie aspekty ponizheniia urovnei voenno-go protivostoianiia v evrope* (Moscow: ISKAN, 1978) *dsp*, p. 6. Typically, Kutovoi drew heavily on IISS, SIPRI, RAND Corporation, and Brookings Institution analyses of Soviet military programs.

210. V. P. Lukin, *Evoliutsiia politiki SShA v otnoshenii KNR na rubezhe 70x godov* (Moscow: ISKAN, 1973) *dsp*, pp. 22–24, 122–23, 128–43, 240–41.

211. Girshfeld was another retired officer and sometime collaborator of Lukin's.

212. V. A. Girshfel'd, *Normalizatsiia otnoshenii i sblizhenie mezhdu KNDR i iuzhnoi koreei v sisteme mezhdunarodnykh otnoshenii v azii* (Moscow: IMEMO, 1973) *sekretno*, pp. 41–42. In 1979, Lukin and his ISKAN colleagues dispensed altogether with class analysis and drew on MacKinder, Spykman, and Mahan to view U.S.-Soviet relations in a "heartland-rimland" framework. From Panama to Thailand, they noted, U.S. military presence declined over the 1970s, even as it leaped ahead of the USSR in development of broader trade and diplomatic ties. V. P. Lukin, V. A. Kremeniuk, and I. B. Bugai, eds., *SShA i problemy tikhogo okeana* (Moscow: ISKAN, 1979).

213. Recall that Orlov was fired at *Izvestiia* for protesting the Prague Spring's fate and then dismissed from Rumyantsev's institute in Trapeznikov's purge of 1972. Hired at INION by Delusin, Orlov was saved again after Delusin's fall by Chernyaev. Boris Orlov (author's interview: Moscow, 25 July 1991). On Chernyaev's own evolving views of social democracy, see A. S. Cherniaev, *Sovremennaia sotsial-demokratiia i proble-my edinstva rabochego dvizheniia* (Moscow: Nauka, 1964) and A. S. Cherniaev and A. A. Galkin, eds., *Sotsial-demokraticheskii i burzhuaznyi reformizm* (Moscow: Nauka, 1980). The latter was printed in an edition of only 1,300 copies.

214. B. S. Orlov, *Sotsial'no-politicheskie korni zapadnogermanskogo neo-fashizma* (Moscow: MGIMO, 1970); B. S. Orlov, *Obshchestvenno-politich-eskie vzgliady V. Brandta* (Moscow: INION, 1973) *dsp*.

215. D. M. Proektor, *Nekotorye novye aspekty politiki FRG v oblasti natsional'noi i evropeiskoi bezopasnosti* (Moscow: IMEMO, 1979).

216. *Osnovnye cherty zapadnoevropeiskoi politicheskoi integratsii na sovremennom etape* (Moscow: IMEMO, 1976); *Rol' i mesto evropeiskogo parlamenta v protsesse zapadnoevropeiskoi integratsii* (Moscow: IMEMO, 1979); M. M. Maksimova, I. S. Kovolev, I. A. Beliiugo, *O tendentsii razvitiia "obshchego rynka"* (Moscow: IMEMO, 1979).

217. On the role of Lev Mendelevich, Anatoly Kovalev, and Yuli Vorontsov (who would later be promoted under Gorbachev), see Yuri Dubinin, "The Road to Helsinki," *International Affairs* (Moscow), no. 7 (1994): 76–94, and Yuri Kashlev, "The CSCE in the Soviet Union's Politics," *International Affairs* (Moscow), nos. 11–12 (1995): 66–72. See also L. Kornilov, "Leonid Il'ich ne znal, chto zapuskaet mekhanizm perestroiki," *Izvestiia*, 21 July 1995.

218. Kornilov, "Leonid Il'ich ne znal." It should be noted that, briefly smitten by the idea of going down in history as a great peacemaker, Brezhnev recalled a new version of his thoughts at the end of World War II. In this telling, he still dreamed of climbing the Eiffel Tower, but now, instead of spitting on Europe, sought to "proclaim for all to hear that the war was over forever." See Dubinin, "The Road to Helsinki," p. 80.

219. Kashlev, "The CSCE in the Soviet Union's Politics," p. 68; see also Leonov, *Likholet'e*, pp. 164–66.

220. Ibid. On Kovalev's difficulties, see also Cherniaev, *Moia zhizn' i moe vremia*, pp. 304–7. On Brezhnev's subsequent embitterment at not receiving the Nobel peace prize, and his rationalization of that failure via a supposed anti-Soviet conspiracy in terms that echo Khrushchev's anger over Pasternak's Nobel literature prize, see Chazov, *Zdorov'e i vlast'*, p. 87.

221. "Only very slowly did the wise men who had formulated the CSCE concept (those were Anatoly Kovalev, Lev Mendelevitch, and a few others) begin to succeed in . . . using our CSCE commitments to make the country drift away from Suslov's ideological orthodoxy, from the 'besieged fortress' philosophy. The 1977 incorporation of the 10 Helsinki Final Act principles into the Soviet Constitution was a major landmark along that road." Kashlev, "The CSCE in the Soviet Union's Politics," p. 68. Also a landmark in the human-rights movement was the reformers' successful persuasion of the leadership to publish the Helsinki Agreement in a mass Russian-language edition; see Grachev, *Kremlevskaia khronika*, p. 64.

222. This was publicly seen in such critical writings and V. G. Kalenskii, *Gosudarstvo kak ob"ekt sotsiologicheskogo analiza* (Moscow: Iuridicheskaia Literatura, 1977), and F. M. Burlatskii and V. E. Chirkin, eds., *Politicheskie sistemy sovremennosti. ocherki* (Moscow: Nauka, 1978). Privately, Chernyaev

proposed to International Department head Ponomarev the creation of a "Committee for the Defense of Human Rights," to which the latter replied, "Are you out of your mind, Anatoly Sergeyevich? And against whom, in your opinion, is it necessary to defend human rights in a socialist society?" Grachev, *Kremlevskaia khronika*, p. 101. See also Shakhnazarov, *Tsena svobody*, p. 352.

223. Ibid., p. 64. Further, "building a united Europe" was "something that they'd unofficially discussed with their social-democratic colleagues in the West for many years." Beyond its boost to establishment reformers, Soviet assent to the Helsinki accords provided an important impetus for other liberals and especially for unofficial human-rights campaigners. Altogether, the process bears strong resemblance to that of the "principled issue networks" that emerged in some other authoritarian systems; see Sikkink, "Human Rights, Principled Issue Networks, and Sovereignty in Latin America."

224. Aleksandr G. Savel'yev and Nikolay N. Detinov, *The Big Five: Arms Control Decision-Making in the Soviet Union* (New York: Praeger, 1995), pp. 16–22.

225. These were the SS-20 medium-range nuclear missiles and the Krasnoyarsk phased-array radar. On warnings by diplomats, civilian analysts and even some military opposition, see B. Surikov, "Stanet li bezopasnei mir?" *Literaturnaia Gazeta*, 24 January 1990; *Lektsiia G. M. Kornienko*, p. 22; Bovin, "Bez illiuzii;" *Moskovskie Novosti*, no. 11 (1990).

226. Velikhov, "Nauka rabotaet na bez"iadernyi mir," pp. 49–53.

227. See Alexander Bovin in *Izvestiia*, 1 July 1979.

228. See *Pravda*, 5 and 22 June, 1979; *Krasnaia Zvezda*, 14 June 1979; *Izvestiia*, 18 July 1979. Credit for these sources is owed Thomas Bjorkman and Thomas Zamostny, "Soviet Politics and Strategy Toward the West: Three Cases," *World Politics* 36, no. 2 (1984): 204.

229. See the critical articles in the series "Materials of an International Conference" on the scientific-technological revolution published in *MEMO*, nos. 6–8 (1979). On Inozemtsev's private appeals to the leadership, see Evgenii Primakov, "Muzhestvo preodeleniia," *Sovetskaia Kul'tura*, 30 March 1991.

230. Quoted from an untitled internal institute document reviewing ISKAN's main policy recommendations of 1968–79 (obtained by the author from ISKAN Deputy Director Sergei Plekhanov in July 1991).

231. V. I. Dashichev, ed., *Problemy vneshnei politiki sotsialisticheskikh stran* (Moscow: IEMSS, 1980), p. 6. This report, written in 1979, was not classified but was published in an edition of only 63 copies.

232. Ibid., pp. 64, 76.

233. Ibid., p. 12.

234. Dashichev cites from this memorandum, and describes its drafting and transmittal to the leadership in April 1979, in "Iz istorii stalinskoi diplomatii," L. G. Beliaeva et al., eds., *Isotriia i stalinizm* (Moscow: Politizdat, 1991), pp. 237–42.

5. The Time of Crisis and Transition

1. For a vivid analysis of the Soviet condition at the beginning of the 1980s, see Tucker, "Swollen State, Spent Society: Stalin's Legacy to Brezhnev's Russia," *Foreign Affairs* 60, no 2 (1981–82).

2. Iakovlev, *Muki prochteniia bytiia*, pp. 9–11. Karpinsky's 1968 observation about the "anachronism" of using "tanks . . . to fire at ideas" was, a decade later, felt all the more acutely.

3. Brezhnev had grown so infirm that by his death in November 1982 a succession struggle had in effect already been under way for two years.

4. The U.S. Strategic Defense Initiative (SDI) was launched in March 1983; KAL 007 was shot down on September 1. The "Euromissile" crisis simmered through the year, culminating in November with the West's response to Soviet SS-20s—deployment of new NATO ballistic and cruise missiles.

5. Literally, "It's impossible to live this way," a reformist refrain of the perestroika era.

6. The "Nixon analogy," that of a lifelong anti-Communist who nevertheless became the architect of U.S.-Soviet détente, was frequently cited.

7. "Real work" was the characterization of Nikolai Shmelev (interview: Moscow, 23 January 1991).

8. *Some Considerations of the Foreign Policy Results of the 1970s (Main Points), Jan. 20, 1980*, cited in "Afghanistan: As Seen in 1980," *Moscow News*, no. 30 (1989): 9. The cited portions of this memo were authored by Vyacheslav Dashichev, head of the foreign-policy section at IEMSS.

9. Ibid.

10. Nikolai I. Bukharin et al., *O prichinakh i sushchnosti krizisa 1980 g. v PNR* (IEMSS: Moscow, June 1981). This report was sent to the Central Committee.

11. On the prevailing hard-line view, blaming "bourgeois propaganda" and "subversion" while fuming at the Poles' ingratitude and their desire to "go over to the West," see the deliberations of the Politburo's Polish Commission described in Shakhnazarov, *Tsena svobody*, p. 115. Confirmation of this—particularly on the persistence of the hostile-isolationist outlook among the leadership as well as on the distorted information and analysis that it was provided—comes from intelligence veteran

Leonov. Summarizing the KGB's "objective" assessments, he stresses two main findings. One was the existence of a split within East European Communist Parties, between those "firmly oriented toward the USSR" and those "seeking to drag their countries to the West." The other was, as in the case of Poland, the insidious influence of "subversive enemy activities" from abroad together with "the strengthening of the kulak class, private property, and capitalist production leading to establishment of a base for anti-Soviet forces" at home. See Leonov, *Likholet'e*, pp. 198–99.

12. Bukharin et al., *O prichinakh*, pp. 1–15. Note here the parallel to Shmelev's mid-1970s critique of Soviet economic policy.

13. Ibid., pp. 15–16.

14. Ibid., pp. 26, 48–49. Of course, six months later repressive measures *were* taken; under intense Soviet pressure, Polish authorities imposed martial law in December 1981.

15. Arbatov, *The System*, p. 202. For recollection of senior diplomats' attempts to modify Soviet SS-20 policy—and of Ustinov's rejection of such initiatives—see Akhromeev and Kornienko, *Glazami marshala i diplomata*, pp. 41–46.

16. Cherniaev, *Moia zhizn' i moe vremia*, pp. 418–20.

17. Primakov, "Muzhestvo preodoleniia." See also N. Inozemtsev, "XXVI s"ezd KPSS i nashi zadachi," *MEMO*, no. 3 (1981) 4–24

18. Donald Maclean, "Some Reflections of a Communist on the Soviet Union" (spring 1981), in Steve Hirsch, ed., *MEMO 3: In Search of Answers in the Post-Soviet Era* (Washington, DC: Bureau of National Affairs, 1992), pp. 203, 208–9.

19. Ibid., pp. 208–9.

20. Ibid., pp. 211–12. Though he was less concerned about Soviet activism in the third world, Maclean also noted that this put him in a minority at IMEMO (p. 212).

21. Also noteworthy was Maclean's analysis of the changing professional-intellectual classes that he saw as vital to future reforms, though these could be launched only from "inside the upper reaches of the party-state hierarchy" through "something in the nature of a palace revolution" (ibid., pp. 203–4 and passim).

22. A. Bovin, "Neprekhodiashchee znachenie Leninskikh idei," *Kommunist*, no. 10 (1980): 70–81. On Afghanistan and the end of Bovin's "illusions," see his interview in "Bez illiuzii," *Sobesednik*, no. 6 (1990).

23. Burlatskii in *Literaturnaia Gazeta*, 28 January 1981; Arbatov in *Der Speigel*, 23 March 1981 (cited in Bjorkman and Zamostny, "Soviet Politics and Strategy," p. 211). Primakov, the former IMEMO deuputy director who now headed the Institue of Oriental Studies, cautiously concurred in his increasingly gloomy assessments of the USSR's prospects in

the third world; see E. Primakov, "Zakon neravnomernosti razvitiia i istoricheskoi sud'by osvobodivshikhsia stran," *MEMO* no. 12 (1980): 27–39.

24. N. S. Kishilov, A. G. Arbatov, Iu. E. Fedotov, *Vliianie vnesneevropeiskikh faktorov na obstanovku v evrope* (Moscow: IMEMO, 1980).

25. V. L. Sheinis, *Sotsial'no-ekonomicheskaia differentsiatsiia razvivaiushikhsia stran. tendentsii i perspektivy* (Moscow: IMEMO, 1981).

26. E. A. Bragina, *Melkoe promyshlennoe proizvodstvo v strategii osvobozhdivshikhsia stran na 80ye gody* (Moscow: IMEMO, 1982).

27. A. Nikiforov, *Sovremennyi podkhod SShA k problemam razvitiia osvobozhdivshikhsia gosudarstv* (Moscow: ISKAN, 1980).

28. V. P. Lukin, *O politike SShA v Azii v nachale 80-x godov*, report at the conference "Aktual'nye problemy sovremennoi Azii" (Moscow, 30 June–2 July 1982). Lukin also noted that the U.S. presence in Southwest Asia was *not* aimed at oil and raw materials—the U.S. had lately reduced its imports and diversified its sources—but rather at "stabilizing" the region.

29. D. M. Proektor, *Problemy bezopasnosti FRG* (Moscow: IMEMO, 1980); A. S. Cherniaev and A. A. Galkin, eds., *Razmezhevaniia i sdvigi v sotsial-reformizme* (Moscow: Nauka, 1983). The latter, though published by the Academy of Sciences as a book and not a classified specialist's report, was permitted an edition of only 1,150 copies.

30. V. V. Potashov, *Teoriia "sderzhivaniia" v iadernoi strategii SShA* (Moscow: ISKAN, 1980) *dsp*; R. G. Tumkovskii, *SShA: kontseptsii i programmy stroitel'stva strategicheskikh sil na rubezhe 80-x godov* (Moscow: ISKAN, 1980) *dsp*; Tumkovskii, *SShA i iadernaia politika anglii i frantsii* (Moscow: ISKAN, 1982) *dsp*.

31. Vladimir Tikhonov, the early advocate of NEP-marketizing measures, warned of a looming "food crisis" that could be prevented only by "cardinal" changes in agriculture; see V. A. Tikhonov, *Ekonomicheskie aspekty prodovol'stvennoi problemy v SSSR* (Moscow: IE, 1982). On cooperative-private enterprise and joint ventures, see respectively *"Maloe predpriiatie" i ego rol' v reshenii sotsial'no-ekonomicheskikh problem v stranakh SEV i SFRIu* (Moscow: IEMSS, 1981) *dsp*; *Sovmestnye predpriiatiia i osnovnye printsipy ikh funktsirovaniia* (Moscow: ISKAN, 1982). See also O. Bogomolov, "Ekonomicheskie sviazi mezhdu sotsialisticheskimi i kapitalisticheskimi stranami," *MEMO*, no. 3 (1980): 41–51.

32. B. P. Kurashvili, "Gosudarstvennoe upravlenie narodnym khoziastvom i perspektivy razvitiia," *Sovetskoe Gosudarstvo i Pravo* no. 6 (1982): 38–39.

33. B. P. Kurashvili, "Ob"ektivnye zakony gosudarstvennogo upravleniia," *Sovetskoe Gosuradrstvo i Pravo* no. 10 (1983): 44.

34. G. Kh. Shakhnazarov, Iu. A. Tikhomirov, eds, *Aktual'nye problemy*

sovremennogo   politicheskogo   razvitiia: ocherki   teorii   (Moscow: Iuridicheskaia Literatura, 1982); Burlatskii and Chirkin, *Politicheskie sistemy sovremennosti.*

35. A. P. Butenko, "Protivorechiia razvitiia sotsializma kak obshchestvennogo stroia," *VF,* no. 10 (1982): 27. Of course "contradictions" plagued capitalism, but under socialism only the existence of "non-antagonistic" contradictions was allowed and these were mostly "vestiges of capitalism." For this official viewpoint—which Butenko criticized—see V. S. Semenov, "Problemy protivorechii v sotsializme," *VF,* no. 7 (1982). For Butenko, the contradictions certainly were antagonistic and, moreover, a problem of the current system that could not simply be blamed on the past.

36. Butenko's IEMSS colleague Yevgeny Ambartsumov, who soon joined in the debate over socialism's contradictions (see below), analyzed their divergent paths under perestroika: "Butenko and I were both for socialism with a human face . . . but went different ways. He never read Western literature, just Marxist-Leninist classics, and remained a prisoner of his paradigm" (author's interview: Moscow, 6 August 1991).

37. As chapter 6 will show, Gorbachev's own evolution from the former to the latter outlook was central to his full embrace of the philosophy of "new thinking."

38. Brezhnev's words came at the 26th CPSU Congress in 1981, the year that nuclear no-first-use was emphasized.

39. V. V. Zagladin, I. T. Frolov, *Global'nye problemy sovremennosti. nauchnyi i sotsial'nyi aspekty* (Moscow: Mezhdunarodnye Otnosheniia, 1981).

40. N. N. Inozemtsev, ed., *Global'nye problemy sovremennosti* (Moscow: Mysl', 1981). See in particular chapter 3 (pp. 76–98) on the developing world by Georgy Mirsky, and chapter 4 (pp. 99–117) on global demographics by Eduard Arab-Olgy.

41. F. Burlatskii, "Filosofiia mira," *VF,* no. 12 (1982): 57–66; Georgi Shakhnazarov, *The Coming World Order* (Moscow: Progress, 1984), translation of *Griadushii miroporiadok* (Moscow: Politizdat, 1981).

42. In this vein, another new work ostensibly unmasking "bourgeois conceptions" but indirectly criticizing socialist practice as well was Khozin's *Global'nye problemy sovremennosti. kritika burzhuaznykh kontseptsii* (Moscow: Mysl', 1982).

43. Shenfield, *Nuclear Predicament,* pp. 61–62.

44. Ibid., p. 62.

45. A. S. Tsipko, *Nekotorye filosofskie aspekty teorii sotsializma* (Moscow: Nauka, 1983). Completed in 1981 after Tsipko's return from study in Poland during the Solidarity epoch, publication was delayed until

1983; even then, it came out only in an edition of 7,150 copies, many of which were subsequently recalled (see below).

46. Ibid., pp. 189–90. For the "Malthusian" critique, see Shakhnazarov, *Coming World Order*, p. 126.

47. Tsipko, *Nekotorye filosofskie aspekty*, pp. 190–91. On the origins of what Tsipko termed his "*Vekhi* worldview," particularly his discussions with dissident Polish intellectuals during the anti-Marxist "bacchanalia" of Solidarity's heyday, see Aleksandr Tsipko, "Gorbachev postavil na 'sotsialisticheskii vybor' i proigral," *Nezavisimaia Gazeta*, 17 October 1996, p. 3.

48. Burlatskii, "Filosofiia mira," p. 45. IMEMO analyst Oleg Bykov also cited Engels, stressing that the overriding priority was now "to ensure preservation of the human race . . . the solution of all other questions—economic, social, political and *ideological*—depends on this." O. Bykov, "Revoliutsionnaia teoriia izbavleniia chelovechestva ot voin," *MEMO*, no. 4 (1983): 3 (italics added).

49. Burlatskii, "Filosofiia mira," p. 57.

50. In addition to the detail offered below, much more is analyzed in Evangelista, *Unarmed Forces*, chapters 7–11.

51. Roald Z. Sagdeev, *The Making of a Soviet Scientist: My Adventures in Nuclear Fusion and Space from Stalin to Star Wars* (New York, Wiley, 1994), p. 266.

52. Chazov, *Zdorove i vlast'*, pp. 90–113. For his efforts, Chazov would later share the Nobel Peace Prize (in 1985) that had eluded Brezhnev.

53. Arbatov, *The System*, p. 302.

54. Roald Sagdeev (author's interview: College Park, MD, 12 April 1997).

55. Evangelista, *Unarmed Forces*, pp. 190–91. See also Elena Agapova, "Nash chelovek v kongresse," *Krasnaia Zvezda*, 15 September 1989.

56. Arbatov, *The System*, p. 303.

57. Extensive recollections of Brezhnev's isolation and decrepitude during his final years are found in the memoirs of Arbatov, Burlatsky, Chazov, and Grachev. Other vivid portrayals of Brezhnev's decline—his confusion of fictional people and events with reality, his insatiable appetite for awards, and his readiness to approve any proposal that his aides recommended—are found in Cherniaev, *Moia zhizn' i moe vremia*, pp. 380–82, 421–39, and Boris El'tsin, *Ispoved' na zadannuiu temu* (Leningrad: Sovetskii Pisatel,' 1990), p. 53.

58. The existence of a "rump" Politburo group that "decided all important issues while other members had little to say" was recalled by long-time Politburo aide Viktor Pribytkov (author's interview: Moscow, 4 July 1991). By most recollections, it was comprised of Brezhnev,

Chernenko, Suslov, Ustinov, Gromyko, and, sometimes, Andropov. Leading up to the latter's accession at the end of the year, 1982 saw the rapid decline or death of the cautious (though dogmatic) Suslov and the (relative) moderates Brezhnev and Chernenko, thus strengthening the hard-line Defense Minister Ustinov (to whom Gromyko usually deferred). On this core group, see also the recollections of others formerly in or near the top leadership, including: Viktor Grishin, "Chto Vam Skazat'? Sami Razbiraites'!" *Nezavisimaia Gazeta* no. 21 (1991); Pechenev, *Gorbachev: k vershinam vlasti*, p. 108; Shevchenko, *Breaking With Moscow*, pp. 207–10.

59. On Gromyko's (and Andropov's) deference to Ustinov and the military, see Akhromeev and Kornienko, *Glazami marshala i diplomata*, pp. 44–46; Arbatov, *Zatianuvsheesia vyzdorovlenie*, pp. 236–37. As Gorbachev recalled, "Nobody in the Politburo dared to oppose him." Gorbachev, *Zhizn' i reformy*, vol. 1, p. 207.

60. On the devolution of initiative to "second echelon" Politburo and Central Committee officials earlier excluded from key decisions, see Viktor Pribytkov, "Pomoshchnik Genseka," *Sovershenno Sekretno*, no. 7 (1990): 16–17; Pechenev, *Gorbachev. k vershinam vlasti*, pp. 10, 31, 80–81, 108–12.

61. Arbatov, *Zatianuvsheesia vyzdorovlenie*, pp. 303–4, 324.

62. Cited in Shenfield, *Nuclear Predicament*, p. 15.

63. Arbatov, *Zatianuvsheesia vyzdorovlenie*, pp. 324–25.

64. See Iakov Etinger, "Ne sleduet uproshchat' slozhnuiu problemu," *Nezavisimaia Gazeta*, 20 March 1993.

65. Andrei Fadin (author's interview: Moscow, 27 November 1990); Kagarlitsky, *Thinking Reed*, p. 350.

66. Arbatov, *Zatianuvsheesia vyzdorovlenie*, pp. 272–73; Gherman Diligensky (author's interview: Moscow, 27 February 1990). Diligensky, Kudyukin's thesis adviser, was fired and only later reinstated to become editor of IMEMO's journal *Mirovaia Ekonomika i Mezhdunarodnye Otnosheniia* (*MEMO*).

67. Arbatov, *Zatianuvsheesia vyzdorovlenie*, p. 273.

68. Inozemtsev died of a heart attack in August 1982; see Cherniaev, *Moia zhizn' i moe vremia*, p. 306.

69. IMEMO deputy director Oleg Bykov recalled that "during the last year of Inozemtsev's life, academic-scientific work basically stopped and we were reduced to a struggle for survival" (author's interview: Moscow, 10 September 1991).

70. Arbatov, *Zatianuvsheesia vyzdorovlenie*, pp. 272–74.

71. Nikolai Bukharin, head of IEMSS Polish section (author's interview: Moscow, 10 August and 30 November 1990; 28 July 1991); Mikhail Gitular, analyst, IEMSS Polish section (author's interview: Moscow, 10 August 1990); Otto Latsis, former head, IEMSS Department for Socialist Countries

(author's interview: Moscow, 12 September 1991); Nikolai Shmelev, former IEMSS analyst (author's interview: Moscow, 23 March 1991).

72. Arbatov, *Zatianuvsheesia vyzdorovlenie*, p. 269. Arbatov recalls that this case prompted a stormy Politburo session and, as in the IMEMO scandal, creation of a Party investigatory commission. Its members included Ustinov, Zimyanin, and Andropov.

73. According to a number of former ISKAN staffers, Arbatov was also criticized for having advised the leadership during the 1980 U.S. presidential elections that a businesslike conservative (Reagan) might be preferable to an erratic human-rights campaigner (Carter). Arbatov himself vehemently denies ever having argued thus (author's interview: Moscow, 6 June 1996).

74. Arbatov also tried, unsuccessfully, to persuade Andropov to end Yakovlev's Canadian "exile" and name him to head state television and radio (*Gosteleradio*); see Cherniaev, *Moia zhizn' i moe vremia*, p. 435.

75. For detail on both Arbatov's and Bovin's woes, see Arbatov, *Zatianuvsheesia vyzdorovlenie*, pp. 324–28.

76. Ibid., p. 324. Also at this time, European-affairs specialist Valentin Falin was fired from a senior Central Committee post for proposing a bold measure to help ameliorate the crisis in Poland—telling the truth about Stalin's Katyn massacre. See Grachev, *Kremlevskaia khronika*, pp. 85–86.

77. Arbatov, *Zatianuvsheesia vyzdorovlenie*, pp. 327–28.

78. Pechenev, *Gorbachev: k vershinam vlasti*, p. 54. Delivered before an assembly of the entire leadership, a more humiliating reprimand is difficult to imagine. The question is, *who* was reprimanded? Pechenev writes that Arbatov was the clear target of Andropov's criticism, while Arbatov himself says that it was in fact Bovin (author's interview: Moscow, 6 June 1996). Perhaps Andropov had both in mind, as well as Chazov, another Central Committee member who regularly consorted with foreigners.

79. The rift was soon healed and Arbatov resumed his practice of informally advising Andropov; see Arbatov, *Zatianuvsheesia vyzdorovlenie*, pp. 328–29.

80. "Experiment" was the Andropov-era code word for reform. For detail on domestic and foreign-policy changes see below.

81. Iu. V. Andropov, "Uchenie Karla Marksa i nekotorye voprosy sotsialisticheskogo stroitel'stva v SSSR," *Kommunist*, no. 3 (1983).

82. *Pravda*, 16 June 1983.

83. Ibid.

84. "It wasn't difficult to create a team that would develop a program for economic perestroika because these people were already well known . . . Aganbegyan, Arbatov, Bogomolov, Zaslavskaya, Tikhonov." See Nikolai Ryzhkov, *Perestroika. istoriia predatel'stv* (Moscow: Novosti, 1992), p. 46.

85. In preparing his report on *The Complex Modernization of Economic*

Management, Shatalin was aided by Zaslavskaya and Leonid Abalkin; see Shatalin, " '500 dnei' i drugie dni moei zhizni."

86. The memo was published in *Survey,* no. 28 (1984). On links to Butenko and the debate about socialism's "contradictions" and "crises," see Elizabeth Teague, *Solidarity and the Soviet Worker: The Impact of the Polish Events of 1980 on Soviet Internal Politics* (London: Croom Helm, 1988), pp. 302–13.

87. V. A. Medvedev, *Upravlenie sotsialistichesim proizvodstvom: problemy teorii i praktiki* (Moscow: Politizdat, 1983). Medvedev worked in the Central Committee apparatus with Yakovlev at the time when Yakovlev supported Gorbachev's local reform efforts (1971) and criticized Russian nationalism (1972).

88. Ryzhkov, *Istoriia predatel'stv;* see also the accounts of Valentin Pavlov, *Izvestiia,* 15 June 1991; and Anatoly Lukyanov in "Interv'iu iz-za reshetki," *Nezavisimaia Gazeta,* 17 September 1992.

89. For detail, see Ryzhkov, *Istoriia predatel'stv,* pp. 37–50.

90. Yegor Ligachev, *Inside Gorbachev's Kremlin: The Memoirs of Yegor Ligachev* (New York: Pantheon, 1993), pp. 9, 17–27.

91. Examples include publishing weekly summaries of Politburo activity, exposés of widespread corruption and alcoholism, and increasingly critical Letters to the editor. On the changes at *Izvestiia* under Tolkunev, see *Moskovskie Novosti* no. 10 (1992): 11. Many examples of emboldened specialist writings are detailed below.

92. Even a majority of U.S. experts believed that development of SDI would violate the ABM treaty and upset the nuclear balance. Regarding Andropov's ignorance of the decision to shoot down KAL 007, see "Taina Koreiskogo 'Boinga-747,'" *Isvestiia,* 23, 29, and 31 May 1991.

93. Kornienko describes a July 1983 meeting between Andropov and Babrak Karmal in which the latter was told "in no uncertain terms . . . not to rely on the long-term presence of Soviet troops in Afghanistan and to [prepare for their exit] by broadening the government's social base through political means." This effort later flagged in tandem with Andropov's health; see Akhromeev and Kornienko, *Glazami marshala i diplomata,* pp. 47–48.

94. An analysis of diplomatic relations under Andropov is Garthoff, *Great Transition,* pp. 85–147.

95. Akhromeev and Kornienko, *Glazami marshala i diplomata,* pp. 41–50.

96. "Andropov remained a man of his times, one of those who couldn't break out of the bounds of old ideas and values—he never resisted [efforts to resurrect Stalin's image] . . . and what about his role in Hungary, Czechoslovakia, in the Afghan war?" Gorbachev, *Zhizn' i reformy,* vol. 1, p. 274.

97. Cited in Wohlforth, *Elusive Balance*, p. 240.

98. *Pravda*, 6 November 1982.

99. Ibid.

100. "Year of Andropov" is the characterization of Kornienko in Akhromeev and Kornienko, *Glazami marshala i diplomata*, p. 48.

101. *USA: Military Production and the Economy* (Moscow: ISKAN, 1983), cited by Shenfield, *Nuclear Predicament*, p. 49.

102. N. P. Shmelev, "SShA v mirovom kapitalisticheskom khoziaistve," *MEMO*, no. 4 (1984): 44.

103. Cited in Wohlforth, *Elusive Balance*, p. 242.

104. See Burlatskii, "Nekotorye voprosy teorii mezhdunarodnykh otnoshenii," *Voprosy filosofii* no. 9 (1983): 36–48; also Burlatskii, "Filosofiia mira."

105. A. V. Kozyrev, "Limitation of the Arms Trade," in *Problems of Common Security* (Moscow: Progress, 1984), pp. 140–56 (translation of *Aktual'nye problemy mezhdunarodnoi bezopasnosti i razoruzheniia*).

106. E. A. Ambartsumov, "Analiz V. I. Leninym prichin krizisa 1921 g. i putei vykhoda iz nego," *Voprosy Istorii*, no. 4 (1984): 15–29.

107. G. Kh. Shakhnazarov, "Logika politicheskogo myshleniia v iadernuiu eru," *VF*, no. 5 (1984): 63–74.

108. Details on his study of East European politico-military affairs, and debates with General Sergei Akhromeev (later Marshal Akhromeev, chief of the general staff), are found in Shakhnazarov, *Tsena svobody*, pp. 84–86.

109. Shakhnazarov, "Logika politicheskogo myshleniia," pp. 64, 66.

110. Ibid., p. 70.

111. Ibid., pp. 67–68. Beyond ecological concerns, Shakhnazarov also approvingly cited Western futurologists' warning of the danger of a third party, possibly a terrorist group, provoking U.S.-Soviet war, a scenario previously downplayed.

112. Ibid., p. 72.

113. For example, in 1983 "Moscow was awash in rumors" over the affair of radio announcer Vladimir Danchev, who, in a broadcast of May 23, spoke of "the struggle against Soviet aggressors" and said that "the Afghan people are defending their country against Soviet occupiers." See "Ego schitali 'chelovekom Andropova'" ["He was considered 'Andropov's man'"] *Sobesednik*, no. 25 (1990): 12. Fueling the belief that Andropov sympathized with such criticism was the treatment accorded Danchev; after being fired and briefly confined in a psychiatric hospital, he was released and offered reinstatement at his job. Sakharov, for his criticism of the Afghan invasion, suffered six years of internal exile. For a broad treatment of Soviet Afghan policy, see Mendelson, *Changing Course*.

114. E. Ambartsumov, "Eshche est' vremia," *Literaturnaia Gazeta*, 16 November 1983, p. 10.

115. "Lichnaia bezopasnost' kazhdogo," *Literaturnaia Gazeta*, 25 April 1990, p. 12.

116. "Dekabristy zastoia," *Moskovskie Novosti*, no. 13 (1990): 11.

117. Gen. Dmitri Volkogonov, at that time deputy chief of the Main Political Administration of the Armed Forces (author's interview: Moscow, 30 May 1991). Volkogonov recalled the affair as a "rebellion."

118. *Reshenie tovarishcheskogo suda chesti starshikh ofitserov voennoi akademii imeni M. V. Frunze ot 8 ianvariia 1986 g.* This document was obtained from Kovalevsky's personal archive, as were more than a dozen student petitions and letters written in his support.

119. My chapter 4 describes how Artsimovich and other scientists defeated a late-1970s military proposal for a Soviet "Star Wars–type" system. Now, with the U.S. program, Soviet strategic-defense advocates were emboldened; Sagdeev recalls the enormous energy spent fighting "the forces that wanted to establish a Soviet SDI." See Sagdeev, *Making of a Soviet Scientist*, p. 320. On Ustinov's hard-line response, see Akhromeev and Kornienko, *Glazami marshala i diplomata*, p. 20.

120. Ambassador Dobrynin described the emergence, as a result of this international cooperation, of "a contemporary Soviet school of foreign policy and military-political research." See A. Dobrynin, "Za bez'iadernyi mir, navstrechu XXI veku," *Kommunist*, no. 9 (1986): 26.

121. Andrei Kokoshin (author's interview: Moscow, 15 August 1991) and Yevgeny Velikhov (author's interview: Moscow, 27 December 1993). In broad outline, the same arguments appeared in such published sources as E. P. Velikhov, "Nauka i aktual'nye problemy borby protiv ugrozy iadernoi voiny," *Vestnik Akademii Nauk SSSR*, no. 9 (1983): 25–26, and *Strategicheskie i mezhdunarodno-politicheskie posledstviia sozdaniia kosmicheskoi protivoraketnoi sistemy s ispol'zovaniem oruzhiia napravlennoi peredachi energii: doklad Komiteta Sovetskikh uchenykh v zashchitu mira, protiv iadernoi ugrozy* (Moscow: Novosti, 1984). See also E. P. Velikhov, A. A. Kokoshin, "Iadernoe oruzhie i dilemma mezhdunarodnoi bezopasnosti," *MEMO*, no. 4 (1985): 33–43.

122. In Sagdeev's words, "Our concept and response to SDI was drafted by the autumn of 1983." Sagdeev, *Making of a Soviet Scientist*, p. 266. These arguments reached Western attention with publication of Yevgeni Velikhov, Roald Sagdeev, and Andrei Kokoshin, *Weaponry in Space: The Dilemma of Security* (Moscow: Izdatel'stvo Mir, 1986). See also R. Z. Sagdeev and S. N. Rodionov, *Space-Based Anti-Missile System: Capabilities Assessment* (Moscow: Space Research Institute, 1986).

123. Velikhov claims that it was the committee that persuaded

Andropov to enact a moratorium on anti-satellite testing in August 1983 (author's interview: Moscow, 30 December 1993).

124. V. V. Aleksandrov and G. L. Stenchikov, *On the Modeling of the Climactic Consequences of the Nuclear Winter* (Moscow, 1983); V. Goldanskii and S. Kapitsa, "Ne dopustit' katastrofy," *Izvestiia*, 25 July 1984; Nikita Moiseev, "Chto vperedi?" *Sovershenno Sekretno*, no. 4 (1991): 2–3. A powerful 1984 address on the folly of nuclear weapons by committee member Boris Raushenbakh, delivered at a meeting of the Soviet Writers' Union, is noted in Dusko Doder, *Shadows and Whispers: Power Politics Inside the Kremlin from Brezhnev to Gorbachev* (New York: Random House, 1985), p. 225.

125. Boris Raushenbakh (author's interview: Moscow, 20 March 1991).

126. Vitaly Goldansky (author's interview: Moscow, 12 December 1990).

127. The contrast between this humanities education and the Brezhnev cohort's hurry-up technical training and harsh indoctrination during the terror and early five-year plans was enormous (see chapter 1). But the difference between a Moscow State law degree and the Ordzhonikidze Aircraft Construction Institute (Ligachev) or the Ural Polytechnical Institute (Ryzhkov, Yeltsin) was also great.

128. For an early example, see the excerpts from his private letters of the mid 1950s—criticizing stagnation and bureaucratism—cited in Gorbacheva, *Ia nadieius'*, pp. 86–88, 102–7.

129. As a regional Party boss in the 1970s, Gorbachev backed the "link" system and other agricultural reforms. Even earlier, he had been involved in efforts to implement some of Gennady Lisichkin's decentralizing plans on a local level. See Brown, *Gorbachev Factor*, pp. 43–46; Gorbachev, *Zhizn' i reformy*, vol. 1, pp. 117–19.

130. Recall (chapter 3) the links between Czechoslovak and Soviet reformers—particularly Sik and Lisichkin—until both were quashed in 1968. Another short-lived "experiment" that attracted Gorbachev's attention was the GDR's mid-1960s effort to increase enterprise autonomy and raise incentives along the lines of the so-called Liberman reforms. See Gorbachev, *Zhizn' i reformy*, vol. 1, pp. 155–56.

131. Mikhail S. Gorbachev, in "Retrospectives at the Gorbachev Foundation," *Demokratizatsiya* 4, no. 1 (1996): 19.

132. Gorbachev, *Zhizn' i reformy*, vol. 1, pp. 118–20.

133. Gorbachev and Mlynar, *Dialog o perestroike*, pp. 31, 36. Note the similarity to Karpinsky's experience in Eastern Europe, after the invasion of Hungary, as described in chapter 2 (n. 160).

134. His experience in Italy, judging by his very detailed and admiring reminiscences, played a special role in Gorbachev's intellectual evolution and his later attraction to Eurocommunist and social-democratic thought.

In fact, his first dealings with the critical, free-thinking Italian Communists—and an acquaintance with Len Karpinsky—came at the 22nd CPSU Congress in 1961; Gorbachev, *Zhizn' i reformy*, vol. 1, pp. 159–64. Also important was Gorbachev's friendship—dating back to a youth festival in the 1960s—with future PCI leader Enrico Berlinguer. Georgy Shakhnazarov (author's interview: Moscow, 28 June 1996).

135. And, it might be added, by his disinterest in studying such aspects of bourgeois decadence as pornography. See Cherniaev, *Shest' let s Gorbachevym*, p. 8.

136. Gorbachev, *Zhizn' i reformy*, vol. 1, p. 169.

137. Gorbachev and Mlynar, *Dialog o perestroika*, p. 38. A more complete listing of the Progress publishers' "white book," limited-circulation translations of Western writings is in chapter 3 at n. 112.

138. Shevardnadze, *Moi vybor*, pp. 60–63, 79.

139. "O nekotorykh merakh posledovatel'nogo osushestvleniia agrarnoi politiki KPSS na sovremennom etape. Iz zapiski v TsK KPSS, mai 1978 goda," in M. S. Gorbachev, *Izbrannye rechi i stat'i*, vol. 1 (Moscow: Politizdat, 1987), pp. 180–200. For analysis of this report, see Brown, *Gorbachev Factor*, pp. 46–47.

140. Stuart Parrott, "Aganbegyan's Press Conference in London," *Radio Liberty Research Report* 486/87, December 1 1987.

141. Vladimir Tikhonov (author's interview: Moscow, 24 May 1990).

142. Cited in Cohen and vanden Heuvel, *Voices of Glasnost*, p. 119. Sagdeev recalls of 1982–83 that "Velikhov, Georgy Arbatov and Abel Aganbegyan . . . mentioned the name of Gorbachev as someone interesting and unusual. I soon discovered that all of my friends . . . had been invited to be regular members of different parallel groups chaired by Gorbachev." See Sagdeev, *Making of a Soviet Scientist*, p. 264.

143. Cohen and vanden Heuvel, *Voices of Glasnost*, p. 160; Yevgeny Velikhov (author's interview: Moscow, 30 December 1993).

144. Cherniaev, *Shest' let s Gorbachevym*, p. 9. Gorbachev's Politburo aide Valery Boldin (whose own views were closer to Andropov's, and who would betray Gorbachev in August 1991) wrote that Gorbachev's meetings with those "who espoused bold ideas" became so frequent that they began to arouse the suspicion of others in the senior leadership. See Valery Boldin, *Ten Years that Shook the World: The Gorbachev Era as Witnessed by his Chief of Staff* (New York: Basic, 1994), p. 37.

145. Cherniaev, *Shest' let s Gorbachevym*, p. 9.

146. Here again, Italy figures prominently. Gorbachev was moved by the outpouring of grief, respect, and national solidarity that he witnessed at the 1984 funeral of PCI leader Enrico Berlinguer: "It all revealed a mentality, a political culture, so different from ours. I had already read the pro-

grammatic documents of the Italian communists, the famous 'Togliatti Memorandum' that surfaced right after the 20th CPSU Congress. I had studied Gramsci's *Prison Notebooks* thoroughly. But still, seeing Berlinguer's funeral was deeply thought-provoking." Gorbachev, *Zhizn' i reformy*, vol. 1, pp. 255–56. Upon his return to Moscow, Gorbachev excitedly told an aide, "You can know a lot about something, but it's still totally different when you see it with your own eyes." Cherniaev, *Shest' let s Gorbachevym*, pp. 15–16; see also pp. 20–21.

147. Vadim Zagladin, cited in Cherniaev, *Shest' let s Gorbachevym*, p. 19.

148. E. Primakov, "Uchenyi, rukovoditel,' chelovek (k 70 letiiu akademika N. N. Inozemtseva)," *MEMO*, no. 4 (1991): 106.

149. Frolov, in "Vokrug sensatsii i bez nego."

150. Shakhazarov, "Vo mnogom poteriannaia zhizn." Further, "For the first time I met a senior official who really read things—and not just Party documents. This was rare . . . we began discussing such issues as the problems of democracy under socialism. I had written about this, about conflicting social interests, but had to get rid of some chapters in order to publish." Georgy Shakhnazarov (author's interview: Moscow, 28 June 1996). On Shakhnazarov's 1972 *Sotsialisticheskaia demokratiia*, see chapter 4 (n. 34).

151. Arbatov, *The System*, pp. 280–81.

152. Sagdeev, *Making of a Soviet Scientist*, p. 266. Chernyaev describes Arbatov's constructive influence on Gorbachev at this time in Cherniaev, *Shest' let s Gorbachevym*, p. 24.

153. Ibid., p. 26.

154. Grachev, *Kremlevskaia khronika*, p. 140.

155. Boldin, *Ten Years That Shook the World*, p. 43.

156. Iakovlev, *Muki prochteniia bytiia*, p. 32. Gorbachev's own writings, on this and other key junctures in the rise of new thinking (and on the role of Yakovlev, Shevardnadze, et al.), are oddly terse. Of his visit to Canada, Gorbachev dwells on agriculture and mentions Yakovlev only as the one who arranged his visit; see Gorbachev, *Zhizn' i reformy*, vol. 1, pp. 237–39.

157. "Konservatizm i dinamizm—ikh adepty," in Iakovlev, *Gorkaia chasha*, pp. 27–38.

158. Ibid., pp. 30–31. A common misperception, based on some of his mass-circulation writings of the early 1980s, is that Yakovlev was deeply anti-American. Not only does this ignore such sources as the above, it also conflates anti-Reaganism with anti-Americanism while forgetting the bitter political climate of that time. In fact, "it was to deflect attention from his real political agenda, that is radical reform, that he felt obliged to adopt the rhetoric of the most orthodox critics of the U.S." See Morton Schwartz, reviewing Richard M. Mills's *As Moscow Sees Us* in *American Political Science Review*, 86, no. 2 (1992): 590.

159. IMEMO analyst Sergei Blagovolin (author's interview: Moscow, 20 May 1991).

160. Martin Malia, "From Under the Rubble, What?" *Problems of Communism*, 41, no. 1 (1992)): 105.

161. S. Chugrov, "Kniga Aleksandra Iakovleva i Lilli Marku vo Frantsii," *MEMO*, no. 12 (1991): 139.

162. Iakovlev, *Muki prochteniia bytiia*, p. 64.

163. S. Blagovolin, *Prostranstvennaia struktura voenno-ekonomichesko-go bloka NATO* (Moscow: IMEMO, 1983) *dsp.*

164. Sergei Blagovolin (author's interview: Moscow, 20 May 1991). In Yakovlev's words, "The top brass insisted that the country be prepared for war 'on all azimuths.' So that's what our 'peaceful coexistence as a particular form of class struggle' means in practice!" Iakovlev, *Gorkaia chasha*, p. 192.

165. Chugrov, "Kniga Aleksandrova Iakovleva," p. 138. On Yakovlev's mobilization of reformist experts and "synthesis" of their recommendations for Gorbachev, see Boldin, *Ten Years*, p. 73.

166. "Gorbachev's team" also included Yevgeny Primakov, Vadim Medvedev, and Georgy Shakhnazarov.

167. Vadim Medvedev, interview with *Le Monde*, from *FBIS-SOV*, 2 June 1989, p. 27.

168. *Pravda*, 7 January 1989. "Nothing happened with the plenum. The only trace it left, the only consolation, were two boxes of studies and reports prepared by the late Academician Nikolai Inosemtsev." Mikhail Gorbachev, "Oglianut'sia nazad, chtoby posmotret' vpered," *Svobodnaia Mysl'*, no. 3 (1995): 5.

169. Chernenko slowed, but did not halt entirely, the turnover of regional Party officials begun under Andropov. Also, by January 1985 it was decided to return to the Geneva nuclear-arms talks; however, progress here remained unlikely as Soviet (and U.S.) positions on substantive issues had not changed.

170. Much like *tak zhit' nel'zia* for reformers, "proven methods" became a mantra of the opponents of perestroika.

171. K. U. Chernenko, "Current Issues of Ideological and Mass-Political Work of the Party" (report at CC CPSU Plenum of 14 June, 1983), *Pravda*, 15 June 1983.

172. A. Butenko, "Eshche raz o protivorechiiakh sotsializma," *VF*, no. 2 (1984); E. Bugaev, "Strannaia pozitsiia," *Kommunist*, no. 14 (1984). On Kosolapov, see Ernst Kux, "Contradictions of Soviet Socialism," *Problems of Communism* 33, no. 6 (1984). In protest against Kosolapov's vicious dogmatism, Chernyaev pointedly resigned from the editorial board of *Kommunist* in 1984.

173. Nikolai Pokrovsky, former assistant editor at the *Nauka* Academy of Sciences publishing house (author's interview: Moscow, 20 June 1990).

174. See the well-scripted 1984 academic show trial of Tsipko, reported in "Na zasedanii nauchnogo soveta MGU po sisteme ekonomicheskikh zakonov i kategorii politicheskoi ekonomii," *Vestnik MGU. Seriia 6 (Ekonomika)*, no. (1985): 72–83.

175. Gorbachev's positive reaction to Tsipko's book—as seen, Gorbachev had a long-standing interest in NEP as a model for new reforms—was noted by Chernyaev (author's interview: Princeton, 26 February 1993). Gorbachev's intercession on Tsipko's behalf was recalled by former Politburo aide Pechenev (author's interview: Moscow, 30 May 1991). See also Tsipko, "Gorbachev postavil na 'sotsialisticheskii vybor.'"

176. Shakhnazarov, *Tsena svobody*, pp. 40–41.

177. Chugrov, "Kniga Aleksandra Iakovleva," p. 139. Among Yakovlev's headaches was the case of IMEMO staffer Girshfeld, the retired army colonel whose criticism of Soviet military policy (he also coined the term *sufficient defenses*, which later became a tenet of Gorbachev's security policy) caused a scandal when it appeared in the Western media. On this episode, see Evangelista, *Unarmed Forces*, pp, 189–90.

178. *New York Times*, 12 February 1992, p. A-8.

179. Nikolai Ogarkov, "Nadezhnaia zashchita mira," *Izvestiia*, 23 September 1983. Gromyko's defense of détente appeared in *Kommunist*, no. 6 (1983): 11–32. Ogarkov was a strong advocate of higher military spending and increased "vigilance." His dismissal, in late 1984, apparently resulted not from policy differences but from a personal clash with Ustinov, and Ogarkov's too-open ambition. Andropov greatly disliked Ogarkov, privately referring to him as "that little Napoleon." See Arbatov, *Zatianuvsheesia vyzdorovlenie*, p. 323.

180. In a less-publicized step, Romanov also took sides with the "Stalinists," against the "Eurocommunists," in an internal Finnish Communist Party dispute. Gorbachev, meanwhile, gave an admiring eulogy at the funeral of Eurocommunist pioneer Berlinguer, while eschewing the worst East-West recriminations and holding out hope of détente's revival. See *Pravda*, 21 and 26 April, 8 November 1983; Gorbachev, *Izbrannye rechi i stat'i*, vol. 1, pp. 445–50. Romanov had recently joined the Central Committee Secretariat (with responsibility for defense and heavy industry) and thus formally became a contender for succession.

181. Compare *Izvestiia* commentary of 24–30 July and 3–8 August 1984, with that of *Pravda*, 21–29 July and 2–11 August 1984. For detail on this issue see also Michael J. Sodaro, *Moscow, Germany, and the West from Khrushchev to Gorbachev* (Ithaca: Cornell University Press, 1990), pp. 265, 288–310.

182. Having supposedly been constant for years, the announced defense budget increase was from 17 to 19 billion rubles.

183. Christopher Andrew and Oleg Gordievsky, *KGB: The Inside Story of its Operations from Lenin to Gorbachev* (New York: Harper-Collins, 1990), pp. 583–605; see also the documents and analysis in Andrew and Gordievsky, eds., *Instructions from the Centre: Top Secret Files from the KGB's Foreign Operations, 1975–1985* (London: Hodder & Stoughton, 1991), pp. 67–90. On exaggerated fears of new NATO medium-range missiles' ability to strike Moscow, see Savel'yev and Detinov, *Big Five*, p. 57.

184. *Literaturnaia Gazeta*, 2 January 1984 (cited in Shenfield, *Nuclear Predicament*, p. 36).

185. A similar argument, in less vivid terms, had recently been made by the foreign minister and International Department head: A. A. Gromyko and B. N. Ponomarev, eds., *Istoriia vneshnei politiki SSSR*, vol. 1 (Moscow: Nauka, 1980), pp. 94–109, 156–58.

186. Neither was this climate eased by such Western statements as Reagan's quip that "we begin bombing in five minutes." See also Vladimir Shlapentokh, "Moscow's War Propaganda and Soviet Public Opinion," *Problems of Communism* 33, no. 5 (1984): 88–94.

187. "Otkrovennyi dialog o perestroike," *Izvestiia*, 29 April 1990.

188. An analysis of Stalin's complex legacy in Soviet society and officialdom is Cohen's "The Stalin Question Since Stalin," in *Rethinking the Soviet Experience*, pp. 93–127.

189. "Worn but worrying refrains from earlier, similar phases of the general line made their reappearance, from xenophobic laws against mixing with foreigners to thinly veiled anti-Semitic propaganda against 'Zionist' influences in Soviet life." Wohlforth, *Elusive Balance*, p. 225.

190. Arbatov, *Zatianuvsheesia vyzdorovlenie*, pp. 324–25.

191. See Tucker, *Soviet Political Mind*, pp. 94–7.

192. For an analysis of Ivan Stadniuk's *Voina* (War), see Dobrenko, "The Literature of the Zhdanov Era," p. 132.

193. Such as the World War II documentary, *Marshal Zhukov*, in which Stalin appeared in a positive light.

194. See the excerpt at the beginning of this chapter, cited from the transcript of a Politburo meeting of 12 July 1984, in the *Cold War International History Project Bulletin*, no. 4 (1994): 81–2.

195. Cited in Chugrov, "Kniga Aleksandra Iakovleva," p. 139.

196. *Izvestiia*, 29 April 1990. See also Shakhnazarov, *Tsena svobody*, p. 92.

197. Arbatov, *Zatianuvsheesia vyzdorovlenie*, p. 337. However, Chernenko still died too soon; the 27th CPSU Congress was held when originally scheduled, in February-March 1986. Others' interpretations of

the initiative to advance the congress vary somewhat. *Pravda* editor Afanasyev saw it simply as an attempt by junior members of Chernenko's entourage to further their careers, possibly gaining places on the Central Committee Secretariat; see Afanas'iev, *4-aia Vlast' i 4 Genseka*, p. 54. Chazov concurs in part, but also emphasizes the interests of such senior hard-liners as Prime Minister Tikhonov and Defense Minister Ustinov in definitively halting reform attempts and strengthening the position of the military-industrial complex; see Chazov, *Zdorov'e i vlast'*, pp. 195–200.

198. Cited in Chugrov, "Kniga Aleksandra Iakovleva," p. 139.

6. The New Thinking Comes to Power

1. Sergei Boguslavsky, "Zagovor akademikov," *Literaturnaia Gazeta*, 28 August 1991, p. 3.

2. Here even polar opposites Yegor Ligachev and Boris Yeltsin agree with Gorbachev's retrospective claim that he could have done nothing, "lived like a tsar, and then come what may." As argued in the introduction, Soviet "crisis" was relative, and the system certainly had sufficient reserves—and society sufficient patience—for at least another decade of muddle-through.

3. Grishin's bid was seen in his staged, publicized efforts to portray himself as Chernenko's right hand (and hence, the obvious successor) as the leader neared death. Yeltsin claims that a list of Grishin's planned Politburo changes was later found; Ligachev denies this, though agreeing that a reactionary alternative did indeed nearly triumph. See El'tsin, *Ispoved' na zadannuiu temu*, pp. 101, 109; Ligachev, *Inside Gorbachev's Kremlin*, pp. 32–33, 66–67. On Romanov's moves to dominate the military-industrial complex, "undermine" Defense Minister Ustinov, and build a "springboard" to the top, see Sagdeev, *Making of a Soviet Scientist*, p. 259. Another version has Romanov backing the older Grishin as a stalking horse for his own later accession; see former Central Committee staffer Valery Legostaev, "Demokrat s radikal'nymi vzgliadami," *Den'*, no. 13 (1991): 4. On Romanov's pretensions, see also Boldin, *Ten Years*, p. 180, and Savel'yev and Detinov, *Big Five*, p. 114.

4. Ryzhkov, *Perestroika. istoriia predatel'stv*, p. 60; Legostaev, "Demokrat s radikal'nymi vzgliadami."

5. Boldin, *Ten Years*, p. 53.

6. On the suppression of Andropov's purported "testament," and the opposition of Defense Minister Ustinov and Prime Minister Tikhonov to Gorbachev, see Arbatov, *Zatianuvsheesia vyzdorovlenie*, p. 334.

7. On the "unprecedented affront" of *Kommnist* editor Kosolapov's refusal to publish a speech by Gorbachev, see Medvedev, *V komande Gorbacheva*, p. 22. On other slights and backstage "maneuvers," see Gorbachev, *Zhizn' i reformy*, vol. 1, pp. 241–72; Boldin, *Ten Years*, pp. 179–81.

8. Ligachev, *Inside Gorbachev's Kremlin*, pp. 74–76. While differing on many details, Yeltsin and Ryzhkov agree that strong support for change came from these new Central Committee members; El'tsin, *Ispoved' na zadannuiu temu*, p. 101; see also Ryzhkov, *Perestroika. istoriia predatel'stv*, p. 79.

9. Insightful here is the memoir of veteran Central Committee staffer and Chernenko aide Vadim Pechenev, *Gorbachev: k vershinam vlasti*, pp. 12–13. Had the Politburo "recommended" another, it is extremely unlikely that the Central Committee would have done anything but accept that choice, too.

10. "Rech' tovarishcha A. A. Gromyko na plenume TsK KPSS 11 marta 1985 goda," *Kommunist*, no. 5 (1985): 6–7.

11. Ryzhkov, *Perestroika. istoriia predatel'stv*, p. 78. Boldin notes that "latent but powerful" opposition to Gorbachev remained. See *Ten Years*, p. 58; also Chazov, *Zdorov'e i vlast'*, pp. 195–201.

12. Anatoly Dobrynin (author's interview: New Jersey Turnpike, 14 June 1993); Alexander Bessmertnykh (author's interview: Moscow, 24 December 1993). Ligachev, in another version of Gromyko's step, again takes credit for the fortunate outcome. But here his depiction of Gromyko's quandary until advised what to do ("At the dramatic moment . . . I was the one with whom Gromyko decided to consult") is surely exaggerated. A discussion likely occurred, even an agreement on nominating strategy. But that the veteran foreign minister and Politburo member was at such a loss without the direction of a relatively junior Central Committee official defies credibility. See Ligachev, *Inside Gorbachev's Kremlin*, pp. 22, 72–73.

13. A third explanation for Gromyko's support of Gorbachev is that he simply wanted to remain foreign minister, and reasoned that his chances were better with a modest reformer as leader—particularly if he helped boost him to power—than with the reactionaries; see Cherniaev, *Shest' let s Gorbachevym*, pp. 30–31.

14. Pechenev, *Gorbachev: k vershinam vlasti*, p. 110. As Pechenev adds, "temporary arrangements have a way of becoming permanent with us."

15. Another conservative and likely Gorbachev opponent, Dinmukhamed Kunaev, could not reach Moscow until after the Politburo's first and decisive meeting, held the evening of Chernenko's death. And Hough reports that Romanov "was not even told about the meeting until after it was over." See Hough, *Democratization and Revolution*, p. 76.

16. Pechenev, *Gorbachev: k vershinam vlasti*, p. 109; see also Legostaev,

"Demokrat s radikal'nymi vzgliadami." In various accounts, it was Ustinov who, together with Tikhonov, led a powerful anti-reform bloc in the Politburo. For detail see Chazov, *Zdorov'e i vlast'*, pp. 195–98.

17. However, citing Ustinov's support for Gromyko's 1984 "compromise" that allowed Gorbachev to serve as second secretary, others argue that, had Ustinov lived, he would have backed Gorbachev again in 1985. See Gorbachev, *Zhizn' i reformy*, vol. 1, pp. 248–53; also Ligachev, *Inside Gorbachev's Kremlin*, p. 77. This seems at odds with Ustinov's role in blocking Gorbachev's outright succession in 1984 and his participation in something of an anti-reform, pro-military-industrial complex "axis" with Prime Minister Tikhonov. Gorbachev's positive words here about Ustinov are also difficult to square with his blistering criticism elsewhere of Ustinov's military advocacy at the expense of the long-suffering civilian economy. If Ustinov had indeed shifted to strong support of Gorbachev by late 1984, this is perhaps explainable via two factors: first, a fairly sudden change of heart about the country's ability to maintain his favored programs under another status-quo leader; and second, that Gorbachev hid well the scope of his reformist intentions. For had Ustinov, or Gromyko, had any real inkling of the latter, they would surely have opposed him strongly. On this point, see Brown, *Gorbachev Factor*, pp. 69–71.

18. Ryzhkov, *Perestroika. istoriia predatel'stv*, p. 79; Shakhnazarov, *Tsena svobody*, p. 37.

19. Pechenev writes that some of the old guard were worried about the influence of Gorbachev's "shadow cabinet," but that Gorbachev himself "always took a centrist position" on major issues; *Gorbachev: k vershinam vlasti*, pp. 90, 92.

20. Gorbachev's "informal advisers," as future KGB director Vladimir Kryuchkov termed them, included some who had previously run afoul of his agency, such as Arbatov and Zaslavskaya, and another whose loyalty was even more seriously doubted, Alexander Yakovlev; see *Sovetskaia Rossiia*, 13 February 1993.

21. Interview with Geidar Aliev in Karaulov, *Vokrug kremlia*, vol. 1, p. 268. Aliev further recalled that "nobody thought that he'd be a reformer. He was simply younger than the others, he was number two in the party, and power was already in his hands . . . Ligachev isn't telling the truth. I don't know where he dreamed up [his version of Gorbachev's succession]. At that time he wasn't even a member of the Politburo" (p. 267).

22. Akhromeev and Kornienko, *Glazami marshala i diplomata*, p. 63.

23. Maclean, "Some Reflections of a Communist," pp. 203, 213.

24. M. S. Gorbachev, "Zhivoe tvorchestvo naroda," 10 December 1984, in *Izbrannye rechi i stat'i*, vol. 2 (Moscow: Politizdat, 1987), pp. 75–108.

25. "Vystuplenie pered chlenami parlamenta Velikobritanii," 18 December 1984, ibid., pp. 109–16.

26. Boldin later wrote that Gorbachev's circumspection was "perfectly understandable" given that "while preparing for his new post, he was anxious not to frighten whose who could not even utter the word *market* without the foulest curses." Boldin, *Ten Years*, pp. 50–51.

27. Oleg Kalugin (author's interview: Moscow, 14 July 1991). See also Oleg Kalugin, *The First Directorate: My 32 Years in Intelligence and Espionage Against the West* (New York: St. Martin's, 1994), pp. 313–14.

28. Cherniaev, *Shest' let s Gorbachevym*, p. 16. Chernyaev, the veteran International Department staffer, became foreign-policy assistant to Gorbachev in February 1986 (see below).

29. Ibid.; Arbatov, *Zatianuvsheesia vyzdorovlenie*, pp. 335–39.

30. "O sozyve ocherednogo XXVII s'ezda KPSS i zadachakh, sviazannykh s ego podgotovkoi i provedenniem," 23 April 1985, in Gorbachev, *Izbrannye rechi i stat'i*, vol. 2, pp. 152–73.

31. Akhromeev and Kornienko, *Glazami marshala i diplomata*, p. 34. Though twice the publicly admitted figure, the defense burden was actually much greater. Ligachev put it at 20 percent of GNP; other estimates approach 30 percent: Yegor Ligachev (Princeton University: public address, 5 November 1991).

32. "Military expenditures grew one-and-one-half to two times faster than the national income. This Moloch devoured everything it could at the cost of enormous labor and merciless exploitation of an aged industrial base. . . . But there was no way to analyze the problem. All data relating to the military-industrial complex were held in strictest secrecy, including from Politburo members. Even a hint that some military enterprise was not working efficiently and Ustinov would tear into the 'immature critic.' " See discussion of agriculture and the abortive "Food Program," in Gorbachev, *Zhizn' i reformy*, vol. 1, pp. 191–212 (quote from p. 207).

33. Even under Andropov, not to mention Chernenko and Brezhnev, comprehensive information on the economy was not available even to most Politburo members (see *Pravda*, 7 December 1990). That information included the fact that some 80 percent of industry was directly or indirectly tied to the military; Mikhail Gorbachev, "Doverie—Vektor Sovremennoi Zhizni," *Svobodnaia mysl'*, no. 9 (1992): 7.

34. A witness recalled Gorbachev saying, "We're all equals now. The Brezhnev doctrine is dead." Anatoly Chernyaev (Princeton University seminar: 24 February 1993).

35. See the analysis in Garthoff, *Great Transition*, p. 214.

36. Dale Herspring, "The Military Factor in East German Soviet Policy," *Slavic Review* 47, no. 1 (1988): 95–96.

37. "Za mirnoe, svobodnoe, protsvetaiushchee budushchee Evropy i vsekh drugikh kontinentov," 3 October 1985, in Gorbachev, *Izbrannye rechi i stat'i*, vol. 2, pp. 459–59.

38. Herspring, "Military Factor": 93–94. On the top brass's perception of Gorbachev's pressure for Soviet concessions as "a genuine and very serious threat," see Savel'yev and Detinov, *Big Five*, p. 92.

39. Akhromeev and Kornienko, *Glazami Marshala i diplomata*, pp. 65–66, 91. On conservative "experts" dismay at Gorbachev's inattention to their recommendations, and his bypassing of established decision-making channels, see also Leonov, *Likholet'e*, pp. 323–29, 333.

40. *Brain trust* is the term of Foreign Ministry staffer and senior interpreter Pavel Palazchenko, *Interpreting the Whirlwind*, p. 203. On these early consultations, see also Arbatov, *The System*, p. 323.

41. Sagdeev, *Making of a Soviet Scientist*, pp. 267–69.

42. Former Central Committee staffer Sergei Grigoriev (author's interview: Princeton, November 28 1991); IMEMO analyst Sergei Blagovolin (author's interview: Moscow, 20 May 1991).

43. Sagdeev, *Making of a Soviet Scientist*, p. 268.

44. Arbatov's published memoirs do not emphasize this role; however, he privately stated that "until Shevardnadze got up to speed in 1986, I was Gorbachev's main foreign-policy adviser. We met many times, usually at his invitation, and I sent him scores of memos" (author's interview: Moscow, 24 December 1993). Chernyaev writes that "Arbatov was one of Gorbachev's first sources" of information and ideas, and one much respected for "his unusual, practical mind, his clear-cut views, his distaste for ideology, his principled positions." Cherniaev, *Shest' let s Gorbachevym*, pp. 24, 44.

45. G. A. Arbatov, *K kontseptsii vneshnei politiki na sovremennom etape*, (personal memorandum to M. S. Gorbachev, April 1985).

46. Summaries of Arbatov's arguments in this unpublished memorandum can be found in Chernyaev, *Shest' let s Gorbachevym*, p. 41, and Arbatov, *The System*, pp. 321–22.

47. Akhromeev and Kornienko, *Glazami marshala i diplomata*, p. 65.

48. Eduard Shevardnadze (author's interview: Moscow, 30 April 1991).

49. "Den' by prostoiat' da noch' proderzhat'sia," *Literaturnaia Gazeta*, 22 January 1992, p. 11.

50. Just as Yakovlev had used his Central Committee position to support Gorbachev's economic experiments in Stavropol in 1971, a decade later Gorbachev aided Shevardnadze's agricultural innovations in Georgia from his Central Committee post. On their cooperation in defense of Georgian "kulaks," see "Eto Ia—Edichka," *Nezavisimaia Gazeta*, 21 November 1991. On Shevardnadze's innovation in Georgia, see also Carolyn McGiffert Ekendahl and Melvin A. Goodman, *The Wars of Eduard*

Shevardnadze (University Park: Pennsylvania State University Press, 1997), pp. 7–28.

51. Ryzhkov, for example, had spent most of his career at the military-dominated Uralmash complex; Ligachev's main experience lay in the Siberian industrial region of Tomsk.

52. Not since another reformer—Khrushchev—had a Soviet leader been so close to agriculture. Brezhnev's main economic experience had been in Eastern Ukraine's mining-industrial regions; his stint in the Virgin Lands campaign, with its enormous investment of resources, military-style mobilization of huge labor brigades, and factory-like state farms *(sovkhozy)* had little in common with the reality of most collective farms (*kolkhozy*).

53. Eduard Shevardnadze, "No One Can Isolate Us, Save Ourselves: Self Isolation Is the Ultimate Danger," *Slavic Review*, 51, no. 1 (1992): 117.

54. A. Cherniaev, *Fenomen Gorbacheva v Kontekste Liderstva* (text of address at the Hebrew University, January 12 1993), p. 15.

55. Levon Mgaloblashvili, former aide to Georgian party boss Shevardnadze (author's interview: Tbilisi, 21 April 1990). Many Georgian figures—journalists, scholars, Party officials, and others, admirers and critics of Shevardnadze alike—recalled his stinging criticism of the war. These include Varlam Keshelava, then editor of *Zaria Vostoka*; foreign-affairs commentator Iosif Tsintsadze; Alexei Chediia, director of the Tbilisi *Znanie* society; and philosopher Merab Mamardashvili (author's interviews: Tbilisi, 17–22 April 1990).

56. Shevardnadze, *Moi vybor*, p. 62. Hough describes the main Georgian daily, *Zarya Vostoka*, as highly unusual for its position "strongly supporting reconciliation with the West" during Shevardnadze's tenure as Party chief of the republic. See Hough, *Democratization and Revolution*, p. 178.

57. Gorbachev's direction of the Politburo's Polish Commission in 1984 was, in Chernyaev's view, another key experience for the future leader (author's interview: Moscow, 5 January 1993). In contrast to the dogmatic gatherings they had been when chaired by Suslov, Andropov, and Chernenko, Gorbachev opened the commission's doors to the reform ideas of IEMSS and other academic institutes. This was described by former commission staffer and Social Sciences Institute rector Yuri Krasin (author's interview: Moscow, 1 August 1990). Pechenev recalls Gorbachev's *open* reaction to the boldest proposals as skeptical (*Gorbachev: k vershinam vlasti*, p. 97).

58. Akhromeev and Kornienko, *Glazami marshala i diplomata*, p. 68.

59. Levon Mgaloblashvili (author's interview: Tbilisi, 21 April 1990); Shevardnadze, *Moi vybor*, pp. 193–97.

60. Shevardnadze himself drew this parallel, complete with reference to Imperial Russia's rule in Georgia; "Ubezhdat' pravdoi," *Ogoniok*, no. 11

(1990): 2–6. An aide recalled that "unlike other Soviet leaders, Shevardnadze was not a man without ethnic memory," and his "extreme sensitivity to national and ethnic feelings" eased his acceptance of German unification and Communism's demise in Eastern Europe; Palazchenko, *Interpreting the Whirlwind*, pp. 191–92, 242; see also Kornilov, "Leonid Il'ich ne znal."

61. Cherniaev, *Shest' let s Gorbachevym*, p. 41.

62. Ibid., p. 37.

63. Ibid., p. 57. This is a summary of Gorbachev's notes (which Chernyaev prepared) for the meeting with Karmal.

64. This infuriated International Department head Boris Ponomarev, who complained, "How can this be? Scores of 'good' communist leaders come, and he only receives the 'bad' Italians." Ibid., pp. 19, 33.

65. Eduard Shevardnadze (author's interview: Moscow, 30 April 1991). The report in question was very possibly one of the IEMSS memos cited in chapters 4 and 5. Shevardnadze also recalled early meetings with Soviet experts on Germany that led him to understand—as early as 1986—that German reunification was inevitable in the not-too-distant future; see Shevardnadze, *Moi vybor*, p. 223.

66. In 1985, Western aid for the Polish Solidarity movement was strong, while deliveries of Stinger anti-aircraft missiles to the Afghan mujahedin were only about to begin.

67. Ceaucescu, whom Gorbachev privately derided as "the Romanian führer," brushed aside Gorbachev's plea that he initiate reform with the argument that "I began my *perestroika* in 1966." Chernyaev (Princeton University seminar, 24 February 1993). Only in Poland and Hungary did Party leaders respond positively to Gorbachev's challenge to reform.

68. *Pravda*, 21 June, 1985.

69. Cherniaev, *Shest' let s Gorbachevym*, p. 68.

70. Shevardnadze, "No One Can Isolate Us," p. 120.

71. Cherniaev, *Shest' let s Gorbachevym*, p. 68.

72. Ibid., p. 101.

73. Cherniaev, *Fenomen Gorbacheva*, p. 17.

74. On this resistance, even from some of Gorbachev's liberal advisers, see the account of Palazchenko in "Monino-Moskva cherez Madrid i Zhenevu," *Nezavisimaia Gazeta*, 11 February 1992. Arbatov also admits his early skepticism on dealing with Reagan; see, for example, his interview in Cohen and vanden Heuvel, *Voices of Glasnost*, p. 311.

75. Shakhnazarov, *Tsena svobody*, pp. 89–91; Palazchenko, *Interpreting the Whirlwind* pp. 132–33.

76. Here Chernyaev is citing from an entry in his journal of early 1986; see *Shest' let s Gorbachevym*, p. 62.

77. "Eduard Shevardnadze's Choice," interview in *International Affairs* (Moscow), no. 11 (1991): 7.

78. *Izvestiia*, 28 November 1985.

79. "Eduard Shevardnadze's Choice," p. 7.

80. See "Gorbachev Meets Soviet Writers: A *Samizdat* Account," *Radio Liberty Research Bulletin* no. 44 (1986): 1–4. On Gorbachev as a listener and learner, see Ivan Frolov, "Al'ternativa," *Zhurnalist*, no. 5 (1994): 45; Anatolii Sobchak, *Khozhdenie vo vlast.'* (Moscow: Novosti, 1991), p. 198. On the development of Gorbachev's ties to the liberal intelligentsia more generally, see Vitaly Tretyakov, "Zagadka Gorbacheva," *Moskovskie Novosti*, 3 December 1989, p. 10; Mikhail Gorbachev, *Perestroika: New Thinking for Our Country and the World* (New York: Harper & Row, 1987), p. 81; and the interviews in Cohen and vanden Heuvel, *Voices of Glasnost*.

81. The 1985–86 arguments of Bogomolov, Shakhnazarov, and others for East European diversity and against Soviet "hegemonistic pretensions" are summarized in Garthoff, *Great Transition*, p. 570.

82. Perhaps the boldest such early call came from Bovin, in *Izvestiia*, 18 January 1986. On Gorbachev's fight against secrecy on defense and foreign policy, see Shakhnazarov, *Tsena svobody*, p. 52.

83. Examples range from the ongoing work of the Soviet Scientists' committee to the pioneering articles of ISKAN analysts Andrei Kokoshin and Igor Malashenko, in venues from popular weeklies to academic journals and books. See, for example, A. A. Kokoshin, " 'Plan Rodzhersa,' al'ternativnye kontseptsii oborony i bezopasnost' v Europe," *S.Sh.A.. Ekonomika Politika, Ideologiia*, no. 9 (1985): 3–14; Committee of Soviet Scientists for Peace, Against the Nuclear Threat, *The Large-Scale Anti-Missile System and International Security* (Moscow: Novosti, 1986); Igor Malashenko, "Reasonable Sufficiency and Illusory Superiority," *New Times* (Moscow), no. 24 (1987): 18–20; and Malashenko, "Parity Reassessed, *New Times*, no. 47 (1987): 9–10.

84. Here, too, the early examples are numerous. One was Gorbachev's mid-1986 intervention on behalf of Alexander Tsipko, to approve his long-delayed appointment as an IEMSS section head and permit his even-longer-delayed receipt of a doctoral degree (going so far as to send Raisa to the dissertation defense, thereby sending a message to Tsipko's critics about his personal support); Tsipko, "Gorbachev postavil na 'sotsialistich-eskii vybor.'" Another was the appointment of the strongly pro-NEP author Sergei Zalygin as editor of *Novy Mir;* see Clark, "Changing

Historical Paradigms," p. 299. As already seen, NEP's significance for Soviet reformers was not limited to domestic affairs.

85. Soon after, Yakovlev also joined the ruling Politburo.

86. An insightful analysis of Yakovlev's career and outlook is Vil' Dorofeev, "Aleksandr Iakovlev: uiti, chtoby ostat'siia," *Dialog*, no. 17 (1990): 90–103.

87. Though the precise extent of Yakovlev's influence on Gorbachev and his reforms is difficult to specify, close observers across the political spectrum agree that it was huge. A liberal describes Yakovlev as "the chief architect of new thinking" (Sagdeev, *Making of a Soviet Scientist*, p. 268), and a conservative notes that "almost every speech the General Secretary made on international affairs was prepared by Yakovlev" (Ligachev, *Inside Gorbachev's Kremlin*, p. 122). Chernyaev judges such views exaggerated, though agreeing that Yakovlev's role was great; see *Fenomen Gorbacheva*, p. 22.

88. He also praised the market, lamented militarization, and wrote that freedom of information was "the locomotive of the economy" while society needed glasnost "like air." This untitled memorandum, dated 3 December 1985, appears in Iakovlev, *Gor'kaia chasha*, pp. 17–23.

89. Yakovlev was instrumental in the appointment of glasnost pioneers Yegor Yakovlev and Vitaly Korotich as editors of *Moskovskie Novosti* and *Ogoniok*. The latter's memoir gives a vivid description of the style as well as substance of Yakovlev's contribution to glasnost; see Korotich, *Zal Ozhidaniia*, pp. 115–22.

90. Akhromeev argued that Yakovlev, with his experience in the West, had "very early formed a negative attitude toward our socio-political system," a source of concern given his "great influence on both foreign and domestic policy." Akhromeev and Kornienko, *Glazami marshala i diplomata*, pp. 65, 111. Of course, Yakovlev was a "Western agent" in only a figurative sense, though some reactionaries later leveled this accusation subsequently—that Yakovlev had originally been co-opted by the FBI and later became a CIA "agent of influence." For example, see Kryuchkov in *Sovetskaia Rossiia*, 13 February 1993.

91. Grachev, *Kremlevskaia khronika*, p. 100.

92. Akhromeev and Kornienko, *Glazami marshala i diplomata*, p. 309. Kornienko soon left the ministry to work as Dobrynin's deputy in the Central Committee's International Department.

93. Yuri Dubinin, "The New Timecount Began at East River," *International Affairs* (Moscow), no. 10 (1995): 87–100. See also Palazchenko, *My Years with Gorbachev and Shevardnadze*, pp. 227–28, 269; Kashlev, "The CSCE in the Soviet Union's Politics," pp. 69–72. Reviewing these key personnel changes is Brown, *Gorbachev Factor*, p. 217.

94. Vyacheslav Dashichev, "On the Road to German Reunification: The View from Moscow," in Gabriel Gorodetsky, ed., *Soviet Foreign Policy, 1917–1991: A Retrospective* (London: Cass, 1994), pp. 170–79.

95. Sergei Kortunov, Foreign Ministry staffer (author's interview: Princeton, 24 October 1991). On the influence of scientists and academics under Shevardnadze, see Savel'yev and Detinov, *Big Five*, p. 116. The particular importance of Shevardnadze's early consultations with Velikhov on SDI and other strategic issues was described by his long-time assitant Teimuraz Stepanov (author's interview: Moscow, 24 July 1991).

96. Sergei Tarasenko, former aide to Foreign Minister Shevardnadze (author's interview: Moscow, 16 August 1991).

97. A. Cherniaev, "Iz dalekoi iunosti," *Vek XX i Mir* nos. 1–2, 1994, pp. 55–56. In one close observer's description, "the two men [Gorbachev and Chernyaev] were practically twins." Boldin, *Ten Years*, p. 113.

98. Shevardnadze, *Moi vybor*, p. 96.

99. On Raisa's central role, and also that of Yakovlev (including his injection of various recent IMEMO analyses into the discussions), see Boldin, *Ten Years*, pp. 73, 115.

100. Ibid., p. 73.

101. For a fascinating account of Tsipko's contribution to the early rethinking of fundamental precepts—and his subsequent cooperation with Yakovlev—see Tsipko, "Gorbachev postavil na 'sotsialisticheskii vybor.'"

102. Shevardnadze, *Moi vybor*, pp. 94, 96.

103. Iakovlev, *Muki prochteniia bytiia*, pp. 181, 188.

104. "Razgovor s Prezidentom SSSR za chashkoi chaia," *Izvestiia*, 20 September 1991.

105. See *The Programme of the Communist Party of the Soviet Union: A New Edition* (Moscow: Novosti, 1986).

106. Mikhail Gorbachev, *Political Report of the CPSU Central Committee to the 27th Party Congress* (Moscow: Novosti, 1986).

107. Shevardnadze, *Moi vybor*, pp. 93–94. See also Kovalev, "Politik poroi obiazan skhodit.'"

108. Earlier, in preparation for 1981's 26th CPSU Congress, Ponomarev drafted the foreign-policy section of the general secretary's report with Brezhnev (or his assistants), making minor changes; now these roles were completely reversed.

109. This precongress debate is cited in Cherniaev, *Shest' let s Gorbachevym*, p. 60.

110. *Izvestiia*, 20 September 1991.

111. Gorbachev, "Doverie," p. 5. Tsipko offers further insight on how radical Gorbachev's perspective already was at the outset of perestroika. "From the very beginning, when Smirnov first invited me [in January 1986]

he insisted on total sincerity. 'Don't think,' Georgy Lukich repeated several times, 'that Gorbachev doesn't understand how high the stakes are. Nearly sixty years have been wasted on nothing. By turning away from NEP, the Party lost its only possible chance. The people were tormented in vain. The country was sacrificed to a view of communism cut off from real life." See Tsipko, "Gorbachev postavil na 'sotsialisticheskii vybor.' "

112. Gorbachev's "insatiable thirst for knowledge" was noted by Chernyaev (author's interview: Princeton, 26 February 1993), and his reading interests were recalled by Dobrynin and Bessmertnykh (author's interviews: 14 June and 24 December 1993). Recall (chapters 2 and 5) Gorbachev's own emphasis on his study, beginning in the 1970s, of "white books" and "white TASS" translations of foreign media. Many reformist experts, from Arbatov to Gaidar, had begun their careers as translator-reviewers of such works, key resources in the rise of a post-Stalin intelligentsia. But never before had they been so utilized by a Soviet leader.

113. Former International Department official Yevgeny Novikov noted the influence of Raisa Gorbacheva's early university ties to "leftist" philosophers, and her affinity for "semi-dissident" scholars of Western Marxism and social democracy (including Zamoshkin, Mamardashvili, Motroshilova, and Nikitich), whom she brought to her husband's attention; see Hamman, "Soviet Defector on Origins of 'New Thinking,'" pp. 14–16. Gorbachev himself noted that, upon returning to Moscow in 1979, Raisa "immediately plugged in . . . to the world of academic discussions, symposia and conferences" and renewed her ties to MGU and the Institute of Philosophy. See Gorbachev, *Zhizn' i reformy*, vol. 1, p. 190. Much like the case of Yakovlev, liberal and conservative observers alike agree on Raisa's enormous influence as one of her husband's most "privileged advisors" and his closest confidant; Grachev, *Kremlevskaia khronika*, p. 137. See also Pechenev, *Gorbachev: k vershinam vlasti*, p. 27; and Leonov, *Likholet'e*, p. 323.

114. Arbatov, *The System*, p. 323. As noted above, Arbatov was a member of the Palme Commission and sponsored the publication of its 1982 report in Moscow, activities that brought him into conflict with Ustinov and Ponomarev.

115. Gorbachev, "Doverie," p. 4.

116. Ibid., p. 5.

117. Cherniaev, *Shest' let s Gorbachevym*, p. 75; Gorbachev, *Perestroika*, pp. 139, 144.

118. Ibid., p. 140.

119. Cherniaev, *Shest' let s Gorbachevym*, p. 102.

120. M. S. Gorbachev, "Doveritel'nyi razgovor," in *Gody trudnykh reshenii. Izbrannoe 1985–1992* (Moscow: Gorbachev-Fond, 1993), p. 235.

121. Ibid., pp. 236–39.

122. Ibid., pp. 239–47. On early discussions with another social democrat (Willy Brandt) and their role in encouraging his embrace of "a common European home," see Gorbachev, *Zhizn' i reformy*, vol. 2, p. 70.

123. Gorbachev, *Perestroika*, p. 140; also pp. 135–39, 215.

124. On such efforts, see Richard Cohn-Lee, "Physicist aims for arms control," *Daily Princetonian*, 3 October 1988.

125. Ibid. Velikhov notes that Gorbachev approved the project (which infuriated the military) without a Politburo vote (author's interview: Moscow, 30 December 1993). On Shevardnadze's support, see Palazchenko, *Interpreting the Whirlwind*, pp. 138–39. Detail on the project is outlined in Thomas B. Cochran, "The NRDC/Soviet Academy of Sciences Joint Nuclear Test Ban Verification Project," *Physics and Society* 16, no. 3 (1987): 5–8.

126. Cherniaev, *Shest' let s Gorbachevym*, p. 62. Gorbachev noted that he agreed to extend the moratorium after "serious study . . . of numerous appeals" from foreign intellectuals; see Gorbachev, *Perestroika*, p. 139. For further detail on all these initiatives, see Evangelista, *Unarmed Forces*, chapters 12–15.

127. As already seen, leading liberal Soviet scientists such as Sagdeyev, Velikhov, and Goldansky had supported early appeals for Sakharov's release. This was also the subject of Gefter's letter that Cherniaev raised with Gorbachev in January 1986; privately, Gorbachev's response was "of course" Sakharov will be freed as soon as politically possible; Cherniaev, "Iz dalekoi iunosti," p. 56. Facilitating Sakharov's release—something bitterly opposed by a Politburo majority—was the first issue addressed by the newly established human-rights sector in Yakovlev's Central Committee Ideology Department. See Grachev, *Kremlevskaia khronika*, p. 100.

128. Chernyaev writes that the evolution of perestroika led Gorbachev to eventual acceptance of Sakharov's idea of a "convergence" of social systems; ibid., p. 142. More immediately, Sakharov was an outspoken proponent of delinking SDI from talks on strategic offensive weapons.

129. Gorbachev, "The Rule of Law."

130. Valery Legostaev, "God 1987-yi—peremena logiki," *Den'*, no. 14 (1991): 2.

131. Ibid. See also Leonov, *Likholet'e*, pp. 323–33.

132. Iuri Prokof'iev, in *Sovetskaia Rossiia*, 27 July 1991.

133. The conspiracy outlook is simultaneously one of the most irritating and revealing aspects of the recollections of Soviet conservatives. It is seen not only in wild charges against certain individuals, and in the near-universal argument that perestroika was planned and manipulated by the West, but also in frequent, usually unsubtle intimations in which every misfortune or untoward event is tied to some dark but unspecified design. In

addition to the works cited above, see the discussions of Arbatov and Yakovlev in Ligachev, *Inside Gorbachev's Kremlin*, pp. 45–47, 94–122.

134. Valery Legostayev, "Nina Andreeva—izgoi pliuralizma," *Den'*, no. 16 (1991): 3.

135. Most conservatives date this turning point to 1987, not 1986 as argued here. This may reflect the faster pace of foreign, over domestic, policy change (the latter being the conservatives' main concern) as well as the lag between Gorbachev's decisions in principle and actual policy implementation. On postdating Gorbachev's turn and the attendant split in the leadership, see Stephen F. Cohen, "Ligachev and the Tragedy of Soviet Conservatism," introduction to Ligachev, *Inside Gorbachev's Kremlin*, pp. xxviii–xxxix.

136. Cherniaev, *Fenomen Gorbacheva*, pp. 9–10.

137. Cited in Greenstein and Wohlforth, eds., *Retrospective on the End of the Cold War*, p. 40.

138. Akhromeev and Kornienko, *Glazami marshala i diplomata*, p. 98.

139. Ibid., pp. 99, 105. For greater detail, see also Ryzhkov, *Perestroika. istoriia predatel'stv*, pp. 133–52.

140. Anatoly Chernyaev (author's interview: Moscow, 16 December 1993).

141. *Izvestiia*, 29 April, 1990; Akhromeev and Kornienko, *Glazami marshala i diplomata*, p. 99.

142. Gorbachev, *Perestroika*, p. 222. Noting the particular horror of Gorbachev and Yakovlev was Vladimir Gubarev, then science correspondent for *Pravda*, whom Yakovlev invited for a private Kremlin briefing after reading his blistering report on the accident (author's interview: Moscow, 10 June 1996). The report was later published as "Zapiska v TsK KPSS: Sovershenno sekretno," in Vladimir Gubarev, *Iadernyi vek Chernobyl'* (Moscow: "Nekos," 1996), pp. 25–29.

143. *Izvestiia*, 29 April 1990.

144. Gorbachev, *Zhizn' i reformy*, vol. 1, p. 302.

145. Shevardnadze, *Moi vybor*, p. 294.

146. Eduard Shevardnadze (author's interview: Moscow, 30 April, 1991). Shevardnadze nearly resigned over this incident. On the coverup, see also Sagdeev, *Making of a Soviet Scientist*, pp. 286–92.

147. Shevardnadze, *Moi vybor*, p. 291; see also Gorbachev, *Perestroika*, p. 221. On Gorbachev and Yakovlev's early, consistent push for greater openness throughout the crisis, see the transcripts of Politburo meetings during late April–early May 1986 appearing in "Chtoby pokoleniia ne zabyli ob etom fakte," *Vestnik*, no. 5 (1996): 87–103.

148. Yevgeny Velikhov (author's interview: Moscow, 30 December 1993).

149. For the best description of the dramatic events of Reykjavik and its aftermath, see Don Oberdorfer, *The Turn* (New York: Poseidon, 1991), pp. 183–209.

150. Gorbachev wrote that he was motivated by a desire to escape the "alien" logic of stubbornness and slow, incremental progress. See Gorbachev, *Zhizn' i reformy*, vol. 2, p. 25.

151. Cherniaev, *Shest' let s Gorbachevym*, p. 110. Gorbachev followed all of these recommendations save that on SDI, though his proposed restrictions on the "Star Wars" program were now more modest.

152. Akhromeev and Kornienko, *Glazami marshala i diplomata*, p. 109.

153. When it was presented to the General Staff Academy in late 1986, the new doctrine met with "incomprehension, confusion, fear . . . and accusations that it was flawed, unacceptable, and bordered on treasonous." Ibid., p. 126.

154. Sagdeev, *Making of a Soviet Scientist*, pp. 272–73.

155. On Chebrikov's alarm sounded at the 27th Party Congress, see ibid., p. 290. On his criticism of anti-Stalinist writers Anatoly Rybakov, Boris Mozhaev, and Bulat Okudzhava, see Cherniaev, *Shest' let s Gorbachevym*, pp. 96–97.

156. Savel'yev and Detinov, *Big Five*, p. 93.

157. Cherniaev, *Shest' let s Gorbachevym*, p. 112.

158. On Shevardnadze's anger at the KGB over Daniloff, and the subsequent "embassy bugging" scandal—in which Chebrikov lied to Shevardnadze concerning penetration of a new U.S. building in Moscow—see Palazchenko, *Interpreting the Whirlwind*, pp. 85–86, 107; also *Literaturnaia Gazeta*, 22 January 1992, p. 11.

159. Cherniaev, *Shest' let s Gorbachevym*, p. 140.

160. Ibid., p. 139.

161. Gorbachev, "Doverie," p. 6.

162. The full text appeared only after the USSR's collapse; see "U perelomnoi cherty," in Gorbachev, *Gody trudnykh reshenii*, pp. 46–55.

163. Ibid., pp. 48–52.

164. Ibid., p. 53.

165. Retrospectively, Gorbachev described this Foreign Ministry conference as the start of "full-scale efforts to put the new thinking into practice." See Gorbachev, *Zhizn' i reformy*, vol. 2, p. 8.

166. Following Gorbachev's speech, a near-euphoric "dissident spirit" spread among Foreign Ministry (and Central Committee) liberals; see Grachev, *Kremlevskaia khronika*, p. 101.

167. Palazchenko, *Interpreting the Whirlwind*, p. 144.

168. Gorbachev's boldest early call for true democratization came at a January 1987 Central Committee plenum, a forum he had sought—and

conservatives had resisted—since 1986. On the advance of democratization through the 19th Party conference of 1988 to the elections of 1989, see Garthoff, *Great Transition*, pp. 302–3; a more detailed analysis is John Gooding, "Gorbachev and Democracy," *Soviet Studies* 42, no. 2 (1990): 195–231.

169. Chernyaev, *Fenomen Gorbacheva*, p. 17. Chernyaev, probably the closest observer of Gorbachev's evolving worldview, argues that this "transformation" was total, sincere, and reflected Gorbachev's outstanding intellectual trait, "an ability to carry out in himself a complete ideological reversal." Ibid., p. 18

170. Gorbachev, "The Crimea Article," in *The August Coup: The Truth and Its Lessons* (New York: HarperCollins, 1991), p. 119. This did not imply the rapid market transition pursued by Gorbachev's successor. But as Shevardnadze noted, while publicly stressing "the socialist choice," Gorbachev now privately saw a European-style social democratic model as the Soviet future; *Literaturnaia Gazeta*, 22 January 1992, p. 11. On the early social-democratic views of Shevardnadze, see Irina Lagunina, "In Tbilisi, Shevardnadze speaks louder," *New Times* (Moscow), no. 17 (1992): 9–11.

171. Two "breakthrough" critiques, stressing Soviet blame for the cold war and the need for a liberal-integrationist policy, were Dashichev, "Vostok-Zapad: poisk novykh otnoshenii," *Literaturnaia Gazeta*, 18 May 1988, p. 14, and Andrei Kozyrev, "Doverie i balans interesov," *Mezhdunarodnaia Zhizn'*, no. 10 (1988): 3–12. The 1987–89 explosion of Soviet foreign-policy debates was well reviewed by Western analysts (see my introduction), though usually with little recognition that such public arguments reflected views quietly developed, discussed, and even published (in the restricted literature) for more than a decade.

172. Though the focus here is on these core East-West issues, Gorbachev's other steps included curbing military aid and supporting democratization and peacemaking efforts among clients in Africa, Asia, and Latin America.

173. A view recognizing the singularity of Gorbachev, Yakovlev, and Shevardnadze as Party leaders (characterizing them as "genetic errors"), as well as that of their contribution to the new thinking, is Adam Michnik, "Tri geneticheskie oshibki," *Novoe Vremia*, no. 1 (1992): 4–7.

174. Besides inattention to the earlier views of new thinkers such as Dashichev and Kozyrev, few Western analysts looked very far beyond their direct perestroika-era arguments to the liberal-integrationist assumptions that underlay them. For example, while blaming Stalin for the cold war, Dashichev stressed not only his "great-power hegemonism" but also the cruel, arbitrary, undemocratic system that made it impossible for the West to trust the USSR in the long run, whatever its policies of the moment.

175. *Literaturnaia Gazeta*, 5 November 1986. Though other such integrationist arguments now followed, Gorbachev's single most comprehensive new-thinking declaration—and thus full Western cognizance—would not come until his famous 1988 UN address. See Mikhail Gorbachev, *Address at the United Nations, New York, December 7, 1988* (Moscow: Novosti, 1989).

176. *Pravda*, 28 January 1987.

177. Sakharov, *Memoirs*, p. 615. The angry-sarcastic reaction of Central Committee bosses to Gorbachev's decision is described in Cherniaev, *Shest' let s Gorbachevym*, p. 126.

178. On the influence of U.S. scientists on Gorbachev as well, see Savely'ev and Detinov, *Big Five*, p. 175. Shevardnadze aide Lev Mendelevich, Kozyrev's early mentor on study of the Soviet arms trade, was perhaps the strongest Foreign Ministry advocate of accepting limited strategic defenses in order to achieve cuts in offensive weapons; see Palazchenko, *Interpreting the Whirlwind*, p. 112.

179. Though Gorbachev's arms-control verification proposals shocked the military on both sides—the United States even balked at some provisions—they were in fact a natural extension of those embodied in the July 1986 Stockholm agreement and no surprise to those who understood the seriousness of his intentions for openness in all areas.

180. Cherniaev, *Shest' let s Gorbachevym*.

181. Oberdorfer, *The Turn*, pp. 235–40.

182. This is the recollection of Alexander Tsipko, at the time a Central Committee consultant for East European affairs (author's interviews: Moscow, 23 May 1990 and 30 August 1991); also Tsipko, *O Prichinakh Krusheniia "Real'nogo Sotsializma" v Stranakh Vostochnoi Evropy* (unpublished MS, 1991), p. 3.

183. Ibid.; see also Garthoff, *Great Transition*, pp. 573–74. Tsipko cites Gorbachev's secret address at a *December* meeting of communist and workers' parties, whereas Garthoff (with Tsipko as one source) describes Gorbachev's closed speech at a *November* gathering of CEMA leaders.

184. The studies were performed in the ministry's Directorate for Assessments and Planning, headed by veteran liberal Lev Mendelevich; Teimuraz Stepanov (author's interview: Moscow, 24 July 1991). Gorbachev's remark to Yazov was noted by Chernyaev (seminar: Princeton, 24 February 1993).

185. This, at least, is the claim of most new thinkers in many private (and some public) interviews.

186. Jacques Levesque, *The Enigma of 1989: The USSR and the Liberation of Eastern Europe* (Berkeley: University of California Press, 1997).

187. Shakhnazarov, *Tsena svobody*, pp. 87–88. Grachev wrote that, even in the Politburo, Gorbachev "was always in the minority, isolated, permanently under threat of being removed." See Grachev, *Kremlevskaia khronika*, p. 136. And Tsipko, a considerably more cynical observer, noted: "Don't forget, all this started in 1986! It was only yesterday that these [Central Committee] corridors were patrolled by Mikhail Suslov and Mikhail Zimianin who would punish you mercilessly for the slightest hint of doubt about the holiness of Soviet history. And now you learn that the General Secretary himself is practically 'anti-Soviet,' rejecting nearly the entire epoch of socialist construction." Tsipko, "Gorbachev postavil na 'sotsialisticheskii vybor.'"

188. On the military's "grave disappointment" and "sharp criticism," see Savel'yev and Detinov, *Big Five*, pp. 135, 138. See also Palazchenko, *Interpreting the Whirlwind*, p. 111. Chernyaev's Politburo notes record Gorbachev's fury at ministerial "inertia" and outright "opposition" that was blocking progress on arms control; see Cherniaev, *Shest' let s Gorbachevym*, pp. 79–80.

189. Tom Nichols, "Volkogonov and Nuclear Victory," *CSIS Soviet News*, 8 September 1987, p. 10.

190. *Pravda*, August 6 1988. In fairness, Ligachev strongly supported efforts to end the Afghan war (as did KGB director Kryuchkov). But their opposition to the broader integrationist goals of new thinking suggests how foreign policy might have evolved without Gorbachev, Shevardnadze, and Yakovlev, under a limited Andropov-style reformism.

191. See the discussion in William C. Wohlforth, "Reality Check: Revising Theories of International Politics in Response to the End of the Cold War," *World Politics* 50, no. 4 (1998): 665.

192. Chernyaev (seminar: Princeton, 24 February 1993). See also A. Cherniaev and A. Galkin, "Pravdu, i tol'ko pravdu," *Svobodnaia mysl'*, nos. 2–3 (1994): 19–29; Cherniaev and Galkin, "M. Gorbachev i vossoedinenie Germanii," *Svobodnaia Mysl'*, no. 1 (1995): 29–37.

193. See Philip Zelikow and Condoleeza Rice, *Germany Unified and Europe Transformed: A Study in Statecraft* (Cambridge: Harvard University Press, 1995), pp. 275–79.

194. See Levesque, *Enigma of 1989*, p. 254; also Wohlforth, "Reality Check," pp. 666–68.

195. Cherniaev, *Shest' let s Gorbachevym*, p. 409. Chernyaev's resignation was withdrawn before it reached Gorbachev.

196. As Gorbachev irritatedly explained to Chernyaev, "You don't understand. . . . it's the army." Ibid., p. 415.

197. Ibid., pp. 409–10. Here Chernyaev employs the tsarist imperial slogan "one and indivisible" (*edinyi i nedelimyi*) to characterize sarcastically Gorbachev's insistence on maintaining the union (empire) at all costs.

198. Ibid., p. 411.
199. Cherniaev, *Fenomen Gorbacheva*, pp. 9–10.
200. Gorbachev, "The Crimea Article," p. 119.

Conclusion

1. "Historical claims for the importance of particular events involve, of necessity, counterfactual analyses of situations in which those events did not occur." Citation from David Sylvan and Stephen Majeski, "A Methodology for the Study of Historical Counterfactuals," *International Studies Quarterly* 42, no. 1 (1998): 79.

2. This assumes that, on the domestic side, Andropov would not have introduced any truly fundamental changes. Hough argues that yet another scenario—sweeping, Chinese-style economic reforms—was a most likely and promising alternative until rejected by Gorbachev in favor of radical political change. This is unconvincing for several reasons, beginning with the far greater structural-bureaucratic and sociocultural obstacles facing the USSR at the outset of reform. Another problem, given that Moscow's entanglements abroad were far more extensive than Peking's, is the incompatibility of Hough's scenario with the improved Soviet-Western relations that he also emphasizes; while suggesting that martial law could have subdued any broad unrest provoked by wrenching economic changes, he ignores the international implications of such a crackdown. Still another problem is a dearth of evidence that such a course had significant high-level support; the retrospective claims of a few embittered conservatives, coupled with Hough's assertions that "they must have been looking at" the Chinese model or "few officials could have been [so] naïve" as to support less radical reforms, are not persuasive (see Hough, *Democratization and Revolution*, pp. 96–97, 106, 118). This is not to say that political, and especially economic, reforms under Gorbachev could not have proceeded differently, but rather to emphasize that the foreign-policy implications of the "Andropov" or "Chinese" models were highly problematic.

3. In addition to the evidence already cited of conservative options and reactionary preferences among the top leadership, there is also the episode of the August 1991 hard-line putsch to consider. Its failure, too, has joined the list of "inevitable" outcomes in another lapse of analytical imagination. But it does not take much to see that, launched a bit earlier and managed a bit better, the putsch could well have prevailed and eventually led to one of the highly conflictual cold war–ending scenarios outlined above.

4. "There is nothing in the character or tradition of the Russian state to suggest that it could ever accept imperial decline gracefully. Indeed, histori-

cally none of the overextended, multinational empires ever retreated to their own ethnic base until they had been defeated in a Great Power war. . . ." Kennedy, *Rise and Fall of the Great Powers*, p. 514. For another pessimistic view on the prevalence of conflict in Great Power transitions, see Robert Gilpin, *War and Change in World Politics* (New York: Cambridge University Press, 1981).

5. Snyder, *Myths of Empire*, pp. 212–54.

6. Ibid., p. 252.

7. Mendelson, *Changing Course*, chapters 1 and 2.

8. Checkel, *Ideas and International Political Change*. This unity, the ideological coherence of a broad Westernizing reform agenda in conjunction with strong personal-professional links among the diverse specialists who advanced it, is central to understanding its influence on innovative leadership and so to explaining what Checkel sees as a paradox: an authoritarian system's resistance to new ideas together with an ability, if so minded, to implement them rapidly.

9. Ibid., p. xiii.

10. In one classic statement, owing to "their concern with rigor and their dissatisfaction with the 'softness' of historical description, generalization and explanation, most social scientists have turned away from the historical movement of ideas. As a result, their own theories, however 'rigorous' they may be, leave out an important explanatory variable and often lead to naïve reductionism." See Robert Dahl, *Polyarchy: Participation and Opposition* (New Haven: Yale University Press, 1971), pp. 182–83.

11. Thomas Risse-Kappen, " 'Ideas Do Not Float Freely,' Transnational Coalitions, Domestic Structures, and the End of the Cold War," *International Organization* 48, no. 2 (1994): 183–214.

12. Evangelista, *Unarmed Forces*. Illustrating the importance of how one defines the new thinking for the conclusions one reaches about its origins is Risse-Kappen's focus on individuals and institutions concerned with arms control from the mid 1970s to the early 1980s. This framework excludes the new thinking's deeper conceptual roots in Soviet intellectuals' broader reappraisal of international relations that began back in the 1950s. Moreover, most rethinking of foreign policy during the 1960s and early 1970s was not, and could not be, conducted openly. Thus it appears that "strategic prescriptions centering around common security were *new* to the Soviet security debate [of the late 1970s], so their intellectual origins must be found *outside* the country and its foreign policy institutes." See Risse-Kappen, "Ideas Do Not Float Freely," pp. 194–95 (emphasis added). Evangelista advances Risse-Kappen by tracing the "transnational movement" back over a decade earlier, though his model, too, cannot capture important influences that are revealed only via the perspective of a broader socio-intellectual process of "Westernization."

13. Herman, "Identity, Norms, and National Security."

14. Beyond what is by now obvious; namely, my argument against too hasty application of models (usually derived from pluralistic political systems) to test putatively independent cases, an effort that actually obscures what—in the real intellectual-political context of the prereform USSR—is better understood as a larger, single case of change. In this regard, see Albert O. Hirschmann, "The Search for Paradigms as a Hindrance to Understanding," *World Politics* 22, no. 3 (1970): 329–43.

15. David Dessler, "Beyond Correlations: Toward a Causal Theory of War," *International Studies Quarterly* 35, no. 3 (1991): 337–55.

16. Jeffrey T. Checkel, "The Constructivist Turn in International Relations Theory," *World Politics* 50, no. 1 (1998): 325.

17. A partial exception for its rather hasty dismissal of cultural approaches to the cold war—despite an otherwise useful analysis of the methodological issues at stake—is Michael C. Desch, "Culture Clash: Assessing the Importance of Ideas in Security Studies," *International Security* 23, no. 1 (1998): 141–70.

18. Wohlforth, "Reality Check," pp. 650–80. See also Ronald L. Jepperson, Alexander Wendt, and Peter J. Katzenstein, "Norms, Identity, and Culture in National Security," in Katzenstein, ed., *Culture of National Security*, pp. 33–75.

19. Wohlforth, *Elusive Balance*.

20. Herrmann laments that analysts of the cold war's end still have yet to undertake "the nitty-gritty work of empirical scholarship" ("Policy-Relevant Theory," p. 137). One who has undertaken such work is Wohlforth, whose materialist interpretation of the cold war's end is probably the strongest argument to date. However, notwithstanding Wohlforth's impressive documentation of the urgency of the Soviet crisis, I argue that Gorbachev and his allies' perceived options in response to that crisis— markedly different from the preferences of others in the senior leadership— were powerfully influenced by ideas whose origins and influence lie largely beyond the material realm.

21. In addition to the works previously cited—most notably Sikkink's study of "principled issue networks"—see the chapters by Price and Tannenwald, Kier, Johnston, Berger, and Barnett in Katzenstein, *Culture of National Security*.

22. A view of Gorbachev as "critical theorist," seeking less to join the prevailing international order than to transform it, is Alexander Wendt, "Anarchy Is What States Make of It: The Social Construction of Power Politics," *International Organization* 46, no. 2 (1992): 391–425 (esp. 418–22). See also Wendt, "Collective Identity Formation and the International State, *American Political Science Review* 88, no. 2 (1994):

384–96; and Rey Koslowski and Friedrich V. Kratochwil, "Understanding Change in International Politics: The Soviet Empire's Demise and the International System," in Lebow and Risse-Kappen, *International Relations Theory and the End of the Cold War*, pp. 126–65.

23. Rather than detailing the main prerequisites (international openness and key elite congregations) and most salient features of the process (simultaneous comparative-interactive and social learning) of belief-identity change, I refer readers to the framework outlined in my introduction. Presented with reference to similar processes in other national experiences, my attempt to specify the how, when, and why of identity transformation is a first-cut attempt to address Checkel's well-reasoned criteria for integrating insights from the case of new thinking into broader efforts at middle-range theorizing about intellectual change and its impact on international relations. See Checkel, "Constructivist Turn," p. 325.

24. Although, in the Chinese case, NATO's bombing of Serbia (and accidental strike against the Chinese embassy) played into the regime's efforts to encourage anti-American nationalism. On similar (but more serious) effects in Russia, see below.

25. Surely greater than what Philpott, struck by such "vastly complex processes whose results are various and contingent" and also depend "on the unpredictable presence of conspiring material and political circumstances," sees as a potential for generalization sharply "bounded in time and place." See Daniel Philpott, "The Possibilities of Ideas," *Security Studies* 5, no. 4 (1996): 195.

26. Herrmann, "Policy-Relevant Theory," p. 137. On this point, Evangelista's *Unarmed Forces* is notable for an empirical depth that surpasses most other recent works on the end of the cold war.

27. Bermeo, "Democracy and the Lessons of Dictatorship," p. 287. On tracing the source of beliefs through the "socialization process," see Johnston, "Thinking About Strategic Culture," pp. 32–64.

28. Brudny, *Reinventing Russia*.

29. It would also temper the optimism of such predictions as "Reformers . . . were able to establish new political institutions, anchor them in a new belief system, and banish traditional Soviet policies once and for all." See Blum, "The Soviet Foreign Policy Belief System," p. 389.

30. Still, the tendency toward a Whiggish interpretation of Russia's post-Soviet fate should be avoided. Just as different choices by Russia's leaders (or different leaders) could have led to a more successful transition, so too might different policies on the part of the West have helped Russia onto a more successful path (and not only in 1992 and after, but back in the critical years 1989–1990, when failure to meet the new thinking halfway and lack of timely aid to perestroika helped defeat Gorbachev's ambitious proj-

ect). Those who view the attempted "Westernization" of Russia as historically doomed—both critics from the Right who see a neo-imperial foreign
policy as predetermined, or those from the Left who argue a cultural
antipathy toward liberal democracy and the market—are guilty of an his-
toricism that fails to consider the contingencies of change and the missed
opportunities for a markedly different outcome. For further discussion of
factors shaping recent Russian foreign policy, see below.

31. For analysis of the sources and nature of anti-Westernism among
various Russian social groups, see Vladimir Shlapentokh, "The Changing
Russian View of the West: From Admiration in the Early 1990s to Hostility
in the Late 1990s," in Tom Casier and Katlijn Malfliet, eds., *Is Russia a
European Power?*
The Position of Russia in a New Europe (Leuven, Belgium: Leuven
University Press, 1998), pp. 67–80.

32. A prominent though superficial view of contemporary Russian
"Eurasianism" is Charles Clover, "Dreams of the Eurasian Heartland,"
Foreign Affairs 78, no. 2 (1999): 9–13. A more thoughtful analysis is David
Kerr, "Eurasianism and Russian Foreign Policy," in Casier and Malfliet, *Is
Russia a European Power?* On most Russians' essential "Europeanness,"
see in the same volume Alexei Bogaturov, "An Inside Outsider," pp. 81–89.

33. In lieu of an extensive discussion of the continuing integrationist,
even "Westernizing" element in most *derzhavnik* opinion, this point can
be made even more forcefully (and briefly) with an illustration from the
most anti-Western camp. Writing in the prominent Russian nationalist
journal *Nash Sovremennik*, Vadim Pechenev argues that national revival can
occur only "through a harmonious combining of the indisputably universal values of world civilization—including those of democracy and a market economy—with Russia's historical peculiarities and contemporary realities." See Vadim Pechenev, "Russkii narod v sud'be gosudarstva
Rossiiskogo," *Nash Sovremennik*, no. 5 (1999): 211.

34. A naivete which indeed characterized some new thinkers' hopes,
but which hardly captures the core beliefs and values of Russia's post-Stalin
"neo-Westernism."

35. Desch, "Culture Clash," pp. 164–65.

36. Sergei A. Romanenko, "The Yugoslav Question in the Foreign
Policy of Russia at the Beginning of the Twentieth Century," in S.
Frederick Starr, ed., *The Legacy of History in Russia and the New States of
Eurasia* (Armonk, NY: Sharpe, 1994), pp. 41–60. See also Jonathan Valdez,
"The Near Abroad, the West, and National Identity in Russian Foreign
Policy," in Adeed and Karen Dawisha, eds., *The Making of Foreign Policy
in Russia and the New States of Eurasia* (Armonk, NY: Sharpe, 1995), pp.
84–109.

37. See Yitzhak M. Brudny, "Neoliberal Economic Reform and the Consolidation of Democracy in Russia: Or Why Institutions and Ideas Might Matter More than Economics" in Karen Dawisha, ed., *The International Dimension of Post-Communist Transitions in Russia and the New States of Eurasia* (Armonk, NY: Sharpe, 1997), pp. 310–14. See also Pavel Kandel's "Kosovskii krizis i etnopoliticheskie konflikty postsovetsko-go prostranstva," in D. Trenin and E. Stepanova, eds., *Kosovo: Mezhdunarodnye Aspekty Krizisa* (Moscow: Tsentr Karnegi, 1999), pp. 280–300. A useful earlier overview is Paul A. Goble, "Dangerous Liaisons: Moscow, the Former Yugoslavia, and the West," in Richard H. Ullman, ed., *The World and Yugoslavia's Wars* (New York: Council on Foreign Relations, 1996), pp. 182–97.

38. Kandel,' "Kosovskii krizis," pp. 288–89; see also L. Batkin in *Vremia MN*, 14 April 1999. For probably the best treatment of the essentially domestic sources of Russia's Serbia policy, see Iurii Davydov, "Problema Kosovo v rossiiskom vnutripoliticheskom kontekste," in Trenin and Stepanova, eds., *Kosovo: Mezhdunarodnye Aspekty Krizisa*, pp. 247–79.

39. See Aleksandr Lukin, "NATO i Rossiia posle Kosovo," *Nezavisimaia Gazeta*, 9 June 1999; also Dmitri Furman, "Nemtsov ne polenilsia poekhat' v Briussel' v fure, *Obshchaia Gazeta*, 17–23 June 1999. Formal legal arguments notwithstanding, it should be emphasized that NATO's eastward expansion violated a clear understanding reached with Gorbachev at the time of agreement on German ratification.

40. Among a growing literature—including works of history, sociology, and psychology as well as political science—especially notable are David D. Laitin, *Identity in Transition: The Russian-Speaking Populations in the Near Abroad* (Ithaca: Cornell University Press, 1998), Ilya Prizel, *National Identity and Foreign Policy: Nationalism and Leadership in Poland, Russia and Ukraine* (New York: Cambridge University Press, 1998) and Casier and Malfliet, *Is Russia a European Power?* See also Roman Szporluk, ed., *National Identity and Ethnicity in Russia and the New States of Eurasia* (Armonk, NY: Sharpe, 1994); Tim McDaniel, *The Agony of the Russian Idea* (Princeton: Princeton University Press, 1996); Ivar B. Neumann, *Russia and the Idea of Europe: A Study in Identity and International Relations* (London: Routledge, 1996); Geoffrey Hosking, *Russia: People and Empire, 1552–1917* (Cambridge: Harvard University Press, 1997); Ian Bremmer and Ray Taras, eds., *New States, New Politics: Building the Post-Soviet Nations* (New York: Cambridge University Press, 1997). Important articles include: Mark Bassin, "Russia Between Europe and Asia: The Ideological Construction of Geographical Space," *Slavic Review* 50, no. 1 (1991): 1–17; George E. Hudson, "Russia's Search for Identity in the Post–Cold War World," *Mershon International Studies Review* 38 (1994):

235–40; Michael Urban, "The Politics of Identity in Russia's Postcommunist Transition: The Nation Against Itself," *Slavic Review* 53, no. 3 (1994): 734–65; and Daniel Rancour-Laferriere, "The Illusion of Russia: One Basis of Russian Ethnonational Identity," *Mind and Human Interaction* 9, no. 2 (1999): 112–27.

41. Tsipko, the *Vekhi*-oriented liberal who as a consequence always stressed the idioscycracies of Russia's political culture, is one who now emphasizes the necessity of forging a national ideology in which "a strong state and great-power might do not contradict democracy and individual liberties." See Aleksandr Tsipko, "Kak sozdaiutsia ideologii," *Nezavisimaia Gazeta*, 1 June 1999. An even earlier and stronger *derzhavnik*, Andrannik Migranyan, argues even more forcefully for the state to "propagandize" and "mobilize" on behalf of a new, unifying "national idea." Andrannik Migranian, "Kontury novoi doktriny," *NG-Tsenarii*, no. 7, 1999, pp. 1, 14. Perhaps ironically—but understandably, given liberals' perceived vulnerability to questioning of their "patriotic" credentials—it is Pechenev writing in the strongly nationalist *Nash Sovremennik* who argues for less a top-down, state-enforced national ideology than a bottom-up, culturally and educationally nourished revived national *idea* or identity. See Pechenev, "Russkii narod," esp. pp. 208–10.

42. The greater concern is that the profession's current disparaging of "area studies" and emphasis on "transitological" approaches discourages deep and nuanced study of that past, and could produce a cohort of specialists with even less facility in Russian history, culture, and language than its predecessors. See Stephen F. Cohen, "Russian Studies Without Russia," *Post-Soviet Affairs* 15, no. 1 (1999): 37–55. See also Valerie Bunce, "Should Transitologists Be Grounded?" *Slavic Review* 54, no. 1 (1995) and the subsequent exchange in issue no. 4.

Bibliography

This bibliography is extensive but not exhaustive. It emphasizes those secondary and especially primary sources that are most central to the book's analysis, most frequently cited therein, and/or least well-known in the emerging literature of which it treats. These sources are divided into four categories: books; articles and chapters; memoirs and published interviews; documents. In some cases, analytical books or articles are included among the memoir sources if used primarily for their contemporaneous observations or historical significance. With the exception of those particularly important or repeatedly cited, shorter articles from Russian periodicals are not noted here (though a list of those publications employed most extensively is included at the end of the bibliography). As in the endnotes—but in contrast to the text, where a more simplified style is used—Russian-language sources are rendered here in a modified Library of Congress system.

Books

Adamov, V. V., ed. *Voprosy istorii kapitalisticheskoi rossii: problema mnogoukladnost'*. Sverdlovsk: Redaktsionno-Izdatel'skii Sovet Ural'skogo Universiteta, 1972.

Afan'asiev, Iu., ed. *Inogo ne dano*. Moscow: Progress, 1988.

Agursky, Mikhail. *The Third Rome: National Bolshevism in the USSR*. Boulder, CO: Westview Press, 1987.

Alexeyeva, Ludmilla. *U.S. Broadcasting to the Soviet Union*. New York: U.S. Helsinki Watch Committee, 1986.

Anderson, Benedict. *Imagined Communities: Reflections on the Origins and Spread of Nationalism*. London: Verso, 1983.

Arbatov, G. *Stroitel'stvo kommunizma i mirovoi revoliutsionnyi protsess*. Moscow: Nauka, 1966.

Aslund, Anders. *Gorbachev's Struggle for Economic Reform: The Soviet Reform Process, 1985–88*. Ithaca: Cornell University Press, 1989.

Bailes, Kendall E. *Technology and Society Under Lenin and Stalin.* Princeton: Princeton University Press, 1978.

Batalov, E. *Filosofiia bunta.* Moscow: Politizdat, 1970.

Bauer, Raymond A., Alex Inkeles, and Clyde Kluckhohn. *How the Soviet System Works.* Cambridge: Harvard University Press, 1959.

Berdyaev, Nicholas. *The Origin of Russian Communism.* Ann Arbor: University of Michigan Press, 1972.

Blacker, Coit D. *Hostage to Revolution: Gorbachev and Soviet Security Policy, 1985–1991.* New York: Council on Foreign Relations Press, 1993.

Blank, Stephen. *The Sorcerer as Apprentice: Stalin as Commissar of Nationalities, 1917–1924.* Westport, CT: Greenwood Press, 1994.

Brown, Archie. *The Gorbachev Factor.* New York: Oxford University Press, 1996.

——, ed. *New Thinking in Soviet Politics.* New York: St. Martin's Press, 1992.

Brudny, Yitzhak M. *Reinventing Russia: Russian Nationalism and the Soviet State, 1953–1991.* Cambridge: Harvard University Press, 1998.

Buganov, A. V. *Russkaia istoriia v pamiati krest'ian XIX veka i natsional'-noe samosoznanie.* Moscow: Institut Etnologii i Antropologii, 1992.

Bukharin, N., and E. Preobrazhensky. *The ABC of Communism.* Ann Arbor: University of Michigan Press, 1966.

Burlatskii, F. M. *Lenin. Gosudarstvo. Politika.* Moscow: Nauka, 1970.

Burlatskii, F. M., and A. A. Galkin. *Sotsiologiia. Politika. Mezhdunarodnye Otnosheniia.* Moscow: Mezhdunarodnye Otnosheniia, 1974.

Burlatskii, F. M., and V. E. Chirkin, eds. *Politicheskie sistemy sovremennosti. ocherki.* Moscow: Nauka, 1978.

Butenko, A. P. *Teoriia i praktika stroitel'stva sotsializma.* Moscow: Nauka, 1975.

Butenko, A. P., A. S. Tsipko, and V. P. Kiselev, eds. *Sotsialisticheskii obraz zhizni. metodologicheskie problemy issledovaniia.* Moscow: IEMSS, 1975.

Byrnes, Robert F. *Soviet-American Academic Exchanges, 1958–1975.* Bloomington: Indiana University Press, 1976.

Chaadaev, Peter. *Philosophical Letters and Apology of a Madman.* Knoxville: University of Tennessee Press, 1969.

Checkel, Jeffrey T. *Ideas and International Political Change: Soviet/Russian Behavior and the End of the Cold War.* New Haven: Yale University Press, 1997.

Cherniaev, A. S. *Sovremennaia sotsial-demokratiia i problemy edinstva rabochego dvizheniia.* Moscow: Nauka, 1964.

Cherniaev, A. S., and A. A. Galkin, *Sotsial-demokraticheskii i burzhuaznyi reformizm v sisteme gosudarstvenno-monopolisticheskogo kapitalizma.* Moscow: Nauka, 1980.

———. *Razmezhevaniia i sdvigi v sotsial-reformizme. kriticheskii analiz levykh techenii v zapadnoevropeiskoi sotsial-demokratii.* Moscow: Nauka, 1983.

———. *Ideologiia mezhdunarodnoi sotsial-demokratii v period mezhdu dvumia mirovymi voinami.* Moscow: Nauka, 1984.

Churchward, L. G. *The Soviet Intelligentsia: An Essay on the Social Structure and Roles of Soviet Intellectuals During the 1960s.* London: Routledge, 1973.

Cohen, Stephen F. *Bukharin and the Bolshevik Revolution: A Political Biography, 1888–1938.* New York: Oxford University Press, 1971.

———. *Rethinking the Soviet Experience: Politics and History Since 1917.* New York: Oxford University Press, 1985.

Danilevskii, N. *Rossiia i Evropa. vzgliad na kul'turnye i politicheskie otnosheniia slavianskogo mira k germano-romanskomu.* Sanktpeterburg: Obshchestvennaia Pol'za, 1871.

Davydov, Iu. *Trud i svoboda.* Moscow: Vysshaia Shkola, 1962.

Doder, Dushko. *Shadows and Whispers: Power Politics Inside the Kremlin from Brezhnev to Gorbachev.* New York: Random House, 1985.

Dudakov, Savelii. *Istoriia odnogo mifa. ocherki Russkoi literatury XIX–XX vv.* Moscow: Nauka, 1993.

Dunlop, John B. *The Faces of Contemporary Russian Nationalism.* Princeton: Princeton University Press, 1983.

———. *The Rise of Russia and the Fall of the Soviet Empire.* Princeton: Princeton University Press, 1993.

Eidel'man, N. Ia. *Tainye korrespondenty "Poliarnoi Zvezdy."* Moscow: Mysl', 1966.

———. *Lunin.* Moscow: Molodaia Gvardiia, 1970.

Ekendahl, Carolyn McGiffert, and Melvin A. Goodman. *The Wars of Eduard Shevardnadze.* University Park: Pennsylvania University Press, 1997.

Ellman, Michael and Kontorovich, Vladimir, eds. *The Disintegration of the Soviet Economic System.* London: Routledge, 1992.

Evangelista, Matthew. *Unarmed Forces: The Transnational Movement to End the Cold War.* Ithaca: Cornell University Press, 1999.

Fitzgerald, T. K. *Metaphors of Identity.* Albany: State University of New York Press, 1993.

Fitzpatrick, Shelia, ed. *Cultural Revolution in Russia, 1928–1931.* Bloomington: Indiana University Press, 1978.

Frierson, Cathy A. *Peasant Icons: Representatives of Rural People in Late Nineteenth-Century Russia.* New York: Oxford University Press, 1993.

Frolov, I. T. *Genetika i dialektika.* Moscow: Nauka, 1969.

Galkin, A. A. *O sovremennoi Sovetskoi diplomatii.* Moscow: Politizdat, 1963.

Garthoff, Raymond L. *Détente and Confrontation: American-Soviet Relations from Nixon to Reagan.* Washington, DC: Brookings Institution Press, 1985.

————. *The Great Transition: American-Soviet Relations and the End of the Cold War.* Washington, DC: Brookings Institution Press, 1994.

Gefter, M. Ia., ed. *Istoricheskaia nauka i nekotorye problemy sovremennosti.* Moscow: Nauka, 1969.

Gellner, Ernest. *Nations and Nationalism.* Ithaca, Cornell University Press, 1983.

Gerasimov, G. I. *Stanet li tesno na zemnom share? Problema narodonaseleniia.* Moscow: Znanie, 1967.

Giddens, Anthony. *Modernity and Self-Identity.* Stanford: Stanford University Press, 1991.

Gildea, Robert. *The Past in French History.* New Haven: Yale University Press, 1994.

Gleason, Abbott. *Young Russia: The Genesis of Russian Radicalism in the 1860s.* New York: Viking Press, 1980.

Gleason, Abbott, Peter Kenez, and Richard Stites, eds. *Bolshevik Culture: Experiment and Order in the Russian Revolution.* Bloomington: Indiana University Press, 1985.

Goldstein, Judith, and Robert O. Keohane, eds. *Ideas and Foreign Policy: Beliefs, Interests, and Political Change.* Ithaca: Cornell University Press, 1993.

Gorbachev, M. S. *Izbrannye Rechi i Stat'i.* 2 vols. Moscow: Politizdat, 1987.

Gorky, Maxim. *Untimely Thoughts.* Ed. Herman Ermolaev. New York: Paul Eriksson, 1968.

Gramsci, Antonio. *Selections from the Prison Notebooks.* Eds. Quintin Hoare and Geoffrey N. Smith. New York: International Publishers, 1971.

Greenfeld, Liah. *Nationalism: Five Roads to Modernity.* Cambridge: Harvard University Press, 1992.

Grushin, B. A. *Mnenia o mire i mir mnenii.* Moscow: Politizdat, 1967.

————. *Sotsialisticheskii obraz zhiznii. poniatie i vozmozhnye napravleniia issledovaniia.* Moscow: TsEMI, 1975.

Grushin, B. A., and V. V. Chikin. *Vo imia shchastia chelovecheskogo.* Moscow: Molodaia Gvardiia, 1960.

————. *Ispoved' pokoleniia.* Moscow: Molodaia Gvardiia, 1962.

Haas, Ernest. *When Knowledge Is Power.* Berkeley: University of California Press, 1990.

Hardeman, Hilde. *Coming to Terms with the Soviet Regime: The "Changing Signposts" Movement Among Russian Emigres in the Early 1920s.* De Kalb: Northern Illinois University Press, 1994.

Herrmann, Richard K. *Perceptions and Behavior in Soviet Foreign Policy.* Pittsburgh: Pittsburgh University Press, 1985.

Hill, Ronald. *Soviet Politics, Political Science and Reform.* London: Martin Robertson, 1980.

History of the Communist Party of the Soviet Union (Bolshevik) Short Course. Moscow: Foreign Languages Publishing, 1944.

Hobsbawm, Eric, and Terence Ranger, eds. *The Invention of Tradition.* New York: Cambridge University Press, 1983.

Holmes, Larry. *The Kremlin and the Schoolhouse.* Bloomington: Indiana University Press, 1991.

Hosking, Geoffrey. *The First Socialist Society: A History of the Soviet Union from Within.* Cambridge: Harvard University Press, 1985.

Hough, Jerry F. *Soviet Leadership in Transition.* Washington, DC: Brookings Institution Press, 1980.

————. *The Struggle for the Third World: Soviet Debates and American Options.* Washington, DC: Brookings Institution Press, 1986.

————. *Russia and the West: Gorbachev and the Politics of Reform.* New York: Simon & Schuster, 1988.

————. *Democratization and Revolution in the USSR, 1985–1991.* Washington, DC: Brookings Institution Press, 1997.

Iadov, V., A. Zdravomyslov, et al., eds. *Man and His Work.* White Plains, NY: International Arts and Sciences Press, 1970.

Iakovlev, Aleksandr N. *Po moshcham i elei.* Moscow: Izdatel'stvo "Evraziia," 1995.

Inkeles, Alex. *Public Opinion in Soviet Russia: A Study in Mass Persuasion.* Cambridge: Harvard University Press, 1951.

————. *Social Change in Soviet Russia.* Cambridge: Harvard University Press, 1968.

Inozemtsev, N. N., ed. *Global'nye problemy sovremennosti.* Moscow: Mysl', 1981.

Inozemtsev, N. N., et al., eds. *Politicheskaia ekonomika sovremennogo monopolisticheskogo kapitalizma.* Moscow: Mysl', 1975.

James, Harold. *A German Identity, 1770–1990.* New York: Routledge, 1989.

Jarausch, Konrad H., ed. *After Unity: Reconfiguring German Identities.* Providence, RI: Berghahn Press, 1997.

Kagarlitsky, Boris. *The Thinking Reed: Intellectuals and the Soviet State from 1917 to the Present.* London: Verso, 1988.

Kalenskii, V. G. *Politicheskaia nauka v S.Sh.A.. Kritika burzhuaznykh kontseptsii vlasti.* Moscow: Iuridicheskaia Literatura, 1969.

————. *Gosudarstvo kak ob"ekt sotsiologicheskogo analiza.* Moscow: Iuridicheskaia Literatura, 1977.

Kapitsa, P. L. *Eksperiment. Teoriia. Praktika.* Moscow: Nauka, 1974.

Kariakin, Iu. F., and E. G. Plimak. *Zapretnaia mysl' obretaet svobodu.* Moscow: Nauka, 1966.

Katzenstein, Peter J., ed. *The Culture of National Security: Norms and Identity in World Politics.* New York: Columbia University Press, 1996.

Kenez, Peter. *The Birth of the Propaganda State: Soviet Methods of Mass Mobilization, 1917–1929.* New York: Cambridge University Press, 1985.

Kennedy, Paul. *The Rise and Fall of the Great Powers: Economic Change and Military Conflict from 1500 to 2000.* New York: Random House, 1987.

Khozin, G. S. *V zashchitu planety. Mezhdunarodnoe sotrudnichestvo v oblasti okruzhaiushchoi sredy.* Moscow: Znanie, 1974.

———. *Global'nye problemy sovremennosti. Kritika burzhuaznykh kontseptsii.* Moscow: Mysl', 1982.

Kim, Samuel S., and Lowell Dittmer, eds. *China's Quest for National Identity.* Ithaca: Cornell University Press, 1993.

Kokoshin, A. A. *O burzhuaznykh prognozakh razvitiia mezhdunarodnykh otnoshenii.* Moscow: Mezhdunarodnye Otnosheniia, 1978.

Kuhn, Thomas. *The Structure of Scientific Revolutions.* Chicago: University of Chicago Press, 1970.

Kull, Stephen. *Burying Lenin: The Revolution in Soviet Ideology and Foreign Policy.* Boulder, CO: Westview Press, 1992.

Lacis, Otto. *The Turning Point.* Moscow: Progress, 1990.

Lahusen, Thomas, ed. *Late Soviet Culture: From Perestroika to Novostroika.* Durham: Duke University Press, 1993.

Lebow, Richard Ned, and Thomas Risse-Kappen, eds. *International Relations Theory and the End of the Cold War.* New York: Columbia University Press, 1995.

Levada, Iu. *Lektsii po sotsiologii.* 2 vols. Moscow: Institut Konkretnykh Sotsial'nykh Issledovanii, 1969.

Levesque, Jacques. *The Enigma of 1989: The USSR and the Liberation of Eastern Europe.* Berkeley: University of California Press, 1997.

Lewin, Moshe. *Political Undercurrents in Soviet Economic Debates.* Princeton: Princeton University Press, 1976.

———. *The Making of the Soviet System: Essays in the Social History of Interwar Russia.* New York: New Press, 1985.

———. *The Gorbachev Phenomenon: An Historical Interpretation.* London: Hutchinson Radius, 1988.

Liehm, Antonin J., and Mira Liehm. *The Most Important Art.* Berkeley: University of California Press, 1977.

Lincoln, Bruce. *In the Vanguard of Reform: Russia's Enlightened Bureaucrats.* De Kalb: University of Northern Illinois Press, 1982.

Linz, Juan J., and Alfred Stepan. *Problems of Democratic Transition and Consolidation: Southern Europe, South America, and Post-*

Communist Europe. Baltimore: Johns Hopkins University Press, 1996.

Lukin, V. *Sotsial-demokratiia v Iuzhnoi i Iugo-Vostochnoi Azii*. Moscow, 1964.

Lynch, Allen. *The Soviet Study of International Relations*. New York: Cambridge University Press, 1987.

Mamardashvili, M. *Formy i soderzhanie myshleniia*. Moscow: Vysshaia Shkola, 1968.

Marcuse, Herbert. *Soviet Marxism: A Critical Analysis*. New York: Vintage, 1961.

Masaryk, Thomas G. *The Spirit of Russia*. 2 vols. London: George Allen & Unwin, 1955.

Matthews, Mervyn. *Education in the Soviet Union: Policies and Institutions Since Stalin*. London: Allen & Unwin, 1982.

Medvedev, Roy. *Let History Judge: The Origins and Consequences of Stalinism*. Revised ed. New York: Columbia University Press, 1989.

———. *Lichnost' i epokha: Politicheskii portret L.I. Brezhneva*. Moscow: Novosti, 1991.

Medvedev, V. A. *Upravlenie sotsialisticheskim proizvodstvom: problemy teorii i praktiki*. Moscow: Politizdat, 1983.

Medvedev, Zhores A. *Soviet Science*. New York: Norton, 1978.

———. *Andropov*. New York: Norton, 1983.

Mehnert, Klaus. *Stalin Versus Marx: The Stalinist Historical Doctrine*. London: Allen & Unwin, 1952.

Mendelson, Sarah. *Changing Course: Ideas, Politics, and the Soviet Withdrawal from Afghanistan*. Princeton: Princeton University Press, 1998.

Nation, R. Craig. *Black Earth, Red Star: A History of Soviet Security Policy, 1917–1991*. Ithaca: Cornell University Press, 1992.

Oberdorfer, Don. *The Turn: From the Cold War to a New Era*. New York: Poseidon Press, 1991.

Pashukanis, E., and M. Spektator. *Desiat' let kapitalisticheskogo okruzheniia SSSR. seriia v semi knigakh*. Moscow: Izdatel'stvo Kommunisticheskoi Akademii, 1928.

Pethybridge, Roger. *The Social Prelude to Stalinism*. New York: St. Martin's Press, 1974.

Pipes, Richard. *The Formation of the Soviet Union*. Cambridge: Harvard University Press, 1964,

Pokrovsky, Mikhail. *Russia in World History*. Ann Arbor: University of Michigan Press, 1970.

Polukhina, Valentina, Joe Andrew, and Robert Reid, eds. *Literary Tradition and Practice in Russian Culture*. Amsterdam: Rodopi, 1993.

Raeff, Mark. *Origins of the Russian Intelligentsia: The Eighteenth Century Nobility.* New York: Harcourt, Brace & World, 1966.

Reiman, Michal. *The Birth of Stalinism: The USSR on the Eve of the "Second Revolution."* Bloomington: Indiana University Press, 1987.

Riasanovsky, Nicholas. *Russia and the West in the Teaching of the Slavophiles.* Cambridge: Harvard University Press, 1952.

Richmond, Yale. *U.S.-Soviet Cultural Exchanges, 1958–1986: Who Wins?* Boulder: Westview Press, 1987.

Rigby, T. H. *Communist Party Membership in the USSR, 1917–1967.* Princeton: Princeton University Press, 1968.

Rosecrance, Richard, and Arthur A. Stein, eds. *The Domestic Bases of Grand Strategy.* Ithaca: Cornell University Press, 1993.

Rotblat, Joseph. *Pugwash–the First Ten Years.* London: Heinemann, 1967.

———. *Scientists in the Quest for Peace: A History of the Pugwash Conferences.* Cambridge: Harvard University Press, 1972.

Rozman, Gilbert. *A Mirror for Socialism: Soviet Criticisms of China.* Princeton: Princeton University Press, 1985.

Rubinstein, Joshua. *Tangled Loyalties: The Life and Times of Ilya Ehrenburg.* New York: Basic Books, 1996.

Sakharov, Andrei D. *Progress, Coexistence, and Intellectual Freedom.* London: Penguin Books, 1968.

Scanlan, James. *Marxism in the USSR.* Ithaca: Cornell University Press, 1985.

Schwartz, Morton. *Soviet Perceptions of the United States.* Berkeley: University of California Press, 1978.

Seniavskaia, E. S. *Frontovoe pokolenie, 1941–1945. Istoriko-psikhologicheskoe issledovanie.* Moscow: Institut Rossiiskoi Istorii, 1995.

Shakhnazarov, G. Kh. *Sotsialisticheskaia demokratiia. nekotorye voprosy teorii.* Moscow: Politizdat, 1972.

———. *Griadushii miroporiadok.* Moscow: Politizdat, 1972. Published in English as *The Coming World Order.* Moscow: Progress, 1984.

Shakhnazarov, G. Kh., and Iu. A. Tikhomirov, eds. *Aktual'nye problemy sovremennogo politicheskogo razvitiia. ocherki teorii.* Moscow: Iuridicheskaia Literatura, 1982.

Sheinis, V. L., ed. *Tretii mir. strategiia razvitiia i upravlenie ekonomiki.* Moscow: Nauka, 1971.

Shenfield, Stephen. *The Nuclear Predicament: Explorations in Soviet Ideology.* London: Routledge & Kegan Paul, 1987.

Shlapentokh, Vladimir. *The Politics of Sociology in the Soviet Union.* Boulder, CO: Westview Press, 1987.

———. *Public and Private Life of the Soviet People: Changing Values in Post-Stalin Russia.* New York: Oxford University Press, 1989.

————. *Soviet Intellectuals and Political Power: The Post-Stalin Era.* London: Tauris, 1990.

Shlykov, V. V. *NATO i sovmestnoe proizvodstvo vooruzhenii.* Moscow: IMEMO, 1970.

————. *NATO i voennyi biznes.* Published under the pseudonym V. V. Repinskii. Moscow: Mezhdunarodnye Otnosheniia, 1970.

Shmelev, Nikolai. *Na Perelome. Perestroika Ekonomike v SSSR.* Moscow: Nauka, 1988.

Snyder, Jack. *Myths of Empire: Domestic Politics and International Ambition.* Ithaca: Cornell University Press, 1991.

Sodaro, Michael J. *Moscow, Germany, and the West from Khrushchev to Gorbachev.* Ithaca: Cornell University Press, 1990.

Somerville, J. *Soviet Marxism and Nuclear War.* London: Aldwych, 1981.

Spechler, Dina R. *Permitted Dissent in the USSR: Novy Mir and the Soviet Regime.* New York: Praeger, 1982.

Stalin, Joseph. *Economic Problems of Socialism in the USSR.* New York: International Publishers, 1952.

Teague, Elizabeth. *Solidarity and the Soviet Worker: The Impact of the Polish Events of 1980 on Soviet Internal Politics.* London: Croom Helm, 1988.

Tsipko, A. *Ideia sotsializma: vekha biografii.* Moscow: Nauka, 1976.

————. *Nekotorye filosofskie aspekty teorii sotsializma.* Moscow: Nauka, 1983.

Tsipko, A., and V. Lukin. *Optimizm istorii.* Moscow: Molodaia Gvardiia, 1974.

Tucker, Robert C. *The Soviet Political Mind.* New York: Norton, 1971.

————. *Stalin as Revolutionary: A Study in History and Personality, 1879–1929.* New York: Norton, 1973.

————. *Stalin in Power: The Revolution from Above, 1928–1941.* New York: Norton, 1990.

—, ed. *The Lenin Anthology.* New York: Norton, 1975.

Turchin, Valentin. *The Inertia of Fear and the Scientific Worldview.* New York: Columbia University Press, 1981.

Ulam, Adam. *Expansion and Coexistence: The History of Soviet Foreign Policy, 1917–1967.* New York: Praeger, 1968.

Vaksberg, Arkady. *Stalin's Prosecutor: The Life of Andrei Vyshinsky.* New York: Grove Weidenfeld, 1990.

Valkenier, Elizabeth. *The Soviet Union and the Third World: An Economic Bind.* New York: Praeger, 1983.

Vasil'iev, V., V. Pisarev, and G. Khozin. *Ekologiia i mezhdunarodnye otnosheniia.* Moscow: Mezhdunarodnye Otnosheniia, 1978.

Vekhi. Sbornik Statei o Russkoi Intelligentsii. Moscow: Novosti, 1990 (orig. publ. 1909).

Velikhov, Yevgeni, Roald Sagdeev, and Andrei Kokoshin. *Weaponry in Space: The Dilemma of Security.* Moscow: Mir, 1986.

Vodolazov, G. *Ot Chernyshevskogo k Plekhanovu.* Moscow: Izdatel'stvo Moskovskogo Universiteta, 1969.

———. *Dialektika i revoliutsiia.* Moscow: Izdatel'stvo Moskovskogo Universiteta, 1975.

Vorozheikin, I. E., et al., eds. *Sovetskaia intelligentsiia. Istoriia formirovaniia i rosta, 1917–1965.* Moscow: Mysl', 1968.

Vucinich, Alexander. *Empire of Knowledge: The Academy of Sciences of the USSR, 1917–1970.* Berkeley: University of California Press, 1984.

Walicki, Andrzej. *A History of Russian Thought.* Stanford: Stanford University Press, 1979.

Westwood, J. N. *Endurance and Endeavor: Russian History, 1812–1986.* New York: Oxford University Press, 1987.

Wittner, Lawrence S. *Resisting the Bomb: A History of the World Nuclear Disarmament Movement, 1947–1970.* vol 1. Stanford: Stanford University Press, 1998.

Wohlforth, William Curti. *The Elusive Balance: Power and Perceptions During the Cold War.* Ithaca: Cornell University Press, 1993.

Wortman, Richard S. *The Development of a Russian Legal Consciousness.* Chicago: University of Chicago Press, 1976.

Yakovlev, Alexander. *The Fate of Marxism in Russia.* New Haven: Yale University Press, 1993.

Yanov, Alexander. *The New Russian Right.* Berkeley: University of California Press, 1978.

Zagladin, N. V. *Istoriia uspekhov i neudach Sovetskoi diplomatii.* Moscow: Mezhdunarodnye Otnosheniia, 1990.

Zagladin, V. V., and I. T. Frolov. *Global'nye problemy sovremennosti. nauchnyi i sotsial'nyi aspekty.* Moscow: Mezhdunarodnye Otnosheniia, 1981.

Zamoshkin, Iu. A. *Krizis burzhuaznogo individualizma i lichnost'.* Moscow: Nauka, 1966.

———, ed. *Amerikanskoe obshchestvennoe mnenie i politika.* Moscow: Nauka, 1978.

Zelikow, Philip, and Condoleeza Rice. *Germany Unified and Europe Transformed: A Study in Statecraft.* Cambridge: Harvard University Press, 1995.

Zimmerman, William. *Soviet Perspectives on International Relations, 1956–1967.* Princeton: Princeton University Press, 1969.

Zubkova, E. Iu. *Obshchestvo i reformy. 1945–1964.* Moscow: Rossiia Molodaia, 1993.

Zubok, Vladislav, and Constantine Pleshakov. *Inside the Kremlin's Cold War: From Stalin to Khrushchev.* Cambridge: Harvard University Press, 1996.

Articles and Chapters

Adler, Emanuel. "The Emergence of Cooperation." *International Organization* 46, no. 1 (1992).

———. "Cognitive Evolution: A Dynamic Approach for the Study of International Relations and Their Progress." In Adler and Beverly Crawford. *Progress in Postwar International Relations.* New York: Columbia University Press, 1991.

Adler, Emanuel, and Michael N. Barnett. "Governing Anarchy: A Research Agenda for the Study of Security Coommunities." *Ethics and International Affairs* 10, no. 4 (1996).

Aksenov, Iu. S. "Poslevoennyi Stalinizm: udar po intelligentsii." *Kentavr* 1, no. 1 (1991).

Ambartsumov, E. "Eshche est' vremia." *Literaturnaia Gazeta*, 16 November 1983.

———. "Analyz V. I. Leninym prichin krizisa 1921 g. i putei vykhoda iz nego." *Voprosy Istorii*, no. 4 (1984).

Arbatov, G. A. "K voprosu o roli narodnykh mass v mezhdunarodnykh otnosheniiakh." *Mezhdunarodnaia Zhizn'*, no. 9 (1955).

Barghoorn, Frederick C. "Some Russian Images of the West." In Cyril E. Black, ed., *The Transformation of Russian Society.* Cambridge: Harvard University Press, 1960.

Barros, Robert. "The Left and Democracy: Recent Debates in Latin America." *Telos* 68, no. 3 (1986).

Bermeo, Nancy. "Democracy and the Lessons of Dictatorship." *Comparative Politics* 24, no. 3 (1992).

Bjorkman, Thomas, and Thomas Zamostny. "Soviet Politics and Strategy Toward the West: Three Cases." *World Politics* 36, no. 2 (1984).

Blum, Douglas. "The Soviet Foreign Policy Belief System: Beliefs, Politics, and Foreign Policy Outcomes." *International Studies Quarterly* 37, no. 4 (1993).

Bogomolov, O. "O vneshne-ekonomicheskikh sviaziakh SSSR." *Kommunist*, no. 5 (1974).

———. "Ekonomicheskie sviazi mezhdu sotsialisticheskimi i kapitalisticheskimi stranami." *Mirovaia Ekonomika i Mezhdunarodnye Otnosheniia*, no. 3 (1980).

Bonnell, Victoria E. "The Representation of Politics and the Politics of Representation." *Russian Review* 47, no. 3 (1988).

Bovin, A. "Nauka i mirovozzrenie." *Kommunist*, no. 5 (1960).

Breslauer, George. "Explaining Soviet Policy Changes: Politics, Ideology and Learning." In Breslauer, ed., *Soviet Policy in Africa*. Berkeley: University of California Press, 1992.

―――. "How Do You Sell a Concessionary Foreign Policy?" *Post-Soviet Affairs* 10, no. 3 (1994).

Brovkin, Vladimir. "Workers' Unrest and the Bolsheviks' Response in 1919." *Slavic Review* 49, no. 3 (1990).

Brown, Archie. "Political Science in the USSR." *International Political Science Review* 7, no. 4 (1986).

Brudny, Yitzhak M. "Neoliberal Economic Reform and the Consolidation of Democracy in Russia: Or Why Institutions and Ideas Might Matter More than Economics." In Karen Dawisha, ed., *The International Dimension of Post-Communist Transitions in Russia and the New States of Eurasia*. Armonk, NY: Sharpe, 1997.

Burg, David [pseud.]. "Observations on Soviet University Students." In Richard Pipes, ed., *The Russian Intelligentsia*. New York: Columbia University Press, 1961.

Burlatskii, F. M. "O sistemnom podkhode k issledovaniiu vneshnei politiki." In *Mezhdunarodnye Otnosheniia, Politika i Lichnost'*. Moscow: Sovetskaia Assotsiatsiia Politicheskikh Nauk, 1976.

―――. "Filosofiia mira." *Voprosy Filosofii* no. 12 (1982).

―――. "Nekotorye voprosy teorii mezhdunarodnykh otnoshenii." *Voprosy Filosofii* no. 9 (1983).

Butenko, A. P. "Protivorechiia razvitiia sotsializma kak obshchestvennogo stroia," *Voprosy Filosofii* no. 10 (1982).

―――. "Esche raz o protivorechiiakh sotsializma." *Voprosy Filosofii* no. 2 (1984).

Byrnes, Robert F. "Attitudes Toward the West." In Ivo J. Lederer, ed., *Russian Foreign Policy*. New Haven: Yale University Press, 1962.

Checkel, Jeffrey. "The Constructivist Turn in International Relations Theory." *World Politics* 50, no. 1 (1998).

Cheng, Li, and Lynn T. White III. "China's Technocratic Movement and the *World Economic Herald*." *Modern China* 17, no. 3 (1991).

Cohen, Stephen F. "Ligachev and the Tragedy of Soviet Conservatism." Introduction to Ligachev, *Inside Gorbachev's Kremlin*.

―――. "Russian Studies Without Russia." *Post-Soviet Affairs* 15, no. 1 (1999).

Daniels, Robert. "Russian Political Culture and the Post-Revolutionary Impasse." *Russian Review* 46, no. 2 (1987).

Dashichev, V. I. "Vostok-Zapad. poisk novykh otnoshenii." *Literaturnaia Gazeta*, 18 May 1988.

Dobrynin, A. "Za bez'iadernyi mir, navstrechu XXI veku." *Kommunist*, no. 9 (1986).

Dorofeev, Vil'. "Aleksandr Iakovlev. uidti, chtoby ostat'siia." *Dialog*, no. 17 (1990).

Druckman, Daniel. "Nationalism, Patriotism, and Group Loyalty: A Social Psychological Perspective." *Mershon International Studies Review* 38, supp. 1 (1994).

Emerson, Caryl. "New Words, New Epochs, Old Thoughts." *Russian Review* 55, no. 3 (1996).

Evangelista, Matthew. "Transnational Relations, Domestic Structures, and Security Policy in the USSR and Russia." In Thomas Risse-Kappen, ed. *Bringing Transnational Relations Back In: Non-State Actors, Domestic Structures and International Institutions.* New York: Cambridge University Press, 1995.

Fedotov, G. P. "Russia and Freedom." *Review of Politics* 8, no. 1 (1946); see also G. Fedotov "Rossiia i Svoboda." *Znamia*, no. 12 (1989).

Feuer, Louis. "Meeting the Philosophers." *Survey*. no. 51 (1964).

Fox, Michael S. "Political Culture, Purges, and Proletarianization at the Institute of Red Professors, 1921–1929." *Russian Review* 52, no. 1 (1993).

Frolov, I. T., and M. K. Mamardashvili. "Soiuz nauki i demokratii." *Problemy Mira i Sotsializma*, no. 4 (1965).

Frolov, I. T., ed. "Chelovek i sreda ego obitaniia." *Voprosy Filosofii*, no. 2 (1973).

Furaev, V. K. "Ob izuchenii istorii mezhdunarodnykh otnoshenii i vneshnei politiki SSSR." *Novaia i Noveishchaia Istoriia*, no. 3 (1992).

Furman, Dmitri. "Ostorozhno s imperiiami." *Vek XX i Mir*, no. 11 (1989).

Galkin, A. A. "Sotsial'naia struktura sovremennogo kapitalisticheskogo obshchestva i burzhuaznaia sotsiologiia." *Voprosy Filosofii*, no. 8 (1972).

Geertz, Clifford. "Ideology as a Cultural System." In David E. Apter, ed., *Ideology and Discontent.* London: Free Press of Gencoe, 1964.

Gefter, M. "Sud'ba Khrushcheva: istoriia odnogo neusvoennogo uroka." *Oktiabr'*, no. 1 (1989).

George, Alexander. "The 'Operational Code': A Neglected Approach to the Study of Political Leaders and Decision-Making." In Erik P. Hoffmann and Frederic J. Fleron, eds., *The Conduct of Soviet Foreign Policy.* Chicago: Aldine, 1971.

Gerasimov, G. "The First-Strike Theory." *International Affairs* (Moscow), no. 3 (1965).

———. "Teoriia igr i mezhdunarodnye otnosheniia." *Mirovaia Ekonomika i Mezhdunarodnye Otnosheniia*, no. 7 (1966).

Gorbachev, Mikhail. "The Crimea Article." In Gorbachev, *The August Coup: The Truth and Its Lessons.* New York: HarperCollins, 1991.

Gould-Davies, Nigel. "Rethinking the Role of Ideology in International Politics During the Cold War." *Journal of Cold War Studies* 1, no. 1 (1999).

Haas, Peter M. "Introduction: Epistemic Communities and International Policy Coordination." *International Organization* 46, no. 1 (1992).

Hall, Peter A. "Policy Paradigms, Social Learning, and the State: The Case of Economic Policymaking in Britain." *Comparative Politics* 25, no. 3 (1993).

Herrmann, Richard K. "Policy-Relevant Theory and the Challenge of Diagnosis: The End of the Cold War as a Case Study." *Political Psychology* 15, no. 1 (1994).

Herspring, Dale R. "The Military Factor in East German Soviet Policy." *Slavic Review* 47, no. 1 (1988).

Hirschmann, Albert O. "The Search for Paradigms as a Hindrance to Understanding." *World Politics* 22, no. 3 (1970).

Hough, Jerry. "The Evolution in the Soviet World View." *World Poltics* 32, no. 4 (1980).

Iakovlev, A. N. "Protiv antiistorizma." *Literaturnaia Gazeta*, 15 November 1972.

Ianov, A. "Zagadka slavianofilskoi kritiki." *Voprosy Literatury*, no. 5 (1969).

Inosemtsev, N. "O novom etape v razvitiii mezhdunarodnykh otnoshenii." *Komminist*, no. 13 (1973).

Johnston, Alastair Iain. "Thinking About Strategic Culture." *International Security* 19, no. 4 (1995).

Kamenka, Eugene. "Philosophers in Moscow." *Survey*, no. 62 (1967).

Karpinskii, L., and F. Burlatskii. "Na puti k prem'ere." *Komsomol'skaia Pravda*, 30 June 1967.

Kneen, Peter. "The Background to *Perestroika*: 'Political Undercurrents' Reconsidered in the Light of Recent Events." In Nick Lampert and Gabor T. Rittersporn, eds. *Stalinism: Its Nature and Aftermath.* New York: Macmillan, 1992.

Kogan, L. A. " 'Vyslat' za granitsu bezzhalostno' (Novoe ob izgnanii dukhovnoi elity)." *Voprosy Filosofii*, no. 9 (1993).

Kon, I. "Razmyshleniia ob Amerikanskoi intelligentsii." *Novy Mir*, no. 1 (1968).

————. "Seks. Obshchestvo. Kul'tura." *Inostrannaia Literatura*, no. 1 (1970).

Kotkin, Stephen. "Coercion and Identity: Workers' Lives in Stalin's Showcase City." In Lewis H. Siegelbaum and Ronald Grigor Suny, eds. *Making Workers Soviet: Power, Class, and Identity*. Ithaca: Cornell University Press, 1994.

Kozhinov, V. "O glavnom v nasledii slavianofilov," *Voprosy Literatury*, no. 10 (1969).

Kozyrev, A. "Doverie i balans interesov." *Mezhdunarodnaia Zhizn'*, no. 10 (1988).

Kozyrev, Andrei. "Limitation of the Arms Trade." In *Problems of Common Security*. Moscow: Progress, 1984.

Kurashvili, B. P. "Gosudarstvennoe upravlenie narodnym khoziastvom i perspektivy razvitiia." *Sovetskoe Gosudartstvo i Pravo*, no. 6 (1982).

————. "Ob"ektivnye zakony gosudarstvennogo upravleniia." *Sovetskoe Gosudarstvo i Pravo*, no. 10 (1983).

Legvold, Robert. "The Revolution in Soviet Foreign Policy." *Foreign Affairs* 68, no. 1 (1988/89).

————. "Observations on International Order: A Comment on MacFarland and Adomeit." *Post-Soviet Affairs* 10, no. 3 (1994).

Levy, Jack. "Learning and Foreign Policy. Sweeping a Conceptual Minefield." *International Organization* 48, no. 2 (1994).

Lukin, V. P. " 'Ideologiia razvitiia' i massovoe soznanie v stranakh 'tret'ego mira.' " *Voprosy Filosofii*, no. 6 (1969).

Malashenko, I. E. *Sotsial'naia Filosofiia Dante*. Moscow: Izdatel'stvo MGU, 1980.

Malia, Martin. "From Under the Rubble, What?" *Problems of Communism* 41, no. 2 (1992).

Marko, Kurt. "History and the Historians." *Survey*, no. 56 (1965).

Markwick, Roger D. "Catalyst of Historiography, Marxism and Dissidence: The Sector of Methodology of the Institute of History, Soviet Academy of Sciences, 1964–68." *Europe-Asia Studies* 46, no. 4 (1994).

Mau, Vladimir. "The Road to Perestroika: Economics in the USSR and the Problems of Reforming the Soviet Economic Order." *Europe-Asia Studies* 48, no. 2 (1996).

McInnes, Neil. "Havemann and the Dialectic." *Survey*, no. 62 (1967).

Michnik, Adam. "Tri geneticheskie oshibki." *Novoe Vremia*, no. 1 (1992).

Murav, Harriet. "The Case Against Andrei Siniavskii: The Letter and the Law." *Russian Review* 53, no. 4 (1994).

Nekrich, Aleksandr M. "The Socio-Political Effects of Khrushchev: His Impact on Soviet Intellectual Life." In R. F. Miller and F. Fehrer, eds., *Khrushchev and the Communist World*. London: Croom Helm, 1984.

Nikitich, L. S. "Nekotorye voprosy sviazi borby za demokratiiu s borboi za sotsializm v trudakh Italianskikh Marksistov." *Vestnik Moskovskogo Universiteta. Seriia VII. Ekonomika, Filosofiia*, no. 4 (1965).

Oduev, S. F. "Zametki o filosofskoi zhizni v Iugoslavii." *Voprosy Filosofii*, no. 5 (1966).

Omel'chenko, N. A. "Spory o evraziistve, opyt istoricheskoi rekonstruktsii." *Polis*, no. 3 (1992).

Packenham, Robert. "The Changing Political Discourse in Brazil, 1964–1985." In Wayne Selcher, ed., *Political Liberation in Brazil*. Boulder, CO: Westview Press, 1986.

Pipes, Richard. "Misinterpreting the Cold War: The Hardliners Had it Right." *Foreign Affairs* 74, no. 1 (1995).

Primakov, E. "Zakon neravnomernosti razvitiia i istoricheskoi sud'by osvobodivshikhsia stran." *Mirovaia Ekonomika i Mezhdunarodnye Otnosheniia*, no. 12 (1980).

Riasanovsky, Nicholas. "Emergence of Eurasianism." *California Slavic Studies* 4 (1967).

Rieber, Alfred J. "Russian Imperialism: Popular, Emblematic, Ambiguous." *Russian Review* 53, no. 3 (1994).

Ripley, Brian. "Psychology, Foreign Policy and International Relations." *Political Psychology* 14, no. 3 (1989).

Rittersporn, Gabor T. "The Omnipresent Conspiracy: On Soviet Imagery of Politics and Social Relations in the 1930s." In J. Arch Getty and Roberta T. Manning, eds., *Stalinist Terror: New Perspectives*. New York: Cambridge University Press, 1993.

Selunin, V., and G. Khanin. "Lukavaia stifra." *Novy Mir*, no. 2 (1987).

Shakhnazarov, G. Kh. "K probleme sootnosheniia sil v mire." *Kommunist*, no. 3 (1974).

———. "Logika politicheskogo myshleniia v iadernuiu eru." *Voprosy Filosofii*, no. 5 (1984).

Shlapentokh, Vladimir. "Moscow's War Propaganda and Soviet Public Opinion." *Problems of Communism* 33, no. 5 (1984).

Shmelev, N. P. "SShA v mirovom kapitalisticheskom khoziastve." *Mirovaia Ekonomika i Mezhdunarodnye Otnosheniia*, no. 4 (1984).

Sikkink, Kathryn. "Human Rights, Principled Issue Networks, and Sovereignty in Latin America." *International Organization* 47, no. 3 (1993).

Sirotkin, V. "Rizhskii mir." *Mezhdunarodnaia Zhizn'*, no. 8 (1988).

Smirnov, Vladimir. "M. K. Mamardashvili: Filosofiia soznaniia." *Kommunist*, no. 8 (1991).

Smith, Steve. "Russian Workers and the Politics of Social Identity." *Russian Review* 56, no. 1 (1997).

Snyder, Jack. "Richness, Rigor and Relevance in the Study of Soviet Foreign Policy." *International Security* 9, no. 3 (1984–85).

Stalin, Joseph. "Foundations of Leninism." In Stalin, *Problems of Leninism*. Moscow: Foreign Languages Publishing, 1953.

Starr, S. Frederick. "New Communications Technologies and Civil Society." In Loren R. Graham, ed. *Science and the Soviet Social Order*. Cambridge: Harvard University Press, 1990.

Stein, Janice Gross. "Political Learning by Doing: Gorbachev as Uncommitted Thinker and Motivated Learner." *International Organization* 48, no. 2 (1994).

Surikov, B. "Stanet li bezopasnei mir?" *Literaturnaia Gazeta*, 24 January 1990.

Tretiakov, Vitalii. "Zagadka Gorbacheva." *Moskovskie Novosti*, 3 December 1989.

Tu Wei-ming. "Intellectual Effervescence in China." *Deadalus* 121, no. 2 (1992).

Tucker, Robert C. "Swollen State, Spent Society: Stalin's Legacy to Brezhnev's Russia." *Foreign Affairs* 60, no. 2 (1981–82).

Velikhov, E. P. "Nauka i aktual'nye problemy borby protiv ugrozy iadernoi voiny." *Vestnik Akademii nauk SSSR*, no. 9 (1983).

———. "Nauka rabotaet ne bez"iadernyi mir." *Mezhdunarodnaia Zhizn'*, no. 10 (1988).

Velikhov, E. P., and A. A. Kokoshin. "Iadernoe oruzhie i dilemma mezhdunarodnoi bezopastnosti." *Mirovaia Ekonomika i Mezhdunarodnye Otnosheniia*, no. 4 (1985).

Verba, Sidney. "Comparative Political Culture." In Lucien Pye and Sidney Verba. *Political Culture and Political Development*. Princeton: Princeton University Press, 1965.

Walt, Stephen M. "The Gorbachev Interlude and International Relations Theory." *Diplomatic History* 21, no. 3 (1997).

Weber, Stephen. "Interactive Learning in U.S.-Soviet Arms Control." In George W. Breslauer and Philip E. Tetlock, eds. *Learning in U.S. and Soviet Foreign Policy*. Boulder, CO: Westview Press, 1991.

Westad, Odd Arne. "Secrets of the Second World: The Russian Archives and the Reinterpretation of Cold War History." *Diplomatic History* 21, no. 2 (1997).

Wohlforth, William C. "Realism and the End of the Cold War." *International Security* 19, no. 3 (1994–95).

———. "Reality Check: Revising Theories of International Politics in Response to the End of the Cold War." *World Politics* 50, no. 4 (1998).

Yanov, Alexander. "In the Grip of the Adversarial Paradigm: The Case of Nikita Sergeevich Khrushchev in Retrospect." In Robert O. Crummey, ed. *Reform in Russia and the USSR*. Urbana: University of Illinois Press, 1989.

Yee, Albert S. "The Causal Effects of Ideas on Politics." *International Organization* 50, no. 1 (1996).

Zubkova, E. Iu. "Lidery i sud'by: 'posadnik' Georgiia Mal'enkova." *Polis*, no. 5 (1991).

Zubok, Vladislav M. "The 'Small' Committee of Information, 1952–1953." *Cold War International History Project Bulletin*, no. 4 (1992).

"Na zasedanii nauchnogo soveta MGU po sisteme ekonomicheskikh zakonov i kategorii politicheskoi ekonomiki." *Vestnik MGU. Seriia 6. Ekonomika*, no. 3 (1985).

"O metodologicheskikh voprosakh istoricheskoi nauki." *Voprosy Istorii*, no. 3 (1964).

Memoirs, Published Interviews, and Transcriptions

Adzhubei, Aleksei. *Te desiat' let*. Moscow: Sovetskaia Rossiia, 1989.

Afanas'iev, Viktor. *4-aia Vlast' i 4 Genseka. Ot Brezhneva do Gorbacheva v "Pravde."* Moscow: Izdatel'stvo KEDR, 1994.

Aganbegyan, Abel. *Moving the Mountain*. London: Bantam Press, 1989.

Agranovskii, Anatolii. "Aprel' v Prage. 1968 god." *Znamia*, no. 1 (1990).

Akhromeev, S. F., and G. M. Kornienko. *Glazami marshala i diplomata. Kriticheskii vzgliad na vneshniuiu politiku SSSR do i posle 1985 goda.* Moscow: Mezhdunarodnye Otnosheniia, 1992.

Alexeyeva, Ludmilla, and Paul Goldberg. *The Thaw Generation: Coming of Age in the Post-Stalin Era*. Boston: Little, Brown, 1990.

Andrew, Christopher, and Oleg Gordievsky. *KGB: The Inside Story of its Operations from Lenin to Gorbachev*. New York: HarperCollins, 1990.

———. *Instructions from the Centre: Top Secret Files from the KGB's Foreign Operations, 1975–1985*. London: Hodder & Stoughton, 1991.

Arbatov, Georgii. *Zatianuvsheesia vyzdorovlenie (1953–1985 gg.) Svidetel'stvo sovremennika*. Moscow: Mezhdunarodnye Otnosheniia, 1991. Published in revised English translation as *The System: An Insider's Life in Soviet Politics*. New York: Times Books, 1992.

Avtorkhanov, Abdurakhman. *Stalin and the Soviet Communist Party*. New York: Praeger, 1959.

Barmine, Alexander. *One Who Survived: The Life Story of a Russian Under the Soviets*. New York: Putnam's, 1945.

Beletskii, Viktor. "Pri otkrytykh granitsakh my ne smozhem tiagat'sia s kapitalizmom." *Izvestiia*, 29 September 1992.

Berkman, Alexander. *The Bolshevik Myth*. London: Boni & Liveright, 1925.

Bobkov, Filipp. *KGB i vlast*.' Moscow: Veteran MP, 1995.

Boguslavskii, Sergei. "Zagovor akademikov." *Literaturnaia Gazeta*, 28 August 1991.

Boldin, Valery. *Ten Years That Shook the World: The Gorbachev Era as Witnessed by his Chief of Staff*. New York: Basic Books, 1994.

Bovin, A. "Bez illiuzii." *Sobesednik*, no. 6 (1990).

Bukovskii, Vladimir. *To Build a Castle: My Life as a Dissenter*. Washington, DC: Ethics and Public Policy Center, 1977.

Burlatskii, Fedor. *Novoe myshlenie*. Moscow: Politizdat, 1989.

———. *Vozhdi i sovetniki. O Khrushchev, Andropove i ne tol'ko o nikh.* Moscow: Politizdat, 1990.

Chazov, Evgenii. *Zdorov'e i vlast'. Vospominaniia "kremlevskogo vracha."* Moscow: Novosti, 1992.

Cherniaev, A. S. *Shest' let s Gorbachevym. Po dnevnikovym zapisiam.* Moscow: Progress-Kul'tura, 1993.

———. *Fenomen Gorbacheva v Kontekste Liderstva.* Unpublished transcript of a speech delivered at the Hebrew University of Jerusalem, 12 January 1993.

———. "Iz dalekoi iunosti." *Vek XX i Mir*, nos. 1–2 (1994).

———. *Moia zhizn' i moe vremia.* Moscow: Mezhdunarodnye Otnosheniia, 1995.

Cherniaev, A., and A. Galkin. "Pravdu, i tol'ko pravdu." *Svobodnaia Mysl'*, nos 2–3 (1994).

———. "M. Gorbachev i vossoedinenie Germanii." *Svobodnaia Mysl'*, no. 1 (1995).

Chugrov, S. "Kniga Aleksandra Iakovleva i Lilli Marku vo Frantsii." *Mirovaia Ekonomika i Mezhdunarodnye Otnosheniia*, no. 12 (1991).

Chuev, F. *Sto sorok besed s Molotovym.* Moscow: Terra, 1991.

Cohen, Stephen F., ed. *An End to Silence: Uncensored Opinion in the Soviet Union*. New York: Norton, 1982.

Cohen, Stephen F., and Katrina vanden Heuvel. *Voices of Glasnost: Interviews with Gorbachev's Reformers*. New York: Norton, 1989.

Dash, Barbara L. *A Defector Reports: The Institute of the USA and Canada*. Falls Church, VA: Delphic Associates, 1982.

Dashichev, V. I. "Iz istorii stalinskoi diplomatii." In L. G. Beliaeva et al., eds., *Istoriia i stalinizm*. Moscow: Politizdat, 1991.

———. "On the Road to German Reunification: The View From Moscow." In Gabriel Gorodetsky, ed. *Soviet Foreign Policy, 1917–1991: A Retrospective*. London: Cass, 1994.

Dobrynin, Anatoly. *In Confidence: Moscow's Ambassador to America's Six Cold War Presidents*. New York: Times Books, 1995.

Dubinin, Yuri. "The Road to Helsinki." *International Affairs* (Moscow), no. 7 (1994).

———. "The New Timecount Began at East River." *International Affairs* (Moscow), no. 10 (1995).

Egorychev, N. G. "Beseda s Egorychevym N. G." In *Neizvestnaia Rossiia XX Vek*, vol 2. Moscow: Istoricheskoe Nasledia, 1992.

Ehrenburg, Ilya. *Memoirs, 1921–1941.* Cleveland, OH: World Publishing, 1963.

El'tsin, Boris. *Ispoved' na zadannuiu temu.* Leningrad: Sovetskii Pisatel', 1990.

Etinger, Iakov. "Ne sleduet uproshchat' slozhnuiu problemu." *Nezavisimaia Gazeta*, 20 March 1993.

Evtushenko, E. A. *Avtobiografiia.* London: Flegon Press, 1964.

Fainberg, Vladimir. "Precursor of Perestroika," *Physics Today* 43, no. 8 (1990).

Falin, V. M. "Tak bylo. Politicheskie vospominaniia. Otryvki iz knigi," *Novaia i Noveishchaia Istoriia*, no. 5 (1995).

Gaidar, Egor. *Dni porazhenii i pobed.* Moscow: Vagrius, 1996.

Gefter, M. Ia. *Iz tekh i etikh let.* Moscow: Progress, 1991.

Gerasimov, G. I. "V range posla." *Sobesednik*, no. 23 (1990).

Ginzburg, Eugenia A. *Journey Into the Whirlwind* New York: Harcourt Brace Jovanovich, 1967.

Gnedin, Evgenii. *Katastrofa i vtoroe rozhdenie. Memuarnye zapiski.* Amsterdam: Fond imeni Gertsena, 1977.

———. *Vykhod iz labirinta.* New York: Chalidze, 1982.

Goldanskii, Vitaly. "Scientist, Thinker, Humanist." *Physics Today* 43, no. 8 (1990).

Gorbachev, Mikhail. *Perestroika: New Thinking for Our Country and the World.* New York: Harper & Row, 1987.

———. "Herman Phelger Lecture on the Rule of Law." *Stanford University Campus Report*, no. 29 (1992).

———. "Doverie–vektor sovremennoi zhizni." *Svobodnaia Mysl'*, no. 9 (1992).

———. *Zhizn' i reformy.* 2 vols. Moscow: Novosti, 1995.

———. "Oglianut'sia nazad, chtoby posmotret' vpered." *Svobodnaia Mysl'*, no. 3 (1995).

Gorbachev, Mikhail, and Zdenek Mlynar. *Dialog o perestroiki, "Prazhskoi vesne" i o sotsializme.* Unpublished MS.

Gorbacheva, R. M. *Ia nadieius.'* Moscow: Novosti, 1991.

Grachev, Andrei. *Kremlevskaia khronika.* Moscow: EKSMO, 1994.

Grigorienko, Petro. *Memoirs.* New York: Farrar, Straus & Giroux, 1982.

Grishin, Viktor. "Chto Vam Skazat'? Sami Razbiraites'!" *Nezavisimaia Gazeta*, no. 21 (1991).

———. *Ot Khrushcheva do Gorbacheva. Politicheskie portrety piati genseka i A. N. Kosygina. Memuary.* Moscow: "ASPOL," 1996.

Gromyko, A. A. *Pamiatnoe*, 2 vols. Moscow: Politizdat, 1990.

Grushin, B. "O liudakh, umevshikh zhit' pod vodoi." *Nezavisimaia Gazeta*, 31 October 1997.

Gukovskii, A. I. "Kak ia stal istorikom." *Istoriia SSSR*, no. 6, 1965.

Hamman, Henry. "Soviet Defector on Origins of 'New Thinking.' " *RFE-RL Report on the USSR*, 20 October 1989.

Iakovlev, Aleksandr. *Muki prochteniia bytiia. Perestroika: nadezhdy i real'nosti.* Moscow: Novosti, 1991.

———. *Gor'kaia chasha. Bol'shevizm i reformatsiia Rossii.* Iaroslavl': Verkhne-Volzhskoe Knizhnoe Izdatel'stvo, 1994.

———. "Vremia podtverdilo moi opaseniia." *Istochnik*, no. 1 (1997).

Ilyichev, Boris. "Indonesia, My Homeland." *International Affairs* (Moscow), no. 3 (1992).

Israelian, Viktor. "O diplomaticheskikh peregovorakh." *Mezhdunarodnaia Zhizn'*, no. 12 (1988).

Israelian, Victor. *Inside the Kremlin During the Yom Kippur War.* University Park: Pennsylvania State University Press, 1995.

Kadomtsev, B. B., ed. *Reminiscences about Academician Lev Artsimovich.* Moscow: Nauka, 1985.

Kalugin, Oleg. *The First Directorate: My 32 Years in Intelligence and Espionage Against the West.* New York: St. Martin's Press, 1994.

Kapitsa, P. L. *Pis'ma o nauke.* Moscow: Moskovskii Rabochii, 1989.

Karaulov, Andrei. *Vokrug Kremlia. Kniga politicheskikh dialogov.* 2 vols. Moscow: Novosti, 1990, 1992.

Karpinskii, Len, and Valery Pisigin. *Zapovednik dlia dinozavrov. Stat'i poslednikh let.* Moscow: EPItsentr, 1996.

Karyagin, Victor. "Berlin After the War." *International Affairs* (Moscow), no. 9 (1991).

———. "Recollections of London." *International Affairs* (Moscow), no. 7 (1992).

Kashlev, Yuri. "The CSCE in the Soviet Union's Politics." *International Affairs* (Moscow), nos. 11–12 (1995).

Katsenelinboigin, Aron. *The Soviet Union: Empire, Nation, and System.* New Brunswick, NJ: Transactions, 1990.

Khrushchev, Nikita. *Khrushchev Remembers.* Boston: Little, Brown, 1970.

———. *Khrushchev Remembers: The Last Testament.* Boston: Little, Brown, 1974.

————. *Khrushchev Remembers: The Glasnost Tapes*. Boston: Little, Brown, 1990.

Khrushchev, Sergei. *Khrushchev on Khrushchev*. Boston: Little, Brown, 1990.

Khrushchev, 1894–1971. Moscow: Rossiiskii Gosudarstvennyi Gumanitarnyi Universitet, 1994.

Kopelev, Lev. *Ease My Sorrows*. New York: Random House, 1983.

Kornienko, G. M. *Lektsiia G. M. Kornienko o dogovore po PRO 1972 g.* Unpublished transcript of a closed lecture at the Institute of USA and Canada, Moscow, 17 November 1989.

Kornilov, L. "Leonid Il'ich ne znal, chto zapuskaet mekhanizm perestroiki." *Izvestiia*, 21 July 1995.

Korotich, Vitalii. *Zal ozhidaniia*. New York: Liberty Publishing, 1991.

Korovinkov, V. I. "Nachalo i pervyi pogrom." *Voprosy Filosofii*. no. 2 (1990).

Kovalev, A. G. *Azbuka diplomatii*. revised edit. Moscow: Interpraks, 1993.

Kozyrev, Andrei. "Osnovnaia opasnost'–v nomenklaturnom revanche," *Nezavisimaia Gazeta*, 10 August 1992.

Lakshin, Vladimir. *Solzhenitsyn, Tvardovsky, and Novy Mir*. Cambridge: Harvard University Press, 1980.

Legostaev, Valery. "Demokrat s radikal'nymi vzgliadami." *Den'*, no. 13 (1991).

————. "God 1987-yi–peremena logiki." *Den'*, no. 14 (1991).

————. "Nina Andreeva–izgoi pliuralizma." *Den'*, no. 16 (1991).

Leonov, N. S. *Likholet'e. Sekretnye missii*. Moscow: Mezhdunarodnye Otnosheniia, 1995.

Ligachev, Yegor. *Inside Gorbachev's Kremlin: The Memoirs of Yegor Ligachev*. New York: Pantheon, 1993.

Lukin, Vladimir. "Tanki na zakate leta." *Literaturnaia Gazeta*, 18 August 1993.

Maclean, Donald. "Some Reflections of a Communist on the Soviet Union." In Steve Hirsch, ed., *MEMO 3: In Search of Answers in the Post-Soviet Era*. Washington, DC: Bureau of National Affairs, 1992.

Maisky, Ivan. *Memoirs of a Soviet Ambassador: The War, 1939–1943*. New York: Scribner's, 1967.

Mamardashvili, Merab. *Kak ia ponimaiu filosofiiu*. Moscow: Progress, 1990.

Medvedev, R., ed. *Politicheskii dnevnik*. 2 vols. Amsterdam: Alexander Herzen Foundation, 1972, 1975.

Medvedev, V. *V komande Gorbacheva*. Moscow: "Bylina," 1994.

Micunovic, Veljko. *Moscow Diary*. London: Chatto & Windus, 1980.

Mihajlov, Mihajlo. *Moscow Summer*. New York: Farrar, Straus & Giroux, 1965.

Mikhailov, F. T. "Slovo ob Il'enkove." *Voprosy Filosofii*, no. 2 (1990).

Mikhailov, V. A. *Ia-"Iastreb."* Moscow: Novosti, 1993.

Moiseev, Nikita. "Chto vperedi?" *Sovershenno Sekretno*, no. 4 (1991.

Motroshilova, N.K. "Pamiati Professora." *Voprosy Filosofii* no. 5 (1988).

Neizvestnaia Rossiia XX Vek. Vols 1–3. Moscow: Istoricheskoe Nasledia, 1990–1992.

Nekrich, Alexander. *Forsake Fear: Memoirs of an Historian.* Boston: Unwin Hyman, 1991.

Nenashev, Mikhail. *Zalozhnik vremeni: Zametki. Razmyshleniia. Svidetel'stva.* Moscow: Progress-Kul'tura, 1993.

Novikov, N. V. *Vospominaniia diplomata. Zapiski 1938–1947.* Moscow: Politizdat, 1989.

Obukhev, A. "Practicioners of Policy." *Vestnik MID*, May 1990.

Orlova, Raisa. *Memoirs.* New York: Random House, 1983.

Palazchenko, Pavel. "Monino-Moskva cherez Madrid i Zhenevu," *Nezavisimaia Gazeta*, 11 February 1992.

———. *Interpreting the Whirlwind.* Unpublished MS, later published in revised form as *My Years with Gorbachev and Shevarduadze: The Memoir of a Soviet Interpreter.* University Park, PA: Penn State Press, 1997.

Pechenev, Vadim. *Gorbachev: k vershinam vlasti.* Moscow: Gospodin Narod, 1991.

Petrov, Vladimir, ed. *"June 22, 1941": Soviet Historians and the German Invasion.* Columbia: University of South Carolina Press, 1968.

Piskotin, M. "Nazyvat' veshchi svoimi imenami." *Narodni Deputat*, no. 11 (1990).

Pokrovskii, N. N. "V prostranstve i vremeni." Introduction to *"Revoliutsiia sverkhu" v Rossii*, by Natan Eidel'man. Moscow: Kniga, 1989.

Pribytkov, Viktor. "Pomoshchnik Genseka." *Sovershenno Sekretno*, no. 7 (1990).

Primakov, E. "Muzhestvo preodeleniia." *Sovetskaia Kultura*, 30 March 1991.

———. "Uchenyi, rukovoditel,' chelovek (k 70 letiiu akademika N. N. Inozemtseva)." *Mirovaia Ekonomika i Mezhdunarodnye Otnosheniia*, no. 4 (1991).

Raushenbakh, B. "Vse ne tak, rebiata." *Literaturnaia Gazeta*, 7 April 1990.

Ryzhkov, Nikolai. *Perestroika. istoriia predatel'stv.* Moscow: Novosti, 1992.

Sagdeev, Roald Z. *The Making of a Soviet Scientist: My Adventures in Nuclear Fusion and Space From Stalin to Star Wars.* New York: Wiley, 1994.

Sakharov, Andrei. *Memoirs.* New York: Vintage Books, 1990.

Saunders, George, ed. *Samizdat: Voices of the Soviet Opposition.* New York: Monad Press, 1974.

Savel'yev, Aleksandr G., and Nikolay N. Detinov. *The Big Five: Arms Control Decision-Making in the Soviet Union*. New York: Praeger, 1995.

Semiryaga, Mikhail. "The Russians in Berlin, 1945." *International Affairs* (Moscow), no. 11 (1994).

Shakhnazarov, Georgii. "Vo mnogom poteriannaia zhizn.' " *Sobesednik*, no. 11 (1992).

———. *Tsena svobody. Reformatsiia Gorbacheva glazami ego pomoshchnika*. Moscow: Rossika-Zevs, 1993.

Shatalin, Stanislav. " '500 dnei' i drugie dni moei zhizni," *Nezavisimaia Gazeta*, 31 March 1992.

———. "Tebe nado byt' prem'erom." In Andrei Karaulov, ed. *Vokrug Kremlia. Kniga politicheskikh dialogov*, vol. 2. Moscow: Novosti, 1992.

Shepilov, D. T. "Vospominaniia." *Voprosy Istorii*, nos. 3–11/12 (1998).

Shevardnadze, Eduard. *Moi vybor. Vzashchitu demokratii i svobody*. Moscow: Novosti, 1991.

———. "Eto Ia–Edichka." *Nezavisimaia Gazeta*, 21 November 1991.

Shevchenko, Arkady. *Breaking With Moscow*. New York: Knopf, 1985.

Shlykov, V. "Mertvye dengi na sluchai voiny." *Demokraticheskaia Rossia*, no. 13 (1991).

Simonov, Konst. *Glazami cheloveka moego pokoleniia. Razmyshleniia o I. V. Staline*. Moscow: Novosti, 1990.

Sobchak, Anatolii. *Khozhdenie vo vlast.'* Moscow: Novosti, 1991.

Tsipko, A. "Pochemu zabludilsia prizrak?" *Sobesednik*, no. 21 (1990).

———. *O Prichinakh Krusheniia "Real'nogo Sotsializma" v Stranakh Vostochnoi Evropy*. Unpublished MS, 1991.

———. "Gorbachev postavil na 'sotsialisticheskii vybor' i proigral." *Nezavisimaia Gazeta*, 17 October 1996.

Vorontsov, Yuli. "The Military-Political Aspects of Security." *International Affairs* (Moscow), no. 10 (1988).

Vorotnikov, V. I. *A bylo tak . . . iz dnevnika chlena Politburo TsK KPSS*. Moscow: Novosti, 1995.

Wohlforth, William C., ed. *Witnesses to the End of the Cold War*. Baltimore: Johns Hopkins University Press, 1996.

York, Herbert. *Making Weapons, Talking Peace: A Physicist's Odyssey from Hiroshima to Geneva*. New York: Basic Books, 1987.

Zamoshkin, Iu. A. "Za novyi podkhod k probleme individualizma." *Voprosy Filosofii*, no. 6 (1989).

Zaslavskaya, Tatyana. *The Second Socialist Revolution: An Alternative Soviet Strategy*. London: Tauris, 1990.

Selected Documents

This section includes classified or limited-circulation reports of various Academy of Sciences Institutes bearing the designation *dsp*, for *dlia sluzhebnogo pol'zovaniia* (for official use only). Where possible, citations include author(s) and institute of origin: the Institute of World Economy and International Relations (IMEMO), the Institute of USA and Canada (ISKAN), the Institute of the Economy of the World Socialist System (IEMSS), the Institute of Economics (IE), and the Central Economic-Mathematical Institute (TsEMI).

Aganbegian, A. G. *Sotsial'no-ekonomicheskie problemy razvitiia Sibiri v desiatoi piatiletke.* Moscow: IE, 1974.

Arbatov, A. G. *Novye programmy strategicheskikh vooruzhennykh sil SShA.* Moscow: IMEMO, 1977; *dsp.*

Arbatov, G. A. *K kontseptsii vneshnei politiki na sovremennom etape.* Unpublished memorandum to Mikhail Gorbachev, April 1985.

Arbatov, G. A., et al. *Uskorenie nauchno-tekhnicheskogo progressa–korennaia strategicheskaia zadacha sovremennogo etapa razvitiia strany.* Unpublished report, Moscow, 17 August 1973.

Bel'chuk, A. A. and E. L. Iakovleva. *Opyt sotsialisticheskikh stran v privlechenii innostrannogo kapitala v forme smeshannykh obshchestv i vozmozhnosti ego ispol'zovaniia v SSSR.* Moscow: IEMSS, 1979.

Blagovolin, S. E. *Prostranstvennaia struktura voenno-ekonomicheskogo bloka NATO.* Moscow: IMEMO, 1983; *dsp.*

Bobrakov, Iu., et al. *Voennoe proizvodstvo SShA i razriadka. ekonomicheskie aspekty problemy konversii.* Moscow: ISKAN, 1978; *dsp.*

Bogomolov, O. T., ed. *Problema razvitiia nauchno-tekhnicheskikh potentsialov stran-chlenov SEV.* Moscow: IEMSS, 1977; *dsp.*

Bukharin, Nikolai I., et al. *O prichinakh i sushchnosti krizisa 1980 g. v PNR.* Moscow: IEMSS, 1981.

Bykov, A. N. *Puti sovershenstvovaniia form i metodov nauchno-tekhnicheskogo obmena SSSR s zarubezhnymi stranami.* Moscow: IEMSS, 1974; *dsp.*

Dashichev, V. I., ed. *Problemy vneshnei politiki sotsialisticheskikh stran.* Moscow: IEMSS, 1980.

Dvenadtsatyi s"ezd RKP (b), April' 1923. stenograficheskii otchet. Moscow: Izdatel'stvo Politicheskoi Literatury, 1968.

Girshfel'd, V. A. *Normalizatsiia otnoshenii i sblizhenie mezhdu KNDR i iuzhnoi koreei v sisteme mezhdunarodnykh otnoshenii v azii.* Moscow: IMEMO, 1973 *sekretno.*

Gorbachev, M. S. *Political Report of the CPSU Central Committee to the 27th Party Congress*. Moscow: Novosti, 1986.

——. *Statement of M. S. Gorbachev at the United Nations, December 7, 1988*. Moscow: Novosti, 1988.

——. "Doveritel'nyi razgovor" and "U perelomnoi cherty." In Gorbachev, *Gody trundykh reshenii. Izbrannoe 1985–1992*. Moscow: Gorbachev-Fond, 1993.

Gubarev, Vladimir. "Zapiska v TsK KPSS. Sovershenno sekretno." In Gubarev, *Iadernyi vek Chernobyl'*. Moscow: "Nekos," 1996, pp. 25–29.

Iashin, B. D. *Voenno-morskaia politika SShA v 70-x godakh*. Moscow: ISKAN, 1977; *dsp*.

Il'ichev, L. F. "S chistym serdtsem priniala politiku partii. zapiska Sekretariia TsK KPSS L. F. Il'icheva o tvorcheskoi intelligentsii." *Vestnik*, no. 6 (1966): 140–51.

Institute of Scientific Information on Social Sciences. Moscow: INION, 1979.

Kapustin, E. I., et al. *Osnovnye problemy ekonomicheskogo razvitiia SSSR v X piatiletke*. Moscow: IE, 1974; *dsp*.

Khozin, G. S. *Razrabotka standartov kachestva vodnykh resursov v SShA*. Moscow: ISKAN, 1977; *dsp*.

"Khronika sobitii po voprosam vnutrennei politiki S.Sh.A." *Arkhiv Vneshnei Politiki SSSR*, Fond Referentura po S.Sh.A. opis. nos. 38, 41, 45 (1952, 1955, 1959).

Kishelev, N. S., A. G. Arbatov, and Iu. E. Fedotov. *Vliianie vneshneevropeiskikh faktorov na obstanovku v evrope*. Moscow: IMEMO, 1980.

Kutovoi, E. G. *Teoreticheskie aspekty ponizheniia urovnei voennogo protivostoianiia v evrope*. Moscow: ISKAN, 1978; *dsp*.

Lukin, V. P. *Evoliutsiia politiki SShA v otnoshenii KNR na rubezhe 70x godov*. Moscow: ISKAN, 1973; *dsp*.

——. *O politike SShA v Azii v nachale 80-x godov*. Moscow: ISKAN. 1982.

Lukin, V. P., V. A. Kremeniuk, and I. B. Bugai, eds. *SShA i problemy tikhogo okeana*. Moscow: ISKAN, 1979.

Maksimova, M. M., I. S. Kovolev, and I. A. Beliugo. *O tendentsii razvitiia "obshchego rynka."* Moscow: IMEMO, 1979.

"Maloe predpriiatiia" i ego rol' v reshenii sotsial'no-ekonomicheskikh problem v stranakh SEV i SFRIu. Moscow: IEMSS, 1981; *dsp*.

Nikiforov, A. *Sovremennyi podkhod SShA k problemam razvitiia osvobozhdivshikhsia stran na 80e gody*. Moscow: IMEMO, 1982.

Nikitin, S. M. *Predlozheniia po uskoreniiu nauchno-tekhnicheskogo progressa i povysheniiu effektivnosti proizvodstva v SSSR (s uchetom opyta SSSR, SShA i Iaponiia)*. Moscow: IMEMO, 1979.

Odinnadtsatyi s"ezd RKP(b). Mart-Aprel' 1922. Stenograficheskii otchet. Moscow: Izdatel'stvo Politicheskoi Literatury, 1961.

Order of the Representative of the Concil of Ministers of the USSR for Protection of Military and State Secrets in the Press, 26 August 1949. From the 1992 U.S. Library of Congress exhibition of declassified Soviet documents.

Orlov, B. S. *Obshchestvenno-politicheskie vzgliady V. Brandta.* Moscow: INION, 1973; *dsp.*

Osnovnye cherty zapadnoevropeiskoi politicheskoi integratsii na sovremennom etape. Moscow: IMEMO, 1976.

Petrakov, N. Ia. *Issledovanie sovremennogo sostoianiia i razrabotka predlozhenii po sovershenstvovaniiu sistemy khozrashchetnykh otnoshenii v promyshlennosti.* Moscow: TsEMI, 1974.

Potashev, V. V. *Teoriia "sderzhivaniia" v iadernoi strategii SShA.* Moscow: ISKAN, 1980; *dsp.*

Proektor, D. M. *Problemy bezopasnosti FRG.* Moscow: IMEMO, 1980.

Reshenie tovarishcheskogo suda chesti starshikh ofitserov voennoi akademii imeni M.V. Frunze ot 8 ianvariia 1986 g. Unpublished Frunze Academy investigation in the matter of Lt. Col. Vladimir Kovalevskii.

Sagdeev, R. Z. and S. N. Rodionov. *Space-Based Anti-Missile System: Capabilities Assessment.* Moscow: Space Research Institute, 1986.

Shatalin, S. S. *Kompleksnyi prognoz narodnogo blagosostoianiia na 1978–80gg.* Moscow: TsEMI, 1974; *dsp.*

Shmelev, N. P. *Ekonomicheskaia strategiia zapada v otnoshenii stran sotsialisticheskogo sodruzhestva.* Moscow: IEMSS, 1974; *dsp.*

———. *Problemy i perspektivy ekonomicheskikh sviazei Sovetskogo soiuza so stranami zapada.* Moscow: IEMSS, 1975; *dsp.*

———. *Ekonomicheskie sviazi vostok-zapad. problemy i vozmozhnosti.* Moscow, 1976.

——, ed. *Osnovnye napravleniia zainteresovannosti zapada v razvitii ekonomicheskikh sviazei so stranami SEV.* Moscow: IEMSS, 1976; *dsp.*

Shmelev, N. P., and V. P. Karavaev. *Osobennosti podkhoda evropeiskikh stran SEV k problemam ekonomicheskikh otnoshenii s zapadom.* Moscow: IEMSS, 1975.

Some Considerations of the Foreign Policy Results of the 1970s (main points), January 20, 1980. IEMSS memorandum to the CPSU Central Committee, cited in *Moscow News,* no. 30 (1989): 9.

Sovmestnye predpriiatiia i osnovnye printsipy ikh funktsirovaniia. Moscow: ISKAN, 1982.

Spisok knig redaktsii Spetsizdanii, peredavaemykh v spravochnuiu biblioteku izdatel'stva "Progress." Moscow, 1993. Unpublished list of foreign works printed in "special edition" closed-circulation Russian translations by Progress publishers.

Starodubrovskaia, V. N. *Analiz opyta kooperativnogo dvizhenii v Vengrii na sovremennom etape.* Moscow: IEMSS, 1974; *dsp.*

Strategicheskie i mezhdunarodno-politicheskie posledstviia sozdaniia kosmicheskoi protivoraketnoi sistemy s ispol'zovaniem oruzhiia napravlennoi peredachi energii: doklad Komiteta Sovetskikh uchenykh v zashchitu mira, protiv iadernoi ugrozy. Moscow: Committee of Soviet Scientists, 1984.

The Program of the Communist Party of the Soviet Union: A New Edition. Moscow: Novosti, 1986.

Tikhonov, V. A. *Problemy Leninskogo kooperativnogo plana v svete novoi konstitutsii SSSR.* Moscow: IE, 1978.

———. *Effektivnost' proizvodztva i spetsifika ee izmereniia primeitel'no k narodnokhoziastvennomu agro-promyshlennomu kompleksu.* Moscow: IE, 1982.

———. *Ekonomicheskie aspekty prodovol'stvennoi problemy v SSSR.* Moscow: IE, 1982.

Trofimenko, G. S., A. A. Kokoshin, and A. V. Nikiforov. *Mezhdunarodnye pozitsii SShA v seredine 70-x godov.* Moscow: ISKAN, 1977; *dsp.*

Tumkovskii, R. G. *Amerikanskie krylatnye rakety.* Moscow: ISKAN, 1978; *dsp.*

———. *SShA i strategicheskie sily velikobritanii. k voprosu ob Amerikanskoi pomoshchi v modernizatsii angliskikh strategicheskikh sil.* Moscow: ISKAN, 1978; *dsp.*

———. *SShA. kontseptsii i programmy stroitel'stva strategicheskikh sil na rubezhe 80-x godov.* Moscow: ISKAN, 1980; *dsp.*

———. *SShA i iadernaia politika anglii i frantsii.* Moscow: ISKAN, 1982; *dsp.*

Volkogonov, D. A., et al., eds. *Neizvestnaia Rossiia XX Vek.* Vols 1–3. Moscow: "Nasledie," 1992–93.

Vos'moi s"ezd RKP(b). Mart 1919. Stenograficheskii otchet. Moscow: Izdatel'stvo Politicheskoi Literatury, 1959.

Vsesoiuznoe soveshchanie istorikov. 18–21 dekabria 1962 g. Moscow: Nauka, 1964.

Vtoroi vsesoiuznyi s"ezd Sovetskikh pisatel'ei. Moscow: Sovetskii Pisatel', 1956.

Vse o MGIMO. Moscow: MGIMO, 1991.

Zapis' Besedy A. N. Kosygina, A. A. Gromyko, D. F. Ustinova, B. N. Ponomareva s N. M. Taraki, 20 Marta 1979 goda: Sov. sekretno: Osobaia papka. 21.III.79g. [No. AK-786cc].

Russian-Language Publications Most Frequently Cited

Den'
Istochnik
Izvestiia
Isvestiia TsK KPSS
Kommunist
Komsol'skaia Pravda
Krasnaia Zvezda
Literaturnaia Gazeta
Mezhdunarodnaia Zhizn' (English edition is titled *International Affairs*)
Moskovskie Novosti (English edition, *Moscow News*)
Mirovaia Ekonomika i Mezhdunarodnye Otnosheniia
Moskovskii Komsomol'ets
Nedel'ia
Nezavisimaia Gazeta
Novaia i Noveishchaia Istoriia
Novoe Vremia (English edition, *New Times*)
Novy Mir
Ogoniok
Polis
Pravda
Problemy Mira i Sotsializma (English edition, *World Marxist Review*)
S.Sh.A.: Ekonomika, Politika, Ideologiia
Sobesednik
Sovershenno Sekretno
Sovetskoe Gosudarstvo i Pravo
Sovetskaia Kul'tura
Sovetskaia Rossiia
Svobodnaia Mysl'
Vek XX i Mir
Vestnik
Vestnik MGU
Vestnik MID
Voprosy Filosofii
Voprosy Istorii
Voprosy Literatury
Znamia

Index

The ABC of Communism (Bukharin and Preobrazhensky), 35, 36, 41–42, 53, 121, 155

ABM Treaty, *see* Anti-Ballistic Missile Treaty

Academic Consultative Council of the USSR Foreign Ministgry, 209

Academic freedom, 34–35, 47

Academy of Sciences, 34, 113

Action Program (Czechoslovak Communist Party), 110

Adamashin, Anatoly, 209

The Administration of Socialist Production (Medvedev), 174

Admissions practices of universities under NEP, 34–35

Adzhubei, Aleksei, 55

Afanasyev, Victor, 188

Afghanistan, 118, 123, 159, 162, 178–79, 203–4, 221, 224

Africa, 57, 120

Aganbegyan, Abel: arguments on Third-World debt, 205; closed session economic report, 99; critique of economic centralization, 79, 80; early meetings with Gorbachev, 182; ideological pressure on, 187; loss of political influence, 236; views on economic data, 96; views on impact of Stalin-era survivors, 94–95; views on Western threat, 100; warnings of socioeconomic ills, 144

Agriculture, 57, 64, 93, 163, 182–84, 200, 202–3

Akademiki (liberal academics), 214

Akhmadulina, Bella, 85

Akhmatova, Anna, 46

Akhromeyev, Sergei, 198, 200, 201, 203, 206, 216

Aksenov, Vasily, 85

Alexander II, 20

Alexandrov-Agentov, Andrei, 209

Alienation, 89–90

Aliev, Geidar, 198, 323n21

Amalrik, Andrei, 81, 91

Ambartsumov, Yevgeny, 177, 178, 187, 264n121

America. *See* United States

American affairs experts, 150

American individualism, 276n91

Andropov, Yuri: accomplishments, 173; address to Central Committee ideology plenum, 173–74; warnings to liberals, 172; central dilemma of reign, 172–73; domestic focus, 180; for

Endnotes are indicated by an "n" after the page number.

Andropov, Yuri *(continued)*
eign policy tasks, 175–76; lack of
support for Arbatov, 163; pro-
motions of younger officials,
174; recruitment of Burlatsky
and consultant group, 72–73;
reformist efforts, 172–80; repression of dissidence, 124, 311n78;
suggestions to foreign-policy
analysts, 176; warnings about
Prague Spring, 259n27
Andropov team, 185–86
Anti-Ballistic Missile Treaty, 107,
118, 148, 236
Anti-intellectualism, 32, , 122–23
Anti-Party Group affair, 82
Antireformists: actions against
Gorbachev, 196; attempt at
hard-line policy turn, 190–91;
bid for power, mid-1980s,
186–91; contenders for succession as general secretary, 196;
long-term foreign agenda, 188;
open foreign-policy disputes,
188; triumph of, 124
Anti-Semitism, 47–48
Anti-Stalinism, 68
Anti-Western nationalism, 26, 237
Anti-Westernism, 18, 32, 33, 36–37,
118, 234–36
Apollo-Soyuz spaceflight, 118, 151
Arab-Olgy, Eduard, 101
Arbatov, Alexei, 152–53, 237
Arbatov, Georgy: attacks on, 170,
187–88; attempts to influence
five-year plan, 163–64; experience at Prague journal, 71; fight
against rehabilitation of Stalin,
286n28; foreign contacts, 148; as
head of USA-Canada Institute,
124, 125; influence, 101, 163, 184,
201–2, 212; influences on, 78;

loss of political influence, 236;
member of "gang of four" of
early Gorbachev advisers,
184–85, 201, 202; participation in
arms control discussions,
168–69; reprimands of, 171–72,
310n73; rescue of Lukin, 113;
response to purge at IMEMO,
171; support for arms control,
156; support for moratorium on
nuclear testing, 213–14; views on
Andropov, 172; views on economy, 143; views on effects of new
thinking, 73; views on excessive
activism abroad, 165; views on
own knowledge, 126; views on
Palme Commission, 169; views
on war, 148
Area studies Sovietologists, 15,
344n40
Arms control, 105, 106, 118, 148,
155, 165, 224
Arms Control and Disarmament
Division of the USSR Foreign
Ministry, 209
Arms race, 1, 117, 168, 206
Arms reduction, 106, 155
Artists, 40
Artsimovich, Lev, 106, 107, 130,
150, 151
Asia, 57, 153, 165
Asian social democracy, 102
Asmus, Valentin, 87
Asymmetric response, 179, 201
Audio technologies, 63
Austria, 54
Autarky, 145
Authoritarian systems, 339n8. *See
also* Closed-dictatorial systems;
Stalinist system

Babi yar (Yevtushenko), 85

Bakradze, Konstantin, 87
Balkans, 22, 237, 238–39
Baltic republics, 226–27
BBC Russian Service, 63
Bell, Daniel, 185
Berdyaev, Nikolai, 23, 139, 140, 294n118. *See also Vekhi*
Berg, Axel, 132
Beria, Lavrenty, 52, 66
Berlinguer, Enrico, 316n146
Bermeo, Nancy G., 234, 243nn19,21, 341n27
Bessmyrtnykh, Alexander, 150, 298n179
Bible of Communism, 36
Biriukov, Nikolai, 300n195
Blagovolin, Sergei, 185
Bloch, Ernst, 88
Bogomolov, Oleg: analysis of détente's demise, 162; attacks on, 171; head of IEMSS, 124, 125; loss of political influence, 236; and Prague journal, 71; Shevardnadze's consultations with, 204; support for Gorbachev's policies, 207; views on economy, 143; views on internationalization process, 156
Bolshevisim, 24, 25, 26–27, 29, 31–37, 249n47,
Botvinnik, Mikhail, 68
Bourgeois democracy, 23
Bourgeois professionals, 34, 40
Bovin, Alexander: attempts to influence five-year plan, 163–64; experience on Andropov's consultant team, 73; firing of, 134; reprimands of, 172; response to purge at IMEMO, 171; support for Gorbachev's policies, 207; views on collapse of détente, 164–65; views on war, 148; warnings about Czech invasion, 112; work in journalism, 124
Brandt, Willy, 102, 331n122
Brest peace, 26, 27
Brezhnev, Leonid: death, 171; dependence on advisers, 122–23; dogmatism, 120; economic experience, 325n52; elevation to Central Committee, 285n16; formative experiences, 121; impact on new thinking, 117; incapacity, 118–19, 169, 309n57; intellectual life under, 124–27; limitations on thaw, 118; reaction to chance of foreign posting, 122; reformers' influence on, 148, 155; response to purge at IMEMO, 171; signing of Helsinki agreement, 154; support for neo-Stalinism, 59; views on foreign trade, 145; views on nuclear victory, 166
Brezhnev cohort. *See* Brezhnev leadership
Brezhnev doctrine, 204
Brezhnev leadership, 119–23; background, 121; influences on, 122, 123; intransigence, 157; outlook of, 198, search for post-Khrushchev identity, 136; views on foreign trade, 145–46;
British imperialism, 36–37, 38
Briusov, Valery, 28
Bukharin, Nikolai, 27, 30, 31, 36, 38, 43
Bukharin, Nikolai (IEMSS analyst), 304n10
Bulgakov, Sergei, 29
Bulletin of the Atomic Scientists (journal), 279n137

Burlatsky, Fedor: appeal for cultural-intellectual freedom, 109; attacks on, 170; intellectual gypsy, 124, 134; *Lenin, the State, and Politics,* 128; "The Philosophy of Peace," 167, 168; proposal for international cooperation, 176–77; support of, 113; views on arms limitation talks, 280n143; views on Andropov consultant team, 72–73; views on economic reform, 166; views on excessive activism abroad, 165; Sakharov and his influence, 130; views on value of peace, 148
Butenko, Anatoly, 128, 166, 187, 307n36
Bykov, Oleg, 134

Cadets (Constitutional Democrats), 25
Camp writers, 86
Capitalism: Berdyaev's views on, 23; end of demonization of, 50; Marxist and Leninist views of, 25, 35; questions of nature of, 166; Stalin's views on, 47
Castro, Fidel, 57
CEMA (Council for Economic Mutual Assistance), 107
Censorship, 67
Center-periphery ties, 30
Central Committee, 70, 72–73, 196, 200. *See also* International Department of the Central Committee
Central Committee apparatus, 125
Central Committee Economics Department, 174
Central Committee plena, 93, 144, 173, 186
Central Committee Secretariat, 197

Central Economic-Mathematical Institute (TsEMI), 71, 76, 96, 125, 142, 187
Central Intelligence Agency (CIA), 99, 178.
Chaadaev, Peter, 246n9
Chauvinism, *see* Russian chauvinism
Chayanov, Alexander, 95
Chazov, Yevgeny, 151, 168, 170
Chebrikov, Viktor, 174, 218
Checkel, Jeffrey T., 231
Chernenko, Konstantin, 186–87, 190
Chernichenko, Yuri, 97, 109
Chernobyl tragedy, 12, 215–18, 220–21
Chernyaev, Anatoly: analysis of fraternal parties, 105; creation of new institutes, 113, 283n191; critique of disarmament proposal, 217–18; experience at *Problemy Mira i Sotsializma,* 71–72; foreign policy discussion with Ponomarev, 211; influence on Gorbachev, 209; letter of resignation, 226–27; observations of Gorbachev's private meetings, 205; replacement of Alexandrov-Agentov by, 209; support for moratorium on nuclear testing, 213–14; views on European social democracy, 102; views on Gorbachev, 182–83, 212
Chicherin, Georgy, 254n135
Children of the 20th Congress, 15, 83. *See also* New intelligentsia
China, 7, 57, 58, 125, 234, 244n24. *See also* Sino-Soviet relations
Chinese, influence on post-Stalin politics, 71–72
Chinese Communists, 38

Chirkin, Veniamin, 129
CISAC (Committee on International Security and Arms Control), 168, 169
Civil war, 26, 27, 32–33, 40
Civilian defense specialists, 207
Closed-dictatorial systems, 234. *See also* Authoritarian systems; Dictatorial systems
Club of Rome, 131, 167
Cognitive punch, 8, 12, 111, 244n28
Cold peace, 234–35
Cold war: importance of intellectual change to end of, 14; initiation of, 53; Molotov's views on, 54; reasons for end, 14, 194; renewal in 1983–84, 177; Stalin's declaration of, 47
Collective farms, 203. *See also* Collectivization
Collective security, 177
Collectivization, 40, 64, 136
Cominform, 47
The Coming World Order (Shakhnazarov), 167
Committee of Soviet Scientists in Defense of Peace and Against the Nuclear Threat, 179–80
Committee on International Security and Arms Control (CISAC), 168, 169
Common Market, 107
Common security, 168, 169
Communications advances, 63
Communist Party, 252n107. *See also* Bolshevism, Party Congresses
Comparative-interactive learning, 7
Complex of revolutionary inadequacy, 120
Conference on Security and Cooperation in Europe (CSCE), 118, 154–55, 303n321

Congress of Czechoslovak Writers, 110
Consciousness, study of, 89–90
Conservatism, era of, 124
Conservative resurgence, 108–9
Conservatives, 208, 214. *See also* Antireformists
Conspiratorial outlook, 22
Constitutional Democrats (Cadets), 25
Constructivism, 233
Consultant groups, 10, 72
Contemporary foreign-policy opinion, 237
Contemporary Global Problems (Frolov and Zagladin), 166–67
Contemporary Global Problems (Inozemtsev), 167
Contemporary Western thought, 89
Contradictions, under socialism, 307n35
Conventional forces, 164
Council for Economic Mutual Assistance (CEMA), 107
Crisis, impetus for change, 3, 229–30
CSCE. *See* Conference on Security and Cooperation in Europe
Cuban Missile Crisis, 50, 82
Cuban Revolution, 57, 65
Cult of culture, 79
Cult of the personality, 68
Cultural exchange agreements, 61
Cultural space, common, 90
Cultural-intellectual life, 82
Culture, political, 18, 21, 23, 24, 28, 31; NEP high culture, 32; popular, 41
Czechoslovak Communist Party, 23–24, 28, 31–32, 36, 40–41, 110

Czechoslovak reforms, 109. *See also*
　Prague Spring

Danchev, Vladimir, 313n113
Daniel, Yuli, 109
Danilevsky, Nikolai, 22
Daniloff, Nicholas, 218
Dartmouth conferences, 107
Dashichev, Vyacheslav, 156, 209,
　283n192
Decembrists, 20, 122
Defense issues, 152. See also *entries
　beginning "Military"*
Delusin, Lev, 113, 124, 125
Democratization, 208, 219, 221,
　222, 235, 334n168
Deportations, 34
Derzhavniki (realist state builders),
　237
De-Stalinization, 52, 60–65,
　65–70, 73–74, 82; of diplomacy,
　73–74
Détente: effects on Soviet scien-
　tists, 150; end of, 118, 120; era of,
　50; during era of stagnation,
　154–57; importance, 14; influ-
　ence, 11, 148, 151; of 1970s, 118;
　rise of, 125
Developed socialism, 136, 137, 144,
　166
Developmental paths, 139–40
Dictatorial systems, 6–8, 233–34.
　See also Authoritarian systems
Diplomatic purge, 43
Diplomats, 74, 103–6, 149, 257n192
Disarmament concerns, 105–6, 107.
　See also Arms control
Disarmament plan, Gorbachev's,
　206
Dissidents, 135. *See also* Sakharov,
　Andrei
Djilas, Milovan, 268n171

Dobrynin, Anatoly, 120, 127, 208,
　213–14
Dobrynin's School, 150
Doctors' Plot, 60, 66
Domestic reforms, 51, 215–16,
　221–22
Domestic travel, 63
Dorosh, Yefim, 84
Dostoevsky, Feodor Mikhailovich,
　22, 28
Dreyfus affair, 84
Dubinin, Nikolai, 132
Dudintsev, Vladimir, 84
Duel of cultures, 32

Early new thinkers, 127. *See also*
　New thinkers
East European reforms, 110, 224
East European scholarship, 89
East Germany, 52
Eastern Europe, 78–79, 204–5, 221,
　224
Eastern European regimes, 224
East-West comparisons, 274n63
East-West relations, 50–51, 58, 169.
　See also Foreign relations
East-West trade, 99–100, 145
Ecology, 288n53
Economic development, 56–57,
　165–67
Economic domestic roots of new
　thinking, 200–207
Economic institutes, 96
Economic isolation, 92
Economic planning, 96–97
*Economic Problems of Socialism in
　the USSR* (Stalin), 47, 94, 190
Economic reformers, early, 142
Economic studies, 93–98
Economics, 93, 141–47
Economics and Law (Skhredov),
　100

Economists, 7, 273n60
Economy: discussions of, 64–65; by
    end of 1950s, 96; Khrushchev's
    reform efforts, 82; need for
    change, 141–42; realistic views
    on, 143; reform currents, 141;
    reports of problems, 144; state
    role in, 275n75
Editorial boards, 10
Education, 34, 67
Ehrenburg, Ilya, 67, 83–84, 86
Eidelman, Natan, 91, 236, 293n104
11th Party Congress, 29
Elite, 18, 42–43
Elite congregations, 51
Elites-identity framework, 5–8,
    236
Encirclement, psychology of,
    60–61
"Enemies," struggle with, 40, 48
Engels, Friedrich, 168
Engineers, 34
Enlightened leadership, 240. See
    also Leadership
Environmentalism, 130
Epistemic community model, 4,
    242n5
Era of stagnation, description of,
    117. See also New thinking, dur-
    ing era of stagnation
The Essentials of Marxism-Leninism
    (Kuusinen), 101
Eurasianism, 28, 237
Euromissile issue, 175, 217
European Marxists, 88–89
European revolution, 26, 39
European social democracy, 102
European ties, 91. See also Foreign
    ties
Europe-oriented Marxists, 24
Evangelista, Matthew, 232, 246n6,
    279nn137, 139, 280n143, 339n12

Exhibitions, U.S., 61
Expansionism, 22, 120, 165
Expert communities, 231
External national identity, 7
Extreme secretiveness, 149–50,
    156

Fadin, Andrei, 170
Falin, Valentin, 310n76
Famine, 33
Faramazian, Rachik, 134
Federal Republic of Germany, 153.
    See also Germany
Federation of American Scientists,
    213
Fedorenko, Nikolai, 132, 144
Fedoseyev, Petr, 46
15th Party Congress, 38–39
Finland, 54
Finnish Communist Party, 319n180
"First Acquaintance" (Nekrasov),
    84
"For the Sake of a Woman's
    Health" (Gerasimov), 130
Forced industrialization, 40
Foreign affairs, 51, 68–69, 100–107.
    See also entries beginning
    "International"
Foreign affairs institutes, 70–71,
    149
Foreign-affairs thought, 71
Foreign contacts, 74–75
Foreign culture, 61–63, 83
Foreign economic studies, 94
Foreign exchanges, 74–75, 125–26,
    150, 151
Foreign-language study, 61
Foreign Ministry, 208–9, 219
Foreign policy: changes in, 26,
    176–77; deideologization of, 211;
    Gorbachev's report on, 210–11;
    Gorbachev's views on, 199;

Foreign policy *(continued)*
impact of Chernobyl tragedy
on, 217; importance of 20th
Party Congress to, 50; intellectual nexus, 207; Khrushchev's,
82; lag in results of decisions on,
224–25; means of determination
of, 226; new priorities, 219;
renewed militancy in, 58; in
service to domestic reform, 207
Foreign-policy analysts, 151–52,
187–88
Foreign-policy hawks, 169–70
Foreign-policy thought, 119,
209–10, 237
Foreign radio broadcasts, 63
Foreign relations, 53, 100–107, 129,
147–53, 180
Foreign-relations theory, 26–27,
102
Foreign students, 62
Foreign threats, 39, 206
Foreign ties, 7, 40, 107
Foreign trade, 99–100, 145
Foundations of Leninism (Stalin),
36
Frank, Semyon, 24
Frolov, Ivan: appointment as editor
of *Voprosy Filosofii,* 131; attacks
on, 289n70; *Contemporary
Global Problems,* 166–67; during
the 1970s, 124; opposition to
Stalinist science, 289n58; promo-
tion of under Gorbachev, 208;
publication of non-Marxist
views, 133; recollections of
Gorbachev, 183

Gagarin, Yuri, 57
Gaidar, Yegor, 275n75, 295n126
Galbraith, John K., 185
Galich, Alexander, 111

Galkin, Alexander, 101–2, 134, 165
"Gang of four"(Gorbachev advisers), 201
Garaudy, Robert, 88
Gefter, Mikhail: Chernyaev calls to
Gorbachev's attention, 209; call
for perestroika of Soviet historiography, 90; challenge to historical schemas of *Short Course,*
91; criticism of scholarly isolation, 78; forced retirement, 135;
death of, 236; response to
crushing of Prague Spring, 112;
views on historical develop-
ment, 139; views on Soviet
development and the interna-
tional community, 140, 141
General secretary (of Politburo),
191, 192, 196–98
Generational change, 291n85
Geneva Summit, 60–61, 205–6, 212
Georgian Public Opinion Center,
291n86
Gerasimov, Gennady, 71, 72, 102,
107, 123, 124, 130, 264n121
German reuinification, 209, 225,
327n65
Germany, 26
Ginzburg, Vladimir, 279n131
Girshfeld, Viktor, 153, 318n177
Glasnost, 207, 223
Glavit (censorship organ), 34
Global outlook, 2, 127–33
Globalistics, 167
Goldansky, Vitaly, 150–51, 279n131
Golikov, Viktor, 122
Gonzalez, Felipe, 213
Gorbachev, Mikhail: acceptance of
reunified Germany's member-
ship in Western alliance, 225;
accomplishments, 2; actions on
human rights, 219; adherence to

old dogmas, 205; and Afghanistan, 203–4, 204; Akhromeyev's views on, 198; ambitions for change, 199; ambivalence on domestic empire, 226–27; appointment of Shevardnadze, 202; and arms control, 205, 206, 223; background, 181, 202–3; characteristics, 181; concern over Eastern Europe, 203; conservatives' views on, 214–15; contradictions in worldview of, 205; cultivation of moderate image, 197–98, 199; debate with Thatcher, 219, 220; defense of reform thinkers, 207–8; early views on international affairs, 183; evolution to social-democratic outlook, 213; extent of changes by, 193; fear of public opinion, 227; foreign activity, 184; foreign policy, 12, 200–201, 209, 210; goals for Soviet Union, 228; initial concerns, 12; loss of political influence, 236; and new thinking, 180–86, 215; opposition to, 196, 218; path to new worldview, 223, 334n169; policies, 200, 222–23, 225; reform characteristics, 192; report for 27th Party Congress, 210–11; response to military burden, 200–201; rethinking of East-West issues, 219–20; skepticism of Western policies, 205; support for agricultural reforms, 315n129, 325n50; support for liberalized Soviet federation, 227

Gorbachev, Mikhail, career: chair of Central Committee secretariat, 197; coming to power of, 195–200; election as general secretary, 192, 196–98; leader of Andropov's protégés, 180; manager of committee on economic issues, 174; on Politburo's Polish Commission, 326n57

Gorbachev, Mikhail, influences on: allegiance with *akademiki*, 214; experiences with Italy, 315n134, 316n146; foreign visits, 181, 182; foreign-policy reformers, 12, 180, 183–84; Gorbacheva, Raisa, 212, 331n113; meetings with foreign representatives, 212–13; meetings with reform economists, 182–83; mentioned, 3, 184; readings, 182; reliance on liberal-Westernizing intelligentsia, 227–28; senior colleagues, 3; study of international relations, 212

Gorbachev, Mikhail, views of: on Chernobyl tragedy, 216; on ending cold war, 205; on foreign policy priorities, 219; on international security, 217–18; on limited conflicts, 216; on new thinking, 214; on West, 182

Gorbacheva, Raisa, 181, 209, 212, 275n85, 331n113

Gorbachev's team, 185. *See also* "Gang of four"

Gorizontov, Boris, 134

Gorky, Maxim, 28

Grachev, Andrei, 112, 208, 286n29

Grain imports, 99

Gramsci, Antonio, 10, 88, 89

Great Patriotic War, cult of, 118

Great Reforms, 20

Great power statists, 237

Great-Russian chauvinism, 18, 30–31

Grigorienko, Petro, 49, 78

Grishin, Victor, 187, 196, 197, 285n15, 321n3
Grodov, Vasily, 44–45
Gromyko, Andrei: biography, 103; declining influence, 169; efforts on behalf of Gorbachev, 196–97, 322n13; Khrushchev-bashing, 190; on struggle with U.S. imperialism, 59; warning to Soviet adversaries, 198
Grushin, Boris, 87, 88, 275n75
Gubarev, Vladimir, 333n142
Guevera, Che, 57

Havemann, Robert, 88
Helsinki Accords, 118, 154–55, 303n221, 303n223. See also CSCE
Herman, Robert G., 232
Herrmann, Richard K., 234
Herz, John, 102
Herzen, Alexander, 22, 111
Higher education, 35, 36. See also Universities
Historians, 90–91
Historical Materialism (Bukharin), 36
Historical studies, 90–92
Historiography, 138–39
History, Russocentrism in, 40, 47
Honecker, Erich, 188
Hostile capitalist encirclement, 18, 26, 38, 42, 50–51, 53, 121
Hostile isolationism, 18, 46, 84, 100, 119–20, 123
Hostile-isolationist identity: characterization of, 9; reasons for persistence of, 121; contribution to demise of détente, 120; critique of, 128; effects on East-West rapprochement, 50–51; importance of Russian nationalism to, 137–38; influences on, 18,

55; under Stalin's terror, 37. See also Old thinking
Hough, Jerry F., 291n85, 338n2
Human rights, 154–55, 219, 220
Human-rights campaigners, 135
Humanities, 34, 40, 83
Humanities institutes, 69–70
Hungarian Diary (Woroszylski), 78
Hungary: agriculture, 142; Burlatsky's views on, 128; foreign policy analysts' visits to, 76; interest in events in, 69, 84; invasion of (1956), 55; market reforms, 97; rebellion of 1848, 263n104; Soviets' shock at anger after invasion of (1956), 78; views of uprising in, 55–56, 65

Ideas, 3, 4, 14, 233
Identity, 5, 6, 238, 239, 243n13. See also National identity
Ideocracy, 121
Ideological entrepreneurs, 7
Ideological insecurity, 120
Ideology, 8–9, 119–20
IEMSS. See Institute of the Economy of the World Socialist System
IISS (International Institute for Strategic Studies), 149
Ilyenkov, Evald, 87, 89
Ilyichev, Boris, 104–5
Ilyichev, L. F., 281n151
IMEMO. See Institute of World Economy and International Relations
Imperial revival, 29
Imperialism, 37, 251n85, 272n46
Imperialism: The Highest Stage of Capitalism (Lenin), 24–25, 26, 71

IMRD (Institute of the International Workers' Movement), 70

In Defense of the Planet (Khozin), 130

Independent Commission on Disarmament and Security (Palme Commission), 168–69

The Individual, 89–90

Individualism, European, 22–23

Indonesian Communist Party, 104

INF (Intermediate-Range Nuclear Forces) Treaty, 206, 223

Information explosion, 74

INION. *See* Institute of Scientific Information on the Social Sciences

Inorodtsy (other peoples), 27

Inostrannaia Literatura (Foreign Literature, journal), 61

Inozemtsev, Nikolai: attempts to influence five-year plan, 163–64; on global problems, 167; leadership of CISAC, 168; shaping of staff at IMEMO, 125; relations with Gorbachev, 183; support for East-West trade, 155–56, 164; victim of purge, 171; views on economy, 143

Institute of Africa, 70

Institute of Concrete Social Research, 98–99, 113, 134

Institute of Economics and Industrial Organization (Novosibirsk Institute): Chernenko's criticism of, 187; continued development, 125; creation of, 70–71; importance of, 96; new school of political economy, 76; younger reformist economists at, 142

Institute of the Economy of the World Socialist System (IEMSS): attacks on, 170, 171, 187; creation of, 70; reformist proposals, 146–47; report on crisis in Poland, 162–63

Institute of the Far East, 70

Institute of History, 69–70, 91

Institute of the International Workers' Movement (IMRD), 70

Institute of Latin America, 70

Institute of Philosophy, 87, 133

Institute of Red Professors, 36

Institute of Scientific Information on the Social Sciences (INION), 113, 125, 151, 290n78

Institute of Theoretical-Experimental Physics, 68

Institute of the USA, 70, 125. *See also* USA-Canada Institute (ISKAN)

Institute of World Economy and International Relations (IMEMO): analysis of third world economies, 165; attacks on, 170–71; creation of, 70; incubator of international economists, 76; influence of, 125; military research section, 152; reformist views, 147; revisions to dogmas about the West, 101; revival under Yakovlev, 185; studies on European integration, 153; U.S.-Soviet Joint Committee on International Issues, 152; views on capitalism, 143; younger reform economists at, 142

Institutes, 10, 70, 98, 124. *See also specific institutes*

Institutional-centered explanation of new thinking, 4

Intellectual change, 17
Intellectual congregations, 8, 233
Intellectual cross-fertilization, 128
Intellectual domestic roots of new
    thinking, 207–15
Intellectual innovation, 240
Intellectual life, 47, 51, 124–27
Intellectual oases, 70–76
Intellectual repression, 133–36
Intellectuals: characteristics, 23;
    freedom of, 66; influences on,
    65, 66; and Prague Spring,
    107–15; renewal of foreign ties,
    51; revival of critical thought,
    65–70; role in establishment of
    national identity, 6; and the
    world, 81–115. See also Policy-
    academic elite; Soviet intellectu-
    al elite
Intelligentsia: Bolsheviks' end of
    cooperation with, 40; historic
    description of, 77; lack of politi-
    cal influence, 247n26; numbers
    of, 266n151; opposition to
    Bolsheviks, 34; rebirth, 76–80;
    targets of Stalinist terror, 46.
    See also Policy-academic elite;
    Soviet intellectual elite
Intelligenty (intelligentsia), 77. See
    also Intelligentsia
Intermediate-Range Nuclear
    Forces (INF) Treaty, 206, 223
Internal migration, 62
Internal national identity, 7
International affairs. See Foreign
    affairs
International class struggle, 50, 55,
    58, 258n23
International cooperation, 176–77
International Department of the
    Central Committee, 112

International exchanges. See for-
    eign exchanges
International Institute for Strategic
    Studies (IISS), 149
International links. See Foreign
    ties
International Organizations
    Department of Foreign
    Ministry, 208–9
International Physicians for the
    Prevention of Nuclear War, 168,
    213
International relations. See Foreign
    relations
International-relations theory. See
    Foreign-relations theory
International scientific community,
    213
International scientific ties, 106
International security, 217–18
International trust, 219, 221, 222,
    227, 335n174
International workers' solidarity,
    24–25
Internatsional'naia Literature
    (journal), 260n49
"The Interrelation of the Natural
    and Social Sciences" (round-
    table), 132
Intrabloc relations, 183, 207. See
    also Eastern Europe
Iron curtain, 65
"Iron Tsar" (Nicholas I), 20
ISKAN. See USA-Canada Institute
Isolation, 18, 100–107, 150
Isolationism: early critiques of
    Stalinist system, 92–100; intel-
    lectuals against, 83–92; role in
    origins of "old thinking," 9;
    Tvardovsky's views on, 86
Israelyan, Viktor, 279n128, 283n192

Italians, defense of critics of Stalinism, 89

Japan, 97
Jews, 47–48
Journalists, 7
June 22, 1941 (Nekrich), 91–92, 109

Kabunin, M., 274n63
KAL 007 airliner tragedy, 175, 188
Kalinin, Mikhail, 27
Kalita, Ivan, 27
Kalugin, Oleg, 199
Kantorovich, Leonid, 95, 97, 132–33
Kapitsa, Peter: criticism of academic isolation, 69; critique of Soviet strategic defenses, 289n56; early critic of scholarly isolation, 150; experience abroad, 106; importance, 131–32; on international scientific cooperation, 78; opposition to Stalinist science, 289n58; support for Sakharov, 288; writings, 288n55–289n55
Karmal, Babrak, 203, 224, 312n93
Karpinsky, Len: appeal for cultural-intellectual freedom, 109; attacks on, 135n113; description of meeting with students in Poland, 267n160; death of, 236; views on post-Prague Spring reaction, 114–15
Karpov, Victor, 209
Karyakin, Yuri, 87, 88, 91, 102, 281n150
Kedrov, Bonifatsy, 68, 87
Keldysh, Mstislav, 113
Khachaturian, Aram, 46
Khanin, Grigory, 97

Khozin, Grigory, 130–31, 132
Khrushchev, Nikita: beginnings of reform efforts, 81; concern for Mao's criticism, 58; De-Stalinization campaign, 82; distrust of West, 56; economic policies, 99; effects of doctrinal changes, 55; influence, 60; responses to fall of, 108; secret speech to 20th Party Congress, 49, 67–68; sensitivity to state of agriculture, 93; during Stalinist terror, 53; suspicions of West, 55; use of U.S. as frame of economic reference, 94; visit to U.S., 56; worldview of, 53, 54
Khrushchev, Nikita, views of: on airing problems, 64; on ignorance and propaganda, 42; on intellectuals, 56; on political process, 39–40; on relationship with Molotov, 54; on Stalin's influence, 60; on Western aggression, 55–56; on Western Europe, 52, 53
Khrushchev, Sergei, 56
Khrushchev cohort, 121
Khrushcheva, Nina, 53
Kirghizia, 95
Klyamkin, Igor, 135
Kokoshin, Andrei, 169, 179
Kompanii (discussion groups), 69, 78
Komsomol (Communist Youth League), 35–36, 68
Kopelev, Lev, 45, 78, 256n176, 267n159
Korean War, 52
Kornai, Janos, 110
Kornienko, Georgy, 103–4, 105–6, 209, 298n173

Kosolapov, Richard, 170, 187, 189, 190, 208
Kosovo-Yugoslavia crisis, 238
Kosygin, Alexei, 59, 144
Kosygin reforms, 100, 109
Kovalev, Anatoly, 154, 209, 263n102
Kovalevsky, Vladimir, 178
Kozyrev, Andrei, 177, 208–9, 236, 299n180
Krasin, Yuri, 102, 290n78
Krasovsky, Viktor, 274n67
Kremenyuk, Victor, 127
Krivosheyev, Vladlen, 112
Kronstadt uprising, 33
Kudyukin, Pavel, 170
Kunaev, Dinmukhamed, 322n15
Kurashvili, Boris, 166
Kurile Islands dispute, 164, 202
Kutovoi, Yevgeny, 153
Kuusinen, Otto, 101
Kuznetsov, Vasily, 259n42
Kvasha, Yakov, 274n67

Labor performance, 96
Laboratory for Concrete Social Research, 98
Latin America, 233–34, 244n21
Latsis, Otto, 98, 135
Leadership: importance of ideology to, 8–9; importance to crisis in USSR, 3; power base, 202. See also Brezhnev leadership; Post-Stalin leaders
Leadership-centered explanation of new thinking, 3–4
Learning, levels of, 7
Lebed, Alexander, 135
Left opposition, 38
Lend-lease aid, 44
Lenin, the State, and Politics (Burlatsky), 128

Lenin, Vladimir: anticapitalism, 9; comparison with Peter the Great, 27; defense of bourgeois specialists, 35; Gonzalez's views on, 213; influence on Stalin, 250n77; as internationalist, 26; messianic claim, 24; views of, contrasted with Plekhanov, 24; views on capitalism, 25; views on chauvinism, 31; views on far-Right support, 29; views on grand designs, 168; views on nationalism question, 30; views on sociology, 98
Lenin Library, 66
Leontiev, Wassily, 185
Let History Judge (Medvedev), 79
Levada, Yuri, 275n75
Liberal economists, 135
Liberal historians, 135–36
Liberal intellectuals, 207–8
Liberal philosophers, 135–36
Liberal sociologists, 135
Liberalization of economic, social, and political life, 107
Liberal-reformist domestic community, 15. See also New thinkers
Liberals, 160
Liberman, Yevsei, 98
Ligachev, Yegor, 174–75, 196, 198, 225
Limited Test Ban Treaty, 50, 58
Linguistics, 47
Lisichkin, Gennady, 98, 109
Literary avant-garde, 85
Literary-cultural thaw, 51
Literature, 30–31, 79, 83–84
Litvinov, Maxim, 43, 282n168
Litvinov, Pavel, 282n168
"The Logic of Political Thinking in the Nuclear Era" (Shakhnazarov), 177

London: Gorbachev's visit to, 199;
    Russian diplomats in, 105
Lotman, Yuri, 90
Lown, Bernard, 168
Lukacs, Georg, 88–89
Lukin, Vladimir: appointment at
    Foreign Ministry, 208;
    Arbatov's rescue of, 113; change
    in political outlook, 237; disser-
    tation, 102; as link to reformers,
    110–11; Prague veteran, 264n121;
    response to invasion of
    Czechoslovakia, 112; review of
    U.S. policy in Asia, 165; study of
    Sino-American rapprochement,
    153; views on totalitarian ideolo-
    gy, 139
Lunacharsky, Anatoly, 28, 29
Lyubimov, Yuri, 79

Maclean, Donald, 164, 198, 306n21
Maisky, Ivan, 91, 283n192
Major cities, population, 62
Malashenko, Igor, 208, 286n29
Malenkov, Georgy, 54
Malinovsky, Rodion, 59
Mamardashvili, Merab: address on
    role of intelligentsia, 268n174;
    criticism of Lenin and Marx, 87;
    death of, 88, 236; lectures on
    European political and social
    thought, 69; popularity, 265n129;
    at Prague journal, 71–72; sanc-
    tions against, 135; views on inter-
    national community, 140–41;
    views on science, 133
"Man and His Habitat" (round-
    table), 131
Manichean outlook, 52, 90
Mao Zedong, 57–58, 59–60
Marcuse, Herbert, 88
Market experiments, 235

Market reformers, 99
Market reforms, 97, 144
Market system, 95
Martov, Yuli, 24
Marx, Karl, 25
Marxism, 23–24, 43
Marxism-Leninism, 122
Marxist-Leninist political literacy,
    35
Masses: growing force in
    Communist party, 32–34; rural,
    19
Materialism, European, 22–23
Mathematical economics, 97. *See
    also* Economics, TsEMI
Mayakovsky, Vladimir, 28, 69
Medunin, A. E., 132
Medvedev, Roy, 79
Medvedev, Vadim, 174, 186, 198
Melamid, Daniil, 283n192
Mendelevich, Lev, 154, 209
Mendelson, Sarah Elizabeth,
    231
Mezhdunarodnaia Zhizn'
    (International Life), 260n50
Mezhdunarodniki (foreign affairs
    experts), 100–107, 147–53
MGIMO (Moscow State Institute
    of International Relations), 74,
    103, 262n93
MGU (Moscow State University),
    67, 87, 181, 271n39
Middle East, 120
Migranyan, Andrannik, 343n39
Mihajlov, Mihajlo, 269n13
Mikhailov, Nikolai, 104
Mikoyan, Anastas, 57, 70, 93
Military defeats, 21–22
Military doctrine, 200, 218, 333n153
Military forces, 118
Military spending, 190, 200,
    324n31, 324n32

Military studies, 152
Military-industrial complex, 201, 202, 218, 324n33
Miliukov, Pavel, 29
Mints, Lev, 274n67
Mitin, Mark, 135
Mitterand, François, 212
Mlynar, Zdenek, 181, 273n57, 281n160
Molotov, Vyacheslav, 54, 190, 258n13
Mongait, A. L., 272n48
Morgenthau, Hans, 102
Moscow, transformation of, 62
Moscow Institute of World Economy, 46, 47
Moscow intelligentsia, 111, 134
Moscow Neo-Slavophilism, 28
Moscow State Institute of International Relations (MGIMO), 74, 103, 262n93
Moscow State University (MGU), 67, 87, 181, 271n39

Najibullah, Muhammed, 224
Napoleonic Wars, 20
Narsky, I. S., 87
National idea, 239
National identity: description, 6; domestic politics of, since perestroika, 238–39; process of change, 5, 6, 7–8, 340n23–341n23
National Resources Defense Council, 213
National-imperial attitudes, 27
Nationalism. See Russian nationalism
Nationalist journals, 292n89
Nations, as historical narratives, 6
NATO, 152, 236, 239, 342n37
Natta, Alessandro, 204
Natural sciences, 34

Nazis, 43
Nekrasov, Viktor, 84
Nekrich, Alexander, 17, 91–92, 109, 283n192
Nemchinov, Vasily, 94–95
Neoliberal explanations of new thinking, 4–5
Neo-realism, 3, 230
Neo-Slavophilism, 28, 136–38, 235
Neo-Stalinism, 58–59
Neo-Stalinists. See Antireformists
Neo-Westernism, 136, 138, 235
NEP. See New Economic Policy
NEP period, 34
New Bolsheviks, 36
New Economic Policy (NEP), 26, 34, 37, 38, 40, 80, 183
New elite, 51
New foreign-affairs thought, 100–101
New industrial workers, 41
New intelligentsia (new intellectuals), 77, 80, 83, 89, 107–8. See also Intelligentsia
New openness, 96
New thinkers: background, 5; beliefs, 5–6; in early 1980s, 161; embrace of global concerns, 129; experience of 1970s, 119; during first post-thaw years, 147; influence of CSCE on, 154–55; internal exile, 134; reconsideration of identity of adversaries, 221; response to conservatives' actions, 221; role, 4; shared social identity, 10, 80; support of efforts to broaden détente, 154; threat of purge against, 190; views on Eastern Europe, 224
New thinking: approaches to nature of, 231–32; broader foundation of, 100; definitions, 5;

description, 2, 3–4, 14; dispersion, 127–28; domestic nexuses,
228; effects of old thinking on,
19; elites-identity explanation of,
5–8; on foreign affairs, 100–107;
Gorbachev's accomplishments
under banner of, 2; impact of
Chernobyl tragedy on, 215–16;
impact of contacts with the West
on, 75–76; institutions important
to, 7; integrationist goal, 222;
lessons of (overview), 13–15;
mobilization of (overview), 11;
nascent centers of, 76; new intellectuals' acceptance of, 114; origins, 2, 3, 9–11, 71, 82, 229–40;
pioneers, 236; political opposition to, 225; sabotage by hard-
line security interests, 218; sociology's contribution to, 99;
transformation, 207; triumph of
(overview), 12–13
New thinking, coming to power
of, 193–228; economic domestic
roots of new thinking, 200–207;
intellectual domestic roots of
new thinking, 207–15; introduction, 193–95; main development
of new thinking, 222–26; openness, democracy, and international trust, 215–22; summary,
226–28
New thinking, during era of stagnation, 117–57; bases for, 126;
Brezhnev cohort and, 119–23;
conservatism, 133–36; debate
over Russia in world civilization, 139–41; détente, levels of,
154–57; economic thought,
141–47; emergence of global
outlook, 127–33; intellectual
life, 124–27; international relations, 147–53; nationalism,
136–39
New thinking, in early 1980s,
159–92; Andropov's reformist
efforts, 172–80; attacks on,
169–72; efforts to save détente,
161–69; introduction, 159–61;
new leadership for, 180–86;
new-Stalinists' bid for power,
186–91; summary, 191–92;
Yakovlev's essay, 184–85; during
year of Andropov, 176
Nicholas I ("Iron Tsar"), 20
Nikiforov, Boris, 113
Nikitich, Lyudmila, 140
1961 Party Program, 136
Nobility, 19–20
Non-aligned movement, 162
Non-Bolshevik scholars, 34–35
Non-Russian periphery, 27
Non-Russians, abuse of, 30
Not by Bread Alone (Dudintsev), 84
Novoe myshlenie. See new thinking
Novosibirsk Institute. See Institute
of Economics and Industrial
Organization
Novosibirsk memorandum
(Zaslavskaya), 174
Novozhilov, Viktor, 95
Novy Mir (reformist journal), 66,
67, 77, 83, 85, 133
Nuclear arms control, 109, 112, 124,
147–49, 168–69, 217. See also
Arms control
Nuclear dilemma, 177, 205
Nuclear forces, 118, 164
Nuclear testing, 200–201, 213–14
Nuclear war, 147–48

Oases of creative thought, 71
Obshchechelovecheskie, see Universal
Human Values

Obukhev, Alexei, 102–3
Offensive détente, 19
Official ideology, 37
Ogarkov, Nikolai, 188, 319n179
Oizerman, Teodor, 87
Okudzhava, Bulat, 79
Old dogmas, 205
Old thinkers, 18
Old thinking, 17–48; basic precepts
    of, 17–18; conspiracy worldview,
    37–43; dangers in evolution of,
    31; duration, 18–19; internation-
    alism vs. nationalism, 25–31; new
    elite for Bolsheviks, 31–37; per-
    petuation, 121; persistence
    (overview), 8–9; during and
    post-WWII, 44–48; reappraisals
    of, 50; role in invasion of
    Afghanistan, 123; Russia's world
    place under old regime, 19–25
"On Sincerity in Literature"
    (Pomerantsev), 67
One Day in the Life of Ivan
    Denisovich (Solzhenitsyn), 8, 78,
    84
"Open Letter" (Solzhenitsyn), 110
Openness, 63–64, 215–22
Oppenheimer, Robert, 106
Optimal planning, 97
Ordinary Fascism (Romm), 269n11
Ordzhonikidze, Sergo, 27–28
Orlov, Boris, 112, 153, 203n213
Orlov, Yuri, 68
Orlova, Raisa, 17, 78
Orwell, George, 10
Ostrovitianov, Yuri, 139
Outside world, 124–25. See also
    Foreign affairs
Overpopulation, 130

Palme, Olof, 102
Palme Commission (Independent

Commission on Disarmament
    and Security), 168–69, 170
Pan-Slavism, 22, 137
Paranoid secretiveness, 149–50, 156
Pariah states, 237
Party Congresses: Eleventh, 29;
    Twelfth, 29; Fifteenth, 38–39;
    Twentieth, 49, 50, 55, 67–68;
    Twenty-second, 82; Twenty-sev-
    enth, 209, 210–11
Party intelligentsia (intellectuals),
    79, 112–13
Party Organizations Department
    of the Central Committee,
    174
Party Program (1961), 136
Pasternak, Boris, 56, 65, 85
Pauling, Linus, 106
Pavlov, Todor, 88
Peaceful coexistence, 37, 38–39, 50,
    58, 82
Peaceful competition, 55
Peasant communes, 21, 24
Pechenev, Vadim, 342n32, 343n39
Perestroika, 195–96, 214, 215–16. See
    also Glasnost; Gorbachev,
    Mikhail
Permanent Western threat, 100
Peter the Great, 19–20
Petrakov, Nikolai, 144, 275n75
Philosophers, young, 89–90
Philosophical-cultural studies, 90
Philosophy, 40, 47, 87–90
"The Philosophy of Peace"
    (Burlatsky), 167
Pilnyak, Boris, 28
Plan and Market (Lisichkin), 98
Planned economy, 146
Plekhanov, Georgy, 24
Plimak, Yevgeny, 87, 91
Podgorny, Nikolai, 120
Pokrovsky, Mikhail, 27, 90

Poland, 26, 33, 38, 160, 162–63
Policy-academic elite, 2–3, 10, 14.
  See also New thinkers
Polish scholarship, 10, 78, 79
Polish war, 33
Politburo: commitment to arms
  control, 149; growing influence
  of second echelon members,
  170; policy arguments in, 218;
  Polish Commission, 305n11;
  responses to illusory prosperity,
  146; support for Gorbachev as
  general secretary, 196. *See also*
  Central Committee
Politgramota (political literacy),
  35
Political climate, 37
Political culture, 18, 41
Political learning, 234
Political liberalization, 221–22
Political philosophers, 23
Political prisoners, 223
Political training, 35–36
Politichskii Dnevnik (Political
  diary), 110
Politics Among Nations
  (Morgenthau), 102
Pomerantsev, Vladimir, 67
Ponomarev, Boris, 122, 170, 176,
  183, 208, 211
Populism, 21, 23
Post-Brezhnev generation,
  198–99
Post-Khrushchev era, 117
Post-Prague decade, 128
Post-Soviet politics, 239–40
Post-Stalin leaders, 52, 55, 56, 198
Post-Stalin reform era, 81
Potashov, Vladimir, 187–88
Power, 14
Power-centered explanation of new
  thinking, 3, 230

Prague, locus of foreign-affairs
  thought, 72. *See also* Prague
  journal
Prague journal *(Problemy Mira i
  Sotsializma*—Problems of Peace
  and Socialism), 70, 71, 72, 73,
  78, 101, 110, 113, 131
Prague Spring: effects of, 11; example of limits of reform, 8; impact
  on Soviet intellectuals, 109;
  legacy, 114–15; mythological sta-
  tus, 114; responses to suppres-
  sion of, 112–14; Soviet intellec-
  tuals and, 107–15
Praktiki (traditional Party man-
  agers), 214
Prejudices of the masses, 32–34
Preobrazhensky, Yevgeny, 35
Pre-Petrine Russia, 19
Pribytkov, Viktor, 309n58
Primakov, Yevgeny, 183, 201, 237,
  286n32
Principled issue network, 242n5,
  303n223
Prison Notebooks (Gramsci), 89
Private salons, 78, 267n157
Problemy Mira i Sotsializma, see
  Prague Journal
Proektor, Daniil, 153, 165
*Progress, Peaceful Coexistence, and
  Intellectual Freedom* (Sakharov),
  130
Proletarian intelligentsia, 10, 35, 80
Proletariat, 253n116
Prompartiia case, 40
Propaganda: anti-NATO, 1; anti-
  Western, reduction in, 60; belief
  in, 254n153; during early 1980s,
  188–89; effects of WWII on, 44;
  importance of ignorance to, 42
Public Opinion Research Institute,
  98

Pugwash movement, 10, 106, 107,
    150, 151, 152, 168, 301n201
Pumpyansky, Alexander, 135
Purge trials, 41. *See also* Show trials
Purges, 124, 170–71
Putsch, attempted, 227, 338n3

Rabfaki (workers' faculties), 35
Radek, Karl, 27
Radical intelligentsia, 140
Radios, 63, 261n64
Radishchev (historian), 91
Rakhmanin, Oleg, 204–5, 208
Rapprochement, 50–51, 119, 127
Raushenbakh, Boris, 151, 180n 126,
    300n190, 314n124
Reactionaries. *See* Antireformists
Reagan, Ronald, 13, 212
Realist analysts, 3, 237–38
Realist state builders *(derzhavniki)*,
    237
Reasonable sufficiency doctrine, 218
Red Imperialist, 45
Red Professors, 43
Red Terror, 34
*Reflections on Progress, Coexistence,
    and Intellectual Freedom*
    (Sakharov), 107, 108
Reform ideas, 4
Reformers, 166, 200. *See also* New
    thinkers
Reformism, 124–25. *See also* New
    thinking
Reformist apparatchiks, 79
Reformist economists, 142, 143,
    144, 146, 182–83
Reformist institutes, 142, 164, 187.
    See also Institutes
Reformist-integrationist thought,
    125–26, 136, 155
Reformist intellectuals, 98. *See also*
    New intelligentsia

Reformists. *See* Liberal-reformist
    domestic community
Regional studies, 153
"Rereading Chekhov"
    (Ehrenburg), 83–84
Research institutes. *See* Institutes
Revolt of the young, 87
Revolution of belief, 41
Revolutionary inadequacy, com-
    plex (syndrome) of, 58, 120
Reykjavik disarmament proposals,
    12, 218
Reykjavik Summit, 217–19
Risse-Kappen, Thomas, 232, 339n12
Romanov, Grigory, 188, 196, 197,
    319n180, 321n3
Romm, Mikhail, 269n11
Rumyantsev, Alexei: aids persecut-
    ed liberals, 88; career, 270n26;
    defeat, 124; as director of
    Institute of Concrete Social
    Research, 98; early experiences,
    265n126; editor of Prague jour-
    nal, 72, 101; publication of calls
    for economic decentralization,
    98; purge of sociology institute,
    134; removal from *Pravda*, 109,
    275n82; role in creations of
    TsEMI, 274n73; support for
    fired reformers, 113, 281n152
Rural incomes, 93
Rural masses, 19
Rural progress, myth of, 64. *See
    also* Collectivization
Rural tragedy, 92
Rusakov, Konstantin, 171
Russia: Asian identity, 25, 28; com-
    mon cultural space with the
    West, 90; military defeats, 21;
    nature of international behavior,
    235–36; place in international
    community, 19, 140–41; prob-

lems of, 3; understanding
Western orientation of, 236;
views of U.S. in 1980s, 1;
Western influence on, 20. *See
also* Soviet Union
Russian chauvinism, 29–30, 83, 85,
250n78. *See also* Russian nation-
alism
Russian Marxists, 24
Russian nationalism: attacks on, 83;
Brezhnev-era resurgence of, 136;
combination with anti-
Westernism, 36–37; dilemma of,
137; as important issue, 27–28,
29–30; Party encouragement of,
118; symbiosis with Soviet patri-
otism, 45; under Stalinism, 43;
Yakovlev's criticism of, 45. *See
also* Neo-Slavophilism
Russocentrism, 40, 47, 256n188
Rutkeevich, Mikhail, 134
Rybalchenko, Filipp, 44–45
Ryzhkov, Nikolai, 174, 196, 198

Sagdeyev, Roald: influences on,
106, 151; loss of political influence, 236; member of
Gorbachev's "gang of four,"
201; influence of Sakharov, 150;
participation in arms control
discussions, 168, 169; and Soviet
Scientists' Committee, 179;
views on Gorbachev's team, 184
St. Petersburg Romance (Galich),
111
Sakharov, Andrei: belief in arms
control, 107; criticism of Afghan
invasion, 313n113; freeing of, 223;
Gorbachev's conversations
about, 214; importance, 129–30;
influence of, 150–51, 288n46;
influences on, 106; *Reflections

on Progress, Coexistence, and
Intellectual Freedom*, 107, 108,
110; support for, 283n187; views
on unity of mankind, 108; views
on war psychology, 48
SALT. *See* Strategic Arms
Limitation Talks
Samizdat (clandestine literature),
79, 105, 266n139
Schaff, Adam, 271n36
Schelling, Thomas, 102
Scholars, suffering of, 34. *See also*
Historians; Scientists
"Science, Ethics, and Humanism"
(roundtable), 133
Scientific exchanges, 106–7
Scientific space, common, 90
*Scientific-Technological Progress
and its Socio-Economic Impact
Through the Year 1990* (Shatalin),
144
Scientific-technological revolution,
143
Scientists, 7, 34, 106–7, 150, 168,
213. *See also* Committee of
Soviet Scientists in Defense of
Peace and Against the Nuclear
Threat
Scythian writers, 25, 28
SDI (Strategic Defense Initiative),
179, 201, 312n92
Secret speech of Khrushchev, 11,
49, 52, 67–68, 81
Secretiveness, 149–50, 156
Self-definition, crisis of, 243n17
Self-determination, 27
Semichastny, Vladimir, 258n18
Separatism, 226–27
Serbia, 238–39
Shakhnazarov, Georgy: *The
Coming World Order*, 167;
demotion, 290n75; disciplining

Shakhnazarov, Georgy *(continued)* of, 134; promotion of, 208; recollections of Gorbachev, 183–84;

Shakhnazarov, Georgy *(continued)* response to crushing of Prague Spring, 112; support for Gorbachev's policies, 207; views on democratization, 166; views on international relations, 287n41; views on military policy, 177; views on political systems, 128; *Tsena svobody*, 193; views on social problems, 177–78; views on weapons production, 134

Shakhty case, 40

Shalapentokh, Vladimir, 96

Shatalin, Stanislav: arguments on Third-World debt, 205; disciplining of, 113, 135, 297n159; initiation of high-level study group, 144; reform proposals under Andropov, 174, 275n75

Shcherbitsky, Vladimir, 197, 206

Sheinis, Viktor, 134, 139, 140, 165

Shelepin, Alexander, 59

Shershnev, Leonid, 178

Shestidesiatniki (those of the sixties), 280n146

Shevardnadze, Eduard: actions supporting Reykjavik Summit, 218–19; Akhromeyev's views on, 198; background, 202–3; concern over Eastern Europe, 203; consultations with Bogomolov, 204; creation of Academic Consultative Council, 209; creation of Arms Control and Disarmament Division, 209; discussion of philosophy of foreign policy, 209, 210; ethnic memory, 326n60; Gorbachev's appointment of, 202; loss of political influence, 236; path to new worldview, 223; relationship with Gorbachev, 3, 12, 182; views on Afghan government, 221; views on Arbatov, 202; views on Chernobyl tragedy, 216

Shkredov, Vladimir, 100

Shlykov, Vitaly, 152, 301n207

Shmelev, Nikolai: analysis of modern capitalism, 176; arguments on Third-World debt, 205; support for market reforms, 276n97; views on foreign trade, 99–100, 145, 146; views on outlook of reformist institutes, 142; views on production enterprises, 144–45

Short Course (Soviet political primer under Stalin), 41–42, 53, 71, 87, 91, 101, 121, 139

Shortwave radios, 63

Shostakovich, Dmitri, 46

Show trials, 40, 41, 64; *see also* purges

Shubkin, Vladimir, 96

Siege mentality, 39

Sik, Ota, 110

Simonov, Konstantin, 46, 83, 85–86, 269n15

Sino-American relations, 153

Sino-Soviet relations, 57–60

Sinyavsky, Andrei, 109

SIPRI (Stockholm International Peace Research Institute), 149

Skrypnik, Mykola, 29, 30

Slavophiles, 9, 21, 23, 292n94

Smena vekh (Change of Signposts) movement, 28–29

Smirnov, Georgy, 210

Snyder, Jack, 230

Social Democracy, 10, 23, 24, 102, 108, 127

Social learning, 7
Social sciences, 34, 83
Socialism, 57, 166
Socialism in one country policy, 38
Socialism with a human face, 88
Socialist democracy, 166
Socialist Democracy
    (Shakhnazarov), 128
Sociological Association, 98
Sociology, 98–100, 129
Solovyev, Vladimir, 25, 270n21
Solzhenitsyn, Alexander, 78, 84,
    110, 111
*Some Philosophical Aspects of the
    Theory of Socialism* (Tsipko),
    167, 187
Southwest Asia, 306n28
Soviet-American Disarmament
    Study (SADS) groups, 107
Soviet Central Statistical
    Administration, 99
Soviet General Staff College, 36–37
Soviet industrial managers, 40
Soviet intellectual elite, 2. *See also*
    Policy-academic elite
Soviet international decline, 230
Soviet nationalism, 83. *See also*
    Russian nationalism
Soviet system, failures of, 141
Soviet Union: need for improved
    international environment, 200;
    overextension in late 1970s, 123;
    paths not taken, 229–30; prob-
    lems in early 1980s, 159–60, 195
Soviet-Western ties, 118
Sovietized workers, 31
Spain, 6–7, 84
Spiritual emancipation, 66
Sputnik, 57
SS-20 missiles, 175, 217
Stalin, Joseph: action against diplo-
    mats, 103; actions, post-WWII,

46; criticisms of foreign policy
of, 91; declaration of permanent
cold war, 47; diplomatic purge,
43; *Economic Problems of
Socialism in the USSR*, 47, 94,
190; efforts to rehabilitate, 117,
124, 190; *Foundations of
Leninism*, 36; growth in authority, 45; influence, 60; interest in
linguistics, 47; legacies, 92; promotion of Russian nationalism,
137; promulgation of revolution
of belief, 41; removal of body
from Lenin mausoleum, 82;
socialism in one country policy,
38; sociology under, 98; speech
to Soviet industrial managers,
40; successors, 52–60; Trotsky's
defeat by, 39; views on, in 1970s,
140; views on chauvinism, 30;
views on European revolution,
39; views on imperialists,
253n131; views on inevitability of
war, 47; views on internationalism, 26
Stalinism, 18, 84–85
Stalinist dogmas, 264n112
Stalinist personality cult, 42
Stalinist regime, 44
Stalinist system, 92–100, 93
Stalinist terror: during Cold War,
47; effects of, 37, 42, 66; post-
WWII, 46; rationalizations for,
41; rethinking after, 63–64
Stalinist worldview, 190
Standards of living, 44
Star Wars defense system (Soviet),
313n119
Star Wars defense system (U.S.),
see Strategic Defense Initiative
START (Strategic Arms Reduction
Talks) Treaty, 206

State and Revolution (Lenin), 24
State-building process, 90–91
Sterbalova, Antonina, 139
Stockholm International Peace
    Research Institute (SIPRI), 149
Stockholm Socialist International,
    102
Stockholm talks, 217
Strategic Arms Limitation Talks
    (SALT) Treaty, 118; talks, 149
Strategic Arms Reduction Talks
    (START) Treaty, 206
Strategic capabilities, 148
Strategic defense initiative (SDI),
    14, 179, 201, 312n92
Strategic defense system, 155
Strategic studies, 152–53
Strategic weapons, 179, 206
Struve, Peter, 23
"Sufficient defenses" doctrine,
    318n177
Superpower relations, in 1980s, 1
Suslov, Mikhail, 122, 154

Tamm, Igor, 69, 78
Tarasenko, Sergei, 299n181
Tartu Semiotics School, 90
Technology, 132
Television, 63
Terkin, Vasily, 86
Territorial settlements, 54
Thatcher, Margaret, 161, 219, 220
The Thaw (Ehrenburg), 67
Thaw era, 49–80; after
    Khrushchev's fall from power,
    82; availability of western litera-
    ture, 94; context for new lead-
    ership, 52–53; critically minded
    Soviets, 77–78; information
    explosion, 74; institutional bases
    for sociology, 98; intellectuals,
    65–70; legacy, 114–15; reappraisal

of socialism in, 65; as time of
    intellectual liberation, 78; views
    on need for economic change,
    141–42; writers of, 83–84
The Theory and Practice of Building
    Socialism (Butenko), 128
Theory building, 232–33
The Theory of Peasant Cooperatives
    (Chayanov), 95
Third world, 118, 165
Third-world debt, 205
Tienanmen massacre, 8
Tikhonov, Nikolai, 197
Tikhonov, Vladimir, 147, 182, 183,
    190, 236
Togliatti, Palmiro, 88
Tolkunev, Lev, 175, 188
Tolstoy, Alexei, 249n62
Tolstoy, Lev, 178
Tourism, 62
"Toward a Revised Approach to
    Foreign Policy" (Arbatov),
    201–2
Trade, East-West, 99–100, 145
Trade schools, 35
Transnational learning model, 4,
    242n6
Trapeznikov, Sergei: adviser to
    Brezhnev, 109; anti-intellectual-
    ism, 122–23, 134; growing influ-
    ence, 170; injury to, 285n21;
    neo-Stalinist directives to
    research institutes, 190; relation
    to Institute of Social Sciences,
    290n78; replaced by Medvedev,
    174; views on 1930s, 109
Troop reductions: in Asia, 153;
    under Gorbachev, 193, 224;
    under Khrushchev, 58
Trotsky, Leon, 26, 38, 39
Trust, international, 219, 221, 222,
    227, 335n174

Truth-telling. *See* Glasnost
Tsipko, Alexander: attacks on, 187; consultations with early Gorbachev team, 210; Gorbachev's interest in, 318n175, 328n84; joins apparat staff under Gorbachev, 208; *Some Philosophical Aspects of the Theory of Socialism,* 167; views on building humanistic socialist society, 140; views on national ideology, 343n39; views on socioeconomic problems, 167–68
Turkey, 54
Tvardovsky, Alexander: firing of, 124; limitations on, 133, publication of reformist works, 109; response to crushing of Prague Spring, 112; support for Western thought, 83; wartime works, 86
12th Party Congress, 29
20th Party Congress, 49, 50, 55, 67–68
22nd Party Congress, 82
27th Party Congress, 209, 210–11

Ukraine, 26
Ukrainian Communists, 91
Ukraintsev, Vasily, 133
Union of Concerned Scientists, 213. *See also* Scientists
United Nations exchanges, 106
United States: aggression, 53; declining military presence, 302n212; economic success, 97; foreign policy, 13; Marxist-Leninist political view of, 35; suppression of socialism, 52–53; views of Russia in 1980s, 1. *See also* USA-Canada Institute
United States-Soviet arms talks, 148

Universal human values (*Obshchechelovecheskie*), 127, 141, 287n45
Universities, as centers of radicalism, 67
University pogrom, 87–88
Urban intelligentsia, 245n33
USA Institute. *See* Institute of the USA
USA-Canada Institute (ISKAN): attacks on, 170, 171–72; creation of, 125; Military Department, 152; report on third world priorities, 165; studies of U.S. economy, 147, 156, 176; study on fall of Bretton Woods order, 143
USSR. *See* Soviet Union
Ustinov, Dmitri, 123, 163, 169, 190, 197, 322n17
Ustrialov, Nikolai, 29
Utopian leaps, 140

Varga, Yevgeny, 46, 47, 70, 79, 80
Vekhi ("Signposts," political philosophers), 23, 24, 139–40, 167, 187
Velikhov, Yevgeny: influence on Gorbachev, 184; influences on, 106, 151; member of "gang of four," 201; mentioned, 169; participation in arms control discussions, 168; relationship with Gorbachev, 183, 184, 185; Soviet Scientists' Committee, 179; verification project at nuclear test sites, 213; views on strategic defense initiative, 179
Verification project, 213
Vezhner, Vladimir, 94–95
Virgin Lands campaign, 93
Vocal minorities, 236

Vodolazov, Grigory, 138, 139
Voice of America, 63
Von Hippel, Frank, 213
Voprosy Filosofii (Philosophical Issues), 131
Vorotnikov, Vitaly, 174
Voznesensky, Andrei, 85
Vydvizhentsy (new elite): backgrounds of, 53, 121; focus of, 37; formation of beliefs of, 43; Khrushchev as member of, 42; rationalization of internal conflicts, 41; suppression of own doubts, 39
Vyshinsky, Andrei, 53–54, 278n120
Vysotsky, Vladimir, 79

Wall newspapers, 68
War, 47, 48, 66, 147–48. *See also* Afghan War; Arms control; Arms race; Cold War; Great Patriotic War; Napoleonic Wars; Polish war; World War II;
War Communism, 26, 35
War Communist militancy, 43
War psychology, 48
War scare, 38, 189
Wartime propaganda, 32–33
Weapons trade, 177
Weinstein, Albert, 274n67
West: aggression, 40; anti-Soviet crusade, 161–62; common cultural space with, 90; cultivation of fear of, 121; culture, 84; demonization of, 41, 48; enemy image of, 251n97; political-economic life, 176; response to Khrushchev's changes, 50; Slavophiles' views on, 21; social and political thought, 89; threatening capitalist, 123. See

also *entries beginning "East-West";* United States
West European Marxists, 101
West European policy analysis, 165
West Germany, 97. *See also* German unification; Germany
Western scholarship, 128–29
Western strategic concepts, 107
Western thought, 79
Westernism, 25, 51
Westernized elite, 18
Westernizers, 2, 9, 21, 22–23
Westernizing liberals, 2, 3, 5, 80, 114, 237
Westernizing socioeconomic critique, 99
Westernizing tradition, 34–35, 90
White book special-edition translations, 102, 277n112, 330n112
Whites, 33
Will the World Become Too Crowded? (Gerasimov), 130
Wohlforth, William C., 233, 340n20
World Economic Herald, 7
World literature, 61
World revolution, 39
World War II, 44–46, 198
World Youth Festival, 62
World-historical process, 91
World's oneness, 216
Worldviews: of archetypal Communists, 32–33; difficulty of changing, 50; Gorbachev's, 205, 223, 334n169; Khrushchev's, 53, 54; of old thinkers, 37–43; Shevardnadze's, 223; Stalinist, 190; Yakovlev's, 184–85, 223
Woroszylski, Wiktor, 78
Writers, 7, 40, 75, 85

Xenophobia, 9, 18, 32, 43

Yagodkin, V. N., 134, 290n74
Yakir, Petr, 282n168
Yakovlev, Alexander: ostensible anti-Americanism, 317n158; appointment as Central Committee Secretary for Ideology, 208; attack on Great-Russian chauvinism, 138; clashes with conservatives, 187; description of neo-Stalinists, 191; as director of IMEMO, 185; discussion of philosophy of foreign policy, 209, 210; dismissal of, 134; evolution of worldview, 184–85, 223; loss of political influence, 236; relationship with Gorbachev, 3, 11, 184, 328n87; support for reformers, 113, 329n89; views on Gorbachev, 199
Yakovlev, Yegor, 109, 112
Yanov, Alexander, 138
Yavlinksy, Grigory, 237
Yazov, Dmitri, Defense Minister, 224
Yegorychev, Nikolai, 257n8

The Yellow River Elegy, 8
Yeltsin, Boris, 227, 234
Yevtushenko, Yevgeny, 85, 112
Youth, political training of, 36
Yugoslavia, 50, 59, 68, 76, 79, 86, 89, 97, 100, 142

Za Rubezhom (Abroad, journal), 61
Zagladin, Vadim, 166–67, 176, 183, 290n78
Zamoshkin, Yuri, 133, 236, 271n37
Zapadniki (Westernizers), 150. See also Westernizers
Zaslavskaya, Tatyana: ideological pressure on, 187; loss of political influence, 236; early discussions with Gorbachev, 182–183; Khrushchev-era research, 96; mentors, 94; Novosibirsk memorandum, 174
Zhdanov, Andrei, 46–47
Dr. Zhivago (Pasternak), 56, 85
Zimyanin, Mikhail, 170–71, 187
Zinoviev, Alexander, 87
Zinoviev, Grigory, 32
Zoshchenko, Mikhail, 46